ANALECTA BIBLICA
INVESTIGATIONES SCIENTIFICAE IN RES BIBLICAS

——— 117. ———

GEORGE MLAKUZHYIL, S.J.
Vidyajyoti, Delhi

THE CHRISTOCENTRIC LITERARY STRUCTURE OF THE FOURTH GOSPEL

EDITRICE PONTIFICIO ISTITUTO BIBLICO – ROMA 1987

Vidimus et approbamus ad normam Statutorum

Pontificia Universitas Gregoriana
Romae, die 29 mensis Ianuarii anni 1987

P. ALBERT VANHOYE, S.J.
P. GERALD O'COLLINS, S.J.

ISBN 88-7653-117-3

© Iura editionis et versionis reservantur

EDITRICE PONTIFICIA UNIVERSITÀ GREGORIANA
EDITRICE PONTIFICIO ISTITUTO BIBLICO
Piazza della Pilotta, 35 - 00187 Roma

*Dedicated
to the Society of Jesus*

GENERAL OUTLINE

Contents	IX
Presentation	XVII
Preface	XIX
0. INTRODUCTION	1
1. DIFFICULTIES AGAINST THE LITERARY UNITY AND STRUCTURE OF THE FOURTH GOSPEL	5
2. SURVEY OF THE STRUCTURES OF THE FOURTH GOSPEL	17
3. CRITERIA FOR THE STRUCTURE OF THE FOURTH GOSPEL	87
3.1 Literary Criteria	87
3.2 Dramatic Techniques	112
3.3 Structural Patterns	121
4. THE LITERARY STRUCTURE OF THE FOURTH GOSPEL	137
4.1 The Main Divisions of the Fourth Gospel	137
4.2 The Sections of the Book of Jesus' Signs and the Book of Jesus' Hour	168
4.3 The Structure of the Sections	191
4.z "The Schema of the Literary Structure of the Fourth Gospel"	239
5. THE LITERARY STRUCTURE AND THE CHRISTOCENTRIC THEOLOGY OF THE FOURTH GOSPEL	243
5.1 Major Theological Themes and the Literary Structure	243
5.2 Christocentric Theological Sketch in the Literary Structure	299
Z. CONCLUSION	349
BIBLIOGRAPHY	353
INDEX OF AUTHORS	367

CONTENTS

Presentation XVII
Preface XIX

0. INTRODUCTION 1

1. DIFFICULTIES AGAINST THE LITERARY UNITY AND STRUCTURE OF THE FOURTH GOSPEL 5

1.1 MAIN PROBLEMS 5
1.11 Interruptions and Inconsistencies in Sequence 5
1.12 Repetitions and/or Passages out of Context 7
1.13 Differences in Greek Vocabulary and Style 7

1.2 PROPOSED SOLUTIONS 8
1.21 Theories of Accidental Displacements 8
1.22 Theories of Multiple Sources 9
1.23 Theories of Multiple Editions/Redactions 11

Excursus: 14
   1) The Aporia at Jn 1,43 and Its Solution 14
   2) The Aporia at Jn 1,51 and Its Solution 15

2. SURVEY OF THE STRUCTURES OF THE FOURTH GOSPEL 17

2.1 GEOGRAPHICAL-CHRONOLOGICAL STRUCTURE (BERNARD) . 18
2.2 CHRONOLOGICAL-LITURGICAL STRUCTURES (MOLLAT, GUILDING, GOULDER) 19
   2.21 Mollat's Chronological-Liturgical Structure 19
   2.22 Guilding's Chronological-Liturgical Structure 21
   2.23 Goulder's Chronological-Liturgical Structure 23
2.3 NUMERICAL-SYMBOLICAL STRUCTURE (LOHMEYER) 26
2.4 LITERARY-CHRONOLOGICAL STRUCTURE (DEFOURNEY) . . . 28
2.5 TYPOLOGICAL STRUCTURE (SAHLIN) 28
2.6 THEOLOGICAL-TYPOLOGICAL-SYMBOLICAL STRUCTURE (MATEOS & BARRETO) 29
2.7 LITURGICAL-SYMBOLICAL-TYPOLOGICAL STRUCTURE (BOISMARD) 31
   2.71 Symbolical-Typological Structure 31
   2.72 Liturgical-Symbolical Structure 33
   2.73 Comparison between the Two Structures 34

CONTENTS

2.8 LITURGICAL-SYMBOLICAL-SIGN STRUCTURE (PUIGDOLLERS) . . 35
2.9 CHIASTIC STRUCTURE (WEBSTER) 37
2.[10] CHIASTIC-SYMBOLIC STRUCTURE (DEEKS). 41
2.[11] SYMMETRICAL-CONCENTRIC STRUCTURE (WILLEMSE) . . . 44
2.[12] RHYTHMICAL-SYMMETRICAL STRUCTURE (RAU) 47
2.[13] CENTRIC-SYMMETRICAL STRUCTURE (KAMMERSTÄTTER) . 49
2.[14] NARRATIVE STRUCTURE (PRETE) 51
2.[15] NARRATIVE-DISCOURSE STRUCTURE (DODD) 53
2.[16] DRAMATIC-CHRONOLOGICAL-GEOGRAPHICAL STRUCTURE (TENNEY) 55
2.[17] DRAMATIC-EPISODIC STRUCTURE (CULPEPPER). 58
2.[18] REVELATORY STRUCTURES (WESTCOTT, VAN DEN BUSSCHE, DE LA POTTERIE) 62

    2.[18]1 Westcott's Revelatory Structure. 62
    2.[18]2 van den Bussche's Revelatory Structure 64
    2.[18]3 de la Potterie's Revelatory Structure. 67

2.[19] REVELATORY-DRAMATIC STRUCTURE (CABA). 69
2.[20] REVELATORY-RESPONSE STRUCTURE (GOURGUES) 71
2.[21] REVELATORY-NARRATIVE STRUCTURE (PASQUETTO) 74
2.[22] REVELATORY-ECLECTIC STRUCTURE (SEGALLA) 76
2.[23] LITERARY-THEMATIC STRUCTURE (BROWN) 79
2.[24] JOURNEY-STRUCTURE (RISSI) 83

3. CRITERIA FOR THE STRUCTURE OF THE FOURTH GOSPEL 87

  3.1 LITERARY CRITERIA 87

    3.11 Conclusions 88
        3.111 Jn 20,30-31 88
        3.112 Jn 21,24-25 89
        3.113 Jn 12,37-43 89
        3.114 Other conclusions 90

    3.12 Introductions. 91
        3.121 Jn 1,1-2,11: introduction to the Gospel as a whole 91
        3.122 Introductions to episodes or pericopes 92

    3.13 Inclusions 93
        3.131 Inclusions for the Fourth Gospel as a whole 94
        3.132 Inclusions for the divisions and subdivisions 94

    3.14 Characteristic Vocabulary 98
        3.141 The vocabulary of 1,35-51 98
        3.142 The vocabulary of 2,1-11 100
        3.143 Comparison of the vocabulary of 1,35-51 and 2,1-11 100

    3.15 Geographical Indications. 101

3.16 Literary-Chronological Indications. 101
    3.161 *Meta tauta* and *meta touto* 101
    3.162 *Tê[i] epaurion* and *tê[i] hêmerâ[i] tê[i] tritê[i]* 102
    3.163 Other literary-chronological indications 102
3.17 Liturgical Feasts 102
3.18 Transitions. 103
3.19 Bridge-Passages. 104
    3.191 Bridge-verses 104
    3.192 Bridge-pericope 106
    3.193 Bridge-section. 106
3.1[10] Hook-Words. 106
    3.1[10]1 Hook-words in 1,1-18 106
    3.1[10]2 Hook-words in 1,35-51 107
    3.1[10]3 Other hook-words. 108
3.1[11] Techniques of Repetition. 108
    3.1[11]1 Repetition of key-terms/expressions 108
    3.1[11]2 Repetition of the *amên amên* formula. 109
    3.1[11]3 Repetition of *egô eimi* sayings 110
    3.1[11]4 Repetition of similar discourses 110
    3.1[11]5 Repetition of the same type-scene 110
3.1[12] Change of Literary 'Genres' 111

3.2 DRAMATIC TECHNIQUES. 112
    3.21 Change of Scenes 112
    3.22 Technique of Alternating Scenes. 113
    3.23 Technique of Double-Stage Action. 113
    3.24 Introduction of Dramatis Personae 114
    3.25 Change of Dramatis Personae. 114
    3.26 The Law of Stage Duality 115
    3.27 Technique of Vanishing Characters 116
    3.28 Technique of Seven Scenes 116
    3.29 Technique of Diptych-Scenes 117
    3.2[10] Sequence of Action-Dialogue-Discourse 117
    3.2[11] Dramatic Development 118
    3.2[12] Dramatic Pattern 119

3.3 STRUCTURAL PATTERNS. 121
    3.31 Parallelism 122
        3.311 Synonymous parallelism 122
        3.312 Antithetic parallelism 123
        3.313 Synthetic parallelism 124
        3.314 Staircase parallelism 124
    3.32 Chiasmus 125
        3.321 Chiasmus in a sentence 126
        3.322 Chiasmus in a pericope 126
        3.323 Chiasmus in a section 129

3.33 Concentric Structure.	129
3.331 Concentric structure in a single sentence	129
3.332 Concentric structure in a pericope	130
3.34 Spiral Structure.	131

4. THE LITERARY STRUCTURE OF THE FOURTH GOSPEL 137

4.1 THE MAIN DIVISIONS OF THE FOURTH GOSPEL 137

4.11 The Introduction and the Conclusion	137
4.111 The conclusion	138
4.112 The introduction	143
4.112,1 Jn 1,1-2,11 as the general introduction.	144
4.112,2 Main divisions of 1,1-2,11 .	145
4.112,3 Chiastic parallelism between 1,1-2,11 and 20,30-31	147
4.112,4 Comparison with other positions	148
4.12 Part I: the Book of Jesus' Signs.	152
4.121 Delimitation of the first part	152
4.122 Designation of Jn 2,1-12,50 as "the Book of Jesus' Signs"	155
4.13 Part II: the Book of Jesus' Hour	156
4.131 Delimitation of the second part	157
4.131,1 The end of the second part	157
4.131,2 The beginning of the second part	157
4.132 Designation of Jn 11,1-20,29 as "the Book of Jesus' Hour"	160
Excursus on the "hour" (*hôra*) in Jn	162
4.14 Appendix (Jn 21) .	167

4.2 THE SECTIONS OF THE BOOK OF JESUS' SIGNS AND THE BOOK OF JESUS' HOUR. 168

4.21 The First Section of the Book of Jesus' Signs	168
4.211 Delimitation of the first section	169
4.211,1 The beginning of the section	169
4.211,2 The end of the section.	170
4.211,3 The unity of the section (Jn 2-4)	173
4.212 Title of Jn 2-4: "Jesus' Initial Signs and Encounters (from Cana to Cana)".	173
4.22 The Second Section of the Book of Jesus' Signs	175
4.221 Delimitation of the second section	175
4.221,1 The beginning of the section	175
4.221,2 The end of the section.	176
4.221,3 The unity of the section (Jn 5-10)	178
4.222 Title of Jn 5-10: "Jesus' Works, Signs and Discussions (at Jewish Feasts)"	179

CONTENTS

4.23 The Third Section of the Book of Jesus' Signs = the First Section of the Book of Jesus' Hour (= the Bridge-Section)   181
    4.231 Delimitation of the bridge-section   181
    4.232 Title of Jn 11-12: "the Climactic Sign and the Coming of Jesus' Hour (Bridge-Section)"   181

4.24 The Second Section of the Book of Jesus' Hour   183
    4.241 Delimitation of the second section   183
    4.242 Title of Jn 13-17: "Jesus' Farewell of the Hour (at the Last Supper)".   184

4.25 The Third Section of the Book of Jesus' Hour   185
    4.251 Delimitation of the third section   185
        4.251,1 Reasons for the unity of Jn 18-19   185
        4.251,2 Reasons for the unity of Jn 18-20   187
    4.252 Title of Jn 18,1-20,29: "the Hour of Jesus' Passion-Death-Resurrection"   188

4.3 THE STRUCTURE OF THE SECTIONS   191

    4.31 The Structure of "Jesus' Initial Signs and Encounters" (Jn 2-4) . . .   191
        4.311 Division of 2,1-4,54 into subsections   191
        4.312 Parallelism between the subsections of 2,1-4,54   195
            4.312,1 Parallelism between 2,1-12 and 4,43-54   195
            4.312,2 Parallelism between 2,13-25 and 4,1-42   196
            4.312,3 Parallelism between 2,23-3,21 and 3,22-4,3   198

    4.32 The Structure of "Jesus' Works, Signs and Discussions" (Jn 5-10) .   200
        4.321 Division of 5,1-10,42 into subsections   200
        4.322 Parallelism between the subsections of 5,1-10,42   210
            4.322,1 Parallelism between 7,1-8,59 and 9,1-41   210
            4.322,2 Parallelism between 5,1-47 and 10,22-42   211
            4.322,3 Parallelism between 6,1-71 and 10,1-21   213

    4.33 The Structure of "the Climactic Sign and the Coming of Jesus' Hour" (Jn 11-12)   215
        4.331 Division of 11,1-12,50 into subsections   215
        4.332 Parallelism between 11,1-54 and 11,55-12,50   217

    4.34 The Structure of "Jesus'. Farewell of the Hour" (Jn 13-17)   221
        4.341 Division of 13,1-17,26 into subsections   221
        4.342 Parallelism between the subsections of 13,1-17,26   226
            4.342,1 Parallelism between 15,1-17 and 15,18-16,4d   226
            4.342,2 Parallelism between 13,31-14,31 and 16,4e-33   226
            4.342,3 Parallelism between 13,1-38 and 17,1-26   227

    4.35 The Structure of "the Hour of Jesus' Passion-Death-Resurrection" (Jn 18,1-20,29)   228
        4.351 Division of 18,1-20,29 into subsections   228

        4.352 Parallelism between the subsections of 18,1-20,29. 233
                4.352,1 Parallelism between 18,28-19,16b and 19,16c-42. . . . 233
                4.352,2 Parallelism between 18,12-27 and 20,1-18 233
                4.352,3 Parallelism between 18,1-14 and 20,19-29 234
    4.36 The Structure of the Appendix (Jn 21,1-25). 235
        4.361 Division and structure of the epilogue (21,1-23) 235
        4.362 Division and structure of the "second (editorial) conclusion"
        (21,24-25) 236

4.z "THE SCHEMA OF THE LITERARY STRUCTURE OF THE
FOURTH GOSPEL". 239

5. THE LITERARY STRUCTURE AND THE CHRISTOCENTRIC THEOLOGY OF THE FOURTH GOSPEL 243

    5.1 MAJOR THEOLOGICAL THEMES AND THE LITERARY
    STRUCTURE 243
        5.11 Christ/Messiah (*Christos/Messias*) 245
        5.12 The Son of God, the Son, the Father, and the Son of Man 256
            5.121 "The Son of God" (*ho hyios tou theou*) 256
            5.122 "The Son" (*ho hyios*) 261
            5.123 "The Father" (*ho patêr*) 264
            5.124 "The Son of Man" (*ho hyios tou anthrôpou*) 267
        5.13 "Signs" and "Works" 271
            5.131 "Sign" (*sêmeion*) 271
            5.132 "Work"/"works"/"to work" (*ergon/erga/ergazesthai*) 276
            5.133 Comparison between "signs" and "works" 278
        5.14 Disciples (*mathêtai*) 279
        5.15 Believing (*pisteuein*) 287
        5.16 (Eternal) Life (*zôê aiônios*) 291

    5.2 CHRISTOCENTRIC THEOLOGICAL SKETCH IN THE LITERARY
    STRUCTURE 299
        5.21 The Christocentric Theological Sketch in the Introduction (1,1-2,11). . . 300
            5.211 Jesus, the divine, creative, revelatory, regenerative, incarnate
            Word, in 1,1-18(C*). 300
            5.212 Jesus, the Messiah, the Son of God, the lamb of God, the king
            of Israel and the Son of Man, in 1,19-51 (B*). 301
            5.213 Jesus, the Messiah, in 2,1-11 (A+) 304
        5.22 The Christocentric Theological Sketch in "Jesus' Initial Signs and
        Encounters" (Jn 2-4) 307
            5.221 Jesus, the Messiah, the life-giver, in 2,1-12 (1A) and 4,43-54
            (1A') 307

5.222 Jesus, the prophet, the Messiah, the Son of God, the temple of God, the Saviour of the world, in 2,13-25 (1B) and 4,1-42 (1B') 308

5.223 Jesus, the Messiah, the bridegroom, the Son of Man, the Son of God, the mediator of the Holy Spirit and eternal life, in 2,23-3,21 (1C) and 3,22-4,3 (1C') 311

5.23 The Christocentric Theological Sketch in "Jesus' Works, Signs and Discussions" (Jn 5-10). 312

5.231 Jesus, the Christ, the Son of God, in 5,1-47 (2B) and 10,22-42 (2B') 313

5.232 Jesus, the prophet-king, the Son of God, the bread of life, the life-giving shepherd, in 6,1-71 (2C) and 10,1-21 (2C') 315

5.233 Jesus, the prophet, the Messiah, the Son of Man, the Son of God, the light of the world, the judge, in 7,1-8,59 (2D) and 9,1-41 (2D') 316

5.24 The Christocentric Theological Sketch in "the Climactic Sign and the Coming of Jesus' Hour" (Jn 11-12) 319

5.241 Jesus, the Christ, the Son of God, the Lord, the resurrection and the life, the life-giving lover, in 11,1-54 (3C). 319

5.242 Jesus, the anointed Messiah-king of Israel and the Son of Man about to be lifted up and glorified during his "hour", but rejected by the people, in 11,55-12,50 (3C') 322

5.25 The Christocentric Theological Sketch in "Jesus' Farewell of the Hour" (Jn 13-17). 324

5.251 Jesus, the exemplar of loving service, "I am", the Son of Man, the Son of God, the revealer of the Father, the mediator of divine life and love, about to be betrayed by Judas but glorified by the Father at "the hour", in 13,1-38 (4C) and 17,1-26 (4C') . 324

5.252 The departure and return of Jesus, the way to the Father and the mediator of the Spirit of truth, in 13,31-14,31 (4D) and 16,4e-33 (4D') 327

5.253 Jesus, the vine, and disciples, the branches, the commandment of love, and the world's hatred, in 15,1-17 (4E) and 15,18-16,4d (4E') 330

5.26 The Christocentric Theological Sketch in "the Hour of Jesus' Passion-Death-Resurrection" (18,1-20,29) 335

5.261 Jesus of Nazareth, "I am", the life-giving shepherd, the sovereign Spirit-giving Lord and God, in 18,1-14 (5C) and 20,19-29 (5C') 336

5.262 Jesus, the man and teacher, tried and denied, but risen as the Lord, lover and brother, in 18,12-27 (5D) and 20,1-18 (5D') . . 338

5.263 Jesus, the man, the Son of God, the king of the Jews, crucified and glorified, the fulfilment of the Scriptures, and the giver of the Spirit, in 18,28-19,16b (5E) and 19,16c-42 (5E'). 339

5.27 The Christocentric Theological Sketch in the Appendix (Jn 21,1-25) . 343

Z. CONCLUSION 349

BIBLIOGRAPHY 353

    A. BIBLIOGRAPHY OF BIBLIOGRAPHY ON THE GOSPEL OF JOHN 353
    B. COMMENTARIES ON THE GOSPEL OF JOHN 353
    C. LITERARY UNITY AND STRUCTURE OF THE GOSPEL OF JOHN 356
    D. OTHER LITERATURE ON THE GOSPEL OF JOHN 362
    E. OTHER BOOKS AND ARTICLES CONSULTED 364

INDEX OF AUTHORS 367

PRESENTATION

The Christocentric orientation of the Fourth Gospel, which is explicitly affirmed by the Evangelist himself, evidently deserves to be studied from diverse points of view. The present study proposes the view-point of literary structure. A work of this type will surely stimulate lively interest and undoubtedly much discussion as well.

It goes without saying that the exegetes are far from unanimous in their attitude towards research on literary structure. While some of them attribute great importance to it, others look at it with suspicion or become quite provoked. It is true that excesses have been committed which risk compromising the entire method. In this case, as in many others, wisdom suggests that one avoid unreasonable generalizations. The study of the literary structure is not a master key which would permit one to open all the doors and resolve all the exegetical problems. Nor is the method justified in examining any text whatsoever. Among living organisms one can distinguish the vertebrates from the invertebrates; in an analogous manner, there are structured texts and those devoid of organic structure. Certain authors apply their concern for composition to each detail, while others tolerate all the negligences which arise from improvisation. In the latter case one loses time searching for a structure which might facilitate the interpretation of the text.

In what category should the Fourth Gospel be placed? Only one who lacks all literary sense would include it in the group of texts which are improvised. Its meditative style, on the contrary, attests to its slow and painstaking elaboration. The trained reader would recognize at every moment the procedures of composition which are characteristic of the Biblical tradition. Therefore, a thorough study of its literary structure promises to be fruitful and in particular provide new insights into Johannine Christology. In effect, if the author of the Gospel has not been inconsistent in carrying out his project, the Christocentric orientation which he intended to give his work would appear in the structure itself. For this reason the subject of the present study is fully justified.

Yet that a certain research is well founded does not mean that it is easy. In the field of Johannine studies the bibliography to be affronted is at present immense, and this fact obliges the scholar to choose wisely from the multitude of opinions. Fr. George Mlakuzhyil was not sparing in his efforts. In his book one finds an extremely comprehensive treatment of the state of the question which is presented in a clear, orderly and sober fashion.

Most of all, however, one will discover the fruits of an intense personal research which avoids the most frequent defect of studies on structure, namely, the insufficiency of the criteria. The greatest merit of the present work in my opinion is precisely that of having had recourse to multiple types of indices with a view to discerning and establishing the structure. Quite often, in order to confirm their intuitions, scholars content themselves with one or other series of indices. Consequently their conclusions remain problematic due to an insufficient convergence of proofs. In contrast, the spectrum of criteria proposed in this work is considerably extensive. The spectrum divides itself into three categories: literary indices, dramatic techniques and structural schemes. To my knowledge, no study of structure has ever assembled such a large variety of criteria. It follows that the conclusions reached often attain a very high degree of probability, bordering on certainty.

One of the most interesting and convincing discoveries is that of "bridge-passages" which belong at once to two successive literary units and form the conclusion of the first and the introduction of the second. The recurrence of this technique, which was recommended by ancient authors, permits one to resolve many problems of composition which otherwise would remain inextricable. As a result of this discovery, the lively flexibility of the structure of the Johannine narrative is considerably enhanced and its dynamism unveiled.

At the same time, the literary structure reveals itself to be rich in Christological significance. In effect, the study of the structure permits one to assert that the intention of the Evangelist, explicitly expressed at the close of his book, has truly guided its composition from beginning to end: to arouse and nourish faith in Jesus who is "the Christ, the Son of God" and the giver of life. From one section to the other a powerful progression becomes evident in unfolding the revelation of Jesus Christ.

Because of the important results which it exposes as well as the discussions which it will generate, the present study will certainly contribute greatly to allowing the literary merits and the inexhaustible spiritual riches of the Johannine Gospel to be ever more appreciated.

Rome, May 30, 1987

Albert Vanhoye S.J.
Rector of the Pontifical
Biblical Institute

PREFACE

This is a doctoral dissertation defended in the Pontifical Gregorian University on 29th January 1987.

Adapting the comment of St. Gregory the Great on the nature of the Sacred Scriptures in general to that of the Gospel of John, the latter may be likened to a lake in which a child can wade and an elephant can swim. If one looks at the waves of Johannine literature in the last few decades, one has the sensation of standing before the surging sea. Diving into the sea in such a situation can be adventurous but also dangerous. But if one is watched over by a professional diver and surrounded by caring friends, the danger recedes and the adventure becomes thrilling. At the end of it all, one turns to the teacher and companions to express one's gratitude for their guidance and support.

I am deeply grateful to Fr. Albert Vanhoye S.J., the Rector of the Pontifical Biblical Institute, for his wise and patient direction and painstaking corrections of my research. Without his invaluable help and insightful suggestions this dissertation would never have come to a happy conclusion.

I also extend my heartfelt gratitude to all my friends and benefactors in Europe, U.S.A. and India (especially Frs. Gerald O'Collins S.J., Philip Rosato S.J., Giorgio Szaszkiewicz S.J., Arij Roest Crollius S.J., Theodor Mulder S.J., M. Francesconi S.J., Eugen Hillengass S.J., Ludwig Wiedenmann S.J., Josef Übelmesser S.J., John Beez S.J., Fr. Abraham Puthumana S.J., Michael Amalados S.J., Noel D'Souza S.J., Patrick Meagher S.J., Fiorello Mascarenhas S.J., Joseph Kallarangatt S.J., Br. Michael Thannivelil S.J., Mgr. H. Michel, Fr. Georg Biesenbach, Srs. Julia Joseph and Elizabeth Michael, Mr. and Mrs. Gaetano Toccafondi, Mr. and Mrs. Marcello Brizi) who have been of great help to me in various ways.

I am grately indebted to my Superiors (particularly the Provincials of Patna Frs. Zacharias Varikamakil S.J., Joseph Knecht S.J., Abraham Puthumana S.J., and John D'Mello S.J.) for their loving care, constant concern, generous support and unfailing encouragement.

My sincere thanks are due to Fr. Luis Alonso Schökel S.J. for accepting this study for publication in the Analecta Biblica series and to Fr. Pasquale Puca S.J. and the employees (especially Mr. Antonio Caporossi) in the Tipografia Poliglotta Gregoriana for printing it well.

Finally, I must thank in a very special way Rev. Fr. Peter-Hans Kolvenbach S.J., the General of the Society of Jesus, the Jesuit Mission Procurators in Nürnberg and Rome, BEA-Stiftung in Munich, the Institute of Missiology in Aachen, the parishes of St. Bernard and Christ the King and the archdiocese of Cologne for their generous financial assistance without which this book would not have seen the light of day.

May 31, 1987

George Mlakuzhyil S.J.
Vidyajyoti, Delhi, India

INTRODUCTION

The literary structure of a number of Biblical books has been detected in the past few decades. These studies have greatly helped the exegesis and the discovery of the theology of the books in question [1]. Although many attempts have been made to establish the structure of the Gospel of John, none so far seems to have succeeded satisfactorily, and the wide variety of the structures proposed is an indication of the differences that divide Johannine scholars. On the other hand, many scholars stress the significance of the structure of the Fourth Gospel for Johannine exegesis. For example, D. M. Smith affirms: "The exegesis of any text must take account of its position and role in the document of which it is a part. Thus our exegesis of Johannine texts must keep *the structure of the Fourth Gospel* in view" [2]. This is equally true with regard to the study of any theological theme in the Gospel of John. In the words of J. Giblet: "Poursuivre l'analyse d'un thème littéraire sans se soucier des particularités et de *la structure de l'évangile johannique*, c'est se condamner à l'échec" [3]. Now one of the peculiarities of the Fourth Gospel is its *Christocentrism*. In fact, the Fourth Evangelist has composed his Gospel for a Christocentric purpose as is explicitly stated in his conclusion: "Now Jesus did many other signs before his disciples which are not written in this book; these are written that you may believe that Jesus is the Christ, the Son of God, and that believing you may have life in his name" (20,30-31). It would be enlightening, therefore, to examine how he has achieved his purpose by structuring his select material into an organic whole.

The *scope* of the dissertation is, as the title itself indicates, primarily to discover and describe *the literary structure of the Fourth Gospel* and secondarily to delineate *the Christocentric theology* of the Gospel in the light of its literary structure. By "literary structure" of the Fourth Gospel we mean "the system of relations obtained thanks to diverse stylistic devices [and dramatic techniques] and to the disposition of the parts" [4]. We do not intend to do a "structuralist

---

[1] E.g. A. VANHOYE, *La Structure Littéraire de l'Épitre aux Hébreux* (Paris 1963), 2 ed. (Paris 1976); U. VANNI, *La Struttura Letteraria dell' Apocalisse* (Brescia 1970), 2 ed. (Brescia 1980).

[2] SMITH, 11 [my italics].

N.B. Every *Commentary* on *the Gospel of John* will be referred to (even the first time) only by the SURNAME of the COMMENTATOR, the Volume Number (if more than one), and the page number (e.g. BROWN, I, 235) (cf. "BIBLIOGRAPHY B: COMMENTARIES ON THE GOSPEL OF JOHN" for full bibliographical details).

[3] J. GIBLET, "Jésus et 'le Père' dans le IVe Évangile", in: *L'Évangile de Jean* (Paris 1958) 111 [my italics].

[4] A. VANHOYE, *Struttura e Teologia nell'Epistola agli Ebrei* (Roma: PIB 1983) 7. Since the dramatic development of the Fourth Gospel forms part of its "literary design", we include also "dramatic techniques" in the description of its "literary structure" (Cf. R. A. CULPEPPER, *Anatomy of the Fourth Gospel. A Study in Literary Design* [Philadelphia 1983]).

analysis" of the Fourth Gospel. Our scope is only to establish its dramatic-literary "surface structure". Nor do we pretend to develop in detail the whole of Johannine theology but only sketch the theology of the Johannine Gospel based on its literary structure.

Before we can begin the investigation of the literary structure of the Fourth Gospel, we have to face the problem of its literary unity, because, if it has no literary unity, it can have no literary structure. In fact, some scholars either doubt or deny the literary unity of the Johannine Gospel because of interruptions and inconsistencies in sequence, repetitions and/or passages out of context, and differences in Greek style and vocabulary. Therefore in the *first chapter* we shall briefly examine these *difficulties* and the different *solutions* that have been proposed, namely, theories of accidental displacements, multiple sources, and multiple editions/redactions.

In the *second chapter* we shall make a critical *survey of the structures* that have been proposed for the Fourth Gospel. We shall do this not in the chronological order (since this has already been done by others) but according to the types of literary criteria used by the various scholars. We shall expose briefly and evaluate about two dozen kinds of literary structures such as: geographical-chronological, chronological-liturgical, liturgical-symbolical-sign, literary-chronological, numerical-symbolical, typological, typological-symbolical-theological, liturgical-symbolical-typological, chiastic, chiastic-symbolical, symmetrical, centric-symmetrical, narrative, narrative-discourse, dramatic-chronological-geographical, dramatic-episodic, revelatory, revelatory-dramatic, revelatory-response, revelatory-narrative, revelatory-eclectic, and literary-thematic.

Since the convergence of diverse kinds of criteria can be a greater guarantee of objectivity in establishing the literary structure than the dependence on a single norm or a couple of criteria, we shall examine in the *third chapter* the numerous and various types of *criteria* found in the Fourth Gospel. We classify them under three categories: 1) *literary criteria* (e.g. introductions, inclusions, conclusions, transitions, characteristic vocabulary, chronological and geographical indications, liturgical feasts, bridge-passages, hook-words, techniques of repetition, change of literary genre such as narrative, dialogue, discourse), 2) *dramatic techniques* (e.g. change of dramatis personae or scenes, techniques of alternating scenes or seven scenes or diptych-scenes or double-stage action or vanishing characters, or law of stage-duality, sequence of action-dialogue-discourse, dramatic development of the plot, dramatic pattern), and 3) *structural patterns* (e.g. parallelism, chiasmus, concentric structure, spiral structure). Though all of these criteria may not be equally important or applicable to every part of the Fourth Gospel, a combination of these norms will enable us to detect the structure of the Gospel as a whole and of its various parts with greater objectivity and certainty than if we were to depend on only one or other of the norms.

Basing ourselves on the above-mentioned criteria we shall establish in the *fourth chapter the literary structure of the Gospel of John*. This we shall do in three stages. First we shall examine the main division of the Johannine Gospel; we shall see that it consists of two closely linked principal parts preceded by an introduction and followed by a conclusion and an appendix. Next we shall show that the two major parts or books are constituted of three sections each in such a way that the third section of the first book is the same as the first section of the second book, that is, the central section functions as a bridge between the two books. Then we shall subdivide the above sections (and the introduction) into their component subsections and demonstrate that the first, second, fourth and fifth sections are composed of six subsections each and the latter are chiastically constructed, while the bridge-section consists of two parallel subsections.

Finally, in the *fifth chapter* we shall study the relation between *the literary structure and the Christocentric theology* of the Fourth Gospel. First we shall examine the development of the major theological themes such as "the Christ", "the Son of God", ("the Son", "the Father", "the Son of Man"), "signs" (and "works"), "faith", "life" and the "disciples" mentioned in the conclusion of the Gospel (20,30-31) and then we shall sketch the Johannine Christocentric theology based on the literary structure of the Gospel.

1
DIFFICULTIES AGAINST THE LITERARY UNITY AND STRUCTURE OF THE FOURTH GOSPEL

The literary structure of a book presupposes its literary unity. Now there are some scholars who deny the literary unity of the Johannine Gospel [1]. If this were true, any attempt at detecting its literary structure would be a futile exercise, since it would be based on a wrong presupposition. Therefore it is necessary first to face the objections of those critics who call into question the literary integrity and unity of the Fourth Gospel, before we can establish its literary structure. Hence the need for this introductory chapter.

We will not, however, discuss in detail all the different difficulties raised against the literary unity (and therefore against the literary structure) of the Gospel of John [2]. We will examine only the major problems and their proposed solutions in so far as they are related to our dissertation on the literary structure of the Fourth Gospel.

1.1 MAIN PROBLEMS

The principal problems connected with the literary unity of the Fourth Gospel may be broadly classified under three headings: 1) interruptions and inconsistencies in sequence, 2) repetitions and/or passages out of context, and 3) differences in Greek vocabulary and style [3].

1.11 Interruptions and Inconsistencies in Sequence [4]

The main "interruptions and inconsistencies in sequence" in the Fourth Gospel are the following:

---

[1] See the authors mentioned in n. 3 below.

[2] The objection that it is impossible to detect the literary structure of the Gospel of John because of the diversity of the numerous structures that have been proposed by various Johannine scholars will be dealt with only in the next chapter.

[3] BROWN, I, xxiv-xxv; BULTMANN, 10; SCHNACKENBURG, I, 44-48; E. SCHWARTZ, "Aporien im vierten Evangelium", *Nachrichten von der königlichen Gesellschaft der Wissenschaften zu Göttingen* (Berlin 1907) 342-72; (1908) 115-88; 497-560; H. M. TEEPLE, *The Literary Origin of the Gospel of John* (Evanston 1974) 1-5; WIKENHAUSER, 50-51. Cf. also BERNARD, I, xvi-xxviii.

[4] We prescind from the pericope on the adulteress (7,53-8,11) which is universally accepted as non-Johannine by textual critics (cf. TCGNT, 219-22). Similarly, Jn 5,3b-4 is established by textual criticism as a later interpolation (cf. TCGNT, 209).

1) Jn 1,6-8 and 1,15 which speak about John the Baptist as a witness to Jesus seem to interrupt the flow of the Prologue (1,1-18), especially since 1,9 seems to continue the theme of 1,4-5, namely, that of the Logos as the light of men, and since 1,16-17 takes up again the themes of "fulness", "grace" and "truth" mentioned in 1,14 [5].

2) The changing of water into wine at Cana (2,1-11) is called the *archê tôn sêmeiôn* of Jesus (2,11) and in 2,23 he is said to have done other signs in Jerusalem; and yet the healing of the royal official's son in 4,46-54 is described as the "second sign" (4,54) [6].

3) In 3,22 and 4,1 we are told that Jesus was baptizing; this is, however, denied in 4,2: "Jesus himself did not baptize, but only his disciples" [7].

4) Jn 3,31-36 appears to be a continuation of the discourse in 3,1-21, since Jesus seems to be the speaker in both the texts and since there are many common elements in their content (e.g. the refusal to accept the testimony of the one who has seen: vv.11 and 32; speaking about earthly things: vv.12 and 31; believing in the Son of God and having eternal life: vv.16 and 36; the sending of the Son: vv.17 and 34) [8]. Therefore 3,22-30, which is mostly a dialogue between John the Baptist and his disciples, seems to be an insertion that interrupts Jesus' discourse consisting of 3,1-21 and 3,31-36 [9].

5) In chapter 5 Jesus is in Jerusalem; and yet at the beginning of chapter 6 we are told: "After this Jesus went to the other side of the Sea of Galilee" (6,1), as if he had been on the opposite shore. Again, even though chapter 6 has been describing Jesus' ministry in Galilee, chapter 7 opens with the observation: "After this Jesus went about in Galilee; he would not go about in Judea, because the Jews sought to kill him". No attempt to kill Jesus has been reported in Jn 6, though it was mentioned in 5,18 [10].

6) In 7,23 Jesus asks the Jews at the feast of Tabernacles if they are angry with him for his having healed a paralytic on the Sabbath during an earlier unnamed feast, which is a reference to 5,1-18. Furthermore, 7,15-24 seems to continue the teaching of 5,41-47. Hence 6,1-7,14 apparently interrupts the discourse consisting of 5,17-47 and 7,15-24 [11].

7) In 13,36 Peter asks Jesus: "Lord, where are you going?" and yet in 16,5 Jesus tells the disciples that none of them asks him: "Where are you going?"

---

[5] H. M. TEEPLE, *op. cit.*, 1; SCHNACKENBURG, I, 48.
[6] W. NICOL, *The Sêmeia in the Fourth Gospel* (Leiden 1972) 28; BROWN, I, xxiv.
[7] H. M. TEEPLE, *op. cit.*, 2.
[8] BROWN, I, 159-60.
[9] BERNARD, I, xxiii; SCHNACKENBURG, I, 47; WIKENHAUSER, 50.
[10] BERNARD, I, xvii; SCHNACKENBURG, I, 46.
[11] SCHNACKENBURG, I, 46-47.

1.1 MAIN PROBLEMS

8) At the end of chapter 14 Jesus tells the disciples: "Rise, let us go hence" (14,31), but the actual departure from the Last Supper room is reported only in 18,1, that is, after the long discourses in Jn 15-16 and the prayer in Jn 17 [12].

9) In 20,30-31 we have clearly the conclusion to the Gospel; yet this is followed by chapter 21 [13].

1.12 Repetitions and/or Passages out of Context

Some passages in the Gospel of John are said to be repetitions and/or out of context. For example:

1) What is said in 5,19-27 about realized eschatology appears to be repeated with slight variations in 5,28-30 about future eschatology [14].

2) The discourse on the bread of life in 6,35-50 seems to be duplicated in the Eucharistic discourse in 6,51-58 [15].

3) There seem to be two farewell discourses in 13,31-14,31 and 15,1-16,33, the second of which repeats many of the themes of the first (e.g. compare 13,33 and 16,16-17: Jesus' going away for a little while; 13,34 and 15,12: the commandment of love; 14,13-14 and 16,23-24: prayer in the name of Jesus; 14,15 and 15,10: loving Jesus and keeping his commandments; 14,16-17,26 and 15,26; 16,13-15: the Paraclete, the Spirit of truth) [16].

4) The parable of the shepherd and the sheep (10,1-18) in its present position after ch. 9 seems to be out of its original context, since it begins without a proper introduction and since the theme of the sheep and the shepherd is repeated in 10,26-29. Furthermore, 10,19-21 which refers back to the cure of the blind man (10,21) appears to be a fitting conclusion to ch. 9 rather than to 10,1-18 [17].

5) Similarly, Jesus' discourse in 12,44-50 apparently without a specific audience seems to be out of context, since it comes immediately after the Evangelist's reflection on the unbelief of the Jews in spite of Jesus' many signs, which may be considered as the conclusion to the first part of the Fourth Gospel [18].

1.13 Differences in Greek Vocabulary and Style

Differences in Greek style and vocabulary are noted in some texts of the Fourth Gospel. For instance:

---

[12] *Ibid.*, 46; BROWN, I, xxiv.
[13] H. M. TEEPLE, *op. cit.*, 4-5.
[14] BROWN, I, xxv.
[15] *Ibid.*
[16] *Ibid.*; cf. also 589-91.
[17] WIKENHAUSER, 50.
[18] *Ibid.*, 50-51.

1) In the Prologue Jesus is called "the Word" (*ho logos*) (1,1.14), whereas such a designation is never again found in the rest of the Fourth Gospel. Similarly the terms "fulness" (*plêroma*) and "grace" (*charis*) (1,14.16.17) never occur outside the Prologue [19].

2) According to Boismard, Jn 12,44-50 contains some peculiar Greek vocabulary and style. For example, *akouein tôn rhêmatôn* is used in 12,47 instead of *akouein ton logon* or *akouein tês phônês*, which occur thrice and 7 times respectively in the Fourth Gospel. Similarly in 12,47 *phylassein* is employed instead of the usual *têrein*, which is used by the Evangelist 11 times to refer to "keeping the commandments" or to "keeping the words". Furthermore, the verb *athetein* in 12,48 is found nowhere else in the Fourth Gospel. Besides, *ex emautou* is employed only in 12,49 instead of the common *ap' emautou* (found 13 times in Jn). Finally, the personal pronoun *autos* is utilized in the *casus pendens* in 12,49 instead of the usual *ekeinos* [20].

3) Some differences in Greek style and vocabulary exist also in the case of Jn 21:

> Features that noticeably do not match the style of the Johannine Gospel include: the mention of the sons of Zebedee in 2; the preposition *syn*, "with," in 3; the word for "daybreak" [*prôïa*] in 4; the causative *apo* and the verb *ischyein*, "to be able," in 6; the partitive *apo* in 10; the verb *epistrephein*, "to turn," in 20 [21].

1.2 PROPOSED SOLUTIONS

The above difficulties have led many Johannine scholars to seek a solution by proposing theories of 1) accidental displacements, 2) multiple sources, and 3) multiple editions/redactions.

1.21 Theories of Accidental Displacements [22]

According to these theories it is supposed that "some accident displaced passages and destroyed the original order, thus creating the confusion that we now find in the Gospel" [23]. The amount of rearrangements proposed varies from scholar to scholar. For example, Bernard and Bultmann have large scale

---

[19] H. M. TEEPLE, *op.cit.*, 2-3.
[20] M.-É. BOISMARD, "Le caractère adventice de Jo., XII,44-50", in: *Sacra Pagina*, II, ed. J. Coppens - A. Descamps - É. Massaux, (Paris 1959) 190-92.
[21] BROWN, II, 1080; cf. also 1067-77; M.-É. BOISMARD, "Le chapitre xxi de saint Jean: essai de critique littéraire", *RB* 54 (1947) 473-501.
[22] BROWN, I, xxvi-xxviii; BARRETT, 21-24; SCHNACKENBURG, I, 44-48; H. M. TEEPLE, *op. cit.*, 106-16; H. THYEN, "Aus der Literatur zum Johannesevangelium", *TRu* 40 (1975) 296-307.
[23] BROWN, I, xxvi. In the words of H. M. TEEPLE: "The fundamental idea in these theories is that the incongruities and poor connections are largely the result of later incorrect arrangement of the writing, so it is necessary to restore the original order before the gospel can be properly understood" (*op. cit.*, 106).

rearrangements in their commentaries [24], while Wikenhauser and Schnackenburg admit some dislocations [25].

Though rearrangement may seem to solve some of the problems mentioned above, it often creates others [26]. For instance, if the order of chapters 5 and 6 is inverted, the apparent geographical inconsistency of 6,1 and 7,1 disappears, but it destroys the succession of bread-water symbolism in Jn 6 and Jn 7. In the words of R. E. Brown: "Geographically ch. vi does go better before v, but the evangelist might have intended the bread theme of vi to be followed immediately by the water theme in vii (37-38) in order to echo the story of the Exodus where God gave Israel bread from heaven and water from the rock" [27].

Rearranging the text always involves the danger of imposing one's own interests on the Gospel, which may be quite different from those of the Evangelist [28]. This danger is amply demonstrated by the differences in the displacements as proposed by the advocates of rearrangements. Furthermore, the presupposition behind all the displacement theories, namely, the Gospel as it now stands does not make sense, cannot be accepted, since it made sense to the one who published it [29]. In fact, later on we shall show that many of the apparent repetitions and seeming inconsistencies underlined by the advocates of displacement theories have a function in the plan of the Fourth Gospel [30].

1.22 Theories of Multiple Sources [31]

Some of the breaks in the sequence, repetitions and stylistic differences noted above (cf. 1.1) are accounted for by source critics who postulate the use of

---

[24] BERNARD, I, xvi-xxviii; BULTMANN, vii-xi.

[25] WIKENHAUSER, 50-51; SCHNACKENBURG, I, 46-48. Cf. also H. M. TEEPLE, *op. cit.*, 106-12 for a history of the theories of displacements starting from F. SPITTA in 1893 up to H. EDWARDS in 1953.

[26] BARRETT makes the following valid observation: "While the proposed alterations generally improve some connections, they often worsen others" (24).

[27] BROWN, I, xxvi-xxvii.

[28] BROWN remarks: "If one indulges in extensive rearrangement, one may be commenting on a hybrid that never existed before it emerged as the brain child of the rearranger" (xxvii). BULTMANN's commentary on the Gospel of John with its numerous rearrangements examplifies the danger of such subjectivism.

[29] BARRETT, 22. After examining the various displacement theories in the history of Johannine studies H. M. TEEPLE concludes: "The arguments against the displacement theories are so strong that most New Testament scholars today rightly reject them" (*op. cit.*, 116).

[30] See ch. 3 and ch. 4 below.

[31] Cf. H. M. TEEPLE, *op. cit.*, for a survey of the source theories of the past two centuries. Some of the more recent and prominent ones are those of BULTMANN, *Das Evangelium des Johannes* (Göttingen 1937); A. Q. MORTON & G. H. C. MACGREGOR, *The Structure of the Fourth Gospel* (London 1961); SCHNACKENBURG, I, 64-68; J. BECKER, "Wunder und Christologie", *NTS* 16 (1969-70) 130-48; R. T. FORTNA, *The Gospel of Signs* (Cambridge 1970); W. NICOL, *op. cit.*; H. M. TEEPLE, *op. cit.* See an excellent evaluation of the last five source theories by R. KYSAR, *The Fourth Evangelist and His Gospel* (Minnesota 1975) 13-37.

written sources by the Evangelist [32]. This is, however, questioned by other Johannine scholars [33]. The source critics themselves are not agreed either about the number and relative importance of the criteria to be used for the detection of the sources or about the number and content of the sources [34]. With regard to the Signs Source, however, a consensus seems to be emerging among the source critics [35].

If this is true, the source critics have still to explain how an intelligent Evangelist could have left the glaring aporias in the final text of the Gospel. R. Kysar asks:

> How can one believe, on the one hand, that the evangelist was an astute enough theologian to sense the weakness of his signs gospel and subtly correct them and yet, on the other hand, was such an inferior editor that he left such glaring flaws in the simple readability of his document? Until that contradiction can be resolved, it seems that the value of the contextual criteria will be seriously impaired [36].

---

[32] BROWN, I,xxviii; see the source critics mentioned in n. 31.

[33] Cf. D. M. SMITH, *The Composition and Order of the Fourth Gospel* (New Haven 1965) for a full-scale criticism of Bultmann's theory of multiple sources (Sêmeia-Quelle, Revelatory Discourse Source, Passion-Resurrection Narrative). For a critical evaluation of the more recent source theories see C. K. BARRETT, "John and the Synoptic Gospels", *ET* 85 (1973-74) 228-33; O. CULLMANN, *The Johannine Circle* (Philadelphia 1976); B. LINDARS, *Behind the Fourth Gospel* (London 1971); F. NEIRYNCK, "John and the Synoptics", in: M. de Jonge (ed.), *L'Évangile de Jean* (Leuven 1977) 73-106; E. RUCKSTUHL, "Johannine Language and Style. The Question of Their Unity", in: M. de Jonge (ed.), *op. cit.*, 125-48. The source theories based on difference in style in the Fourth Gospel were strongly attacked by E. SCHWEIZER, *Ego Eimi. Die religionsgeschichtliche Herkunft und theologiche Bedeutung der joh. Bildreden, zugleich ein Beitrag zur Quellenfrage des vierten Evangeliums* (Göttingen 1939). J. JEREMIAS, "Joh. Literarkritik", *ThB* 20 (1941) 33-46; P.-H. MENOUD, *L'Évangile de Jean d'après les recherches récentes*, 2 ed. (Paris 1947); E. RUCKSTUHL, *Die literarische Einheit des Johannesevangeliums* (Freiburg 1951).

[34] After examining the different norms (aporias, style, form, ideological tensions) employed by the different source critics (Fortna, Nicol, Teeple, Becker, Schnackenburg), R. KYSAR concludes: "While one would not want to press these differences too far, it would seem fair to conclude that the method of source criticism of the fourth gospel is somewhat in shambles" (*op. cit.*, 24). Cf. also B. LINDARS *op. cit.*, 54; E. RUCKSTUHL, *art. cit.*, 125-47.

[35] Cf. R. KYSAR, "The Source Analysis of the Fourth Gospel. A Growing Consensus?" *NovTest* 15 (1973) 134-52. The seven miracles in the Gospel of John (2,1-11; 4,46-54; 5,1-9; 6,1-15; 6,16-21; 9,1-7; 11,1-44) form the common ground for the source critics like Becker, Fortna, Nicol, Schnackenburg and Teeple, though they do not agree among themselves which verses of these narratives belong to the Signs Source (cf. R. KYSAR, *op. cit.*, 25-29 and especially the table on pp. 26-27). E. RUCKSTUHL, however, is critical of this consensus of the source critics concerning the Signs Source, for he says:

> I cannot deny the possibility of a Sêmeia-Quelle if I hold that our evangelist most likely drew on oral and written traditions. Nevertheless I am not sure that there ever existed a Sêmeia-Quelle which would have related just seven miracles. Am I wrong in guessing that we shall never know exactly what were the sources which our evangelist drew upon and how he drew upon them? (*art. cit.*, 146).

Likewise BARRETT is skeptical of a Signs Source: "It must be plainly said that there is nothing at all incredible in the suggestion that there was available to John a source containing a sequence of miracle stories described as signs... It may have been so; but I see no evidence that proves, or indeed could prove, that it was so..." (19).

[36] R. KYSAR, *op. cit.*, 36.

Even if the Evangelist used some sources, he has reworked them so much that a scissor-and-paste method cannot be applied to the Fourth Gospel to recapture the original sources, because "the creative composition places the precise underlying traditions beyond recovery"[37].

At this point it may be worth noting that at least some of the aporias may be the creations of the critics themselves. For instance, the enumeration of the two Cana signs, which is claimed to be the ace in the hands of the source critics, is regarded by them as a real aporia[38]. But let us examine the texts to see if this is true. First of all, John does not call the changing of water into wine "the first sign" (*prôton sêmeion*) but the "beginning of the signs" (*archê tôn sêmeiôn*) (2,11). Secondly, in chapters 2-4 John does not describe but only mentions in passing "the signs" that Jesus did in Jerusalem (2,23; 4,45; cf. also 3,2). Thirdly, the healing of the royal official's son is not simply called "the second sign", but is qualified as follows: *touto [de] palin deuteron sêmeion epoiêsen ho Iêsous elthôn ek tês Ioudaias eis tên Galilaian* (4,54), which may be translated as: "[Now] this second sign again Jesus did when he came from Judea into Galilee". It does not mean, as the source critics claim, that this was the second sign that Jesus ever performed (which would contradict 2,23; 3,2 and 4,45), but that this second sign too, like the first, was done on Jesus' return from Judea into Galilee. Jesus' coming "from Judea into Galilee" is underlined already at the beginning of the pericope (4,47). One may object that the first Cana sign was not explicitly stated by the Evangelist to have been done by Jesus on his return from Judea. But this seems to be implied in 1,43 and 2,1.11[39]. If the above interpretation is accepted, the apparent aporia at 4,54 disappears and there is no need of appealing to a hypothetical Signs Source to solve the problem[40].

1.23 Theories of Multiple Editions/Redactions

According to these theories, the difficulties described in 1.1 above are the result of many editions by the Evangelist[41] and/or revision by one or more

---

[37] B. LINDARS, *op. cit.*, 54.

[38] E.g. BULTMANN, 113; R. T. FORTNA, *op. cit.*, 19-20; W. NICOL, *op. cit.*, 28.

[39] It is true that in 1,35-51 we are not told where Jesus' dwelling-place was (cf. 1,39), from where he decided to go to Galilee (1,43), even though the first two disciples began to follow him (1,35-38) probably from Bethany beyond the Jordan where John was baptizing (1,28). That Judea is Jesus' *patris* is hinted at 4,44 and he is twice reported as staying in Judea (3,22; 4,3). Judea is Jesus' *patris* also in a spiritual sense, since the temple, his Father's house (2,16), is in the Judean capital, Jerusalem. This is confirmed by the fact that most of Jesus' ministry, according to John, takes place in and around Jerusalem (2,13-4,3; 5,1-47; 7,14-12,50).

[40] Cf. F. NEIRYNCK *Jean et les Synoptiques*, 173-74.

[41] Some scholars like BROWN, WILKENS, LINDARS, BOISMARD, have proposed "developmental theories of composition" according to which a gradual process of composition is postulated (Cf. R. KYSAR, *op. cit.*, 38-54, for a good critical evaluation of the first three scholars mentioned above). The questions KYSAR has asked them are quite pertinent:

Finally, one is still left with the Johannine literary puzzle, even after the advancement of these three process theories of composition: Why does the gospel in its final stage still present its

redactors[42]. For instance, 1,6-8 and 1,15 (about John the Baptist) in the Prologue are attributed to a redactor[43]. Some of the other problem-passages ascribed to a redactor(s) are: the discourse in 3,31-36[44]; the parenthetical comment about Jesus' not baptizing in 4,2[45]; the future-eschatological verses in 5,28-29; 6,39.40.44.54[46]; the Eucharistic discourse in 6,51c-58[47]; the inversion of chs. 5 and 6[48]; the summary-discourse in 12,44-50[49]; the so-called second farewell discourse and priestly prayer in chs. 15-17[50]; and ch. 21[51].

---

reader with incongruities, intrusions, and breaks in the narrative?... why after the long process of editing did the gospel not emerge as a polished work? (*ibid.*, 54).

For a thorough criticism of Boismard's theory of composition in stages ("Document C, Jean II-A, Jean II-B, Jean III") cf. F. NEIRYNCK, *op. cit.*, 66-283.

We cannot be certain whether the Evangelist produced different editions of his Gospel or not, since we do not have any manuscript evidence. Even if he did, it does not necessarily create a real difficulty against the structure of the Gospel, since we are concerned about the structure of the final edition as we have it today.

[42] Cf. H. M. TEEPLE, *op. cit.*, 84-105, for an excellent survey of various redaction theories during the last one and a half centuries (from 1839 up to 1970).

[43] E. HAENCHEN, "Probleme des johanneischen 'Prologs'", *ZTK* 60 (1963) 305-34. According to him the Evangelist could not have written vv.6-8, because here John the Baptist is spoken of as (1) a "witness", (2) "sent from God", (3) in order "that all might believe through him", while in the rest of the Fourth Gospel the Baptist is not described as a witness (5,34), nor do "all" believe through his testimony, and only Jesus is said to be sent from God. But one who examines the Gospel carefully will find that John the Baptist is repeatedly presented as bearing witness to Jesus (1,19.26-27. 29-31.32-34.35-37; 3,26-30; 5,33.36; 10,41) and his testimony helps many to believe in Jesus (cf. 10,41-42; 1,35-42). It is also not true that only Jesus is described in the Fourth Gospel as sent from God, for the Holy Spirit is spoken of as sent by the Father (14,26). Furthermore, *apestalmenos para theou* (without the article) at 1,6 may refer to the Baptist's mission from the Word, since the latter is called *theos* (without the article) at 1,1 (cf. also *monogenês theos* at 1,18), whereas the Father is normally called *ho theos* (1,1.2).

[44] BROWN, I, 160.

[45] H. J. FLOWERS, "Interpolations in the Fourth Gospel", *JBL* 40 (1921) 146-58. According to him 2,21-22; 4,2; 5,28-29; 6,39.40.44.54; 7,39; 12,33; 18,9; 19,35 and 21,1-25 are all interpolations by the redactor.

[46] *Ibid.*; WELLHAUSEN, 71; SPITTA, 151; BULTMANN, 219-20; SCHNACKENBURG, II, 48.

[47] E. LOHSE, "Wort und Sakrament im Johannesevangelium", *NTS* 7 (1960-61) 110-25. Cf. SCHNACKENBURG, II, 56-59 for arguments for and against the theory of redactional addition of 6,51c-58.

[48] Cf. H. THYEN, "Aus der Literatur zum Johannesevangelium", *TRu* 43 (1978) 329-36, for a survey of the theories of accidental displacement and of redactional inversion of Jn 5 and 6, where he discusses the positions of R. BULTMANN, H. STRATHMANN, S. SCHULZ, R. SCHNACKENBURG, W. WILKENS, B. LINDARS, J. WELLHAUSEN, P. PARKER, C. H. DODD, D. H. SMITH, W. LANGBRANDTNER. Cf.also M.-É. BOISMARD and A. LAMOUILLE, *Synopse des Quatre Évangiles*, Tome III, *L'Évangile de Jean* (Paris 1977) 44.

[49] E. SCHWARTZ, "Aporien im vierten Evangelium", *Nachrichten* (Berlin 1907) 324-72; (Berlin 1908) 115-88; 497-560 [as reported by H. M. TEEPLE, *op. cit.*, 86]; M.-É. BOISMARD *art. cit.*, in: *Sacra Pagina*, II, 192.

[50] J. WELLHAUSEN, *Erweiterungen und Änderungen im vierten Evangelium* (Berlin 1907); BROWN, II, 594.

[51] *Ibid.*, II, 1077-82.

The presence of Jn 21 (which contains a number of stylistic variations) after the conclusion to the Gospel (20,30-31) clearly points to the probability, if not the certainty, of a redactor who added this chapter to the original Gospel [52].

It is possible that the redactor(s) added 12,44-50 and some glosses like 4,2, which contain some stylistic differences [53]. But when such differences in style cannot be established for certain, we do not think it right to attribute to a later redactor, as is done by some scholars [54], passages which appear to be repetitions (e.g. 3,31-36) [55] or which seem to mention a different theological point of view (e.g. the future eschatology in 5,28-29) [56].

1z. Since there is no manuscript evidence for the accidental displacement theories and since the dislocations create more problems than they solve, we do not accept displacements in the Johannine Gospel. Besides, many of the aporias in the Fourth Gospel are only apparent or are creations of the critics themselves (e.g. 1,43 and 1,51) [57]. Whether or not the Fourth Evangelist used sources in composing his Gospel does not affect our dissertation on the literary structure of the Gospel, since what we are interested in is to discover the structure of the end-product of his literary activity, whatever might have been the sources used by him. The differences in the Greek style in 21,1-25; 12,44-50 and 4,2 probably point to the hand of one or more redactors who added those passages, which, however, as we shall see later (in ch. 4), do not disturb the overall structure of the Johannine Gospel. Since there is unity of style and thought in the rest of the Gospel, it is not necessary to relegate other passages to the status of interpolations by later redactors. Hence the problem posed by the literary critics need not detain us from discovering the literary structure of the Fourth Gospel.

---

[52] Cf. H. M. TEEPLE, *op. cit.*, 92-93. This is the view of most of the Johannine scholars today (cf. BROWN, II, 1078, for some of the reasons). Whether Jn 21 was actually composed by the redactor or whether it was a Johannine passage coming from the Evangelist himself, which was added here by the redactor (perhaps with some modifications), or in other words, whether the redactor or the Evangelist was the actual author is still a matter of debate among Johannine experts. The Evangelist's authorship is held by scholars like BERNARD, KRAGERUD, LAGRANGE, PLUMMER, RUCKSTUHL, SCHLATTER, WESTCOTT, WILKENS, while the redactor's authorship is maintained by BARRETT, BROWN, BULTMANN, DIBELIUS, DODD, GOGUEL, KÄSEMANN, KÜMMEL, MICHAELIS, SCHNACKENBURG, STRATHMANN, and WIKENHAUSER (cf. BROWN, II, 1080).

[53] Cf. H. M. TEEPLE, *op. cit.*, 84-105 for the different authors who hold such a view.

[54] E.g. BROWN proposes as redactor's additions not only 12,44-50 and 21,1-25 but also 3,31-36; 6,51-58; 11-12; 15-17.

[55] We shall see below (in ch. 4) that most of such passages have a vital role to play in the carefully constructed structure of the Fourth Gospel (e.g. parallel passages in a chiastic structure), which we prefer to attribute to the Evangelist rather than to a later redactor. Once the literary structure of the Gospel is understood, many of the difficulties mentioned earlier will disappear.

[56] Realized eschatology (5,24-25) and future eschatology (5,28-29) are not contradictory but complementary.

[57] We have explained above the example of the numbering of the Cana-signs (2,11; 4,54). We add below an excursus on the aporias in 1,43 and 1,51 to illustrate how we can find satisfactory solutions to them without appealing to source or redaction theories.

Excursus

1) *The Aporia at Jn 1,43 and Its Solution*

1,43a: Tê[i] epaurion *êthelêsen* exelthein eis tên Galilaian
b: kai *heuriskei* Philippon
c: kai *legei* autô[i] ho *Iêsous*:
d: akolouthei moi.

Here there is a problem of syntax. First of all, it is not quite clear who is the subject of the verbs *êthelêsen* in v.43a and *heuriskei* in v.43b. Secondly, even though the subject is not specified both in v.43a and in v.43b, the subject of the verb *legei* in v.43c is expressly stated to be Jesus, whereas the normal Johannine custom is to mention the subject in the first clause or sentence, especially when a confusion might otherwise arise (e.g. 1,35; 2,13; 3,22; 4,1).

According to some source critics the aporia at 1,43 is the outcome of the Evangelist's having used a source for the composition of the verse [58], while according to some redaction critics it is the result of an interpolation by a later redactor [59].

Now the whole of 1,43 cannot be either from a source or from a later redactor, since the verse begins with a Johannine literary-chronological device (*tê[i] epaurion*) used to structure 1,19-51 (cf. vv.29.35.43), and since v.43c has a typically Johannine construction (*legei* + *autô[i]* + *ho Iêsous*), which occurs 27 times in Jn [60].

Furthermore, without having recourse to a source-theory or an interpolation hypothesis, the difficulty about the mention of "Jesus" only in v.43c (and not in v.43ab) can be explained, since sometimes in Jn the subject of the first sentence of a new subsection or transition is not explicitly given but is expressed in the second sentence in order to emphasize the latter (e.g. 2,23-24; 4,43-44). Thus, 1,43 may be rendered as: "The next day, after having *decided* to go to Galilee and *finding* Philip, Jesus *says* to him: 'Follow me'". This would underline not so much Jesus' decision to go to Galilee nor his finding Philip but his asking the latter to follow him. It is for the sake of this emphasis that "Jesus" is explicitly mentioned in v.43c. Hence there is no need to postulate a source or redaction (interpolation) hypothesis to account for the apparent aporia at 1,43.

---

[58] E.g. S. TEMPLE, *The Core of the Fourth Gospel* (London 1975) 85; H. M. TEEPLE, *op. cit.*, 170; R. T. FORTNA, *op. cit.*, 236; BOISMARD, III, 88.

[59] E.g. H. THYEN, "Entwicklungen innerhalb der johanneischen Theologie und Kirche im Spiegel von Joh. 21 und der Lieblingsjüngertexte des Evangeliums", in: *L'Évangile de Jean*, ed. M. de Jonge, 275; cf. also WELLHAUSEN, 12-13; E. SCHWARTZ, *art. cit.*, (1908) 515.

[60] Cf. BOISMARD, III, 507.

2) *The Aporia at Jn 1,51 and Its Solution*

1,51a: *kai legei autô[i]*:
  b: amên amên legô *hymin*,
  c: *opsesthe* ton ouranon aneô[i]gota kai tous angelous tou theou anabainontas kai katabainontas epi ton hyion tou anthrôpou.

Most Johannine source critics[61] and commentators[62] admit the presence of an aporia at 1,51 for the following reasons: 1) although Jesus has been talking to Nathanael in the immediately preceding v.50, verse 51 begins with *kai legei autô[i]*; 2) even though the *amên amên* saying is addressed to Nathanael (cf. the singular *autô[i]* in v.51a), the plural *hymin* of v.51b and *opsesthe* of v.51c suggest that Jesus has a wider audience in mind; 3) after the *meizô toutôn opsê[i]* of v.50 which could be an indirect reference to the Cana miracle that follows in the next pericope, v.51 with its *opsesthe ton ouranon aneô[i]gota ktl* which, if taken literally, does not seem to be fulfilled in the Fourth Gospel, seems to interrupt the smooth sequence of 1,50 and 2,1-11.

Before proposing a solution to the problem posed by v.51, it must be borne in mind that, in spite of the difficulties described above, the Johannine character of the verse cannot be denied because: 1) it contains the typically Johannine double "amen" saying (found only in Jn in the entire NT, which is, therefore, an exclusive characteristic of Johannine style)[63]; 2) the interruption of direct speech by means of a reporting formula especially before an important statement or command is found elsewhere in Jn (e.g. 11,11; 21,19), the purpose of which is to underline what is going to be said (which may be compared to the modern journalistic interruptions while reporting a direct speech by means of such parenthetical formulas as "the Pope continued" or "the Pope emphasized"); 3) the change from singular to plural is also not rare in Jn (e.g. 3,11-12; 4,48; 14,9-11.23), which is made in order to extend the application of what is said to one individual to all the members of his class.

Now we propose our solution to the apparent aporia present in v.51. The reason why the sentence in 1,51 is begun with a singular (*autô[i]*) is to show continuity with Jesus' conversation with Nathanael, whereas the plural (*hymin* and *opsesthe*) indicates the wider applicability of Jesus' promise to all the disciples who have begun to believe in him. Furthermore, from the structural point of view, *opsesthe* of v.51 is not a useless repetition of *opsê[i]* of v.50[64] but rather they are the hook-words which connect vv.47-50 and v.51. Again, v.51 not only does not break the sequence between the promise of the vision of

---

[61] E.g. R. T. FORTNA, *op. cit.*, 187; W. NICOL, *op. cit.*, 39-40. 103; H. M. TEEPLE, *op. cit.*, 171; S. TEMPLE, *op. cit.*, 58. 89; B. LINDARS, *op. cit.*, 44-52.

[62] E.g. BERNARD, I, 66; BROWN, I, 88-89; BULTMANN, 105; SCHNACKENBURG, I, 319-20.

[63] Cf. BOISMARD, III, 492; E. RUCKSTUHL, *Die literarische Einheit des Johannesevangeliums* (Freiburg 1951) 203-5.

[64] *Pace* BROWN, I, 89.

"greater things" of v.50 and the beginning of its realization in the first sign at Cana (2,1-11)[65], but establishes a better sequence by providing the disciples a hermeneutical key to the deeper significance of the "greater things" they are going to see starting with the sign at Cana and continued in the rest of the Fourth Gospel, since "the whole Gospel will be a gradual unfolding of the promise of 1,51"[66].

Thus we conclude that we can make good sense of Jn 1,43 and 1,51, if we pay proper attention to the way the Evangelist has composed them, and we need not desperately appeal to a hypothetical source theory or a redaction (interpolation) theory to explain an apparent aporia there.

---

[65] *Pace* BROWN, I, 89.
[66] F. J. MOLONEY, *The Johannine Son of Man*, 2 ed., (Rome 1978) 37.

2

SURVEY OF THE STRUCTURES OF THE FOURTH GOSPEL

Before we can suggest a structure for the Fourth Gospel, it is necessary to examine the actual state of research on the subject, for a large number and variety of structures have been proposed by different Johannine scholars[1]. Of course, it is not possible, within the space of a single chapter, to describe and discuss in detail all the different structures suggested by various authors[2]. We leave out from our study all the purely thematic plans that have been proposed, since they are mostly subjective and not based on objective literary criteria. We shall briefly survey and critically examine the significant and representative literary structures.

We may classify the various literary structures according to the criteria used by the different scholars as follows: 1) geographical-chronological structure (J. H. Bernard); 2) chronological-liturgical structure (D. Mollat, A. Guilding, M. D. Goulder); 3) numerical-symbolical structure (E. Lohmeyer); 4) literary-chronological structure (P. Defourney); 5) typological structure (H. Sahlin); 6) theological-typological-symbolical structure (J. Mateos & J. Barreto); 7) liturgical-symbolical-typological structure (M.-É. Boismard); 8) liturgical-symbolical-sign structure (R. Puigdollers); 9) chiastic structure (E. C. Webster); 10) chiastic-symbolic structure (D. Deeks); 11) symmetrical-concentric structure

---

[1] I. DE LA POTTERIE remarks: "Piani di ogni genere sono stati proposti per l'evangelo di Giovanni; questa diversità è non poco sconcertante e pone una questione di metodo" ("L'Evangelo di San Giovanni", in: *Introduzione al Nuovo Testamento*, 2 ed., G. Rinaldi & P. de Benedetti [Brescia 1971] 893).

[2] J. J. C. WILLEMSE gives a good chronological account of the various structures that have been proposed from 1844 untill 1964 (*Het vierde evangelie. Een onderzoek naar zijn structuur* [Antwerpen 1965] 24-98).

D. MOLLAT mentions "plans chronologiques et géographiques", "plans dramatiques", "plans logiques", "plans thématiques", "plans cycliques", "plans numériques" and "plans symboliques" ("L'Évangile selon Saint Jean", in: *L'Évangile selon Saint Jean et les Épitres de Saint Jean* (La Sainte Bible), 2 ed., D. Mollat & F.-M. Braun [Paris 1960] 27-31).

J. KAMMERSTÄTTER classifies summarily 16 proposed structures under five headings: (1) "die zweiteilige...", (2) typologische..., (3) symbolische..., (4) kultische und festchronologische..., (5) konzentrische Struktur des Johannesevangeliums..." (*Zur Struktur des Johannesevangeliums. Seine zentrierte Symmetrie als Träger des kerygmatischen Aktualismus* [Wien 1970] [an unpublished doctoral thesis at the Catholic Theological Faculty of the University of Vienna] 40-48).

Cf. also PRETE, 62-74 and PASQUETTO, 97-109 for summaries of structures suggested by some recent scholars.

(J. J. C. Willemse); 12) rhythmical-symmetrical structure (C. Rau); 13) centric-symmetrical structure (J. Kammerstätter); 14) narrative structure (B. Prete); 15) narrative-discourse structure (C. H. Dodd); 16) dramatic-chronological-geographical structure (M. C. Tenney); 17) dramatic-episodic structure (R. A. Culpepper); 18) revelatory structure (B. F. Westcott, H. van den Bussche, I. de la Potterie); 19) revelatory-dramatic structure (J. Caba); 20) revelatory-response structure (M. Gourgues); 21) revelatory-narrative structure (V. Pasquetto); 22) revelatory-eclectic structure (G. Segalla); 23) literary-thematic structure (R. E. Brown); 24) journey-structure (M. Rissi).

In order to present the position of each scholar as accurately and faithfully as possible, we shall first give the outline of each structure in the original language, abbreviating it, however, if it is too long and elaborate, and then we shall make a few critical remarks highlighting some of the salient positive points and pointing out some of the weaknesses of the structure in question. Space will not permit us to make an exhaustive evaluation of each structure.

2.1 GEOGRAPHICAL-CHRONOLOGICAL STRUCTURE (BERNARD)

J. H. Bernard proposes a structure of the Fourth Gospel based mostly on geographical and chronological indications:

THE STRUCTURE OF THE GOSPEL

The Gospel falls into three parts, preceded by a Prologue and followed by an Appendix.

Part I (cc. 1,19-4,54 with c. 6) begins at Bethany beyond the Jordan, goes on to Galilee, thence to Jerusalem, and back to Samaria and Galilee. It deals with the ministry of a little more than one year.

Part II (cc. 5, 7, 8-12) has to do with the Jerusalem ministry of Jesus, and extends over a second year.

Part III (cc. 13-20) is wholly concerned with the Passion and Resurrection[3].

It must be noted that, in order to sustain this geographical-chronological division of the Gospel, Bernard has to remove ch. 6 from its actual position and place it between chs. 4 and 5[4], for which, however, there is no manuscript evidence.

Secondly, the whole of Part II cannot be, strictly speaking, termed "Jerusalem ministry", since there are passages in it which deal with Jesus' ministry elsewhere (e.g. 7,1-9: Galilee; 10,40-42: [Bethany] beyond the Jordan; 11,1-44: Bethany; 11,54: Ephraim; 12,1-11: Bethany).

---

[3] BERNARD, I, xxx (cf. also xxxiii). The principal parts of the Fourth Gospel are further divided according to the change of place, time, or feasts and themes (cf. xxx-xxxii).

[4] BERNARD follows the theory of accidental displacement and hence relocates a number of chapters and pericopes (cf. xvi-xxx).

Thirdly, "the Passion" of Jesus in the Fourth Gospel begins already in ch. 12 (cf. 12,27: "Now my soul is troubled. And what shall I say? 'Father, save me from this hour'?").

Finally, it may be remarked that, although the chronological and geographical criteria have a role to play in the plan of the Fourth Gospel, they must not be used alone but together with other literary criteria, since the abundance of discourses, for instance, draws our attention away from the chronological and geographical data [5].

2.2 CHRONOLOGICAL-LITURGICAL STRUCTURES (MOLLAT, GUILDING AND GOULDER)

Basing themselves mostly on the mention of the temporal elements and of the Jewish feasts in the Fourth Gospel, D. Mollat, A. Guilding and M. D. Goulder claim to find chronological-liturgical structures.

2.21 Mollat's Chronological-Liturgical Structure

Mollat maintains that the Evangelist himself has given us two clear indications for the division of the Fourth Gospel, namely, 1) the Jewish liturgical feasts (three Passovers: 2,13; 6,4; 11,55; an unnamed feast: 5,1; a feast of Tabernacles: 7,2; a feast of Dedication: 10,22) and 2) the mention of the weeks and days (e.g. the first week of Jesus' ministry: 1,19-2,11; the week of the feast of Tabernacles: 7,2.14.37; the Passion week: 12,1.12; 19,31.42) [6].

Applying the above two norms of "feasts" and "weeks", Mollat proposes the following structure for the Fourth Gospel:

> *Prologue, 1* 1-18: "Au commencement..."
>
> I. La *première semaine* du ministère messianique: Jésus est manifesté come Messie; elle se termine par le miracle de Cana, *1* 19-*2* 11.
>
> II. Les événements qui gravitent autour de la *première Pâque* et qui se terminent par le second miracle de Cana, *2* 12-*4* 54.

---

[5] Another advocate of a geographical-chronological structure is E. B. ALLO who divides the Fourth Gospel into five principal parts: 1) the period of preparation, mostly in Judea (1,19-4,44); 2) ministry in Galilee (4,45-7,9); 3) Jesus' solemn declarations in Jerusalem (7,10-11,57); 4) the great week of the Passion (12-19); 5) resurrection and apparitions (20-21) ("Jean", in: *Dictionnaire de la Bible Supplément*, IV [Paris 1949] 817-21).

R. KIEFFER employs the geographical preposition *peran* to divide the Gospel of John into four parts (1,19-3,21; 3,22-5,47; 6,1-10,39; 10,40-21,23) ("Rum och tid i johannesevangeliets teologiska struktur [Space and Time in the Theological Structure of the Gospel of John]", *SvExAb* 49 [1984] 109-25). But *peran* is found in the Fourth Gospel not only at 1,28; 3,22; 6,1 and 10,40 but also at 6,17.22.25 and 18,1. If *peran* at 6,1, for instance, can indicate the beginning of a major part of the Gospel of John, one wonders why the use of the same preposition at 18,1 cannot have the same function.

[6] D. MOLLAT, *La Sainte Bible (Oecuménique)*, 150.

III. Le *sabbat du paralytique*: Jésus guérit un infirme à la piscine de Bézatha, *5* 1-47.

IV. La *Pâque du pain de vie*, *6* 1-71: Jésus opère le miracle de la multiplication des pains.

V. La *fête des Tentes* et la guérison de l'aveugle-né, *7* 1-*10* 21.

VI. La *fête de la Dédicace* et la résurrection de Lazare, *10* 22-*11* 54.

VII. La *Semaine Sainte* et la Pâque de la crucifixion, *11* 55-*19* 42.

VIII. La *Résurrection* et la semaine des apparitions, *20* 1-29.

IX. Appendice, *21*: l'annonce de la vie de l'Eglise et l'attente du retour de Jésus [7].

According to Mollat the guiding principle of the plan of the Gospel is the idea that Jesus put an end to the Jewish institutions by bringing them to fulfilment [8]. But one wonders whether the replacement of the Jewish feasts by Jesus was the primary concern of the Evangelist (cf. 20,30-31) [9].

Mollat himself has modified his view in a later publication and has given a different division of the Fourth Gospel, which may be called a "liturgical-revelatory structure", whose outline is given below [10]:

PROLOGUE (1,1-18)

LE MINISTERE DE JÉSUS (1,19-12,50)...

I. L'annonce de la nouvelle économie (1,19-4,54)...

II. Deuxième fête, un jour de sabbat, à Jérusalem: première opposition à la révélation (5,1-47)...

III. En Galilée, deuxième Pâque: nouvelle opposition à la révélation (6,1-71)...

IV. La fête des Tentes: la grande révélation messianique; le grand refus (7,1-10,21)...

V. La fête de la Dédicace: décision de tuer Jésus (10,22-11,54)...

VI. Fin du ministère public de Jésus et préliminaires de la dernière Pâque (11,55-12,50)...

---

[7] *Ibid.* MOLLAT gives a slightly different plan of the Fourth Gospel in "L'Évangile selon Saint Jean", in: *La Sainte Bible* [Bible de Jérusalem] 2 ed. (Paris 1960) 35-36, where he takes 1,19-4,54 as one major unit (I) instead of two (I & II). Cf. also n. 10 below.

[8] "Une idée se dégage de ce plan: Jésus met fin aux institutions juives en les accomplissant" (*La Sainte Bible [Oecuménique]* 150). But see n. 10 below.

[9] J. CABA critically remarks:

La struttura liturgica, concentrata intorno alle sei feste, presenta la garanzia di trovarsi appoggiata dallo stesso testo. Tuttavia ha un aspetto debole, poiché un vangelo cosi dottrinale difficilmente può essere racchiuso nella cornice giudaica e avere come idea primordiale la fine della liturgia dell' antica alleanza (*Dai Vangeli al Gesù Storico* [Roma 1974] 338-39).

[10] MOLLAT says:

Le but propre de l'évangile johannique n'est pas de signifier que Jésus est venu mettre fin à la liturgie de l'ancienne alliance. L'auteur du quatrième évangile a des visées plus profondes. Il a voulu mettre en pleine lumière la personne de Jésus, "Messie, Fils de Dieu", révélateur du Père et source de vie pour les hommes (20,31), c'est le but même de son écrit. Mais précisément, il n'était pas cadre plus approprié à la manifestation du mystère du Christ que les grandes célébrations liturgiques juives... ("L'Évangile selon Saint Jean", in: D. Mollat & F.-M. Braun, *L'Évangile et les Épîtres de Saint Jean*, 3 ed., [Paris 1973] 40).

Cf. *ibid.*, 35-40 for the schema of the structure.

L'HEURE DE JÉSUS. LA PAQUE DE L'AGNEAU DE DIEU (13,1-20,31)...
  I. Le dernier repas de Jésus avec ses disciples (13,1-17,26)...
  II. La Passion (18-19)...
  III. Les récits de la résurrection et la béatitude de la foi (20,1-29)...
  IV. Première conclusion de l'évangile (20,30s)...
EPILOGUE (21,1-25).

Notice that here Mollat has a bipartite division of the Fourth Gospel (1,19-12,50; 13,1-20,31), the first part being subdivided into six sections (1,19-4,54; 5,1-47; 6,1-71; 7,1-10,21; 10,22-11,54; 11,55-12,50) and the second into four (13-17; 18-19; 20,1-29; 20,30-31). Note that whereas in the first structure 1,19-2,11 and 2,12-4,54 were regarded as two units (I & II), here they are combined to form only one unit (1,19-4,54). Similarly, what was a single unit (VII: 11,55-19,42) in the first structure has now become three units (11,55-12,50; 13-17; 18-19), one of which belongs to the first major division (1,19-12,50) and two to the second (13,1-20,31).

It is, however, to Mollat's credit that the two criteria that he has employed for the division of the Gospel of John are found in the Gospel itself and hence are objectively verifiable, except some of the "weeks" which are not clearly indicated in the Gospel.

2.22 Guilding's Chronological-Liturgical Structure

Another advocate of a chronological-liturgical plan is A. Guilding, according to whom the sequence of the Gospel corresponds exactly to that of a three-year lectionary (used in the synagogues of Palestine on the Jewish feasts and Sabbaths). In her own words:

> It is suggested, then, that the Fourth Gospel appears to be a Christian commentary on the Old Testament lectionary readings as they were arranged for the synagogue in a three-year cycle. The order of the Gospel follows the cycle of the Jewish lectionary year, which was so arranged that a suitable portion of Scripture was read at each of the feasts, and the Evangelist's many allusions to Jewish festivals are not merely casual references but are fundamental to the structure of the Gospel[11].

Talking about the Johannine chronology, Guilding states that "for the Fourth Evangelist time is at once historic time and *lectionary time*... It is lectionary time that is all-important to him"[12].

Guilding gives the following threefold division of the Gospel of John which corresponds to the three-year cycle of the Jewish lectionary[13]:

---

[11] A. GUILDING, *The Fourth Gospel and Jewish Worship* (Oxford 1960) 3; cf. also p. 231.
[12] *Ibid.*, 4. Again on the same page she insists: "Historical time is subordinated to the liturgical cycle..."
[13] *Ibid.*, 46. The themes of the three divisions of the Gospel are explained on pp. 50-53.

Prologue	1.1-18
(1) manifestation of the Messiah to the world	1.19-4.54
(2) manifestation of the Messiah to the Jews	6,5,7-12
(3) manifestation of the Messiah to the Church	13-20
Epilogue	21

The above threefold division is, in the opinion of Guilding, supported by the fact that in the first division Jesus manifests himself to all types of people (Galileans, Judeans, Samaritans, Jews and Gentiles), while in the second division Jesus reveals himself only to the Jews and particularly in Jerusalem, whereas in the third division the self-revelation of Jesus is made only to the disciples [14]. This is further confirmed, affirms Guilding, by the mention of belief or unbelief at the end of each division (cf. 4,42.45.53; 12,37; 20,30-31) [15].

Guilding illustrates the division of the Gospel by means of a "diagram", "a plan of the Gospel arranged for three and a half lectionary years" [16]. According to this "diagram" each of the three sections or cycles of the Fourth Gospel (1,19-4,54; 5,1-12,50; 13,1-20,31) contains readings arranged according to the six major Jewish feasts (New Year, Tabernacles, Dedication, Purim, Passover and Pentecost).

Now comparing Guilding's "diagram" with the text of the Gospel we find that three different Passovers (the word *pascha* occurs ten times: 2,13.23; 6,4; 11,55.55; 12,1; 13,1; 18,28.39; 19,14), one feast of Tabernacles (7,2) and one feast of Dedication (10,22) are found in the Fourth Gospel, but nothing is said (explicitly) about the other Jewish feasts like Pentecost, New Year and Purim, while Guilding's "diagram" is built around all of them. If the Evangelist wanted to structure his Gospel according to the annual Jewish feasts during the three years, one wonders why some of the feasts are not mentioned at all, while others are!

Secondly, in order to fit the text of the Gospel to the "triennial cycle" Guilding has to transpose Jn 5 and Jn 6 [17], and the unnamed "feast of the Jews" in 5,1 is identified as the feast of the New Year [18], which is questionable.

---

[14] *Ibid.*, 46-47. This, however, is not fully true, since Jesus reveals himself to the Greeks in 12,20-36 and to the Jews in 18,1-19,42.

[15] *Ibid.*, 47. This is not a valid proof of the threefold division of the Gospel, since faith and unbelief are mentioned throughout the Gospel (e.g. 2,11.23; 6,69; etc.).

[16] *Ibid.*, 47-48.

[17] *Ibid.*, 45-46.

[18] *Ibid.*, 69-72. But other scholars are of the opinion that the "feast" of 5,1 is Pentecost (cf. F.-M. BRAUN, *RevThom* 52 (1952) 263-65; B. NOACK, "The Day of Pentecost in Jubilees, Qumran, and Acts", *Annual of the Jewish Theological Institute* 1 (1962) 72-95; SCHNACKENBURG, II, 93). GUILDING herself admits the possibility that the feast in question could be Pentecost (cf. 69-70; 72), although she prefers the New Year. Most probably the primary concern of the Evangelist was neither Pentecost nor the New Year (since he does not mention them explicitly), but the Sabbath (5,9) (cf. BROWN, I, 206).

Thirdly, the attribution of certain Johannine passages to certain Jewish feasts seems to be arbitrary and inconsistent. For example, 2,1-12 is put in the period of the feast of Dedication[19]. The cleansing of the temple (2,13-22) is placed in the section of Purim, though the Evangelist explicitly states in 2,13 that the feast of the Passover was near, whereas Jn 6 with a similar introduction (cf. 6,4) is rightly put by Guilding in the context of the Passover[20].

Finally, it is precarious to build the structure of the Gospel on the unreliable foundation of a first-century, uniform, Palestinian "triennial cycle" which is disputed or refuted by most scholars today[21].

2.23 Goulder's Chronological-Liturgical Structure

M. D. Goulder claims that the Gospel of John had a liturgical origin and he divides it into a "Fifty Day Reading Cycle" for the season of Lent and Easter and compares his liturgical divisions with those of a "Greek Church Lectionary" of A. D. 900[22]:

St. John as a Fifty Day Reading Cycle

Greek Church Lectionary A.D.900			St. John		
EASTER	I.1-17	LENT I	I.1-28		Logos, Light, Witness
M	I.18-28		I.29-34		Two Baptisms - "On the next day"
T	Lk.XXIV.12-35		I.35-42		X, Andrew, Peter - "On the next day"
W	Jn.I.35-42		I.43-end		Philip, Nathanael - "On the next day"
Th	III.1-15		—		
F	II.12-22		II.1-12		Cana Marriage - "On the third day"
S	III.22-33		II.13-22		*Temple Cleansed* - "Passover was near"
EASTER I	XX.19-31	LENT II	II.23-III.21		Nicodemus - "At the Passover Feast"
M	II.1-11		III.22-end		Aenon
T	III.16-21		IV.1-42		Samaritaness

[19] A. GUILDING, *op. cit.*, 48 (see **2a** in the "diagram" on p. 48).
[20] *Ibid.* (see **2b** in the "diagram" on p. 48).
[21] Cf. K. P. BLAND, "Rabbinic Lectionary Cycle", in: *IDB, Supplementary* Volume (Nashville 1976) 538. GUILDING herself admits that the use of the triennial lectionary cycle in the first century A.D. is not certain, for she says: "although there is a strong presumption that the triennial cycle was already in use by the first century A.D., this is *incapable of strict proof, since nearly all the evidence is later than the first century*" (*op. cit.*, 24; my italics).
[22] M. D. GOULDER, "The Liturgical Origin of St. John's Gospel", in: *Studia Evangelica*, VII, ed. E. A. Livingstone (Berlin 1982) 205-21. The chart is found on pp. 220-21.

Greek Church Lectionary A.D.900			St. John	
W	V.17-24		—	
Th	V.24-30		—	
F	V.30-VI.2		IV.43-end	Officer's Son - "After Two Days" (4,43)
S	VI.14-27		V	Bethzatha - "The Feast of the Jews"
EASTER II	Mk.XV.43-XVI.8	LENT III	VI.1-21	5000, *Walking Water* - "Passover was near"
M	Jn.IV.46-54		VI.22-40	Bread of Life - "On the next day"
T	VI.27-33		—	
W	VI.48-54		—	
Th	VI.40-44		—	
F	VI.35-39		—	
S	XV.17-XVI.1		VI.41-end	In the Synagogue
EASTER III	V.1-15	LENT IV	VII.1-13	*Brothers to Feast* - "Tabernacles near"
M	VI.56-69		—	
T	VII.1-13		—	
W	VII.14-30		VII.14-36	*Jesus to the Feast* - "The middle of Feast"
Th	VIII.21-30		—	
F	VIII.21-30		—	
S	VIII.31-42		VII.37-X.21	Light of World - "Last Day of Feast"
EASTER IV	IV.5-42	LENT V	X.22-39	*Good Shepherd* - "Dedication"
M	VIII.42-51		X.40-XI.16	Lazarus Sick ("Stayed two days where he was")
T	VIII.51-59		—	
W	VI.5-14		—	
Th	IX.39-X.9		XI.17-46	Lazarus Raised - "Four days already"
F	X.17-28		XI.47-54	Caiaphas' Plot
EASTER V	IX.1-38	LENT VI	XI.55-XII.11	Bethany Anointing - "six days to Pass."
M	XI.47-54		XII.12-19	Palm Entry - "On the next day"
T	XII.19-36		XII.20-end	Greeks
W	XII.36-47		MOVEABLE TO FIT 14th NISAN	
Th	Lk.XXIV.36-53 (Asc.)		XIII-XVII	*Last Supper Discourses*
F	Jn.XIV.1-10		XVIII-XIX	Passion
S	XIV.10-21			

2.2 CHRONOLOGICAL-LITURGICAL STRUCTURES

Greek Church Lectionary A.D.900		St. John		
EASTER VI	XVII.1-13	EASTER	XX.1-18	Mary at Tomb "On the first day of the week"
			XX.19-25	Evening Appearance "On the evening"
M	XIV.27-XV.7		—	
T	XVI.2-13		—	
W	XVI.15-23		—	
Th	XVI.23-33		—	
F	XVII.18-26		—	
S	XXI.14-25		—	
PENTECOST	XX.19-23 VII.37-VIII.12	EASTER I	XX.26-31	Thomas - "Eight Days later"

Goulder believes the chronological and liturgical indications in the Gospel to refer not primarily to the historical time of Jesus and the Jewish feasts that he attended, but rather to the specific days when there was a Lenten or Easter reading of the Fourth Gospel in the Johannine community. For instance, the temporal specification "on the third day" at 2,1 indicates that the reading of the Gospel was resumed only on the third day (Friday) after a day (Thursday) without any reading! Similarly, the chronological indication "after two days" at 4,43 points to the resumption of reading after an interval of two days! Likewise, the remark about Jesus' going up into the temple "about the middle of the feast" (7,14) tells us that the reading of this passage was done about the middle of the week, namely, on Wednesday! [23]

It must also be noted that, while the readings for certain days consist of just a few verses (e.g. 7,1-13 for the Sunday of Lent IV; 12,12-19 for the Monday of Lent VI), the readings for other days consist of many long chapters (e.g. 7,37-10,31; 13-17; 18-19) [24].

Finally the careful comparison of Goulder's "Fifty Day Reading Cycle" with that of the 9th-century "Greek Church Lectionary" not only does not confirm his position but contradicts it. While the Greek Lectionary uses the Fourth Gospel for the readings of only the Easter season (47 out of the 50 days from Easter to Pentecost), Goulder's cycle consists of Lent and Easter (and it has no readings for 21 days!). Notice also that Jn 21 is omitted from his cycle.

2.2z The critical examination of the chronological-liturgical structures proposed by Mollat, Guilding and Goulder warns us against the danger of depending on a single criterion for determining the structure of the Fourth Gospel, because sometimes it leads to subjective and fanciful conclusions.

---

[23] See the chart on pp. 220-21, where there is no reading for some days of the week!
[24] *Ibid.*, 220-221.

2.3 NUMERICAL-SYMBOLICAL STRUCTURE (LOHMEYER) [25]

E. Lohmeyer finds the key to the structure of the Fourth Gospel in the symbolism of the numbers "seven" and "three", and proposes a sevenfold division as follows [26]:

I. Der Prolog 1 1-18.
   a) 1-5. b) 6-13. c) 14-18.

II. Eingang 1 19-51.
   1. Die Botschaft der Priester 1 19-23.
   2. Die Botschaft der Pharisäer 1 24-28.   Der Vorläufer.
   3. Das Zeugnis des Täufers 1 29-34.
   4. Andreas und der Ungennante 1 35-39.
   5. Simon Petrus 1 40-42.   Die ersten
   6. Philippus 1 43-44.   Jünger.
   7. Nathanael 1 45-51.

III. Jesus auf Wanderungen in jüdischen Ländern c. 2-6.
   1. In Kana 2 1-11.
   2. In Jerusalem 2 12-3 21 [...].
   3. In Ainon bei Salem 3 22-36.
   4. Am Brunnen zu Sychar 4 1-42 [.......].
   5. Jesus in Kana 4 43-54.
   6. Jesus in Jerusalem 5 1-47 [...].
   7. Jesus am Galiläischen Meer 6 1-71 [.......].

IV. Jesus auf Wanderungen in Judäa c. 7-12.
   1. Aufbruch nach Jerusalem 7 1-13.
   2. Jesus auf dem Laubhüttenfest 7 14- 8 59 [.......].
   3. Jesus und der Blindgeborene 9 1- 10 21.
   4. Jesus auf dem Tempelweihfest 10 22-42 [...].
   5. Die Auferweckung des Lazarus 11 1-57 [.......].
   6. Die Salbung in Bethanien 12 1-8.
   7. Jesus in Jerusalem 12 9-50 [...].

---

[25] E. LOHMEYER, "über Aufbau und Gliederung des vierten Evangeliums", *ZNW* 27 (1928) 11-36. We do not examine N. KOULOMZINE's symbolical plan of the Fourth Gospel based on the symbolism of the numbers "seven" and "three" (*La Sainte Bible [Oecuménique]*, 146-50), since he does not divide the Gospel accordingly. Similarly we exclude from our study F. QUIÉVREUX's "La structure symbolique de l'évangile de St. Jean" (*RHPR* 33 [1953] 123-65), since he does not divide the Fourth Gospel into different units but only examines the frequency of occurrence of different Johannine terms (e.g. *agapê*), and finds a symbolic meaning in each number. For instance, he says: "Le nombre 6 exprime l'harmonie divine" (p. 147) and so *eirênê* occurs 6 times. "Le nombre 7 signifie la perfection" (p. 148) and hence *agapê* is found 7 times in the Gospel of John.

[26] E. LOHMEYER, *art. cit.*, 30-32. The threefold or sevenfold subdivisions of the units have been left out from the outline which, however, are indirectly indicated by means of three or seven dots enclosed in square brackets e.g. [...] at III.2 and [.......] at III.4.

V. Die Passionsgeschichte c. 13-19.
  1. Die Fusswaschung 13 1-20.
  2. Die Bezeichnung des Verräters 13 21-30.
  3. Die Abschiedsreden 13 31- 17 26.
     a) Der Reden erster Teil 13 31- 14 31 [.......].
     b) Der Reden zweiter Teil 15 1- 16 33 [.......].
     c) Das hohepriesterliche Gebet 17 1-26.
  4. Die Gefangennahme 18 1-11.
  5. Das Verhör Jesu und die Verleugnung des Petrus 18 12-26.
  6. Jesus und Pilatus 18 28- 19 16 [.......].
  7. Jesus auf Golgotha 19 17-42 [.......].

VI. Der Auferstandene c. 20.
     a) Vor Maria Magdalena 20 1-18.
     b) Vor den Zwölfen 20 19-23.
     c) Thomas 20 24-29.
        Schlussworte 20 30-31.

VII. Der Epilog c. 21.

Note that, according to Lohmeyer, not only does the entire Fourth Gospel comprise of seven main divisions (I-VII) but also that four of the latter (II, III, IV, V) consist of seven units each; and the first and the sixth main divisions are made up of three units each. Many of these units are further divided into seven or three subunits [27].

Lohmeyer sums up the results of his investigation in the following words:

A thorough ordering determines the structure and the division of the 4th Gospel. It rests in the first place on the *schema of seven*, in the second place also on that of *three*. It embraces not only the large main sections but also the smallest units [28].

But Lohmeyer himself admits that the numerical ordering is not explicitly emphasized by the Evangelist himself [29].

Notice also the lack of proportion in the length of the units. For instance, while IV.1 (7,1-13) consists of just 13 verses, IV.2 (7,14-8,59) contains 86 verses; whereas IV.6 (12,1-8) has only 8 verses, IV.7 (12,9-50) has 42 verses. Again, while V.2 (13,21-30) contains only 10 verses, the next unit V.3 (13,31-17,26) consists of 155 verses! Hence, but for a few Johannine units (e.g. 18,28-19,16; 19,17-42) [30] whose sevenfold subdivisions (18,28-32.33-38.38-40; 19,1-3.4-8.8-12.12-16;

---

[27] III.4; III.7; IV.2; IV.3; IV.5; V.6; V.7 have sevenfold subdivisions. III.2; III.6; IV.4; IV.7; V.3 have threefold subdivisions (*ibid.*, 14-32).

[28] "Eine durchgängige Ordnung bestimmt den Aufbau und die Gliederung des 4. Evangeliums. Sie ruht in erster Linie auf dem *Schema der Sieben*, in zweiter Linie auch auf dem der *Drei*. Sie umfasst nicht nur die grossen Hauptabschnitte, sondern auch die kleinsten Gebilde" (*ibid.*, 33) [my italics].

[29] "Sie dringt durch alle Schilderung, ohne doch jemals irgendwie betont zu sein" (*ibid.*, 33).

[30] See V.6 and V.7 in the outline given above.

19,17-18.19-22.23-24.25-27.28-30.31-37.38-42) are correct and interesting, Lohmeyer seems to have followed a numerical mirage or *ignis fatuus* in structuring the Fourth Gospel on a fixed pattern of "seven's" and "three's" [31].

2.4 LITERARY-CHRONOLOGICAL STRUCTURE (DEFOURNEY)

P. Defourney bases the structure of the Gospel of John on the literary-chronological expressions *meta touto* (2,12) and *meta tauta* (3,22; 5,1; 6,1; 7,1; 21,1). These are taken to be the "beginning formula" of the seven "episodes" of which the Fourth Gospel is made up. The first episode is preceded by the Prologue. Thus we get the following division of the Gospel [32]:

Prologue: 1,1-18
1st episode: 1,19-2,11
2nd episode: 2,12-3,21 (*meta touto* : 2,12)
3rd episode: 3,22-4,54 (*meta tauta* : 3,22)
4th episode: ch. 5   ("   "   : 5,1)
5th episode: ch. 6   ("   "   : 6,1)
6th episode: chs. 7-20 ("   "   : 7,1)
7th episode: ch. 21   ("   "   : 21,1)

Now it is true that the expression "after this" is found in the places indicated above, but it must be noted that it occurs in many other places not mentioned by Defourney (e.g. *meta tauta* at 5,14; 19,38; *meta touto* at 19,28; cf. also 11,7.11). Furthermore, the "6th episode" (Jn 7-20) is disproportionately long (14 chapters) as compared to the other episodes (many of which consist of just one chapter). Finally, Defourney, like Lohmeyer, seems to be under the spell of the magic number "seven"!

2.5 TYPOLOGICAL STRUCTURE (SAHLIN)

According to H. Sahlin, "the Fourth Gospel as a whole forms a typological parallel to the Exodus-tradition" [33]. He admits, however, that Jn 15-17 and 20-21 do not have typological parallels in Exodus [34]. Making use of the "types" in the books of Exodus, Leviticus, Numbers, Joshua and 1 Kings, Sahlin defends the thesis that the Johannine Jesus is presented as the new Moses, Joshua and Solomon, and finds a corresponding threefold division of the Fourth Gospel (Jn 1-9; 10-11; 12-19) [35].

---

[31] W. BAUER's criticism of LOHMEYER's numerical structure is worth quoting: "Lohmeyer zieht einem Irrlicht nach, das ihn vom festen Boden fortlockt" ("Johnnnesevangelium und Johannesbriefe", *TRu* NF 1 (1929) 144, as cited by J. KAMMERSTÄTTER, *op. cit.*, 42).

[32] P. DEFOURNEY, "Au sujet de la composition du quatrième évangile", *Collectanea Mechliniensia* 11 (1937) 359-67. Cf. also J. J. C. WILLEMSE, *op. cit.*, 65-67.

[33] H. SAHLIN, *Zur Typologie des Johannesevangeliums* (Uppsala 1950) 74; cf. also 8-58.

[34] *Ibid.*, 52; 59.

[35] *Ibid.*, 64-78; cf. also p. 5 where he states the scope of his book.

Now granting that there are some Exodus themes in the Gospel of John (e.g. Moses: 1,17; 3,14; 5,45.46; 6,32; etc.; manna: 6,32), one cannot say that Sahlin demonstrates convincingly that the Fourth Gospel is patterned on the Exodus-typology [36]. For instance, one does not see any justification from the text of the Gospel for Sahlin's designation of Jn 10-11 as the "Joshua-phase", especially since Joshua is never mentioned in these chapters (nor in the entire Gospel) [37]. This is true also for his "Solomon-phase" (Jn 12-19) [38].

2.6 THEOLOGICAL-TYPOLOGICAL-SYMBOLICAL STRUCTURE (MATEOS & BARRETO)

J. Mateos and J. Barreto propose a theological structure based on the typology of creation and the Passover-covenant and on the symbolism of the number six [39]. They outline the main structure in the following manner [40]:

I. Prólogo: El designio creador (1,1-18).
II. Sección introductoria: De Juan a Jesús (1,19-51).
III. Primera parte: El día sexto. La obra del Mesías (2,1-19,42).
  A. El día del Mesías (2,1-11,54).
    1. Ciclo de las instituciones: "Los suyos no lo acogieron" (2,1-4,46a).
    2. Ciclo del hombre: El éxodo del Mesías (4,46b-11,54).
  B. La Hora final: La Pascua del Mesías (11,55-19,42).
    1. Primera sección: La opción ante el Mesías (11,55-12,50).
    2. Segunda sección: La Cena. La nueva comunidad humana (13,1-17,26).
    3. Tercera sección: Entrega, muerte y sepultura de Jesús. La manifestación de la gloria (18,1-19,42).
IV. Segunda parte: El día primero. La nueva creación (20,1-31).
V. Epílogo: La misión de la comunidad y Jesús (21,1-25).

---

[36] J. KAMMERSTÄTTER remarks: "Seine typologischen Gegenüberstellungen können aber kaum voll überzeugen" (*op. cit.*, 42).

[37] Cf. J. J. C. WILLEMSE, *op. cit.*, 74.

[38] Compare SAHLIN's thesis with G. ZIENER's proposal of a typology between the Book of Wisdom and the Gospel of John (G. ZIENER, "Weisheitsbuch und Johannesevangelium", *Bib* 38 [1957] 396-418; 39 [1958] 37-60), according to whom the order of the miracles in the Fourth Gospel is the same as that of the Exodus-miracles as narrated [not in the Book of Exodus but] in the Book of Wisdom, for he says that "das Johannesevangelium die Wunder Jesu fast in derselben Reihenfolge berichtet wie das Weiheitsbuch die Exoduswunder..." (*Bib* 38 [1957] 415).

[39] MATEOS & BARRETO, 13-17. They affirm in the introduction to their commentary:

De hecho, el plan que estructura el evangelio de Juan es teológico...
Las líneas maestras de la teología de Juan son dos: el tema de la creación y el de la Pascua-alianza...
Se notará la insistencia de Jn en el número seis: día sexto, hora sexta, seis días antes de Pascua, seis fiestas, seis tinajas. Este número indica lo incompleto, lo preparatorio, el período de actividad que mira a un resultado (*ibid.*, 14-16).

[40] *Ibid.*, 34.

One of the first things to be noted about the above structure is the disproportion between the first part consisting of 18 chapters (Jn 2-19) and the second part comprising only a single chapter (Jn 20). It is also precarious to base this major division on a fragile chronological indication at 20,1: "the first day of the week".

Again, "the third day" at 2,1, which occurs at the end of a literary-chronological series of "the next day" (1,29.35.43), is said to refer to "the sixth day" of creation, namely, "that of the creation of man" [41] (cf. Gen 1,26-31), since creation is attributed to the Word in the Prologue (1,3: *panta di' autou egeneto*) and since the "power to become children of God" is the gift of the incarnate Word to the believers (1,12). But if the Evangelist had intended to insist on the sixth day, he would have written "the sixth day" instead of "the third day" in 2,1.

Furthermore, it is doubtful whether one can reasonably affirm with Mateos and Barreto that "the theme of the creation, which opens in the Prologue (1,1ff), dominates the chronology and provides an interpretative key to the work of Jesus" [42], because the theme of "creation" is not explicitly mentioned in the rest of the Gospel. The six-day-chronology in 12,1-19,42 is not primarily, *pace* Mateos and Barreto [43], a creation-chronology but a Passover-chronology (12,1.12; 13,1; 19,14.31.42). Hence it seems to be an exaggeration to say that "the whole activity of Jesus, until his death, rests under the sign of 'the sixth day'" [44].

The division of "the sixth day" (2,1-19,42) into two periods, namely, "the Day of the Messiah" (2,1-11,54) and "the final Hour" (11,55-19,42) [45] does not make sense, since "the final Hour" is an integral part of "the Day of the Messiah", just as the last hour of a 24-hour day is part of that day. (One does not normally divide a "day" into a "day" and "final hour" but rather into "hours".) Secondly, "the hour" of Jesus is the hour of his "glorification" (cf. 12,23.27-29; 13,1; 17,1) which refers not only to his death but also to his resurrection. Therefore the delimitation of "the final Hour" to 11,55-19,42 goes against the Johannine understanding of "the hour".

---

[41] *Ibid.*, 15.

[42] *Ibid.*: "El tema de la creación, que se abre en el prólogo (1,1ss), domina la cronología y da una clave de interpretación de la obra de Jesús."

[43] *Ibid.*

[44] *Ibid.*: "De ahí que toda actividad de Jesús, hasta su muerte, quede bajo el segno de "el día sexto", indicando el designio que la preside: dar remate a la obra creadora, completando al hombre con el Espíritu de Dios (cf. 19,30; 20,22)."

[45] *Ibid.*: "El día sexto encierra dos períodos: el de la actividad de Jesús, "el Día del Mesías" (2,1-11,54; cf. 8,56), y "la Hora final", que lo consuma y que coincide con el período de la última Pascua (11,55-19,42;...)."

MATEOS & BARRETO argue that Jn 8,56 (*tên hêmeran tên emên*) supports their designation of the public ministry or activity of Jesus as "the Day of the Messiah" (*ibid.*, 427) but it should be noted that other Johannine scholars do not agree on the interpretation of 8,56 (cf. BERNARD, II, 320-21; BARRETT, 352; BROWN, I, 359-60; SCHNACKENBURG, II, 221-22).

Again, the subdivision of 2,1-11,54 into two sections, namely, the "Cycle of the institutions: His own did not receive him (2,1-4,46a)" and the "Cycle of man: The exodus of the Messiah (4,46b-11,54)" is not quite convincing, because 2,1-11 and 4,46-54 have many inclusions and parallelisms (e.g. 2,1.11; 4,46.53-54) and hence they form integral parts of the same section (2,1-4,54). Furthermore, it is not true to the text to say that 2,1-4,46a represents the rejection of Jesus by his own, since many (e.g. the disciples in 2,1-11; the Jerusalemites in 2,23; the many who became disciples of Jesus in 4,1; the Samaritan woman and people in 4,4-42) do believe in him.

It is true that there are some similarities in the vocabulary of 4,46b-54; 5,1-47 and 11,1-54 [46], but similar vocabulary alone is not sufficient to decide whether the pericopes in question belong to the same section; one must look for a convergence of criteria to determine the delimitation of the sections in the structure of the Gospel [47].

Finally, one suspects that Mateos' and Barreto's structure based on the theological themes of "creation" and "the Passover-covenant" is the result of reading the Johannine Gospel through Pauline spectacles, since the terms (new) "creation" and "covenant" are never found in the Fourth Gospel.

2.7 LITURGICAL-SYMBOLICAL-TYPOLOGICAL STRUCTURE (BOISMARD)

Boismard has proposed two different structures for the Fourth Gospel which may be named as "symbolical-typological structure" and "liturgical-symbolical structure" respectively.

2.71 Symbolical-Typological Structure [48]

This structure is based on the symbolism of the number "seven" and the typology of "creation" and "covenant" in the Gospel of John.

Concerning the symbolism of "seven" Boismard affirms: "This number was for the ancients a symbol of perfection; in the Fourth Gospel it is the appropriate number of the Messiah and is like the seal which authenticates his work" [49].

Boismard finds in the Fourth Gospel 7 discourses (3,2-21; 4,5-27; 5,19-47; 6,27-44.; 7-8; 10,1ff.; 14-17), 7 miracles (2,1-11; 4,46-54; 5,1-13; 6,1-15; 6,16-21; 9,1-7; 11,1-44), 7 "I am" sayings (6,35; 8,12; 10,7; 10,11; 11,25; 14,6; 15,1), 7 Messianic titles for Jesus in 1,29-51 (1,29.36: "lamb of God"; 1,34: "Son of God"; 1,38.49: "Rabbi"; 1,41: "Messiah"; 1,45: "Jesus of Nazareth"; 1,49: "king

---

[46] Cf. MATEOS & BARRETO, 252.
[47] See 4.211; 4.221; 4.231 below.
[48] M.-É. BOISMARD, "L'évangile à quatre dimensions", *Lumière* V 1 (1951) 94-114.
[49] *Ibid.*, 99: "Ce chiffre était, pour les anciens, symbole de perfection; dans le quatrième évangile, c'est le chiffre propre du Messie, et comme le sceau qui authentique son oeuvre."

of Israel"; 1,51: "Son of man") [50], and 7 periods in the life of Jesus joined to the Jewish feasts and often consisting of a week of seven days:

> 1) la première semaine du ministère messianique... [1,19-2,12]; 2) les événements qui gravitent autour de la première Pâque (2,13-4,54); 3) ceux qui gravitent autour de la deuxième Pâque (5-6); 4) les sept jours de la fête des Tabernacles (7-9); 5) les discours tenus par le Christ lors de la fête de la Dédicace, avec la guérison de Lazare, qui la suit de peu (10-11); 6) la Semaine Sainte, termineé par la mort du Christ, lors de la troisième Pâque (12-19); 7) enfin la semaine pascale (20) [51].

Now the above 7 divisions of the Gospel are, in the opinion of Boismard, parallel to the 7 days of creation in Gen 1,1-2,4. Just as in the creation the first three days are devoted to the work of separation (Gen 1,1-13), the first three sections of the Fourth Gospel deal with the separation of the old from the new economy: 1) baptism in the Spirit (1,29-34), and the new wine (2,1-11); 2) the new temple (2,13-21), the new birth (3,3-21), and the new worship (4,20-24); 3) the new sabbath of divine work (ch. 5), and the new manna (ch. 6). Just as the next three days in the creation account are devoted to the work of "populating" the world with lights (4th day) and life (5th and 6th day) (Gen 1,14-31), so the 4th, 5th and 6th sections of the Fourth Gospel speak about the new "light of the world" (chs. 7-9), the new "life" (chs. 10-11), and the "gestation of the new man" (chs. 12-19) [52].

Regarding the purpose of the symbolism of the number "seven" and of the parallelism between the work of creation and the work of Christ, Boismard makes the following concluding remark: "L'intention de Jean est donc claire: par le symbolisme du chiffre sept, il veut présenter l'oeuvre du Messie comme une nouvelle création, reprenant, ou plus exactement recommençant la création première" [53].

Concerning the "new covenant" in the Gospel of John, Boismard affirms that Jesus is presented as the new Moses, the leader of the new Exodus and the mediator of the new covenant. This is clear for Boismard from the comparison between Moses and Jesus in 1,17; 3,14; 6,32-35; 7,22-23. This is supported by the parallelism between Jn 1-7 and Ex 3-17; 33-34: for instance, 1) Jn 1,29-34 (Jesus, "the lamb of God who takes away the sin of the world") and Ex 3,7-10.16-17 (the call of Moses to liberate the people of Israel from the slavery of Egypt); 2) Jn 1,35-2,11 (Jesus' gathering of the first disciples and his performance of the first miracle) and Ex 4,1-31 (Moses' authorization to gather the elders of

---

[50] *Ibid.*, 100.

[51] *Ibid.*, 101. J. GOETTMANN also gives the same sevenfold division of the Gospel of John (*Saint Jean. Évangile de la Nouvelle Genèse* [Paris 1982]).

[52] *Le Prologue de Saint Jean* (Lectio Divina 11) (Paris 1953) 137-38. Cf. also *Lumière V* 1 (1951) 101-5.

[53] *Art. cit.*, 104. M. GIRARD also finds a sevenfold structure in the Fourth Gospel patterned according to Gen 1,1-2,4 ("La structure heptapartite du quatrième évangile", *SR* 5 [1975-76] 350-59). Cf. also T. BARROSSE, "The Seven Days of the New Creation in St. John's Gospel", *CBQ* 21 (1959) 507-16.

the people and to perform miracles); 3) Jn 2,13-21 (celebration of the first Passover by Jesus, the new Paschal lamb) and Ex 11-12 (the celebration of the first Passover with the smearing of the blood of the lamb on the doorposts); 4) Jn 3 (baptism with water and Spirit: v.5) and Ex 14-15 (the crossing of the Red Sea, the symbol of baptism); 5) Jn 4,1-26 (Jesus and the Samaritan woman at the well of Jacob) and Ex 15,22-25 (cf. Num 21,16-17) (Moses and the people at the well of Marah); 6) Jn 6 (Jesus, the new manna) and Ex 16 (the miracle of the manna); 7) Jn 7,1.37-39 (the threat to kill Jesus and the promise of "living water") and Ex 17,1-7 (the threat to stone Moses and the promise of water: cf. also Num 20,7-13); 8) Jn 1,14-18 (theophany of the "transfiguration") and Ex 33-34 (theophany at Sinai)[54]. In short, in the opinion of Boismard, the mission of the Johannine Jesus is to mediate "the new covenant"[55].

2.72 Liturgical-Symbolical Structure

Besides the "symbolical-typological structure" based on the symbolism of the number "seven" and the typology of "creation" and "covenant", Boismard has proposed a new structure which may be called "liturgical-symbolical", since it is built on the Jewish feasts mentioned in the Fourth Gospel (three Passovers: 2,13; 6,4; 11,55; 12,1; 13,1; Pentecost: 5,1; Tabernacles: 7,2; Dedication: 10,22) and on the symbolism of the numbers "six" (namely, imperfection) and "seven" (namely, perfection or totality). Thus there are only *six* Jewish liturgical feasts but the last Passover is also the Passover of Jesus and the word "Passover" occurs seven times during this feast (11,55a; 11,55b; 12,1; 13,1; 18,28; 18,39; 19,14), which means that the Passover of Christ replaces all the Jewish feasts. Similarly, Jesus performs only *six* "signs" during his public ministry, which manifest his glory only imperfectly, but his resurrection is the seventh sign which reveals his divine glory in its fulness. Finally, since John often speaks of weeks of seven or eight days (1,19-2,11; 7,2.14;37; 12,1.12; 19,31.42; 20,1.26), the whole Gospel can be divided into eight weeks, preceded by the Prologue and followed by a conclusion[56]:

Prologue: *1* 1-18.
Première semaine: *1* 19 - *2* 12.
    Pas de fête.
    Signe: le vin des noces de Cana (*2* 1-11).
Deuxième semaine: *2* 13 - *4* 54.
    Première Pâque (*2* 13).
    Signe: guérison d'un enfant à Capharnaum (*4* 46-54).

---

[54] *Art. cit.*, 105-113. (Cf. also the schematic presentation of the parallelisms between Jn 1-7 and Ex 3-17; 33-34 in: PASQUETTO, 99).
[55] *Art. cit.*, 110: "Et c'est cette Alliance Nouvelle [foretold by Jer 31,32-33] que le Christ est venu réaliser."
[56] BOISMARD, III, 38-39. (The divisions of the structure are given on p. 39).

Troisième semaine: 6 1-71.
    Deuxième Pâque (6 4).
    Signe: multiplication des pains (6 1-13).

Quatrième semaine: 5 1-47.
    Pentecôte (*5* 1).
    Signe: guérison d'un infirme (*5* 2-16).

Cinquième semaine: 7 1 - 10 21.
    Tentes (*7* 2.14.37).
    Signe: guérison de l'aveugle-né (*9* 1ss).

Sixième semaine: 10 22 - 11 54.
    Dédicace (*10* 22).
    Signe: résurrection de Lazare (*11* 1-44).

Septième semaine: 11 55 - 19 42.
    Troisième Pâque (*11* 55; *12* 1; *13* 1).
    Pas de signe.

Huitième semaine: 20 1-31.
    Pas de fête.
    Signe: Jésus ressuscité (cf. *2* 18-19).

Conclusion: 21 1-25.
    Pas de fête.
    Signe: Pêche miraculeuse (*21* 1-14).

Boismard is convinced that the reason why Jesus does not do any sign during the seventh week is because it corresponds to the seventh day of creation, which is a day of rest [57].

2.73 Comparison between the Two Structures

Now let us compare the two structures proposed by Boismard to see on what points they agree or disagree. First of all, both of them underline the importance of the symbolism of numbers, but, while the first structure is constructed on the sacred "seven" (cf. the 7 miracles, 7 discourses, etc. and the sevenfold division of the Fourth Gospel) [58], the foundation of the second structure is the imperfect number "six" (cf. 6 "signs" and 6 Jewish feasts) [59]! Secondly, both the structures stress the role of Jewish feasts but, whereas in the

---

[57] Trying to integrate his first structure based on the typology of creation BOISMARD affirms: "Dans la perspective de la création nouvelle, Jésus n'accomplit aucun "signe" durant la septième semaine; il ne "travaille" pas puisque cette semaine correspond au septième jour du récit de la création durant lequel Dieu "chôma après tout l'ouvrage qu'il avait fait" (Gn *2* 2)" (*ibid*.,39).

[58] Cf. 2.271 above.

[59] It must be noted that while Jesus' walking on the water (6,16-21) was regarded as a miracle in the first structure, it ceases to be a "sign" in the second structure, since BOISMARD now has to find the imperfect number "six", instead of the perfect number "seven"! Thus, instead of adjusting his theory to the text, the text is adjusted to his theory.

first structure the unnamed feast of 5,1 was linked to the Passover of Jn 6[60], the same feast is identified as Pentecost in the second structure (in which Jn 5 is placed after Jn 6, for which there is no manuscript evidence). Similarly, 10,1-21 is attached to the feast of Dedication in the first structure but to the feast of Tabernacles in the second structure. Thirdly, according to the first structure Jn 20 (the Easter week) corresponds to the day of "rest" (the 7th day) in creation; but according to the second structure it is 11,55-19,42 (and not Jn 20) which is parallel to the day of repose[61]! Thus the two structures of Boismard contradict each other on a number of points.

Furthermore, it must be noted that very few of the seven or eight "weeks" of Boismard have an explicit basis in the Johannine text.

Though some of the observations of Boismard about the liturgical, symbolical and typological aspects of the Fourth Gospel are interesting, it is difficult to establish the Gospel's structure on the symbolism of "six" or "seven" or on the typology of "creation" and/or "covenant"[62].

2.8 LITURGICAL-SYMBOLICAL-SIGN STRUCTURE (PUIGDOLLERS)

A structure which is similar to the liturgical-symbolical structure of Boismard is proposed by R. Puigdollers who bases it primarily on the liturgical feasts and signs mentioned in the Gospel[63] and secondarily on the symbolism of the number "seven"[64]. Thus the Fourth Gospel is divided into seven "nuclei" preceded by a Prologue and followed by a conclusion[65]:

---

[60] Cf. the divisions of the two structures.

[61] In the second structure the resurrection is considered as "the signe par excellence effectué par Jésus" (Synopse, III, 39).

[62] BROWN, I, cxlii. Cf. also F.-M. BRAUN's criticism of symbolical structures in *Jean le Théologien*, I, (Paris 1959) 13-16.

[63] R. PUIGDOLLERS, "Notas sobre la estructura del cuarto evangelio", *NatGrac* 19 (1972) 123-51. He states on p. 131:

"Para determinar los núcleos que constituyen la unidad del cuarto evangelio adopto el siguiente *criterio literario*: dividir el evangelio en tantas partes cuantas *fiestas* y *signos-milagros* haya." [my italics].

[64] *Ibid.*, 141-42:

Yo creo que se debe mantener una *división en siete partes con carácter simbólico*. El comparar el cuarto evangelio con la semana de la creación, encuentra su apoyo en el principio del prólogo: *en arjé* con referencia a *berêsit* en Gén 1,1. Igualmente ha sido señalado el paralelismo de la semana inaugural con la semana de la teofanía en el Sinaí, a través del Targum del Pseudo-Jonatán. Tampoco podemos olvidar que el cuarto evangelio empieza con una semana inaugural y termina con una semana santa.

[65] *Ibid.*, 133.

Prólogo		1,1-18
I. núcleo:	Bodas en Caná Conversión del agua en vino	1,19-2,11
II. núcleo:	La pascua de los judíos Curación del hijo moribundo	2,12-4,54
III. núcleo:	Una fiesta de los judíos Curación de un paralítico	5,1-47
IV. núcleo:	La pascua de los judíos Multipl. panes y paso sobre el mar	6,1-71
V. núcleo:	La fiesta judía de las Tiendas Curación de un ciego	7,1-10,21
VI. núcleo:	La fiesta de la Dedicación Resurrección de Lázaro	10,22-11,53
VII. núcleo:	La pascua de los judíos Resurrección de Jesús	11,54-20,29 (30-31) 21,1-23
Conclusión		21,24-25.

The text of the Fourth Gospel mentions six liturgical feasts (2,13; 5,1; 6,4; 7,2; 10,22; 11,55) but Puigdollers proposes the marriage at Cana (2,1) as the seventh feast because of its symbolism and its conjunction with a "sign-miracle", though it is not a liturgical feast [66].

Similarly, "the signs-miracles which at first sight appear to be seven..." [67] are reduced to six by taking the multiplication of the loaves (6,1-15) and the walking on the sea (6,16-21) as a single unit [68], so that the resurrection of Christ may be presented as the seventh sign [69].

The sevenfold "nuclear" structure is further qualified respectively as "linear", "concentric" and "parabolic" to express its dynamic character tending towards the "seventh nucleus" (VII), to underline the centrality of the middle "nucleus" (IV) and to combine the dynamic and symmetrical aspects of the structure simultaneously [70].

It is true that the Fourth Gospel mentions six liturgical feasts and seven signs but it is not certain whether the Evangelist intended each unit to consist of a feast and a sign, as Puigdollers has concluded. For instance, the resurrection of Lazarus (11,1-54) is not connected with the feast of the Dedication (10,22-42) but rather with the following Passover (11,1-12,50), since there are many cross-references and parallel elements (e.g. the mention of Martha, Mary and Lazarus at 11,1 and 12,1-3, of Mary's anointing of Jesus at 11,2 and 12,3, and of Jesus' raising of Lazarus from the dead at 11,43-44 and 12,1.9.17).

---

[66] *Ibid.*, 132: "Aunque no sea una fiesta litúrgica, las bodas de Caná son una fiesta simbolica y su unión a un signo-milagro lo confirma."
[67] *Ibid.*: "Los signos-milagros que aparecen a primera vista son siete..."
[68] *Ibid.*, 132-33.
[69] *Ibid.*, 133.
[70] *Ibid.*, 134-38.

Again, the designation of the whole of 11,54-21,23 as "the Passover of the Jews: the Resurrection of Jesus" (VII) seems to be inadequate, since the farewell discourses (Jn 13-17) and the Passion of Jesus are passed over in silence. Furthermore, the seventh division is disproportionately long (10 chapters) in comparison with the other divisions some of which consist of a single chapter (e.g. III, IV). Hence the attempt to construct a concentric structure around Jn 6 (nucleus IV) as the centre is neither successful nor acceptable. Here again we see the danger of depending on only one or two literary criteria for establishing the structure.

2.9 CHIASTIC STRUCTURE (WEBSTER)

E. C. Webster finds a chiastic structure for the Fourth Gospel as a whole [71]. According to him, "the Gospel, as a literary whole, is meticulously constructed on the basis of symmetrical design and balanced units" [72]. In his opinion, the following devices are employed by the Evangelist to achieve literary symmetry [73]:

1. a balancing of incident against incident and theme against theme in paired complementary units;
2. triadic (with some quadratic) arrangements of paired units in consecutive (a,a' - b,b' - c,c'), sequential (a,b,c - a',b',c'), or chiastic order (a-b-c-b'-a')...;
3. parallel sequences within complementary units;
4. word or formula repetitions to mark units;
5. a close balance as to length between complementary units.

Combining some of the episodes of Dodd's sevenfold division of the Book of Signs [74], Webster makes a fivefold division of the Fourth Gospel as follows [75]:

   I. chs.1-5 - from the opening of the Gospel to the healing of the paralytic at the pool (the 1st and 2nd episodes of Dodd);
   II. chs. 6-8 - the events in Galilee at Passover and those in Jerusalem at Tabernacles (Dodd's 3rd and 4th episodes);
   III. chs. 9-12 - the healing of the man born blind and the raising of Lazarus (Dodd's 5th, 6th, and 7th episodes);
   IV. chs. 13-17 - the dialogues at supper;
   V. chs. 18-21 - the passion and resurrection narratives.

---

[71] E. C. WEBSTER, "Pattern in the Fourth Gospel", in: D. J. A. Clines, D. M. Gunn & A. J. Hauser (ed.), *Art and Meaning: Rhetoric in Biblical Literature* (JSOT Supplement Series, 19), (Sheffield 1982) 230-57.
[72] *Ibid.*, 230.
[73] *Ibid.*, 231.
[74] *Ibid.* (See 2.[15] below for DODD's division of the Book of Signs).
[75] *Ibid.*

The above five sections are further divided in the following manner[76]:

THE GOSPEL ACCORDING TO ST. JOHN

Christological statement *i*: The pre-existent Son 1:1-18

I. Jesus: the source and giver of life
    A. The coming of the Christ
        1. John: men of Jer. 1:19-34   2. Galilean disciples 1:35-51
    B. His authority manifested
        1. Wedding feast 2:1-12   2. Passover: temple 2:13-25
    C. Baptismal dialogues & ministry
        1. Jerusalem & Judea   2. Samaria
          a. Nicodemus 3:1-21   a. Samaritan woman 4:4-26
          b. John's ministry closes;   b. Disciples' ministry opens;
             Jesus' ministry proclaimed   the Samaritan response to Jesus
             3:22-4:3   4:27-44
    D. Gifts of new life: healing signs
        1. Official's son 4:45-54   2. Paralytic 5:1-18

Christological statement *ii*: The Son of man, judge of all 5:19-47

II. Jesus: sustainer of life amidst the hostility of the world
        1. Passover - manna   2. Tabernacles - law
          a. Signs: feeding 6:1-27   a. Teachings & threats 7:1-30
          b. Living bread 6:28-59   b. Signs to come: departure & Spirit
                                        7:31-8:20
          c. The Holy One of God 6:60-71   c. "I am he" 8:21-30

Christological statement *iii*: The Son who frees from sin & death 8:31-59

III. Jesus: light & life, the penultimate signs
        1. Jerusalem   2. Countryside to Jerusalem
          a. Man born blind 9:1-10:6   a. Lazarus 11:1-46
          b. Door & Shepherd 10:7-21   b. False shepherds: the council
                                        11:47-57
          c. Feast of Dedication 10:22-42   c. Entry before Passover 12:1-12

Christological statement *iv*: The Son of man, lifted up 12:23-50

IV. Example & promise: abiding love & the Counselor
        1. Jesus & the disciples   2. The disciples & the world
          a. Washing the feet 13:1-20   a. Vine & branches 15:1-16
          b. Judas' departure 13:21-32   b. The world's hatred 15:17-27
          c. Dialogue 13:33-14:31   c. Dialogue 16:1-33

Christological statement *v*: The Son glorified ch. 17

---

[76] *Ibid.*, 249-50.

2.9 CHIASTIC STRUCTURE

V. Death & resurrection
   A. Jesus, abandoned & rejected
      1. The garden 18:1-14   2. The court 18:15-32
   B. Jesus before Pilate
      1. The first judgement   2. The second judgement
         18:33-19:7   19:8-16
   C. Obedience & triumph
      1. Execution   2. Burial & resurrection
        a. The cross 19:17-27   a. The tomb 19:38-20:18
        b. Death 19:28-37   b. The Risen Lord & the disciples
                                              20:19-31
   D. The figures of the Church: the third appearance
      1. The drag-net 21:1-14   2. Shepherd & flock 21:15-25.

Besides the Prologue at the beginning of the Gospel, Webster maintains that there are four "christological statements" at the end of sections I-IV, namely, 5,19-47; 8,31-59; 12,23-50; 17,1-26, which are thematically and structurally parallel to each other [77].

Thematically, the first division of each unit is supposed to contain "a complete christology of the Lord's person"; the second, "Witnesses to His Coming"; the third, "the Effect of His Coming" [78].

According to Webster, the five "christological statements" are linked to one another "chiastically" (a-b-c-b'-a') [79].

Webster claims that the "christological statements" have a similar function. "In John the christological statements open the Gospel and separate the narrative sections. They thus have a structural role similar to that of Matthew's collections of sayings and parables" [80].

Webster finds a pairing pattern in all the five narrative sections: "The five narrative sections are composed of paired complementary units" [81]. Thus section II consists of 6,1-71 and 7,1-8,30; section III is composed of 9,1-10,42 and 11,1-12,22; section IV contains a pair: 13,1-14,31 and 15,1-16,33. Sections I and V "are each composed of four shorter pairs" [82].

The paired units of each section are said to be parallel to one another and are subdivided in such a manner as to have a similar structural pattern. For instance, the two units of sections II (6,1-71; 7,1-8,30) have both an a-b-c pattern [83].

Furthermore, the five sections (I-V) form, in the opinion of Webster, a large "chiasmus" (ABCB'A'), for he says: "In addition to the parallelism within the

---

[77] *Ibid.*, 232.
[78] *Ibid.*
[79] *Ibid.*, 233.
[80] *Ibid.*
[81] *Ibid.*, 235.
[82] *Ibid.* (See I.A.B.C.D. and V.A.B.C.D. in the outline given above.)
[83] See the outline given above.

pairs of each section, there are indications of chiastic symmetry among the sections"[84]. The pairing pattern and the chiastic scheme are again underlined in the following words[85]:

> It has been argued that the structure of the johannine Gospel follows a regular pattern of paired complementary units which themselves appear to be arranged in an over-all chiastic scheme. The sections are separated by a series of structurally similar christological statements which also fall into a chiastic pattern.

From the above quotation it is quite clear that Webster's primary criterion for the division of the Gospel into five sections (I-V) is the presence of the five "christological statements" (*i-v*). But there are many other christological passages elsewhere (e.g. 3,11-21; 3,31-36; 6,22-59; 8,12-20; 8,21-30; 10,1-21; 10,22-42; 13,31-16,33, all of which are included in the narrative sections by Webster). Similarly, the triadic division of the five "christological statements" is sometimes subjective (e.g. the Prologue is divided into 1,1-5.6-8.9-18, whereas vv.6-8 are clearly parallel to v.15, since both deal with the Baptist's witness to Christ)[86]. Hence all of them cannot be said to have a triadic structural form[87]. Nor do they form a true chiasmus, since 1,1-18 ("christological statement *i*"), for instance, is parallel not only to 17,1-26 ("christological statement *v*") but also to 12,23-50 ("christological statement *iv*")[88].

Again, the pairing of some of the narrative sections does not seem to be true to the Johannine text. For example, section IV (13,1-16,33) is said to be composed of two complementary units (13,1-14,31; 15,1-16,33), the first of which is given the title "Jesus & the disciples", and the second, "the disciples & the world". But 15,1-17 (Jesus, the vine, and disciples, the branches) belongs rather under the first title than the second. Similarly, Jesus' trial before Pilate (18,28-19,16), which consists of seven alternating scenes[89], is reduced to two "judgements" (18,33-19,7 & 19,8-16).

Finally, the "chiastic symmetry among the sections" which Webster has suggested seems to be rather subjective, since it is not clear, for instance, why 2,1-24 (the changing of water into wine and the cleansing of the temple) should be regarded as parallel to 18,33-19,16 (the trial of Christ, the king, before Pilate)[90], since Jesus' kingship is not even mentioned in 2,1-24.

Because of the above reasons, the "chiastic" structure Webster has proposed seems to be subjective.

---

[84] E. C. WEBSTER, *art. cit.*, 247.
[85] *Ibid.*, 248.
[86] See 3.34 below for the division of the Prologue.
[87] E. C. WEBSTER, *art. cit.*, 232 (see especially the outline there).
[88] *Ibid.*, 248-49.
[89] Cf. A. JANSSENS DE VAREBEKE, "La structure des scènes du récit de la passion en Joh. xviii-xix", *ETL* 38 (1962) 504-22; cf. also BROWN, II, 802-3.
[90] E. C. WEBSTER, *art. cit.*, 247.

2.[10] CHIASTIC-SYMBOLIC STRUCTURE (DEEKS)

D. Deeks divides the Fourth Gospel into four parts, for he states: "St. John's Gospel consists of four sections, as follows: (A) i.1-18; (B) i.19-iv.54; (C) v.1-xii.50; and (D) xiii.1-xx.31. (John xxi, as usual, is regarded as a later appendix.)"[91]. These are further divided into subsections as given in the following figure[92]:

Fig. 1. Structure of the Fourth Gospel

A i.1-18		B i.19-iv.54				C v.1-xii.50		D xiii.1-xx.31	
Cosmological	A1								
Witness of John	A2							Resurrection and Worship	D3
The Coming of Light	A3								
Economy of Salvation	A4								
		John the Baptist	Lamb of God					Pascal Lamb / Crucifixion	D2
		B1							
		B2	Disciples	Discipleship				Jesus and His Disciples	D1
					d / c				
		B3	Purification Rites	Marriage Feast		Worship	C7		
		B4	Temple	Resurrection		Resurrection	C6		
					b				
		B5	Pharisaical Jew	Baptism		Baptism	C5		
					a / Med	Apologetic	C4		
		B6	Samaritan	Living Water		Eucharist	C3		
						Witness (a,b,c,d)	C2		
		B7	Gentile	Healing		Healing	C1		

☐ Indicates footnotes

---

[91] D. DEEKS, "The Structure of the Fourth Gospel", *NTS* 15 (1968-69) 107-29. The quotation is from p. 110.

[92] *Ibid.*, 110-20. The chart is found on p. 109, where
A = 1,1-18; B = 1,19-4,54; C = 5,1-12,50; D = 13,1-20,31; and
A1 = 1,1-5; A2 = 1,6-8; A3 = 1,9-13; A4 = 1,14-18;
B1 = 1,19-34; B2 = 1,35-51; B3 = 2,1-11; B4 = 2,13-25; B5 = 3,1-21; B6 = 4,1-42;
B7 = 4,46-54;

Note that section A (1,1-18) is divided into 4 subsections (A1-A4), sections B (1,19-4,54) and C (5,1-12,50) into 7 subsections each (B1-B7 and C1-C7 respectively), and section D (13,1-20,31) into 3 subsections (D1-D3), so that the first and the last sections make up 7 subsections.

Deeks not only follows unquestioningly C. K. Barrett's fourfold division of the Prologue (1,1-5.6-8.9-13.14-18) but also contends that the four subsections of the Prologue "provide summaries of the contents of the four main sections of the gospel, A, B, C and D"[93]. Now, since Barrett's division of the Prologue is not accepted by most Johannine scholars who have examined its literary structure more closely than Barrett[94], Deeks' claim that the four main sections of the Fourth Gospel correspond to the four subsections of the Prologue cannot be uncritically accepted. Therefore the very basis of his thesis is problematic.

Secondly, except for the arguments which are often subjective because they are based on the contents of the supposed sections[95], Deeks does not provide any literary criteria for his division of the Fourth Gospel into four main sections.

Thirdly, in order to assure a sevenfold subdivision of sections B and C, Deeks has to relegate certain parts of the Gospel to the status of "footnotes" (e.g. 3,22-36; 10,22-42; 12,37-50)[96], and artificially separate passages which form a unit (e.g. 5,1-47 is divided into two subsections C1: 5,1-30 and C2: 5,31-47[97].

C1 = 5,1-30; C2 = 5,31-47; C3 = 6,1-71; C4 = 7,1-8,59; C5 = 9,1-10,21;C6 = 11,1-57; C7 = 12,1-26;
D1 = 13,1-17,26; D2 = 18,1-19,42; D3 = 20,1-31.

[93] *Ibid.*, 110. Even the titles of the subsections of the Prologue in the chart given above have been borrowed by DEEKS from C. K. BARRETT (*The Gospel according to St. John*, 1st ed., pp. 125-26).

[94] Cf. S. A. PANIMOLLE, *Il Dono della Legge e la Grazia della Verità* (Roma 1973) 71-105. See below also our structure of the Prologue in 3.34.

[95] D. DEEKS, *op. cit.*, 110-19. The Sections A, B, C, and D are given the following "comprehensive titles":
A: "Cosmological" (110).
B: "Witness to Christ; Christ supersedes all earlier expectations" (111).
C: "The public work of Christ (the Church) in the world and the world's reaction to Christ (the Church)" (113).
D: "Economy of Salvation and the inner life of the Church which is grounded upon the saving work of Christ" (119).

How inadequate the "comprehensive titles" are and how subjective the arguments on which they are based may be seen, for instance, from DEEKS' statement about the title of Section A:

It is apparent that 'Cosmological' will serve as an adequate heading for section A as a whole. For, as we have already noted, it is much more philosophical in character than the rest of the gospel, and it attempts to relate the Incarnate One and His significance to the pre-existent being of God and His Will (*ibid.*, 110).

It must be noted that the Prologue is neither 'cosmological' nor 'philosophical' but through and through Christological and soteriological. Therefore Section A is not 'philosophy' but 'Economy of Salvation' like Section D (and Sections B and C), which DEEKS himself admits later on: "the first [section]... brings together the themes elaborated in the subsequent sections" (*ibid.*, 121).

[96] See 'a', 'b', 'c', 'd' placed in a rectangle in the diagram of the "Structure of the Fourth Gospel" given above. About 'a' DEEKS affirms: "iii.22-36 is clearly a footnote to the story about Nicodemus" (*ibid.*, 112). Likewise he says about 'b', and 'c' & 'd': "At this stage it will be tentatively suggested that x.22-42 and xii.27-50 are appendices to the basic sevenfold substructure of section C" (*ibid.*, 114).

[97] *Ibid.*, 114.

Fourthly, Deeks makes a "much more speculative" proposal that the Fourth Gospel has a "chiastic structure": "St John has arranged his material so that the latter two sections (C, D) repeat in reverse order the themes of the first two sections (A, B), and *vice versa*. That is, the gospel is arranged as a huge chiasmus: A, B; B'(=C), A' (=D)"[98]. And Deeks sets out in a table the parallel themes of A & B and C & D[99]:

Subsidiary themes in A,B	Chiastic reversal in C,D
i. 1-18 Prologue	xx. 1-31
i. 19-34 Lamb of God	xviii. 1-xix. 42
i. 35-51 Discipleship	xiii. 1-xvii. 26
ii. 1-12 Marriage Feast	xii. 1-26*
ii. 13-25 Death and Resurrection	xi. 1-57
iii. 1-21*Baptism	ix. 1-x. 21*
iii. 31-6 Meditation	vii. 1-viii. 59
iv. 1-45 Living Water and Worship	vi. 1-71
iv. 46-54 Healing	v. 1-30+

Only a few of the parallel passages in the table above have common themes; others do not. For example, one fails to see how 2,1-12 and 12,1-26 can be said to have the same theme of "marriage feast"[100]. Again, how can the discourse in 3,31-36 and the controversies in 7,1-8,59 be both called "meditations"?

Furthermore, some of the parallel themes are also found elsewhere in the Fourth Gospel. For instance, "discipleship" is described not only in 1,35-51 and 13,1-17,26 but also in 6,1-71; 7,1-8,59; 9,1-10,21; 11,1-57; 12,1-26; 18,1-19,42; 20,1-31. Or again, "living water" is explicitly mentioned not only in 4,1-45 but also in 7,1-8,59 (cf. 7,38), whereas it is not to be found in 6,1-71. Healing is narrated not merely in 4,46-54 and 5,1-30 but also in 9,1-10,21.

Besides, it must be noted that the members of Deeks' chiasmus are quite unequal in length, for while A & B consist of only 4 chapters, B' & A' (=C & D) have 16 chapters.

Finally, Deeks' chiastic-symbolic structure is quite "complicated" as he himself has admitted[101].

---

[98] *Ibid.*, 122; cf. also 126. See also the diagram on p. 109.
[99] *Ibid.*, 122; see also the explanations of the parallel themes on pp. 123-26.
[100] The reasons given on pp. 124-25 are not convincing.
[101] *Ibid.*, 121. Again on p. 126 DEEKS affirms that "the Fourth Gospel has imposed upon its *complicated* ground-plan a chiastic structure" [my italics]. Perhaps it is Deeks, not the Evangelist, who has imposed upon the Fourth Gospel a complicated chiastic structure! B. PRETE rightly remarks: "Indubbiamente l'indagine del Deeks sulla struttura del quarto vangelo appare complicata e macchinosa..." ("Vangelo di Giovanni", in: *Il Messaggio della Salvezza*, Vol. VIII, 74).
Another person who proposes a symmetrical structure for the entire Gospel patterned on that of the Prologue is J. STALEY for he states: "just as the first strophe of the prologue sets the tone for the symmetrical, rhythmic shape of the entire prologue, so also the symmetrical shape of the prologue sets the tone for the structure of the narrative to follow" ("The Structure of John's Prologue: Its Implications for the Gospel's Narrative Structure", *CBQ* 48 [1986] 242). And he suggests a chiastic

2.[11] SYMMETRICAL-CONCENTRIC STRUCTURE (WILLEMSE)

After having surveyed the various attempts to determine the structure of the Fourth Gospel by different Johannine scholars from 1844 until 1964 [102], J. J. C. Willemse proposes a symmetrical-concentric structure with its centre in Jn 9 (the healing of the blind man) [103]. He claims to detect three types of indications of criteria, which he calls "the literary-'historical' phases", "the literary-'chronological' accents" and "the literary-'theological' schemes" [104].

Because of the mention of "the beginning of the signs" at 2,11 and of "many signs" in 20,30-31, Willemse calls Jn 2-20 "the book of signs" and divides the whole Gospel into Jn 1 and 2-20 [105]. Since, however, the Gospel begins with the phrase "in the begining" (1,1) and since Jesus on the cross says: "it is finished" (19,30), Jn 1-19 is called "the book of works" and so the whole Gospel is divided into Jn 1-19 and 20 [106]. He also finds many elements which form

---

structure (A)(B)(B)(A) for the first strophe (1,1-2) (*ibid.*, 243) and a concentric structure for the Prologue: A (vv.1-5), B (vv.6-8), C (vv.9-11), D (vv.12-13), C' (v.14), B' (v.15), A' (vv.16-18) (*ibid.*, 245-49). And taking the Prologue's concentric structure as the key to the literary structure of the Gospel as a whole and the journey motif as the central element in the metaphorical-theological structure of the Gospel, he divides 1,19-21,25 into four "Ministry Tours" of Jesus (1,19-3,36; 4,1-6,71; 7,1-10,42; 11,1-21,25) (*ibid.*, 249-264; cf. especially his conclusion on p. 262 and the chart on p. 164: "The Concentric Structure of the Fourth Gospel"). First of all, it must be observed that the Prologue's first strophe does not have a chiastic but a synthetic parallel structure (see 3.313 below) and the structure of the Prologue is more spiral than concentric (see 3.34 below). Since the structure of the Gospel as a whole is based on a disputable concentric structure of the Prologue, and since it is doubtful whether the "journey motif" is central to the Fourth Gospel (e.g. one fails to see how 1,14 can be described as "The journey of the Logos into our midst" or 21,15-23 as "The journey of Jesus (metaphorical)" [*ibid*, 264]), STALEY's narrative-concentric structure of the Gospel is not convincing.

[102] J. J. C. WILLEMSE, *op. cit.*, 24-98.

[103] *Ibid.*, 99-326. See below the concentric/symmetrical structures of C. E. LUTHARDT, W. HÖNIG and A. WILD as given by WILLEMSE on p. 40:

Luthard (1951):
          Joh. i-xx
  i-x   ///   xi-xii   ///   xiii-xx
i-iii   //   iv-x   //   xi   //   xii   //   xiii-xvii   //   xviii-xx
    iv-vi/vii-ix/x   xiii/xiv-xvi/xvii

Hönig (1851):
          Joh. ii-xx
  ii-vi   //   vii-xii   //   xiii-xx
ii-iv,46/iv,46-v/vi   /   vii/viii-ix/x-xii   /   xiii-xvii/xviii-xix/xx

Wild (1877):
          Joh. i-xx
  i   //   ii-xii   //   xiii-xx
i,1-18/19-36/37-51   /   ii-iv,42/iv,43-vi/vii-xii   /   xiii-xvii/xviii-xix/xx

See 2.[12] below where C. RAU's rhythmical-symmetrical structure with its centre in Jn 11 (raising of Lazarus) is given.

[104] J. J. C. WILLEMSE, *op. cit.*, 105-43; 144-220; 221-326.

[105] *Ibid.*, 107; cf. also p. 124.

[106] *Ibid.*, 112: "De inhoudelijke bepaling van Joh.ii-xx als 'het boek der tekenen' nodigt ons als het ware uit om nu van Joh.i-xix te spreken als 'het boek der werken'".

2.[11] SYMMETRICAL-CONCENTRIC STRUCTURE 45

inclusions between Jn 1 and 20 [107] and says that Jn 20 is not an end but a new beginning because of the mention of "the first day of the week" (20,1.19), which corresponds to "the beginning" (1,1) of the Prologue [108].

Furthermore, Willemse claims that the Gospel of John is developed in six "overlapping" phases (Jn 2; 2-4; 2-6; 1,19-10,42; 1/2-12; 1/2-20) [109]. These phases are indicated, according to him, by the inclusions in the text [110]. It is a fact that some of the inclusions he gives are real (e.g. 1,1-5 & 12,46.48.50; 1,1 & 20,28) [111], while others cannot be called literary inclusions (e.g. "on the third day" at 2,1 and "in three days" at 2,19.20; "wine-sign" in 2,1-11 and "bread-sign" in 6,1-15) [112].

Willemse considers as "literary-'chronological' criteria" not only the Jewish feasts (three Passovers: 2,13; 6,4; 11,55; Tabernacles: 7,2; Dedication: 10,22), but also the "first day of the week" as the Lord's day (Sunday) and claims to find 6 Sundays in the Fourth Gospel (1,1-18; 2,1-11; Jn 6; Jn 11; 20,1-23; 20,26-29) [113]. But "the first day of the week" is explicitly mentioned only at 20,1.19.(26) and hence only these may be regarded as references to Sunday.

Finally, according to Willemse, there are four "revelation-diptychs" in the Gospel of John (2,1-11 & 2,13-22; 5,1-18 & 6,1-15; 11,1-44 & 12,1-19; 18 & 20). And the two members of each diptych underline respectively the twofold basic creed of the Fourth Gospel, namely, Jesus is "the Christ" and "the Son of God" [114]. These two Christological titles correspond respectively to the twin themes: Jesus "crucified" and "risen" [115].

The chapters between the above four "revelation-diptychs" are called "intervals" (Jn 3-4; 7-10; 13-17), in each of which "dialogue" and "sign" alternate, thus forming a symmetrical construction [116]:

a - gesprek: Joh.iii,1-iv,42
b - teken: Joh.iv,46-54
    a - gesprek: Joh.vii,1-viii,59
    b - teken: Joh.ix,1-7
    a - gesprek: Joh.ix,8-x,39
b - 'voorbeeld': Joh.xiii,1-17
a - gesprek: Joh.xiii,18-xvii,26

---

[107] *Ibid.*, 115-16.
[108] *Ibid.*, 117: "Het gaat niet over een einde, maar over een nieuw begin." See also the footnote 18 on p. 117.
[109] *Ibid.*, 122-24.
[110] *Ibid.*
[111] *Ibid.*, 123-24; 115.
[112] *Ibid.*, 124-25. But a mere similarity between two expressions or episodes is not enough to constitute a literary inclusion.
[113] *Ibid.*, 145-220.
[114] *Ibid.*, 276-90.
[115] *Ibid.*, 291-300.
[116] *Ibid.*, 301-2.

The first "interval" (Jn 3-4) is described as "the dialogue with faith-candidates", the second (Jn 7-10) as "dialogue with the unbelievers", and the third (Jn 13-17) as "the dialogue with the believers"[117].

Willemse gives the following graphical representation of the symmetrical-concentric structure of the Fourth Gospel[118]:

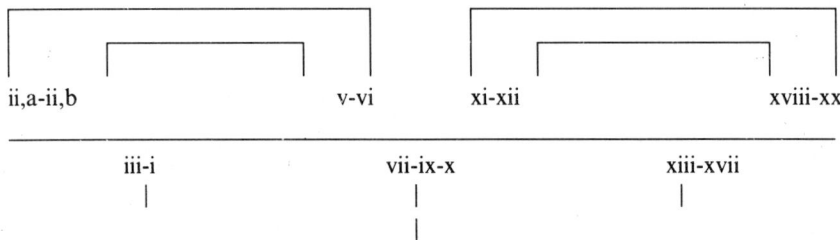

Without entering into a detailed discussion of this symmetrical structure consisting of four "revelation-diptychs" and three "intervals", we may make the following critical remarks: 1) If it is true that 2,1-11 and 2,13-22 form a diptych of two revelatory scenes, it is equally true that 6,1-15 and 6,16-21 form another similar diptych, and a third diptych is formed by 12,1-11 and 12,12-19, and so on. 2) One fails to see why 5,1-18 & 6,1-15; 11,1-44 & 12,1-19, and 18 & 20 should be regarded as diptychs, since the two members of each diptych do not succeed each other immediately but are separated from each other by a discourse or narrative (5,19-47; 11,45-57; 19). 3) The basic creed of the Fourth Gospel is not simply that Jesus is the Christ and the Son of God, as is supposed by Willemse, but that Jesus is also the life-giver or the life of the believers (cf. 20,31). While it is true that some pericopes underline one of the Christological themes mentioned above (e.g. "the Son of God": 2,13-22; 5,1-18), it is difficult to prove that each member of Willemse's diptychs has only one theme (e.g. 11,1-44 contains all the three themes [cf. 11,25-27]). 4) Similarly, "the crucified Christ" and "the risen Son of God" cannot be ascribed only to one of the members of each diptych (as Willemse does)[119], because often the same pericope contains both the aspects (e.g. 2,19: "Destroy this temple, and in three days I will raise it up"). 5) It may be granted that some of the parallelisms given by Willemse are valid (e.g. between 2,13-22 and 5,1-18; 11,1-44 and 20,1-29). But some of the "phases" (e.g. Jn 2; 2-6) seem to be artificially imposed on the Gospel. For instance, 2,23-25 is intimately related to 3,1-21, and hence 2,1-25 should not be considered as the first phase or unit[120].

---

[117] *Ibid.*, 302-8; 308-17; 3,17-21.
[118] *Ibid.*, 326. In the scheme ii,a = Jn 2,1-11 and ii,b = 2,13-22.
[119] *Ibid.*, 323.
[120] See 3.191 below.

2.[12] RHYTHMICAL-SYMMETRICAL STRUCTURE (RAU)

C. Rau proposes a rhythmical-symmetrical structure, for which he employs basically the principle of thematic correspondence between the events in the first half of the Gospel (1,19-10,39) and those in the second half (11,54-21,24), which are arranged symmetrically around the central event of the raising of Lazarus (10,40-11,53) [121]. Besides the Prologue, the Fourth Gospel is divided into "*17 Sections*" [122]. The beginning of each of these Sections is marked by a stylistic sign such as the expression *meta touto/tauta* (2,12; 3,22; 5,1; 6,1; 7,1; 19,38; 21,1) or the identification of a place or the name of a Jewish feast [123].

Rau claims also to detect three great "rhythms" within the above 17 Sections: (1) the seven "sign-deeds", (2) the seven "I-Am-Sayings", and (3) the seven "Agape-centres", which reveal respectively Christ's deed, word and being [124]. We give below the chart of "the three great rhythms within the 17 Sections" [125] (cf. also "the reflected [mirror-image-like] construction of the Gospel of John" [126]).

Die drei grossen Rhythmen innerhalb der 17 Abschnitte

Prolog	(1,1-18)	
I	(1,19-2,11)	1. Hochzeit zu Kana
II	(2,12-3,21)	—
III	(3,22-4,54)	2. Heilung des Knaben

---

[121] C. RAU, *Struktur und Rhythmus im Johannes-Evangelium* (Stuttgart 1972) 18-42. On p. 20 he states "the principle of correspondence":

Im Folgenden wenden wir *das Prinzip der Entsprechung* auf alle im Johannes-Evangelium geschilderten Ereignisse an. *Paarweise gruppieren sie sich um das Zentralereignis, die Auferweckung des Lazarus.* Ein Abschnitt der ersten Evangelienhälfte steht jeweils einem Abschnitt der zweiten Evangelienhälfte gegenüber, und zwar in umgekehrter Reihenfolge: Der Beginn der ersten Hälfte entspricht dem Schluss der zweiten Hälfte, und so fort. Wie die Säulen einer Tropfsteinhöhle von oben und von unten aufeinander zuwachsen, so wächst das Evangelium zugleich vom Anfang und vom Schluss zur Mitte zu, bis beide Richtungen sich treffen. Von vorn und von hinten zielt die kompositorische Anlage des gesamten Werkes auf das zentrale Ereignis: die Auferweckung des Lazarus. Die beiden besprochnen Sätze [1,19 & 21,24] bilden eine Art Rahmen für die übrigen spiegelbildlichen Entsprechungen, welche uns Einblick gewähren in die grossartige Komposition dieses Werkes. [my italics].

[122] *Ibid.*, 43: "Die im Vorangehenden gezeigten thematischen Entsprechungen lassen erkennen, dass das Johannes-Evangelium aus ingesamt *17 Abschnitten* besteht. Ihnen ist ein *Prolog* vorangestellt."

[123] *Ibid.*, 43-52. The 17 Sections are said to begin with the following verses: 1) 1,19; 2) 2,12; 3) 3,22; 4) 5,1; 5) 6,1; 6) 7,1; 7) 7,53; 8) 9,1; 9) 10,40; 10) 11,54; 11) 12,36; 12) 13,31; 13) 14,31b; 14) 17,1; 15) 18,1; 16) 19,38; 17) 21,1 (pp.50-52).

[124] *Ibid.*, 53-109. Cf. also p. 116:
die sieben Zeichen: die Werk-Offenbarung Christi
die sieben Ich-Bin-Worte: die Wort-Offenbarung Christi
die sieben Agape-Zentren: die Wesens-Offenbarung Christi.

[125] *Ibid.*, 108-9. [A comma has been added by me between the chapters and verses.]

[126] *Ibid.* See also the attached sheet ("Der spiegelbildliche Aufbau des Johannes-Evangeliums") at the end of the book.

IV	(5,1-5,47)	3. Heilung des Gelähmten	
V	(6,1-6,71)	4. Speisung der Fünftausend	Ich bin das Brot des Lebens
		5. Wandeln auf dem Meer	
VI	(7,1-7,52)	—	—
VII	(7,53-8,59)	—	Ich bin das Licht der Welt
VIII	(9,1-10,39)	6. Heilung des Blinden	Ich bin die Tür/ Ich bin der rechte Hirte
IX	(10,40-11,53)	1) Liebe als Fundament der Geist-Gemeinschaft	Ich bin die Auferstehung und das Leben
		7. Auferstehung des Lazarus	
X	(11,54-12,36a)	—	—
XI	(12,36b-13,30)	—	—
XII	(13,31-14,31a)	2) Liebe als Erkennungsmerkmal	Ich bin der Weg, die Wahrheit, das Leben
		3) Liebe als Zugang zum Vater	
XIII	(14,31b-16,33)	4) Liebe als Bleiben beim Vater	Ich bin der wahre Weinstock
		5) Liebe als Todes-Durchgangs-Kraft	
XIV	(17,1-17,26)	6) Liebe als Gotteserkenntnis	
XV	(18,1-19,37)	—	
XVI	(19,38-20,31)	—	
XVII	(21,1-21,23)	7) Liebe als Lebenswegzehrung	

Even though some of Rau's criteria are objective (e.g. *meta tauta/touto*, liturgical and geographical indications), they are often applied arbitrarily (e.g. *meta tauta* at 5,14 is not mentioned) or mechanically (e.g. *meta touto* at 2,12 is taken as the beginning of the second Section [2,12-3,21], though 2,12 is a transition between 2,1-11 and 2,13-22; *meta de tauta* at 19,38 is (mis)understood as indicating a new Section [19,38-20,31], though the burial of Jesus [19,38-42] is linked more with the other scenes on Calvary [19,16c-37] than with the resurrection scenes [20,1-29]). Similarly, 12,36b (Jesus' hiding) and 14,31b (Jesus' saying: "Rise, let us go hence"), which clearly point to the end of the episode or discourse, are (mis)taken by Rau as the beginning of new Sections (12,36b-13,30; 14,31b-16,33), which shows his arbitrariness regarding the delimitations of the Sections. Often a Section is said to be parallel to another merely because the name of a person (e.g. Nicodemus in Sections II [2,12-3,21] and XVI [19,38-20,31] or "the Spirit" in Sections VI [7,1-52] and XII [13,31-14,31a]) or a term (e.g. "light" in Sections VIII [9,1-10,39] and X [11,54-12,36a]) occurs in both of them, though it is found also in other Sections, which are passed over in silence by Rau (e.g. Nicodemus at 7,50; "the Spirit" at 1,32-33; 3,5-8; 6,63; etc.). Thus, although some of Rau's observations are interesting (e.g. the role of the miracles in structuring the Gospel), many of his findings are far-fetched and fantastic (e.g. the parallelism between many Sections) and his conclusions about the rhythmical-symmetrical structure of the Fourth Gospel are unconvincing [127].

2.[13] CENTRIC-SYMMETRICAL STRUCTURE (KAMMERSTÄTTER)

J. Kammerstätter defends the thesis: "The Gospel of John consists of planned units of text which are arranged in centred symmetry around central sentences" [128]. The entire Fourth Gospel is divided into 23 units or Sections (*"Grossabschnitte"*) followed by a conclusion (20,30-31) and an appendix (Jn 21) [129]. Each of the 23 Sections is composed of an odd number of paragraphs (*"Teilabschnitte"*) which are symmetrically arranged around a central proposition (*"Zentralsatz"*). We give below the Sections and their divisions into paragraphs with their central verses [130]:

Sections	*Divisions of the Sections*
1) 1,1-18:	1,1-5. 6-7. 8-10. *11.* 12-13. 14. 15-18
2) 1,19-34:	1,19-20. 21-23. 24-25. *26-28.* 29. 30-32. 33-34
3) 1,35-2,12:	1,35-40. 41-42. 43-46. 47-48. *49.* 50-51; 2,1-5. 6-8. 9-12
4) 2,13-25:	2,13-17. 18. *19.* 20. 21-25
5) 3,1-21:	3,1-2. 3-4. 5-9. 10. *11.* 12. 13-17. 18-19b. 19c-21
6) 3,22-36:	3,22-24. 25-27. *28-30.* 31-33. 34-36
7) 4,1-42:	4,1-6a. 6b-7. 8-12. 13-15. 16-18. *19-23b.* 23c-26. 27-30. 31-36. 37-38. 39-42
8) 4,43-54:	4,43-46b. *46c-51.* 52-54
9) 5,1-47:	5,1-9. 10-18. 19-20. 21-23. *24.* 25-27. 28-30. 31-38. 39-47
10) 6,1-71:	6,1-13. 14-21. 22-25. 26-31. 32-35. *36.* 37-40. 41-46. 47-52. 53-59. 60-71

---

[127] H. LEROY concludes the review of RAU's book with the following critical remark:
   Er stellt in phantastischer Analyse drei grosse Rhythmen heraus, die ineinander verschränkt sind: die sieben Zeichentaten, die sieben Ich-Bin-Worte, die sieben Agapezentren. Sie bedeuten die Werkoffenbarung, die Wortoffernbarung, die Wesenoffenbarung Christi. - Rezensent gesteht, dass er das Buch interessiert gelesen hat, den Beobachtungen und Schlussfolgerungen des Verf. indes letzlich nicht zu folgen vermag. (*TRu* 70 [1974] 23).

[128] J. KAMMERSTÄTTER, *op. cit.*, 56:
   "THESE: DAS JOHANNESEVANGELIUM BESTEHT AUS GEPLANTEN TEXTEINHEITEN, DIE IN ZENTRIERTER SYMMETRIE UM ZENTRALSÄTZE ANGEORDNET SIND."
   Again at the conclusion of the dissertation the author affirms: "jeder Grossabschnitt des Johev hat einen Zentralsatz, um den einander symmetrisch entsprechende Teilabschnitte angeordnet sind" (308).

[129] *Ibid.*, 58.

[130] *Ibid.*, 58-62; 282-305. (The *"Zentralsätze"* are written in italics e.g. Jn 1,*11.*)

Sections	Divisions of the Sections
11) 7,1-52:	7,1-8. 9-13. 14-20. 21-24. 25-26. *27*. 28-29. 30-32. 33-38. 39-42. 43-52
12) 8,12-59:	8,12-16. 17-20. 21-22. 23-29. 30-33. 34-35. *36*. 37-38. 39-41. 42-47. 48-50. 51-53. 54-59
13) 9,1-10,42:	9,1-9. 10-12. 13-17. 18-21. 22-23. 24-34. 35-41; *10,1-6*. 7-16. 17-18. 19-24. 25-31. 32-33. 34-42
14) 11,1-54:	11,1-4. 5-10. 11-13. 14-16. 17-22. 23-24. *25-32*. 33-34. 35-40. 41-42. 43-44. 45-50. 51-54
15) 11,55-12,50:	11,55-57; 12,1-3. 4-6. 7-11. 12-16. 17-19. 20-23. *24-25*. 26-28. 29-32. 33-36c. 36d-40. 41-43. 44-47. 48-50
16) 13,1-30:	13,1-9. 10-11. 12-13. *14-15*. 16-17. 18-19. 20-30
17) 13,31-14,31c:	13,31-33. 34-37. 38-14,5. 6-8. 9-11. *12*. 13-17. 18-20. 21-24. 25-28b. 28c-31c
18) 14,31d-15,27:	14,31d-15,8. 9-10. 11-13. *14-15*. 16-17. 18-19. 20-27
19) 16,1-33:	16,1-4b. 4c-11. 12-13. 14-15. 16-18. *19*. 20-21. 22-23a. 23b-24. 25-30. 31-33
20) 17,1-26:	17,1-3. 4-8. 9-11c. *11d-15*. 16-19. 20-23. 24-26
21) 18,1-40:	18,1-2. 3-9. 10-11. 12-16. 17-18. *19-24*. 25-27. 28-30. 31-37. 38-42
22) 19,1-42:	19,1-6. 7-12. 13-14. 15-18. 19-21. *22*. 23-24. 25-27. 28-30. 31-37. 38-42
23) 20,1-29:	20,1-8. 9-10. 11-13. *14-18*. 19-21. 22-23. 24-29
[24] 20,30-31:	[Conclusion]
[25] 21,1-25:	21,1-2.3-7b. 7c-13. *14*. 15-191. 19b-23. 24-25

Now looking carefully at Kammerstätter's division of the Fourth Gospel into Sections and paragraphs, one realizes the arbitrariness of some of the divisions (e.g. 9,1-10,42 is regarded as one unit, although there is a new beginning [the feast of Dedication] indicated clearly at 10,22; similarly, 18,1-40 is considered as an independent Section separate from 19,1-42, but 18,28-19,16b certainly forms a unit which describes Jesus' trial before Pilate). The divisions of some of the Sections are even more arbitrary (e.g. the Prologue is divided into 7 paragraphs as follows; 1,1-5.6-7.8-10. 11.12-13.14.15-18). Again, some of the central sentences ("*Zentralsätze*"), around which the Sections are supposed to be symmetrically constructed, are not always the most significant statements in the Sections concerned (e.g. 6,36; 7,27; 19,22).

Although some of the criteria Kammerstätter has used are valid (e.g. repetitions, inclusions, introductions, framing)[131], the validity of some others[132]

---

[131] *Ibid.*, 56.
[132] KAMMERSTÄTTER states unambiguously:

Das Johev selbst bietet folgende Kriterien für eine Strukturanalyse an: die formale Funktion der AMHN- und EGO EIMI-Sätze, der AT-Zitate, der Jesusworte mit syn Anklängen und der Stileigentümlichkeiten des Vf. Weitere formale Kriterien sind z.B. alte Einteilungen in griechischen Kodizes oder Nahtstellen des Textes, für die psychologische Erklärungen versucht wurden. In fast allen Grossabschnitten des Johev treten mehrere Kriterien zugleich auf und untermauern die Konzentrik auch im statischen Wortbestand (*ibid.*, 149).

for the structure can be questioned. For instance, while it is true that the double *Amên* formula emphasizes the saying of Jesus, it is doubtful whether it is always employed to underline "the central propositions" or the beginning or end of paragraphs, as is claimed by Kammerstätter[133]. Again, his conclusion concerning the formal function of the *Egô eimi* sayings that the absolute form is always used to conclude a paragraph (4,26; 8,24.28; 13,19) or Section (8,58) and that the others always form the beginning of the paragraphs[134], is not quite true (cf. 8,24 and 11,25, for instance).

Similarly, whether all the OT quotations, except those spoken by Jesus, have the formal function of concluding the paragraphs[135] is open to question, since many OT citations are found in the middle of Johannine units (e.g. 6,31; 7,42; 12,15).

Finally, one wonders whether the Fourth Evangelist was such an unimaginative author as to use only the concentric structure for all the Sections as Kammerstätter would like us to believe[136].

2.[14] NARRATIVE STRUCTURE (PRETE)

B. Prete proposes a narrative structure of the Fourth Gospel which tells the story of the life of Jesus Christ (his public ministry, passion, death and resurrection). It is divided into four principal blocks (1,1-18; 1,19-12,50; 13,1-20,31; 21,1-25), which are further subdivided into sections and subsections as follows[137]:

I) PROLOGO: 1,1-18

II) PRIMA PARTE: 1,19-12,50, la quale a sua volta è divisa nelle seguenti sezioni:

1) Preparazione all'attività di Gesù: 1,19-51
   a. la testimonianza del Battista: 1,19-34
   b. i primi discepoli di Gesù: 1,35-51

2) Inizi dell'attività di Gesù: 2,1-4,54
   a. le nozze di Cana (primo miracolo): 2,1-12
   b. Gesù a Gerusalemme (prima Pasqua): 2,13-3,21
      - la purificazione del tempio: 2,13-25
      - incontro con Nicodemo: 3,1-21

---

[133] *Ibid.*, 182.
[134] *Ibid.*, 194.
[135] *Ibid.*, 239.
[136] We shall see later that the Fourth Evangelist has used a variety of structures (parallel, chiastic, concentric, spiral) for the composition of the Gospel.
[137] B. PRETE, "Vangelo di Giovanni", in: *Il Messaggio della Salvezza*, VIII, 4 ed., (Torino 1978) 62-66. [We have left out the subdivisions of a, b, c, etc.].

c. ultima testimonianza del Battista: 3,22-36
   d. Gesù in Samaria: incontro con la Samaritana: 4,1-42
   e. ritorno di Gesù in Galilea e guarigione del figlio di un funzionario regio (secondo miracolo): 4,43-54

3) Pienezza dell'attività taumaturgica e rivelatrice di Gesù: 5,1-10,39
   a. guarigione del paralitico alla piscina di Betzata a Gerusalemme e rivelazione della missione di Gesù da parte del Padre (seconda Pasqua oppure festa della Pentecoste): 5,1-47
   b. moltiplicazione dei pani e discorso sul pane di vita in Galilea: 6,1-71
   c. la grande rivelazione messianica di Gesù nella festa dei Tabernacoli: 7,1-52
   d. altre importanti rivelazioni di Gesù e forti reazioni dei giudei: 8,12-59
   e. guarigione del cieco nato: 9,1-41
   f. il discorso sul buon pastore: 10,1-21
   g. ultima rivelazione di Gesù nella festa della Dedicazione: 10,22-39

4) Ultimi fatti dell'attività pubblica di Gesù: 10,40-12,50
   a. risurrezione di Lazzaro (settimo miracolo) e decisione del sinedrio di uccidere Gesù: 10,40-11,54
   b. ultimo viaggio di Gesù a Gerusalemme (terza Pasqua): 11,55-12,50

III) SECONDA PARTE: 13,1-20,31; questo blocco narrativo contiene le seguenti sezioni:

1) Ultima cena e discorsi di addio: 13,1-17,26
   a. i fatti dell'ultima cena: 13,1-30
      - lavanda dei piedi e suo significato: 13,1-20
      - Gesù predice il tradimento di Giuda e svela l'apostolo che lo tradirà: 13,21-30
   b. i discorsi di addio: 13,31-17,26
      - primo discorso di addio: 13,31-14,31
      - secondo discorso di addio: 15,1-16,33
      - la preghiera di addio: 17,1-26

2) Passione e morte di Gesù: 18,1-19,42
   a. Gesù davanti alle autorità giudaiche: 18,1-27
   b. Gesù davanti a Pilato: 18,28-19,16a
   c. crocifissione, morte e sepoltura di Gesù: 19,16b-42

3) Risurrezione ed apparizioni del Risorto: 20,1-31
   a. la tomba vuota: 20,1-10
   b. l'apparizione a Maria di Magdala: 20,11-18
   c. l'apparizione ai discepoli: 20,19-25
   d. l'apparizione a Tommaso: 20,26-29
   e. conclusione del vangelo: 20,30-31

IV) APPENDICE: 21,1-25
   a. l'apparizione del Risorto sulle rive del lago e pesca miracolosa: 21,1-14
   b. conferimento del potere pastorale a Pietro e predizione del suo martirio: 21,15-19
   c. la sorte del discepolo che Gesù amava: 21,20-23
   d. altra conclusione del vangelo: 21,24-25.

Prete does not tell us explicitly about the criteria he has used in detecting the structure or the coordinating principle which, in his opinion, the Evangelist has employed in structuring the Gospel. Prete seems to have based his structure on the "narrative" aspect of the Gospel, since the first part (1,19-12,50) is divided into four sections described in terms of Jesus' "activity": 1) "Preparation to the activity of Jesus" (1,19-51), 2) "Beginning of the activity of Jesus" (2,1-4,54), 3) "Fulness of the miraculous and revelatory activity of Jesus" (5,1-10,39), and 4) "Final facts of the public activity of Jesus" (10,40-12,50), and since the second part (13,1-20,31) is called a "narrative block" which contains the three sections entitled 1) "Last supper and farewell discourses" (13,1-17,26), 2) "Passion and death of Jesus" (18,1-19,42), and 3) "Resurrection and apparitions of the Risen one" (20,1-31)[138]. However, this "narrative" aspect is common to all the four Gospels, since they "narrate" the life, death and resurrection of Jesus.

Secondly, Prete's structure does not sufficiently stress other aspects of the Fourth Gospel such as the dramatic aspect[139] and the role of discourses[140].

Thirdly, some of the divisions and subdivisions of the structure are questionable. For instance, 1,19-51 is taken by Prete as belonging only to the first part (1,19-12,50), although it functions as part of the introduction to the Gospel as a whole[140a]. Similarly, 20,30-31, which is clearly the conclusion of the whole Gospel, is regarded as part of the third section (20,1-31) of the second part (13,1-20,31)[140b].

2.[15] NARRATIVE-DISCOURSE STRUCTURE (DODD)

C. H. Dodd divides the Fourth Gospel into three principal parts (1,1-51; 2,1-12,50; 13,1-20,31), followed by an Appendix (Jn 21). These are subdivided as follows[141]:

A. THE PROEM: PROLOGUE AND TESTIMONY (1,1-51)
    1) the Prologue (1,1-18)
    2) the Testimony (1,19-51)

B. THE BOOK OF SIGNS (2,1-12,50)
    1) First Episode. The New Beginning (2,1-4,42)
        (a) The miracle of Cana (2,1-12)
        (b) The cleansing of the temple (2,13-25)
        (c) Discourse with Nicodemus (3,1-21)
        --- Appendix (3,22-36)
        (d) Discourse with the Samaritan woman (4,1-42)

---

[138] *Ibid.* V. PASQUETTO characterizes PRETE's structure as "Struttura secondo l'aspetto 'narrativo'" (*Da Gesù al Padre*, 102).
[139] Cf. 2.[16-18] below.
[140] Cf. C. H. DODD's "narrative-discourse" structure below (2.[15]).
[140a] See 4.112 below.
[140b] See 4.111 below.
[141] C. H. DODD, *The Interpretation of the Fourth Gospel* (Cambridge 1953) 289-443.

2) Second Episode. The Life-giving Word (4,46-5,47)
   (a) The healing of the nobleman's son (4,46-54)
   (b) The healing of the paralytic (5,1-18)
   (c) Discourse on the Son's activity of giving life (5,19-47)
3) Third Episode. Bread of Life (6,1-71)
   (a) The feeding of the multitude (6,1-15)
   (b) The walking on the water (6,16-21)
   (c) Discourse on the bread of life (6,22-59)
   --- Appendix (6,60-71)
4) Fourth Episode. Light and Life: Manifestation and Rejection (7,1-8,59)
   (a) Introductory (7,1-10)
   (b) Scene at the Feast of Tabernacles in the absence of Jesus (7,11-13)
   (c) Jesus at the Feast. First dialogue: theme, Moses and Christ (7,14-24)
   (d) Second dialogue: the messianic claims of Jesus... (7,25-36)
   (e) Third dialogue..., the messianic claims of Jesus (7,37-44)
   (f) Fourth dialogue. The same theme continued... (7,45-52)
   (g) Fifth dialogue..., the nature and value of the evidence for the claims of Jesus (8,12-20)
   (h) Sixth dialogue..., the challenge of Jesus to the Jewish leaders (8,21-30)
   (i) Seventh and closing dialogue..., Abraham, his 'seed' and Christ... (8,31-59)
5) Fifth Episode. Judgement by the Light (9,1-10,39)
   (a) The healing of the blind man (9,1-12)
   (b) Dialogue in the form of a trial scene (9,13-41)
   (c) Discourse on the shepherd and the flock (10,1-21)
   --- Appendix (10,22-39)
6) Sixth Episode. The Victory of Life over Death (11,1-53)
   (a) The raising of Lazarus (narrative and dialogue interwoven) (11,1-44)
   (b) The meeting of the Sanhedrin (11,47-53)
7) Seventh Episode. Life through Death. The Meaning of the Cross (12,1-36)
   (a) The anointing at Bethany (12,1-8)
   (b) The triumphal entry into Jerusalem (12,12-19)
   (c) Discourse on the approaching Passion (12,20-36)
   -- Epilogue to the Book of Signs (12,37-50)
   (i) The Evangelist's comment on the story of Jesus (12,37-43)
   (ii) *Résumé* of the salient points of the preaching of Jesus (12,44-50)

C. THE BOOK OF THE PASSION (13,1-20,31)
   I. The Farewell Discourses (13,1-17,26)
      (a) Opening dramatic scene (13,1-20)
      (b) Dialogue on Christ's departure and return (13,31-14,31)
      (c) Discourse on Christ and His Church (15,1-16,33)
      (d) The Prayer of Christ (17,1-26)
   II. The Passion-Narrative (18,1-20,31)

D. APPENDIX (21,1-25)[142].

---

[142] Jn 21 is not discussed in detail, since it is taken as a "postscript", for DODD says: "Ch. xxi, whether the work of the evangelist or of another, has the character of a postscript, and falls outside the design of the book as a whole" (*ibid.*,290).

Dodd has undoubtedly discovered a characteristic feature of the composition of the Fourth Gospel in the connection between narratives and discourses. This is considered as the criterion for the division of the Book of Signs into episodes: "This seems naturally to divide itself into seven episodes, each consisting of one or more narratives of significant acts of Jesus, accompanied by one or more discourses"[143].

Dodd detects a similar pattern of narrative and discourse in the Book of the Passion, where, however, the discourses are followed by the narrative, while the narratives are followed by the discourses in the Book of Signs[144].

Although it is true that the Fourth Evangelist often places the narrative first and then explains its significance by means of a discourse (e.g. the multiplication of the loaves in 6,1-15 and the discourse on the bread of life in 6,22-59), he also feels free to end an episode with a discourse (e.g. 5,19-47) or with a dialogue (e.g. 6,67-71) or with a narrative (e.g. 4,46-54) or to interweave a narrative and a dialogue/discourse into one tightly knit episode (e.g. 11,1-44). So Dodd's relegation of a number of Johannine passages to the status of "appendixes" (3,22-36; 6,60-71; 10,22-39) in order apparently to end the episodes with a discourse seems to be unwarranted and does violence to the organic structure of the Johannine Gospel. Secondly, Dodd appears to be much too interested in the number "seven", since he seems to be determined to find seven episodes in the Book of Signs (but to obtain seven episodes he has to denote Jn 10,22-39 as a mere "appendix") and only seven dialogues in the fourth episode (7,1-8,59). Thirdly, some of the divisions according to themes (e.g. 4,46-5,47; 15,1-16,33) seem to be subjective and open to different interpretations[145].

2.[16] DRAMATIC-CHRONOLOGICAL-GEOGRAPHICAL STRUCTURE (TENNEY)

M. C. Tenney thinks that the Fourth Gospel has a dramatic structure, since it contains a plot which "reveals the perennial struggle between good and evil evinced in the contest of belief and unbelief directed towards the person of the Lord Jesus"[146]. The stages of the development of the plot are as follows[147]:

---

[143] *Ibid.*, 290. In the conclusion of his "argument and structure" of the Book of Signs he affirms unambiguously: "The unit of structure is the single episode composed of narrative and discourse, both related to a single dominant theme" (*ibid.*, 384).

[144] *Ibid.*, 290-91.

[145] J. CABA designates DODD's structure of the Fourth Gospel as a "thematic structure" (*struttura tematica*) and critically remarks: "La strutturazione per temi si presta più facilmente a interpretazioni personali" (*Dai Vangeli al Gesù Storico*, 343). Cf. also p. 339.

[146] M. C. TENNEY, *John: The Gospel of Belief* (Michigan 1953) 36-53. The quotation is from p. 51.

[147] *Ibid.*, 36.

Prologue	1:1-18
The Period of Consideration	1:19-4:54
The Period of Controversy	5:1-6:71
The Period of Conflict	7:1-11:53
The Period of Crisis	11:54-12,36a
The Period of Conference	12:36b-17:26
The Period of Consummation	18:1-20:31
Epilogue	21:1-25

The validity of the logical sequence of the dramatic divisions is confirmed, in the opinion of Tenney, by the chronological and geographical indications in the text of the Gospel [148]:

THE STRUCTURE OF THE GOSPEL OF JOHN BY DIVISIONS

ACTION	CHRONOLOGICAL		GEOGRAPHICAL	
Prologue 1:1-18				
Period of Consideration 1:19-4:54	Day One	1:19-28	Bethany beyond Jordan	1:28
	"On the morrow"	1:29-34		
	"On the morrow"	1:35-42		
	"On the morrow"	1:43-51		
	Day Three	2:1-11	Cana of Galilee	2:1-11
	"After this"	2:12	Capernaum	2:12
	"Abode not many days"			
	The *Passover* at hand	2:13-22	Jerusalem	2:13-3:21
	During *Passover*	2:23-3:21		
	"After these things"	3:22-36	Land of Judea	3:22-36
	During activity of John	4:1	Aenon near Salim	3:23
	"After two days"	4:43	Samaria	4:1-42
			Galilee	4:43
			Cana	4:46
Period of Controversy 5:1-6:71	"After these things" A *Feast*	5:1-47	Jerusalem	5:1
	"After these things"	6:1-21	Other side of Galilee	6:1
	Passover at hand	6:4	Proceeded to Capernaum	
				6:16,17
	"On the morrow"	6:22-59	Synagogue at Capernaum	6:59

[148] *Ibid.*, 40-48. The outline is found on pp. 40-41.

ACTION	CHRONOLOGICAL		GEOGRAPHICAL	
Period of Conflict 7:1-11:53	"After these things" Feast of Tabernacles at hand 7:2	7:1-13	Galilee	7:1-13
	"The midst of the Feast" 7:14		Jerusalem	7:14-10:39
			Jerusalem	7:53-8:11
	Feast of Dedication		Aenon (?)	10:40-11:16
		10:22-39	Bethany	11:17-53
Period of Crisis 11:54-12,36a	Passover at hand	11:54-57	Ephraim	11:54-57
	"Six days before the Passover"	12:1-11	Bethany	12:1-11
	"On the morrow"	12:12-36	Jerusalem	12:12
Period of Conference 12:36b-17:26	"Before the Feast of the Passover"	13:1	Room in city	13:1-14:31a
			Removal	14:31b-17:26
Period of Consummation 18:1-20:31			Crossing Kidron Garden	18:1-11
			House of Annas Court of Caiaphas (?)	18:12-14
				18:15-27
	"Sixth hour"	19:14	Praetorium	18:28-19:16
			Golgotha	19:17-30
	"Preparation	19:31	Garden burial	19:31-42
	First Day	20:1-18	Garden tomb	20:1-18
	Evening	20:19-25	Upper room	20:19-25
	Eighth Day	20:26-29	Upper room	20:26-29
Epilogue 21:1-25	"After these things"	21:1-23	Sea of Tiberias	21:1-23

It is true that there is a plot in the Gospel of John, illustrated by the vocabulary, built upon the characters and expressed in the action[149], but whether the stages of the plot are those given by Tenney is questionable. For instance, 7,1-11,53 is called "the Period of Conflict", because he says: "The Period of Conflict, 7:1-11:53, records events which illustrate definite hostility

---

[149] *Ibid.*, 51.

between Jesus and His critics which had sharpened to bitter hatred. No less than four times was it stated that the Jews sought to kill Jesus (7:19,25, 8:37, 11:53)"[150]. But Jewish attempts to kill Jesus were already reported at 5,18. Similarly, one wonders why 12,36b-50 is combined with 13,1-17,26, since the former does not speak of any "conference" of Jesus with the disciples. Furthermore, though the table of the chronological and geographical indications in the Fourth Gospel is useful, its division seems to be rather arbitrary. For instance, talking about the unity of 1,19-2,11 Tenney states:

> Actual chronology begins with John 1:19. From this beginning of the ministry of John the Baptist to the close of the marriage at Cana there is *one group of events tied together by a single chronological thread.* Three times in this text the phrase "on the morrow" occurs... One thing is clear: they *unite the sections into one consecutive line of thought* which is continued by 2:1-11, opening with the phrase "on the third day." This group of five units... incorporates the initial presentation of Jesus to the men who became His disciples, and records their reactions to Him. *Chronologically and topically the units coincide* [151].

It is surprising then that, although Tenney explicitly states that 1,19-2,11 is a unit, the latter is combined with 2,12-4,54 to form "the Period of Consideration".

Finally, it seems to us that Tenney is carried away by the desire to describe all the stages of the drama in periods which begin with the letter 'C' ("Consideration", "Controversy", "Conflict", "Crisis", "Conference", and "Consum--mation") but unfortunately the divisions do not often depend on literary criteria[152].

2.[17] DRAMATIC-EPISODIC STRUCTURE (CULPEPPER)

Another author who examines in detail the plot of the drama of the Fourth Gospel is R. A. Culpepper[153]. Even though his primary purpose is not to establish the literary structure of the Gospel but to study it as a narrative text[154] by employing modern methods of literary criticism of fiction[155], yet

---

[150] *Ibid.*, 38.
[151] *Ibid.*, 42-43 [my italics].
[152] See ch. 3 below.
[153] R. A. CULPEPPER, *Anatomy of the Fourth Gospel. A Study in Literary Design* (Philadelphia 1983). See especially Ch. 4: "Plot" (pp. 77-98). He accepts M. H. ABRAMS' definition of "plot": "The plot in a dramatic or narrative work is the structure of its actions, as these are ordered and rendered toward achieving particular emotional and artistic effects." (quoted on p. 80 from M. H. ABRAMS' *A Glossary of Literary Terms*, p. 127).
[154] The purpose of his book is stated as follows: "Our aim is to contribute to understanding the gospel as a narrative text, what it is, and how it works." (*Anatomy of the Fourth Gospel*, 5).
[155] CULPEPPER observes:

> John is, at points at least, "novelistic, realistic narrative." In the gospel narratives, individual units of the Jesus tradition, whether oral or written, became parts of a larger entity in which

many of his observations on the existence and development of the plot in the Fourth Gospel are useful in detecting its literary structure. For instance, he adduces the evidence of a plot in John in the following words [156]:

> Several literary features point to the shaping of John's plot. First, events are put in a different order from the synoptic accounts. Jesus moves back and forth between Judea and Galilee, and the confrontation in the temple is his first public act rather than his final provocation, as it is in the synoptics... Second, John's dialogues are noticeably more contrived and less realistic than those of the synoptics... the dialogue is often impelled by misunderstanding, inept questions, and double entendre. Both Jesus and his opponents speak in the Johannine idiom, and the same themes recur repetitively. The more repetition there is in a work the more evident it is that the author is using repetition to make a point, and there is a great deal of repetition in John. Images, terms, themes, signs, confrontations over the law and Jesus' identity, appearances at feasts in Jerusalem, and dialogues with followers and opponents are repeated throughout. Together these features point unmistakably to the careful crafting of a unified sequence and a logic of causality which is developed through the repetition of scenes and dialogues in the gospel.

After establishing the existence of a plot Culpepper describes its development around the central figure, Jesus Christ, the divine Logos who became a human being to reveal the Father and who was rejected by the "Jews" and welcomed in faith by a few. The progressive but episodic character of the development of the Johannine plot is underlined, for example, in the following paragraph [157]:

> Plot development in John, then, is a matter of how Jesus' identity comes to be recognized and how it fails to be recognized. Not only is Jesus' identity *progressively revealed by the repetitive signs and discourses and the progressive enhancement of metaphorical and symbolic images*, but *each episode has essentially the same plot as the story as whole*. Will Nicodemus, the Samaritan woman, or the lame man recognize Jesus and thereby receive eternal life? The story is repeated over and over. No one can miss it. Individual episodes can almost convey the message of the whole; at least they suggest or recall it for those who know the story.

Culpepper analyzes in detail the development of John's plot chapter by chapter [158].

The Prologue both presents Jesus as the incarnate Word of God with the mission of revealing the Father, and provides plenty of clues to the Gospel's plot (cf. 1,11-12) [159].

---

they perform functions they did not have previously; they build characterization and have a place in the development of themes and the plot... Literary criticism can help us to understand how the units of tradition cohere and function together within the gospel... (*ibid.*, 8-9).

[156] *Ibid.*, 86-87.
[157] *Ibid.*, 89 [my italics].
[158] *Ibid.*, 89-97.
[159] *Ibid.*, 89.

Jn 1,19-2,11 is regarded as "a dramatic introduction to Jesus and his work"[160].

Jesus' cleansing of the temple in Jerusalem and the ensuing discussion with the Jews on the issue of the destruction and rebuilding of the "temple", which is an allusion to Jesus' death and resurrection, move the plot forward (2,13-22). The problem posed by Jesus' reluctance to trust those who believed in his name (2,23-25) complicates the plot somewhat and sounds a less optimistic note than the first chapter[161].

The dialogues and discourses in Jn 3 disclose further dimensions of Jesus' identity, mission and significance and the causes and consequences of belief and unbelief[162].

Except for an allusion to the adverse reaction of the Pharisees to Jesus (4,1.3) and a reference to the further rejection of Jesus (4,44), the characters of chapter 4 react positively to Jesus' revelation through words and deeds (e.g. the Samaritan woman, the Samaritans, the royal official)[163].

Jn 5 presents a new phase in the development of the plot, since there is open conflict between Jesus and the Jews over the issues of his identity and work (5,18)[164].

Jn 6 shows the escalation of Christ's conflict with unbelief, for, as he reveals himself as the bread of life, the unbelief of the Jews spreads to the disciples, since many of them not only murmur against Jesus but dissociate themselves from him (6,60-66)[165].

The Jews' frequent unsuccessful attempts to arrest Jesus before his hour increase dramatic tension in Jn 7[166].

The hostility between Jesus and the Jews hardens in Jn 8, bursts out into the most virulent verbal attacks and culminates in the Jews' attempt at stoning him (8,59)[167].

Culpepper considers 9,1-10,21 as "an interpretative interlude" in which there is thematic development[168]. The dramatic action is resumed in 10,22-39, since the Jews try again to stone (10,31) and arrest Jesus (10,39) so that he has to leave Jerusalem[169].

In Jn 11, Jesus, the resurrection and the life, returns to Judea to raise his dead friend Lazarus to life, which will cost Jesus his own life, since the Sanhedrin decides to do away with him[170].

---

[160] *Ibid.*, 89-90.
[161] *Ibid.*, 90.
[162] *Ibid.*, 90-91.
[163] *Ibid.*, 91.
[164] *Ibid.*
[165] *Ibid.*, 91-92.
[166] *Ibid.*, 92.
[167] *Ibid.*, 93.
[168] *Ibid.*, 93-94.
[169] *Ibid.*, 94.
[170] *Ibid.*

Jn 12 is regarded by Culpepper as a "link" chapter: "In many ways chapter 12 is a transitional chapter. It brings Jesus' public ministry to a close, describes the final preliminary steps towards his arrest and death, and forms a solid link between chapters 11 and 13"[171].

Jn 13-17 narrates the washing of the disciples' feet by Jesus and describes his discourses and prayer of the hour[172].

"With chapter 18 the waiting is over," comments Culpepper, "and events begin to move quickly toward Jesus' death"[173]. First of all, Jesus voluntarily allows himself to be arrested. After a thwarted attempt to defend him with a sword, Peter denies his discipleship (18,1-27).

The dramatic description of the trial before Pilate, the crucifixion and the burial of "the king of the Jews" are given in 18,28-19,42[174].

Jn 20, which narrates the finding of the empty tomb and the appearances of the risen Jesus to Mary Magdalene, the disciples and Thomas, brings the Gospel to a happy ending[175].

Jn 21 is taken to be an epilogue, which completes the characterization of Peter and the Beloved Disciple[176].

Some of the characteristic features of the Johannine plot such as the "conflict between belief and unbelief", its "episodic repetition", the role of dialogues in the development of themes, characterization and plot, the "sequence" of the episodes, the "causality" of the conflict, the "unity" of the story, and the "affective power of the narrative" are highlighted by Culpepper[177].

---

[171] *Ibid.*

[172] *Ibid.*, 94-95. Jn 13-17 seems to be treated by CULPEPPER as a unit, since those five chapters are dealt with in one paragraph, while he has till now devoted an entire paragraph for each of the earlier chapters (cf. pp. 89-94).

[173] *Ibid.*, 95.

[174] *Ibid.*, 95-96.

[175] *Ibid.*, 96.

[176] *Ibid.*

[177] *Ibid.*, 97-98. CULPEPPER's observations about the four features of the Johannine plot are worth citing:

> The *four constitutive features* of a plot... are present in John in ascending order of importance. *Sequence or order*, a feature which some commentators have found remarkably lacking in John, allows each episode to have a meaningful place in the story. *Causality*, though it is less important than thematic development, contributes to the story's *unity*. The *affective power* of the narrative, however, is the most important feature of its plot. By showing Jesus confronting a wide variety of individuals in everyday situations, the gospel dramatizes the message that the Word has become flesh and dwelt among us. At a wedding and a well, at the temple among the religious and at a pool among the wretched and lame, ordinary persons come step by step to recognize glory enfleshed. The gospel is the testimony of one who speaks for all those who recognized the Word in Jesus... The effect of this narrative structure, with its prologue followed by episodic repetition of the conflict between belief and unbelief, is to enclose the reader in the company of faith. The gospel's plot, therefore, is controlled by thematic development and a strategy for wooing readers to accept its interpretation of Jesus (*ibid.*, 97-98) [my italics].

His careful analysis of the dramatic-episodic plot is instructive and most of his conclusions are valid. But one of the weaknesses of the analysis is that it is mostly done chapter by chapter[178], as though the Fourth Evangelist had divided the Gospel into 21 chapters. Culpepper does not sufficiently stress the principal phases of the development of the plot, though some of them are hinted at[179]. Such Semitic literary devices as "inclusion" for the division of a narrative are hardly ever mentioned. Although the repetitive episodic character of the Johannine drama is well brought out, the divisions of the literary structure of the Fourth Gospel are not established[180].

2.[18] REVELATORY STRUCTURES (WESTCOTT, VAN DEN BUSSCHE, DE LA POTTERIE)

A number of Johannine scholars are of the opinion that the central issue around which the Fourth Gospel is structured is the revelation of Jesus Christ. We discuss below the revelatory structures proposed by B. F. Westcott, H. van den Bussche and I. de la Potterie[181].

2.[18]1 Westcott's Revelatory Structure

B. F. Westcott gives the following plan of the Fourth Gospel in his Commentary[182]:

---

[178] *Ibid.*, 89-94. Only a few chapters are grouped together (1,19-2,11; 9-10; 13-17; 18,28-19,42).

[179] Thus regarding Jn 1-4 he remarks: "These chapters have a powerful 'primacy effect,' that is, they firmly establish the reader's first impression of Jesus' identity and mission" (*ibid.*, 91). Similarly he calls Jn 5-9 "five chapters of escalating hostility" (*ibid.*, 94). Yet it is surprising that nothing is said in the conclusion (pp. 97-98) about the major divisions of the plot (except its repetitive episodic character).

[180] Of course the primary purpose of CULPEPPER's creative book is not to establish the literary structure of the Fourth Gospel but rather to study its literary design as the subtitle of the book ("A Study in Literary Design") clearly indicates. So the above observation is made not to point out a defect in his original and valuable study but only to show its (necessary) limitation and hence the need of complementing his literary-design approach with a literary-structural one.

[181] Since the *revelatory* aspect of the Gospel of John is highlighted in these structures, they are called, for lack of a better expression, "revelatory structures".

We do not include R. BULTMANN who also regards "the revelation of the *doxa*" of Jesus Christ to be the central theme of Jn and who calls Jn 2-12 "the Revelation of the *doxa* to the World" and Jn 13-20 "the Revelation of the *doxa* before the Community" (vii; x), since he rearranges the text of the Gospel.

We do not discuss the position of G. GHIBERTI who likewise admits the progressive revelation of Jesus and divides the Fourth Gospel into seven revelatory cycles (1,19-4,54; 5; 6; 7,1-10,21; 10,22-11,54; 11,55-12,50; 13,1-20,31) preceded by a prologue (1,1-18) and followed by an appendix (21), since the author does not give literary criteria for his sevenfold division (cf. *La Bibbia: parola di Dio scritta per noi*, Vol III [Torino 1980] 328-29).

We shall examine later (see 2.[19] below) the position of J. CABA who proposes a "revelatory-dramatic structure".

[182] B. F. WESTCOTT, xlii-xliii.

THE PROLOGUE, i.1-18.
   The Word in His absolute, eternal Being; and in relation to Creation.
THE NARRATIVE, i.19-xxi.23.
   The Self-revelation of Christ to the world and to the Disciples.

I.-THE SELF-REVELATION OF CHRIST TO THE WORLD (i.19-xii.50).
   1. *The Proclamation* (i.19-iv.54).
      i. The testimony to Christ (i.19-ii.11)
         of *the Baptist*, i.19-34,
            disciples, i.35-51,
            signs (water turned to wine), ii.1-11.
      ii. The work of Christ (ii.13-iv.54)
         in Judea (Nicodemus), ii.13-iii.36,
            Samaria (the woman of Samaria), iv.1-42,
            Galilee (the nobleman's son healed), iv.43-54.
               Unbelief as yet passive.
   2. *The Conflict* (v.1-xii.50).
      i. The Prelude (v., vi.),
         (a) *In Jerusalem* (the impotent man healed on the Sabbath), v.
             The Son and the Father.
         (b) *In Galilee* (the five thousand fed), vi.
             Christ and men.
      ii. The great Controversy (vii.-xii.).
         (a) *The Revelation of faith and unbelief*, vii.-x.
             The Feast of Tabernacles, vii, viii.
             The Feast of Dedication (the blind man healed on the Sabbath), ix., x.
         (b) *The decisive Judgement*, xi., xii.
             The final sign and its issues (the raising of Lazarus), xi.
             The close of Christ's public ministry, xii.

II.-THE SELF-REVELATION OF CHRIST TO THE DISCIPLES (xiii.-xxi.)
   1. *The last ministry of love* (xiii.-xvii.).
      i. The last acts of love (xiii.1-30).
      ii. The last discourses (xiii.31-xvi.33),
         In the chamber, xiii.31-xiv.,
         On the way, xv., xvi.
      iii. The prayer of consecration, xvii.
   2. *The Victory through death* (xviii.-xx.).
      i. The Betrayal (xviii.1-11).
      ii. The double Trial (xviii.12-xix.16).
      iii. The end (xix.17-42).
      iv. The new life (xx.).
   3. *The Epilogue*, xxi.
      i. The Lord and the body of disciples (the miraculous draught of fishes), xxi.1-14.
      ii. The Lord and individual disciples (xxi.15-23).
         Concluding notes, xxi.24,25.

Looking carefully at this plan one recognizes the importance attached to "the self-revelation of Christ" in the structure, as 1,19-21,23 is given the title "The Self-revelation of Christ to the World and to the Disciples". This is divided into two parts: I. "The Self-revelation of Christ to the World" (1,19-12,50), and II. "The Self-revelation of Christ to the Disciples" (13-21)[183]. One may reasonably doubt whether this division is fully justifiable, since there are many pericopes in the first part where Jesus reveals himself exclusively to the disciples (e.g. 1,35-51; 6,16-21) and at least one episode in the second part where the disciples are not mentioned at all (18,28-19,16b). Furthermore, some of the subdivisions seem to be rather arbitrary. For example, Jn 5-6 is called "the prelude" to "the great controversy" in Jn 7-12, although we are told already in 5,16-18 that the Jews were not only persecuting Jesus but also seeking to kill him.

While explaining the plan of John's Gospel, Westcott maintains that three pairs of themes are vital for its development: "witness and truth, glory and light, judgement and life" and states that "the narrative may be fairly described as the simultaneous unfolding of these three themes, into which the great theme of faith and unbelief is divided"[184]. It is true that these themes appear often in the Fourth Gospel[185], but there are other themes which are as important as these (e.g. love). There is always the danger of subjectivism when one decides the structure by basing oneself exclusively or primarily on Johannine themes[186].

2.[18]2 H. van den Bussche's Revelatory Structure

H. van den Bussche provides a detailed revelatory structure[187]. He lists the following simple and controllable criteria for the divisions and subdivisions

---

[183] *Ibid.* It must also be noted that elsewhere WESTCOTT maintains that "conflict between faith and unbelief... is the main subject of St. John's Gospel" (*ibid.*, xlix). But this does not contradict the centrality of Christ's self-revelation, since belief and unbelief are the two responses to the revelation as is admitted by Westcott himself at the end of his discussion of the plan of the Fourth Gospel: "Even from this rapid summary it will be seen that the self-revelation of Christ became stage by stage the occasion of fuller personal trust and more open personal antagonism" (*ibid.*, l).

[184] *Ibid.*, xliv.

[185] Cf. *ibid.*, xliv-l for WESTCOTT's discussion of these pairs of ideas. He states at the beginning: "There is the manifold attestation of the divine mission: there is the progressive manifestation of the inherent majesty of the Son: there is the continuous and necessary effect which this manifestation produces on those to whom it is made..." (*ibid.*, xliv).

[186] See, for instance, the plan proposed by É. COTHENET ("Le quatrième Évangile", in: *Introduction à la Bible*, Tome III, Vol. IV: *La tradition johannique* [Paris 1977] 136-37). H. VAN DEN BUSSCHE comments: "Une comparaison des tables des matières des commentaires et des titres des fragments démontre le danger d'options purement subjectives" (*Jean*, 53). We admit, however, that themes can have a supportive or confirmatory role in detecting the literary structure, as we shall see in ch. 5 below.

[187] H. VAN DEN BUSSCHE, "La structure de Jean I-XII", in: *L'Évangile de Jean. Etudes et Problèmes* (Recherches Bibliques, III) (Desclée de Brouwer 1958) 61-109; *Jean*, 53-59.

of the structure: 1) introductions, 2) conclusions, 3) inclusions, and 4) theological themes[188]. We give below the outline of his revelatory structure[189]:

A. PROLOGUE (1,1-18)

B. PREMIERE PARTIE: LE JOUR DE JESUS
SA VIE PUBLIQUE, REVELATION VOILEE DE LA GLOIRE (ch. 2-12)

1. *Introduction à la première partie: du Baptiste à Jésus* (1,19-51)

   a) *Le témoignage officiel* du Baptiste aux envoyés de Jérusalem (1,19-28)
   b) *Le lendemain*, le Baptiste rend un témoignage privé à ses disciples (1,29-34)
   c) *Le lendemain*, les deux disciples de Jean suivent l'Agneau de Dieu... (1,35-42)
   d) *Le lendemain*, c'est le recrutement en Galilée (1,43-51)

2. *La section des signes: la révélation du Messie* (ch. 2 à 4)

   a) *Diptyque de Révélation* (2,1-25)
      Le miracle du vin à Cana (2,1-12)
      Le signe du Temple à Jérusalem (2,13-22)
   b) *Transition: la révélation doit conduire à la foi* (2,23-25)
   c) *Le défilé des candidats à la foi* (3,1-4,54)...

3. *La section des oeuvres: la révélation du Fils de l'Homme* (ch. 5 à 10)

   a) *Diptyque de révélation* (5,1-6,71)...
   b) *"Ensuite": Le procès contre les Juifs...* (ch. 7-10)...

4. *La montée vers Jérusalem* (ch. 11 à 12)

   a) La marche à la mort apporte la vie: Lazare (11,1-44)
   b) La résurrection de Lazare, occasion de la mort de Jésus (11,45-54)
   c) La Pâque approche. Onction à Béthanie (11,55-12,11)
   d) La joyeuse entrée du Messie à Jérusalem (12,12-19)
   e) L'église des païens entre en scène (12,20-26)
   f) Jésus accepte l'Heure (12,27-36)
   g) Méditation de l'évangéliste sur l'aveuglement des Juifs (12,37-43)

5. *Epilogue de la première partie* (12,44-50)

C. DEUXIEME PARTIE: L'HEURE DE JESUS
LA REVELATION DE SA GLOIRE (ch. 13-20)

1. *Les discours d'adieu* (13-17)

   a) Le lavement des pieds (13,1-30)
   b) Premier discours d'adieu: Je ne vous laisse pas seuls (13,31-14,31)
   c) Second discours d'adieu: l'union et la communauté de vie avec Jésus (15-16)
   d) Prière sacerdotale (17)

---

[188] "Divisions et subdivisions, partie ou sections sont marquées par des introductions et des conclusions, souvent des inclusions sémitiques. Elles sont en outre dominées par un même thème théologique" ("La structure de Jean I-XII", 63). Cf. also *Jean*, 52.

[189] *Jean*, 53-59; cf. also "La structure de Jean I-XII", 61-109 and especially pp. 108-9; *Het Vierde Evangelie I, Het Boek der Tekens* (Tielt 1961) 66-74. [In giving the outline we have reproduced the exact words of VAN DEN BUSSCHE in *Jean*, 53-59, but we have left out the detailed subdivisions of B.2.c), B.3.a), and B.3.b) and the explanations found often within the outline.]

2. *La Passion et les apparitions du Ressuscité* (18-20)
   a) La Passion (18-19)
      1. Jésus se constitue prisonnier (18,1-11)
      2. Jésus devant les Juifs (18,12-27)
      3. Jésus proclamé Roi des Juifs (18,28-19,22)
      4. Tout est accompli (19,23-42)
   b) La Résurrection (20,1-29)
      1. Le tombeau vide et l'intelligence chrétienne (20,1-9)
      2. Marie de Magdala et la présence véritable de Jésus (20,10-18)
      3. Les disciples et la présence efficace de Jésus (20,19-23)
      4. Thomas et la présence permanente de Jésus (20,24-29)

3. Fin de l'Evangile (20,30-31)

D. APPENDICE DE L'EDITEUR (21,1-25)

According to van den Bussche the Fourth Gospel falls into two principal parts (chs. 2-12 and 13-20), preceded by the Prologue (1,1-18) and followed by an Appendix (ch. 21). He calls Jn 2-12 "the Day of Jesus" and Jn 13-20 "the Hour of Jesus"[190]. But the arrival of "the hour" of Jesus is mentioned not only in Jn 13-20 but already in Jn 12 (cf. vv. 23.27).

Although the division of Jn 2-12 into three sections (Jn 2-4; 5-10; 11-12) is correct, their designations are not exact. Jn 2-4 is called "the section of signs" and Jn 5-10 "the section of works", though the "sign" of the multiplication of the loaves is narrated in 6,1-15 and the word "sign" is found only six times in Jn 2-4, whereas it occurs seven times in Jn 5-10. Furthermore, it is not exact to say that Jn 2-4 deals with "the revelation of the Messiah", while Jn 5-10 gives "the revelation of the Son of Man", since the word *Christos* occurs only three times in Jn 2-4 but eight times in Jn 5-10. Similarly, "the ascent to Jerusalem"[191] is not an apt title for Jn 11-12, since Jesus' "going up to Jerusalem" is often explicitly mentioned in the earlier chapters (e.g. 2,13; 5,1; 7,10.14).

It must also be noted that van den Bussche's divisions of some of the sections are quite questionable. For instance, Jn 5-10 is subdivided into a) Jn 5-6, and b) Jn 7-10, although Jn 5, Jn 6 and Jn 7 begin with *meta tauta* (cf. also 5,14).

It is, however, to his credit that he has tried to use some literary criteria (introductions, conclusions and inclusions) besides theological themes to determine the structure[192]. But he has neither detected nor employed all the criteria necessary for establishing the structure more objectively[193].

---

[190] See the outline given above. Concerning "the hour of Jesus" VAN DEN BUSSCHE says:
Désigne-t-elle succesivement la mort, puis la résurrection, enfin l'ascension, cette Heure, si souvent évoquée? Nullement! Mais bien l'événement global, indivisible, qui s'accomplit de la mort à l'ascension et qui marque l'effusion de l'Esprit. Dans la mort de Jésus, nous voyons souvent la condition de sa glorification; au regard de Jean, cette mort elle-même apparaît comme le triomphe du Christ, *hupsôsis*: l'élévation sur la croix, c'est l'élévation dans la gloire (*Jean*, 37).

[191] *Ibid.*, 58: "La montée vers Jérusalem".
[192] See n. 188 above.
[193] See ch. 3 below.

2.[18]3 I. de la Potterie's Revelatory Structure

I. de la Potterie states in unambiguous terms that "the central idea that dominates the whole Gospel" of John is "the progressive revelation of the Word incarnate, Messiah and Son of God"[194], to which men respond either positively through faith or negatively through unbelief.

The entire Fourth Gospel is divided by de la Potterie into two parts (Jn 1-12 and 13-20)[195], which are subdivided in the following manner:

I. *revelatio coram mundo* (1-12)[196]
  Prologus: Jesus, unigenitus Filius (1,1-18).
  Introductio historica: testimonia (praesertim Joh -B.) de Jesu Messia (1,19-51).

  A. *Primum diptychum revelationis et diversae responsiones fidei* (2,1-4,54).

  1. *Diptychum revelationis* (2,1-22).
     a. Signum "vini" in Cana Galilaeae (2,1-12).
     b. Signum "templi" in Jerusalem (2,13-22).

  2. *Tres responsiones fidei* (2,23-4,54).
     a. Nicodemus Iudaeus in Jerusalem (2,23-3,36).
     b. Mulier Samaritana (4,1-42).
     c. Regulus in Cana Galilaeae (4,43-54).

  B. *Alterum diptychum revelationis et incredulitas Iudaeorum* (5,1-10,42).

  1. *Diptychum revelationis* (5-6).
     a. Sanatio languidi in Jerusalem et apologia Christi (5,1-47).
     b. Signum panis in Galilaea et sermo Christi de pane vitae (6,1-71).

  2. *Progressus fidei et incredulitatis apud Iudaeos in Jerusalem* (7-10).
     a. Introductio (7,1-13).
     b. Mediante festo Tabernaculorum, prima controversia cum Iudaeis (7,14-36).
     c. Die magno novissimo festivitatis, magna revelatio publica ("clamabat") (7,37-10,21):
        – relatio aperta (7,37-8,59);
        – illuminatio caeci nati (Jesus est "lux mundi") et caecitas Iudaeorum (9,1-41);

---

[194] I. DE LA POTTERIE, "L'Evangelo di San Giovanni", in: *Introduzione al Nuovo Testamento*, G. Rinaldi & P. de Benedetti (ed.), (Brescia 1971) 893:

È importante prima di tutto, ci sembra, scoprire l'idea centrale che domina tutto l'evangelo, poiché la disposizione dei racconti e dei discorsi è comandata dallo sviluppo di questo tema. Ora, il prologo (1,1-18), l'epilogo della vita publica (12,37-50) e la conclusione di tutto l'evangelo (20,30-31) indicano chiaramente questa grande idea: la rivelazione progressiva del Verbo incarnato, Messia e Figlio di Dio. In corrispondenza, a ogni tappa è notata l'accoglienza riservata dagli uomini a questa rivelazione: rifiuto e incredulità da parte degli uni, accettazione e fede da parte degli altri.

[195] I. DE LA POTTERIE, *Exegesis Quarti Evangelii. Capita III-IV* (Romae, PIB, 1972-73), 2:
"Ut a plerisque admittitur, *totum evangelium* dividitur in duas partes:
  1-12: revelatio coram mundo;
  13-20: culmen revelationis in hora Jesu."

[196] *Ibid.*, 2-4. [The italics of *revelatio coram mundo* is mine.] The same structural division of Jn 1-12 is given also in "Structura primae partis Evangelii Johannis", *VD* 47 (1969) 132-33.

- revelatio velata (paroimia de bono Pastore) (10,1-21).
"Schisma" erat inter eos (7,43; 9,16; 10,19).

    d. In festo Dedicationis, ultima controversia cum Iudaeis (10,22-39).
    e. Conclusio (10,40-42).

C. *Praeparationes et praefigurationes horae Jesu* (11-12).

    1. Resurrectio Lazari, causa mortis Jesu, sed praefiguratio resurrectionis (11,1-56).
    2. Unctio in Bethania, praefiguratio mortis et sepulturae Jesu (12,1-11).
    3. Ingressus Regis-Messiae in civitatem mortis (12,12-19).
    4. Adventus Graecorum praefigurat adventum horae Jesu, i.e. horae mortis, exaltationis et glorificationis eius (12,20-36).
    5. Reflexio evangelistae de incredulitate Iudaeorum (12,37-43).
    Epilogus (12,44-50).

II. *Culmen revelationis in hora Jesu* (13-20)[197].

    A. *Il discorso dopo la Cena* (13-17)[198].

        1. lavanda dei piedi e l'annuncio della debolezza dei suoi apostoli (13,1-38).
        2. primo discorso (14,1-31).
        3. il secondo discorso (15,1-16,33).
        4. la preghiera dell'"ora" (17,1-26).

    B. *Passio et Mors Christi* (18-19)[199].

        1. (18,1-11). In "horto". Introductio: Iesus coram adversis suis
        2. (18,12-27). Iesus coram Pontifice
        3. (18,28-19,16a). Iesus coram Pilato
        4. (19,16b-37). Ad Calvariam
        5. (19,38-42). In "horto" (inclusio cum 18,1-11).
        Epilogus: sepultura.

    C. *Resurrectio Christi* (20).

        1. Les deux disciples au tombeau (20,1-10)[200].
        2. L'apparition à Marie de Magdala (20,11-18).
        3. L'apparition aux disciples (20,19-25).
        4. L'apparition en présence de Thomas (20,26-29).

---

[197] I. DE LA POTTERIE, *Exegesis Quarti Evangelii. Capita III-IV*, 2 [my italics].

[198] I. DE LA POTTERIE, "L'Evangelo di San Giovanni", 897 [my italics]. [Since no titles of the divisions of "the discourse after Supper" are given by DE LA POTTERIE, relevant phrases from the corresponding explanatory paragraphs in Italian are taken verbatim and given by me as titles.]

[199] I. DE LA POTTERIE, *Exegesis IVi Evangelii. De narratione Passionis et Mortis Christi. Joh. 18-19*, quarta editio (Romae, PIB, 1978-79), 41-42. [The italics of the subdivisions has been left out.]

[200] The fourfold division of Jn 20 is given by I. DE LA POTTERIE, "Genèse de la foi pascale d'après Jn. 20", *NTS* 30 (1984) 26-49, especially p. 28, where the four episodes of Jn 20 are presented as forming a chiastic structure:

    A (20,1-10)   A' (20,26-29)
        B (20,11-18)   B' (20,19-25)

Literary criteria (e.g. inclusions, introductions and conclusions) and thematic unity are the two types of norms used by de la Potterie for the delimitation of the sections of the Gospel [201]. But some of the applications are not acceptable, since they are opposed to one another. For instance, the unity of 2,1-4,54 is defended in one place [202], whereas the unity of 1,19-4,54 is preferred in another [203], for each of which positions a number of arguments are given [204]. Again, in order to arrive at the proposed structure, some of the passages are passed over in silence. For example, in order to present 2,23-4,54 as "three responses of faith", the pericope on John the Baptist's final testimony to Christ in 3,22-36 is not mentioned as a subsection but is understood as part of the Nicodemus-pericope (2,23-3,36) [205]. Similarly, in order to have a "diptych of revelation" in Jn 5-6, Jesus' walking on the water is bypassed [206]. However, it must be admitted that de la Potterie rightly highlights the relation between the literary structure and the central theme of Jesus' revelation [207].

2.[19] REVELATORY-DRAMATIC STRUCTURE (CABA)

Following in the footsteps of de la Potterie [208], J. Caba constructs a "progressively revelatory-dramatic structure" [209] and agrees with him that there is a "progressive revelation" of Jesus in the Fourth Gospel [210]. Caba underlines the dramatic effect of the diverse "reactions" to the "manifestation of Jesus" [211]. He outlines the Gospel's structure as follows [212]:

---

[201] I. DE LA POTTERIE, *Exegesis Quarti Evangelii. Capita III-IV*, 3.

[202] *Ibid.*, 5-8. He states on p. 5: "Nobis tamen melius videtur totam sectionem 2,1-4,54 ut unitatem litterariam et theologicam considerare (cum van den Bussche, Brown et Willemse)". Compare, however, this statement with the quotation in the next note n. 203.

[203] I. DE LA POTTERIE, *Exegesis Quarti Evangelii. De Matre Iesu in IV Evangelio* (Romae, PIB, 1976-77), 24-25. On p. 24 he affirms:

> Cum aliis auctoribus (Boismard, Mollat, Thurian, Lightfoot, Barrett, Grassi, Serra, Olsson) preferimus connexionem nostrae pericopae [2,1-12] cum 1,19-51. Tota sectio 1,19-2,12 tunc constituit aliquam "hebdomadam inauguralem" cuius dies clare indicantur.

But see, however, the previous note n. 202 for the opposite view.

[204] For instance, in *Exegesis Quarti Evangelii. Capita III-IV* DE LA POTTERIE argues that the first two signs at Cana (2,1-11 and 4,43-54) form an inclusion (pp. 6-8), while in *De Matre Iesu* he refutes this position of his (pp. 24-25).

[205] *Capita III-IV*, 4 and "L'Evangelo di San Giovanni", 895.

[206] *Capita III-IV*, 4.

[207] See the titles of the divisions of the structure.

[208] J. CABA, *Dai Vangeli al Gesù Storico*, 344, n. 160: "Lo schema proposto segue, nelle sue linee generali, la struttura proposta da I. de la Potterie" [in "Evangelo di San Giovanni"].

[209] *Ibid.*, 343-49.

[210] *Ibid.*, 343: "Tutto il quarto vangelo è una progressiva rivelazione e manifestazione di Gesù." Cf. also 344-48.

[211] *Ibid.*, 344: "La diversità di atteggiamenti determinati dalla manifestazione progressiva di Gesù costituisce il drammatismo del quarto vangelo." Cf. also 345-49.

[212] *Ibid.*, 343-49. [Since the structure is too long, it has been abbreviated by leaving out Caba's detailed explanation of each section in terms of "a) Manifestation of Jesus" and "b) Reactions".]

PROLOGO (1,1-18)...

I. VITA PUBBLICA (1,19-12,50): Progressiva manifestazione di Gesù e reazioni che suscita

   A. *Introduzione al ministero* (1,19-2,12)...

   B. *Sette sezioni* attorno alle feste ebraiche (2,13-12,36)
      1. *Prima sezione* (2,13-4,54): Prima *Pasqua* (2,13)...
      2. *Seconda sezione* (5,1-47): In *giorno di festa dei giudei* (v.1)..
      3. *Terza sezione* (6,1-71): in Galilea e in prossimità della *Pasqua* (vv.1.4)...
      4. *Quarta sezione*, centrale (7,1-10,21): durante la *festa dei Tabernacoli*, nel tempio...
      5. *Quinta sezione* (10,22-42): durante la *festa della Dedicazione*, in Gerusalemme...
      6. *Sesta sezione* (11,1-56): verso la fine si fa allusione alla prossima *festa della Pasqua* (v.55)...
      7. *Settima sezione* (12,1-36): alcuni giorni prima dell'ultima *Pasqua* (v.1)...

   C. *Epilogo* della vita pubblica (12,37-50)...

II. ULTIMA CENA, PASSIONE, RISURREZIONE (13,1-20,31): Suprema manifestazione di Gesù e specificazione delle due reazioni

   1. La *manifestazione suprema* di Gesù:
      a) Nell'intimità del *cenacolo* (c. 13-17)...
      b) La *passione* (c. 18-19): è il momento culminante della rivelazione di Gesù...
      c) La *risurrezione* (20,1-31): è il culmine dell'opera rivelatrice di Gesù...

   2. Reazioni di fronte alla suprema manifestazione di Gesù: continuano e si accentuano le due reazioni segnalate nella vita pubblica:
      a) di ostilità...
      b) di accettazione...

EPILOGO: 21,1-25...

It is true that the theme of the manifestation of Jesus, together with the reactions it produces, returns again and again in the development of the Fourth Gospel[213]. But Caba does not explain how "the manifestation of Jesus" and the "reactions", which are certainly present in every section, are decisive in the division of the Gospel into the sections he proposes. The two themes mentioned above are found not only in the sections but also in almost every subsection or pericope (e.g. the revelation of Jesus as the new temple and the disciples' faith in 2,13-22).

Evidently the liturgical feasts mentioned in the Gospel of John have played a decisive role in Caba's division of 2,13-12,36 into seven sections, since the names of feasts are underlined at the beginning of each section. One is also surprised to see that in order to get "seven sections around the Jewish feasts", he has to connect the raising of Lazarus (11,1-54) with the last Passover, mentioned

---

[213] *Ibid.*, 349.

in 11,55, though 11,54 is clearly the conclusion of the Lazarus-episode, and 11,55-57 is the introduction or transition to the next section (cf. "Passover" at 12,1).

Again, one may rightly object to his division of Jn 18-20 into 18-19 (the passion) and 20 (the resurrection) and their designation as "the culminating moment of the revelation of Jesus" and "the climax of the revelatory work of Jesus" respectively [214].

It is also open to discussion whether 2,1-12 should be regarded as an integral part of the introduction, as is maintained by Caba, or as part of the first section (from Cana to Cana) as is held by others, or as a bridge-pericope [215].

Finally, while the subdivisions of some of the sections are in general right (e.g. 2,13-4,54 = 2,13-25; 3,1-21; 3,22-36; 4,1-42; 4,43-54), the subsections of others are not always clearly indicated (e.g. the fourth section: 7,1-10,21; the Passion: 18-19) or convincingly established [216].

2.[20] REVELATORY-RESPONSE STRUCTURE (GOURGUES)

Another author who advocates a revelatory-response structure is M. Gourgues [217]. He accepts "the classical bipartite division" of the Gospel of John into the "Book of Signs" (1,19-12,50) and the "Book of the Hour" (Jn 13-20/21) [218], which, in turn, are subdivided as follows [219]:

PROLOGUE	1,1-18
LE "LIVRE DES SIGNES"	1,19-12,50
La première phase de la manifestation de Jésus, ou le temps des options	1,19-6,71
1. Le témoignage initial et les options premières	1,19-4,54
a) Témoignage de Jean	1,19-31
b) Jésus se manifeste	2,1-3,21
a') Témoignage de Jean	3,22-36
b') Jésus se manifeste	4,1-54

---

[214] *Ibid.*, 348.

[215] See 4.112 below.

[216] It is true that CABA does not claim his proposed structure to be the last word, for he admits:

Questa strutturazione non pretende di rinchiudere in uno schema rigoroso il profondo contenuto del quarto vangelo, ma piuttosto delineare il concetto unitario che permea tutta l'opera e raccoglie gli elementi principali e fondati dalle altre sistemazioni (*ibid.*, 349).

[217] M. GOURGUES, *Pour que vous croyiez. Pistes d'exploration de l'évangile de Jean* (Paris 1982) 73-101.

[218] *Ibid.*, 73-74. He gives the following reason on p. 77: "Livre des signes' figure ici entre guillemets. La désignation est devenue tellement classique qu'on n'ose guère la mettre de côté." But because of the importance of *ergon* throughout the Fourth Gospel, Gourgues suggests the following titles for the so-called "Book of Signs" and "the Book of the Hour":

"1,19-12,50: L'oeuvre accomplie avant la venue de l'heure;

13-20: L'oeuvre achevée avec la venue de l'heure" (*ibid.*, 78).

[219] *Ibid.*, 85; 97; 98; 100.

2. Le témoignage réitéré et la consolidation des options
　　　　premières   chap. 5-6
　　　　　a) Signe (à Jérusalem)   5,1-18
　　　　　b) Discours   5,19-47
　　　　　a') Signe (en Galilee)   6,1-24
　　　　　b') Discours   6,25-71

La seconde phase de la manifestation de Jésus, ou le temps du refus   chap. 7-12

　　　1. Le témoignage de la dernière chance rencontre l'opposition   chap. 7-8
　　　　Préambule   7,1-13
　　　　　a) Enseignement et réactions   7,14-36
　　　　　b) Enseignement et réactions   7,37-51
　　　　La femme adultère   8,1-11
　　　　　a) Controverse avec les pharisiens et réaction défavorable   8,12-19
　　　　　b) Controverse avec les Juifs et réaction favorable   8,21-30
　　　　　c) Controverse avec les Juifs qui ont cru et réaction
　　　　　　favorable   8,31-59
　　　2. L'ultime manifestation de la lumière se heurte au refus   9,1-11,54
　　　　　a) Signe à Jérusalem (aveugle-né)   9,1-8
　　　　　b) Réactions partagées   9,9-41
　　　　　a') Discours à Jérusalem (berger)   10,1-18
　　　　　b') Réactions partagées   10,19-39
　　　　　a) Signe à Béthanie (Lazare)   11,1-44
　　　　　b) Réactions partagées   11,45-54
　　　3. L'heure de la glorification est venue   11,55-12,36
　　　　　a) L'évocation "événementielle" de la glorification   11,55-12,19
　　　　　　- Transition   11,55-57
　　　　　　- L'onction à Béthanie et l'évocation de la mort   12,1-11
　　　　　　- L'accueil à Jérusalem et l'évocation de la résurrection   12,12-19
　　　　　b) La proclamation de la glorification   12,20-36
　　　4. "Bilan" final. Conclusion de la première partie   12,37-50

LE "LIVRE DE L'HEURE"   13-20/21

Les adieux: avec "ceux qui l'ont reçu"   13-17
　　　1. Le dernier repas   13,1-30
　　　2. Le dernier témoignage   13,31-17,26
　　　　　a) Entretien   13,31-14,31
　　　　　b) Discours   chap. 15-16
　　　　　c) Prière   chap. 17

L'élévation   18-20/21
　　　1. La passion et la mort   18,1-19,42
　　　　　a) Vers la mort: arrestation et condamnation   18,1-19,16a
　　　　　b) La mort   19,16b-30
　　　　　c) Après la mort: côté transpercé et mise au tombeau   19,31-42

2. La résurrection	20,1-29
a) Le tombeau vide	20,1-10
b) Les apparitions	20,11-29
- à Marie	20,11-18
- aux disciples	20,19-29
3. Finale	20,30-31
Appendice	chap. 21

Gourgues gives the following four reasons for the bipartite division: 1) the signs are mentioned only in the first twelve chapters (the only exception being 20,30); 2) the coming of the "hour" marks the end of a section in Jn 12 and the beginning of a new one in Jn 13; 3) Jn 12,37-50 is an epilogue or evaluation of the ministry of Jesus; 4) while Jn 1-12 reports Jesus' public activity, he is alone with his disciples in Jn 13-21.

While reasons 1) and 3) are valid, 2) and 4) need qualification. The insistence on the arrival of "the hour" both in Jn 12 (cf. vv. 23.27) and in Jn 13-17 (cf. 13,1; 17,1) indicates not a clear-cut division between Jn 12 and Jn 13 but rather their intended interrelationship. This is confirmed by the many parallel elements in Jn 11-12 and 13-21 (e.g. the raising of Lazarus is a prefiguration of the resurrection of Christ; the anointing of Jesus at Bethany is a preparation for his burial; etc.)[220]. It is not quite exact to say that the manifestation of Jesus in Jn 1-12 is public, while that in Jn 13-20/21 is private or reserved only to the disciples. The latter is true only of Jn 13-17 and 20-21; Jesus reveals himself publicly in Jn 18-19. There are also entire pericopes in Jn 1-12 in which Jesus reveals himself exclusively to the disciples (e.g. 1,35-51; 6,60-71; 11,1-27; 12,1-8).

Hardly any valid reason has been given by Gourgues for the division of the "Book of Signs" (1,19-12,50) into 1,19-6,71 and 7,1-12,50[221]. Also some of the subsections of the above divisions are open to question. For instance, 1,19-6,71 is subdivided into two sections (1,19-4,54; 5,1-6,71) on account of a "symmetrical organization of the materials"[222]. But the "symmetry" is the

---

[220] See 4.13 and 4.23 below.

[221] With regard to the division of 1,19-12,50 he says:

> Quant à la première partie, il nous semble que, tout bien pesé, elle se subdivise à son tour en deux grandes sections:
> 1. La première phase de la manifestation de Jésus, ou le temps des options (1,19-6,71);
> 2. La seconde phase de la manifestation de Jésus, ou le temps du refus (chap. 7-12).
> Ces titres manifestent une attention portée à ce que nous avions appelé plus haut la grille "action/réaction" (= manifestation/options, refus), d'une part, et la grille "témoins", d'autre part (*ibid.*, 78).

But there are "refusals" of Jesus already in 1,19-6,71 (e.g. the Jews seek to kill him in 5,18; many of the disciples desert him in 6,66); and "options" for Jesus continue in 7,1-12,50 (e.g. the cured blind man in Jn 9; Martha and Mary in Jn 11; the Greeks in 12,20-21).

[222] *Ibid.*, 79; 82. (See sections 1 and 2 of the first phase in the outline given above.)

result of an oversimplification by Gourgues. For example, "Jesus manifests himself" not only in 2,1-3,21 but already in 1,35-51, and the "testimony of John" is, strictly speaking, restricted to 1,19-37 and does not include 1,38-51 which describes the disciples' discovery of the Messiah.

Likewise one fails to see the literary parallelism between the miracle of curing the blind man in 9,1-8 and the parabolic discourse in 10,1-18 [223]. Similarly, because a few themes (connected with the shepherd and the sheep) of the preceding pericope (10,1-18) are recalled in 10,26-28, which is a normal procedure in Jn (e.g. the theme of "life" in Jn 5 is taken up in Jn 6), Gourgues joins 10,1-21 with 10,22-39. However, the Evangelist has clearly distinguished it from the former by explicitly mentioning a change of place (temple) and time (during the feast of Dedication) at 10,22, just as such a change is given also in Jn 5 and Jn 6.

Finally, while Gourgues' basic insight is valid, namely, in order to determine the literary structure one must use multiple criteria and take into account not only the content but also the arrangement of the material, yet he has utilized only a couple of criteria. Hence the structure he has suggested is not completely convincing.

2.[21] REVELATORY-NARRATIVE STRUCTURE (PASQUETTO)

V. Pasquetto proposes a revelatory-narrative structure which stresses both the revelatory and the narrative aspects of the Gospel of John [224]. According to him, besides the introduction (1,1-51), the Fourth Gospel narrates seven successive manifestations of Jesus (2,1-4,54; 5,1-6,71; 7,1-11,54; 12,1-50; 13,1-17,26; 18,1-19,42; 20,1-29), which are followed by the conclusion to the Gospel (20,30-31) and by a non-Johannine Epilogue (21,1-25) [225]:

— INTRODUZIONE ALLA COMPARSA DI GESÙ RIVELATORE (1,1-51).

    a) Presentazione di Gesù e della sua opera (1,1-18)
    b) Movimento degli uomini verso Gesù (1,19-50)

        1) testimonianza del Battista in ordine a se stesso (1,19-28)
        2) testimonianza del B. in ordine a Gesù (1,29-34)
        3) passaggio dei discepoli del B. a Gesù (1,35-50)

    c) Gesù come "luogo privilegiato" della rivelazione divina (1,51).

A) PRIMA MANIFESTAZIONE DI GESÙ (= DA CANA A CANA: 2,1-4,54).

    a) Presenza di due segni (2,1-22)
        1) segno di Cana (2,1-11)
        2) segno di Gesù-tempio (2,12-22)

---

[223] Note that in the outline "a) Signe à Jérusalem (aveugle-né)" (9,1-8) is presented as being parallel to "a') Discours à Jérusalem (berger)" (10,1-18).
[224] V. PASQUETTO, 107-9.
[225] Ibid.

b) Diversità di risposta in ordine ai due segni (2,23-4,54)
   1) Nicodemo (2,23-3,36)
   2) i Samaritani (4,1-42)
   3) il funzionario regio (4,46-54; 4,43-45: "transizione").

B) SECONDA MANIFESTAZIONE DI GESÙ (= ALTRI DUE SEGNI + DUE DISCORSI: 5,1-6,71).

   a) Primo segno (= guarigione del paralitico: 5,1-15)
   b) Primo discorso (5,16-47)
   c) Secondo segno (= moltiplicazione dei pani: 6,1-15)
   d) Secondo discorso (6,26-71; 6,16-25: "transizione").

C) TERZA MANIFESTAZIONE DI GESÙ (= FESTE DEI TABERNACOLI E DELLA DEDICAZIONE: 7,1-11,54)

   a) Introduzione (7,1-13)
   b) Manifestazione di Gesù durante la Festa dei Tabernacoli (7,14-10,21)
   c) Manifestazione di Gesù durante la Festa della Dedicazione (10,22-11,54).

D) VERSO LA MORTE (12,1-50).

   a) Unzione a Betania (12,1-8)
   b) Ingresso in Gerusalemme (12,9-19)
   c) Venuta dei "Greci" e compimento dell'"Ora" (12,20-36)
   d) Rifiuto del popolo eletto a credere in Gesù (12,37-43)
   e) Riepilogo del ministero pubblico di Gesù (12,44-50).

E) MANIFESTAZIONE DI GESÙ AI "SUOI" PRIMA DELLA MORTE (13,1-17,26).

   a) Lavanda dei piedi (13,1-20)
   b) Separazione di Giuda (=demonio) dai "suoi" (13,21-30)
   c) Discorso sulla sua dipartita e sul suo ritorno (13,31-14,31)
   d) Discorso sul destino dei discepoli nel mondo dopo la sua dipartita (15,1-16,33)
   e) Preghiera "di commiato" al Padre (17,1-26)
      1) per sé (17,1-8)
      2) per i discepoli (17,9-19)
      3) per tutti i credenti (17,20-26).

F) CAMMINO VERSO LA GLORIA DELLA CROCE (= LA PASSIONE E LA MORTE DI GESÙ COME "SEGNO" E "ATTUAZIONE" DELLA SUA REGALITA (18,1-19,42).

   a) Arresto e interrogatorio di Gesù davanti al tribunale giudaico (18,1-27)
   b) Processo di Gesù davanti al tribunale pagano di Pilato (18,28-19,16a)
   c) Crocifissione - Morte - Sepoltura di Gesù (19,16b-42).

G) NUOVA MANIFESTAZIONE DI GESÙ AI "SUOI" COME RISORTO (20,1-29).

   a) Nell'ambito del sepolcro (20,1-10.11-18)
   b) Nel Cenacolo senza Tommaso (20,19-25)
   c) Nel Cenacolo con Tommaso (20,26-29).

CHIUSURA DEL VANGELO SU GESÙ-RIVELATORE (20,30-31).

EPILOGO (21,1-25 = non giovanneo).

While it is true that there is a certain progression both in the narrative and in the self-revelation of Jesus from the first manifestation to the last, the division of the Fourth Gospel into seven successive manifestations does not seem always to be based on objective, unquestionable literary criteria. For instance, one does not see why Jn 11 must be taken together with Jn 7-10 to form a single manifestation of Jesus (7,1-11,54), and why Jn 12 (which is closely connected with Jn 11) should be separated from Jn 11 and regarded as the fourth manifestation. Again, the outline of the structure proposed passes over in silence some passages, and is sometimes even contradicted by the author when he explains the outline in the course of his book. For example, the pericope on John the Baptist (3,22-36) is given in the outline as part of the pericope on Nicodemus (2,23-3,36), although it is admitted elsewhere that strictly speaking only 2,23-3,21 deals with Jesus' encounter with Nicodemus and that 3,3-21 and 3,22-36 are parallel to each other [226].

2.[22] REVELATORY-ECLECTIC STRUCTURE (SEGALLA)

After examining briefly the different types of structures that have been proposed, G. Segalla suggests an "eclectic" structure [227], based on the guiding principle of "the historical revelation of the Word Incarnate, Messiah and Son of God, who gives life through faith" [228] and on various other criteria for the determination of the different literary units [229]. He divides the Gospel of John into four parts or "books" preceded by a Prologue and followed by an epilogue [230]:

---

[226] *Ibid.*, 159-60.
[227] SEGALLA, 130: "La struttura che proponiamo sembrerà *eclettica*; e in realtà lo è." [my italics].
[228] SEGALLA states:

   L'idea fondamentale che guida l'evangelista è *la rivelazione storica* del Verbo Incarnato, Messia e Figlio di Dio, mediante segni e discorsi, ed infine mediante il suo innalzamento alla croce e la sua elevazione alla gloria per suscitare la fede e così donare la vita all'uomo. Lo scopo o fine di un opera è quello che guida la struttura, e lo scopo dichiarato del vangelo si trova proprio nella sua conclusione (Gv 20,30-31). Qui ci sembra di scoprire *l'idea-guida* (130-31; my italics).

[229] *Ibid.*, 131-33.
[230] *Ibid.*, 133-37.

Prologo - 1,1-18...

I. Il libro dei segni - 1,19-12,50:
rivelazione di Gesù al popolo mediante segni e discorsi

PARTE PRIMA - 1,19-51: la prima rivelazione di Gesù
  19-34: la rivelazione
  35-51: i primi discepoli vanno a Gesù (= credono)

PARTE SECONDA - 2-4: da Cana a Cana - il nuovo inizio
  1) 2,1-11: inizio dei segni a Cana
      12: *sommario storico*
  2) 2,13-22: il tempio e il corpo di Gesù
      23-25: *sommario storico-teologico*
  3) 3,1-21: il dialogo con Nicodemo
      22-30: l'ultima testimonianza del Battista
      31-36: conclusione del dialogo-monologo con Nicodemo
      4,1-3: *sommario storico*
  4) 4,4-42: il colloquio con la samaritana
      43-45: *sommario storico*
  5) 4,46-53: il funzionario regio e il figlio guarito, mentre Gesù è a Cana
      54: *conclusione redazionale*

PARTE TERZA - 5-10: Gesù e le feste giudaiche
  1) 5,1-47: il sabato
      1-9a: il miracolo
      16-47: disputa (9b-18) e discorso interpretativo (19-30 e 31-47)
  2) 6,1-71: la Pasqua e Gesù vera manna, pane di vita
      1-21: i due segni
      22-71: introduzione storica (22-25), discorso rivelatorio (26-59) e reazione (60-71)
  3) 7,1-9,41: la festa delle Capanne e Gesù che sostituisce l'aqua e la luce...
  4) 10,1-42: la festa della Dedicazione e Gesù buon pastore...

PARTE QUARTA - 11-12: Gesù va verso l'ora della morte e glorificazione
  1) 11,1-54: Gesù dà la vita e i giudei lo condannano a morte...
  2) 11,55-12,36: scene che introducono alla Passione e concludono il ministero pubblico...

Conclusione - 12,37-50: valutazione conclusiva del ministero rivelatorio di Gesù...

II. Il libro degli addii - 13,1-17,26:
rivelazione di Gesù ai suoi

PARTE PRIMA - 13,1-35: cena, lavanda dei piedi e suo significato...

PARTE SECONDA - 13,36-14,31: primo discorso sulla fede e l'amore come risposta al turbamento per la prossima partenza di Gesù...

PARTE TERZA - 15,1-16,33: il secondo discorso sull'amore e la fede come risposta all'odio del mondo

1) 15,1-17: l'amore a Gesù che si fonda sull'immanenza in lui e produce frutti...
2) 15,18-16,4a: l'odio del mondo contro Gesù e la testimonianza...
3) 16,4b-15: la missione del Paraclito
4) 16,16-33: il ritorno di Gesù porterà ai discepoli gioia, pace e conferma della loro fede

PARTE QUARTA - 17,1-26: la preghiera conclusiva al Padre...

III. Il libro della Passione - 18,1-19,42:
la rivelazione di Gesù, re-Messia al mondo

1) 18,1-11: Gesù al Getsemani si rivela ai discepoli e riceve il calice
2) 18,12-27: Gesù davanti ad Anna, e le tre negazioni di Pietro
3) 18,28-19,16a: il processo davanti a Pilato...
4) 19,16b-30: la crocifissione
5) 19,31-42: colpo di lancia e sepoltura

IV. Il libro della risurrezione - 20,1-29:
la rivelazione del Signore risorto ai suoi

1) 20,1-18: i fatti avvenuti al sepolcro
   1-10: la Maddalena, Pietro e il discepolo che Gesù amava
   11-18: incontro della Maddalena con il Risorto
2) 20,19-29: apparizioni ai discepoli
   19-23: prima apparizione con la missione e lo Spirito
   24-29: seconda apparizione e professione solenne di fede

Conclusione generale - 20,30-31:
scopo dell'evangelista

Epilogo (nell'intenzione del redattore finale) - 21,1-23: futuro della Chiesa e del mondo...

Conclusione finale - 21,24-25...

Note that the four parts or "books" are related to the "guiding idea" of "revelation" and are distinguished from one another according to the content of each "book" and the destination of the revelation (namely, I. "to the people", II. "to his own", III. "to the world", and IV. "to his own")[231].

"The Book of Signs" (1,19-12,50) is further divided into four parts (1,19-51; 2-4; 5-10; 11-12), each part having a different structuring principle. Thus, the literary units of the first part (1,19-51) and third part (Jn 5-10) are *"chronologically"* structured (cf. *tê[i] epaurion* at 1,29.35.43; *meta tauta* at 5,1; 6,1; 7,1), while those of the second (Jn 2-4) and the fourth parts (Jn 11-12) are marked by "historical summaries" (2,12; 2,23-25; 4,13; 4,43-45) and "summaries of transition" (11,55-57; 12,9-11) or "conclusion" (12,37-50)[232]. But it must be noted that Segalla has overlooked or left out some "chronological" connections

---

[231] *Ibid.*, 131-32. See also the titles and subtitles of the four "books".
[232] *Ibid.*, 132.

(e.g. *tê[i] hêmera[i] tê[i] tritê[i]* at 2,1 which joins 2,1-11 with the previous pericopes which begin with *tê[i] epaurion*) or "general chronological indications" (e.g. *meta tauta* at 5,14) and some "historical summaries" (e.g. 3,22-24). Besides, though it is explicitly stated that the third part (Jn 5-10) is "divided by means of *general chronological indications*"[233], *de facto* Segalla seems to have divided it according to "the Jewish feasts" (Sabbath, Passover, Tabernacles and Dedication).

"The Book of Farewells" (Jn 13-17) is divided "*thematically*" (faith and love) into four parts[234]. There is always danger of subjectivism in dividing the structure according to themes alone. Thus Segalla's division of Jn 13-17 overlooks the evident parallelism between 13,31-14,31 and 16,4b-33[235].

The fivefold division of "the Book of the Passion" (Jn 18-19) is made according to the number of "*successive scenes*", while "the Book of the Resurrection" (Jn 20) is divided into two units according to the "*different places*": the empty tomb and the cenacle[235a]. But different places are mentioned not only in Jn 20 but also in Jn 18-19 (e.g. 18,1.15.28; 19,17) and "successive scenes" are painted not only in Jn 18-19 but also in Jn 20 (e.g. 20,1-10.11-18.19-23.24-25.26-29).

In conclusion we may say that while Segalla's attempt at detecting and using different literary criteria is praiseworthy, the structure he has given is "eclectic" as he himself has admitted. Instead of choosing one or other of the criteria for each one of the "books", one must employ different types of criteria and use the convergence of criteria as a more secure way of establishing the literary structure. Secondly, while "the Book of Signs" and "the Book of Farewells" consist of twelve and five chapters respectively, "the Book of the Passion" and "the Book of the Resurrection" are composed of just two and one respectively. Hence one wonders whether the Evangelist intended them to be regarded as "books" or major divisions. The division of Jn 13-20 into three "books" does not take into account the parallelism between Jn 13-17 and 18-20, since the first explains the significance of the passion-resurrection (Jn 18-20) as a single mystery.

2.[23] LITERARY-THEMATIC STRUCTURE (BROWN)[236]

R. E. Brown in his excellent two-volume commentary on Jn presents the following "GENERAL OUTLINE OF THE GOSPEL"[237]:

---

[233] *Ibid.*
[234] *Ibid.*
[235] Cf. BROWN, II, 588-91 and see 4.342,2 below.
[235a] SEGALLA, 132.
[236] For lack of a better term we designate BROWN's outline as "thematic-literary structure", since he uses both themes and literary criteria. Though these two types of norms have been used also by other authors we have discussed above, however, they emphasized some (one or more) specific literary criteria on which they based their structure.
[237] BROWN, I, cxxxviii.

i 1-18: THE PROLOGUE...
i 19-xii 50: THE BOOK OF SIGNS...
xiii 1-xx 31: THE BOOK OF GLORY...
xxi 1-25: THE EPILOGUE...

Brown gives a detailed division of "the Book of Signs" and "the Book of Glory" as follows [238]:

DIVISION OF THE BOOK OF SIGNS
(i 19-xii 50)

Part One: The Opening Days of the Revelation of Jesus (i 19-51, plus ii 1-11)
A. i 19-34   The Testimony of John the Baptist...
B. i 35-51   The Baptist's Disciples come to Jesus as he manifests himself...
    (ii 1-11 The Disciples Come to Believe in Jesus as He Manifests His Glory at Cana - this scene both closes Part One and opens Part Two)

Part Two: From Cana to Cana - various responses to Jesus' ministry in the different sections of Palestine (ii-iv)

A. ii 1-11   The First Sign at Cana in Galilee - water into wine.
    12   Transition - Jesus goes to Capernaum.
B. ii 13-22   Cleansing of the Temple in Jerusalem.
    23-25   Transition - Reaction to Jesus in Jerusalem.
C. iii 1-21   Discourse with Nicodemus in Jerusalem.
    22-30   The Baptist's final Witness to Jesus.
    31-36   Discourse of Jesus completing the preceding.
    iv 1-3   Transition - Jesus leaves Judea.
D. iv 4-42   Discourse with the Samaritan Woman at Jacob's Well.
    43-45   Transition - Jesus enters Galilee.
E. iv 46-54   The Second Sign at Cana in Galilee - healing the official's son; the household become believers.
    (This scene both closes Part Two and opens Part Three)

Part Three: Jesus and the principal feasts of the Jews
    (v-x, introduced by iv 46-54)
    iv 46-54   (Jesus gives life to the official's son at Cana)
A. v 1-47   THE SABBATH - Jesus performs works that only God can do on the Sabbath...
B. vi 1-71   PASSOVER - Jesus gives bread replacing the manna of the Exodus...

---

[238] *Ibid.*, cxl-cxli; II, 785-86; 965. [We have left out the detailed subdivisions of A, B, C, D of the Sections of the Book of Signs and the Book of Glory.]

C. vii 1-viii 59   TABERNACLES - Jesus replaces the water and light ceremonies...
    ix 1-x 21   Aftermath of Tabernacles...
D.   x 22-39   DEDICATION - Jesus, the Messiah and Son of God, is consecrated in place of the temple altar...
    40-42   Apparent Conclusion to the public ministry.

Part Four: Jesus moves toward the hour of death and glory (xi-xii)

A.   xi 1-54   Jesus gives men life; men condemn Jesus to death...
    55-57   Transition - Will Jesus come to Jerusalem for Passover?
B.   xii 1-36   Scenes preparatory to Passover and death...

Conclusion: Evaluation and summation of Jesus' ministry (xii 37-50)...

DIVISION OF THE BOOK OF GLORY
(chs. XIII-XX)

PART ONE: THE LAST SUPPER (chs. XIII-XVII)

A.   xiii 1-30:   THE MEAL.
    (1-20) The footwashing...
    (21-30) Prediction of betrayal.

B. xiii 31-xvii 26:   THE LAST DISCOURSE.
   (xiii 31-
   xiv 31)   *Division 1*: The departure of Jesus and the future of the disciples...
   (xv-xvi)   *Division 2*: The life of the disciples and their encounter with the world after Jesus shall have departed...
   xv 1-17:   *Subdivision 1*: The vine and the branches...
   xv 18-
   xvi 4a: *Subdivision 2*: The world's hatred for Jesus and his disciples...
   xvi 4b-33:   *Subdivision 3*: Duplicate of Division 1...
   (xvii)   *Division 3*: The concluding prayer of Jesus...

PART TWO: THE PASSION NARRATIVE (chs. XVIII-XIX)

A.   xviii 1-27   *Division 1*: THE ARREST AND INTERROGATION OF JESUS...
B.   xviii 28-
    xix 16a   *Division 2*: THE TRIAL OF JESUS BEFORE PILATE...
C.   xix 16b-42   *Division 3*: THE EXECUTION OF JESUS ON THE CROSS AND HIS BURIAL...

PART THREE: THE RISEN JESUS (XX 1-29)

A.   xx 1-18:   *Scene One*: AT THE TOMB...
B.   xx 19-29:   *Scene Two*: WHERE THE DISCIPLES ARE GATHERED...

The division of the Fourth Gospel into "the Book of Signs" (1,19-12,50) and "the Book of Glory" (13,1-20,31) is claimed by Brown to be suggested by the Gospel itself, since there is a break in the narrative at the end of Jn 12 (cf. 12,37-43 and 12,44-50) and since Jesus' words in Jn 13-17 are addressed to the disciples[239]. But there is not only a break between Jn 12 and 13 but also a connection between them, since both chapters speak of the arrival of "the hour" of Jesus (12,23; 13,1) and his glorification (12,23; 13,31.32) and both describe episodes before the Passover (12,1; 13,1).

Also the designation of the whole of 1,19-12,50 as "the Book of Signs" is not quite exact, since nothing is said about "signs" in 1,19-51. Similarly, "glory" and the "glorification" of Jesus are spoken about already in Jn 2-12 (cf. 2,11; 11,4; 12,23) and therefore the designation of only Jn 13-20 as "the Book of Glory" is not quite correct.

Regarding Brown's division of the Book of Signs, we may note that Jn 2-4 certainly forms a well defined unit ("From Cana to Cana"). And his insight that the first Cana sign (2,1-11) both closes 1,19-2,11 and opens Jn 2-4 is quite valid. Whether the second Cana sign (4,46-54) also has the same "closing-opening" function is at least open to discussion[240]. Jn 5-10 ("Jesus and the principal feasts of the Jews") is another well demarcated division. Similarly, Jn 11-12 ("Jesus moves toward the hour of death and glory") has a unity of its own.

With regard to the subdivisions of the parts of the Book of Signs, we may make the general remark that most of them are based on objective criteria like the transitions (e.g. the divisions of Part Two into A B C D E) and Jewish feasts (e.g. the divisions of Part Three into A B C D). But the application of the criteria is not always rigorous or exact. For instance, 3,22 is a transition like 2,23-25; 4,1-3 and 4,43-45 but Brown does not mention it as a transition perhaps because he would like to combine 3,22-36 with 3,1-21 to form a single unit. Likewise, although "Sabbath" is explicitly mentioned in Jn 9 (cf. v.14) and "Tabernacles" does not feature in 9,1-10,21, yet the latter passage is entitled "Aftermath of Tabernacles" and is joined to Jn 7-8.

Like many other Johannine commentators Brown divides "the Book of Glory" (Jn 13-20) into three parts ("the Last Supper": 13-17; "the Passion Narrative": 18-19; "the Risen Jesus": 20). Although merely at the narrative level this threefold division can perhaps be defended, it seems to go against the Johannine understanding of "the hour" of Jesus as the supreme moment of his return to the Father (13,1) or of his glorification (17,1) through his passion-death-resurrection-ascension interpreted as one event[241], and not as successive events, as is the case in the Synoptic Gospels.

---

[239] *Ibid.*, I, cxxxviii.
[240] See 4.211 below.
[241] Cf. G. FERRARO, *L'"Ora" di Cristo nel Quarto Vangelo* (Roma 1974) 301. BROWN himself admits the indivisible unity of "the action of glorification" described in Jn 18-20 and interpreted in Jn 13-17:

Again, Part One (Jn 13-17) is divided into 13,1-30 ("the Meal") and 13,31-17,26 ("the Last Discourse"), even though the meal is only the setting for the footwashing, the dialogues and the discourses that follow. Furthermore, the three divisions of the Last Discourse (13,31-14,31; 15,1-16,33; 17,1-26) are based on a hypothetical "theory of Gospel composition" in five stages [242]. This is all the more surprising, since Brown himself admits the strict parallelism between 13,31-14,31 and 16,4b-33 [243]. Here his hypothesis seems to have prevented him from noting the chiastic structure of the actual text we now have in Jn 13-17 [244].

Divisions 2 ("the Trial of Jesus before Pilate") and 3 ("the Execution of Jesus on the Cross and His Burial") of Part Two ("the Passion Narrative") are well defined units. But one does not see why "the arrest and interrogation of Jesus" should be regarded as one division rather than two (i.e. Jesus before the arrest-party, and Jesus before the high priest), since there is a change of scene in 18,12-14.

Brown provides a number of interesting insights into the divisions and subdivisions of the Fourth Gospel, and he has tried to arrive at them by following the "indications in the Gospel itself". Yet he seems sometimes to have fallen into "the danger of imposing insights on the evangelist" [245] and sometimes to have failed to draw the right conclusions from the literary indications he has correctly detected (e.g. the parallelism between 13,31-14,31 and 16,4b-33). This is due to his hypothesis of a 5-stage composition of the Fourth Gospel.

2.[24] JOURNEY-STRUCTURE (RISSI)

M. Rissi proposes a structure based on the journeys of Jesus in the Gospel of John, for he says:

> Es ist meines Wissens bisher nicht beachtet worden, dass die *Reisen Jesu* im vierten Evangelium nach einem bestimmten Plan gestaltet sind, und dass dieses Schema die Struktur des ganzen Buches bestimmt... Das Johannesevangelium kennt vier Reisen Jesu, und *alle vier führen Ihn zum selben Ziel: Judäa und näherhin Jerusalem...* [246].

In the Book of Signs we saw the phenomenon whereby Jesus' discourses, coming after the signs, served to interpret the signs. In the Book of Glory the Last Supper and the Discourse that precede the action of glorification serve to interpret that action (II, 542).

If this is true, then Jn 13-20 should not be divided into three major parts (Jn 13-17; 18-19; 20) as Brown does, but only into two (Jn 13-17 and 18-20). This twofold division is supported also by the chiastic parallelism between Jn 13-17 (4C D E E' D' C') and Jn 18-20 (5C D E E' D' C'). (See 4.34 and 4.35 below.)

[242] BROWN, II, 586.
[243] *Ibid.*, 588-94 (cf. especially "Chart I" on pp. 589-91). BROWN notes that not only are there many parallels between the two units but also "the over-all structure of the two is roughly the same" (p. 588).
[244] See 4.34 below.
[245] BROWN, I, cxlii (e.g. the linking function of 4,46-54 as "closing" the previous section Jn 2-4 and "opening" the next section Jn 5-10).
[246] M. RISSI, "Der Aufbau des vierten Evangeliums", *NTS* 29 (1983) 48 [my italics].

Rissi regards as important for the structure not only the goal of Jesus' journeys (Judea-Jerusalem) but also their successive stages, for he says about the first three journeys: "Und zwar beginnen die Wanderungen je in einem heidnischen oder halbheidnischen Ort - führen dann jedesmal nach Galiläa und von dort ins 'heilige Land'"[247].

Applying the above criteria Rissi finds that the first three journeys of Jesus are narrated in 1,19-3,36; 4,1-5,47 and 6,1-10,39. These three journeys together with the Prologue (1,1-18) constitute, according to Rissi, the first major part (*Hauptteil*) of the Fourth Gospel (1,1-10,39)[248].

The second major part (*Hauptteil*) consists of 10,40-20,31 because of the following reasons: (1) The "hour" of Jesus arrives already in 12,23ff. (2) Jesus is condemned to death by the Sanhedrin already in 11,47-57. (3) The Jewish condemnation of Jesus is connected to the raising of Lazarus in Jn 11. (4) Jn 13 is linked to Jn 12 and Jn 11 through the mention of "the Passover" (cf. 11,55; 12,1; 13,1), which coincides with Jesus' passing over from this world to the Father (13,1). It is also to be noted that in 11,8-11 Jesus returns to Judea ready to face death[249].

The second principal part of the Fourth Gospel (10,40-20,31) consists of three sections: 1) Jesus' last journey to Jerusalem (10,40-12,41), 2) Jesus' farewell to his disciples (13,31-14,31), and 3) the return home of the Son to the Father (18,1-20,31)[250]. Jn 12,42-50; Jn 15-17 and Jn 21 are left out as later interpolations[251].

In short, the structure of the Fourth Gospel according to Rissi is as follows[252]:

1. Hauptteil 1. Der Prolog 1.1-18
              2. Die erste Wanderung 1.19-3.36
              3. Die zweite Wanderung 4.1-5.47
              4. Die dritte Wanderung 6.1-10.39
2. Hauptteil 5. Die letzte Wanderung 10.40-12.41
              6. Jesu Abschied von seinen Jüngern 13.1-14.31
              7. Der Heimgang des Sohnes zum Vater 18.1-20.31.

Now the four reasons given by Rissi for taking Jn 11-12 as part of the second major part of the Fourth Gospel are quite valid but he has not examined the close connection between Jn 11-12 and the first principal part of the Gospel (cf. for instance the concluding character of 12,37-43). That is, he has failed to

---

[247] *Ibid.*, 49.
[248] *Ibid.*
[249] *Ibid.*, 50-51.
[250] *Ibid.*, 51-52.
[251] *Ibid.*, 52 and 54, n. 22.
[252] *Ibid.*, 52.

see the "bridging" function of Jn 11-12[253]. Using Rissi's own criterion of the "journeys" of Jesus, one would have expected Rissi to regard "the last journey" as related to the first three "journeys"!

No reason is given by Rissi for taking the Prologue as belonging exclusively to the first major part of the Gospel. Secondly, it is questionable whether 12,42-50 and especially Jn 15-17 can be discarded as later interpolations. Thirdly, while it is true that the Gospel of John mentions many journeys of Jesus (1,43; 2,12.13; 3,22; 4,3-4.43.45.46; 5,1; 6,1; 7,10; 10,40; 11,7.17.54; 12,1.12; 18,1), it is doubtful whether the Gospel's structure can be determined by using the journey-criterion alone. Fourthly, Rissi's affirmation that the first three journeys of Jesus always begin in a pagan or half-pagan place, then continue every time through Galilee and finally end in the "holy land" (namely, Judea- Jerusalem)[254] is very subjective. For instance, the Evangelist does not give any indication that Jesus reached his journey's end at 3,36; 5,47; 10,39 and 12,41 respectively (as Rissi maintains). Furthermore, instead of linking Bethany in Perea with Judea (cf. Rissi's "first journey": 1,19-3,36), the Evangelist explicitly connects the two Cana-signs (2,1-11; 4,46-54; cf. 4,46) and expressly states that the second Cana-sign too was done when Jesus "came from Judea into Galilee" (4,54). Hence one wonders whether Rissi's "Wanderung-Schema" is not perhaps a "wandering" in the wilderness led by the shooting star of "Jesus' journeys"!

Rissi's contribution consists, not in the "journey-structure" he has proposed for the Fourth Gospel but in his insight that the second major part of the Gospel includes Jn 11-12 because of the close connection between Jn 11-12 and Jn 13-20 (cf. his four reasons given above). However he has not noticed the link between the first major part and Jn 11-12.

2.7 We may sum up the survey of the structures of the Fourth Gospel by noting that many of the authors we have examined (more than two dozen of them) have employed one or more literary criteria (highlighted in our titles) for the structural analysis, and some have combined them with Johannine themes for the determination of the divisions of the structure. The weakness of most of the structures proposed by different scholars is that they have not examined the various kinds of criteria the Johannine author has employed and hence have sometimes been led astray. This accounts for the wide variety of the structures suggested and the marked differences in the division and subdivision of the Gospel of John.

---

[253] See 3.19; 4.12; 4.13; 4.23 below.
[254] *Art. cit.*, 49.

3
CRITERIA FOR THE STRUCTURE OF THE FOURTH GOSPEL

Our discussion of the various structures of the Fourth Gospel proposed by the different Johannine scholars has convinced us of the need to discover as many different types of criteria as possible in order to detect the structure objectively. In the words of S. Lyonnet: "plus nombreux et plus variés seront les critères, plus la probabilité s'approchera d'une véritable certitude"[1], for convergence of criteria of diverse natures can guarantee greater objectivity than can dependence on a single norm which might mesmerize a scholar and lead him to subjective conclusions.

By examining carefully the Greek text of the Fourth Gospel[2] from various angles, we find three different categories of criteria for the determination of its structure, namely, 1) literary criteria, 2) dramatic techniques, and 3) structural patterns.

3.1 LITERARY CRITERIA

We may conveniently classify the literary or linguistic criteria under the following twelve headings: 1) conclusions, 2) introductions, 3) inclusions, 4) charac-

---

[1] These are the words of S. LYONNET in the "Preface" to A. VANHOYE's *La Structure Littéraire de l'Épitre aux Hebreux* (Paris 1963) 8. The latter uses five different literary criteria for establishing the Epistle's structure, namely, announcement of the subject, hook-words, genre, characteristic terms, and inclusions (*ibid.*, 37).

Similarly, U. VANNI insists on the importance of multiple literary elements for detecting the true structure of the Apocalypse:

> Parliamo intenzionalmente di *elementi* al plurale. Senza pretendere di individuare tutti i fatti letterari, che possano avere un rapporto con la struttura del libro, insistiamo su una molteplicità più larga che ci sarà possibile. Infatti, sarà proprio questa molteplicità di elementi a permetterci di completare i singoli indizi che ricaveremo, di integrarli, di consolidarne, sommandole insieme, le conclusioni verso cui essi convergeranno. (*La Struttura Letteraria dell'Apocalisse*, 2 ed., [Brescia 1980] 106).

The above observation of Vanni about the multiplicity of criteria is equally important and valid for establishing the literary structure of the Fourth Gospel. For, in the words of S. P. KEALY: "To discover John's plan we must try to look for his own criteria, e.g. his introduction, conclusions, inclusions..., his change of audience, themes, etc." (*That You may Believe* [Slough 1978] 32).

We do not claim to have discovered *all* the criteria useful to determine the literary structure of Jn but we have found numerous and various types of criteria on whose convergence our proposed structure will be based.

[2] We use NESTLE-ALAND's *Greek-English New Testament*, 2nd ed., (Stuttgart 1985), whose text is the same as that of *The Greek New Testament*, 3rd ed., ed. by K. ALAND *et alii* (Stuttgart 1983).

teristic vocabulary, 5) geographical indications, 6) chronological indications, 7) liturgical feasts, 8) transitions, 9) bridge-passages, 10) hook-words, 11) techniques of repetition, and 12) change of literary genres (narrative, dialogue, discourse).

3.11 Conclusions

We shall start with the conclusion to the whole Gospel, which is found at the end of chapter 20 (vv.30-31). Then we shall consider the conclusion(s) at the end of Jn 21 by the final redactor(s) (21,24-25). Thirdly, we shall examine the conclusion to the first part of the Gospel (12,37-43). Finally, we shall mention some of the other conclusions of episodes or pericopes.

3.111 *Jn 20,30-31*

Reading through the Fourth Gospel from the beginning, one has the impression that one has come to the end when one reaches Jn 20,30-31: "Now Jesus did many other signs in the presence of the disciples, which are not written in this book; but these are written that you may believe that Jesus is the Christ, the Son of God, and that believing you may have life in his name." A close examination of these verses confirms the first impression, since the first verse states the selective character or limits of the book, and the second, the double scope or purpose of the writer, namely, that the readers may believe in Jesus as the Christ and the Son of God and continuing to believe may have eternal life.

Similar concluding statements are found also in some other books of the Bible. For instance, the First Letter of John concludes by stating its purpose: "I have written this to you who believe in the name of the Son of God, that you may know that you have eternal life" (5,13). This surely resembles the statement of purpose of the Gospel of John in 20,30-31. A statement about the limits of the narrative quite similar to Jn 20,30 is found in 1 Mac 9,22: "Now the rest of the acts of Judas, and his wars and the brave deeds that he did, and his greatness, have not been recorded, for they were very many"[3].

The concluding character of Jn 20,30-31 is confirmed by the presence there of many of the same Johannine terms already found in the introduction (1,1-2,11): e.g. *zôê* (1,4.4; 20,31), *pisteuein* (1,6.12.50; 20,31.31), *to onoma autou* (1,12; 20,31), *Christos* (1,17.20.25.41; 20,31), *ho hyios tou theou* (1,34.49; 20,31), *sêmeia* (2,11; 20,30), *mathêtai* (1,35.37; 2,2.11; 20,30). All these terms also occur repeatedly in the body of the Fourth Gospel. Outside the introduction and the conclusion *zôê* occurs 33 times, *pisteuein* 93 times, Jesus' *onoma* 9 times (and the

---

[3] It is true that 1 Mac 9,22 is not the conclusion of the whole book but only of the part that describes the life and death of Judas Maccabeus (1 Mac 3-9). Nevertheless, it may be taken as a statement similar to Jn 20,30, since both of them occur at the end of the narrative that recounts the deeds and death of Judas and Jesus respectively.

Cf. BULTMANN, 697, n. 2 for non-biblical examples of conclusions.

Father's *onoma* 7 times), *Christos* 14 times (and *Messias* twice), *ho hyios tou theou* 6 times (*sou ho hyios* once, and the absolute *ho hyios* 17 times), *sêmeion* 16 times, Jesus' *mathêtai* 65 times (and 10 times in Jn 21).

We may also mention here that Johannine scholars and commentators are almost unanimous in affirming that 20,30-31 is intended by the Evangelist to be his conclusion to the Gospel as a whole [4].

3.112 *Jn 21,24-25*

We have a second conclusion to the Fourth Gospel in the last two verses of chapter 21.

The purpose of 21,24 is to establish the identity of the author as the Beloved Disciple ("this is the disciple who is bearing witness to these things, and who has written these things") [5] and to attest to the truthfulness and reliability of his testimony ("and we know that his testimony is true"). In other words, 21,24 is essentially a testimonial conclusion or colophon. It was added, most probably after the death of the Beloved Disciple (cf. 21,23), by the redactor (who was responsible for the addition of Jn 21) and his fellow Johannine disciples (cf. *hêmeis* in 21,24) [6].

Jn 21,25 is a hyperbolic conclusion, which may be an imitation of 20,30 by the final redactor or publisher of our Gospel [7].

3.113 *Jn 12,37-50*

The last two pericopes at the end of Jn 12 (vv.37-43.44-50) may be considered as a double conclusion to the first part of the Gospel (Jn 2-12) [8] for the following reasons: 1) In 12,37-43 the Evangelist states and explains the fact of the unbelief of the Jews in spite of the many signs that Jesus did during his public ministry. This is all the more significant, since Jesus' "signs" and "works" and the Jews' "unbelief" are given much prominence in Jn 2-12 [9]. 2) In

---

[4] For example, BULTMANN states in unambiguous terms: "20.30f. is a *clear conclusion* to the Gospel, in which *the selective character of the narrative* is stressed and *its purpose* declared" (697; my italics).
In the words of BROWN: "The air of *finality* in these two verses justifies their being called a *conclusion* despite the fact that in the present form of the Gospel a whole chapter follows" (II, 1057; my italics).
Cf. also the many authors mentioned in ch. 2 above and in n. 2 of ch. 4 below.

[5] Cf. BROWN, II, 1123-24 for the different interpretations of *grapsas tauta* of 21,24.

[6] *Ibid.*, 1124-25; BARRETT, 587-88; LINDARS, 641; SCHNACKENBURG, III, 372-74.

[7] SCHNACKENBURG, III, 374; BROWN, II, 1129-30. Similar hyperbolic concluding statements are found also in rabbinic writings (cf. STRACK-BILLERBECK [on Jn 21,25], II, 587).

[8] See ch. 4 below for the division of the Fourth Gospel.

[9] Not only the term *sêmeion* occurs 16 times (2,11.18.23; 3,2; 4,48.54; 6,2.14.26.30; 7,31; 9,16; 10,41; 11,47; 12,18.37) and Jesus' *erga* are mentioned 13 times (5,20.36.36; 7,3.21; 9,3.4; 10,25.32. 32.33.37.38) in Jn 2-12, but also seven signs/works are described in detail in these chapters (2,1-11; 4,46-54; 5,1-9; 6,1-15; 6,16-21; 9,1-7; 11,1-44). Similarly, the Jews' refusal to believe in Jesus is progressively revealed in Jn 2-12 (e.g. 2,18-20; 3,11-12; 5,10-18.38.44; 6,30-31.41-42.52; 7,15.19.30; 8,46.59; 9,18; 10,19-20.25.31.39; 11,53; 12,19.37).

12,44-50 the Johannine Jesus sums up the message of his earlier revelatory discourses (e.g. believing in Jesus and in God who sent him: 5,24; 12,44; Jesus, the light of the world: 3,19; 8,12; 9,5; 12,46; not walking/remaining in darkness: 8,12; 12,46; Jesus' mission of not judging the world but saving the world: 3,17; 12,47; not doing/speaking on his own authority: 5,19.30; 7,17; 12,49.50). It is also worthy of note that he makes this final public proclamation (cf. *ekraxen*: 12,44), as it were, from behind the curtain for dramatic effect[9a]. 3) Many of the main themes of 12,37-50 are found also in the introduction (1,1-2,11) and/or in the conclusion of the whole Gospel (20,30-31). Some of the most important common terms and expressions are: *sêmeia poiein* (2,11; 12,37; 20,30), *pisteuein* (1,6.12.50; 2,11; 12,37.38.39.42.44.44.46; 20,31.31), *zôê (aiôniôs)* (1,4.4; 12,50; 20,31), *phôs* (1,4.5.7.8.8.9; 12,46), *phôs eis ton kosmon erchesthai* (1,9; 12,46), *kosmos* (1,9.10.10.10; 12,46.47.47), *en tê[i] skotia[i]* (1,5; 12,46), *homologein* (1,20; 12,42)[10], *doxa* (1,14.14; 2,11; 12,41.43.43), *(ho) patêr* (1,14.18; 12,49.50), *Esaïas ho prophêtês* (1,23; 12,38.39.41)[11], and *Kyrios* (1,23; 12,38)[12]. The presence of so many same Johannine terms in 12,37-50 and in 1,1-2,11, which comprises the introduction[13], and in 20,30-31, which is the conclusion to the Gospel as a whole[13a], confirms our position that 12,37-43 and 12,44-50 form a double conclusion to the first part of the Johannine Gospel (Jn 2-12). Note that 12,37-43 emphasizes Jesus' revelation through deeds (the many signs which he did) and 12,44-50 stresses his revelation through words, both of which have been described in Jn 2-12.

3.114 *Other conclusions*

The Fourth Gospel provides numerous examples of different types of conclusions to episodes or pericopes:

1) The Evangelist concludes the pericope of the testimony of John the Baptist on the first day (1,19-27) with the following historical information: "This took place in Bethany beyond the Jordan, where John was baptizing" (1,28).

2) Similarly at the end of Jesus' discourse on the bread of life (6,22-58) we are told: "This he said in the synagogue, as he taught in Capernaum" (6,59).

3) Sometimes a pericope is concluded by combining historical information with an observation which creates dramatic tension. For example, Jesus' self-revelation as the light of the world and the ensuing discussion with the Jews

---

[9a] See 4.331 below for the dramatic technique of speaking from behind the stage.

[10] It is found elsewhere in the Fourth Gospel only once (9,22).

[11] This occurs nowhere else in this Gospel.

[12] We shall see later (3.13 below) that many of these terms and expressions form inclusions with the introduction (1,1-2,11).

It must be also remarked that 12,37-50, besides concluding Jn 2-12, contains some terms and phrases which point forward to the subsequent part of the Gospel (see 4.331 below).

[13] See 3.121 below.

[13a] See 3.111 above.

(8,12-19) end with the Evangelist's remark: "These words he spoke in the treasury, as he taught in the temple; but no one arrested him, because his hour had not yet come" (8,20).

4) At times a pericope ends with a longer and more complex conclusion. Thus at the end of the narrative of Jesus' first miracle (2,1-10) the Evangelist interprets its meaning and describes the disciples' reaction to it, while also mentioning the place at which it occurred: "This beginning of the signs Jesus made in Cana of Galilee and manifested his glory; and his disciples believed in him" (2,11: my translation).

5) The second sign at Cana (the healing of the royal official's son: 4,46-54) concludes with an observation about the circumstances in which the miracle took place: "This second sign again Jesus did when he came from Judea into Galilee" (4,54: my translation).

6) Often a pericope or episode ends with the reaction of the people present on the occasion. a) One of Jesus' dialogues with the Jews in Jerusalem during the feast of Tabernacles (8,21-29) concludes with the remark: "As he spoke thus, many believed in him" (8,30; cf. also 2,11). b) Some pericopes end with a hostile reaction of the Jews to Jesus: for instance, (i) at the end of a controversy between Jesus and the Jews during the feast of Tabernacles (8,31-58) we read: "So they took up stones to throw at him; but Jesus hid himself, and went out of the temple" (8,59); (ii) similarly, at the end of Jesus' discourse on his divine Sonship during the feast of Dedication (10,31-38) we are told about the Jews' attempt to arrest him: "Again they tried to arrest him, but he escaped from their hands" (10,39). c) At times a mixed reaction of the audience is given as the conclusion of a pericope. Thus at the end of Jesus' parable of the good shepherd (10,7-18) there was "a division among the Jews", some accusing him of being possessed or mad and others opposing this view (10,19-21).

3.11z There are conclusions not only at the end of the Gospel (20,30-31; 21,24-25) and at the end of the public life of Jesus (12,37-50) but also at the end of many individual episodes or pericopes (1,28; 2,11; 4,54; 6,59; 8,20.30.59; 10,6.19-21.39; 12,36de; 19,16ab.27c; 20,10.18; 21,14)[14].

3.12 Introductions

Here we shall examine briefly the introduction to the Fourth Gospel as a whole and shall mention some of the introductions to episodes or pericopes.

3.121 *Jn 1,1-2,11: introduction to the Gospel as a whole*

Most Johannine scholars agree that the Fourth Gospel has an introduction, but they disagree about the exact limits of the introduction. The debate is

---

[14] See ch. 4 below.

whether 1,1-18 [15] or 1,1-51 [16] or 1,1-2,11 [17] is to be taken as the introduction. It may also be noted here that some take 1,19-51 [18] or 1,19-2,11(12) [19] as an introduction only to Jn 2-12 (and not to the Gospel as a whole). Later we shall discuss the delimitation, division and nature of the introduction [20]. Here we are concerned only about the fact or existence of an introduction.

We may arrive at a provisional conclusion about the existence and extent of the introduction by comparing it with the conclusion (20,30-31). We have seen above that there the Evangelist explicitly mentions Jesus' "signs" (*sêmeia*) done in the presence of the "disciples" (*mathêtai*), and underlines the importance of "believing" (*pisteuein*) that Jesus is "the Christ, the Son of God" (*ho Christos, ho hyios tou theou*) in order to "have eternal life in his name" (*hina... zôên echête en tô[i] onomati autou*). Looking at the beginning of the Gospel of John we find that *pisteuein* is mentioned in 1,1-18 (vv.7.12), 1,19-51 (v.50) and 2,1-11 (v.11), but Jesus' *sêmeia* and his *mathêtai* are mentioned only in 2,1-11 (v.11 and vv.2.11 respectively), the Christological titles *ho Christos* and *ho hyios tou theou* occur only in 1,19-51 (vv.20.25.41 and 34.49 respectively) [21], while the term *zôê* and the expression *en tô[i] onomati autou* are found only in 1,1-18 (v.4 and v.11 respectively) [22]. In other words, if 20,30-31 is, as we have seen above, the conclusion to the Fourth Gospel, the whole of 1,1-2,11 may rightly be understood as the introduction [23].

Having an introduction is not a peculiarity of the Johannine Gospel; the Synoptic Gospels too have their introductions, e.g. Mk 1,1-15 [24].

3.122 *Introductions to episodes or pericopes*

Besides the introduction to the whole Gospel (1,1-2,11), a number of instances of introductions to pericopes or episodes may be cited:

---

[15] So BERNARD, GUILDING, LOHMEYER, DEFOURNEY, BOISMARD, PUIGDOLLERS, WEBSTER, DEEKS, RAU, KAMMERSTÄTTER, PRETE, TENNEY, WESTCOTT, VAN DEN BUSSCHE, CABA, GOURGUES, SEGALLA, BROWN (see ch. 2 above). [The names are given in the same order as in ch. 2.]

[16] So WILLEMSE, DODD, PASQUETTO (see ch. 2 above).

[17] This is our view (see 4.112 for our reasons).

[18] So VAN DEN BUSSCHE, DE LA POTTERIE (see ch. 2 above).

[19] So CULPEPPER, DE LA POTTERIE, CABA (see ch. 2 above).

[20] See 4.112 below.

[21] It is true that the name "Jesus Christ" occurs at 1,17 but it is not used there as a Christological title but as a personal name. Similarly, *monogenês/hyios* is mentioned at 1,14.18 but, though it refers to the same filial reality of Jesus in relation to the Father, the expression is not the same as *ho hyios tou theou*.

[22] We shall show later (in ch. 4) that these Johannine terms and most of the others present in the Prologue (e.g. *phôs*) are frequently found in the body of the Fourth Gospel.

[23] We shall see later that these Johannine terms in the introduction and the conclusion form *inclusions* (see 3.13 below) and that 1,1-2,11 and 20,30-31 are constructed as a chiasmus (C*B*A⁺ AzBzCz) (see 4.112,3 below). These will confirm our conclusion concerning the introductory character of 1,1-2,11.

[24] We shall see below (cf. n. 39a) that Mk 1,14-15 is, like Jn 2,1-11, a bridge-passage belonging to the introduction and to the first part of the Gospel.

1) At the beginning of the first sign at Cana, the occasion ("there was a marriage": 2,1), the place ("Cana in Galilee": 2,1) and some persons ("Jesus", his "mother", and his "disciples": 2,1-2) are mentioned. These two verses, therefore, serve as an introduction to the whole narrative (2,1-11).

2) Similarly, the sign of the multiplication of the loaves (6,3-15) begins with the mention of Jesus' going up to the mountain and sitting there with his disciples and of the fact that the feast of Passover was near (6,3-4). These two verses have an introductory function, since the persons named there (Jesus and the disciples) play a prominent role in the pericope and only in the context of the Passover can the miracle of the multiplication of the loaves be correctly understood.

3) Likewise, the episode during the feast of Dedication (10,22-39) is introduced by the first three verses, for v.22 names the feast (Dedication), the city (Jerusalem) and the season of the year (winter); v.23 specifies the place where Jesus was walking ("in the temple, in the portico of Solomon"); v.24 describes what the Jews did ("gathered round him") and said to him ("How long will you keep us in suspense? If you are the Christ tell us plainly").

4) Again, Jesus' discourse in 12,23-36 is introduced by 12,20-22 which describes the Greeks' request to see Jesus reported to him by Philip and Andrew.

5) The whole of Jn 13-17(20) is introduced by 13,1 which mentions the time before Passover, Jesus' awareness of the arrival of the hour of his return to the Father and his unlimited love for his own, in the light of which alone his words and deeds at the Last Supper (and during his passion-death-resurrection) can be understood.

6) Jesus' trial before Pilate (18,28-19,16b) is introduced by 18,28 which describes how the Jewish authorities brought Jesus from the house of Caiaphas to the praetorium early in the morning and their refusal to enter the praetorium in order not to be defiled before the Passover.

7) Similarly, Mary Magdalene's arrival at the tomb of Jesus very early in the morning on the first day of the week, her discovery that the stone was removed and her running to Peter and the Beloved Disciple with the words that Jesus' body has been taken away (20,1-2), introduce the scene of the disciples at the empty tomb (20,3-10).

3.12z Besides the introduction to the Fourth Gospel as a whole (1,1-2,11), many of the episodes or pericopes begin with a proper introduction (2,1-2; 3,1-2; 3,22-24; 4,4-6; 4,46; 5,1-5; 6,3-4; 6,22-24; 7,14-15; 9,1; 10,22-24; 11,1-3; 12,1-2; 12,20-22; 13,1.2-5; 17,1; 18,1; 18,28; 20,1-2; 21,1).

3.13 Inclusions

This literary procedure of enclosing a literary unit (a book, section, pericope, or paragraph) between two important and identical words or phrases at the beginning and end of the unit, is frequently found in the Fourth Gospel.

These inclusions indicate the boundaries of the literary unit under examination[25]. There are inclusions in the Fourth Gospel which are valid 1) for the whole book, and 2) for its divisions and subdivisions.

3.131 *Inclusions for the Fourth Gospel as a whole*

We have seen above that all the important Johannine terms in the conclusion (20,30-31) are present also in the introduction (1,1-2,11). Although some of these do not occur at the very beginning of the introduction but only towards its middle or end, they may still be regarded as forming a sort of literary inclusion with the identical terms in the conclusion, since they are found at the beginning (introduction) and end (conclusion) of the book as a whole: *zôê* (1,4; 20,31), *pisteuein* (1,7 [cf. also 1,12.50; 2,11]; 20,31.31), *onoma autou* (1,12; 20,31), *Christos* (1,20.25.41; 20,31), *ho hyios tou theou* (1,34.49; 20,31), *mathêtai* (1,35.37; 2,2.11; 20,30) and *sêmeia* (2,11; 20,30).

3.132 *Inclusions for the divisions and subdivisions*

Inclusions often indicate the divisions and subdivisions of the Gospel. We give below some examples of such Johannine inclusions:

1) The first verse of the Prologue (1,1-18) and the last verse of the first sign at Cana (2,1-11) are most probably intended by the Evangelist to form an inclusion for the introduction (1,1-2,11) to the Fourth Gospel as a whole, since they contain the term *archê*[26]:

---

[25] A. VANHOYE defines an inclusion as "ce procédé qui consiste à reprendre à la fin d'un passage donné un terme ou une formule utilisée en son début et qui indique donc de manière très concrète les limites du développement" (*op. cit.*, 37). He gives another (more concise) definition as follows: "Au sens propre, une inclusion consiste en une correspondence verbale entre le début et la fin d'une unité littéraire" ("Discussions sur la structure de l'Épître aux Hébreux", *Bib* 55 [1974] 365). This literary device was defined by QUINTILIAN in the words: "respondent primis et ultima" (*Inst. Orat.* 9,3,34) (cited by A. VANHOYE, *art. cit.*, 365, n. 1). We may note here that inclusion is an important criterion (one of the five norms) used by VANHOYE to establish the structure of the Epistle to the Hebrews and its divisions and subdivisions (cf. *op. cit.*, 38-58).

Inclusions play a prominent role also in the structures of *The Epistles of John. Greek Text and English Translation Schematically Arranged* (Rome 1973) by E. MALATESTA.

Inclusions, which signal the delimitation of a literary unit or division, must be distinguished from *cross-references*, which indicate the "interconnectedness" of the Gospel of John (cf. S. P. KEALY, *That You may Believe*, 32-33). In fact, the *forward-looking* and *backward-looking* cross-references, which occur throughout the Fourth Fospel, underscore its unity (e.g. "the lifting up of the Son of Man": 3,14; 8,28; 12,34 [cf. Jn 18-20]; Judas' betrayal: 6,64.71; 12,4; 13,2.11.21 [cf. 18,1-11]; the anointing of Jesus by Mary: 11,2 [cf. 12,3]; John the Baptist's testimony: 3,26.28; 5,33; 10,40-41 [cf. 1,19-28]; the healing of the blind man: 10,21; 11,37 [cf. 9,1-7]; the raising of Lazarus: 12,1.9.17 [cf. 11,43-44]; not losing those whom the Father has given Jesus: 18,8-9 [cf. 6,69; 17,12]; Peter's denials before the cock crows: 18,17.25.27 [cf. 13,38]; reference to Jesus' death on the cross: 18,32 [cf. 12,32-33]; "making himself (equal to)/(Son of) God": 19,7 [cf. 5.18; 10,33.36]).

[26] Precisely because the changing of water into wine is denoted not as *prôton tôn sêmeiôn* but as *archê tôn sêmeiôn* (2,11), G. FERRARO concludes:

3.1 LITERARY CRITERIA

1,1 : En ***archê[i]*** ên ho logos... (cf. also 1,2).
2,11: tautên epoiêsen ***archên*** tôn sêmeiôn ho Iêsous...

2) There is a name-inclusion between the beginning of the first Cana-sign (2,1-11) and the end of the second (4,46-54), which shows that Jn 2-4 forms a unit or section:

2,1 : Kai... gamos egeneto en Kana *tês Galilaias* (cf. also 2,11).
4,54: ... elthôn ek tês Ioudaias eis *tên Galilaian* (cf. also 4,46) [27].

3) Similarly, the emphasis on "love" (*agapan/agapê*) in the first verse of Jn 13 and the last verse of Jn 17 shows that we certainly have here a literary inclusion for the whole section of Jn 13-17:

13,1 : ... ***agapêsas*** tous idious tous en tô[i] kosmô[i],
eis telos ***êgapêsen autous***.
17,26: ... hina hê ***agapê*** hên ***êgapêsas*** me en *autois* ê[i]...

4) The two pericopes of testimony by John the Baptist (1,19-28 and 1,29-34) are enclosed in an inclusion formed by the first and last verses of the passage:

1,19: kai hautê estin hê **martyria** *tou Iôannou*...
1,34: *kagô* heôraka kai **memartyrêka**...

5) Similarly, the verbs of "saying" and "seeing" at the beginning and end of the passage about the disciples' discovery of the Messiah (1,35-51) form a double inclusion:

1,36: kai emblepsas to[i] Iesou peripatounti *legei* [28]:
IDE ho amnos *TOU THEOU*.
1,51: kai *legei* autô[i]: amên amên *legô* hymin,
OPSESTHE... tous angelous *TOU THEOU*.

Quindi l'*archê* di 2,11 è in relazione con l'*archê* di 1,1 con cui comincia il vangelo, il "principio" in cui il Verbo era. Ma mentre l'*archê* del Verbo ci fa entrare nell'eternità stessa in cui il Figlio è congiunto con il Padre, l'*archê* di 2,11 ha carattere storico e temporale (*L'"Ora" del Cristo nel Quarto Vangelo* [Roma 1974] 110).

That the author of the Fourth Gospel intended this inclusion between the Prologue (1,1-18) and the first sign at Cana (2,1-11) is supported by the presence of some of the other expressions of the Prologue at 2,11 (*pisteuein eis*: 1,12; *hê doxa autou*: 1,14). Note that even the construction of 1,14c and 2,11b is strikingly similar:

1,14c: *kai etheasametha* **tên doxan autou**
2,11b: *kai ephanerôsen* **tên doxan autou**.

[27] That the name of "Galilee" at 2,1 and 4,54 is intended as an inclusion is confirmed by the parallelism between 2,1-11 and 4,46-54 (cf. especially the resumptive parallelism at 4,46).

[28] One may object that the "saying"-inclusion is not valid, since *legein* is too frequent in the passage to be truly significant. But it must be remembered that if the Fourth Evangelist has employed the verbs of "saying" 22 times in just 17 verses, he has done so in order to underline their

Notice that, besides the verbal inclusions, the genitive *TOU THEOU* in 1,36 and 1,51 may be taken as another inclusion.

6) Another good example of a multiple inclusion between two connected pericopes is found in 20,1-2.18:

20,1 : **Maria hê Magdalênê** ERCHETAI prôï...
20,2 : ERCHETAI pros Simôna Petron kai pros ton allon *mathêtên*...
kai legei autois: êran *TON KYRION*...
20,18: ERCHETAI **Maria hê Magdalênê** angellousa tois *mathêtais*
hoti heôraka *TON KYRION*...

7) The Fourth Gospel also contains many instances of inclusions which delimit single pericopes. For example:

a) The triple mention of *THEOS* in the first two verses of the Prologue and its double occurrence in the last verse certainly form an inclusion:

1,1bc: kai ho logos ên pros ton *THEON*, kai *THEOS* ên ho logos.
1,2 : houtos ên en archê[i] pros ton *THEON*.
1,18 : *THEON* oudeis heôraken pôpote; monogenês *THEOS*... exêgêsato.

b) The introductory and concluding verses of the first Cana-sign (2,1-11) contain a number of inclusions:

2,1 : Kai... gamos egeneto en KANA tês GALILAIAS...
2,2 : eklêthê de kai *ho Iêsous* kai **hoi mathêtai autou** eis ton gamon.
2,11 : tautên epoiêsen archên tôn sêmeiôn *ho Iêsous* en KANA tês GALILAIAS...
kai episteusan eis auton **hoi mathêtai autou**.

c) Similarly, the second Cana-sign (4,46-54) contains many inclusions in its first and last verses:

4,46: *êlthen* oun **PALIN eis tên Kana tês GALILAIAS**,
hopou *epoiêsen* to hydôr oinon...
4,47: *Iêsous* hêkei **ek tês IOUDAIAS eis tên GALILAIAN**...
4,54: touto [de] **PALIN** deuteron sêmeion *epoiêsen*
ho *Iêsous* **elthôn ek tês IOUDAIAS eis tên GALILAIAN**.

d) Finally, we may give an example of multiple inclusions in a longer episode, namely, the healing of the man born blind (9,1-41). The double repetition of the terms "blind" and "sin" in the initial and final verses (vv.1-3.40-41) clearly forms a double inclusion:

---

importance, and therefore their occurrence at the beginning and end of the passage is intended to be an inclusion. This is confirmed by the emphatic solemn statement of Jesus ("Amen amen I say to you") in the last verse. This is also supported by the fact that the Jesus of the Fourth Gospel reveals himself not only through deeds ("signs" and "works") but also through words (dialogues and discourses). It may be noted also that the Baptist's testimony in 1,36 (*ide ho amnos TOU THEOU*) may be thought of as forming another inclusion with Nathanael's confession in 1,49 (*sy ei ho hyios TOU THEOU*), since *TOU THEOU* is common and since *ide* may be regarded as parallel to *sy ei*.

9,1 : Kai paragôn eiden anthrôpon TYPHLON ek genetês.
9,2 : kai êrôtêsan auton hoi mathêtai autou legontes:
       rhabbi, tis **hêmarten**... hina TYPHLOS gennêthê?
9,3 : apekrithê *Iêsous*:
       oute houtos **hêmarten** oute hoi goneis autou...
9,40: êkousan ek tôn Pharisaiôn tauta... kai eipon autô[i]:
       mê kai hêmeis TYPHLOI esmen?
9,41: eipen autois ho *Iêsous*:
       ei TYPHLOI ête, ouk an eichete **hamartian**;
       nyn de legete hoti blepomen, hê **hamartia** hymôn menei.

8) Inclusions are employed not only to delimit an episode or pericope (as we have seen above) but also to indicate the divisions of an episode. Let us take for example the Lazarus-episode (11,1-54). The first part of the episode is demarcated by a multiple inclusion between v.1 and v.5:

11,1 : ên de tis asthenôn, **LAZAROS** apo Bêthanias,
       ek tês komês Marias kai *MARTHAS* **tês adelphês autês**.
11,5 : êgapa de ho Iêsous tên *MARTHAN* kai **tên adelphên autês**
       kai ton **LAZARON**.

Similarly, the second event of the episode is marked by a double inclusion between v.7 and v.16:

11,7 : epeita meta touto *legei* **tois mathêtais**:
       agômen eis tên Ioudaian palin.
11,16: *eipen* oun Thomas... **tois synmathêtais**:
       agômen kai hêmeis hina apothanômen met' autou.

Other examples of the use of inclusions to divide episodes/discourses are: a) *polloi ek tôn mathêtôn autou* at 6,60.66; b) *hoi dôdeka* at 6,67.71; c) *ho patêr mou* at 15,1.8, and *karpon pleiona/polyn pherein* at 15,2.8; d) *agapan/agapê* at 15,9.10; e) *entolê/entellomai* at 15,12.17, and *hina agapate allêlous* at 15,12.17; f) *misein* at 15,18.25; g) *pater* and *doxazein* at 17,1.5; h) *ho Iêsous* at 19,16.18; i) *graphein* at 19,19.22; j) *stratiôtai* at 19,23.24; k) *mêtêr* at 19,25.27; l) *tetelestai* at 19,28.30; m) *phaneroô... tois mathêtais* at 21,1.14.

3.13z Besides the major inclusions between the introduction (1,1-2,11) and the conclusion (20,30-31) (cf. *zôê*: 1,4; 20,31; *pisteuein*: 1,7; 20,31; *to onoma autou*: 1,12; 20,31; *Christos*: 1,20.25.41; 20,31; *ho hyios tou theou*: 1,34.49; 20,31; *mathêtai*: 1,35.37; 2,2.11; 20,30; *sêmeion*: 2,11; 20,30), there are many inclusions which delimit the sections, episodes, pericopes and their subdivisions. They are found in the following passages: 1,1 & 1,18; 1,1 & 2,11; 1,19 & 1,34; 1,36 & 1,51; 2,1 & 4,54; 2,1-2 & 2,11; 4,46-47 & 4,53-54; 6,60 & 6,66; 6,67 & 6,71; 7,4 & 8,59; 9,1-3 & 9,40-41; 11,1 & 11,5; 11,7 & 11,16; 13,1 & 17,26; 15,2 & 15,8; 15,12 & 15,17; 15,18 & 15,25; 17,1 & 17,5; 19,16 & 19,18; 19,19 & 19,22; 19,23 & 19,24; 19,25 & 19,27; 19,28 & 19,30; 20,1-2 & 20,18; 21,1 & 21,14.

3.14 Characteristic Vocabulary

Most of the episodes or pericopes have characteristic vocabulary which distinguishes them from the neighbouring units. In order to illustrate this point we shall examine and compare the characteristic vocabulary of two neighbouring narratives, namely, 1,35-51 and 2,1-11.

3.141 *The characteristic vocabulary of 1,35-51*

The typical vocabulary of 1,35-51 may be conveniently classified under the following headings:

1) Disciples' names

Although the word *mathētai* occurs only twice (1,35.37) in our pericope, the names of four disciples are mentioned 18 times in just 17 verses (Andrew: 1,40.44; Simon, Simon Peter, Peter/Cephas: 1,40.41.42.42.42.44; Philip: 1,43.44. 45.46.48; Nathanael: 1,45.46.47.48.49), that is, about one name per verse. Such a proportionately high frequency of the names of the disciples is not found in any other pericope in the entire Gospel.

2) "Coming", "following" and "remaining"

Connected with the Johannine concept of discipleship are the terms *akolouthein* (1,37.38.40.43), *erchesthai* (1,39.39.46.47) and *menein* (1,38.39.39).

3) Verbs of "seeing"

It is interesting to note that many verbs of "seeing" are mentioned a number of times (13 times in all) in the passage under consideration (*horan*: 1,39.50.51; *idein*: 1,39.46.47.48.50, to which is related the revelatory-exclamatory *ide*: 1,36.47; *emblepein*: 1,36.42; *theasthai*: 1,38). This high frequency of the verbs of "seeing" highlights their importance in our text.

4) ("Seeking" and) "discovering"

Although the verb *zētein* occurs only once (1,38) in our pericope, it is important since *ti zēteite* are the first words of Jesus in the Fourth Gospel.

Related to "seeing" and "seeking" is the concept of "discovering" (*heuriskein*) which occurs 5 times in our pericope (1,41.41.43.45.45). This is certainly significant when it is remembered that the term is found only 19 times in a total of 21 chapters and in no other pericope is it repeated so often as here. It is also worth noting that nowhere else in the gospel of John does the perfect *heurēkamen* (1,41.45) occur.

5) Verbs of "saying"

Like the verbs of "seeing", the verbs of "saying" (*legein, apokrinesthai, lalein*) too are frequently found in 1,35-51. In fact, *legein* is employed 12 times (1,36.38.38.39.41.43.45.46.47.48.51.51) and *eipein* 6 times (1,38.42.46.48.50.50).

Apokrinesthai is used alone or together with *eipein* thrice (1,49.48.50). Finally the revelatory verb *lalein* occurs once (1,37). This amounts to 22 occurrences of the verbs of "saying" in just 17 verses.

In response to the possible objection that the high frequency of the verbs of "saying" is bound to be found in any dialogue and hence is not peculiar to the pericope we are studying, we note that it was the Fourth Evangelist who decided to present the vocation of the first disciples in the form of dialogues, there being very little dialogue in the Synoptic accounts of the call of the disciples (cf. Mt 4,18-22; Mk 1,16-20; Lk 5,1-11).

Notice also that the historic present *legei* is used (except once in 1,48) only of Jesus (1,38.39.43.47.51) and of those who bear witness to him (1,36.41.45.46). This gives not only a dramatic effect to the dialogues but also an added emphasis to what Jesus or his witnesses say, thus underlining the enduring value of their testimony. Jesus' use of *amên amên legô hymin* (1,51), found only on his lips in the Gospel of John, further highlights the importance and assures the truth of his statement [28a].

6) Jesus and the Messianic titles

In our pericope the name of "Jesus" (*Iêsous*) is found 10 times (1,36.37. 37.42.42.43.45.47.48.50) and 8 different Christological titles are employed 11 times (*ho amnos tou theou*: 1,36; *rhabbi/didaskalos*: 1,38.49; *Messias/Christos*: 1,41.41; *hon egrapsen Môüsês en tô[i] nomô[i] kai hoi prophêtai*: 1,45; *hyios tou Iôsêph*: 1,45; *ho hyios tou theou*: 1,49; *basileus tou Israêl*: 1,49; *ho hyios tou anthrôpou*: 1,51), which are distributed throughout the pericope. Such an intense concentration of the Messianic titles applied to Jesus renders our pericope a unique phenomenon in the whole Gospel. It is also worth noting that *hyios* occurs in three of the titles applied to Jesus ("son of Joseph", "the Son of God", and "the Son of Man"), which underscore different aspects of Jesus' identity and function.

7) God

Even though *ho Patêr* does not occur in 1,35-51, the Father is referred to by means of the expression *ho theos* (1,36.49.51), since *theos* with the article *ho* is used absolutely (that is, without any qualification as at 20,28: *ho theos mou*) in the Fourth Gospel to denote only the Father. It is also interesting to note that the genitive *tou theou* is found in all the three occurrences of *ho theos* in 1,35-51 two of which form part of two Messianic titles of Jesus (*ho amnos tou theou*: 1,36; *ho hyios tou theou*: 1,49) and the third is closely connected with a third title *ho hyios tou anthrôpou* on whom "the angels *of God*" ascend and descend (1,51).

[28a] See 3.1[11]2 below.

3.142 *The characteristic vocabulary of 2,1-11*

This small pericope about the first sign of Jesus at Cana contains the following terms which occur two or more times (arranged in the decreasing order of frequency): *legein* 7 times (2,3.4.5.5.7.8.10); *Iêsous* 6 times (2,1.2.3.4.7.11); *oinos* 5 times (2,3.3.9.10.10); *hydôr* (2,7.9.9), *architriklinos* (2,8.9.9), and *hê mêtêr tou Iêsou/autou* (2,1.3.5) thrice each; *gamos* (2,1.2), *Kana tês Galilaias* (2,1.11), *hoi mathêtai autou* (2,2.11), *diakonoi* (2,5.8), *hydriai* (2,6.7), *gemizein* (2,7.7), *antlein* (2,8.9), *pherein* (2,8.8), *oida* (2,9.9), *kalos* (2,10.10), *poiein* (2,5.11) twice each.

3.143 *Comparison of the vocabulary of 1,35-51 and 2,1-11*

Now comparing the vocabulary of the two episodes we find that the name "Jesus" is mentioned quite frequently in both the texts (10 times in 1,35-51 and 7 times in 2,1-11), which underlines their Christocentric character. But note that none of the eight Christological titles present in 1,35-51 is found in 2,1-11, which shows that the Christocentric functions of these texts are different, as we shall see below.

Again, *legein* is employed a number of times (12 times and 7 times respectively) in the two pericopes, which may be due to the dialogues in the two texts. But there is also a difference, namely, while only *legei* (the historical present) is used in 2,1-11, *legei* and other verbs of "saying" (*eipein, apokrinesthai, lalein*) are employed in 1,35-51.

Likewise, although "his disciples" are mentioned twice each in 1,35-51 and 2,1-11 (which shows the continuity between the two passages), in 1,35.37 "his disciples" refers to the Baptist's disciples (who are about to become those of Jesus), whereas in 2,2.11 they are already Jesus' disciples. Moreover, no names of individual disciples are given in 2,1-11, and the emphasis is on the disciples as a group.

For the rest, the vocabulary is quite different in 1,35-51 and 2,1-11 [29]. Whereas the first passage contains many Messianic titles and a number of terms related to discipleship (e.g. "following", "coming", "discovering"), the Cana-sign has its own characteristic vocabulary connected with the context and content of the miracle (e.g. "marriage", "Cana", "the mother of Jesus", "the steward of the feast", "servants", "water", "wine", "jars", "fill", "draw", "take"), which clearly distinguishes the pericope from the preceding and following passages.

---

[29] The only terms (besides the ones mentioned above) which are common to both the pericopes are *hôra* (1,39; 2,4) and *pisteuein* (1,50; 2,11), but even here there is a real difference both in their use and in their significance in the two episodes. Thus while in 1,39 *hôra* is without the article *hê* and is qualified by a numeral (*dekatê*) (cf. also 4,6.52; 11,9; 19,14) and it refers to the time of the day when the disciples encountered Jesus, *hôra* at 2,4 is used with the article and is modified by *mou*, and this cryptic expression (*hê hôra mou*) refers to Jesus' passion-death-resurrection (cf. 7,30; 8,20; 13,1; 17,1). Similarly, whereas *pisteuein* in 1,50 is used absolutely and may be translated as "to become a believer" (cf. 4,53; 20,29), *pisteuein* in 2,11 is combined with *eis auton* and it means "to believe in him" which underlines the aspect of commitment in faith to Christ (cf. 3,16.18; 4,39; 6,40; etc.).

3.14z The examination, comparison and contrast between the vocabulary of 1,35-51 and 2,1-11 demonstrate the value of this criterion of characteristic vocabulary for understanding individual episodes and for distinguishing them from one another in the structure of the Gospel, provided the study is made not in a merely mechanical and statistical manner.

3.15 Geographical Indications [30]

The names of a number of places are mentioned in the Gospel of John often in connection with the journeys of Jesus, his actions, dialogues and discourses: e.g. Cana of Galilee (2,1.11; 4,46), Galilee (1,43; 4,3.43.45.47.54; 7,1.9), the Sea of Galilee/Tiberias (6,1; 21,1), Capernaum (2,12; 6,59), Samaria (4,4), Sychar (4,5), Jerusalem (2,13.23; 4,45; 5,1.2; 10,22; 12,12), Judea (4,3.47.54; 7,1.3; 11,7; cf. also 3,22), Bethany (11,17; 12,1), Ephraim (11,54), the Kidron valley (18,1), Golgotha (19,17) [31]. Some place-names are given in connection with the ministry of John the Baptist (Bethany beyond the Jordan: 1,28; cf. also 10,40 [32]; Aenon near Salim: 3,23).

3.15z These geographical indications at 1,28.43; 2,1.11.12.13.23; 3,23; 4,3. 4.5.43.45.46.47.54; 5,1.2; 6,1.59; 7,1.3.9; 10,22.40; 11,7.17.54; 12,1.12; 18,1; 19,17; 21,1 will be of some help in determining the structure of the Fourth Gospel, provided they are used together with other literary criteria.

3.16 Literary-Chronological Indications [33]

We shall examine briefly the literary-chronological indications *meta tauta* and *meta touto*, *tê[i] epaurion* and *tê[i] hêmera[i] tê[i] tritê[i]*, and mention some others which are found in the Fourth Gospel.

3.161 *Meta tauta* and *meta touto*

Often a new episode in the Gospel of John begins with the general literary-chronological indication *meta tauta* (3,22; 5,1; 6,1; 7,1; 21,1) [34], whose function is *primarily* literary (namely, to signal the beginning of the new episode) and not chronological (that is, to date the event), although it refers to an unspecified period of time. The same literary-chronological device (*meta tauta*) is used sometimes to indicate a division of an episode (5,14; 19,38) [34a].

---

[30] Cf. M. C. TENNEY, *op. cit.*, 40-41 (see 2.[16] above).

[31] Bethlehem (7,42) and Galilee (7,52) are mentioned during the controversy among the Jews about the place of origin of Jesus, the Christ (7,42), the prophet (7,52). Similarly, the native place of Philip, Andrew and Peter is given as Bethsaida (1,43) and that of Nathanael as Cana of Galilee (21,2). These occurrences of the names of places do not seem to be important for the structure.

[32] Jesus' journey to this place "across the Jordan" is explicitly stated here (10,40).

[33] Cf. M. C. TENNEY, *op. cit.*, 40-41 (see 2.[16] above).

[34] P. DEFOURNEY (see 2.4 above) and C. RAU (see 2.[11] above).

[34a] Hence it must not be used as an infallible guide to the division of the Gospel into episodes

At times *meta touto* is employed to introduce a transition or a scene connected with the immediately preceding one (2,12; 19,28; 11,7.11)[35].

3.162 *Tê[i] epaurion* and *tê[i] hêmera[i] tê[i] tritê[i]*

The very first words of five Johannine pericopes are the literary-chronological expression *tê[i] epaurion* (1,29.35.43; 6,22; 12,12) which indicates not only the chronological succession of days but also the beginning of a connected but distinct pericope. Hence it is a reliable criterion for the division of one major passage into pericopes (e.g. 1,19-51 divides itself into 1,19-28.29-34.35-42.43-51).

Similarly, *kai tê[i] hêmera[i] tê[i] tritê[i]* at 2,1 both connects and distinguishes the first Cana-sign from the preceding pericope (1,43-51).

3.163 *Other literary-chronological indications*

At times the duration of a person's stay in a particular place is given in terms of the number of days (mentioned normally towards the end of an episode or pericope or paragraph: 1,39; 4,40; 11,6).

Occasionally the hour of the day when the event took place is specified (e.g. "tenth hour": 1,39; "sixth hour": 4,6; 19,14).

At times the day of the week and/or the part of the day are given at the beginning of the pericope (e.g. "on the first day of the week... early": 20,1; "on the evening of that day, the first day of the week": 20,19; "when evening came": 6,16).

Some events are introduced in chronological relation to Jewish feasts (e.g. "about the middle of the feast [of Tabernacles]": 7,14; "on the last day of the feast": 7,37; "six days before the Passover": 12,1).

3.16z Most of these literary-chronological indications at 1,29.35.39.43; 2,1.12; 3,22; 4,6.40; 5,1.14; 6,1.16.22; 7,1.14.37; 11,6.7.11; 12,1.12; 19,14.28.38; 20,1.19.26; 21,1 can serve as signals for the division and subdivision of the text, provided they are employed in conjunction with other criteria.

3.17 Liturgical Feasts [36]

Many of the episodes are narrated in the context of the Jewish feasts such as the Passover (*to pascha*: 2,13.23; 6,4; 11,55; 12,1; 13,1; 18,28.39; 19,14), the

---

(*pace* P. DEFOURNEY and C. RAU). We may also note that, unlike at 5,1; 6,1 and 7,1 where *meta tauta* is followed by a verb in the past tense, at 5,14 it is followed by an historical present (*heuriskei*). It is also noteworthy that only at 19,38 we find *meta de tauta* (i.e. *de* inserted between *meta* and *tauta*).

[35] At 11,7 we have *epeita meta touto* and at 11,11 *kai meta touto*. They indicate the beginning of the first and second dialogues between Jesus and the disciples (11,7-10.11-16) in the same scene (11,7-16).

[36] Cf. M. C. TENNEY, *op. cit.*, 40-41.

Tabernacles (*hê skênopêgia*: 7,2), the Dedication (*ta enkainia*: 10,22), and the Sabbath (*sabbaton*: 5,9.10.16.18; 9,14.16; 19,31)[37]. In fact, except for the Sabbath, the feasts are explicitly mentioned at the very beginning of the episode, pericope or transition, which is a great help for their delimitation.

3.18 Transitions

Sometimes two successive units (pericopes or episodes) are separated from one another by means of a few verses which serve as a passage from one unit to the next. For instance, between Jesus' sign of changing water into wine (2,1-11) and his cleansing of the temple (2,13-22), his descent to Capernaum with his mother, brothers and disciples, and his short stay there are reported in passing in 2,12, which, therefore, forms a transition from the Cana-sign (cf. *meta touto*: 2,12a) to the temple-scene (cf. *kai ekei emeinen ou pollas hêmeras*: 2,12b).

Similarly, after the Samaritan episode (4,4-42), the Evangelist reports Jesus' departure from Samaria to Galilee, his saying about a prophet in his own country and his reception by the Galileans (4,43-45). These verses function as a link with the previous pericope (cf. 4,40: *kai emeinen ekei dyo hêmeras* and 4,43: *meta de tas dyo hêmeras*) and prepare the reader for the following event in Galilee (the second sign at Cana: 4,46-54). Note that in place of a *meta touto* as at 2,12, we have *meta de tas dyo hêmeras* at 4,43, which confirms the transitional character of 4,43-45.

Sometimes a summary serves simultaneously as a transition and as an introduction. Thus 3,22-24, which reports the baptizing ministry of Jesus in the Judean countryside and that of John the Baptist in Aenon near Salim, functions both as a transition from the Nicodemus-episode (3,1-21) (cf. *meta tauta* at 3,22) to the Baptist-episode (3,25-36) and as an introduction to the latter (cf. *ebaptizen* at 3,22 and *baptizei* at 3,26 both of which refer to Jesus' baptizing, which is the starting-point for the discussion between the Baptist and his own disciples in 3,25-30).

Other examples of summaries which are at the same time transitions and introductions are 6,1-2 and 7,1, both of which begin with *meta tauta* as in 3,22.

We may also mention 5,1 as another example of a transitional (cf. *meta tauta*) introduction (since it brings Jesus to Jerusalem, the scene of his next action). (It is worth noting that the first words of Jn 5, Jn 6, Jn 7 are *meta tauta* with which the three transitions begin.)

Sometimes a summary functions both as a transition and as a conclusion. For example, 10,40-42, which mentions Jesus' departure from Jerusalem for a place beyond the Jordan and his stay there where many believe in him, serves as a sort of conclusion to the temple-episode in 10,22-39 and as a transition to the Lazarus-episode in 11,1-53.

---

[37] An unnamed feast of the Jews is mentioned at 5,1.

Finally 11,54 at the end of the Lazarus-episode (11,1-53) may be mentioned as another instance of a summary-statement which is a transitional conclusion. This is somewhat similar to the transition (2,12) at the end of the first Cana-sign (2,1-11).

3.18z It is noteworthy that all the transitions (2,12; 3,22-24; 4,43-45; 5,1; 6,1-2; 7,1; 10,40-42; 11,54) mention the movement of Jesus from one place to another. The transitional summaries serve also as introductions (3,22-24; 4,43-45; 6,1-2; 7,1) or conclusions (2,12; 10,40-42; 11,54).

3.19 Bridge-Passages

A "bridge-passage" is one which "bridges" or connects two successive units by concluding the first and by introducing the second. Thus a "bridge-passage" is more than a mere transition, since it serves simultaneously as a conclusion to the first unit and as an introduction to the second. In other words, it belongs to both the units, just as a bridge over a river belongs to both the banks of the river. This was a literary device used by ancient authors like Lucian to join the different parts of a well-planned book [38].

A "bridge-passage" may consist of one or more verses or an entire pericope or a whole section, which may then be called "bridge-verse(s)", a "bridge-pericope", and a "bridge-section" respectively.

3.191 *Bridge-verses*

The simplest example of a bridge-verse is 1,42a: *êgagen auton pros ton Iêsoun*. Here Andrew's bringing his brother Simon Peter to Jesus (1,42a) both ends the scene of Andrew's announcement of the Messianic discovery to his brother (1,40-42a) and opens the door to the scene of Peter's encounter with Christ (1,42), so that 1,42a belongs to both the scenes [39].

---

[38] In *How to Write History* (*Pôs dei historian syngraphein*) LUCIAN explains how the different parts of a composition must be linked together:

> Der Autor wird zunächst alles Einzelne getrennt und in sich abgerundet ausarbeiten; hat er dann den ersten Teil abgeschlossen, so fügt er den zweiten daran; dieser soll sich *so anschliessen und anpassen wie ein Kettenglied [halyseos tropon synêrmosmenon]* an das andere, sodass das Ganze nicht abgehackt in viele nebeneinanderstehende Einzelerzählungen zerfällt - nein, der vorangehende Teil soll stets dem nächstfolgenden nicht nur benachbart sein, sondern auch *zu ihm gehören und sich ihm lückenlos anfügen [kai koinônein kai anakekrasthai kata ta akra]* (N. 55, transl. H. HOMEYER, *Lukian. Wie man Geschichte schreiben soll*, Griechisch und Deutsch [München 1965] 159) [my italics].

LUCIAN himself follows this "Kettenglied" rule in composing his *How to Write History*. For example, ch. 33 simultaneously concludes the first part (7-32) and introduces the second part (34-60). Similarly, ch. 42 which ends the first section (34-42) of the second part (34-60) "leads over to" the second section (43-60) (Cf. H. HOMEYER, *op. cit.*, 13-14).

See n. 39a below for Biblical examples of "bridge-passages".

[39] Jn 1,37 may be another bridge-verse which concludes the revelatory testimony of the Baptist (1,35-37; cf. *autou lalountos* in v.37) and introduces the following of the disciples (1,37-39; cf. *êkolouthêsan tô[i] Iêsou* in v.37 and v.38).

A good example of a few verses forming a "bridge" between two adjacent pericopes is found in 2,23-25, which joins Jesus' cleansing of the temple (2,13-22) to his dialogue-discourse with Nicodemus (3,1-21). First of all, the names of the city "Jerusalem" and of the feast "Passover" in 2,23 point back to the same names in 2,13. Secondly, the expression *autou ta sêmeia ha epoiei* of 2,23 bridges the Jews' question to Jesus in 2,18: *ti sêmeion deiknyeis hêmin, hoti tauta poieis?* with Nicodemus' words to Jesus in 3,2: *oudeis gar dynatai tauta ta sêmeia poiein ha sy poieis*. Note that *sêmeion* is a key-term in all the three sentences. Thirdly, *pisteuein eis to onoma* is common to both 2,23 and 3,18 (cf. *pisteuein* also at 2,22; 3,12.15.16). Fourthly, the hook-word *anthrôpos* at the very end of 2,25 and at the beginning of 3,1 links 2,23-25 with 3,1-21.

Jn 4,27-30 is an excellent example of bridge-verses which, like the connecting link of a chain, join two pericopes in the same episode, since these verses are equally linked to the immediately preceding pericope of Jesus' dialogue-discourse with the Samaritan woman (4,7-26) and to the pericope which immediately follows, namely, Jesus' dialogue-discourse with his disciples (4,31-38). Notice that *hoi mathêtai (autou)* is explicitly mentioned at the beginning of 4,7-26 (cf. v.8) and of 4,31-38 (cf. vv.31.33). Secondly, 4,27-30 both concludes the Samaritan woman's encounter with Jesus (4,7-26) by reporting her return to the town to announce her Messianic discovery to her people (4,28-29) and introduces the next scene (4,31-38) by mentioning the disciples' return from the town and their amazement at Jesus' talking with a woman (4,27). Therefore 4,27-30 functions as a bridge between the two scenes (4,7-26 and 4,31-38).

Other examples of Johannine bridge-verses are 4,1-3; 5,14-18; 13,31-38; 15,9-11; 18,12-14 and 20,24-25 [39a].

[39a] "Bridge-verses" are found also in other books of the Bible. Cf. H. VAN DYKE PARUNAK, "Transitional Techniques in the Bible", *JBL* 102 (1983) 525-48; "Oral Typesetting: Some Uses of Biblical Structure", *Bib* 62 (1981) 153-68. Parunak calls a "bridging" transition-unit a "hinge" which may be either direct (A/a b/B) or inverted (A/b a/B).

Although the term ("bridge-verse") itself has not been used, the reality of a *transition* which *simultaneously concludes* one section and *introduces* another has been detected, for instance, by A. VANHOYE in Heb 4,14-16, for in the second edition of his *La Structure Littéraire de l'Épître aux Hébreux* (1976) he says:

> On peut, si on le préfère, considérer 4,14-16 comme un court paragraphe de *transition* entre les deux sections de la Deuxième Partie. Il reste que cette transition se divise nettement en deux parts: la première phrase (4,14) *conclut* la section précédente, elle évoque l'autorité du Christ glorifié et ne dit pas un mot de sa compassion; les deux versets suivants (4,15-16) forment *l'introduction* de la seconde section, ils parlent de la compassion du Christ et n'insistent pas sur sa glorification (264) [my italics].

Perhaps the dispute among the Marcan scholars about the position of Mk 1,14-15 in the structure of the Gospel of Mark (i.e. whether 1,14-15 is an integral part of the introduction or of the first part of the Gospel) can be settled, if Mk 1,14-15 would be regarded as bridge-verses. (Many Marcan commentators like E. LOHMEYER, D.E. NINEHAM, V. TAYLOR, take Mk 1,14-15 as part of the first section of the Gospel, while L. KECK and R. PESCH consider those verses to be part of the introduction. Cf. K. STOCK, *Le Pericopi Iniziali del Vangelo di San Marco* [Rome, PIB, 1976] 6-7.) A. STOCK regards Mk 1,14-15 as a "hinge" ("Hinge Transitions in Mark's Gospel", *BibTB* 15 [1985] 27-31 especially p. 28).

3.192 Bridge-pericope

An example of a bridge-pericope is 2,1-11, which both concludes the introduction to the Fourth Gospel (2,1-11) and introduces the first part of the Gospel (Jn 2-12) and its first section (Jn 2-4)[40].

3.193 Bridge-section

Jn 11,1-12,50 may be looked upon as a bridge-section which connects the first part (Jn 2-12) and the second part (11,1-20,29)[41] of the Fourth Gospel.

3.19z There are a number of bridge-verses (1,42a; 2,23-25; 4,1-3; 4,27-30; 5,14-18; 13,31-38; 15,9-11; 18,12-14; 20,24-25). Furthermore, a bridge-pericope (2,1-11) concludes the introduction (1,1-2,11) and introduces the first part (Jn 2-12), and a bridge-section (Jn 11-12) concludes the first part (Jn 2-12) and introduces the second part (11,1-20,29), thus underlining the close connection between the major parts of the Fourth Gospel.

3.1[10] Hook-Words

A hook-word is a literary-mnemonic device of suturing two neighbouring literary units (e.g. sentences, paragraphs or pericopes) by means of the repetition of the same word or phrase (normally) from (the end of) the first unit at the beginning of the next[42]. Hook-words are found frequently in the Fourth Gospel. To illustrate this we shall examine the hook-words in 1,1-18 and 1,35-51, and mention a few others from the rest of the Gospel.

3.1[10]1 Hook-words in the Prologue

The first five verses of the Prologue contain many hook-words (cf. the s p a c e d words below):

1,1: En archê[i] ên h o   l o g o s,
    kai h o   l o g o s ên pros ton t h e o n,
    kai t h e o s ên ho logos.
1,2: houtos ên en archê[i] pros ton t h e o n.
1,3: panta di' autou e g e n e t o,
    kai chôris autou e g e n e t o oude hen.
1,4: ho g e g o n e n en autô[i] z ô ê ê n,
    kai hê z ô ê ê n t o p h ô s tôn anthrôpôn;
1,5: kai t o p h ô s en t ê [i] s k o t i a [i] phainei,
    kai h ê s k o t i a auto ou katelaben.

---

[40] See 4.112 and 4.121 below for the reasons.
[41] See 4.121 and 4.131 below for the reasons.
[42] Cf. L. VAGANAY, "Le plan de l'Épître aux Hébreux", in: *Mémorial Lagrange* (Paris 1940) 269-77, where the author uses hook-words ("mot-crochets") as the only criterion for the structure of the Epistle to the Hebrews. Cf. A. VANHOYE, *op. cit.*, 24-58 for a valid criticism of Vaganay's exclusive use of hook-words for the division of the Epistle and Vanhoye's own use of hook-words as one of the five criteria.

There are a number of hook-words also in 1,8-11:

1,8 : ouk ên ekeinos to p h ô s,
    all' hina martyrêsê[i] peri t o u p h ô t o s.
1,9 : ên t o p h ô s to alêthinon,
    ho p h ô t i z e i panta anthrôpon,
    erchomenon eis t o n k o s m o n.
1,10: en t ô [i] k o s m ô [i] ên,
    kai ho kosmos di' autou egeneto,
    kai ho kosmos auton ouk egnô.
1,11: eis ta i d i a êlthen,
    kai hoi i d i o i auton ou parelabon.

It may be noted here that while most of the hook-words in the Prologue are used to build well-knit units (e.g. 1,1-5) or subunits (e.g. 1,9-11), the hook-word *p h ô s* at the end of v.8 and at the beginning of v.9 is employed to bind the two neighbouring units (vv.6-8 and 9-14)[43].

3.1[10]2 *Hook-words in 1,35-51*

Hook-words are skillfully used by the Evangelist to construct two well-knit pericopes (1,35-42 and 1,43-51) which describe the first disciples' discovery of Jesus, the Messiah. We give below the verses which contain the main hook-words:

1,37b : kai ê k o l o u t h ê s a n t ô I ê s o u.
1,38a : strapheis de h o I ê s o u s [44]
    kai theasamenos autous a k o l o u t h o u n t a s ...
1,38e : p o u m e n e i s ?
1,39bc: e r c h e s t h e k a i o p s e s t h e.
    de: ê l t h a n oun k a i e i d a n
    fg: p o u m e n e i kai par' autô[i] e m e i n a n...
1,40 : ên Andreas h o a d e l p h o s S i m ô n o s ...
1,41a : heuriskei... t o n a d e l p h o n... S i m ô n a...
1,42a : êgagen auton pros t o n I ê s o u n.
    b : emblepsas autô[i] h o I ê s o u s eipen...
1,44 : ên de ho P h i l i p p o s...
1,45a : heuriskei P h i l i p p o s...
1,45d : apo N a z a r e t h.
1,46b : ek N a z a r e t h...
1,46de: e r c h o u kai i d e.
1,47a : e i d e n... e r c h o m e n o n...
1,50b : kai e i p e n autô[i]
    c : hoti e i p o n soi
1,50f : meizô toutôn o p s ê [i].
1,51c : o p s e s t h e ton ouranon...

---

[43] This shows that hook-words alone are not sufficient to decide the division of a pericope into smaller units, since hook-words can be present in the same unit or in the neighbouring units.

[44] Note that here a proper name (*Iêsous*) is used as a hook-word (cf. also 1,42.44-45).

It is noteworthy that there are 17 hook-words in just 17 verses, which shows how well-constructed an episode 1,35-51 is and how the numerous hook-words are used to bind together the successive parts of the pericopes.

3.1[10]3 *Other hook-words*

We may mention a few other hook-words which link the neighbouring units of a connected episode. Thus *anthrôpos* at the very end of 2,25 and at the beginning of 3,1 hooks 2,23-25 and 3,1-21. Similarly, *pisteuein* at 8,30 and 8,31 connects 8,21-30 and 8,31-59. Likewise the sentence *exebalon auton exô* at the end of 9,34 is repeated at the beginning of 9,35. Again, Judas' departure (*exêlthen*) from the Last Supper room is mentioned both at the end of 13,30 and at the beginning of 13,31 [45].

3.1[11] Techniques of Repetition [46]

One of the characteristic features of the Fourth Gospel is its repetitiveness. The same key-words and parallel phrases, similar revelatory statements and identical discourse-formulas, and same type-scenes appear again and again in the course of the Gospel. Their repetition seems at first sight to be haphazard, which creates problems for many a modern reader. In the words of R. Alter: "One of the most imposing barriers that stands between the modern reader and the imaginative subtlety of biblical narrative is the extraordinary prominence of verbatim repetition in the Bible" [47].

3.1[11]1 *Repetition of the same key-term/expression*

Let us take, for instance, the simple example of the key-term "light". The word *phôs* occurs 23 times in the Gospel of John (all of them in Jn 1-12), while it is found only 7 times each in Mt and Lk, and only once in Mk. The Prologue presents the Logos as "the light of men" (1,5), "the true light that enlightens every man" (1,9), to which John the Baptist bears witness (1,7-8). In Jesus' discourse with Nicodemus we are told that "the light has come into the world" (3,19b; cf. also 1,9: "the true light... was coming into the world" and 12,46: "I have come as light into the world") but that "men have loved darkness rather than light" (3,19c). While 1,9 and 3,19 mention "the coming of the light into the world", 3,20-21 comments on "the coming of men to the light" ("For every one

---

[45] Another similar hook-word in a discourse is *gongyzein* at 6,41 and 6,43.

[46] Cf. R. ALTER, *The Art of Biblical Narrative* (New York 1981) 88-113, for "the technique of repetition" used in the OT narratives. (Repetition is an essential element of many of the literary criteria we have studied above, e.g. inclusions, characteristic vocabulary, hook-words.)

[47] *Ibid.*, 88. Many seem to miss the "'Oriental' sense of the intrinsic pleasingness of repetition in the underlying aesthetic of the Bible" (*ibid.*). This may be one of the reasons why many Western Johannine scholars have resorted to various hypotheses of displacement, sources and redactions to account for the repetitions in the Fourth Gospel (cf. ch. 1 above).

who does evil hates the light, and does not come to the light... But he who does the truth, comes to the light..."). Again, the revelatory statement of Jesus at 8,12: "I am the light of the world" is repeated at 9,5 (cf. also 12,46). While according to the Prologue "the life was the light of men" (1,4), according to Jesus' proclamation at 8,12 the men who follow him "will have the light of life". Before going to Bethany to raise his friend Lazarus from the dead Jesus tells the disciples: "If any one walks in the day, he does not stumble, because he sees the light of this world. But if any one walks in the night, he stumbles, because the light is not in him" (11,9-10). Finally Jesus tells the crowd in 12,35-36: "The light is with you for a little longer. Walk while you have the light... While you have the light, believe in the light, that you may become sons of light."

Thus we see that there is repetition not only of the symbolic word "light" (*phôs*) but also of the expression "the light of the world" (8,12; 9,5; 11,9; 12,46), "the coming of the light into the world" (1,9; 3,19; 12,46), man's "coming to the light" (3,20.21) and "having the light" (8,12; 12,35.36). We also find the antithetical parallel phrases "walking in the day" (11,9) and "walking in the night" (11,10). Besides the repetition of the same words and/or parallel phrases, the entire revelatory statement: "I am the light of the world" is repeated twice (8,12; 9,5; cf. also 12,46). While sometimes the parallel statements are found in the neighbouring verses (e.g. 3,20-21; 11,9-10; 12,35-36), at other times they occur in different chapters near to one another (8,12 & 9,5; 11,9-10 & 12,35-36) or far apart from one another (1,9 & 3,19 & 12,46). We must examine in the next chapter if these repetitions are chance occurrences or the result of careful structural planning, since they recur in parallel parts of the Fourth Gospel[48].

3.1[11]2 *Repetition of the amên amên formula*

The double *amên* is a typical and exclusive characteristic of Johannine style, since it is found 25 times in the Fourth Gospel and it is not used at all in the rest of the New Testament[49].

It must be observed that only Jesus employs the emphatic solemn formula *amên amên legô hymin/soi*. Normally he uses it at the beginning and/or end of a dialogue or discourse or a division thereof. Thus the first statement of Jesus during his dialogue with Nicodemus is an *amên amên* saying (3,3; cf. also 6,26). The discourse proper begins with another *amên amên* saying at 3,11 (cf. also 5,19; 6,53; 10,1.7; 12,24). Jesus concludes his dialogue with Nathanael (and the other disciples) with an important *amên amên* statement (1,51; cf. also 6,32.33; 8,58; 13,38; 21,18).

---

[48] The only other place in which the term "light" (*phôs*) occurs is 5,34, which speaks about the light of John the Baptist (*en tô[i] phôti autou*) who is called a "lamp" (*lychnos*) and not "the light" (*to phôs*). In fact, in 1,8 it is explicitly stated that "he was not the light".
See 5.1 below for the recurrence of other key-terms like "life", "believe", etc.

[49] *Amên amên legô hymin* is found 20 times in Jn (1,51; 5,19.24.25; 6,26.32.47.53; 8,34.51.58; 10,1.7; 12,24; 13,16.20.21; 14,12; 16,20.23) and *amên amên legô soi* 5 times (3,3.5.11; 13,38; 21,18).

Sometimes a well-constructed dialogue or discourse which contains an *amên amên* saying at the beginning (e.g. at 3,3 in 3,1-10; at 5,19 in 5,19-30) has another or others at the centre (e.g. 3,5; 5,24.25).

At other times it is difficult to decide the function of the double *amên* sayings (e.g. 13,16.20.21) without the help of other criteria.

3.1[11]3 *Repetition of egô eimi sayings*

Jesus' self-revelatory *egô eimi* sayings provide us with another type of Johannine repetition. These may be classified into two categories: a) the absolute *egô eimi* sayings (6,20; 8,24.28.58; 13,19; cf. also 18,5.6.8), and b) *egô eimi* followed by a predicate which describes what Jesus is. The following seven kinds of "I am" sayings belonging to the second category are found in the Fourth Gospel: 1) "I am the bread of life" (6,35.48; cf. also 6,41.51); 2) "I am the light of the world" (8,12; 9,5); 3) "I am the door of the sheep" (10,7.9); 4) "I am the good shepherd" (10,11.14); 5) "I am the resurrection and the life" (11,25); 6) "I am the way, the truth and the life" (14,6); 7) "I am the true vine" (15,1.5). Besides the dramatic quality of these self-revelatory sayings, we shall see in the next chapter that some of these proclamatory statements of Jesus occur in parallel parts of the structure of the Fourth Gospel (e.g. "I am the bread of life" in 2C, and "I am the resurrection and the life" in 3C) [50].

3.1[11]4 *Repetition of similar discourses*

Besides the repetitions of the same key-terms, expressions, formulas, and similar sayings, we find also some so-called "duplicate discourses". The classical examples are 3,11-21 & 3,31-36; 13,31-14,31 & 16,4e-33, which, we shall see later, are parallel to each other and have definite roles to play in the structure of the Gospel [51].

3.1[11]5 *Repetition of the same type-scene*

We find in the Gospel of John another kind of repetition which is not verbatim but which consists in the recurrence of the same "type-scene". This is a well-known compositional convention in Biblical narratives [52]. Such a type-

---

[50] See 4.3 below.
[51] See 3.31 and 4.3 below.
[52] Cf. R. ALTER, *op. cit.*, 47-62: "Biblical Type-Scenes and the Uses of Convention". The author affirms that the "type-scene" "constitutes a central organizing convention of biblical narrative" (*ibid.*, 181). Some of the most common biblical type-scenes are: "the annunciation... of the birth of the hero to his barren mother; the encounter with the future betrothed at a well; the epiphany in the field; the initiatory trial; danger in the desert and the discovery of a well or other source of sustenance; the testimony of the dying hero" (*ibid.*, 51). (Cf. *ibid.*, 51-62, for an interesting and instructive discussion of the OT examples of betrothal type-scene [e.g. Gen 24,10-61: Rebekah; Gen 29,1-20: Rachel; etc.]).

scene in the Fourth Gospel is the "miracle story"[53]. Two types of miracles are narrated in the Johannine Gospel, namely, nature and healing miracles[54]. The changing of water into wine (2,1-11), the multiplication of the loaves (6,3-15), Jesus' walking on the water (6,16-21)[55], and the miraculous catch of fish (21,1-14) belong to the first category, while the healing of the royal official's son (4,46-54), the curing of the cripple (5,1-9), the giving of sight to the man born blind (9,1-12) and the raising of Lazarus to life (11,1-54) belong to the second group. Whether they appertain to the first or second category, all the miracles narrated in the Fourth Gospel have a basic common pattern consisting of at least four connected elements[56]: 1) the setting (cf. 2,1-2; 4,46-47; 5,1-3; 6,3-5; 6,16-17; 9,1-2; 11,1-2; 21,1-3); 2) the description of a difficult situation or serious sickness (cf. 2,3; 4,46-47; 5,5; 6,5-9; 6,18-19; 9,1-2; 11,3; 21,3-5); 3) Jesus' intervention (cf. 2,7-8; 4,50; 5,8; 6,10-11; 6,19-20; 9,6-7; 11,43; 21,6); 4) the confirmation of the miracle (cf. 2,9-10; 4,51-53; 5,9; 6,12-14; 6,21; 9,8-12; 11,45-53; 21,6.11)[57].

3.1[12] Change of Literary 'Genres'

The different literary genres such as narratives, dialogues, discourses, hymns and prayers, employed in the Fourth Gospel can serve as useful criteria for the correct division of a section or pericope into smaller units.

Thus the first sign at Cana (2,1-11) is a miracle narrative, while the cleansing of the temple (2,13-22) is a conflict-narrative. Both the Nicodemus-episode (2,23-3,21) and the Baptist-episode (3,22-36) contain a short transitional narrative (2,23-25; 3,22-25), a dialogue (3,1-10; 3,26-30) and a discourse (3,11-21; 3,31-36), whereas the Samaritan episode (4,4-42) consists primarily of two dialogues (4,7-26; 4,31-38) inserted between three small narratives (4,4-7; 4,27-30; 4,39-42), while the second Cana-sign (4,46-54) is a miracle-narrative.

---

[53] "Miracle story" is a literary form which the form critics like Bultmann find abundantly present in the Gospels (cf. R. BULTMANN, *History of the Synoptic Tradition*, tr. by J. Marsh [1963] 209ff).

[54] Unlike the Synoptic Gospels, the Johannine Gospel has no exorcism.

[55] A few Johannine scholars (e.g. SANDERS & MASTIN, 182-83) do not regard this to be a miracle, since they interpret *peripatounta epi tês thalasês* (6,19) as "walking by the sea" and not as "walking on the sea".

[56] J. L. MARTYN mentions only three elements (the last three in our list) in "the miracle story form" (*op. cit.*, 24-25). We include also the "setting", since it is found in most miracles. These four parts of the narrative pattern are found also in the Synoptic parallels of these miracles (e.g. the multiplication of the loaves in Mt 14,13-21 // Mk 6,32-44 // Lk 9,10-17).

[57] Sometimes the fourth element is dramatically expanded by the Evangelist into a different scene(s) (e.g. 4,51-53: the royal official and his servants; 5,19-13: the cured cripple and the Jews; 9,8-41: the scenes following the curing of the blind man; 11,45-53: the Jews' reaction to Jesus' raising Lazarus to life). J. L. MARTYN remarks about 9,8-41:

> That the man's neighbours somehow confirm the miracle may have been the third element in an earlier form of the story. In the present form of the text, however, the neighbours are employed as actors who come on stage only in a separate scene, and who introduce, therefore, what we should probably term a *dramatic expansion* of the original miracle story (vv. 8-41) (*op. cit.*, 25-26).

Often the action in the narrative provokes the dialogue which, in turn, leads to the ensuing discourse or monologue. For example, the healing of the lame man on a Sabbath (5,1-9) is accompanied by a dialogue between him and the critical Jews (5,10-13), which is followed by a discourse of Jesus (5,14-47)[58]. Likewise, the miracle-narrative of the multiplication of the loaves (6,3-15) and the epiphany-narrative of Jesus' walking on the water (6,16-21) are followed by a dialogue between Jesus and the crowd (6,22-34) which flows into his discourse on the bread of life (6,35-58).

The Prologue (1,1-18) provides us with an example of a hymn, and 17,1-26 an instance of a prolonged prayer of Jesus in the Fourth Gospel.

3.1[12]z The above examples illustrate how the change of the literary genre in the development of a section (e.g. Jn 2-4) or an episode (e.g. Jn 5 or Jn 6) can denote its division.

3.1z Thus we find that the Gospel of John contains at least a **dozen literary criteria** which can be helpful in detecting the structure of the Gospel. Some of them are more important (e.g. introductions, inclusions, conclusions) than others (e.g. hook-words). All of them are useful if employed in conjunction with others.

3.2 DRAMATIC TECHNIQUES

We have seen in the last chapter that many scholars have already noted the dramatic character of the Fourth Gospel[59]. Here we do not intend to examine in detail all its dramatic features. Our only scope is briefly to survey those dramatic techniques which can help us detect the literary-dramatic structure and its divisions.

We shall examine rapidly the following twelve dramatic techniques: 1) change of scenes, 2) technique of alternating scenes, 3) technique of double-stage action, 4) introduction of dramatis personae, 5) change of dramatis personae, 6) law of stage-duality, 7) technique of vanishing characters, 8) technique of seven scenes, 9) technique of diptych-scenes, 10) sequence of action-dialogue-discourse, 11) dramatic development, and 12) dramatic pattern.

3.21 Change of Scenes

A scene may be defined as part of an act (of a play) involving the same persons (actors) in the same place and time[60]. The Gospel of John contains many such dramatic scenes.

---

[58] The narrative in 5,14-18 forms a bridge between the dialogue (5,9d-13) and the discourse proper (5,19-47).

[59] See 2.[16], 2.[17] and 2.[19] above. Cf. also C. R. BOWEN, "The Fourth Gospel as Dramatic Material", *JBL* 49 (1930) 292-305; E. K. LEE, "The Drama of the Fourth Gospel", *ExpTim* 65 1953-54) 173-76; W. R. DOMERIS, "The Johannine Drama", *JournTheolSAfrica* 42 (1983) 29-35.

[60] There is a change of scene, if one of the main characters or the place or time is changed.

For example, if we examine Jn 2-4, we find the following main scenes: the wedding at Cana (2,1-11), the cleansing of the temple in Jerusalem (2,13-22), the discussion between Jesus and Nicodemus (3,1-21), a Messianic discussion between the Baptist and his disciples at Aenon near Salim (3,23-36), Jesus' dialogue with the Samaritan woman at Jacob's well at Sychar (4,4-26), Jesus' dialogue-discourse with his disciples (4,31-38), Jesus and the Samaritans (4,39-42), Jesus and the royal official (4,46-50), the latter and his servants (4,51-53).

Sometimes a single episode is made up of a series of scenes. For example, the multiplication of the loaves on the eastern side of the Sea of Galilee (6,1-15), Jesus' walking on the water (6,16-21), the crowd's coming to Capernaum in search of Jesus the next day (6,22-24), his discourse on the bread of life in the synagogue (6,25-59) with the consequent defection of many of his disciples (6,60-66) and the confession of Simon Peter (6,67-71) constitute the Johannine episode of "Jesus, the bread of life" (6,1-71). Note that the first four scenes depict four different places (the eastern side of the Sea of Galilee, the Sea of Galilee, from the eastern side of the Sea to Capernaum, and the synagogue at Capernaum), while the last two scenes apparently belong to the same place.

Different scenes may be enacted on the same stage by changing the dramatis personae. Thus Jesus' dialogues with the Samaritan woman (4,7-26) and with his disciples (4,31-38) take place at Jacob's well at Sychar. Similarly, the risen Jesus appears to the disciples (20,19-23) and to Thomas (20,26-29) seemingly in the same place where the disciples are gathered together behind closed doors (20,19.26). Here there is also change of time ("eight days later": 20,26).

3.22 Technique of Alternating Scenes

The trial of Jesus before Pilate is presented in seven alternating scenes, namely, outside and inside the praetorium (18,28-32.33-38b.38c-40; 19,1-3.4-7.8-11.12-16b)[61]. The alternation of scenes is clearly indicated by Pilate's "going out" (*exêlthen*: 18,29.38c; 19,4; cf. also *êgagen exô*: 19,13) and "entering" (*eisêlthen*: 18,33; 19,9) the praetorium[62].

3.23 Technique of Double-Stage Action

Sometimes action takes place simultaneously on two stages. We find a good illustration of this in 4,27-38, where, as the Samaritan woman returns to the town of Sychar and brings the people to Jesus still at Jacob's well (4,27-30), Jesus is engaged in a dialogue with his disciples (4,31-38). Likewise, in 3,22-23 the simultaneous baptizing activity of Jesus in the Judean countryside and that of

---

[61] A. JANSSENS DE VAREBEKE, "La structure des scènes du récit de la passion en Joh., xviii-xix", *ETL* 38 (1962) 504-22. The division of the trial before Pilate is given on p. 521.
[62] *Ibid.*, 521.

the Baptist at Aenon near Salim are reported (cf. also 4,1-3). Similarly, as Jesus after his arrest is questioned by the high priest in his palace (18,19-24), Jesus is denied by Peter in the palace-courtyard (18,15-18.25-27).

3.24 Introduction of Dramatis Personae

Often at the beginning of a Johannine episode some of the major characters who will be involved in the event are introduced to the reader. Thus the first two verses of the first sign at Cana (2,1-11) present the mother of Jesus, Jesus and his disciples at a marriage feast (2,1-2). Similarly, the first two verses of the cleansing of the temple (2,13-22) mention the principal protagonists, namely, Jesus, those who were selling oxen, sheep and pigeons, and the money-changers (2,13-14). Likewise at 3,1 Nicodemus is introduced as "a man of the Pharisees..., a ruler of the Jews".

Other examples of this dramatic technique which indicates the beginning of an episode are found at 4,4-7 (Jesus and the Samaritan woman); 4,46 (Jesus and the royal official); 5,1-5 (Jesus and the cripple); 9,1-2 (Jesus, the man born blind and the disciples); 10,22-24 (Jesus and the Jews in Jerusalem); 11,1-3 (Lazarus, Martha, Mary and Jesus); 18,1-3 (Jesus, his disciples, Judas and the arrest-party); 18,28-29 (the Jews, Jesus and Pilate); 20,1-2 (Mary Magdalene, Simon Peter and the Beloved Disciple); 20,19 (the disciples and the risen Jesus).

3.25 Change of Dramatis Personae

Since Jesus is the hero of the Johannine drama, he is actively present in most of the scenes, while the other characters often enter or exit at a change of scene. Thus we find the Samaritan woman in 4,4-42, the royal official in 4,46-54, the paralytic in 5,1-9, etc. Sometimes the stage remains the same but the characters are gradually changed in such a way that the plot of the pericope can progress. Thus at the wedding at Cana (2,1-11) the actors appear on the stage in the following order:

1) the mother of Jesus and Jesus with his disciples (vv.1-2),
2) the mother of Jesus and Jesus (vv.3-4),
3) the mother of Jesus and the servants (v.5),
4) Jesus and the servants (vv.6-8),
5) the steward of the feast and the bridegroom (vv.9-10)[63],
6) Jesus and the disciples (v.11).

---

[63] The "servants" are mentioned in a parenthetical clause in v.9 (*hoi de diakonoi ê[i]deisan hoi êntlêkotes to hydôr*). Similarly, the "steward of the feast" is mentioned in Jesus' command to the servants in v.8 (*antlêsate nyn kai pherete tô[i] architrichlinô[i]*). But we are here concerned not with the occurrence of the words but with the appearance or active presence of the characters.

3.26 The Law of Stage Duality

In constructing a dramatic episode the Evangelist frequently follows "the law of stage duality"[64], which is an "ancient maxim that no more than two active characters shall normally appear on stage at one time"[65]. A very good example of the application of this rule is found in the structuring of the first Cana-sign (2,1-11)[66].

This law appears also to be adhered to in the division of the story of the cured blind man into seven successive scenes in Jn 9, in each of which (except the first) only two active characters are present[67]:

1. Jesus, his disciples, and the blind man   vv. 1-7
2. The blind man and his neighbours   8-12
3. The blind man and the Pharisees   13-17
4. The Jews and the blind man's parents   18-23
5. The Jews and the blind man   24-34
6. Jesus and the blind man   35-38
7. Jesus and some Pharisees   39-41.

The law of stage duality seems operative also in 1,35-51 which describes the discovery of Jesus Christ by the first disciples, in which the actors appear in twos (except in the first scene in which there are three characters)[68]:

1) The Baptist with two of his disciples and Jesus (vv.35-37)
2) Jesus and the two disciples (vv.37-39)
3) Andrew and Simon Peter (vv.40-42a)
4) Simon Peter and Jesus (v.42)

---

[64] R. BULTMANN, *History of the Synoptic Tradition*, tr. by John Marsh (London 1963) 188.

[65] J. L. MARTYN, *History and Theology in the Fourth Gospel*, 2 ed., (New York 1979) 26.

[66] See 3.25 above. "Jesus and his disciples" in 2,2 are to be understood as a single dramatic character (namely, Jesus with his disciples). This is suggested by the singular verb *eklêthê* (see a similar phenomenon at 1,35: *heistêkei*). Secondly, here the disciples are mentioned only in passing; they are not *actively* present.

[67] J. L. MARTYN, *op. cit.*, 26-27. It is true that in the first scene (9,1-7) there are three characters (Jesus, his disciples, and the blind man); in fact, B. NOACK divides 9,1-7 into two scenes: 1) Jesus and his disciples (vv.1-5), and 2) Jesus and the blind man (vv.6-7) (*Zur johanneischen Tradition* [1954] 115, mentioned by J. L. MARTYN, *op. cit.*, 27, n. 18). Instead of regarding 9,1-5 and 9,6-7 as separate scenes, the whole of 9,1-7 can be thought of as a single scene composed of two *sub-scenes* (9,1-5.6-7) in the same place. The first introduces the characters (see 3.24 above) and the second describes the miracle of healing, in each of which the law of stage duality is observed, since in 9,1-5 the blind man, though present, is not active, and in 9,6-7 the disciples, though present, do not intervene.

[68] If we take vv.35-37 as a unit, then three active characters (the Baptist, his disciples and Jesus) appear in it. But we have seen above (cf. n. 39) that v.37 may be a bridge-verse which concludes the first unit (vv.35-37) and introduces the second (vv.37-39). This may be the reason why the law of stage duality is not strictly adhered to in vv.35-37 (cf. also 4,27-30; 5,14-18). It is also possible that in the introductory scene the Evangelist does not observe the law of stage duality, since he often introduces in the first scene many of the representative characters of the episode (see 3.24 above). This shows that the law of stage duality is not an absolute rule.

5) Jesus and Philip (vv.43-44)
6) Philip and Nathanael (vv.45-46)
7) Nathanael and Jesus (vv.47-50)
8) Jesus and (the disciples) (v.50)[69].

In all the above cases the law of stage duality is strictly followed, except in the introductory scene, where another literary dramatic technique (of introducing the representative characters)[70] seems to take precedence over the rule of stage duality.

3.27 Technique of Vanishing Characters

The author of the Fourth Gospel sometimes combines "the law of stage duality" with what could be called "the law of vanishing characters" according to which an active character of the previous scene is instrumental in introducing the next scene and then practically disappears or vanishes from the stage.

The application of this technique is evident, for instance, in 1,37 where John the Baptist who has borne witness to Jesus (1,35-36) and thus has helped his disciples to follow Jesus (1,37) disappears, as it were, from the scene, leaving Jesus and the disciples alone on the stage. A similar phenomenon happens also in 1,42a where Andrew brings his brother Simon to Jesus and withdraws, as it were, into the background, so that Jesus and Peter are in the foreground[71].

Again, the neighbours of the cured blind man who question him in 9,8-12 bring him to the Pharisees in 9,13 and disappear from the stage[72].

3.28 Technique of Seven Scenes

Often the author of the Fourth Gospel builds a dramatic episode in seven successive scenes. This is best seen in the description of Jesus' trial before Pilate in seven alternating scenes (18,28-32.33-38b.38c-40; 19,1-3.4-7.8-11.12-16b)[73]. Again, 19,16c-42 which depicts Christ on Calvary contains seven episodes (19,16c-18.19-22.23-24.25-27.28-30.31-37.38-42)[74]. Another illustration of this

---

[69] In 1,51 all the disciples present seem to be implied, since Jesus' promise is meant not only for Nathanael (cf. *autô[i]*) but also for the others (cf. the plural *hymin* and *opsesthe*).

[70] See n. 59 above.

[71] Note that in 1,35-42 the "vanishing" of the characters takes place in the bridge-verses (vv. 37 and 42a) (cf. 3.191 above).

[72] Similarly, the disciples mentioned in the first scene (9,1-7) do not appear again in the rest of Jn 9.

[73] See 3.22 above. Cf. A. JANSSENS DE VAREBECKE, *art.cit.*, 504-22; BROWN, II, 785; 859.

[74] BROWN, II, 786. He calls the first and the last subdivisions not episodes but "introduction" and "conclusion" respectively. We prefer the designation "episodes" for all the seven subdivisions, since they describe different events.

A. JANSSENS DE VAREBECKE too divides 19,16-42 into seven episodes, the last two, in his opinion, being 19,38-40 and 19,41-42 (*art. cit.*, 803). But since the whole of 19,38-42 deals with the burial of Jesus, it is to be regarded as one episode (see n. 419 in ch. 4 below).

dramatic technique is found in the sevenfold division of the healing of the blind man (9,1-7.8-12.13-17.18-23.24-34.35-38.39-41)[75].

3.29 Technique of Diptych-Scenes

Sometimes two adjacent scenes are painted in such a way that they form a diptych, namely, two distinct but matching pictures are joined or hinged together to form a bigger unit. Thus the two testimonies of John the Baptist on two successive days (his negative testimony about himself in 1,19-28 and his positive testimony about Jesus in 1,29-34) form a "testimony-diptych". The close connection between the two pericopes is indicated also by the inclusion between *hê martyria tou Iôannou* at 1,19 and *kagô... memartyrêka* at 1,34.

We find a "discovery-diptych" in 1,35-51, whose parallel panels present the Messianic discovery by the anonymous disciple, Andrew and Peter on the first day (vv.35-42) and by Philip and Nathanael on the next day (vv.43-51).

Just as at the beginning we have two diptychs (1,19-28 & 1,29-34; 1,35-42 & 1,43-51), so at the end the Evangelist has painted two "resurrection-diptychs" (20,1-10 & 20,11-18; 20,19-25 & 20,24-29). The first diptych depicts the discovery of the empty tomb by Mary Magdalene, the Beloved Disciple and Peter, and the subsequent appearance of Jesus to Mary at the tomb (20,1-18). The second diptych contains Jesus' appearances to the disciples, first without Thomas and then with him, gathered in a locked room (20,19-29).

3.2[10] Sequence of Action-Dialogue-Discourse

Many of the episodes in the Fourth Gospel have the dramatic sequence of action-dialogue-discourse, that is, often an episode begins with an action of Jesus which sparks off a dialogue between him and another character, which, in turn, ends in a discourse by Jesus. Or looking at the episodes from the literary point of view, that is, examining their literary 'genres', the episodes may be said to follow the pattern of narrative-dialogue-discourse. In the words of C. H. Dodd:

> The episodes are constructed upon a common pattern, subject to endless variations. Each of them tends to move from narrative, through dialogue, to monologue, or at least to form a dialogue in which comparatively long speeches are allotted to the chief speaker[76].

This pattern is quite evident in Jn 5, where the action/narrative of Jesus' healing of the paralytic (5,1-9c) leads to a dialogue between the latter and the Jews (5,9d-13), which, in turn, is followed by Jesus' discourse on the Son's authority and his witnesses (5,14-47). This discourse explains the significance of his "work" on the Sabbath, which points to his divine identity and authority testified by many witnesses[77].

---

[75] See 3.25 above for the division of 9,1-41 into seven scenes.
[76] C. H. DODD, *The Interpretation of the Fourth Gospel*, 384.
[77] See 5.122 below.

Similarly, in Jn 6 Jesus' sign of feeding the five thousand (6,3-15) and his walking on the water (6,16-21) are followed by his dialogue with the crowd (6,22-34) and the discourse on the bread of life (6,35-59)[78].

The same pattern of action-dialogue-discourse can be noticed also in 2,23-3,21 and 3,22-36, though here the narrative parts (2,23-25 and 3,22-24) are relatively short and serve only to introduce the ensuing dialogues. Notice that in both these cases the dialogues (3,1-10 and 3,25-30) slide smoothly into the discourse (3,11-21 and 3,31-36) without a clear indication of the change from dialogue to discourse[79]. A similar pattern is vaguely discernible also in Jn 13-17 (narrative: 13,1-11; dialogue: 13,12-38; discourse/prayer: 14,1-17,26)[80].

3.2[11] Dramatic Development

We have seen in the last chapter that in the opinion of many Johannine scholars the main plot of the Fourth Gospel is developed dramatically from beginning to end[81].

There is a dramatic development not only in the Gospel as a whole but also in individual episodes. For instance, a carefully planned plot is discernible in the seven successive scenes in Jn 9 which describe the healing of the man born blind, the consequent discussions and disputes between him and his neighbours and the Jewish authorities, his expulsion from the synagogue, his confession of faith in Christ and Jesus' judgement of the unbelieving Jews[82]. Likewise the curing of the cripple and the subsequent dialogues and discourse(s) demonstrate the dramatic power and literary composition of Jn 5[83]. Other examples of detailed dramatic development of individual episodes are: the disciples' discovery of the Messiah (1,35-51), Jesus and the Samaritan woman (4,4-42), Jesus, the bread of life (6,1-71), Jesus in Jerusalem during the

---

[78] The discourse is then followed by two other dialogues, the first with his disciples (6,60-66) and the second with the Twelve (6,67-71). Jn 6,60-71 is regarded by C. H. DODD as "an appendix or epilogue" (*op. cit.*, 340) but we shall see later in ch. 4 that it is an integral part of Jn 6 and has a dramatic and theological role in the organization of Jn 6.

[79] C. H. DODD rightly remarks:

What we constantly observe is that dramatic *dialogue*, often marked by vivid characterization of the interlocutors, *melts imperceptibly into monologue*, with certain variations of style, it is true, but without any change so marked that we can say with confidence, 'Here Jesus, or the Baptist, is speaking, and here the evangelist' (*op. cit.*, 308) [my italics].

[80] It may be noted here that the whole of Jn 14-16 is not a pure discourse, since it contains some dialogues between Jesus and his disciples (14,5-9.22-23; 16,29-33). This, however, is not a rare phenomenon in Jn (cf. for example the dialogues in the discourses of Jn 6 and Jn 7-8).

In Jn 13-17 the narrative is reduced to a minimum probably because it is meant primarily to be the theological interpretation of the passion-death-resurrection narrative in Jn 18-20 (*ibid.*, 423).

[81] See 2.[16] (TENNEY); 2.[17] (CULPEPPER); 2.[19] (CABA) above. Cf. also W. R. DOMERIS, *art. cit.*, 29-35.

[82] J. L. MARTYN, *op. cit.*, 24-36.

[83] *Ibid.*, 68-73.

feast of Tabernacles (7,1-8,59), the raising of Lazarus (11,1-54), Jesus' trial before Pilate (18,28-19,16b), and Jesus on Calvary (19,16c-42) [84].

3.2[12] Dramatic Pattern

The Fourth Gospel has not only a dramatic development of the plot around the hero Jesus Christ but also a dramatic pattern similar to classical Greek tragedies [85].

A typical Greek tragedy consisted of the following parts:

(a) the prologue (*prologos*), the part before the entrance of the chorus, in monologue or dialogue, setting forth the subject of the drama and the situation from which it starts...

(b) the *parodos*, the song accompanying the entrance of the chorus.

(c) the episodes (*epeisodia*), scenes in which one or more actors took part, with the chorus...

(d) *stasima*, songs of the chorus 'in one place', i.e. in the orchestra, as opposed to the *parodos* when the chorus was entering...

(e) ... the *exodos* or final scene [86].

Examining carefully the Gospel of John we find that it begins with a Prologue (1,1-18) which introduces the plot and denouement of the drama (cf. especially 1,11-14) [87].

---

[84] See 4.3 below.

[85] W. R. DOMERIS affirms:
John has deliberately fashioned his Gospel after the model of the Greek dramas and particularly the Tragedies. He does not abandon the form of the Gospel, but sets out to present the life of Jesus in such a way that someone familiar with the pattern of the Classical Tragedies would recognize the form" (*art. cit.*, 29-30).

The above hypothesis is supported by "the prologue, conclusion, use of discourses and dialogues, forensic setting, naming of characters, introduction of representative characters and views, general use of direct speech rather than reported speech, lack of a series of miracles and above all, the focus on Jesus at all times" (*ibid.*, 35).

[86] P. HARVEY, *The Oxford Companion to Classical Literature* (Oxford 1937) 435: "Divisions and construction of a Greek tragedy"; cf. also M. CROISET, *Histoire de la Littérature Grecque*, III, *Période Attique: Tragédie - Comédie - Genres Secondaires*, 3 éd., (Paris 1913) 114-24.

Thirty out of the 32 extant tragedies of AESCHYLUS, SOPHOCLES and EURIPIDES have the five parts mentioned above, the only exceptions being the two earliest tragedies of Aeschylus (*Persians* and *Suppliants*) which do not have a prologue (cf. C. DIANO [ed.], *Il Teatro Greco: Tutte le Tragedie* [Firenze 1970]).

[87] W. R. DOMERIS observes: "John does not use a poetical metre, but prefers instead to follow the traditional prose of the Gospel genre. However, he does start with a *prologue*, which may be compared to the traditional opening lines of a typical Greek tragedy" (*art. cit.*, 30) [my italics].

The function of this Johannine Prologue is quite similar to that of the Euripidean prologues. M. CROISET comments on the role of the latter: "Très souvent, ils indiquent le sujet essentiel de la pièce, ils signalent d'avance au spectateur ce qu'il devra regarder, ils lui laissent entrevoir ou lui annoncent même d'une manière formelle le dénouement" (*op. cit.*, 338). These words are equally applicable to Jn 1,1-18 (cf. especially 1,11-18).

Immediately after the Prologue the Fourth Gospel contains a passage which describes the testimony of John the Baptist and the disciples's discovery of Jesus, the Messiah (1,19-51), which may be compared to the *parodos* of the Greek tragedies [88] and particularly to the dialogic *parodos* found, for instance, in *Oedipus at Colonus* by Sophocles [89], in which the *parodos* consists of two pairs of alternating strophes and antistrophes in the form of dialogues between the chorus, the chorus-leader (*coriphaeus*), Oedipus and his daughter Antigone [90].

It is also interesting to note that, just as the Sophoclean *parodos* in *Oedipus at Colonus* flows naturally into the first episode in which, besides the characters of the *parodos*, other actors like Ismea (daughter of Oedipus) and Theseos (king of Athens) appear [91], the Johannine *parodos* (1,19-51) is linked to the first Cana-sign (2,1-11) in which, besides Jesus and the first disciples (mentioned already in 1,35-51), others like the mother of Jesus, the servants, the steward of the feast come on stage.

We shall see below that the body of the Fourth Gospel (2,1-20,29) is divided into five sections or acts (Jn 2-4; 5-10; 11-12; 13-17; 18-20) [92] which are similar to the fivefold division (four episodes + *exodos* [= the final episode]) of the majority of the Sophoclean and Euripidian tragedies [93].

It must be admitted, however, that the Gospel of John does not contain *stasima* (the songs of the chorus), which usually indicated the divisions in the dramatic action in a classical Greek tragedy [94]. Since a chorus, in the strict sense of the term, does not appear in the Fourth Gospel, it is not surprising to see the absence of *stasima* in the Johannine drama. And yet, some of the questions and responses, reactions and remarks of the "crowds" (*ochlos* or *polloi*) in the Gospel of John may be reminiscent of the Greek chorus [95]. For example, at the end of Jn 10 "many" (*polloi*) make a comparative observation about John the Baptist

---

[88] ARISTOTLE defines *parodos* as "the first speaking of the whole chorus" (*parodos men hê prôtê lexis holou chorou*) (*Poetics*, c. 12, cited by M. CROISET, *op. cit.*, 117, n. 2).

[89] M. CROISET mentions other examples of dialogic *parodos* from AESCHYLUS, SOPHOCLES and EURIPIDES:

> Au lieu d'une parodos proprement dite, nous voyons dans le *Prométhée enchaîné* un dialogue lyrique entre Prométhée et les Océanides. Il en est encore ainsi dans l'*Électre* de Sophocle, dans... ses *Trachiniennes*. Euripide à son tour use du même procédé dans *Hélène*, dans *Électre*, dans *Héraclides*, dans *Ion*, dans *Médée*, dans *Oreste*, dans les *Troyennes*... (*op. cit.*, 117-18).

[90] C. DIANO (ed.), *op. cit.*, 357-58.
[91] *Ibid.*, 359-65.
[92] See 4.2z and n. 288 there.
[93] C. DIANO (ed.), *op. cit.*, 359-65.
[94] M. CROISET, *op. cit.*, 118. The absence of *stasima* in Jn may be accounted for, if their use in dramas had gone out of vogue before the time of the Evangelist. According to P. HARVEY, already AGATHON (who died c. 400 B.C.), the most important Greek tragedian after Aeschylus, Sophocles and Euripides, had "made the songs of the chorus [*stasima*] mere interludes (*embolima*) without reference to the subject of the play, thus preparing the way for the division of the tragedy into acts" (*op. cit.*, 13). Cf. also M. CROISET, *op. cit.*, 119.
[95] W. R. DOMERIS sees vestiges of the Greek chorus in the "crowds" in the Fourth Gospel, for he says: "We see in these crowds the dramatic use of the chorus, sometimes confessing Jesus, sometimes raising questions devoid of real insight into his being" (*art. cit.*, 33).

and Jesus Christ: "John did no sign, but everything that John said about this man was true" (10,41), which, though it is too short to be a *stasimon*, seems to serve the same function of separating the sections or episodes [96]. In some other places in Jn (e.g. 7,12.20.31.40-43; 12,12-14.29.34) the crowd (*ochlos*) intervenes *during* the episodes as the chorus does in most of the Greek tragedies.

We must also note that the passion-resurrection in Jn 18-20, which is dramatically constructed (cf. the many dialogues there compared to the Synoptic accounts of the passion-resurrection) may be considered as the *exodos* similar to that of the Greek tragedies.

Finally, it is noteworthy that the conclusion of the Fourth Gospel in which the Evangelist summarizes Jesus' life in terms of the "signs" he did and appeals to the readers to believe in his Messiahship and divine Sonship and thus to have eternal life (20,30-31) sounds like the concluding words of some of the Greek tragedies in which the chorus-leader highlights the tragic hero's greatness and tells the audience the moral lesson to be learned (e.g. in Sophocles' *Oedipus Tyrannus*) [97].

3.2[12]z Besides the dramatic development of the plot in the Fourth Gospel, which some Johannine scholars have highlighted, we find that at least four of the five principal parts of a typical classical Greek tragedy (namely, *prologos, parodos, epeisodia* and *exodos*) are applicable, *mutatis mutandis*, to the Gospel of John, though it is not written as a drama to be staged in a theatre. In other words, we suggest that the Fourth Gospel has not only a dramatic development of the plot but also a dramatic pattern similar to that of the Greek tragedies [98].

3.3 STRUCTURAL PATTERNS

Besides the literary criteria and the dramatic techniques discussed above, the Evangelist has employed a number of structural patterns based on the principles of repetition and balance [99]. We find in the Fourth Gospel the following four formal structural patterns: 1) parallelism, 2) chiasmus, 3) concentric structure, and 4) spiral structure [100].

---

[96] We cannot, however, be quite sure of this, since John does not seem to have used the "crowds" in the same way between other sections of the Gospel.

[97] The chorus-leader's concluding words are the following:

O Abitanti di Tebe mia patria, guardate: ecco qui Edipo, il sapiente che sciolse l'enigma famoso, il signore sopra tutti potenti, l'uomo alla cui fortuna tutti i concittadini mirarono con invidia. E voi vedete ora in che paurosa procella di sventure è caduto. Nessun uomo mortale puoi reputare felice fintanto che di sua vita aspetti l'ultimo giorno, bensì dopo ch'egli ne abbia varcato il termine senza patire dolori (tr. by M. Valgimigli, in: C. DIANO [ed.], *op. cit.*, 313).

Cf. also EURIPIDES' *Medea, Electra, Helen* (*ibid.*, 452; 770; 865 respectively).

[98] This is intended only as a modest suggestion and hence is open to correction by experts on ancient dramas.

[99] Cf. C. H. TALBERT, *Literary Patterns, Theological Themes and the Genre of Luke-Acts* (SBL 20) (Montana 1974) 15-65 for an excellent study of the literary patterns or archetectonic designs such as parallelism and chiasmus in Lk-Ac.

[100] Cf. *ibid.*, 14, n. 70, for the flexible nomenclature of some of these structural patterns. See also 3.31; 3.32; 3.33 and 3.34 below, where the names are explained.

3.31 Parallelism

Different types of parallelism (synonymous, antithetic, synthetic and staircase) are frequently employed in the dialogues and discourses of Jesus [101].

3.311 Synonymous parallelism

Synonymous parallelism consists in the repetition of the same words or of the same idea in different but synonymous words. An instance of the first type is found in 1,39:

A (a b) : **erchesthe** *kai opsesthe* (v.39bc)
A' (a' b'): **êlthan** oun *kai eidan* (v.39de).

Note that A and A' contain identical terms ("coming" and "seeing") and have even the same construction (a b // a' b'). This type of parallelism where the words repeated are identical is very easily detected and we need not give more examples. Often, however, diverse but synonymous terms are used to repeat the same basic idea. This is clearly seen in Jesus' saying in 6,35:

ho erchomenos pros eme *ou mê peinasê[i]*,
kai **ho pisteuôn eis eme** *ou mê dipsêsei* pôpote.

Here the first line is parallel to the second, since "coming to me" is equivalent to "believing in me" (cf. 7,37), and "hunger" and "thirst" correspond to each other. Other instances of such synonymous parallelism are found in 6,55; 7,37 and 13,16 [102].

Often a synonymous parallelism occurs not in the same verse but in two neighbouring verses of the same pericope. Take, for instance, 3,3 and 3,5:

3,3: a m ê n a m ê n l e g ô s o i,
    ean mê tis gennêthê[i] *anôthen*,
    ou dynatai **idein tên basileian tou theou**.
3,5: a m ê n a m ê n l e g ô s o i,
    ean mê tis gennêthê[i] *ex hydatos kai pneumatos*,
    ou dynatai **eiselthein eis tên basileian tou theou**.

Notice that the two sayings are the same except for *anôthen* which corresponds to *ex hydatos kai pneumatos* and *idein* which is parallel to *eiselthein eis*. Other examples of synonymous parallelism in nearby verses are found in 6,54.56; 10,11.14; 12,35.36; 12,44.45.

---

[101] Cf. BROWN, I, cxxxii; A.-J. FESTUGIÈRE, *Observations stylistiques sur l'Évangile de S. Jean* (Paris 1974) 48-63; 91-93. Cf. also C. F. BURNEY, *The Poetry of Our Lord* (Oxford 1925) 63-99, for the presence of the same types of parallelism in the discourses of Jesus in the Gospel of John and in the Synoptics.
[102] BROWN, I, cxxxii; A.-J. FESTUGIÈRE, *op. cit.*, 92-93.

Synonymous parallelism may be present also in two different but parallel pericopes or episodes. Jn 2,23-3,21 and 3,22-36 provide us with excellent examples:

3,11: ho oidamen laloumen kai *ho heôrakamen* **martyroumen,**
kai tên martyrian hêmôn *ou lambanete.*
3,32: *ho heôraken* kai êkousen touto **martyrei,**
kai tên martyrian autou *oudeis lambanei.*
3,13: **ho ek tou ouranou** *katabas*
3,31: **ho ek tou ouranou** *erchomenos*
3,16: houtôs gar **êgapêsen** *ho theos* ton kosmon,
hôste *ton hyion* ton monogenê e d ô k e n...
3,35: *ho patêr* **agapa[i]** *ton hyion,*
kai panta d e d ô k e n en tê[i] cheiri autou.
3,16: hina pas **ho pisteuôn eis** *auton... echê[i] zôên aiônion.*
3,36: **ho pisteuôn eis** *ton hyion echei zôên aiônion.*
3,17: ou **gar apesteilen ho theos** *ton hyion* eis ton kosmon...
3,34: *hon* **gar apesteilen ho theos** ta rhêmata tou theou lalei...

Because of the above unmistakable parallelisms the two discourses in 3,11-21 and 3,31-36 are certainly parallel.

Other examples of synonymous parallelism of pericopes or episodes are: 2,1-11 & 4,46-54; 5,1-47 & 10,22-42; 6,1-71 & 10,1-21; 13,1-38 & 17,1-26; 13,31-14,31 & 16,4e-33 [103].

3.312 *Antithetic parallelism*

In antithetic parallelism one part is contrasted with the second. It may be found in two lines of the same sentence or verse. For example,

3,18: **ho pisteuôn** eis auton *ou krinetai*;
ho [de] mê pisteuôn *êdê kekritai...*

Unlike in 3,18 where the terms of the antithetical parallelism are identical (*pisteuein* and *krinesthai*), we may have an antithetical parallelism in the same verse where the terms are not the same but synonymous or similar as in 3,36:

ho pisteuôn eis **ton hyion** *echei* **zôên** *aiônion*;
ho de apeithôn **tô[i] hyiô[i]** *ouk opsetai* **zôên**...

Other examples of antithetical parallelism in the same verse are found in 6,27.32; 7,18; 8,14.35; 9,39; 15,15 [104].

---

[103] These examples of synonymous parallelism of pericopes or episodes will be discussed in detail in ch. 4 below.
[104] BROWN, I, cxxxii; A.-J. FESTUGIÈRE, *op. cit.*, 91-92.

Sometimes two adjacent verses are antithetically constructed e.g. 3,20-21:

3,20: pas gar *ho phaula prassôn* misei to phôs
      kai **ouk erchetai pros to phôs**,
        h i n a *mê elenchthê[i]* ***ta erga autou***.
3,21: *ho de poiôn tên alêtheian*
      erchetai pros to phôs,
        h i n a *phanerôthê[i]* ***autou ta erga***...

The Fourth Gospel contains many other examples of antithetical parallelism in two immediately neighbouring verses (e.g. 4,13.14; 6,49.50; 7,28.29; 10,4.5; 10,11.12) [105].

Two parallel pericopes or episodes may be antithetically arranged by contrasting the characters in them. Thus the unbelieving Jews of Jerusalem in 2,13-22 (cf. v.18) seem to be contrasted with the Samaritan woman and the people of Sychar who believe in Jesus in 4,4-42 (cf. v.42). Similarly, the spiritually blind Pharisees (not only in Jn 9 but also in Jn 7-8) who refuse to receive Jesus, the light of the world (8,12), seem to be contrasted with the man born blind who receives both physical and spiritual sight through faith in Jesus (9,1-41) [106].

3.313 *Synthetic parallelism*

Some synthetic parallelisms are also found in the Fourth Gospel. For instance, the second verse of the Prologue (1,2) is synthetically parallel to the first verse:

1,1: **En archê[i]** *ên* h o l o g o s,
      kai h o l o g o s *ên* ***pros ton theon***,
      kai theos *ên* h o l o g o s.
1,2: h o u t o s *ên* **en archê[i]** ***pros ton theon*** [107].

3.314 *Staircase parallelism*

Staircase parallelism, which is a special case of synthetic parallelism, where the successive lines are connected by means of hook-words and are constructed, as it were, to form the steps of a staircase, is quite frequent in the Gospel of John. This is well illustrated in 1,4-5:

1,4: ho gegonen en autô[i] z ô ê ên,
      kai hê z ô ê ên to *p h ô s* tôn anthrôpôn;
1,5:   kai to *p h ô s* en tê[i] s k o t i a [i] phainei,
      kai hê s k o t i a auto ou katelaben.

---

[105] *Ibid.*
[106] See 4.322,1 below for the reasons for the contrast.
[107] BROWN, I, cxxxii. He gives 8,44 as another example of synthetic parallelism.

The Prologue itself contains many other examples of such staircase parallelism (e.g. 1,1.10.11). Other instances are 6,37; 8,32; 13,20; 14,21 [108].

3.32 Chiasmus

Chiasmus is a structural pattern employed widely in antiquity both in the Bible and in the non-biblical literature [109]. It is basically an "inverted parallelism" or "a passage in which the second part is inverted and balanced against the first" [110]. The simplest example of this is Jesus' saying about the Sabbath: "The Sabbath is made for man, not man for the Sabbath" (Mk 2,27).

Though this literary phenomenon, involving inversion and balance, is recognized by many, there is no fixed nomenclature in scholarly circles. "In modern times, chiasmus has been exposited under the names of *epanodos*, introverted parallelism, extended introversion, concentrism, the *chi*-form, palistrope, envelope construction, the *delta*-form, recursion, as well as simple, compound, and complex chiasmus" [111]. We prefer the term "chiasmus" to other designations, since this is the older and more commonly used term [112].

Unlike many authors who include the "concentric structure" in the "chiasmus" [113], we would like to distinguish them, since they have two different structural patterns, for while chiasmus has two inverted parallel panels (e.g. A B //

---

[108] *Ibid.*

[109] Cf. N. W. LUND, *Chiasmus in the New Testament* (Chapel Hill 1942); A. DI MARCO, *Il Chiasmo nella Bibbia. Contributi di Stilistica Strutturale* (Torino 1980). (He makes a useful but uncritical collection of chiasms [proposed by various authors] in the different books of the Bible from Genesis to Revelation.) J. W. WELCH (ed.), *Chiasmus in Antiquity. Structures, Analyses, Exegesis* (Hildesheim 1981). This book contains many valuable essays by different scholars on chiasmus in: Sumero-Akkadian (R. F. SMITH), Ugaritic (J. W. WELCH), Hebrew Biblical Narrative (Y. T. RADDAY), Biblical Hebrew Poetry (W. G. E. WATSON), Aramaic Contracts and Letters (B. PORTEN), Talmudic-Aggadic Narrative (J. FRAENKEL), the Book of Mormon (J. W. WELCH), and Ancient Greek and Latin Literatures (J. W. WELCH). Cf. also the rich bibliography on chiasmus on pp. 269-86 and the very useful "Index" on pp. 287-352 (see especially pp. 341-52 which mention the main books and articles on chiasmus in each of the books of the NT classified according to chapter and verse). Cf. also A. STOCK, "Chiastic Awareness and Education in Antiquity", *BibTB* 14 (1984) 23-35.

[110] YELLAND's *Handbook of Literary Terms*, p. 32, cited by J. W. WELCH, *op. cit.*, 9. Cf. also M. DAHOOD, "Chiasmus", in: IDB, Supplementary Volume, (Nashville 1976) 145.

[111] *Ibid.*, 9-10. (The references to these designations are found in the footnotes 2-11 at the end of the chapter, namely, on pp. 15-16 of the book.)

CHIASMO viene chiamato anche INCLUSIONE (semitica), STRUTTURA CONCENTRICA, SIMMETRIA CONCENTRICA, PARALLELISMO INVERTITO, PALINDROMIA o PALINDROME, REGRESSIONE, "ENVELOPE FIGURE", RING COMPOSITION, PALISTROFA, LOGICA CIRCOLARE, PARALLELISMO ANTITETICO, ALL'INDIETRO, etc... (A. DI MARCO, *op. cit.*, 6).

Cf. also R. MEYNET, "Comment établir un chiasme", *NRT* 100 (1978) 234.

[112] Cf. the books mentioned in n. 109 above. "Chiasmus" is also the earliest term used first by J. A. BENGEL in: *Gnomon Novi Testamenti* (Tübingen 1742), cited by R. MEYNET, *art. cit.*, 234 and N. W. LUND, *op. cit.*, 35; 38).

[113] Cf. the authors mentioned in n. 109 above and the different names including "concentric structure" given to "chiasmus" in n. 111 above.

B'A'; A B C // C' B' A'; etc.), the concentric structure has a unique central element around which other elements are arranged in a parallel manner (e.g. A *B* A'; A B *C* B'A'; etc.)[114].

The Gospel of John contains a number of chiastic constructions in 1) single sentences, 2) individual pericopes, and 3) whole sections.

3.321 *Chiasmus in a sentence*

The simplest example of the chiastic construction of a single verse is found in 3,31b which has an A B B'A' pattern:

3,31b: A   *ho ôn*
        B   *ek tês gês*
        B' *ek tês gês*
      A' *estim...*

Jn 3,32d-33a and 18,36bc are two instances of chiastic pattern consisting of three parallel elements (A B C C' B'A'):

3,32d: A   kai **tên martyrian**
        B   *autou*
          C   **oudeis lambanei.**
3,33a: C' **ho labôn**
        B' *autou*
      A' **tên martyrian...**

18,36b: A   **hê basileia hê emê**
        B   *ouk estin*
          C   **ek tou kosmou toutou**;
18,36c: C' **ei ek tou kosmou toutou**
        B' *ên*
      A' **hê basileia hê emê...**

3.322 *Chiasmus in a pericope*

An excellent example of a large chiasmus (A B C D D' C' B'A') involving a number of verses is found in Jesus' discourse in 5,19-30[115]:

---

[114] We shall discuss the "concentric structure" separately (see 3.33 below).

[115] A. VANHOYE, "La composition de Jn 5,19-30", in: *Mélanges Bibliques. En hommage au R. P. Béda Rigaux*, ed. A. Descamps & A. de Halleux (Duculot 1970) 259-74. The author of the article does a detailed analysis of the text and we find his conclusions convincing. X. LÉON-DUFOUR, "Trois chiasmes johanniques", *NTS* 7 (1960-61) 249-55, also considers 5,19-30 as a chiasmus built around a central verse: "Le v.24 forme entre les vv.19 and 30 le point médian d'un chiasme" (p. 254). (In our terminology this would not be called a "chiasmus" but a "concentric structure": see 3.33 below.) But a careful comparison of vv.24 and 25 makes it clear, as VANHOYE has shown, that they are parallel to each other in form and in content.

3.3 STRUCTURAL PATTERNS

A 19: Apekrinato oun ho Iêsous kai elegen autois:
amên amên legô hymin,
OU DYNATAI ho hyios **POIEIN** *APH' HEAUTOU OUDEN*
ean mê ti *blepê[i] ton patera* **poiounta**;
ha gar an ekeinos **poiê[i]**, tauta kai *ho hyios* homoiôs **poiei**.

B 20: ho gar patêr philei ton hyion
kai *panta* deiknysin autô[i] ha autos poiei,
kai meizona toutôn deixei autô[i] erga,
hina hymeis **thaumazête**.

C 21: **hôsper gar** *ho patêr* egeirei tous nekrous kai **zô[i]opoiei**,
houtôs kai *ho hyios* hous thelei **zô[i]opoiei**.
22: oude gar *ho patêr* ***krinei*** oudena,
alla tên ***krisin*** pasan ***dedôken*** *tô[i] hyiô[i]*,
23: hina pantes timôsi *ton hyion* kathôs timôsi *ton patera*.
ho mê timôn *ton hyion* ou tima[i] *ton patera* ton pempsanta auton.

D 24: *amên amên legô hymin hoti* ho *ton logon mou akouôn*
kai pisteuôn tô[i] pempsanti me **echei zôên aiônion**
kai eis krisin ouk erchetai
alla metabebêken ek tou thanatou eis **tên zôên**.

D' 25: *amên amên legô hymin hoti* erchetai hôra kai nyn estin
hote hoi nekroi *akousousin tês phônês tou hyiou* tou theou
kai hoi *akousantes* **zêsousin**.

C' 26: **hôsper gar** *ho patêr* **echei zôên** en heautô[i],
houtôs kai *tô[i] hyiô[i]* ***edôken*** **zôên echein** en heautô[i];
27: kai exousian ***edôken*** autô[i] ***krisin poiein***,
hoti *hyios* anthrôpou estin.

B' 28: mê **thaumazete** touto hoti erchetai hôra en hê[i]
pantes hoi en tois mnêmeiois akousousin tês phônês autou
29: kai ekporeusontai hoi ta agatha poiêsantes eis anastasin zôês,
hoi de ta phaula praxantes eis anastasin kriseôs.

A' 30: *OU DYNAMAI* egô **POIEIN** *AP' EMAUTOU OUDEN*;
kathôs *akouô* ***krinô***, kai hê ***krisis*** hê emê dikaia estin,
hoti ou zêtô to thelêma to emon
alla to thelêma tou pempsantos me.

It is to be noted that besides the parallelisms between the corresponding elements A (v.19) and A' (v.30), B (v.20) and B' (vv.28-29), C (vv.21-23) and C' (vv.26-27), D (v.24) and D' (v.25), which have been explained by Vanhoye[116], there are also some correspondences between the extreme elements A A' and D D' (cf. *amên amên legô hymin* in vv.19.24.25, that is, in A, D, and D', on the one hand, and *akouein* in vv.24.25.30, that is, in D, D', and A', on the

---

[116] Cf. A. VANHOYE, *art. cit.*

other hand). Again, some of the alternating elements have some similarities between them. For instance, A and C are somewhat similar:

A 19: ha *gar* an *ekeinos* **poiê[i]**,
tauta *kai ho hyios* homoiôs **poiei**.
C 21: hôsper *gar ho patêr* egeirei tous nekrous kai zô[i]o**poiei**,
houtôs *kai ho hyios* hous thelei zô[i]o**poiei**.

Similarly, D' is parallel to B':

D' 25: ***hoti erchetai hôra*** kai nyn estin
hote *hoi nekroi* **akousousin tês phônês** *tou hyiou tou theou*
kai hoi **akousantes** *zêsousin*.
B' 28: ***hoti erchetai hôra*** en hê[i]
pantes *hoi en tois mnêmeiois* **akousousin tês phônês** *autou*
kai ekporeusontai... eis anastasin *zôês*...

Likewise, C' corresponds to some extent to A', since ***krisin poiein*** in v.27 (C') is equivalent to ***krinô*** (cf. also ***krisis***) in v.30 (A').

Notice also that just in 12 verses (19-30) the word *hyios* occurs 10 times and the term *patêr* 7 times, which underline the basic theme of the discourse, namely, the unity of the Son with the Father.

The parallelisms and correspondences between the parallel elements (A A', B B', C C', D D'), between the extreme and the central elements (A D D', D D'A'), and between the alternating elements (A C, D'B', C'A') and the underlying theme of the intimate relation between Jesus, the Son, and God, the Father, indicate the interconnections between the different elements in a Johannine chiasmus [117].

A chiastic pattern may be noted also in other Johannine pericopes. For instance, the first sign at Cana (2,1-11) seems to be chiastically constructed (A B C C'B'A'), for *en Kana tês Galilaias* and *hoi mathêtai autou* are found only in the verses that begin (vv.1-2) and end (v.11) the pericope, that is, only in A and A'; the word *oinos* occurs only in v.3 (twice) and vv.9-10 (thrice), that is, only in B (vv.3-4) and B' (vv.9-10); and the advice of the mother of Jesus to the servants (*ho ti an legê[i] hymin poiêsate*: v.5) corresponds to the exact execution of Jesus' commands by the servants (*gemisate... egemisan* and *pherete... ênenkan*: vv.7-8), that is to say, C (v.5) may be taken to be somewhat parallel to C' (vv.6-8) [118].

---

[117] This phenomenon is present also in the chiastic arrangement of the sections of the Gospel of John (see 4.3 below).

[118] It is true that the terms used in v.4 and v.7 are not identical but the underlying idea is the same, since the following of Jesus' concrete commands ("Fill the jars with water" and "now draw some out and take it to the steward") is implicitly contained in Mary's general advice to the servants ("Do whatever he tells you"). Therefore v.4 (C) may be regarded as parallel to vv.6-8 (C'). Here N. W. LUND's observation about the different kinds of inversions found in various types of chiasms may be cited: "We observe that there are inversions of *identical terms* (cf. Mk 2:27), but more often of *similar ideas* (cf. Ps 51:7), and not infrequently the inversion consists in the proper arrangement of *nouns* and *verbs* in couplets (cf. Ps 20:2-5)" (*op. cit.*, 32).

3.323 *Chiasmus in a section*

We shall see later that not only some verses and pericopes but four of the five sections of the Fourth Gospel (Jn 2-4; 5-10; 13-17; 18-20) are constructed chiastically [119].

3.33 Concentric Structure

This is a structural pattern which is somewhat similar to the chiastic structure we have discussed above [120]. Both involve inversion of parallel elements, but, while in a chiasmus every element in the first panel has a corresponding inverted element in the second panel (e.g. A B // B'A'), in a concentric structure the parallel elements are arranged around a common centre (e.g. A B C B'A') [120a]. Like chiasmus, concentric structure is also quite common in the Bible [121]. A single sentence or (part of) a pericope may be structured concentrically in Jn.

3.331 *Concentric structure in a single sentence*

A simple Johannine example is found in 3,13:

A   *kai oudeis*
  B   **anabebêken**
    C   *eis ton ouranon*
      D   *ei mê ho*
    C'   *ek tou ouranou*
  B'   **katabas**
A'   *ho hyios tou anthrôpou.*

Note that A and A' are connected through the central element D (*"no one... except... the Son of Man"*). B (**anabebêken**) corresponds to B' (**katabas**), and C (*eis ton ouranon*) is parallel to C' (*ek tou ouranou*).

---

[119] See 4.3 below.

[120] In fact, many authors do not distinguish between them and both are often called chiasms (cf. the authors cited in 3.32 above).

[120a] Such a structure *"constructed symmetrically about a central idea"* is called chiasmus by J. BRECK ("Biblical Chiasmus: Exploring Structure for Meaning", *BTB* 17 [1987] 71). But since it has a *"centre"*, it is better to call it *"concentric structure"*.

[121] Many of the Biblical examples of chiasmus given by the authors mentioned in n. 109 are, strictly speaking, examples of concentric structure. For example, N. W. LUND gives Col 3,3.4 and Mt 9,17 as examples of chiasmus with "a *single* line at the centre" and remarks: "But there are many such examples in the Old Testament" (*op. cit.*, 35).

Some OT examples with "a single central line" given by LUND are: Amos 5,4b-6a (A B C *D* C'B'A') (p. 42), Num 15,35-36 (A B C D *E* D' C' B' A') (p. 42), Is 28,15-18 (A B C *D* C'B'A') (p. 45).

For more of such examples from the OT, see "Chiasmus in Hebrew Biblical Narrative" by Y. T. RADDAY, and "Chiastic Patterns in Biblical Hebrew Poetry" by W. G. E. WATSON, in: J. W. WELCH (ed.), *op. cit.*, 50-117 and 118-68 respectively.

3.332 *Concentric structure in part of a pericope*

Not only a single verse but also part of a pericope may have a concentric structure in the Fourth Gospel. For instance, 6,35-42 is concentrically constructed [122]:

A 35a : *EIPEN* autois ho Iêsous:
    b : ***EGÔ EIMI HO ARTOS*** tês zôês;

  B 35c : *ho erchomenos pros eme ou mê peinasê[i]*
      d : kai **ho pisteuôn eis eme** *ou mê dipsêsei pôpote*.
    36ab: all' eipon hymin hoti kai *heôrakate [me]*
      c : kai ou **pisteuete**.

    C 37ab: **pan ho didôsin moi** ho patêr pros eme hêxei,
        c : kai ton erchomenon pros eme *ou mê ekbalô exô*,

      D 38a: hoti **katabebêka apo tou ouranou**
          b: ouch hina poiô to thelêma to emon
          alla to thelêma tou pempsantos me.

    C' 39a : touto de estin to thelêma tou pempsantos me,
        bc: hina **pan ho dedôken moi** mê apolesô ex autou
        d : alla anastêsô auto [en] tê[i] eschatê[i] hêmera[i].

  B' 40a : touto gar estin to thelêma tou patros mou,
      b : hina pas *ho theôrôn ton hyion*
        kai **pisteuôn eis auton** eche[i] *zôên aiônion*,
      c : kai anastêsô auton egô [en] tê[i] eschatê[i] hêmera[i].

A' 41ab: egongyzon oun hoi Ioudaioi peri autou hoti *EIPEN*:
    c : ***EGÔ EIMI HO ARTOS*** ho **katabas ek tou ouranou**,
  42ab: kai elegon: ouch houtos estin Iêsous ho hyios Iôsêph,
    c : hou hêmeis oidamen ton patera kai tên mêtera?
    de: pôs nyn *LEGEI* hoti **ek tou ouranou katabebêka**?

It must be observed that A' is not only parallel to A and forms a double inclusion with A (*EIPEN*... ***EGÔ EIMI HO ARTOS***: vv.35ab.41) but also combines Jesus' revelatory statement in A (***EGÔ EIMI HO ARTOS***...: v.35b) with that in the central unit D (**katabebêka apo tou ouranou**: v.38a). Thus in A' we have ***EGÔ EIMI HO ARTOS* ho katabas ek tou ouranou** (v.41c), which is a combination of A and D. This shows the importance of the central and extreme elements and their interconnection in a concentric structure.

Note also that B' is clearly parallel to B, since both speak about "seeing" the Son (vv.36b.40b) and "believing" in him (vv.35d.36c.40b) and since *echê[i] zôên aiônion* (v.40b) of B' may be regarded as equivalent to *ou mê peinasê[i]* and

---

[122] Cf. X. LÉON-DUFOUR, *art. cit.*, 249-55. According to him the central verse is v.38 (cf. p. 252), but note that he leaves out v.35 from the structure he proposes: "Le v.35 semble n'avoir pas de rapport littéraure avec les vv.36-40" (p. 252).

ou mê dipsêsei pôpote (v.35cd) of B. Again, C' is parallel to C, since **pan ho didôsin moi** (v.37a) of C is surely intended to be parallel to **pan ho dedôken moi** (v.39b) of C', and since *ou mê ekbalô exô* (v.37c) of C corresponds to *mê apolesô ex autou* (v.39c) of C'.

We must also note the interconnectedness between the various units, besides the ones we have seen above, of the concentric structure of 6,35-42. Thus the expression *ho erchomenos pros eme* (vv.35c.37c) is common to B and C. Again, *to thelêma* (vv.38b.39a.40a) is found in D, C' and B'. In fact, *to thelêma tou pempsantos me* (vv.38b.39a) in D and C' is a "hook-phrase" that links D and C'. Notice also that C' and B' begin with an almost identical clause: *touto... estin to thelêma... hina...* (vv.39ab.40ab) and end with *alla/kai anastêsô auto/n (egô) [en] tê[i] eschatê[i] hêmera[i]* (vv.39d.40c).

The above-mentioned inclusions, parallelisms and interconnections indicate how well-constructed the concentric structure of 6,35-42 is [123].

3.34 Spiral Structure

Many authors affirm that the Johannine development of thought is not linear but spiral. For instance, R. Kysar says: "Far from a straightforward linear argument, the evangelist's thought seems to move in circles (more optimistically, spirals), doubling back upon itself" [124]. A spiral structure may be compared also to a winding staircase, climbing which one goes round and round, on the one hand, but higher and higher, on the other [125].

A whole pericope may be spirally constructed. For example, the Prologue (1,1-18) seems to have a spiral structure, which may be represented as a*b*c* b**c**:

---

[123] Other examples of concentric structure are 15,1-8 (A = 1-2; B = 3-4a; C = 4bcd; D = 5; C' = 6; B' = 7; A' = 8) and 17,1-5 (A = 1-2; B = 3; A' = 4-5).

According to J. KAMMERSTÄTTER, every pericope in the Fourth Gospel has a (con)centric structure constructed around a central sentence (*op. cit.*, 56), which, as we have seen above (2.[13]), is an exaggeration.

[124] R. KYSAR, *The Fourth Evangelist and His Gospel* (Minneapolis 1975) 176. Cf. also SCHNACKENBURG, II, 65.

[125] I. DE LA POTTERIE compares the Johannine manner of composition to a spiral or to an advancing wave in the sea ("L'evangelo di san Giovanni", in: *Introduzione al Nuovo Testamento*, ed. G. Rinaldi & P. Benedetti (Brescia 1971) 894.

Cf. also H. CLAVIER, "La structure du quatrième évangile", *RHPR* 35 (1955) 178; H. BECKER, *Die Reden des Johev. und der Stil der gnostischen Offenbarungsrede*, ed. R. Bultmann, (Göttingen 1956), calls the Johannine development of thought a "spiralige Entwicklung von Gedanken" (p. 55).

Spiral development is not an exclusive characteristic of the Gospel of John; it is found also in the Epistle of John, for R. LAW states:

> The word that, to my mind, might best describe St. John's mode of thinking and writing in his Epistle is "*spiral*".
> The course of thought does not move from point to point in a straight line. It is like a *winding staircase* always revolving around the same centre, always recurring to the same topics, but at a higher level (*The Tests of Life. A Study of the First Letter of St. John* [Edinburgh 1909] 5) [my italics].

a*   (1,1-5)   : The divine, creative, revelatory Word
   b*   (1,6-8)   : The Baptist's mission of testimony to the revelatory Word
      c*   (1,9-14) : The revelatory, regenerative, incarnate Word
   b** (1,15)   : The Baptist's testimony to the divine, incarnate Word
      c** (1,16-18): The incarnate, revelatory, divine Word.

Note that b* (1,6-8: "the Baptist's mission of testimony to the revelatory Word") is parallel to b** (1,15: "the Baptist's testimony to the incarnate Word") (cf. *Iôannês*: vv.6.15; *martyrein*: vv.7.8.15); similarly c* (1,9-14: "the revelatory, regenerative, incarnate Word") and c** (1,16-18: "the incarnate, revelatory, divine Word") are parallel to each other (cf. *lambanein*: vv.12.16; *didômi*: vv.12.17; *monogenês*: vv.14.18; *patêr*: vv.14.18; *plêrês/plêrôma*: vv.14.16; *charis kai alêtheia*: vv.14.17; cf. also *charis* in v.16).

The spiral development of the Prologue becomes evident if we study the subdivisions of a*, c*, c** and their interconnections.

THE SPIRAL STRUCTURE OF THE PROLOGUE (1,1-18)

a*   (1,1-5) : The Divine, Creative, Revelatory Word

a   (1-2)   : The divine Word with God
   b   (3ab)   : The mediation of the divine Word in creation
      c   (3c-5) : The life-giving, revelatory Word opposed

b*   (1,6-8) : The Baptist's Mission of Testimony to the Revelatory Word

c*   (1,9-14) : The Revelatory, Regenerative, Incarnate Word

   c'   (9-11) : The revelatory Word rejected
      d   (12-13) : The mediation of the revelatory Word in regeneration
         e   (14)   : The incarnate, revelatory Word contemplated

b (1,15) : The Baptist's Testimony to the Divine, Incarnate Word**

c (1,16-18): The Incarnate, Revelatory, Divine Word**

            e'   (16)   : The incarnate, revelatory Word participated
               f   (17)   : The mediation of Jesus Christ in revelation
                  g   (18)   : The only divine revealer of God [126].

---

[126] "The Spiral Structure of the Prologue" given in the text is somewhat similar to the "schema della struttura" of Jn 1,1-18 (in three parts) as proposed by S. A. PANIMOLLE (*Il Dono della Legge e la Grazia della Verità* [Gv 1,17] [Roma 1973] 96), which is given below:

I parte (vv.1-5): Il Verbo e la sua opera rivelatrice:
A) (vv.1s): il Logos nella sua vita divina prima della creazione;
B) (v.3): La mediazione del Verbo nella creazione;
C) (vv.4s): L'azione rivelatrice del Logos fonte di vita e luce.

II parte (vv.6-14): La incarnazione del Verbo Rivelatore:
AI) (vv.6-8): La testimonianza di Giovanni Battista alla Luce;
C') (vv.9ss): La rivelazione cosmica e storica della Luce;
D) (vv.12s): Il dono riservato a chi accoglie la Rivelazione del Logos;
A') (v.14): La incarnazione del Verbo Rivelatore.

Note that the theme of the opposition to the revelation mentioned in the last subunit of a* (c: "the life-giving, revelatory Word opposed") is taken up and deepened in the first subunit of c* (c': "the revelatory Word rejected") through the concatenation of three terms (*phôs*: vv.4.5.9; *anthrôpos*: vv.4.9; *ou katelaben*: v.5 and *ou parelabon*: v.11). Similarly, the theme of the incarnate Word's "fullness of grace and truth" mentioned for the first time in the last subunit of c* (e: *plêrês charitos kai alêtheias*: v.14) is resumed and developed in the first two subunits of c** (e': *plêrôma*: v.16; f: *hê charis kai hê alêtheia*: v.17). Thus there is not only parallelism but also dynamic progression between c (vv.3c-5) and c' (vv.9-11). Likewise, there is both parallelism and progression between e (v.14) and e' (v.16), since whereas "the incarnate, revelatory Word" is "contemplated" by the contemporary eye-witnesses in e (*kai etheasametha tên doxan autou... plêrês charitos kai alêtheias*: v.14c), his fullness is shared by all the believers in e' (*hoti ek tou plêrômatos autou hêmeis pantes elabomen*: (v.16).

It must also be observed that the central subunits of a*, c* and c** deal with the triple **mediation** of the Word in **creation** (b: *panta di' autou egeneto...*: v.3), **divine regeneration** (d: *edôken autois exousian tekna theou genesthai... ek theou egennêthêsan*: vv.12-13) and **revelation** (f: *hê charis kai hê alêtheia dia Iêsou Christou egeneto*: v.17) respectively.

At times two neighbouring pericopes, which at first sight appear to be parallel, are on closer examination found to have a spiral relationship. For instance, 1,35-42 and 1,43-51, both of which describe the disciples' discovery of the Messiah, are globally parallel to each other (like the panels of a diptych) but have internal structures which may be spirally represented as b c d e and c'd'e'f respectively:

```
b    (1,35-37+)  : the Baptist's testimony to Jesus
  c   (1,37-39)  : the call of the first two disciples
    d  (1,40-42a) : Andrew's proclamation of the Messianic discovery to Simon
      e (1,42)     : the encounter of Simon Peter with Jesus
  c'  (1,43-44)  : the call of Philip
    d' (1,45-46)  : Philip's proclamation of the Messianic discovery to Nathanael
      e' (1,47-50)  : the encounter of Nathanael with Jesus
        f (1,51)     : Jesus' promise of a future revelatory vision.
```

III parte (vv.15-18): Il dono della Rivelazione escatologica totale:
AI') (v.15): La testimonianza di Giovanni Battista al Logos Incarnato;
D') (v.16): La nuova "grazia" (*charis*) del Verbo Rivelatore;
B') (v.17): La mediazione di Gesù nella Rivelazione escatologica;
A'') (v.18): Gesù l'unico Rivelatore perfetto, perché Unigenito di Dio.
    Cf. *ibid.*, 7-85 for other structures of the Prologue and their evaluation by PANIMOLLE.

Now it is indisputable that d (1,40-42a) is parallel to d' (1,45-46) because of the many parallel elements in those subunits:

1,41: **heuriskei** houtos... Simôna
 kai legei autô[i]: **heurêkamen**...
1,45: **heuriskei** Philippos ton Nathanaêl
 kai legei autô[i]: ... **heurêkamen**...

Similarly, c (1,37-39) is parallel to c' (1,43-44) because both speak about "following Jesus" (*êkolouthêsan tô[i] Iêsou*: 1,37; cf. also 1,38; *akolouthei moi*: 1,43).

Likewise e (1,42) is parallel to e' (1,47-50), since both begin by describing how Jesus looks at (sees) the person coming to him and makes a revelatory statement about him:

1,42: êgagen auton *pros* **ton Iêsoun**
 emblepsas autô[i] **ho Iêsous** *eipen*: sy ei Simôn...
1,47: *eiden* **ho Iêsous** ton Nathanaêl erchomenon *pros* **auton**
 kai *eipen* peri autou: ide alêthôs Israêlitês...

Observe that just as b (1,35-37: the Baptist's testimony to Jesus) has no parallel in 1,43-51, so f (1,51: Jesus' promise of a future revelatory vision) has no parallel in 1,35-42. In other words, there is a spiral progression from b c d e to c'd'e'f.

3.3z The Fourth Evangelist has used at least **four** different (Biblical) **structural patterns** (parallelism, chiasmus, concentric structure and spiral structure) in the construction of several sentences and pericopes or parts thereof. This points to the probability that the Fourth Gospel as a whole may have a definite, detectable structure.

3z We may now conclude this chapter on the criteria to be used to discover the structure of the Fourth Gospel by summarizing the results of our investigation. We have examined *three* **different kinds of criteria** (literary criteria, dramatic techniques and structural patterns). We have found a *dozen* **literary criteria** (introductions, conclusions, inclusions, characteristic vocabulary, geographical and chronological indications, liturgical feasts, transitions, bridge-passages, hook-words, techniques of repetition of the same terms or formulae or type-scene or similar sayings or discourses of Jesus, change of literary genres such as narrative, dialogue, discourse). Besides, we have discovered a *dozen* **dramatic techniques** (introduction of dramatis personae, change of dramatis personae or scenes, techniques of diptych-scenes or alternating scenes or seven scenes, techniques of double-stage action or stage-duality or vanishing characters, sequence of action-dialogue-discourse, dramatic development of the plot and dramatic pattern). We have also detected *four* **structural patterns** (parallelism, chiasmus, concentric structure, and spiral structure) based on the principles of repetition and balance, which govern the construction of many Johannine units. In short, we have given above not only a large number (about 30) but also a great variety of criteria in order to establish the structure of the Johannine Gospel.

It must be remembered, however, that all these criteria are not of equal importance or value for determining the structure of the Gospel as a whole or that of a unit. For example, inclusions play a greater role in the delimitation and division of the structure of a literary unit than do hook-words.

It must also be noted that all the criteria cannot be applied equally, everywhere in the Fourth Gospel. For instance, the geographical and chronological indications are more frequent in narratives than in discourses.

Furthermore, while some of the criteria may be connected with one another (e.g. introductions, conclusions and inclusions), others exclude one another (e.g. if a particular pericope has a chiastic structure, it cannot have a spiral or concentric structure).

Finally, we do not claim to have discovered *all* the criteria used (consciously or unconsciously) by the Fourth Evangelist in structuring his Gospel, but we believe that we have found enough (all of them based on the text of the Gospel) to be able to detect objectively the structure of the Johannine Gospel.

4
THE LITERARY STRUCTURE OF THE FOURTH GOSPEL

In the second chapter we examined the variety of structures proposed for the Fourth Gospel and arrived at the conclusion that one of the reasons for the wide divergence in the proposed structures was the dependence of scholars on a single criterion or a very restricted number of criteria. Therefore in the last chapter we examined a large number of criteria (about 30) belonging to three different categories (namely, literary, dramatic and structural). In this chapter we shall apply these criteria so as to determine the literary structure of the Fourth Gospel. It must be recalled that all the criteria studied in the third chapter are not of the same value and cannot be applied to all the parts of the Johannine Gospel. Whenever possible, we shall look for the convergence of different kinds of criteria. This will guarantee a greater objectivity and certainty for the structure we propose than if we were to rely on a single criterion.

We shall study the structure of the Gospel in three stages: 1) we shall examine its *main divisions*; 2) we shall divide these principal component parts into *sections*; 3) we shall establish the *structure of these sections* by subdividing them into subsections and comparing them with one another. Then in the conclusion we shall present the *whole structure schematically*.

4.1 THE MAIN DIVISIONS OF THE FOURTH GOSPEL

Initially we shall examine the *introduction* and the *conclusion*, and then establish the *two principal parts* of the body of the Gospel. Finally we shall briefly look at the appendix.

4.11 The Introduction and the Conclusion

It is important to start the structural study of a literary work by analyzing its introduction and conclusion, since they may afford us a proper perspective to the author's purpose and invaluable clues to his plan of the book.

Since the Evangelist has stated his purpose in the last two verses of Jn 20 (which look like his *conclusion*), we shall start our investigation there. (We begin with the conclusion also because it is easier to establish its limits than those of the introduction.)

4.111 *The conclusion*

In order to determine whether 20,30-31 is the general conclusion to the Fourth Gospel as a whole, we shall first examine its literary unity and structure and then its function in the Gospel.

First of all, 20,30-31 has a literary unity of its own, since v.30 is linked to v.31 by means of *men oun... de*. Not only are the opening words of the two verses (*polla men oun kai alla...* and *tauta de*) contrasted with each other but also the negative çlause (*ha ouk estin gegrammena...*) at the end of v.30 is opposed to the positive proposition (*tauta de gegraptai*) at the beginning of v.31. Note that *gegrammena* and *gegraptai* may be regarded as hook-words which bind the two contrasting verses together. Furthermore, the phrase *en tô[i] bibliô[i] toutô[i]*, which follows *gegrammena*, is to be understood after *gegraptai*. In other words, *tauta de gegraptai* really stands for *tauta de gegraptai en tô[i] bibliô[i] toutô[i]* (see the structure of 20,30-31 given below). Similarly, the *hoti*-clause after *pistueu[s]ête* is to be understood after *pisteuontes*. We may also note that the name *Iêsous* occurs once each in v.30 and in v.31 (cf. also *autou* in *en tô[i] onomati autou* at the end of v.31), which underlines the importance of Jesus in these two verses. In fact, the first verse tells us what Jesus did (*polla men oun kai alla sêmeia epoiêsen ho Iêsous*) and the second who Jesus is (*Iêsous estin ho Christos ho hyios tou theou*). In the light of the link between "signs" and revelation, this implies that the "signs" that he "did" before the disciples revealed to them his identity as "the Christ" and "the Son of God". And the Fourth Gospel is written that the readers may believe in this Jesus who is the Messiah and the divine Son of God, and through this faith (*pisteuontes*) "may have life in his name" (*kai hina pisteuontes zôên echête en tô[i] onomati autou*). Thus from the point of view both of its literary structure and of its content, it is evident that vv.30-31 form a small compact Christocentric unit.

The literary unity of this small pericope is confirmed by its carefully constructed structure, for, although grammatically the two verses consist of two complex sentences, structurally they may be represented as follows:

```
Az  a   Polla men oun kai alla sêmeia epoiêsen ho Iêsous
        enôpion tôn mathêtôn [autou],
    b   ha ouk estin gegrammena en tô[i] bibliô[i] toutô[i];
Bz  b'  tauta de gegraptai      ["  "  "  "  "  "  "]
    c   hina pisteu[s]ête       hoti Iêsous estin ho Christos
                                     ho hyios tou theou,
Cz  c'  kai hina pisteuontes    ["  "  "  "  "  "  "  "  "]
    d   z ô ê n  echête         en tô[i] onomati autou.
```

Notice that Az, Bz and Cz contain two structural elements each (Az = **a b**; Bz = **b' c**; Cz = **c' d**) and that **b** is linked to **b'** through the hook-word (*gegrammena/gegraptai*) and **c** is connected to **c'** by means of another hook-word (*pisteuein*). Az (v.30) tells us the limits of the Gospel, since it says that only a small number of Jesus' signs has been included in the book. Bz (v.31abc) states the immediate Christological purpose of writing the Gospel ("that [*hina*] you may believe that Jesus is the Christ, the Son of God"). Cz (v.31d) reveals the ultimate soteriological purpose ("and that [*hina*] believing you may have life in his name"). In short, the literary structure of 20,30-31 underscores its *Christocentric* character.

Besides having a literary structural unity, 20,30-31 is also clearly separated from the following episode of the risen Jesus' appearance to the seven disciples at the Sea of Tiberias (21,1-14), since this episode begins with the literary-chronological device *meta tauta* (21,1) which signals a new beginning (cf. 3,22; 5,1; 6,1; 7,1)[1].

Jn 20,30-31 is distinguished not only from the following episode but also from the immediately preceding pericope on the risen Jesus' appearance to Thomas (20,26-29), which ends with the Johannine beatitude: "Blessed are those who have not seen and yet have believed" (20,29). Although the name of Jesus and two of the terms of 20,30-31 occur also in 20,26-29 (*Iēsous*: 20,26.29.30.31; *hoi mathētai autou*: 20,26.30; *pisteuein*: 20,29.29.31.31), a number of Johannine expressions found in 20,30-31 (*sēmeion poiein*: 20,30; *ho Christos*: 20,31; *ho hyios tou theou*: 20,31; *zōēn echein*: 20,31)[2] do not appear in 20,26-29. This means that, although there is some link between the two adjacent pericopes, they are distinct from one another.

Now that we have established the limits and the literary unity of the pericope (20,30-31), we must examine its function in relation to the rest of the Gospel. In other words, is 20,30-31 the conclusion to the Gospel as a whole[3] or only to a part thereof?

Most Johannine commentators take 20,30-31 to be the conclusion to the whole Gospel[4]. A few, however, understand it to be the conclusion of the second part of the Gospel (Jn 13-20) or only of Jn 20. For instance, R. E. Brown writes concerning the function of 20,30-31:

> This conclusion at the end of the Book of Glory is meant to match the conclusion at the end of the Book of Signs (xii 37...). There the writer was concerned with the fact that Jesus had performed so many signs before "the Jews", and yet they refused to believe in him. Here he is concerned with the signs performed before his disciples which lead to faith in Jesus as the Messiah, the Son of God[5].

But this parallelism between 12,37 and 20,30-31 does not exclude the latter from being the general conclusion to the Gospel as a whole, since it occurs at the

---

[1] See 3.161.
[2] See 5.13; 5.11; 5.12; 5.16 below.
[3] See 3.111.
[4] So BECKER, II, 632; BERNARD, II, 685; BULTMANN, 697-99; DE BOOR, II, 248-50; LINDARS, 616-18; MARSH, 649; SANDERS & MASTIN, 438-39; SCHNACKENBURG, III, 335-40; SCHULZ, 247-48; SEGALLA, 473; WESTCOTT, 297-98.
[5] BROWN, II, 1058.

end of the book (*en tô[i] bibliô[i] toutô[i]*: 20,30) and since it explicitly mentions many of the Johannine terms employed in the introduction [6].

E. Hoskyns and P. S. Minear maintain that 20,30-31 is the conclusion not of the whole Gospel but only of Jn 20 [7].

Hoskyns gives an *a priori* argument about how the Gospel must end, for he says:

> But a Christian gospel ends properly, not with the appearance of the risen Lord to His disciples, and their belief in Him, but with a confident statement that this mission to the world, undertaken at His command and under His authority, will be the means by which many are saved [8].

Hoskyns appeals also to the ending of Matthew, which describes the commissioning of the disciples and the promise of the permanent presence of Jesus with them (Mt 28,20), and to the longer ending of Mark which mentions the mission of the disciples (Mk 16,20), and concludes that Jn 21, which narrates symbolically the mission of the Church, must be the conclusion of the Gospel of John [9].

First of all, it is not necessary that the Johannine Gospel must have a conclusion similar to that of the Synoptic Gospels, especially since both its introduction and its development (contrast, for instance, the many journeys of the Johannine Jesus to Jerusalem with the single journey of the Synoptic Jesus to the holy city) are quite different from those of the Synoptic Gospels. Secondly, the disciples are commissioned in 20,21: "As the Father has sent me, even so I send you", which is somewhat similar to Mt 28,20. Finally, after the beatitude of those who believe without seeing (20,29) one would not expect the Evangelist to narrate other appearances of the risen Jesus [9a]. Hence we do not see the validity of Hoskyns' view that Jn 21, and not 20,30-31, must be the conclusion of the Gospel of John.

P. S. Minear is another advocate of "the theses that in the original design of the [Johannine] gospel the last two verses of chapter 20 served only as the

---

[6] See 3.111 and 3.131. In fact, BROWN himself admits the above position as probable:
> In xx 30-31 John probably does not mean to exclude the signs described in chs. i-xii (especially a sign such as the first Cana miracle which was performed before his disciples that they might believe in him [ii 11], but he must mean also to include the appearances to the disciples in xx 1-28 that led them to confess Jesus as Lord (II, 1058).

[7] HOSKYNS, 549-50; P. S. MINEAR, "The Original Functions of John 21", *JBL* 102 (1983) 85-98, especially 87-90 and 98. K. H. RENGSTORF, on the other hand, holds exactly the opposite view, namely, the "signs" in 20,30 do not at all refer to the appearances of the risen Jesus but only to the signs described in Jn 2-12 (*TDNT*, VII, 254-55). LAGRANGE suggests that originally 20,30-31 stood after 21,23 but was moved to its present place by the disciples of the Evangelist, when they added 21,24-25 (p. 520). But since there is no manuscript evidence for this view, we do not discuss it.

[8] HOSKYNS, 550.

[9] *Ibid.*

[9a] BROWN, II, 1078.

conclusion of that chapter and that the last chapter served as the conclusion of the entire document"[10]. He advances the following arguments in defence of his first thesis, namely, 20,30-31 is the conclusion only of Jn 20: 1) Jn 20,30-31 is "very closely linked to verse 29, in which the central motif is that of seeing and believing. The Evangelist has drawn a sharp contrast here between Thomas who believed because of seeing, and those later disciples, who would believe without seeing"[11]. 2) Jn 20,30-31 speaks about the signs done "in the presence of the disciples". This must refer "to the four episodes in chapter 20", where the disciples are present, but "not true of many of the earlier signs"[12]. 3) The "signs" mentioned in 20,30-31 could not refer to "the earlier signs" (that is, those during Jesus' public ministry), since they did not produce "perfect faith"[13].

Now we shall briefly answer the three difficulties. 1) Though 20,30-31 is connected to 20,29 because both passages insist on "believing", yet, unlike 20,29, there is no contrast between seeing and believing in 20,30-31. 2) The disciples may be said to be present at all the four episodes of Jn 20, if we include Mary Magdalene among the disciples (since it is to her that the risen Jesus appears in 20,11-18). However, it is not true to the Johannine account of the signs to affirm that the disciples were not present during "many of the earlier signs", for the disciples are explicitly mentioned in five (2,1-11; 6,1-15.16-21; 9,1-41; 11,1-54) of the seven miracles narrated in Jn 2-20. They are presumed to be present in the others too (4,46-54; 5,1-47), since they are with Jesus from the beginning (1,35-51; 2,2.11), continue to accompany him (2,12.17.22; 3,22; 4,2.8.27. 31-38; 6,3., etc.) and Jesus himself tells them during the Last Supper that they would be his witnesses "because you have been with me from the beginning" (*hoti ap' archês met' emou este*: 15,27)[14]. 3) If by "perfect faith" is meant the Christian faith in Jesus' divinity (as in Thomas' confession: "My Lord and my God": 20,28), then the "signs" during Jesus' earthly ministry did not and could not produce such "perfect faith", for even the disciples understood the deeper meaning of Jesus' deeds and words only after the resurrection (cf. 2,22; 12,16) under the guidance of the Holy Spirit (14,26; 16,12-15)[15]. But already during Jesus' public ministry the signs helped the disciples and others to believe in him as the Messiah (cf. 2,11; 4,54; 6,14; 7,31; 11,27.45.47.48). Furthermore, if the "signs" in 20,30 were intended to refer only to the resurrection appearances

---

[10] P. S. MINEAR, *art. cit.*, 98.
[11] *Ibid.*, 87.
[12] *Ibid.*, 88.
[13] *Ibid.*, 89-90.
[14] There may be a structural-theological reason why the disciples are not explicitly said to be present during the healing of the official's son (4,46-54) and the cripple (5,1-47) (see 4.3 below).
[15] Cf. W. NICOL, *The Sêmeia in the Fourth Gospel* (Leiden 1972) 129: "the meaning of all the miracles is not limited to what would have been obvious during the life of Jesus, but their full meaning can be grasped in the light of the fact that Jesus is glorified and therefore present, in the light of the Paraclete".

recounted in Jn 20, the Evangelist would have made it clear by stating, for instance, that Jesus did many other signs "after he was raised from the dead" (*egertheis ek nekrôn*) as at 21,14. Moreover, Minear's position is directly opposed to the views of some Johannine source critics like R. T. Fortna who regard 20,30-31 to have been originally the conclusion of the Signs Source or "the Gospel of Signs"[16]. Because of the reasons stated here we hold that the "signs" in 20,30 do not refer only to the resurrection appearances but also to all the signs of Jesus, for "the concept of *sêmeion* is *widened* to include the appearances"[17], and therefore the earlier "signs" are not excluded from the *sêmeia* of 20,30.

Now we may examine Minear's second thesis "that the last chapter [Jn 21] served as the conclusion to the entire document"[17a]. He finds the following three functions of Jn 21 in defence of his thesis: (1) "only in chapter 21 do we find an adequate end to the story of the two disciples who, from chapter 13 on, have played the most conspicuous supporting roles in the gospel: Simon Peter and the beloved disciple"[17b]; (2) "the chapter expresses a strong and continuing interest in the disciples of the second generation"[17c]; (3) a third function of Jn 21 is "to make clear to readers the relationship of the Evangelist to the beloved disciple"[17d].

It may be granted that these arguments contain an element of truth and that these might have been the reasons why the redactor added Jn 21 after the original conclusion of the Gospel (20,30-31), but these functions of Jn 21 do not prove that it was placed here by the Evangelist himself and intended to be the conclusion.

Regarding reason (1), it must be remarked that the Evangelist's primary interest in writing the Gospel was to emphasize Christological and soteriological motifs (cf. the Christocentric statement of purpose in 20,30-31) and not to present stories of the individual figures like Simon Peter or the Beloved Disciple. Secondly, Minear's view that Jn 21 is needed "to provide an edifying end to the story of these two men"[17e], is not quite true, since such "an edifying end" is already given in 20,1-10, where Simon Peter and the Beloved Disciple are described as running to the tomb of Jesus (evidently because both of them loved him).

---

[16] Cf. R. T. FORTNA, *The Gospel of Signs*, 197-99.

[17] W. NICOL, *op. cit.*, 115 [my italics]; cf. BROWN, II, 1058. See also 5.13 below. That the passion-resurrection is included in the extended meaning of *sêmeion* is indicated by Jesus' reply to the Jews who ask for a sign, for when they ask: *ti sêmeion deiknyeis hêmin?* (2,18), Jesus answers: *lysate ton naon touton kai en trisin hêmerais egerô auton* (2,19). And the Evangelist's remarks in 2,21-22 make the meaning of Jesus' reply quite clear.

[17a] P. S. MINEAR, *art. cit.*, 98.
[17b] *Ibid.*, 91.
[17c] *Ibid.*, 94.
[17d] *Ibid.*, 95.
[17e] *Ibid.*, 91.

Concerning the second argument (2), it may be said that not merely the Evangelist but even the redactor may reasonably be thought to have an "interest in the disciples of the second generation" and hence it is not a compelling argument for attributing to the Evangelist the addition of Jn 21 to the Gospel.

Regarding the third reason (3), it would seem that a redactor would be more interested in revealing the identity of the Evangelist than the Evangelist himself, since the latter has tried to remain anonymous in Jn 1-20.

Finally, there are a number of stylistic differences between Jn 21 and the rest of the Gospel, which suggest that chapter 21 was probably added by a redactor as an appendix or epilogue [17f].

In short, the arguments of neither Hoskyns nor Minear prove that Jn 21 was intended by the Evangelist as the conclusion to the original Gospel.

That 20,30-31 is the Christocentric conclusion of the entire Gospel follows from 1) the presence (already noted) of some important Johannine terms in 20,30-31 (*sēmeion, Christos, ho hyios tou theou, zôê*) which are not found in 20,1-29 but occur frequently in the rest of the Gospel [18], 2) the many inclusions between 20,30-31 and the beginning of the Gospel (1,1-2,11) [19], and 3) the convention in antiquity of having a general conclusion in Biblical and non-biblical writings [20].

This assertion that 20,30-31 is the Christocentric conclusion to the entire Gospel is confirmed by the configuration of the three constituent parts of this passage and their relative functions (which, we shall see later, correspond chiastically to the three parts of the introduction) [21]:

    Az (20,30) : Historical sign-conclusion
        Bz (20,31abc): Christological conclusion
            Cz (20,31d) : Soteriological conclusion.

4.11z Because of the reasons given above we conclude that the distinct literary unit formed by the last two verses of Jn 20 (vv.30-31) is the *Christocentric conclusion* of the Gospel as a *whole* and not merely of the second part or of Jn 20.

4.112 *The Introduction*

In the last chapter we arrived at the provisional conclusion that 1,1-2,11 forms an introduction to the Fourth Gospel [22]. But there is very little agreement among Johannine scholars on the extent of the introduction [23]. They may be broadly classified into the following groups: those who regard 1,1-18 as

---

[17f] See 4.15 below.
[18] See 3.111 above; see also 5.11; 5.12; 5.13 and 5.16 below.
[19] See 3.131.
[20] See 3.111. Cf. also BECKER, II, 632; BULTMANN, 697, n. 2.
[21] See 4.112 below for the structure of 1,1-2,11 (C*B*A+).
[22] See 3.121.
[23] See ch. 2.

the introduction/prologue to the whole Gospel[24], and those who take the whole of 1,1-51 as the general introduction[25]. There are also a few who consider 1,19-51 as an introduction to the first part of the Gospel (1,19-12,50)[26] or to the Gospel as a whole[27], and still others who propose 1,19-2,11(12) as an "introduction to the ministry" of Jesus[28] or as "a dramatic introduction to Jesus and his work" in the entire Gospel[29]. There are again others who understand 1,19-2,11(12) as the first major division of the Gospel (and not as an introduction)[30].

In short, the debate is about the extent of the introduction. Does 1,1-18 or 1,1-51 or 1,1-2,11(12) function as the introduction to the whole Gospel? Does 1,19-51 or 1,19-2,11(12) have an introductory role (if it has one) only for a part of the Gospel or for its entirety? Since the correct understanding of these Johannine passages and of the Gospel as a whole depends on the right answer to these questions, we shall look for a convergence of criteria for the delimitation of the introduction.

4.112,1 Jn 1,1-2,11 as the general introduction

First of all, the Fourth Gospel begins with the words *en archê[i]* (1,1; cf. Gen 1,1) which are repeated in the next verse (1,2), showing that they are emphasized by the Evangelist himself. The next time we find the term *archê* is at 2,11, that is, at the end of the sign of changing water into wine at Cana (2,1-11), which, in fact, is called not the "first sign" (*prôton sêmeion*) but the "beginning of the signs" (*archê tôn sêmeiôn*: 2,11). Now this *archê* could be understood as forming an inclusion with the *archê* at the beginning of the Prologue, or the *archê tôn sêmeiôn* could be thought of as the beginning of the first part of the Gospel. Since, on the one hand, many of Jesus' signs are narrated in Jn 2-12 (e.g. 4,46-54; 6,3-15; 11,1-45; cf. also the reference to the "many signs" of Jesus at 12,37), the mention of the "beginning of the signs" at 2,11 must indicate the beginning of "the Book of Jesus' Signs" (Jn 2-12)[31]. On the other hand, the Cana-sign (2,1-11) is connected to the preceding pericope (1,43-51) by means of the literary-chronological indication *tê[i] hêmera[i] tê[i] tritê[i]* (2,1) which is certainly linked to *tê[i] epaurion* at 1,43 (cf. also 1,29.35)[31a]. Since 1,19-34 is

---

[24] So BERNARD, BOISMARD, BROWN, CABA, DEEKS, DEFOURNEY, GOURGUES, GUILDING, KAMMERSTÄTTER, LOHMEYER, MOLLAT, PRETE, PUIGDOLLERS, RAU, SEGALLA, TENNEY, VAN DEN BUSSCHE, WEBSTER, WESTCOTT (see ch. 2 above).
[25] So DODD (see 2.[15]), PASQUETTO (see 2.[21]), WILLEMSE (see 2.[11]).
[26] So DE LA POTTERIE (see 2.[18]3), PRETE (see 2.[14]), VAN DEN BUSSCHE (see 2.[18]).
[27] So LOHMEYER ("Eingang": see 2.3), MATEOS & BARRETO ("Sección introductoria": see 2.6).
[28] So CABA (see 2.[19]); cf. also LIGHTFOOT, 11, 92-93.
[29] So CULPEPPER (see 2.[17]).
[30] So BOISMARD (see 2.7), DEFOURNEY (see 2.4), MOLLAT (see 2.21), PUIGDOLLERS (see 2.8).
[31] See 4.13 below.
[31a] See 3.162. These are some of the reasons why 2,1-11 must be regarded as a "bridge-pericope" (see 3.192 above and 4.12 below).

closely connected to the Prologue by means of the testimony of John the Baptist (*Iôannês*: 1,6.15.19.26.28.32.35.40; *martyria*: 1,7.19; *martyrein*: 1,7.8.15. 32.34), the whole of 1,1-2,11 must be considered as a literary unit. The connection between 2,1-11 and 1,1-18 is confirmed by the presence of some of the key Johannine terms, expressions and themes of 2,11 in 1,1-18 (e.g. *doxa*: 1,14.14; 2,11; *pisteuein eis*: 1,12; 2,11; the theme of revelation: *exêgêsato*: 1,18; *ephanerôsen*: 2,11; cf. also the inclusion formed by *archê* at 1,1 and 2,11)[32].

That 1,1-2,11 is intended by the Evangelist to be the Christocentric introduction to his Gospel can be seen from the correspondence between 1,1-2,11 and the Christocentric conclusion (20,30-31). We have seen above that all the major themes of 20,30-31 are found also in 1,1-2,11 (*sêmeion*: 2,11; 20,30; *hoi mathêtai autou*: 2,2.11; 20,30; *pisteuein*: 1,7.12.50; 2,11; 20,31.31; *Christos*: 1,20.25.41; 20,31; *ho hyios tou theou*: 1,34.49; 20,31; *zôê*: 1,4.4; 20,31; *to onoma autou*: 1,12; 20,31)[33]. These form many major inclusions between the beginning and end of the Gospel[34]. It may also be recalled that the name *Iêsous* is found 17 times in 1,1-2,11 (cf. also *Iêsous Christos* at 1,17) and twice in 20,30-31.

We may also note some other interesting, though minor, elements in 1,1-2,11 which correspond to those in 20,30-31. For instance, the same verb (in the aorist) *epoiêsen* is used in connection with Jesus' doing signs both in 2,11 and in 20,30. Again *graphein en* is found at 1,45 and 20,30 (cf. also 20,31). Finally, the confessional formulas *houtos estin ho hyios tou theou* at 1,34, *sy ei ho hyios tou theou* at 1,49 and *Iêsous estin... ho hyios tou theou* at 20,31 not only deal with the same Christological titles but also have the same form or construction (pronoun or noun as the subject + verb *einai* in the present tense + the complement). All these are clear literary indications that 1,1-2,11 corresponds to 20,30-31, and since the latter is the general conclusion, the former must be the general introduction to the Gospel of John as a whole[35].

But since many regard only part of 1,1-2,11 as the general introduction, we have to establish its main divisions and determine their nature and function.

4.112,2 Main divisions of 1,1-2,11

The main divisions of 1,1-2,11 can be readily detected by applying carefully the different criteria discussed in the last chapter.

First of all, the triple occurrence of *theos* in 1,1-2 and its double occurrence in 1,18 form an inclusion for the Prologue (1,1-18)[36]. This inclusion is strengthened by the correspondence between *kai ho logos ên pros ton theon* of

---

[32] See 3.132,1.
[33] See 3.121.
[34] See 3.131.
[35] This will be confirmed by the inverse parallelism (or chiastic relationship) between the threefold division of 20,30-31 (AzBzCz) and that of 1,1-2,11 (C*B*A+) (see below).
[36] See 3.132,7a.

1,1b and *monogenês theos ho ôn eis ton kolpon tou patros* of 1,18b, both of which emphasize the dynamic, personal, intimate relationship between the Logos/Jesus and God/the Father.

Similarly, the first Cana-sign is enclosed in a triple inclusion (*en Kana tês Galilaias*: 2,1.11; *ho Iêsous*: 2,2.11; *hoi mathêtai autou*: 2,2.11)[37].

The text (1,19-51) situated between the Prologue (1,1-18) and the first sign at Cana (2,1-11) forms another unit, since the four episodes described in it are connected by means of the same literary-chronological device *tê[i] epaurion* (1,29.35.43)[38].

The distinction between the three related units (1,1-18; 1,19-51; 2,1-11) is seen also from the change of their literary genres. Jn 1,1-18 is basically a hymn to the incarnate Logos (cf. 1,1.14) in which is inserted the testimony of John the Baptist to Jesus Christ (cf. 1,6-8.15: *martyria/martyrein*: vv.7.7.8.15). So 1,1-18 may be called "an hymnic-testimonial introduction"[39]. The next section (1,19-51) consists essentially of the testimony/kerygma of the Baptist (cf. *martyria/martyrein*: 1,19.32.34; the kerygmatic statements in 1,26-27.29.30.34.36) and that of the disciples (cf. 1,41: *heurêkamen ton Messian*; cf. also 1,45; 1,49: *rhabbi, sy ei ho hyios tou theou, sy basileus ei tou Israêl*). Hence 1,19-51 may be designated as "a testimonial-kerygmatic introduction". Jn 2,1-11 narrates an historical event, namely, Jesus' sign of changing water into wine at a wedding at Cana. Therefore it may be called "an historical sign-introduction", which is different from the literary genres of 1,1-18 and 1,19-51[40].

The definite geographical indication ("Cana of Galilee") at 2,1.11[41] and the change of scene in 2,1-11[42] (cf. the new characters: the mother of Jesus, the servants, the steward of the feast, and the bridegroom in the Cana-pericope) distinguish 2,1-11 from the preceding pericopes.

The literary-chronological indication *tê[i] hêmera[i] tê[i] tritê[i]* (2,1) at the beginning of 2,1-11 both links and distinguishes it from the previous episodes connected together by a different literary-chronological indication *tê[i] epaurion* (1,29.35.43)[43].

---

[37] See 3.132,7b.

[38] See 3.162.

[39] See 3.1[12]. From the dramatic point of view, it may be called a "Prologue" similar to the *prologos* of classical Greek tragedies. In fact, 5 of the 7 extant tragedies of AESCHYLUS, all the 7 (extant) tragedies of SOPHOCLES and all the 18 (extant) tragedies of EURIPIDES have a "prologue" (cf. C. DIANO, ed., *Il Teatro Greco: Tutte le Tragedie* [Firenze 1970]).

Some scholars call the Prologue (Jn 1,1-18) an "overture". For example, T. E. POLLARD explains:

> The Prologue provides a summary of the Gospel, or perhaps rather an *overture* in which the stage is set and the atmosphere created for the drama of the Gospel, and the main themes of the Gospel are announced (*Johannine Christology and the Early Church* [Cambridge 1970] 14).

[40] *Ibid.*

[41] See 3.15.

[42] See 3.21.

[43] See 3.162.

Furthermore, the characteristic vocabulary of 2,1-11 differs from that of the preceding pericopes (which we have discussed in detail in the last chapter)[44]. The vocabulary of the Prologue is also different from that of the following passages. For example, *ho logos* (1,1.1.1.14), *zôê* (1,4.4), *phôs* (1,4.5.7.8.8.9), *skotia* (1,5.5), *monogenês* (1,14.18), *plêrês/plêrôma* (1,14.16), *charis* (1,14.16.16.17) and *alêtheia* (1,14.17) do not occur at all in 1,19-51 and 2,1-11, whereas the Christological titles *ho Christos* (1,20.25.41), *ho amnos tou theou* (1,29.36), *ho hyios tou theou* (1,34.49), *rhabbi* (1,38.49), *basileus tou Israêl* (1,49) and *ho hyios tou anthrôpou* (1,51) are not found in 1,1-18 or 2,1-11.

4.112,2z Because of the above reasons the introduction (1,1-2,11) may be said to divide itself into three connected but distinct subunits, which may be called "hymnic-testimonial introduction" (1,1-18), "testimonial-kerygmatic introduction" (1,19-51) and "historical sign-introduction" (2,1-11) respectively. This triple division will be confirmed by its parallelism with the conclusion[45].

4.112,3 Chiastic parallelism between 1,1-2,11 and 20,30-31

It is interesting to note that the threefold division of the introduction (1,1-2,11) corresponds chiastically to the threefold division of the Christocentric conclusion (20,30-31):

   C* (1,1-18) : Hymnic-testimonial introduction
      B* (1,19-51) : Testimonial-kerygmatic introduction
         A+ (2,1-11) : Historical sign-introduction

         Az (20,30) : Historical sign-conclusion
      Bz (20,31abc) : Christological conclusion
   Cz (20,31d) : Soteriological conclusion.

Notice that 1) the "hymnic-testimonial introduction" C* (1,1-18) is parallel to the "soteriological conclusion" Cz (20,31d) (cf. *zôê*:1,4.4; 20,31d; *pisteuein*: 1,7.12; 20,31d; *to onoma autou*: 1,12; 20,31d), 2) the "testimonial-kerygmatic introduction" B* (1,19-51) corresponds to the "Christological conclusion" Bz (20,31abc) (cf. *pisteuein*: 1,50; 20,31b; *hoti houtos/Iêsous estin*: 1,34; 20,31c; *Christos*: 1,41; 20,31c; *ho hyios tou theou*: 1,34.49; 20,31c), 3) the "historical sign-introduction" A+ (2,1-11) parallels the "historical sign-conclusion" Az (20,30) (cf. *epoiêsen*: 2,11a; 20,30a; *sêmeia*: 2,11a; 20,30a; *ho Iêsous*: 2,11a; 20,30a; *hoi mathêtai autou*: 2,11c; 20,30a). Observe also the Christocentric nature of all the constituent parts of both the introduction and the conclusion (cf. the terms given above and their relation to the person and mission of Jesus). In short, the Christocentric introduction and conclusion are *chiastically* constructed in relation to each other (C*B*A+/AzBzCz).

---

[44] See 3.14.
[45] See 4.112,3 below.

4.112,4 Comparison with other positions

Now that we have established that 1,1-2,11 is a tripartite Christocentric introduction to the Fourth Gospel as a whole, we may briefly compare and contrast our position with the different opinions of the Johannine scholars mentioned at the beginning of our discussion (4.112)[46].

Those who propose that the Prologue (1,1-18) is separate from the rest of the Gospel have noted correctly its distinct vocabulary and its different literary genre (a hymn to the Logos)[47]. But they have not noticed or taken seriously the close connections between the Prologue and the immediately following pericopes (e.g. between the Baptist's testimony to Jesus in 1,6-8.15 and in 1,19-34: note, for instance, the frequent occurrence of *martyria/martyrein* at 1,7.7.8.15.19.32.34 and the almost verbatim repetition of v.15cdef in v.30). Hence, while the differences between the Prologue and the following pericopes help to distinguish them, their similarities and links indicate their interconnectedness. Both the distinction and the connection between 1,1-18 and 1,19-51 are revealed in our designation of them as the "hymnic-testimonial introduction" and "testimonial-kerygmatic introduction" respectively[48].

Perhaps "Prologue" could be added (in parenthesis) as a subtitle to our title "hymnic-testimonial introduction" in order to show its similarity to the prologues in Greek tragedies.

Those who take 1,1-51 as the general introduction rightly stress the introductory character of and the connection between 1,1-18 and 1,19-51[49]. Thus, C. H. Dodd says: "Chapter 1 forms a proem to the whole Gospel. It falls into two parts: 1-18, commonly designated the Prologue, and 19-51, which we may, from the nature of its contents, conveniently call the Testimony"[50]. While Dodd's division of Jn 1 into two parts is valid, his designation of 1,19-51 as "Testimony" does not seem to be quite exact, since the "testimony" of John the Baptist is emphasized also in the Prologue (cf. *martyria/martyrein* in 1,6-8.15) and the terms for "testimony" (*martyria/martyrein*) do not occur, strictly speaking, in the last two pericopes (1,35-42.43-51) which narrate the disciples' discovery and proclamation of Jesus, the Messiah (cf. Andrew's and Philip's *heurêkamen* at 1,41.45 and Nathanael's confession in 1,49). Hence we suggest that 1,19-51 be called not "testimony" but the "testimonial-kerygmatic introduction". Again, although Dodd admits that the sign at Cana (2,1-11) has links with the Prologue (e.g. *kai ephanerôsen tên doxan autou* of 2,11b "are clearly intended to recall" the words *kai etheasametha tên doxan autou* of

---

[46] Cf. ns. 22-30.
[47] Cf. n. 24.
[48] The opinion of I. DE LA POTTERIE that 1,1-18 is an introduction only to Jn 1-12 (see 2.[18]3) will be discussed later.
[49] Cf. n. 25.
[50] C. H. DODD, *The Interpretation of the Fourth Gospel*, 292.

1,14c)⁵¹, he does not consider 2,1-11 as part of the introduction to the Gospel but only as part of the first episode (2,1-4,42)⁵². We have seen above that the Cana-sign is connected not only to the Prologue (e.g. through the inclusion formed by *archê* found at the very beginning of the Prologue [1,1a] and at the end of the sign at Cana [2,11]) but also to the immediately preceding pericope (through the literary-chronological device *tê[i] hêmera[i] tê[i] tritê[i]* [2,1] which links it to *tê[i] epaurion* of 1,43). Hence 2,1-11 is the concluding part of the general introduction (1,1-2,11). It is at the same time also the "beginning of the signs" (2,11) narrated in "the Book of Jesus' Signs" (Jn 2-12)⁵³. Since it both concludes the introduction and introduces "the Book of Jesus' Signs", 2,1-11 is a *"bridge-pericope"*⁵⁴.

Now there are a few who hold the view that 1,19-51 is an introduction only to the first part of the Gospel (1,19-12,50)⁵⁵. For instance, H. van den Bussche calls 1,19-51 "Introduction à la première partie: du Baptiste à Jésus"⁵⁶ and affirms that 1,51 indicates the end of that introduction⁵⁷. But he seems to contradict himself when he explains the saying on the Son of Man in 1,51 in terms of the ascension⁵⁸, since the ascension is mentioned not only in the first part (3,13; 6,62) but also in the second part of the Gospel of John (20,17). Furthermore, the Son of Man sayings occur not only in the first part but also in the second (e.g. 13,31).

Similarly, I. de la Potterie proposes 1,19-51 as a part of Jesus' *"revelatio coram mundo (1-12)"* and as *"Introductio historica: testimonia (praesertim Joh - B.) de Jesu Messia"*⁵⁹. It is true that some historical persons (Jesus, John the Baptist, Andrew, Simon Peter, Philip, Nathanael) and places (Bethany beyond the Jordan, Galilee, Bethsaida) are mentioned in 1,19-51, but the historical aspect of the episodes described does not seem to be stressed, since precise geographical information about the places where some events took place is not given (e.g. the places where Jesus was staying: 1,39.42; where Andrew found Peter: 1,41; where Jesus called Philip: 1,43; where Philip found Nathanael: 1,45.48). Hence to designate 1,19-51 as a "historical introduction" underlines an aspect of the introduction not emphasized by the Evangelist. Furthermore, de la Potterie's restriction of 1,19-51 as an introduction only to Jesus' "revelation before the world" (Jn 1-12) is not borne out by the content and function of the Johannine text in question. We note that 1) the Baptist's testimony in 1,19-34

---

⁵¹ *Ibid.*, 297.
⁵² *Ibid.*
⁵³ See 4.13 below.
⁵⁴ See 3.192.
⁵⁵ Cf. n. 26.
⁵⁶ VAN DEN BUSSCHE, 53.
⁵⁷ *Ibid.*, 54.
⁵⁸ *Ibid.*, 129.
⁵⁹ See 2.[18]3.

relates the revelation of Jesus not primarily to the world but to Israel, for the Baptist himself says: "for this I came baptizing with water, that he might be revealed to Israel" (1,31); 2) the last two pericopes (1,35-42.43-51) deal exclusively with Jesus' revelation to and discovery by the disciples (and not by the world); 3) Jesus' solemn promise of a heavenly revelation at 1,51 ("Truly, truly I say to you, you will see heaven opened, and the angels of God ascending and descending upon the Son of Man"), with which 1,19-51 ends, refers to Jesus' revelation to the disciples (and not to the world) which points to his self-disclosure in the entire Gospel (and not merely its first part, as de la Potterie maintains); 4) finally it is reasonable to regard 1,19-51, in which the disciples play a prominent part (cf. 1,35-51), as an introduction not only to Jn 2-12 but also to Jn 13-20 where they have an important role in the Johannine drama (e.g. during the Last Supper in Jn 13-17; at Gethsemane in 18,1-11; during the trial of Jesus before the high priests in 18,12-27; on Calvary in 19,25-27; at the tomb in 20,1-18; and during Jesus' appearances in 20,19-29).

We agree with those who judge that 1,19-51 is an introduction to the Gospel as a whole (e.g. Lohmeyer, Mateos & Barreto)[60], but disagree with them in so far as they see it as an independent, major section (for instance, Lohmeyer takes 1,19-51 as one of the seven major divisions of the Fourth Gospel)[61]. It is surprising that, though Mateos & Barreto admit the close connections between the Prologue, 1,19-51 and 2,1-11, they present 1,19-51 as an independent "introductory section"[62] rather than as a part of 1,1-2,11.

Caba considers 1,19-2,12 as an "introduction to the ministry" of Jesus[63]. We have seen above that 1,19-51 forms a "testimonial-kerygmatic introduction" consisting of parts which are both linked together and distinguished from one another, and that they form integral parts of the general introduction to the entire Gospel. Therefore Caba's designation of 1,19-2,12 as an introduction only to the ministry of Jesus seems to be too restrictive[64].

---

[60] See 2.3 and 2.6.
[61] See 2.3.
[62] MATEOS & BARRETO, 31:

Después del Prólogo y en conexión con él por las menciones hechas de Juan Bautista (1,6.14) y de Jesús (1,17), se encuentra una *sección introductoria* (1,19-51), que puede titularse: "De Juan a Jesús". Su unidad y, al mismo tiempo, su carácter introductorio están indicados, por una parte, por la sucesión cronológica de los episodios, que desembocará en la escena de Caná (1,19.29.35.42; 2,1), y, por otra, por la temática, el desplazamiento de la expectación mesiánica desde Juan a Jesús, apoyada en declaraciones del mismo Juan...

If "the chronological succession of the episodes" "flows into the scene of Cana", 1,19-2,11 forms a large unit, and therefore one does not see why the authors consider only 1,19-51 as the "introductory section".

[63] See 2.[19].
[64] Regarding the numerous Christological titles in 1,19-51 I. DE LA POTTERIE writes: "Magnum momentum habent tituli Christologici in tota hac sectione 1,19-51... Habetur in 1,19-51 quasi completa manifestatio Iesu" ("De Matre Iesu in IV Evangelio" [Roma, PIB, 1976-77] 26). Therefore it must be an introduction to the revelation not only during his "ministry" (Jn 2-12) but also during his farewell and passion-death-resurrection (Jn 13-20).

We are in agreement with Culpepper concerning the dramatic, introductory character of 1,1-2,11[65]. But it must be noted that he has not sufficiently stressed the distinction between 1,19-51 and 2,1-11 (see, for example, the many Christological titles in 1,19-51, none of which is found in 2,1-11), nor has he shown the literary-thematic connection between the Prologue and the following pericopes (e.g John the Baptist's testimony in 1,6-8.15 and 1,19-36).

Perhaps we could compare 1,1-18; 1,19-51 and 2,1-11 with the prologue (*prologos*), the *parodos* (the entrance song of the chorus), and the first episode (*epeisodion*) of the classical Greek tragedies of Aeschylus, Sophocles and Euripides. For instance, the *prologos*, the *parodos* and the first *epeisodion* of *Eumenides* of Aeschylus are not only distinguished from one another but also linked together, because the chorus (*choros*) consisting of the (sleeping) Furies is present already during the prologue (where the different actors, namely, Pizia, Apollo, Oreste and the shadow of Clitemnestra are presented) and after the *parodos* the *coryphaeus* (the leader of the chorus) dialogues with Apollo during the first episode. Similarly, in the Sophoclean tragedy *Electra*, the heroine Electra, who has appeared on the scene already in the prologue, sings the *kommoi* (lamentations) with the chorus during the *parodos* and dialogues with the chorus in the first episode, which shows that, though the first three parts of the Sophoclean drama (*prologos*, *parodos*, first *epeisodion*) are distinct, they are closely connected. Such a distinction and connection between the prologue, *parodos* and first episode are verified also in some Euripidian tragedies like *Electra* (in which Electra is the principal character in the prologue, *parodos* and the first episode)[66]. These examples illustrate that the Johannine manner of simultaneously distinguishing and linking 1,1-18; 1,19-51 and 2,1-11 was a common dramatic device used by authors in antiquity.

Since it is quite clear from the above discussion that 1,1-2,11 is basically introductory in character, we need not bring new arguments against the positions of those who regard 1,19-2,11/12) as the first section ("first week"[67], "first episode"[68], or "first nucleus"[69]) of the Fourth Gospel and not as the Gospel's introduction[70].

---

[65] Cf. n. 160 of ch. 2.
[66] Cf. C. DIANO, ed., *op. cit.*, 157-61; 223-31; 725-39.
[67] BOISMARD (see 2.7) and MOLLAT (see 2.21).
[68] DEFOURNEY (see 2.4).
[69] PUIGDOLLERS (see 2.8).
[70] We have seen in ch. 2 that all these authors (BOISMARD, MOLLAT, DEFOURNEY, PUIGDOLLERS) seem to be mesmerized by the symbolic number "seven" and have used only one or two criteria for their structural division of the Fourth Gospel. None of them has examined the characteristically introductory function of 1,1-2,11 or the close links between the Prologue and 1,19-2,11. Therefore they have concluded that 1,19-2,11(12) is the first section in a series of similar sections.

The chiastic parallelism between the triple introduction (1,1-2,11) and the conclusion (20,30-31) is another argument against the positions of the above-mentioned authors (see 4.113).

4.11z Since there is a convergence of different kinds of criteria (literary, dramatic, structural criteria), we conclude that *1,1-2,11* is a *tripartite Christocentirc introduction* to the entire Fourth Gospel, that *20,30-31* is the *Christocentric conclusion* of the Gospel, and that the three parts of the former are *chiastically* related to those of the latter (C*B*A$^+$/AzBzCz).

4.12 Part I: the Book of Jesus' Signs [71]

Here we shall discuss 1) the delimitation of the first principal part of the Fourth Gospel, and 2) the designation of the first part as "the Book of Jesus' Signs".

4.121 *Delimitation of the First Part*

Ten of the 28 Johannine authors we examined in ch. 2 divide the Fourth Gospel into two principal parts, and eight of these agree that the division occurs at the end of Jn 12 [72]. In the words of C. H. Dodd: "The book naturally divides itself at the end of ch. xii. The division corresponds to that which is made in all the Gospels before the beginning of the Passion-narrative" [73]. This division, in Dodd's opinion, is supported by the summary statement and evaluation of Jesus' public ministry and of the Jews' reaction to it in 12,37: "Though he had done so many signs before them, yet they did not believe in him" [74]. Likewise R. E. Brown brings the following arguments for "a break in the narrative" between the end of ch. 12 and the beginning of ch. 13: "In xii 37-43 there is a summary description and analysis of Jesus' public ministry and its effect on the people; xii 44-50 are the last words of Jesus directed to the people in general. In xiii 1-3 there is a shift in emphasis..." [75].

The above reasons of Dodd and Brown for the division at the end of ch. 12 are valid, provided, as we shall see later, it is not regarded as "an absolute division" [76].

---

[71] Here and in the next section (4.13) the term "book" is not to be understood as a complete work but only as "a major division of a literary work" (*Webster's New Collegiate Dictionary*, 127). Ancient authors used to divide their works into "books" in the above sense. For example, JOSEPHUS divides his *History of the Jewish War* into seven "books".

[72] BROWN (see 2.[23]), CABA (see 2.[19]), DE LA POTTERIE (see 2.[18]3), DODD (see 2.[15]), GOURGUES (see 2.[20]), PRETE (see 2.[14]), VAN DEN BUSSCHE (2.[18]2), WESTCOTT (2.[18]1).
The division between Jn 12 and Jn 13 is held also by the commentators like BRAUN, LIGHTFOOT, SCHNACKENBURG, SCHNEIDER, SCHULZ, WIKENHAUSER.

[73] C. H. DODD, *op. cit.*, 289.

[74] *Ibid.*; SCHNACKENBURG, II, 411.

[75] BROWN, I, cxxxviii.

[76] LIGHTFOOT, 11.

4.1 MAIN DIVISIONS

Although many scholars agree on a bipartite division between Jn 12 and Jn 13, there is hardly any agreement about the beginning of the first part. Jn 1,1 [77] or 1,19 [78] or 2,1 [79] or 2,12 [80] has been proposed as the beginning.

I. de la Potterie defends his view that the first part of the Gospel comprises 1,1-12,50 arguing that "the fundamental theme" of Jesus' revelation and man's faith or unbelief is present throughout Jn 1-12, and that 1,1-18 and 12,44-50 form a "grand inclusion" [81]. In so far as 1,1-18 is part of the introduction to the whole Gospel [82], it is natural that some of the major themes of the Prologue would be found also in the first part of the Gospel, just as they are found in the second part (e.g. *pisteuein, zôê, doxa*). Furthermore, we shall see below that the Prologue is parallel not only to 12,44-50 but also to 3,11-21.31-36; 17,1-26 and 20,19-29 [83]. Besides, the confession of the divinity of Jesus Christ both at the beginning of the Prologue (*kai theos ên ho logos*: 1,1; cf. also 1,18: *monogenês theos*) and at the end of the risen Jesus' appearance to Thomas (*ho kyrios mou kai ho theos mou*: 20,28) certainly forms an inclusion for the whole Gospel. Finally, if 1,1-18 and 12,44-50 form a "grand inclusion", the Prologue forms a number of inclusions also with the conclusion of the Gospel of John (*zôê*: 1,4.4; 20,31; *pisteuein*: 1,6.12; 20,30.31; *to onoma autou*: 1,12; 20,31). In short, because of the above reasons 1,1-18 cannot be considered the introduction exclusively of the first major part of the Gospel.

Since we have explained above why we regard 1,19-51 as a "testimonial-kerygmatic introduction" [84] and as an integral part of the introduction to the whole Gospel [85], and since we have given many reasons why 1,19-51 should not be regarded as an introduction exclusively of the first part [86], it follows that

---

[77] DE LA POTTERIE (see 2.[18]3).
[78] BROWN (see 2.[23]), CABA (see 2.[19]), GOURGUES (see 2.[20]), PRETE (see 2.[14]), WESTCOTT (see 2.[18]1).
[79] DODD (see 2.[15]).
[80] LIGHTFOOT, 11; 92-94.
[81] Concerning the "Prima pars evangelii (1-12)" I. DE LA POTTERIE says:

Thema fundamentale est: dialectica inter r e v e l a t i o n e m (ex parte Jesu) et f i d e m vel i n c r e d u l i t a t e m (ex parte hominum)."

Hoc thema recurrit per totam primam partem evangelii, in variis sectionibus ubi alternantur sectiones narrativae et longi sermones. Praeterea, thema illud quasi programmatice enuntiatur in prologo (1,1-18) et in conclusione vitae publicae (12,44-50): hae due sectiones, magnam inclusionem efficere videntur (*VD* 47 [1969] 131).

Comparing 1,1-18 and 12,44-50 (and 12,35-36) he finds the following inclusions: 1) *kekragen* (1,15) and *ekraxen* (12,44); 2) *phôs/skotia* (1,4-5.9; 12,46.35-36); 3) *logos* (1,1.14; 12,48); 4) *zôê* (1,4; 12,49).

[82] See 4.112.
[83] See 4.3 below.
[84] See 4.112,2.
[85] See 4.112,1.
[86] See 4.112,3.

1,19-51 is not, in our opinion, a constituent element of the first major part of the Gospel [87].

So we come to the third view that the first part consists of chs. 2-12 because of the following reasons: 1) the miracle of changing water into wine at Cana (2,1-11) is called the "beginning of the signs" (*archê tôn sêmeiôn*: 2,11); 2) other signs, besides the first Cana-sign, are described in Jn 2-12 (the healing of the royal official's son [4,46-54; cf. *sêmeion* in 4,54], the multiplication of the loaves [6,1-15; cf. *sêmeion* in 6,14]; the raising of Lazarus [11,1-54; called *sêmeion* in 12,18]); 3) the term *sêmeion* is found almost exclusively in Jn 2-12 (16 out of 17 times in Jn); 4) Jesus' public ministry is summed up in Jn 12 in terms of the "many signs" he did (*tosauta... sêmeia*: 12,37); 5) there are a number of parallels between 2,1-11 and 12,37-43, which may be thought of as forming a sort of inclusion [88]:

2,11a: tautên *epoiêsen* archên tôn **sêmeiôn** ho Iêsous...
12,37: tosauta de *autou* **sêmeia** pepoiêkotos...

2,11c: kai **episteusan eis auton**...
12,37: ouk **episteuon eis auton**...

2,11b: kai *ephanerôsen* **tên doxan autou**
12,41: *eiden* **tên doxan autou**.

But we have seen above that 2,1-11 is an integral part of the introduction (1,1-2,11) as well [89]. Therefore the first Cana-sign (2,1-11) must be regarded as a "bridge-pericope" which simultaneously concludes the introduction (1,1-2,11) and introduces the first part of the Gospel (2,1-12,50) [90].

Since 2,1-11 is a "bridge-pericope", the first principal part of the Gospel begins not with 2,12, as Lightfoot maintains [91], but with 2,1.

4.121z Thus we conclude that the first major part of the Gospel of John consists of chs. 2-12 [91a].

---

[87] This is all the more true, if the first part is designated as "the Book of Signs" (cf. BROWN, cxxxviii-cxxxiv), since no "sign" is mentioned in 1,19-51 (the first "sign" being described only in 2,1-11).

[88] These are not inclusions in the strict sense of the word, since 2,11 does not occur at the beginning of the pericope (2,1-11). But because the whole Cana-sign is a single pericope, the striking parallelisms between 2,11 and 12,37.41 may be said to form "a sort of inclusion".

[89] See 4.112.

[90] See 3.192. BROWN (I, cxl; 106) too admits that 2,1-11 has a bridging character: according to him the Cana-sign "closes" 1,19-2,11 and "opens" Jn 2-4. But in our opinion it "closes" not only 1,19-2,11 but also 1,1-2,11 (see above); similarly, it "opens" not only Jn 2-4 but the whole of Jn 2-12 (see above).

[91] LIGHTFOOT, 11.

[91a] The delimitation of the first part (Jn 2-12) will be confirmed by other criteria (see 4.122 and 4.13 below).

4.122 Designation of Jn 2-12 as "the Book of Jesus' Signs"

Various names have been given to this part of the Gospel (Jn 2-12) which stress different aspects of its content such as the public ministry of Jesus, his revelation, the signs he did, and some combinations of these. Thus some of the titles given are: "the public life"[92], "the public manifestation of the Lord"[93], "the revelation before the world"[94], "the revelation of the *doxa* to the world"[95], "the self-revelation of Christ to the world"[96], "the day of Jesus: his public life; veiled revelation of his glory"[97], "the work of Jesus in the world"[98], "the Book of Signs"[99], "the Book of Signs: revelation of Jesus to the people through signs and discourses"[100].

All the titles given above correspond to some extent to the content of the first part. However, the title "the public life" does not account for the typically Johannine emphasis on signs in the first part of the Gospel. Other titles, while underlining correctly the revelatory aspect, do not seem to be exact in restricting Jesus' revelation (in the first part of the Gospel) to "the world", since this may give the (wrong) impression that Jesus revealed himself only to the world (and not to the disciples, but see 2,1-11; 4,31-38; 6,16-21.60-71; 11,6-16 and many other places where the "disciples" are explicitly mentioned e.g. 2,12.17.22; 3,22; 4,2; 6,3.8.12; 9,2; 11,54; 12,4.16), or that Jesus did not manifest himself to the world in the second part of the Gospel (but see Jn 18-19 where Jesus' revelation is not, unlike Jn 13-17 and Jn 20, directed exclusively to the disciples).

The designation "the Book of Signs" seems to be a good title for Jn 2-12, since it highlights the typically Johannine perspective in which the public ministry of Jesus is described. In the words of C. H. Dodd:

> The earlier chapters [Jn 2-12] correspond to the account of the Ministry in the other gospels. The way in which John regards it may be gathered from the opening words of the epilogue which he has supplied in xii.37-50 *tosauta de autou sêmeia pepoiêkotos...* We may fitly call it *The Book of Signs*[101].

---

[92] LAGRANGE, lxxiv: "La vie publique (I,19-XII)"; I. DE LA POTTERIE, "L'Evangelo di San Giovanni", in: G. Rinaldi & P. de Benedetti (ed.), *op. cit.*, 894: "la vita pubblica" (1,19-12,50); CABA (see 2.[19]).

[93] LIGHTFOOT, 107; cf. also p. 11, where 2,12-12,50 is designated as "the Lord's public ministry".

[94] DE LA POTTERIE (see 2.[18]3). CABA combines "public life" with "progressive manifestation of Jesus and the reactions which it arouses" in his long title for 1,19-12,50 (see 2.[19]).

[95] BULTMANN, vii.

[96] WESTCOTT (see 2.[18]1).

[97] VAN DEN BUSSCHE (see 2.[18]2).

[98] WIKENHAUSER, 81: "L'opera di Gesù nel Mondo".

[99] DODD (see 2.[15]), BROWN (see 2.[23]), GOURGUES (see 2.[20]).

[100] SEGALLA (see 2.[22]). Cf. S. MIGLIASSO, *La presenza dell' Assente: Saggio di analisi letterario-strutturale e di sintesi teologica di Gv. 13,31-14,31* (Roma 1979) 43, for other titles.

[101] DODD, *op. cit.*, 289 [my italics].

It must be noted that *sêmeia* at 12,37 include all the miracles done by Jesus in Jn 2-12, whether they are called "signs" (*sêmeia*) or "works" (*erga*)[101a]. R. E. Brown explains the title "the Book of Signs" as follows:

> We have designated i 19-xii 50 as "The Book of Signs" because these chapters largely concern Jesus' miracles, referred to as "signs", and discourses which interpret the signs. By contrast, the word "sign" occurs in the second division of the Gospel only in the summary statement of xx 30[102].

Instead of the designation "the Book of Signs", we prefer to call Jn 2-12 "the Book of Jesus' Signs" in order to underscore the fact that the signs spoken of are those done by Jesus.

"The Book of Jesus' Signs" not only corresponds broadly to the content of Jn 2-12 but also contains the typically Johannine term "signs", which has a revelatory function[103], and which is often related to Jesus' dialogues and discourses in Jn 2-12 (e.g. the sign of healing the royal official's son in 4,46-54 and the dialogues therein; the sign of the multiplication of the loaves and the dialogue/discourse on Jesus, the bread of life, in Jn 6; the sign of raising Lazarus to life and the dialogue/discourse on Jesus, the resurrection and the life, in Jn 11)[104]. Hence the short title "the Book of Jesus' Signs" stands actually for a longer title "the Book of Jesus' Signs, Works, Dialogues and Discourses". The title "the Book of Jesus' Signs" also helps the reader to recall the related theme of "faith" which is the response to Jesus' revelation through "signs" (and works, dialogues and discourses) (cf. the correlative terms *sêmeion* and *pisteuein* in 2,11 and 12,37)[104a].

4.13 Part II: the Book of Jesus' Hour [105]

We shall now discuss both the delimitation and the designation of the second principal part of the Gospel.

[101a] See 5.13 below.

[102] BROWN, I, cxxxviii-cxxxix. Cf. n. 87 above.

[103] See 5.13 below.

[104] It is true that SEGALLA's designation of the first division of the Gospel of John as "the Book of Signs: revelation of Jesus to the people through signs and discourses" (see 2.[22]) is a more complete title than "the Book of Signs" alone, since it explicitates how Jesus reveals himself in Jn 2-12, namely, "through signs and discourses". But since Segalla's title is too long to be a proper title, we prefer the short title "the Book of Jesus' Signs", which may be looked upon as standing for the more adequate designation of Jn 2-12 as "the Book of Jesus' Signs, Works, Discussions and Discourses", just as "heads" can stand for whole "persons" (e.g. in the expression "count heads" in the context of a meeting of persons). The correctness of this interpretation is confirmed by the Johannine conclusion of Jn 2-12, in which Jesus's public ministry is summarized in terms of the "many signs he did" (12,37) without explicitly mentioning his works, discussions and discourses (see 5.13 below).

[104a] See 5.15 below.

[105] The reasons for the designation of the second part of the Fourth Gospel as "the Book of Jesus' Hour" will be given below (see 4.132).

4.131 *Delimitation of the second part*

Most scholars who suggest a bipartite division of the Fourth Gospel take, as we have seen in ch. 2, the second part to consist of Jn 13-20 [106], while a few include also Jn 21 in the second division (Jn 13-21) [107].

4.131,1 The end of the second part

Since we have a general conclusion to the Gospel in 20,30-31 [108], and since, as we shall show below, ch. 21 is an appendix [109], we conclude that the second major division of the Gospel ends at 20,29 [110].

4.131,2 The beginning of the second part

Now we shall examine where the second part of the Gospel begins. Since the first part ends with Jn 12, it would seem that the second would naturally begin with Jn 13, and this is the almost unanimous view of scholars who propose a bipartite division [111].

It has been argued that 13,1 indicates "a shift in emphasis", since it mentions "the Passover feast" and Jesus' awareness of the arrival of "the hour" [112] and since his revelation in Jn 13-20/21 is directed only to his disciples (and not to the Jews or to the world as in Jn 2-12) [113]. But these reasons are only partly true, since both "the Passover feast" and the arrival of "the hour" are explicitly mentioned already in 11,55-12,50 (*to pascha*: 11,55.55; 12,1; *hê heortê* [of Passover]: 11,56; 12,20; *elêlythen hê hôra*: 12,23; cf. also *hê hôra* at 12,27.27), and since Jesus manifests himself exclusively to the disciples only in Jn 13-17 and 20 (unlike 18-19, where the Jews are very much present).

Again, it has been suggested by Dodd that Jn 13-20/21 corresponds to "the Passion-narrative" in the Synoptic Gospels [114]. This is, however, to be

---

[106] So DODD (see 2.[15]), PRETE (see 2.[14]), VAN DEN BUSSCHE (see 2.[18]2), DE LA POTTERIE (see 2.[18]3), CABA (see 2.[19]), BROWN (see 2.[23]). Cf. also the next note.

[107] GOURGUES seems to be indecisive about whether the second major division ends with Jn 20 or Jn 21, since his division is given as 13,1-20,31/21,25 (see 2.[2])). WESTCOTT concludes the second part only at Jn 21 (see 2.[18]1).

[108] See 4.111.

[109] See 4.14 below.

[110] We have seen above (4.111) that 20,30-31 is the conclusion to the whole Gospel and not primarily to the second part. Hence, strictly speaking, the second division ends with 20,29. This does not mean that 20,30-31 has no connection with the preceding chapter(s). It functions as the conclusion to the whole Gospel, and therefore also to the second part as well as the last section of the second part.

[111] So BROWN (see 2.[23]), CABA (see 2.[19]), DE LA POTTERIE (see 2.[18]3), DODD (see 2.[15]), GOURGUES (see 2.[20]), PRETE (see 2.[14]), VAN DEN BUSSCHE (see 2.[18]2), WESTCOTT (see 2.[18]1). (MATEOS & BARRETO, however, consider only Jn 20 as the second division [see 2.6].)

[112] BROWN, I, cxxxviii.

[113] WESTCOTT, xlii-xliii; BROWN, I, cxxxviii.

[114] DODD, *op. cit.*, 289.

qualified, since the Johannine parallel to the Synoptic scene of Jesus' agony in the garden of Gethsemane is given not in Jn 18,1-11 but already in Jn 12,20-36 ("Now is my soul troubled. And what shall I say, 'Father, save me from this hour'? No, for this purpose I have come to this hour": 12,27; cf. Mt 26,38-39 // Mk 14,34-36 // Lk 22,41-43). Therefore 11,55-12,50 must be regarded as an integral part of what follows. In fact, this is the position of some scholars like Mollat and Boismard who take 11,55-19,42 as forming "the Holy week and the Passover of the crucifixion"[115].

It must be noted, however, that 11,55-12,50 is linked not only to the following chapters but also to the immediately preceding passage 11,1-54 because there are explicit cross-references: e.g. *Lazaros, hon êgeiren ek nekrôn Iêsous* at 12,1 refers back to Jn 11 which has described Jesus' raising Lazarus from the dead (cf. also 12,9.17); similarly Mary is introduced in 11,2 as: *ên de Mariam hê aleipsasa ton kyrion myrô[i] kai ekmaxasa tous podas autou tais thrixin autês*, which is almost a verbatim anticipation of the description of her anointing of Jesus described in 12,3: *hê oun Mariam labousa litran myrou nardou pistikês polytimou êleipsen tous podas tou Iêsou kai exemaxen tais thrixin autês tous podas autou*[116]. There are numerous other parallel elements between Jn 11 and Jn 12[117]. For instance, compare 11,40 (*opsê[i] tên doxan tou theou*) and 12,41 (*eiden tên doxan autou*; cf. also *doxa tou theou* at 11,4 and 12,43) or 11,45 (*polloi oun ek tôn Ioudaiôn... episteusan eis auton*) and 12,42 (*ek tôn archontôn polloi episteusan eis auton*), or 11,9-10 and 12,35-36[118].

Thus we see that, on the one hand, 11,55-12,50 is intimately linked to the following chapters and, on the other hand, it is closely connected to 11,1-54 through cross-references and numerous parallels[119]. Therefore the second principal part of the Fourth Gospel must be thought of as beginning not at 13,1 nor at 11,55 but at 11,1.

Jn 11,1-54 has also many characteristic terms and expressions in common with 11,55-20,29. For instance, Jesus speaks about "the glorification (*doxazein*) of the Son of God/Man" (*ho hyios tou theou/anthrôpou*) at 11,4; 12,23; 13,1; 17,1.

---

[115] So MOLLAT (see 2.21). BOISMARD too regards 11,55-19,42 as "la Semaine Sainte, terminée par la mort du Christ, lors de la troisième Pâque" (see 2.71). MATEOS & BARRETO understand 11,55-19,42 as "La Hora final: La Pascua del Mesías" (see 2.6).

[116] See 3.1[11].

[117] Cf. P. MOURLON BEERNAERT, "Parallelisme entre Jean 11 et 12. Étude de structure littéraire et théologique", in: A.-L. Descamps et al. (ed.), *Genèse et structure d'un texte du Nouveau Testament. Étude interdisciplinaire du Chapitre 11 de l'Évangile de Jean* (Paris 1981) 123-49. He finds that "plus de cinquante éléments du ch. 11" have parallels in ch. 12 (p. 132).

[118] P. MOURLON BEERNAERT takes "marcher" (*peripatein*: 11,9; 12,35), "la lumière" (*to phôs*: 11,9.10; 12,35.36), "de nuit" (*en tê[i] nykti*: 11,10) and "dans les ténèbres" (*en tê[i] skotia[i]*: 12,35) as three inclusions between Jn 11 and 12 (*art. cit.*, 130). These, however, cannot be called inclusions (at least in the strict sense of the term), since the expressions are not found at the beginning and end of the section. They are, strictly speaking, parallels.

[119] Other parallels will be examined later (see 4.3 below).

Jesus' being "troubled" (*tarassein*) in spirit is mentioned at 11,33 and 13,21. The imminent "death" (*apothnêskein*) of Jesus is spoken of for the first time in the Fourth Gospel in Jn 11. Thomas' words at 11,16 (*agômen kai hêmeis hina apothanômen met' autou*) imply that Jesus will die in Judea. This premonition of Thomas is confirmed by Caiaphas' prediction of Jesus' death at 11,50 (*sympherei hymin hina heis anthrôpos apothanê[i] hyper tou laou*) and the Evangelist's remark at 11,51 (*eprophêteusen hoti emellen Iêsous apothnêskein hyper tou ethnous...*). This prophecy of the high priest about Jesus' death is explicitly recalled by the Evangelist during the trial of Jesus before the high priests (18,14). Starting from Jn 11 there are a number of references to Jesus' death (*apothnêskein*) at 12,24.24.33; 18,32; 19,7 which show that Jn 11 is intimately related to Jn 12-19.

Lazarus' death, burial and resurrection in Jn 11 symbolically represents Jesus' own death, burial and resurrection, since Jn 11 contains many terms connected with death, burial and resurrection found also in Jn 19-20 (e.g. *apothnêskein*: 11,14.21.32.37; 19,7; *anastênai*: 11,23.24.31; 20,29 and nowhere else in the Gospel of John; *tithêmi auton/Iêsoun* to signify the burial of Lazarus/Jesus at 11,34; 19,42). Note also that Jesus' words to Mary and Martha at 11,34: *pou tetheikate auton?* are almost verbatim repeated by Mary Magdalene to Jesus who appeared to her at his tomb as a gardener: *pou ethêkas auton* (20,15; cf. also 20,2.13: *pou ethêkan auton*). Connected with the burial of Lazarus and of Jesus are *mnêmeion* (11,17.32.38; 12,17; 19,41.42; cf. also 20,1.1.2.3.4.6.8.11; elsewhere only once at 5,28), and *soudarion* (11,44; 20,7 and nowhere else in Jn). Again, taking away the tomb-stone (*airein ton lithon*) is mentioned both at 11,39.41 (before raising Lazarus from the dead) and at 20,1 (in connection with the resurrection of Jesus). We may also note the repeated reference to the "weeping" (*klaiein*) of Mary at 11,31.31 and Mary Magdalene at 20,11.11.13.15.

The unity of 11,1-20,29 is supported also by the quasi-chiastic correspondence between Jn 11-12 and 13-20: 1) the raising of Lazarus in Jn 11 is parallel to the resurrection of Jesus in Jn 20 (cf. *anastênai*: 11,23.24.31; 20,9); 2) the anointing of Jesus at Bethany narrated in 12,1-8 is presented as an anticipatory rite for his burial (cf. *entaphiasmos*: 12,7; *entaphiazein*: 19,40) described in 19,38-42; 3) the triumphal entry of Jesus into Jerusalem (12,12-19) corresponds broadly to his arrest, trial and death (18,1-19,37), since both the passages emphasize the kingship of Christ (cf. *basileus*: 12,13.15; 18,33.37.37.39; 19,3.12.14.15.21.21); 4) there are a number of parallel elements between 12,20-36 and Jn 13-17 (and especially Jn 13 and 17) e.g. the arrival of the hour (*elêlythen hê hôra*: 12,23; 17,1; cf. also 13,1: *êlthen autou hê hôra*); the glorification of the Son of Man (*doxazthê[i]/edoxasthê ho hyios tou anthrôpou*: 12,23; 13,31); Jesus' being troubled (*hê psychê mou tetaraktai*: 12,27; *ho Iêsous etarachthê*: 13,21); his prayer to the Father for glorification (*pater, doxason*: 12,28; 17,1.5). This quasi-chiastic parallelism between Jn 11-12 and Jn 13-20 may be represented as follows:

1) The *resurrection* of Lazarus (Jn 11)
2) The anointing for the *burial* of Jesus (12,1-8)
3) The triumphal entry of Jesus, the *king* (12,12-19)
4) The *arrival of the hour* and the *prayer for glorification* (12,20-36)

8) The *resurrection* of Jesus (Jn 20)
7) The *burial* of Jesus (19,38-42)
6) The trial and death of Jesus, the *king* (18,1-19,37)
5) The *arrival of the hour* and the *prayer for glorification* (13,1-17,26)

4.131z Because of the above reasons we conclude that the second major division of Jn consists of 11,1-20,29, the overlapping between the first part (2,1-12,50) and the second part (11,1-20,29) being caused by the **bridge-section** (11,1-12,50) which concludes the first part and introduces the second simultaneously [120]. This Johannine "bridge-section" is similar to the Markan "bridge-section" (Mk 8,27-33: Peter's confession of Jesus as the Messiah [8,27-30] and Jesus' prediction of the passion of the Son of Man [8,31-33], which are mutually linked like Jn 11 and Jn 12) not only concluding the first principal part of Mk: "the Mystery of the Messiah" (1,14-8,33) but also introducing the second part of Mk: "the Mystery of the Son of Man" (8,27-16,8) [121].

4.132 *Designation of Jn 11,1-20,29 as "the Book of Jesus' Hour"*

Most scholars who propose a bipartite division of the Gospel of John take the second part to consist of Jn 13-20/21 (and not 11,1-20,29, as we have seen above), but they designate it by different names such as "the Book of the

---

[120] See 3.193.

[121] E. J. MALLY gives the following outline of the Gospel of Mark ("The Gospel according to Mark", in: *The Jerome Biblical Commentary*, Vol II, eds., R. E. Brown & J. A. Fitzmyer & R. E. Murphy [London 1970] 23-24):

(I) Prologue (1:1-13)
(II) The Mystery of the Messiah (1:14-8:33)
(III) Conclusion of Part II and Transition to Part IV:
    Peter's Profession and Jesus' Correction (8:27-33)
(IV) The Mystery of the Son of Man (8:31-16:8)
(V) The Ending of the Marcan Gospel (16:9-20).

MALLY explains the function of (III) Mk 8,27-33 as follows:

This passage is the turning point of Mk, for it climaxes Jesus' self-revelation with the disciples' first recognition of him as the Messiah. It also introduces the theme of the suffering Messiah, which will be developed in the succeeding chapters. Both Peter's confession and the first prediction of the passion form a logical and structural unit in Mk... This section really *belongs at once to the preceding and the following parts of Mk*, for it is the climax of chs. 1-8 and also the transition to the new section; hence the overlapping of the outline (p. 40) [my italics].

Passion"[122], "the Book of Glory"[123], "the Book of the Hour"[124], "the Self-Revelation of Christ to the Disciples"[125], "the Hour of Jesus, the Revelation of His Glory"[126], "the Climax of Revelation in the Hour of Jesus"[127], etc.[128].

All these titles emphasize one aspect or other of Jn 13-20/21 but some seem to be less suitable than others. For instance, C. H. Dodd's designation of Jn 13-20/21 as "the Book of the Passion" seems to be the result of assimilating the Johannine text with the Synoptic "Passion-narrative"[129], and brings out neither the Johannine unity of the passion-resurrection nor the Johannine emphasis on "the hour" of Jesus. R. E. Brown bases his title "the Book of Glory" on "Jesus' return to his Father (xiii 1, xiv 2, 28, xv 26, xvii 5, 11, xx 17)", which "means the glorification of Jesus (xiii 31, xiv 14, xvii 1, 5, 24), so that the resurrected Jesus appears to his disciples as Lord and God (xx 25, 28)"[130]. This is true, but Jesus' "glory" and "glorification" are spoken

---

Again he affirms in unambiguous terms: "it is at once *impossible to separate 8:27-33 from the first part of the Gospel as it is from the second part*. And yet the episode itself functions as *the hinge* of the two" (p.41).

If Mk 8,27-33 is truly a "hinge" or a bridge between 1,14-8,33 and 8,27-16,8, then it would be better to regard those seven verses not as forming a complete part (III) by itself, as Mally does, but as forming a "bridge-section" which belongs to the two principal parts (Mk 1,14-8,33; 8,27-16,8).

We suggested in the last chapter (see n. 39a there) that Mk 1,14-15 is probably intended as a bridge-pericope between the introduction (1,1-15) and the first part of Mk (1,14-8,33). Taking these factors into account we may divide Mark's Gospel as follows:

Introduction (1,1-15)
    [1,14-15 = bridge-pericope]
Part I   (1,14-8,33)
    [8,27-33 = bridge-section]
Part II (8,27-16,8)
Appendix (16,9-20).

Notice that, just as there is a "bridge-section" (Mk 8,27-33) between the first part of Mk (1,14-8,33) and the second part (8,27-16,8), so there is a "bridge-section" between the first part of Jn (2,1-12,50) and the second part (11,1-20,29). (Similarly, both the Gospels have a "bridge-pericope" [Mk 1,14-15; Jn 2,1-11] between the introduction and the first part.)

[122] C. H. DODD, *op. cit.*, 289. CABA calls 13,1-20,31 "Ultima cena, Passione, Resurrezione" (see 2.[19]).

[123] BROWN, I, cxxxix.

[124] M. GOURGUES, *op. cit.*, 98. É. COTHENET vacillates between "the Book of the Hour" and "the Book of Glory" (in: A. George & P. Grelot [eds.], *Introduction à la Bible*, Tome III, *Introduction critique au Nouveau Testament*, Vol. IV, *La tradition johannique* [Paris 1977] 137).

[125] WESTCOTT (see 2.[18]1).

[126] VAN DEN BUSSCHE (see 2.[18]2).

[127] DE LA POTTERIE (see 2.[18]3).

[128] Cf. S. MIGLIASSO, *op. cit.*, 43 for other designations of Jn 13-20/21 by different authors.

[129] C. H. DODD, *op. cit.*, 289.

[130] BROWN, I, cxxxix.

of already in Jn 1-12 (e.g. *hê doxa autou/mou*: 1,14; 2,11; 8,50.54; 12,41; *doxazein*: 8,54; 11,4; 12,23). Therefore the designation of Jn 13-20 as "the Book of Glory" is not quite exact. The titles proposed by Westcott, van den Bussche and de la Potterie rightly stress the "revelation" of Jesus in Jn 13-20/21. But Westcott's specification of Jesus' self-revelation "to the disciples" is not quite correct, since Jesus is alone with them only in Jn 13-17 and 20 (but not in 18-19). Similarly, while van den Bussche's title "the Hour of Jesus, the Revelation of His Glory" emphasizes correctly the relation between Jesus' revelation and his "Hour", the distinction (or the contrast) between this title and the title for Jn 2-12 ("the Day of Jesus, His Public Life, Veiled Revelation of His Glory")[131] is not quite exact, since the glory of God/Jesus is always "veiled" (even during "the Hour") to those who refuse to believe (12,38) and is seen only by the eyes of faith (cf. 11,40: "Did I not tell you that if you believe, you would see the glory of God?"). Perhaps de la Potterie's designation "Culmen revelationis in hora Jesu" brings out better the relation between the "revelation" and "the hour" of Jesus[132] but the restriction of "the hour" only to Jn 13-20/21 is unfortunate, since it excludes Jn 12 which mentions explicitly the arrival of the hour of Jesus (cf. 12,23. 27.27).

We prefer to designate 11,1-20,29 (not 13,1-20,31)[133] "the Book of Jesus' Hour"[134]. In order to justify this title, it is necessary to examine briefly the occurrences of the "hour" (*hôra*) in the entire Gospel[135].

Excursus on the "hour" (*hôra*) in Jn

The word *hôra* occurs 26 times in Jn[136]. Sometimes it refers to the time of the day (when the "hour" is qualified by a number e.g. "tenth hour": 1,39; "sixth hour": 4,6; 19,14; "seventh hour": 4,52.53) when an event took place[137].

---

[131] VAN DEN BUSSCHE, 53.
[132] DE LA POTTERIE (see 2.[18]3).
[133] M. GOURGUES and É. COTHENET call 13,1-20,31 "the Book of the Hour" (cf. n. 124 above).
[134] Here again, as in the case of "the Book of Jesus' Signs", "book" is understood not as a complete work but as a major division of a literary work.
[135] Cf. G. FERRARO, *L'"Ora" di Cristo nel Quarto Vangelo* (Roma 1974); W. THÜSSING, *Die Erhöhung und der Verherrlichung Jesu im Johannesevangelium* (NTA XXI 1/2) (Münster 1959) 75-100 (cf. also the earlier bibliography on "the hour" given in the above two works); I. DE LA POTTERIE, *De narratione Passionis et Mortis Christi: Ioh 18-19* (Roma, PIB, 1978-79) 17-23: "Hora Iesu".
[136] In the Synoptics: Mt = 21, Mk = 12, Lk = 17. In most of these texts *hôra* refers to the time (hour) of the day and does not have a deeper theological significance.
[137] G. FERRARO (*op. cit.*, 93-99; 117-27; 152-58; 301) finds a deeper Christological significance for these numerical hours of the day, for he says: "Gesù è sempre sullo sfondo, sono le dodici ore del

Hê hôra (mou/autou) is used a number of times to denote "the hour" of Jesus (2,4; 7,30; 8,20; 12,23; 13,1; 17,1)[138]. Jesus' first enigmatic reference to his hour (*oupô hêkei hê hôra mou*: 2,4) before working the first Cana-miracle seems to point to an important time in his life but its meaning remains mysterious for the reader[139]. The Evangelist's remark during Jesus' controversy with the Jews at the feast of Tabernacles that they did not arrest him "because his hour had not yet come" (7,30; 8,20) gives the reader a clue that Jesus' hour includes his arrest. Jesus' own earlier reference to his hour (2,4) at the beginning of his public ministry and the Jews' failure to arrest him during the feast of Tabernacles because the divinely determined hour had not yet arrived (7,30; 8,20) show that Jesus' whole life gradually and irrevocably tends towards it and all the hostile human endeavours to kill him before the hour will be futile (11,9). In Jn 12 Jesus reveals for the first time that the hour has come (*elêlythen hê hôra*: 12,23) that he may be glorified (*hina doxasthê[i] ho hyios tou anthrôpou*: 12,23) through his "being lifted up" (*hypsothênai*: 12,32), that is, through his death on the cross (12,33). Jesus accepts "this hour" during his agonizing prayer (12,27) because it will glorify the Father (12,28). This is confirmed by Jesus' prayer to the Father during the Last Supper: "Father, the hour has come; glorify your Son that the Son may glorify you" (17,1), which makes it clear that both the Son and the Father are going to be glorified in and through "the hour" of Jesus'

---

giorno in cui Gesù cammina e lavora. Queste ore, così segnate e determinate, scandiscono il periodo dell'esistenza di Gesù dall'inizio al termine del suo ministero pubblico" (*ibid.*, 301). But in spite of Jesus' reference to "12 hours of the day" (11,9), it is doubtful whether the Evangelist intended to present Jesus' life or public ministry under the rubric of a "day" of "12 hours", since the "hours" do not always increase as the drama of the Gospel develops (e.g. the "tenth hour" at 1,39 is followed not by the "eleventh hour" but by the "sixth hour" at 4,6).

[138] *Ibid.*, 100-16; 159-221; 260-75; W. THÜSSING, *op. cit.*, 75-100.

[139] *Hê hôra mou* is understood differently by various scholars depending on whether *oupô hêkei hê hôra mou* (2,4) is taken as a question ("Has not my hour come?") or as a negative statement ("My hour has not yet come"). Some like M.-É. BOISMARD (*Du Baptême à Cana* [Paris 1956] 149-59) and A. VANHOYE ("Interrogation johannique et exégèse de Cana [Jn 2,4]", *Bib* 55 (1974) 157-67) interpret 2,4c as a question, while others like BROWN (I, 99), P. BRAUN (*La Mère des Fidèles. Essai de théologie johannique*, 2 ed. [Paris 1954], P. GÄCHTER (*Maria im Erdenleben* [Innsbruck 1954] 180-91), SCHNACKENBURG (I, 327-31), A. FEUILLET ("L'heure de Jésus et le signe de Cana", in: *Études Johanniques* [Paris 1962] 13) take it as a negative statement.

BOISMARD (*op. cit.*, 156) argues that *oupô hêkei hê hôra mou* (2,4c) must be a question, since it is preceded by another question (*ti emoi kai soi*: 2,4b) as in Mt 16,9; Mk 8,17, while others like BROWN (I, 99) take 2,4c as a negative statement, since *oupô* is always used negatively in Jn and since the construction of 2,4c is similar to 7,30 and 8,20 (cf. also SCHNACKENBURG, I, 328-331; A. FEUILLET, *art. cit.*, 13). This is questioned by A. VANHOYE, for he says: "non seulement parce qu'elle [la construction de 2,4c] est la seule à suivre une proposition interrogative, mais aussi parce qu'elle est la seule qui soit privée de toute liaison; ailleurs on a *oupô gar* (3,24; 7,39; 20,17), *oupô de* (11,30) ou *kai oupô* (6,17) ou bien *oupô* à l'intérieur de la phrase (7,6.8.30.39b; 8,20.57). En Jn 2,4 on a un *oupô* asyndétique" (*art. cit.*, 160).

death-resurrection. That "the hour" involves Jesus' return to the Father is underscored by the Evangelist in the opening verse of Jn 13, which states that "Jesus knew that his hour had come to depart out of this world to the Father" (13,1) [140].

The non-numerical "hour" is mentioned only once (19,27) in the passion-resurrection narrative (Jn 18-20) [141]. The revelatory words of Jesus to his mother ("Woman, behold you son!": 19,26) and to his Beloved Disciple ("Behold your mother!": 19,27) and the Evangelist's observation in the following verse that after this Jesus knew that *êdê panta tetelestai* (19,28) and Jesus' last word on the cross (*tetelestai*) at 19,30 show that the expression *ap' ekeinês tês hôras* in 19,27 is not simply a chronological indication but refers to "the theological hour" [142], namely, the decisive hour of Jesus' glorifying and Spirit-giving death (cf. 19,30: *kai klinas tên kephalên paredôken to pneuma*) which coincides with the hour when the mother of Jesus becomes the mother of the disciple, and when the disciple of Jesus becomes the son of Jesus' mother [143]. Thus the last mention of "the hour" in the Fourth Gospel (19,27) seems all at once to contain "the hour of Christ, the hour of Mary, the hour of the Church" [144]. In other words, the hour of Jesus' death-resurrection coincides with the hour of the spiritual maternity of Mary and inaugurates the time of the Church. In short, with "the hour" of Christ "the last day" has dawned (cf.

---

[140] These two verses (13,1 and 17,1) on the arrival of "the hour" may be regarded as a sort of inclusion for the whole section (Jn 13-17), since 13,1 is the introduction to the whole of Jn 13-17 and Jesus' prayer of "the hour" in Jn 17 may be considered as the conclusion of his farewell discourse in the immediately preceding chapters. (Here we are using the term "inclusion" not in the strict sense of the term but only in the wide sense.) Note that this is the only section which mentions "the hour" at the beginning and towards the end of the section, while the first section (Jn 2-4) has "the hour" at the beginning alone (2,4), the second section (Jn 5-10) in the middle (7,30; 8,20), the third section (Jn 11-12) towards the end (12,23.27), and the fifth section (Jn 18-20) in the middle (19,27). (See 4.2 below for the division of the Fourth Gospel into sections.)

[141] At 19,14 *hôra* is followed by the number *hektê*, which refers to the hour when Pilate proclaimed Jesus "king of the Jews", the hour when the Paschal lambs were being killed in the temple. Hence the sixth hour here seems to have a symbolic meaning. Although the term "hour" does not occur elsewhere in Jn 18-20 except at 19,27, the whole section describes the chronological succession of the events of "the hour" of Jesus (the betrayal, arrest, trials before the high priest and Pilate, crucifixion, resurrection and ascension), whose theological significance has been highlighted in the previous section (Jn 13-17).

[142] A. FEUILLET, "L'heure de la femme (Jn 16,21) et l'heure de la Mère de Jésus (Jn 19,25-27)", *Bib* 47 (1966) 169-84; 361-80; 557-73 especially 179. Similarly, BROWN understands "that hour" at 19,27 as "the hour of Jesus' return to the Father" (II, 907).

[143] "Questa ora, in cui Gesù proclama il rapporto maternità-filiazione tra Maria e il discepolo e in cui questo rapporto si realizza, è insieme l'ora del Figlio di Dio in cui egli sa che tutto è compiuto, e l'ora della madre" (G. FERRARO, *op. cit.*, 279-80).

[144] *Ibid.*, 280: "ora di Cristo, ora di Maria, ora della Chiesa".

6,39.40.44.54; 12,48)[145], just as with the hour of parturition of a woman (16,21). dawns the day of the child in the world.

Probably it is this eschatological time of the Church that Jesus refers to primarily, 1) when he tells the Samaritan woman: "*erchetai hôra* when neither on this mountain nor in Jerusalem will you worship the Father" (4,21) and "*erchetai hôra kai nyn estin* when the true worshippers will worship the Father in Spirit and truth" (4,23; cf. the addition here of *kai nyn estin* to *erchetai hôra*), 2) when Jesus tells the Jews in Jerusalem: "*erchetai hôra kai nyn estin* when the dead will hear the voice of the Son of God, and those who hear will live" (5,25; cf. also 5,28), 3) when Jesus forewarns the disciples during the Last Supper: "*erchetai hôra* when whoever kills you will think he is offering service to God" (16,2; cf. also 16,4), and 4) when Jesus promises them: "*erchetai hôra* when I shall no longer speak to you in figures but tell you plainly of the Father" (16,25)[146].

We may sum up the results of our brief study of the "hour" in the Fourth Gospel. 1) "The hour" of Jesus refers to his passion-glorification and is of central importance in the Johannine Gospel. Its arrival is mentioned positively for the first time at the centre of the Gospel (12,23.27). While the first part of the Gospel tends towards "the hour" (cf. 2,4; 7,30; 8,20), the second part explains its theological meaning and its soteriological and chronological content (cf. 13,1; 17,1; 19,27). In the words of G. Ferraro:

> L'"*hôra*" è anzitutto l'"*hôra*" di Gesù, è l'"*hôra*" per eccellenza, il culmine della terminologia temporale. È l'"*hôra*" di cui si dice che - non è venuta - e che - è venuta-; è l'"*hôra*" della glorificazione che comprende in se stessa la passione, l'"*hôra*" dell' arresto, l'"*hôra*" del passaggio di Gesù al Padre[147].

2) Besides this primarily Christocentric dimension of the "hour", there is also an ecclesial dimension[148]. "The hour" of Jesus inaugurates the "hour" of

---

[145] Cf. *ibid.*, 297-99 for the Christocentric theology of the Gospel of John.

[146] So W. THÜSSING, *op. cit.*, 97-99. Notice that in all the above instances (4,21.23; 5,25.28; 16,2.25) *hôra* is anarthrous, whereas when *hora* is applied to Jesus it is used with the article (*hê hôra*). *Hôra* is anarthrously used also in the combined expression *idou erchetai hôra kai elêlythen* (16,32), which refers to the time when the disciples "will be scattered" (*skorpisthête*: 16,32). Note that, although this "hour" of the "scattering" of the disciples coincides with "the hour" of the passion of Jesus, the emphasis is on the disciples' being "scattered" on the occasion of the passion of Jesus. This may be the reason for the anarthrous use of *hôra* (cf. 16,2).

[147] G. FERRARO, *op. cit.*, 300; cf. also p. 301. Similarly J. M. ROVIRA BELLOSO states: "La 'hora' de la glorificación comprende la pasión, muerte, resurrección y donación del Espíritu entendidos todos estos momentos como fases interiores de un mismo acontecimiento" (*Revelación de Dios, Salvación del Hombre* [Salamanca 1979] 252).

[148] G. FERRARO, *op. cit.*, 301.

the Church (*tempus Ecclesiae*) during which the Father will be openly revealed (16,25) and worshipped in Spirit and truth (4,21.23), when the dead will live again (5,25) and when the disciples will be persecuted and killed (16,2.4) [149].

3) Since the second major division of the Gospel of John (11,1-20,29) deals with the arrival and significance of "the hour" of Jesus, to which the first part ("the Book of Jesus' Signs") progressively and dramatically tends [150], we may rightly designate the second part as "the Book of Jesus' Hour", 11,1-12,50 being understood as the "bridge-section" [151] which concludes "the Book of Jesus' Signs" and introduces "the Book of Jesus' Hour" [151a].

---

[149] *Ibid.*, 302. The double expression *erchetai hôra kai nyn estin* at 4,23 and 5,25 seems to have double-level significance, namely, the time of Jesus and the time of the Church. Thus regarding 4,23 G. FERRARO affirms:

> L'ora della vera adorazione può essere proclamata presente *"kai nyn estin"* perché è presente Gesù *"egô eimi"*... Questa ora è il tempo sacramentale della Chiesa nella quale si svolge il vero culto, un tempo che viene inaugurato dalla presenza di Gesù che si prolunga nella continuazione di lui attraverso la Chiesa. Perciò vi è la dialettica del duplice annunzio: "viene l'ora" - "viene l'ora ed è adesso" (*ibid.*, 138).

Cf. *ibid.*, 148 for a similar interpretation of 5,25.28. So also W. THÜSSING, *op. cit.*, 98.

[150] J. SEYNAEVE says: "Ainsi la vie publique (ch. 1,19-12,50) peut et doit être considérée comme une longue préparation, comme une réelle anticipation de "l'heure" finale. Y mènent tous les événements décrits dans le récit de la vie publique" ("Le Thème de "l'Heure" dans le Quatrième Évangile", *RAfrT* 13 (1983) 35.

According to A. FEUILLET: "It is evident that all the happenings of Jesus' public life are oriented toward the Hour, as toward a point of consummation" ("The Hour of Jesus and the Sign of Cana", in: *Johannine Studies* [New York 1964] 20).

Similarly H. VAN DEN BUSSCHE writes:

> Evangelium Johannis manifeste stat in prospectu alicuius horae mysteriosae, quae punctum centrale constituit vitae Jesu. Hora illa dat vitae ipsius totum suum sensum, et simul dividit evangelium in duas partes: tota prima pars (cc. 1-12) modo constanti tendit versus illam horam et ab ipsa quasi attrahitur; seconda pars (cc. 13-20) in extenso explicat significationem illius horae ("De Betekenis van het Uur in het vierde Evnagelie", *CollGand* 2 [1952] 97, cited and trans. by I. DE LA POTTERIE, *Exegesis IV Evangelii: De narratione Passionis et Mortis Christi Ioh 18-19*, [Romae, PIB, 1978-79] 17).

But it must be noted that the second part of the Gospel which "explains in detail the significance of that hour" consists not of Jn 13-20 as van den Bussche affirms but of Jn 11-20, since Jesus himself affirms the arrival of "the hour" already at 12,23.27-28 and explains its significance in terms of the glorification of the Son of Man (12,23) and of God (12,27-28), which, as we shall see below, is parallel to 11,4.

[151] See 3.193.

[151a] "The Book of Jesus' Hour" may also be called "the Book of Love" or "the Book of Loving", since the terms *agapê, agapan* and *philein* occur much more frequently in the second book than in the first (*agapê* is found 6 times in Jn 11-20 out of a total of 7 times in Jn, *agapan* 25 out of 36 times, *philein* 7 out of 13 times, and *philos* 5 out of 6 times). Jesus' love for his disciples and friends and the mutual love of the disciples are mentioned for the first time in the second book and are frequently emphasized there (cf. Jesus' love for the disciples: 11,3.5.36; 13,1.1.23.34; 14,21; 15,9.10.12.13; 19,26; 20,2; the disciples' love for Jesus: 14,15. 21.21.23.24.28; 16,27; the disciples' love for one another: 13,34.34.35; 15,12.14.17; the Father's love for the disciples: 14,21.23; 16,27; 17,23). But since "the hour" refers to the passion-death-resurrection which is the greatest revelation of Jesus' love (cf. 13,1), we prefer the title "the Book of Jesus' Hour" to "the Book of Love".

4.14 Appendix (Jn 21)

Since we have already examined and rejected the position of those who propose that Jn 21 is the conclusion of the Gospel as a whole [152], we accept the view of the vast majority of commentators and scholars who consider Jn 21 as an addition to the Gospel of John [153]. We do not enter into the scholarly debate whether Jn 21 was added by the Evangelist or by a redactor [154], though the latter seems more probable 1) because of the differences in style between Jn 21 and the rest of the Gospel [155], 2) because of the presence of the conclusion (20,30-31) before Jn 21 [156], and 3) because of the "ecclesiastical point of view" in Jn 21 [157] as compared to the Christocentric view of the Evangelist in the rest of the Gospel.

If Jn 21 has been added by the redactor, it is an "appendix" as far as the original Gospel is concerned, since the Evangelist had considered the Gospel complete without ch. 21 [158]. But it is probable that the reason why the redactor added Jn 21 to the Gospel was because he regarded 21,1-23 as an "epilogue" to the Johannine drama and wanted 21,24-25 to be a "second (editorial) conclusion" [159].

4.14z In short, Jn 21 may be called an "appendix" which consists of an "epilogue" (21,1-23) and a "second (editorial) conclusion" (21,24-25).

4.1z We may sum up the main results of our study of the principal divisions of the Gospel of John in the following schematic outline:

---

[152] See 4.111.

[153] BARRETT, 576-77; BERNARD, II, 187-92; BULTMANN, 700-2; LIGHTFOOT, 338-42; LINDARS, 618-24; SCHNACKENBURG, III, 341-51; WIKENHAUSER, 452-53. Cf. also CABA (see 2.[19]); CULPEPPER (see 2.[17]); DEEKS (see 2.[10]); DE LA POTTERIE (see 2.[18]3); DODD (see 2.[15]); GUILDING (see 2.22); KAMMERSTÄTTER (see 2.[13]); MOLLAT (see 2.21); PASQUETTO (see 2.[21]); SEGALLA (see 2.[22]); TENNEY (see 2.[16]; VAN DEN BUSSCHE (see 2.[18]2).

[154] See the list of the scholars for each of these positions in BROWN, II, 1080.

[155] So M.-É. BOISMARD, "Le chapitre xxi de saint Jean: essai de critique littéraire", *RB* 54 (1947) 473-501.

[156] So BROWN, II, 1080; SCHNACKENBURG, III, 343.

[157] So SCHNACKENBURG, III, 344. Cf. also S. B. MARROW, *John 21: An Essay in Johannine Ecclesiology* (Rome 1968).

[158] But according to BROWN (III, 1078-79) Jn 21 should not be called an "appendix" but an "epilogue". According to SCHNACKENBURG (III, 344): "None of these designations fully applies". He prefers to call Jn 21 an "editorial conclusion" (III, 341). In our opinion such a phrase is a fitting designation not of the whole of Jn 21 but only of 21,24-25.

If it is remembered, however, that the designation one gives depends on one's viewpoint, a compromise solution can be found. If one's standpoint is that of the Evangelist, Jn 21 may rightly be designated as an "appendix" but, if one's point of view is that of the redactor, 21,1-23 may be named an "epilogue" and 21,24-25 an "editorial conclusion".

[159] Cf. the last note.

THE MAIN DIVISIONS OF THE FOURTH GOSPEL

O. CHRISTOCENTRIC INTRODUCTION (1,1-2,11)
                                     [2,1-11: bridge-pericope]
I. THE BOOK OF JESUS' SIGNS (2,1-12,50)
                                       [11,1-12,50: bridge-section]
II. THE BOOK OF JESUS' HOUR (11,1-20,29)
Z. CHRISTOCENTRIC CONCLUSION (20,30-31)
X. APPENDIX (21,1-25)[160].

4.2 THE SECTIONS OF THE BOOK OF JESUS' SIGNS AND THE BOOK OF JESUS' HOUR

We have seen above that the Gospel of John consists of two closely linked parts which may be called "the Book of Jesus' Signs" (2,1-12,50) and "the Book of Jesus' Hour" (11,1-20,29) which are preceded by an introduction (1,1-2,11) and followed by a conclusion (20,30-31) and an appendix (21,1-25). Now we shall study how these two books are further divided into sections and how these may be designated by proper Johannine titles which point to their content and nature and indicate their interconnections.

4.21 The First Section of the Book of Jesus' Signs

We saw in ch. 2 above how differently Jn 1/2-12 has been divided by various Johannine scholars and commentators. They have divided Jn 2-12 (if Jn 1 is

---

[160] Such a bipartite division with an introduction and a conclusion and with a bridge-passage between the two major parts is also found elsewhere in ancient literature. An excellent example is given in LUCIAN's *How to Write History* (*Pôs dei historian syngraphein*) which divides itself as follows:

O. *Introduction* (1-6)
I. *Part One* (7-33)
     [33 = bridge-passage]
II. *Part Two* (33-60)
Z. *Conclusion* (61-63).

Such a division of Lucian's work is our modification of the outline given by H. HOMEYER (*Lukian, Wie man Geschichte schreiben soll*, Griechisch und Deutsch, herausgegeben, übersetzt und erläutert [München 1965] 13-14) who says: "Die Schrift gliedert sich deutlich in drei Hauptteile: Einleitung (1-6), Durchführung (7-60), Epilogue (61-63)" (*ibid.*, 13). Homeyer divides the "Durchführung (7-60)" into two parts (7-32; 34-60) which are linked together by chapter 33 about whose nature and function he remarks: "Ein Satz, in dem der Autor persönlich hervortritt, und ein Kapitel (33), das durch einen Rückverweis auf den Anfang (Kap. 4: *oikodomia*) die Gliederung unterstreicht, *leiten über* zum zweiten Teil (34-60)..." (*ibid.*, 13) [my italics].

Since chapter 33 refers back to and forms an inclusion with chapter 4 (*oikodomia*) and since chapter 33 simultaneously concludes the first part and introduces the second, it is a "bridge-passage" and hence belongs to both the parts (see 3.19 and especially our quotation of this rule in n. 38a there).

excluded)[161] into two[162], three[163], four[164], five[165], six[166], seven[167], eleven[168], twelve[169], thirteen[170], or twenty[171] sections. Except for the triple division about which at least three or four authors agree[172], there is hardly any agreement among the others with regard to the delimitation of the sections[173]. It is worth noting, however, that many of the above authors regard 4,54 as the end of one section and 5,1 as the beginning of the next[174], even though there is great difference of opinion as to where the first section begins and the second ends.

We shall now carefully apply the different kinds of criteria[175] in order to detect the delimitation of the first section of the Book of Jesus' Signs.

4.211 *Delimitation of the first section*

4.211,1 The beginning of the section

We have seen above that the Book of Jesus' Signs (2,1-12,50) begins with the first sign at Cana (2,1-11)[176] and hence the first section must have its

---

[161] Many include 1,19-51 as part of the first section (1,19-2,11/12). We have included this in the number of sections as reported below.

[162] BERNARD (see 2.1); DEEKS (see 2.[10]); GOURGUES (see 2.[20]); GUILDING (see 2.22); LOHMEYER (see 2.3); WESTCOTT (see 2.[18]1).

[163] BROWN (see 2.[23]); DE LA POTTERIE (see 2.[18]3); SEGALLA (see 2.[22]); WEBSTER (see 2.9).

[164] PASQUETTO (see 2.[21]); VAN DEN BUSSCHE (see 2.[18]2).

[165] TENNEY (see 2.[16]).

[166] BOISMARD (see 2.71); DEFOURNEY (see 2.4).

[167] BOISMARD (see 2.72); DODD (see 2.[15]; MOLLAT (see 2.21); PUIGDOLLERS (see 2.8).

[168] RAU (see 2.[12]).

[169] CULPEPPER (see 2.[17]).

[170] KAMMERSTÄTTER (see 2.[13]).

[171] GOULDER (see 2.23).

[172] BROWN (see 2.[23]), DE LA POTTERIE (see 2.[18]3) and SEGALLA (see 2.[22]) divide Jn 2-12 into three sections (Jn 2-4; 5-10; 11-12) to which is added an introductory section (1,19-51). PRETE's division differs only slightly from those given above, the difference being in the beginning of the last section at 10,40 instead of 11,1, and in the ending of the last but one section at 10,39 instead of 10,42.

[173] Notice, for instance, the divergence in the twofold division according to: 1) BERNARD (1,19-4,54 + 6,1-71; 5,1-47 + 7,1-12,50); 2) DEEKS (1,19-4,54; 5,1-12,50); 3) GOURGUES (1,19-6,71; 7,1-12,50); 4) GUILDING (1,19-4,54; 6,1-71 + 5,1-47 + 7,1-12,50); 5) LOHMEYER (2,1-6,71; 7,1-12,50); 6) WESTCOTT (1,19-4,54; 5,1-12,50) (see ch. 2 above).

Similarly, those who propose a sevenfold division differ widely among themselves with regard to the extension of each section: 1) BOISMARD (1,19-2,12; 2,13-4,54; 5,1-47; 6,1-71; 7,1-10,21; 10,22-11,54; 11,55-19,42); 2) DODD (2,1-4,42; 4,46-5,47; 6,1-71; 7,1-8,59; 9,1-10,39; 11,1-53; 12,1-36 [+ 12,37-50]; 3) MOLLAT (1,19-2,11; 2,12-4,54; 5,1-47; 6,1-71; 7,1-10,21; 10,22-11,54; 11,55-19,42); 4) PUIGDOLLERS (1,19-2,11; 2,12-4,54; 5,1-47; 6,1-71; 7,1-10,21; 10,22-11,53; 11,54-20,29) (see ch. 2 above).

We shall see below that some of these sections (e.g. 5,1-47; 6,1-71) are, in fact, not sections but subsections of larger units or sections (e.g. 5,1-10,42).

[174] So BOISMARD, BROWN, CULPEPPER, DEEKS, DEFOURNEY, DE LA POTTERIE, GOULDER, GOURGUES, KAMMERSTÄTTER, MOLLAT, PASQUETTO, PRETE, PUIGDOLLERS, RAU, SEGALLA, TENNEY, VAN DEN BUSSCHE, WESTCOTT (see ch. 2 above).

[175] See ch. 3 above.

[176] See 4.121.

beginning at 2,1 [177]. This is confirmed by the designation of the changing of the water into wine at Cana as the "beginning of the signs" (*archê tôn sêmeiôn*: 2,11) of Jesus [178].

4.211,2 The end of the section

While many scholars hold the view that the first section ends with the second Cana-sign, a few are of the opinion that the latter (4,46-54) is the beginning of the second section and not the end of the first section [179]. So we must examine briefly the reasons for and against each position.

4.211,21 Reasons for regarding 4,46-54 as the end of the first section

The principal arguments for taking 4,46-54 as the end of the first section and not the beginning of the second section are: 1) Whereas the royal official and his household respond favourably, through faith, to Jesus' word and sign in 4,46-54, the hostility of the Jews towards Jesus is mentioned for the first time in Jn 5 (vv.16.18). This means that a new phase in the public life of Jesus has begun with Jn 5, since such hostile reactions have not been reported in Jn 2-4 [180]. 2) The curing of the cripple in Jn 5 is considered as a "work" (*ergon*: 7,21; *ergazomai*: 5,17) of Jesus, while the healing of the official's son is called a "sign"

---

[177] So BROWN, DODD, LOHMEYER, MATEOS & BARRETO, PASQUETTO, PRETE, SEGALLA, VAN DEN BUSSCHE, WILLEMSE (see ch. 2 above). But some like BOISMARD, CABA, DEFOURNEY, MOLLAT, PUIGDOLLERS begin the section at 2,12 (13) because they take 2,1-11(12) as belonging exclusively to the preceding pericopes (1,19-51) (see ch. 2 above). But we have seen that 2,1-11 is a "bridge-pericope" and hence it simultaneously concludes the introduction (1,1-2,11) and introduces the Book of Jesus' Signs (2,1-12,50) (see 4.112 and 4.121).

[178] So I. DE LA POTTERIE, *Exegesis Quarti Evangelii: capita III-IV* (Romae, PIB, 1972-73) 5: "cum ipse Johannes hunc eventum [primum signum Canae] vocet *initium* signorum (2,11), difficile est illum considerare ut conclusionem introductionis; ergo potius connectendus est cum sequentibus". It may be noted, however, that in another place DE LA POTTERIE holds exactly the opposite view, for he affirms: "preferimus connexionem nostrae pericopae [2,1-12] cum 1,19-51. Tota sectio 1,19-2,12 tunc constituit aliquam 'hebdomadam inauguralem' cujus dies clare indicantur" (*Exegesis Quarti Evangelii: De Matre Iesu in IV Evangelio* [Romae, PIB, 1976-77] 24). Such a contradiction can be avoided if 2,1-11 is considered as a "bridge-pericope" (see 4.112).

[179] E.g. DODD (see 2.[15]); cf. also A. FEUILLET, *Études Johanniques*, 34-46 especially 39-46.

[180] A. FEUILLET rightly remarks:

La plupart du temps la guérison du fils de l'officier de Capharnaüm est rattachée au contexte antécédent. L'argument le plus fort en faveur de cette connexion, c'est qu'avec le chapitre v le ministère public de Jésus prend un nouveau départ: Jésus monte à Jérusalem et y guérit un paralytique un jour de sabbat; à cette occasion il se heurte pour la première fois à l'hostilité déclarée de Juifs, hostilité qui le conduira à la mort (*ibid.*, 34-35).

Similarly, I. DE LA POTTERIE remarks: "Inde a ca. V sumus in contextu *hostilitatis* et polemicae" (*Capita III-IV*, 7). He notes also the radical difference between the faith of the royal official in 4,50.53 and the unbelief of the Jews in Jn 5 (vv. 38.44.46.47) (*ibid.*).

From the dramatic point of view R. A. CULPEPPER finds that "John 5 brings a fresh development" (*op. cit.*, 91).

(*sêmeion*: 4,54)¹⁸¹. 3) While in Jn 4 Jesus reveals himself mostly as the Messiah (4,25-26) and the prophet (4,44; cf. also 4,19), in the discourse in Jn 5 Jesus openly manifests his divinity (5,17-30)¹⁸². 4) Sin (5,14), judgement (5,22.27. 29.30) and testimony (5,31.32.33.34.36.37.39) found often in Jn 5 are missing from 4,46-54¹⁸³. 5) The two Cana-signs form an inclusion for the whole section of Jn 2-4¹⁸⁴. 6) The inclusive character of the two Cana-miracles is confirmed not only by the Evangelist's explicit reference to the first sign both at the beginning and end of the second sign¹⁸⁵ but also by the common pattern of the two signs¹⁸⁶. 7) Finally, the episodes in Jn 2-4 have a chiastic structure (A B C C'B'A')¹⁸⁷, where the first Cana-sign (A) corresponds to the second Cana-sign (A').

4.211,22 Reasons for regarding 4,46-54 as the beginning of the second section

We shall now critically examine the main arguments for connecting the second Cana-sign with the next episode in Jn 5.

1) Jesus' saying in 4,44: "a prophet has no honour in his own country" points forward to the Jerusalemite Jews' adverse reaction to him in Jn 5¹⁸⁸. While it is true that Jesus' "own country" at 4,44 refers to Judea or Jerusalem, the saying in 4,44 does not tell us about the rejection of Jesus by the Jerusalemite Jews in Jn 5 but about the Jews' reaction as compared to that of the Samaritans described in the immediately preceding pericope (cf. *dyo hêmeras* at 4,40 and 4,43); similarly 4,45 clearly refers *back* to 2,23. Since both the immediately preceding verse (4,43) and the following verse (4,45) refer back to the preceding episodes, the middle verse (4,44) too would naturally be expected to do the same (cf. the reluctance or refusal to believe or welcome Jesus at 2,18; 3,11-12).

2) Jesus' complaint to the royal official: "Unless you see signs and wonders you will not believe" (4,48) is understood to be "addressed to the Jews [in Jn 5]

---

[181] SCHNACKENBURG, I, 476; see 5.133 below for the difference between *sêmeia* and *erga*. Cf. also L. CERFAUX, "Les miracles, signes messianiques de Jésus et oeuvres de Dieu, selon l'évangile de saint Jean", in: *L'attente du Messie* (Mélanges J. Coppens) (Bruges 1954) 131-38.

[182] A. FEUILLET says:

Or dans le discours du chapitre v... c'est la personne même de Jésus qui est en cause, et pas seulement sa dignité messianique, mais sa divinité proprement dite, ses relations avec le Pére: pour la première fois Jésus s'affirme avec netteté source de vie conjointement avec le Pére. Cela étant, il semble normal de mettre une coupure entre les chapitres iv et v, et de voir dans le miracle de la piscine (v,1-18), occasion immédiate des enseignements nouveaux du chapitre v, l'introduction à une nouvelle section (*op. cit.*, 35-36).

[183] SCHNACKENBURG, I, 477; I. DE LA POTTERIE, *Capita III-IV*, 7.

[184] See 3.132,2. Cf. also I. DE LA POTTERIE, *Capita III-IV*, 6; A. FEUILLET, *op. cit.*, 38.

[185] SCHNACKENBURG says: "In the narrative sequence the story [of the healing of the official's son] is connected with the preceding (cf. 4:43-46) and 4:54 points back to 2:11" (I, 476).

[186] BROWN, I, 194; see 4.312,1 and n. 317 below.

[187] See 4.32 below.

[188] A. FEUILLET says: "la préface des versets 43-44 annonce ce heurt" (*op. cit.*, 40).

over the head of the royal official"¹⁸⁹. But this is not true, since the Jews in Jn 5 do not believe even after seeing the miracle of the healing of the paralytic (5,1-18.38.44.46.47). The saying of Jesus at 4,48 seems to be intended to raise the royal official from the lower level of faith based on the marvelous aspect of miracles (*sêmeia kai terata*: 4,48; cf. also 2,23) to a more perfect faith based on Jesus' word (4,50: *pisteuein tô[i] logô[i]*; cf. 4,41).

3) The most important argument advanced for taking the healing of the official's son with the curing of the cripple is that "both narratives tell how the word of Christ gave life to those who were as good as dead, either in the sense of being at the point of death or in the sense of living chronically in a state of suspended vitality. In each case the life-giving word is the pivot of the story"¹⁹⁰. It is true that both the stories contain the theme of "living" (*zên*: 4,50.51.53) or "life" (*zôê*: 5,24.26.29.40; *zên*: 5,21; *zôopoiein*: 5,21), but, while *zên* in 4,46-54 refers primarily to physical life, *zên* and *zôê* in Jn 5 denote eternal life. If restoring health/physical life is symbolic of Jesus' power to give eternal life, the latter (*zôê*) has been emphasized already in 3,16.36 and 4,14 (cf. also *hydôr zôn* at 4,10.11) and hence it is not a theme introduced for the first time in 4,46-54 and developed in 5,1-47. In fact, we shall see later that, though the terms connected with "eternal life" (*zôê, zên, zôopoiein*) are frequent in Jn 5, the central point of the episode is not eternal life but the unity of the Son with the Father (cf. 5,17.19-30)¹⁹¹. It is also true that Jesus' word has an important role in the two healing pericopes (*ho logos*: 4,50; 5,24) but obedience to his word is insisted upon also in the first Cana-sign (cf. Mary's instruction to the servants at 2,4: "Do whatever he tells you" and their perfect obedience to Jesus' commands in 2,7-8: *gemisate... egemisan... pherete... ênenkan*, which is similar to the royal official's reaction to Jesus' command at 4,50: *poreuou... eporeueto*). Finally, "believing" is equally underlined in 4,46-54 (cf. vv.50.53) as in 2,1-11 (cf. 2,11), since both the Cana-signs end with faith in Jesus, faith being "a major theme in chs. ii-iv"¹⁹².

4.211,2z Since there are more numerous and more substantial arguments based on different types of criteria in favour of joining 4,46-54 with the preceding pericopes than with the following episode in Jn 5¹⁹³, we prefer to look upon the second Cana-sign (4,46-54) as the conclusion of the first section of the Book of Jesus' Signs than as the beginning of the second section.

---

[189] *Ibid.*, 41.
[190] C. H. DODD, *op. cit.*, 318; cf. also A. FEUILLET, *op. cit.*, 41-44.
[191] See 4.322,2 below [and 3.322 above].
[192] BROWN, I, 197.
[193] BROWN concludes his critical evaluation of A. Feuillet's position that 4,46-54 belongs to the following section:

> We believe that *structurally* the evangelist wished *iv 46-54* to serve *primarily as the conclusion of Part Two* (chs. ii-iv) and only secondarily as the introduction to Part Three. The strong emphasis that this is the second Cana miracle and the similarities that it has with the first Cana miracle make it an obvious *inclusion* with ii 1-11, and inclusion is the Johannine way of marking off parts (I, 198) [my italics].

4.211,3 The unity of the section (Jn 2-4)

Apart from the many parallelisms and/or inclusions between the opening and concluding pericopes (2,1-11; 4,46-54), there are also other factors which point to the unity of Jn 2-4: 1) Besides the description of the two Cana-signs, the term *sêmeion* is often mentioned in Jn 2-4 (2,11.18.23; 3,2; 4.48.54)[193a]. 2) In this first section Jesus travels to and manifests himself in the principal parts of Palestine (cf. "Galilee": 2,1.11; 4,3.43.45.46.47.54; "Judea": 3,22; 4,3.47.54; "Samaria": 4,4.5.7; cf. also the names of villages or towns in Galilee, Judea and Samaria: "Cana": 2,1.22; 4,46; "Jerusalem": 2,13.23; 4,45; "Sychar": 4,5)[193b] thus completing, as it were, the first round of revelation from Cana to Cana. 3) In general the reaction to Jesus' revelation in Jn 2-4 is positive. Thus at the end of the first sign at Cana the disciples believe in him (2,11); during the feast of the Passover many believe in his name (2,23); Nicodemus accepts him as a teacher from God (3,2); many in Judea go to Jesus to be baptized (3,26); many become his disciples there (4,1); the Samaritan woman acknowledges Jesus to be a prophet (4,19) and probably the Messiah/Christ (4,25.29); the Samaritans confess that he is the Saviour of the world (4,42; cf. also 4,39.41); the royal official believes Jesus' word (4,50) and he and his household become believers (4,53). Unlike in the following chapters there is hardly any hostility to Jesus in Jn 2-4. 4) We shall see below that Jn 2-4 has a chiastic structure (A B C C' B' A')[193c].

4.211z Because 2,1 is the beginning of the first section and 4,54 its end, and because the text bounded by these two limits has a unity of its own, we conclude that the first section consists of 2,1-4,54.

4.212 *Title of Jn 2-4: "Jesus' Initial Signs and Encounters (from Cana to Cana)"*

Jn 2-4 has been called by different names such as "The Section of Signs"[194], "From Cana to Cana"[195], "From Cana to Cana - the New Beginning"[196], "Beginnings of the Activity of Jesus"[197], "First Manifestation of Jesus (= From Cana to Cana)"[198], "First Diptych of Revelation and Different Responses of Faith"[199], and many others[200].

[193a] See 5.131 below.
[193b] See 3.15.
[193c] See 4.31 below.
[194] H. VAN DEN BUSSCHE, "La structure de Jean I-XII", 76.
[195] BROWN, I, 93.
[196] SEGALLA, 133.
[197] PRETE (see 2.[14]).
[198] PASQUETTO (see 2.[21]).
[199] DE LA POTTERIE (see 2.[18]3).
[200] See ch. 2 for other titles given by different scholars to Jn 2-4.

Each one of these designations contains an element of truth and underlines an aspect emphasized in Jn 2-4.

H. van den Bussche's title ("the Section of the Signs") refers to the section bounded by the first two signs described in 2,1-11 and 4,46-54 and underscores their importance in Jn 2-4, while his subtitle ("the revelation of the Messiah")[201] highlights an important function of chs. 2-4. But the title and subtitle are not quite exact and may be misleading, since other signs are described in later sections (e.g. the sign of feeding the five thousand in 6,1-15; the sign of raising Lazarus to life in Jn 11) and Jesus' Messiahship is manifested also elsewhere (e.g. *Christos* at 7,31.41; 11,27).

R. E. Brown's designation ("From Cana to Cana - various responses to Jesus' ministry in the different sections of Palestine")[202] gives too much emphasis to the geographical aspect of the first phase of Jesus' ministry and the differences in response.

G. Segalla's title ("From Cana to Cana - the New Beginning") seems to be a combination of Brown's and Dodd's designations of Jn 2-4[203]. Since Segalla does not explain his title, it is difficult to know for certain his reasons for choosing it.

B. Prete's proposal ("Beginnings of the Activity of Jesus") appears to be based on the mention of the "beginning of the signs" at 2,11 but his title remains too general and vague, since "the Activity of Jesus" is not specified or qualified.

V. Pasquetto's appellation ("First Manifestation of Jesus") rightly underlines the revelation of Jesus in Jn 2-4 but does not sufficiently distinguish this from Jesus' subsequent manifestations except by means of the numerical qualification ("first") and a geographical subtitle ("From Cana to Cana"), whereas at 2,11 the Evangelist explicitly states that Jesus "manifested his glory" through performing a "sign".

I. de la Potterie's designation ("First Diptych of Revelation and Different Responses of Faith") highlights the dimension of revelation and that of faith-response. But it gives the impression that there is "revelation" only or mainly in the "diptych" (2,1-12 and 2,13-22) and "responses of faith" only in the rest of the section (2,23-4,54)[204]. This is not quite true to the Johannine text (e.g. the disciples' faith in 2,11).

Granting that it is impossible to include every important aspect of a section in its title, we propose to designate Jn 2-4 as "Jesus' Initial Signs and Encounters". There are two basic reasons: 1) the whole section is enclosed between the wine miracle (2,1-11) called the "beginning of the signs" (*archê tôn*

---

[201] See n. 194.

[202] BROWN, I, cxl.

[203] C. H. DODD, *op. cit.*, 297. He calls 2,1-4,42 the "First Episode. The New Beginning".

[204] This impression is confirmed by DE LA POTTERIE's division of Jn 2-4 into two subsections: "1. Diptychum revelationis (2,1-22)" and "2. Tres responsiones fidei (2,23-4,54)" (see 2.[18]3). (We shall see below that 2,1-4,54 consists of six subdivisions arranged chiastically [1ABC C'B'A'].)

sêmeiôn: 2,11) and the healing of the royal official's son (4,46-54) reported as the "second sign" (*deuteron sêmeion*: 4,54); 2) this section also recounts Jesus' encounters with different kinds of individuals and categories of people e.g. the mother of Jesus, the Jews, Nicodemus (a ruler of the Jews), the Samaritan woman, the royal official (probably a Gentile). Our title has also the merit of containing a central Johannine term ("sign")[205] which the Evangelist himself has employed to describe the two Cana miracles which form an inclusion for the section in question. The adjective "initial" which qualifies "signs and encounters" helps us to distinguish these from those in the following sections and gives us a hint that Jn 2-4 is, in a sense, the "beginning" of Jesus' manifestation through "signs" and personal encounters[206].

We may add a subtitle "from Cana to Cana" (in parenthesis), since the Evangelist explicitly mentions Cana in connection with the two signs. Such a subtitle can also help the reader to remember that the initial round of Jesus' revelation through signs and encounters starts and ends at Cana. In other words, the subtitle indicates the geographical delimitation of the first section of the Book of Jesus' Signs.

4.212z It follows from what has been said above that our title of Jn 2-4 is: *"Jesus' Initial Signs and Encounters (from Cana to Cana)"*.

4.22 The Second Section of the Book of Jesus' Signs

4.221 *Delimitation of the second section*

4.221,1 The beginning of the section

Since we have established above that the first section ends with the last verse of Jn 4 (v.54), the second section must begin with the first verse of Jn 5[207]. A new beginning is indicated at 5,1 by the literary-chronological device *meta tauta*[208] and the mention of Jesus' movement to a new place (Jerusalem)[209] on the

---

[205] See 5.13 below for the different dimensions of "signs" (e.g. the "revelatory", the "Messianic" and the "symbolic" aspects of "signs"). The use of this pregnant term "signs" in the title reminds the readers of those important dimensions in Jn 2-4.

[206] The addition of the adjective "initial" in the title will also answer the main objection (to H. VAN DEN BUSSCHE's designation of Jn 2-4 as "the Section of the Signs") that other "signs" are described in the subsequent sections. It may be objected that Jesus' first encounters (with the disciples) are recounted in 1,35-51 (and not in Jn 2-4). This is true to a certain extent; but what is most emphasized there is the "kerygmatic" aspect (see 4.112 above). Secondly, our subtitle for Jn 2-4 ("from Cana to Cana") further specifies the "signs and encounters" described there (see below).

[207] See 4.211 for the reasons why we do not regard 4,46-54 as the beginning of the second section.

[208] See 3.161.

[209] See 3.15 for the criterion of "geographical indications".

occasion of a feast of the Jews [210]. Four other reasons for regarding Jn 5 as the beginning of a new phase in the development of the Fourth Gospel have been given above [211]. On the basis on this convergence of a number of criteria we conclude that Jn 5 begins the second section.

4.221,2 The end of the second section

Now we have to determine the end-limit of the second section [212]. A number of prominent Johannine scholars have suggested 10,42 as the end of the section [213]. The following arguments may be advanced in its support:

1) There are a number of inclusions and/or parallels between Jn 5,1-47 and 10,22-42:

a) It is instructive to compare, for instance, the insistence on the "works" (*erga*) in Jesus' dialogue-discourses in 5,15-47 and 10,25-39 [214]:

5,36bc : **ta** gar **erga** ha dedôken moi *ho patêr* hina teleiôsô auta,
    de : auta **ta erga ha poiô** *m a r t y r e i   p e r i   e m o u.*
10,25de: **ta erga ha egô poiô**... *m a r t y r e i   p e r i   e m o u.*
10,37ab: ei ou **poiô ta erga** *tou patros* mou, mê pisteuete moi;
10,38ac: ei de **poiô**... **tois ergois** pisteuete...

5,17bc : *ho patêr mou* heôs arti **ergazetai** kagô **ergazomai**.
10,37a : ei ou poiô **ta erga** *tou patros mou...*

5,20d : kai meizona toutôn *deixei* autô[i] **erga**...
10,32b : polla **erga** kala *edeixa* hymin ek *tou patros.*

Notice that not only the term **erga** is repeated many times in both the discourses but also some of the expressions connected with the "works" are identical (e.g. **ta erga ha [egô] poiô** *martyrei peri emou* at 5,36de and 10,25de; cf. also **poiô ta erga** at 10,37a; *deixei...* **erga** at 5,20d and **erga...** *edeixa* at 10,32b).

b) Note also that Jesus refers to God the Father as *ho patêr (mou)* 14 times in 5,1-47 and 9 times in 10,22-42, which is relatively much more frequent than in the intervening episodes [215]. Furthermore, Jesus reveals himself as *(ho) hyios (tou) theou* at 5,25 and 10,36 [216].

---

[210] See 3.17 for the criterion of "liturgical feasts".
[211] See the first four arguments in 4,211,21.
[212] We do not wish to determine where the individual episode which begins at 5,1 ends (which we shall discuss later in 4.3) but where the second major section (which may consist of a number of episodes as in the first section of the Book of Jesus' Signs) ends.
[213] So BROWN (see 2.[23]; DE LA POTTERIE (see 2.[18]3); SEGALLA (see 2.[22]); VAN DEN BUSSCHE (see 2.[18]2). PRETE proposes 10,39 as signaling the end of the section (see 2.[14]).
[214] See 3.132,3 and 3.311.
[215] Jn 5,17.18.19.20.21.22.23.23.26.36.36.37.43.45 and 10,25.29.30.32.36.37.38.38. It is noteworthy that, while *ho patêr (mou)* occurs in 30% of the verses of 5,1-47 and in 43% of the verses of 10,22-42, it is found much less frequently in 6,1-71 (14%); 7,1-8,59 (13%); 9,1-41 (0%); 10,1-21 (19%). Also its occurrence is only 2% in 11,1-54 and 9% in 11,55-12,50.
[216] See 5.121 below. The absolute *ho hyios* is used by Jesus 8 times with reference to himself in 5,19-26 (vv.19.19.20.21.22.23.23.26). And often *egô* on the lips of Jesus (in the context of the

c) Again, the Evangelist's explanation at 5,18 as to why the Jews were trying to kill Jesus is parallel to the Jews' answer to Jesus at 10,33 as to why they want to stone him ("because of blasphemy"):

5,18bc: h o t i... *patera idion elegen ton theon,*
   ison heauton poiôn tô[i] theô[i].
10,33c: h o t i *sy anthrôpos ôn*
   poieis seauton theon.

d) Similarly, the redactional remarks of the Evangelist at 5,18a and 10,39a are parallel to each other. (They may even be thought of as forming a sort of inclusion for the section Jn 5-10 [217], since 5,18a occurs at the beginning of the first discourse and 10,39a at the end of the last discourse, both dealing with the unity of action and being between the Son and the Father.)

5,18a : dia touto *oun* mallon **ezêtoun auton** hoi Ioudaioi *apokteinai*
10,39a: **ezêtoun** [*oun*] palin **auton** *piasai.*

e) We may also note that 5,33 and 10,41 make a similar back-reference to John the Baptist's testimony to Jesus (which was reported in the introduction at 1,19-28):

5,33ab: hymeis apestalkate pros **Iôannên**,
   kai *memartyrêka* tê[i] **alêtheia[i]**.
10,41d: panta de hosa *eipen* **Iôannês**
   peri autou **alêthê** ên.

2) Jn 10,40-42 looks like a double conclusion to Jn 5-10 and to "the public ministry of Jesus" [218].

3) These concluding verses of Jn 10 may be thought of as forming a kind of inclusion with the "testimonial introduction" in which John the Baptist bears witness to Jesus (1,19-34; cf. also 1,6-8.15.35-36) [219]. This is supported by the fact that 10,40 is almost a verbatim repetition of 1,28:

---

controversies with the Jews who accuse him of blasphemy cf. 5,18; 10,33.36) is equivalent to *ho hyios*. For instance, *ou dynamai egô poiein ap' emautou ouden* at 5,30 is parallel to *ou dynatai ho hyios poiein aph' heautou ouden* at 5,19, since 5,19 and 5,30 are the extreme elements of the chiastic structure (ABCC'B'A') of 5,19-30 (see 3.322). Again, *egô* stands for *ho hyios* in Jesus' statements: *egô elêlytha en tô[i] onomati tou patros mou* (5,43), *egô katêgorêsô hymôn pros ton patera* (5,45), *ta erga ha egô poiô en tô[i] onomati tou patros mou* (10,25), *egô kai ho patêr hen esmen* (10,30), since *egô* and *ho patêr* go together in all of them.

[217] H. VAN DEN BUSSCHE, "La structure de Jean I-XII", 97. He regards the inclusion between 5,17-18 and 10,31-39 as a "perfect inclusion", for he concludes: "L'inclusion de la section des oeuvres est parfaite" (*ibid.*, 103). It must, however, be admitted that the inclusion is not "perfect", since it does not occur at the beginning of Jn 5 (namely, at 5,1).

[218] Regarding 10,40-42 BROWN says: "These verses supply a conclusion for... chs. v-x; and, indeed, by their tone they seem to bring to an end the public ministry of Jesus" (I, 414).

[219] See 4.112. It must be observed that the very purpose of the Baptist's testimony stated in 1,7 ("that all may *believe* through him") is (at least partially) fulfilled in 10,40-42, since "many" are said to have "*believed* in him" [Jesus] (10,42) because of the testimony of John (10,41).

1,28 : tauta en Bêthania[i] egeneto *peran tou Iordanou*,
hopou ên ho **Iôannês baptizôn**.
10,40: kai apêlthen palin *peran tou Iordanou* eis ton topon
hopou ên **Iôannês** to prôton **baptizôn**... [220].

It is also worth noting that the acknowledgement of the many who believe in Jesus at Bethany beyond the Jordan (10,41: "everything that John said about this man was true") refers to the total testimony of the Baptist in 1,1-36 [221].

4.221,2z Because of these reasons we may conclude that 10,42 indicates the end of the second section (5,1-10,42) of the Book of Jesus' Signs [222].

4.221,3 The unity of the section (Jn 5-10).

Besides the numerous inclusions and/or parallels between the episodes which begin and end the section (5,1-47; 10,22-42), its unity is underlined by other factors as well:

1) Unlike in the previous section (Jn 2-4) where Jesus' miracles were generally referred to as "signs" (*sêmeia*), in Jn 5-10 some of his miracles are called "works" (*erga*: 5,20.36.36; 7,3.21; 9,3.4; 10,25.32.32.33.37.38) [223], though others are still called "signs" (*sêmeia*: 6,2.14.26.30; 7,31;9,16) [224].

2) All the miracle narratives in Jn 5-10 (unlike those in Jn 2-4) are followed by a dialogue and/or discourse which deals with the miracle. Thus the curing of the cripple at Bethzatha (5,1-9c) leads to a dialogue between the cured man and the Jews (5,9d-13) and another between him, Jesus and the Jews (5,14-18) which turns into a discourse of Jesus on the unity of the Son with the Father (5,19-30) and on the witnesses to Jesus (5,31-47). Similarly, after the sign of feeding the five thousand (6,1-15) and Jesus' walking on the water (6,16-21) there follows a dialogue/discourse on the bread of life (6,22-59). Finally, after the healing of the man born blind (9,1-7) there ensues a series of dialogues (connected with the healing) between the cured blind man and his neighbours (9,8-12), the man and the Pharisees (9,13-17.24-34), the Pharisees and the parents of the man (9,18-23),

---

[220] Cf. H. VAN DEN BUSSCHE, *art. cit.*, 97. According to BROWN (I, 414) 10,40-42 forms an inclusion only with 1,19-28. But since 10,41 refers back to the entire testimony of John ("everything that John said about this man was true"), 10,40-42 may be said to form an inclusion not only with 1,19-28 but with the whole of 1,1-34 (cf. 1,6-8.15).

[221] Because of this inclusion WILLEMSE regards 1,19-10,42 as one of the "phases" in the structure of the Fourth Gospel (see 2.[11]).

[222] See ch. 2 for a critical evaluation of those who divide the Book of Jesus' Signs differently. For instance, DODD divides the Book of Signs into seven "episodes" (2,1-4,42; 4,46-5,47; 6,1-71; 7,1-8,59; 9,1-10,39/42) (see 2.[15] for our criticism of this division). We shall see below that some of these "episodes" correspond to our subsections (e.g. 6,1-71; 7,1-8,59) (see 4.3).

[223] See 5.13 below.

[224] See 5.133 below for the distinction between "signs" and "works".

the man and Jesus (9,35-38), and finally Jesus and the Pharisees (9,39-41)[225]. This pattern of miracle-dialogue/discourse is a characteristic feature only of the second section[226].

3) In Jn 5-10 it is in the context of Jewish feasts such as the Sabbath (5,9; 9,14), the Passover (6,4), Tabernacles (7,2), and the Dedication (10,22)[227] that Jesus reveals himself through works and signs, dialogues, controversies and discourses[228]. During an unnamed feast which coincides with a Sabbath, Jesus cures a cripple (5,1-9) and on another Sabbath he gives sight to a man born blind (9,1-7.14). When the Passover is near, he feeds the crowd (6,1-15) and walks on the sea (6,16-21). During the feast of Tabernacles and Dedication Jesus engages in controversies with the unbelieving Jews (7,1-8,59; 10,22-39).

4) There is a strong opposition and hostility to Jesus and his revelation through word and deed in the second section, which we do not find in Jn 2-4. His words and actions cause divisions (*schisma*: 7,43; 9,16; 10,19) among the Jews. In Jn 5-10 the Evangelist mentions repeated Jewish attempts to arrest Jesus (7,30. 32.44; 8,20; 10,39), stone him (8,59; 10,31.31.33) and kill him (5,18; 7,1.19.25; 8,37.40). The Jews' hostility towards Jesus and yet their failure to harm him because his "hour" has not yet come (7,30; 8,20) heighten the dramatic tension and indicate a new stage in the dramatic development of the Fourth Gospel[229].

5) We shall show below that Jn 5-10 has a chiastic structure (2B C D D' C' B')[230] which confirms the unity of the section.

4.212,13z These reasons are sufficiently compelling to acknowledge that the second section of the Book of Signs (Jn 5-10) is a well-knit unit.

4.222 *Title of Jn 5-10: "Jesus' Works, Signs and Discussions (at Jewish Feasts)"*

Jn 5-10 has been called "the Section of Works"[231], "Jesus and the principal feasts of the Jews"[232], "Fulness of the miraculous and revelatory

---

[225] See 3.1[12]).

[226] We shall see later that in the next section (11,1-12,50) Jesus' dialogue/discourse precedes the miracle (cf. the raising of Lazarus in Jn 11). We have seen above that the signs in the first section (2,1-11; 4,46-54) are not followed by any dialogue/discourse dealing with the theme of the miracle.

[227] See 3.17. It is true that the feast of "the Passover" is mentioned also at 2,13.23. But note that the other Jewish feasts are mentioned only in Jn 5-10.

[228] In the first section (Jn 2-4) 2,23 mentions the "signs" that Jesus did in Jerusalem during the feast of Passover, but they are not described there. Nor is there any discourse connected with the two Cana-signs.

[229] See 3.2[12].

[230] See 4.32 below.

[231] So VAN DEN BUSSCHE (see 2.[18]2).

[232] So BROWN (see 2.[23]). Similarly SEGALLA calls Jn 5-10 "Gesù e le feste giudaiche" (see 2.[22]).

activity of Jesus"[233], and "Second diptych of revelation and unbelief of the Jews"[234]. It is true that each one of these titles underlines an aspect of Jn 5-10.

H. van den Bussche's designation of Jn 5-10 as "the Section of the Works" underscores the importance of the "works" (*erga*) in the higher revelation of Jesus in Jn 5-10[235]. But since Jn 5-10 includes not only "works" but also "signs" (cf. the sign of feeding the five thousand in 6,1-15 and Jesus' reference to it at 6,26), discussions and discourses which are of capital importance for the correct understanding of the section in question but are not included in van den Bussche's title, the latter is not adequate[236].

While it is true that some important feasts of the Jews (the Passover, Tabernacles and Dedication) are, as we have seen above, mentioned in Jn 5-10, R. E. Brown's designation of the entire section as "Jesus and the principal feasts of the Jews" seems to overstress their relative importance in the Johannine Gospel in which all "the principal feasts of the Jews" (e.g. the Pentecost) are not mentioned[237].

While there is "miraculous and revelatory activity of Jesus" in Jn 5-10, it is an exaggeration to call it the "fulness" of such activity, as Prete does[238]. If Jn 5-10 already provides the "fulness", the following chapters are redundant.

Whereas it is correct to call attention to the revelation of Jesus and the unbelief of the Jews in Jn 5-10, one finds it difficult to see the section as a "second diptych of revelation and unbelief of the Jews" as I. de la Potterie suggests[239], since Jn 5 and Jn 6 do not form a "diptych" as there are many scenes in them[240], whereas a diptych, in the strict sense, contains only two scenes.

We suggest the title "Jesus' Works, Signs and Discussions", since the section contains the "works", "signs" and "discussions" of Jesus, all of which have a revelatory role. Such a designation also indicates the link with and dif-

---

[233] Prete proposes to name 5,1-10,39 "Pienezza dell'attività taumaturgica e rivelazione di Gesù" (see 2.[14]).

[234] So de la Potterie (see 2.[14]).

[235] H. van den Bussche, *art. cit.*, 88-103. According to him, the revelation of Jesus through the works in Jn 5-10 is higher than the Messianic revelation through the signs in Jn 2-4, for he says: "la révélation par les oeuvres est supérieure à l'attente du peuple juif..." (*ibid.*, 89). While the signs manifest Jesus as the Jewish Messiah, the works reveal him as the divine "Son of Man" and the "Son of God" (*ibid.*).

[236] See 2.[18]2 above for our criticism of van den Bussche and see 5.133 below for the similarities and differences between "signs" and "works".

[237] That all the principal feasts of the Jews were not so important for John is seen by his mention of a "feast" without a name at 5,1. Some have suggested that this unnamed feast could be Pentecost but others prefer to see it as New Year (cf. A. Guilding, *op. cit.*, 69-72). But one wonders why the Evangelist did not specify this feast, if it was important for him, since he identifies the other feasts elsewhere (e.g. 2,13; 6,4; 7,2; 10,22). What is important for the Evangelist is rather that the day Jesus cured the cripple was a Sabbath (cf. 5,9.16.18).

[238] See n. 233.

[239] See 2.[18]3.

[240] See 4.32 below for the division of Jn 5-10 into subsections.

ference from the first section of "Jesus' Initial Signs and Encounters" (Jn 2-4). Our short title includes not only the "works" and "signs" done by Jesus and described in Jn 5-10 but also all the dialogues, discourses and controversies, many of which are in close connection with the "works" and the "signs" [241]. So the title ("Jesus' Works, Signs and Discussions") must be understood as a short form for a longer title such as "Jesus' Works and Signs, Dialogues, Discourses and Controversies".

Since some Jewish feasts have a secondary role in Jn 5-10, a subtitle ("at Jewish Feasts") could be added to the title ("Jesus' Works, Signs and Discussions") [242].

4.222z Thus our title and subtitle for the second section (Jn 5-10) are: *"Jesus' Works, Signs and Discussions (at Jewish Feasts)"*.

4.23 The Third Section of the Book of Jesus' Signs = the First Section of the Book of Jesus' Hour (= the Bridge-Section)

4.231 *Delimitation of the bridge-section*

We have seen above that the Book of Jesus' Signs extends from 2,1 to 12,50 and the Book of Jesus' Hour from 11,1 to 20,29, which means that the last section of the first book coincides with the first section of the second book [243]. In other words, 11,1-12,50 is a *bridge-section* [244] common to both the books. It is clear that, if the the Book of Jesus' Signs ends with 12,50 and the Book of Jesus' Hour begins at 11,1, those two verses (11,1 and 12,50) indicate the limits of the bridge-section (11,1-12,50).

The unity of this section (Jn 11,1-12,50) is supported by the numerous cross-references [244a] and parallel elements in 11,1-54 and 11,55-12,50 [244b].

4.232 *Title of Jn 11-12: "the Climactic Sign and the Coming of Jesus' Hour (Bridge-Section)*

B. Prete calls 10,40-12,50 the "last facts of the public activity of Jesus" [245]. While this is factually true, it is a colourless title which does not bring out the particular hue of the Johannine presentation of these "last facts of the public activity of Jesus".

---

[241] See 3.1[12] above and 5.13 below.

[242] By adding this subtitle ("at Jewish Feasts") the reader is reminded that most of "Jesus' Works and Signs" and the (accompanying) dialogues, discourses and controversies occurred on the occasion of some Jewish feasts.

[243] See 4.121 and especially 4.131,2.

[244] See 4.131z. Cf. BROWN, I, 429 for the transitional role of Jn 11.

[244a] See ch.3, n. 25.

[244b] See 4.33 below. Cf. P. MOURLON BEERNAERT, *art. cit.*, 123-49.

[245] See 2.[14].

H. van den Bussche gives Jn 11-12 the title "la montée finale à Jérusalem"[246]. It is correct to say that in this section Jesus goes up to Jerusalem for the last time. But strictly speaking, Jesus' going up to Jerusalem is spoken of only in the second subsection (11,55-12,50) (cf. 11,56; 12,12), whereas his going to Judea/Bethany is emphasized in Jn 11 (e.g. at 11,7: "Let us go into Judea again"; cf. also 11,8.11.15.16.17.20)[247]. Secondly, van den Bussche's title is silent about Jesus' greatest sign, namely, raising Lazarus to life (Jn 11), and its relation to the arrival of "the hour" of Jesus (Jn 12), although this theme may be implicit in his title.

At least three Johannine scholars rightly give Jn 11-12 a title that contains an explicit reference to "the hour". Thus I. de la Potterie designates Jn 11-12 "preparations and prefigurations of the hour of Jesus"[248]. It is certainly a good insight to link Jn 11-12 with "the hour", but the title neither indicates the connection of Jn 11-12 with the preceding section(s) nor underlines (although it is implied) the role of the final sign of raising Lazarus from the dead, which leads to Jesus' death.

R. E. Brown and G. Segalla give almost identical titles: "Jesus moves towards the hour of death and glory"[249], and "Jesus goes towards the hour of death and glorification"[250]. These titles rightly stress the movement in Jn 11-12 towards "the hour" of Jesus' death-glorification. But a more suitable title can still be found[251].

We suggest the title "the Climactic Sign and the Coming of Jesus' Hour", since the dramatic development of the Fourth Gospel reaches a "climax" with the "sign" of the raising of Lazarus (11,1-44) and the consequent decision of the Sanhedrin to kill Jesus (11,45-54), and since the anointing at Bethany (11,55-12,11), the triumphal entry into Jerusalem (12,12-19) and the coming of the Greeks (12,20-36) announce the imminence or arrival of "the hour" of Jesus (cf. 12,7.16.23.27). The title also indicates the bridging character of the section, since the mention of "sign" tells the reader that this section belongs to the Book of Jesus' Signs (Jn 2-12) and the mention of "the hour" hints that the present section is also part of the Book of Jesus' Hour (11,1-20,29).

In order to underline the "bridging" function of Jn 11-12, we may add a subtitle "Bridge-Section".

---

[246] H. VAN DEN BUSSCHE, "La Structure de Jean I-XII", 103. He explains the title in the following words: "Jésus monte à Jérusalem, c'est une marche à la mort. Mais avant de mourir, il ressuscite un mort à la vie" (*ibid.*).

[247] In his commentary on Jn VAN DEN BUSSCHE designates Jn 11-12 as "la montée vers Jérusalem" (see 2.[18]1), which implicitly includes Jesus' going to Judea/Bethany.

[248] See 2.[13]3.

[249] See 2.[23].

[250] See 2.[22].

[251] See below our title "the Climactic Sign and the Coming of Jesus' Hour".

4.232z To sum up, we propose to name Jn 11-12 (the third section of the Book of Jesus' Signs which is the same as the first section of the Book of Jesus' Hour) *"the Climactic Sign and the Coming of Jesus' Hour (Bridge-Section)"*.

4.24 The Second Section of the Book of Jesus' Hour

4.241 Delimitation of the second section

First of all, 13,1 is a solemn introduction: "Now before the feast of the Passover, when Jesus knew that his hour had come to depart out of this world to the Father, having loved his own who were in the world, he loved them to the end" [252].

The delimitation of this section is clearly marked by the indisputable inclusion between the first verse of ch. 13 and the last verse of ch. 17, both of which insist upon "love":

13,1: **agapêsas** *tou idious... eis telos* **êgapêsen** *autous*
17,26: *hina hê* **agapê** *hên* **êgapêsas** *me en autois ê[i]*... [253].

The inclusive character of the beginning of Jn 13 and the end of Jn 17 is reinforced by the repetition of other Johannine terms there (*patêr*: 13,1; 17,24.25; *kosmos*: 13,1.1; 17,24.25).

The unity of Jn 13-17 is confirmed by the criteria of *time* (13,2: *deipnou ginomenou*, that is, during the Last Supper before the Passion), *audience* (the disciples of Jesus) and *literary genre* (*"farewell"*: cf. Jesus' announcement of his imminent departure: 13,33; 14,2-4; 16,16; his reassurance of his disciples: 14,1.27; 16,6-7.22; his directive to the disciples to keep his commandments: 14,15.21; 15,10.14; and especially his commandment of mutual love: 13,34; 15,12.17; his desire for unity among his followers: 17,11.21-23; his prediction of future persecutions: 15,18.20; 16,2-3; his gift of peace: 14,27; 16,23; his promise of joy: 15,11; 16,22.24; his assurance of the disciples' prayers being heard: 14,13.14; 15,16; 16,24.26; his promise of sending the Spirit/Paraclete: 14,16-17.26; 15,26; 16,7-11.13-15; his final prayer: 17,1-26) [254].

---

[252] See 3.122,5.
[253] See 3.132,5. In the words of Y. SIMOENS:

L'appui formel qui permet de définir Jn 13-17 comme un ensemble en soi est la répétition insistante de l'agapê à son début (13,1) et à son terme (17,26)...
L'inclusion est d'autant plus nette qu'elle ne se limite point à la simple reprise d'un seul term... Mais elle est formée de l'attirance mutuelle qui joue entre un double emploi du verbe *agapan* en 13,1 et un emploi du même verbe, accompagné d'un complement interne de même racine, *agapê*, en 17,26 (*La gloire d'aimer. Structures stylistiques et interprétatives dans le Discours de la Cène (Jn 13-17)* [AnBib 90] [Rome 1981] 55-56).

[254] BROWN, II, 597-601; E. CORTES, *Los Discursos de Adiós de Gn 49 a Jn 13-17* (Barcelona 1976) 366-84; J. MUNCK, "Discours d'adieu dans le Nouveau Testament et dans la littérature biblique", *Aux sources de la tradition chrétienne* (Mélanges M. Goguel) (Neuchâtel 1950) 155-70.

The unity of Jn 13-17 is supported also by its chiastic structure, as we shall see later [255].

Since most of the Johannine scholars understand Jn 13-17 as a large literary unit [256], it is not necessary, it seems to us, to explain the obvious any further.

4.242 Title of Jn 13-17: "Jesus' Farewell of the Hour (at the Last Supper)"

Some of the headings suggested by different scholars are: "the Last Supper"[257], "the dialogues at supper"[258], "the discourse after the supper"[259], "the last supper and farewell discourses"[260], "the Farewell Discourses"[261], "the book of farewells"[262], "the last ministry of love"[263], "the supreme manifestation of Jesus in the intimacy of the cenacle"[264], "manifestation of Jesus to 'his own' before death"[265], and "the testament of Jesus to his disciples"[266].

The diversity of the titles cited above demonstrates the difficulty of expressing the occasion, literary genre and nature (and content) of Jn 13-17 in a few words. "The Last Supper" suggests the occasion; "Farewell Discourses" and "the testament" indicate the literary genre; "manifestation of Jesus" expresses the revelatory nature. All the titles given above validly represent an important aspect of Jn 13-17.

Without claiming to give a title that would contain all the aspects, we propose "Jesus' Farewell of the Hour". First of all, this title underlines "the hour" of Jesus emphasized by the Evangelist himself in the very first verse of the section (13,1) and in the opening words of the prayer of the hour (17,1: "the hour has come")[267]. Secondly, it hints at the literary genre ("farewell") of

---

BROWN concludes his study of the literary genre of Jn 13-17 in the following words: "From this survey of parallel themes it seems certain that the Last Discourse of the Fourth Gospel belongs to the *literary genre* of the *farewell speech*" (II, 600-601) [my italics].

PANIMOLLE prefers to designate Jn 13-17 "the testament of Jesus", for he writes: "In realtà Gv 13-17 è la sezione del quarto vangelo che contiene *il testamento di Gesù* o i suoi discorsi di addio..." (III, 154).

[255] See 4.34 below.

[256] BROWN, CABA, CULPEPPER, DE LA POTTERIE, DODD, GOULDER, GOURGUES, PASQUETTO, PRETE, SEGALLA, VAN DEN BUSSCHE, WEBSTER, WESTCOTT (see ch. 2). Cf. also PANIMOLLE, III, 151-370.

[257] BROWN (see 2.[23]).

[258] WEBSTER (see 2.9).

[259] DE LA POTTERIE (see 2.[18]3).

[260] PRETE (see 2.[14]).

[261] DODD (see 2.[15]); VAN DEN BUSSCHE (see 2.[18]2).

[262] SEGALLA (see 2.[22]).

[263] WESTCOTT (see 2.[18]1).

[264] CABA (see 2.[19]).

[265] PASQUETTO (see 2.[21]).

[266] PANIMOLLE, III, 151. Cf. the other titles of Jn 13-17 given by various authors grouped together by S. MIGLIASSO, *La presenza dell' Assente. Saggio di analisi letterario-strutturale e di sintesi teologica di Gv. 13,31-14,31* (Roma 1979) 44.

[267] See 4.13.

these chapters. Thirdly, it is general enough to include the symbolic action of the hour (the washing of the disciples' feet), the dialogues, discourses and prayer of the hour. Fourthly, "Jesus' Farewell of the Hour" underscores the dramatic moment in the life of Jesus at which he bids farewell to his own (13,1). Fifthly, it reminds the reader of the revelatory aspect of these chapters, in which Jesus reveals the secrets of his heart to his own. Finally, the mention of "the hour" in the title indicates the links between this section (Jn 13-17) and the preceding section of "the Climactic Sign and the Coming of Jesus' Hour" (11,1-12,50) on the one hand, and between the present section and the following section of "the Hour of Jesus' Passion-Death-Resurrection" (Jn 18-20) on the other [268].

Since it was during Jesus' last supper (*deipnou ginomenou*: 13,2) with his disciples that he bade them farewell, we suggest "at the Last Supper" as the subtitle for Jn 13-17.

4.242z In short, the second section of the Book of Jesus' Hour or the fourth section of the Fourth Gospel as a whole (13,1-17,26) may be called *"Jesus' Farewell of the Hour (at the Last Supper)"*.

4.25 The Third Section of the Book of Jesus' Hour

4.251 *Delimitation of the section*

The beginning of the section is clearly marked by the Evangelist, since at 18,1 he paints the picture of Jesus leaving the cenacle with his disciples, crossing the Kidron valley and entering a garden, which is a transitional introduction to his betrayal and arrest in Gethsemane (18,2-12).

Although Johannine scholars are almost unanimous in affirming the beginning of a new section at 18,1 [269], there is great divergence of opinion among them regarding its end. According to some, the end of ch. 19 indicates the end of the section [270], while according to others the section concludes only at the end of Jn 20 [271]. Now let us examine the main reasons for these two positions.

4.251,1 Reasons for the unity of Jn 18-19

An important argument for regarding Jn 18-19 as an independent unit (ending at 19,42) is that it contains the Johannine "Passion Narrative" which is

---

[268] See 4.25.

[269] See ch. 2 above. Most of the scholars we examined there agree that 18,1 signals the beginning of a new unit, although the length of the unit is determined differently by different authors.

[270] E.g. BROWN, CABA, DE LA POTTERIE, PASQUETTO, PRETE, SEGALLA (see ch. 2). SEGALLA takes Jn 18-19 not as a section but rather as the fourth principal part of the Fourth Gospel which he calls "il libro della Passione" (132; 136).

[271] E.g. DODD, VAN DEN BUSSCHE, WESTCOTT (see ch. 2). Cf. also TENNEY and WEBSTER who regard Jn 18-20 not as a section but as a major part of the Fourth Gospel (see ch. 2).

said to be similar to the Synoptic narrative of the Passion [272]. Secondly, 18,1-11 and 19,38-42 are thought of as the "introduction" and "epilogue" of the Passion because of a topographical inclusion (*kêpos* at 18,1; 19,41) [273].

Regarding the first reason, though there may be some similarity between the Johannine and Synoptic Passion Narratives especially in the order of the major events narrated (the arrest, the Jewish trial, the Roman trial, the crucifixion and the burial), this *"grosso modo"* similarity does not prove the dependence of John on the Synoptics [274], and hence the question of the unity of Jn 18-19 cannot be settled by appealing to some Synoptic similarity. Secondly, the Synoptics themselves differ in their presentation of the Passion of Jesus. For instance, whereas Mark separates Jesus' burial (Mk 15,42-47) from the episode of the empty tomb (Mk 16,1-8), Luke unites them (Lk 23,50-24,11; cf. *to men... tê[i] de* at 23,56-24,1). Thirdly there are many narrative, dramatic and theological differences between the Johannine and Synoptic Narratives of the Passion [275]. Finally, reading the Johannine Passion Narrative through Synoptic spectacles does not help us to appreciate the Johannine perspective of the intimate interpenetration of the Passion and Resurrection of Jesus in Jn 18-20 [276].

Regarding the second argument based on the occurrence of a "garden" (*kêpos*) at 18,1 and 19,41, it is doubtful whether this is intended as an inclusion, since the term refers to two different gardens in two different places (the one across the Kidron valley: 18,1, and the other on Calvary where Jesus was crucified: 19,41). Furthermore, it must be noted that there is a cross-reference at 18,26 to the "garden" (*kêpos*) of 18,1. Similarly, there is an indirect reference to the second "garden" (*kêpos*) of 19,41, when the "gardener" (*kêpouros*) is mentioned at 20,15 [277].

---

[272] PANIMOLLE, III, 371; 375.

[273] I. DE LA POTTERIE, *De narratione Passionis et Mortis Christi: Ioh 18-19* (Romae, PIB, 1978-79) 42. Concerning 18,1-11 and 19,38-42 he says: "Prima et quinta scaena (ambae in 'horto') sunt aliquo sensu extra ipsam narrationem, et constituunt potius *introductionem* et *epilogum*" (*ibid.*, 42). The mention of a "garden" (*kêpos*) at 18,1 and 19,41 is regarded by him as an inclusion (*ibid.*).
Similarly, PASQUETTO takes 18,1-11 as "Introduzione (= Gesù nell'Orto)" and 19,38-42 as "Conclusione (Sepoltura di Gesù nell'Orto)" (*op. cit.*, 329-30). Cf. also PANIMOLLE, III, 376.

[274] In the words of R. E. BROWN: "John does not draw to any extent on the existing Synoptic Gospels or on their sources as reconstructed by scholars. The Johannine Passion Narrative is based on an independent tradition that has similarities to the Synoptic sources" (II, 791).

[275] Cf. A. VANHOYE & I. DE LA POTTERIE & C. DUQUOC & É. CHARPENTIER, *La Passion selon les quatre Évangiles* (Paris 1981) 11-63; 65-87; 107-123; especially 66-77. Cf. also C. H. DODD, *op. cit.*, 423-43.

[276] See 4.251,2.

[277] The scholars who see an inclusion created by *kêpos* at 18,1 and 19,41 (see n. 273 above) do not mention its occurrence at 18,26 nor the presence of *kêpouros* at 20,15. PANIMOLLE mentions also *topos* at 18,2 and 19,41 as inclusive in character (III, 376). But *topos* at 19,41 is rather a back-reference to (or inclusion with) *Kraniou Topos* at 19,17, since *topos* in each instance is qualified as the place where Jesus was crucified:

19,17-18: ... Kraniou **Topon**... *hopou* auton *estaurôsan*
19,41 : ên de en tô[i] **topô[i]** *hopou estaurôthê*...

4.251,2 Reasons for the unity of Jn 18-20

1) C. H. Dodd has demonstrated that many individual episodes (e.g. Jn 5) of the Book of Signs follow the *pattern* of *narrative* and *discourse* and that Jn 13-20 has the same pattern but in the reverse order, since Jn 13-17 is basically a *discourse* which interprets the *narrative* of the passion-death-resurrection of Jesus in Jn 18-20[278]. If, then, as we have seen above, the interpretative discourse in Jn 13-17 is a literary unit ("Jesus' Farewell of the Hour")[279], it is natural to expect the continuous narrative in Jn 18-20 to be a corresponding literary unit.

2) Secondly, we have seen above that "the hour" of Jesus consists not only of his death but also his resurrection, or rather his death and resurrection are seen as the single event of his going to the Father (13,1) or of his glorification (12,23; 17,1)[280]. Since the Evangelist does not separate death from resurrection, crucifixion from exaltation (cf. "the lifting up of the Son of Man" at 3,14; 8,28; 12,32.34), the Passion-narrative (Jn 18-19) should not be separated from the Resurrection-narrative (Jn 20).

3) The above conclusion is confirmed by the inclusion between the beginning and end of Jn 18-20 (*hoi mathētai autou*: 18,1.1.2; 20,30)[281].

4) Jn 18-19 and Jn 20 are intimately interlinked. Consider, for instance, the terms common to the last scene of Jn 19 (the burial of Jesus: 19,38-42) and the first episode of Jn 20 (at the tomb of Jesus: 20,1-18):

Common Terms	Jn 19,38-42	Jn 20,1-18
mathētēs	38	2.3.4.8.10.18
airein	38.38	1.2.13.15
to sōma tou Iēsou	38.40	12
erchesthai	38.39.39	1.2.3.4.6.18
othonia	40	5.6.7
mnēmeion	41.42	1.1.2.3.4.6.8.11.11
tithēmi	41.42	2.13.15

It should also be noted that the principal actors in 20,1-10 were mentioned already in Jn 18-19 (*Maria hē Magdalēnē*: 19,25; 20,1; *[Simōn] Petros*: 18,10.

---

[278] C. H. DODD, *op. cit.*, 290; 423. Regarding the relation between Jn 13-17 and Jn 18-20 on the one hand, and the function of the narrative of the Passion-Resurrection (Jn 18-20) on the other hand DODD says:

> It is as though the evangelist, having sufficiently set forth the meaning of the death and resurrection of Christ, turned to the reader and said, 'And now I will tell you what actually happened, and you will see that the facts themselves bear out my interpretation' (*ibid.*, 431-32).

[279] See 4.24.
[280] See 4.132.
[281] It is quite normal that the general inclusion for the whole book serves as one also for the final section.

11.15.16.16.17.18.25.26.27; 20,2.3.4.6; *allos mathêtês*: 18,15.16; 20,2.3.4.8; cf. also 19,26.27.27). Besides, the Beloved Disciple and Simon Peter are together both in 20,1-10 and in 18,15-16.

The episodes of the crucifixion (in Jn 19) and those of the resurrection (in Jn 20) are connected through some important common terms and expressions (e.g. *pleura*: 19,34; 20,20.25.27; *hê graphê*: 19,24.28.36.37; 20,9; *(to) pneuma*: 19,30; 20,22; *horaô... pisteuô*: 19,35; 20,8.25.29.29).

5) Finally, we shall see later that 18,1-20,29 has a chiastic structure (5C D E E' D' C') parallel to the chiastic structure of 13,1-17,26 (4CDE E' D' C')[282], which confirms the literary unity of the former.

4.251z Since there are more solid and valid reasons for the unity of 18,1-20,29 than for Jn 18-19, we conclude that the third section of the Book of Jesus' Hour consists of 18,1-20,29.

4.252 Title of Jn 18,1-20,29: "The Hour of Jesus' Passion-Death-Resurrection"

Dodd designates Jn 18-20 as "the Passion-narrative"[283]; van den Bussche, "the Passion and the Apparitions of the Risen" [Jesus][284]; Westcott, "the Victory through Death"[285]; and Tenney, "Period of Consummation"[286].

"The Passion-narrative" emphasizes the central significance of the Passion or death of Jesus in the narrative of Jn 18-20, but it may be misleading as a title for the whole section, since it could be understood as referring only to Jn 18-19 where the Passion proper (the arrest, trials, crucifixion) is narrated.

The title "the Passion and the Apparitions of the Risen" [Jesus] rightly describes the content of Jn 18-19 and Jn 20 respectively, but gives the impression of a succession of events without sufficiently stressing the Johannine perspective of the Passion-Resurrection as the indivisible event of glorification.

Westcott's heading for Jn 18-20 "the Victory over Death" underscores the paradoxical triumph of Jesus over death through his very death, but one wonders whether the aspect of "victory" is as much stressed by the Evangelist in Jn 18-20 as Westcott's title implies, since the term *nikaô* does not occur at all in the Johannine chapters on the Passion-Resurrection (*nikaô* is found only once in the Fourth Gospel at 16,33).

Tenney's proposal "Period of Consummation" highlights the dramatic and perfect completion of Jesus' work of salvation, and yet another title containing the Johannine term "the hour" would be preferable[287].

---

[282] See 4.34 and 4.35 below.
[283] See 2.[15].
[284] See 2.[18]2.
[285] See 2.[18]1.
[286] See 2.[16].
[287] See our designation of Jn 18-20 below.

Combining the main insights of the authors mentioned above, we suggest the title "the Hour of Jesus' Passion-Death-Resurrection". The hyphenated "Passion-Death-Resurrection" indicates the Johannine understanding of the passion, death and resurrection of Jesus as a single, integral, soteriological event. The mention of "the hour" links 18,1-20,29 with the previous section (Jn 13-17) and hints at the glorification of Jesus during "the hour" of his passion-death-resurrection.

4.252z To sum up, 18,1-20,29 may be called *"the Hour of Jesus' Passion-Death-Resurrection"*.

4.2z We present the results of our investigation of the sections of the Book of Jesus' Signs and the Book of Jesus' Hour through the following schema:

I. THE BOOK OF JESUS' SIGNS (2,1-12,50)
 1. *Jesus' Initial Signs and Encounters* (from Cana to Cana) (2,1-4,54)
 2. *Jesus' Works, Signs and Discussions* (at Jewish Feasts) (5,1-10,42)
 3+. *The Climactic Sign and the Coming of Jesus' Hour* (Bridge-Section)+ (11,1-12,50)+

II. THE BOOK OF JESUS' HOUR (11,1-20,29)
 3+. *The Climactic Sign and the Coming of Jesus' Hour* (Bridge-Section)+ (11,1-12,50)+
 4. *Jesus' Farewell of the Hour* (at the Last Supper) (13,1-17,26)
 5. *The Hour of Jesus' Passion-Death-Resurrection* (18,1-20,29)

In short, the body of the Fourth Gospel (i.e., the Book of Jesus' Signs + the Book of Jesus' Hour) is divided into *five sections* (2,1-4,54; 5,1-10,42; 11,1-12,50; 13,1 17,26; 18,1 20,29), the central section (Jn 11-12) being a bridge-section belonging both to the Book of Jesus' Signs (2,1-12,50) and to the Book of Jesus' Hour (11,1-20,29).

It should also be noted that from the dramatic point of view these *five sections* of the Gospel of John may be compared to the *five episodes* (*epeisodia*) of the majority of the classical Greek tragedies of Sophocles and Euripides [288] and to the *five acts* of Roman tragedies, since by the time of Horace (65-8 B.C.) the fivefold division of drama had become the formal rule, for he writes to Pisones in *Ars Poetica*:

---

[288] In fact, four out of the seven extant Sophoclean tragedies (*Electra, Trachiniae, Oedipus Tyrannus, Oedipus at Colonus*) and twelve of the eighteen Euripidean tragedies (*Alcestis, Hippolytus, Children of Heracles, Andromache, Madness of Heracles, Ion, Electra, Iphigenia in Tauris, Phoenissae, Orestes, Rhesus, Iphigenia at Aulis*) have, besides the Prologue (*prologos*) and *parodos* (the entrance song of the chorus), *five parts* or sections (that is, *four episodes* separated by *stasima* [songs of the chorus on the orchestra] + one *exodos*, which is the last episode) (Cf. Diano, ed., *Il Teatro Greco: Tutte le Tragedie* [Firenze 1970] 175-382; 391-1112).

It is true that only one (*Suppliants*) out of the seven extant dramas of the earliest Greek tragedian AESCHYLUS (525-456 B.C.) has five episodes. But it seems that by the time of EURIPIDES

4. THE LITERARY STRUCTURE OF THE FOURTH GOSPEL

Neve minor neu sit quinto productior actu
Fabula, quae posci vult et spectata reponi[289].

The Fourth Gospel may, therefore, be thought of as a *five-act drama*.

Notice also that the first, third and fifth sections are equal in length (2,1-4,54 = 115 verses; 11,1-12,50 = 107 verses; and 18,1-20,29 = 111 verses) and that the two longest sections (Jn 5-10 and Jn 13-17) are found at the centre of the Book of Jesus' Signs (2,1-12,50) and the Book of Jesus' Hour (11,1-20,29) respectively[290].

It is also remarkable that the central (third) section (11,1-12,50) really functions as a "bridge" between the Book of Jesus' Signs and the Book of Jesus' Hour, since Jesus performs the last and the greatest "sign" of raising Lazarus to life (Jn 11) and since "the hour" of Jesus, towards which the earlier sections have been tending (cf. 2,4; 7,30; 8,20) and which is the central topic of the following sections (cf. 13,1; 17,1), is now said for the first time to have arrived (*elêlythen hê hôra*: 12,23). Again, it is in the "bridge-section" that Jesus reveals himself unambiguously for the first time as "the life" (cf. 11,25), towards which his self-revelation in the previous sections has been moving (e.g. the "living water" in Jn 4 and "the living bread" or "the bread of life" in Jn 6), and which will be taken up in the fourth section (cf. 14,6; 17,2.3). Furthermore, faith in Jesus reaches a climax in Jn 11-12, since here (11,27) we have for the first time the confession that Jesus is "the Christ, the Son of God" (the same formula used in the conclusion of the Gospel at 20,31). Thomas' confession of faith ("My Lord and my God": 20,28) in the last section will be the final climax of faith. Likewise, unbelief also reaches its peak in the "bridge-section", since the Sanhedrin decides

---

(480-406 B.C.) the division of the drama into *five episodes* (preceded by the Prologue) had become a general dramatic convention, though not a rigid one. M. CROISET concludes his study of the division of the classical Greek tragedies by stating:

> On voit par là que *ce nombre de cinq*, sans s'imposer regoureusement aux poètes du siècle de Périclès [c. 500-429 B.C.], tendait pourtant à se faire accepter par eux comme *le plus convenable* (*Histoire de la Littérature Grecque* III: *Periode Attique: Tragédie - Comédie - Genres Secondaires* 3 ed., [Paris 1913] 121) [my italics].

[289] HORACE, *Ad Pisones*, 189, cited by M. CROISET, *op. cit.*, 121. The latter comments on this law of the fivefold division: "Il est évident par là que, de son temps, cette division était à peu près incontenstée dans la tragédie romaine" (*ibid.*).

[290] One may object that these two sections (Jn 5-10 = 301 verses; Jn 13-17 = 155 verses) are not of the same length. This is true, since Jn 5-10 consists of about double the number of verses of Jn 13-17, but it must be remembered that the episodes in ancient dramas were not and did not have to be all of equal length. M. CROISET observes:

> Une première remarque à faire au sujet des épisodes de la tragédie grecque, c'est qu'ils n'ont jamais été assujettis, comme les actes de nos pièces modernes, à une mesure commune. S'il y en a de très longs, il y en a aussi de très courts, et cela dans une même tragédie. Dans les Sept contre Thèbes, le second épisode a 350 vers, tandis que le troisième en a 29 (*op. cit.*, 120).

to kill Jesus (11,50) precisely because he does many signs (11,47)[291] and at the end of this section the Evangelist laments that "though he had done so many signs before them, yet they did not believe in him" (12,37).

4.3 THE STRUCTURE OF THE SECTIONS

Here we shall examine successively how the five sections of the Gospel of John (2,1-4,54; 5,1-10,42; 11,1-12,50; 13,1-17,26; 18,1-20,29) are subdivided into subsections (namely, episodes or pericopes) and how they are structurally related to each other. In other words, what we intend to do in the following paragraphs is to determine, with the help of the criteria given in the last chapter, the overall structure of each section [292].

4.31 The Structure of "Jesus' Initial Signs and Encounters" (Jn 2-4) [293]

First we shall determine the division of 2,1-4,54 into sub-sections. Secondly we shall compare these to decide on the internal structure of the section as a whole.

4.311 *Division of 2,1-4,54 into subsections*

The division of the first section is indicated by means of transitions, bridge-verses, and transitional conclusions between the different episodes. Between the first episode (the sign of changing water into wine at Cana: 2,1-11) and the second (the cleansing of the temple at Jerusalem: 2,13-22) there is a transition which mentions Jesus' going down to Capernaum and his short stay there (2,12). Likewise there is another transition (about Jesus' leaving Samaria for Galilee and the welcome accorded him by the Galileans: 4,43-45) between Jesus' encounter with the Samaritan woman (4,4-42) and the second sign at Cana (the healing of the royal official's son: 4,46-54)[294]. Notice also that these two transitions

---

[291] This decision of the Jewish authorities to put Jesus to death may be compared to the *peripeteia* in a Greek tragedy, namely, the "*sudden reversal of circumstances* on which the plot in the tragedy hinges, such as Oedipus' discovery of his parentage" (LIDDELL-SCOTT, *A Greek-English Lexicon*, 9 ed., [Oxford 1940] 1382: *peripeteia*: I, 2). Also Jesus' realization that his "hour" has come (12,23) may be considered similar to the "recognition" (*anagnôrisis*) in Sophoclean and Euripidean tragedies. Just as the *peripeteia*/"recognition" in a typical Greek tragedy divides the drama into two parts, namely, the "knot" (*desis*) and the "denouement" (*lysis*), that is, the chain of events before and after the *peripeteia* (cf. M. CROISET, *op. cit.*, 127), so the first two sections and the last two sections of the Gospel of John may be regarded as the Johannine *desis* and *lysis* respectively.

[292] The main divisions of the introduction (1,1-2,11) have been established earlier (see 4.112).

[293] We will discuss only briefly the reasons for the division of Jn 2-4, since the majority of Johannine scholars agree on the delimitation of most of the subsections. We shall examine more in detail those points about which there is disagreement.

[294] See 3.18.

contain a literary-chronological indication (*meta touto*: 2,12; *meta de tas dyo hêmeras*: 4,43)[295] and a new geographical name ("Capernaum": 2,12; "Galilee": 4,43.45)[296] which signal a change of scene[297].

Jesus' cleansing of the temple (the second episode: 2,13-22) and his dialogue with Nicodemus (the third episode: 3,1-21) are linked together by means of bridge-verses (2,23-25)[298].

Similarly, the fourth episode (John the Baptist's dialogue with his disciples: 3,22-36) and the fifth (Jesus' dialogue with the Samaritan woman: 4,4-42) are joined together by means of bridge-verses (4,1-3) which refer explicitly back to 3,22-23 and point forward to 4,43-45. For example, the baptizing activity of both Jesus and John the Baptist recorded at 3,22-23 is recalled in 4,1 (cf. *baptizein* at 3,22.23.23; 4,1)[299]. Besides, "Judea" is named in both the passages (3,22; 4,3). Again, Jesus' "making more disciples and baptizing than John" (4,1) refers back to 3,22-23[300] and to 3,26 ("Behold he is baptizing and all are going to him"). Notice that Jesus' "disciples" are mentioned not only at 3,22 and 4,1.2 but also in the next episode (cf. 4,8.27.31-38). It must be noted that the Samaritan episode (4,4-42) is enclosed or framed between 4,1-2 and 4,43-45, for, while Jesus' leaving Judea for Galilee is reported at 4,3 (*aphêken tên Ioudaian kai apêlthen palin eis tên Galilaian*), his arrival in Galilee is mentioned only in 4,43-45 (*êlthen eis tên Galilaian*: 4,45). In short, 4,1-3 contains back-references to the beginning of the Baptist-episode (3,22-23), forward-looking references to the Samaritan episode (4,4-42; cf. 4,27.31-38) and to the next transition (4,43-45)[301]. Hence instead of describing 4,1-3 as a mere transition or a "historical summary"[302], they may be more aptly called "bridge-verses"[303], since

---

[295] See 3.16.
[296] See 3.15.
[297] See 3.21.
[298] See 3.191, where the bridging character of 2,23-25 is explained.
[299] The parenthetical sentence at 4,2 (*kaitoige Iêsous autos ouk ebaptizen all' hoi mathêtai autou*), which apparently contradicts 3,22 according to which Jesus "was baptizing" (*ebaptizen*), is taken by many scholars to be an addition by a later redactor for fear "that the sectarians of John the Baptist would use Jesus' baptizing as an argument that he was only an imitator of John the Baptist" (BROWN, I, 164). But this could have been added by the Evangelist himself to show that, while at the beginning Jesus himself was baptizing (3,22.26), later so many began to go to him to become his disciples (4,1) and to be baptized (4,1) that he was only instructing them about discipleship while his disciples actually baptized the people. We could argue that it would have been difficult for Jesus to do both for large crowds (4,1) and he would have liked his disciples to share in his work (cf. 4,38: "I sent you to reap for that which you did not labor"). If this interpretation is accepted, there would be no real contradiction between 3,22 and 4,2.
[300] Because of these cross-references some scholars take 4,1-3 as the conclusion of the Baptist-episode (3,22-4,3). For example, R. INFANTE holds this view ("L'amico dello sposo, figura del ministero di Giovanni Battista nel Quarto Vangelo", *RivB* 31 (1983) 3-19, especially 4-5).
[301] Cf. ch. 3, n. 25.
[302] SEGALLA, 133.
[303] See 3.19.

they serve both as a conclusion to 3,22-36 and prepare the reader for the Samaritan episode (4,4-42). One of the reasons why 4,1-3 was added just before 4,4-42 might have been to hint at the conversion of the Samaritans (cf. 4,39-42) as an instance of Jesus' "making disciples" (*mathētas poiein*) mentioned at 4,1. This may be compared to the "sowing" spoken of by Jesus in 4,36-37, while the "baptizing" mentioned at 4,1-2 may be likened to the "harvesting" in 4,35-38 [304].

The distinction between the third episode (Jesus and Nicodemus: 3,1-21) and the fourth (the Baptist and his disciples: 3,22-36) [305] is clearly indicated by the literary-chronological device *meta tauta* (3,22), which normally signals the beginning of a new section or subsection (cf. 5,1; 6,1; 7,1). It must be recalled that 3,22-24 functions more as an introduction to the Baptist-episode than as a transition, since Jesus' baptizing activity reported at 3,22 (*ebaptizen*) is the starting point of the dialogue between the Baptist and his disciples (cf. the disciples' complaint to him at 3,26: *ide houtos baptizei*...) [306].

From our examination of the transitions (2,12; 4,43-45), bridge-verses (2,23-25; 4,1-3), and the transitional introduction (3,22-24), it is clear that 2,1-4,54 divides itself into six pericopes (2,1-11; 2,13-22; 3,1-21; 3,22-36; 4,4-42; 4,46-54) separated or joined by the above transitions or bridge-verses. (Notice that *meta tauta* [3,22] occurs only between the central episodes [3,1-21; 3,22-36]).

The above sixfold division is confirmed by other literary criteria. Thus all the six pericopes begin with a proper *introduction* (2,1-2.13; 3,1-2.22-24; 4,4-6. 46) [307]. The first two and the last two episodes end with a clear *conclusion* (2,11.22; 4,39-42.53-54) [308]. Each one of the six subsections is enclosed in one or more *inclusions* which indicate the limits of the pericope in question (*en Kana tēs Galilaias*: 2,1.11; *Iēsous*: 2,1.2.11; *hoi mathētai autou*: 2,2.11; *to pascha*: 2,13.23; *Hierosolyma*: 2,13.23; *erchesthai pros*: 3,2.21; *ēlthen*: 3,22 and *apēlthen*: 4,3; *Iēsous*: 3,22; 4,1.1.2; *mathētēs*: 3,22; 4,1.2; *Ioudaia*: 3,22; 4,3; *baptizein*: 3,22.23.23; 4,1.2; *Iōannēs*: 3,23.24; 4,1; *Samareia*: 4,4.5 and *Samaritai*: 4,39.40; *erchesthai*: 4,5.40; *polis*: 4,5.39; *erchesthai*: 4,46.54; *palin*: 4,46.54; *Galilaia*: 4,46.54; *epoiēsen to hydōr oinon*: 4,46 and *sēmeion epoiēsen*: 4,54; *hyios*: 4,46.53) [309]. At the beginning of each of the six episodes a *geographical name* of a part of Palestine or of a town is given (Cana of Galilee: 2,1; Jerusalem: 2,13.23; Judea: 3,22; Samaria: 4,4; Sychar: 4,5; Cana of Galilee: 4,46) [310]. The cleansing

---

[304] This is another reason for regarding 4,1-3 as bridge-verses.

[305] Some authors do not regard 3,22-36 as an integral episode but only as "an explanatory appendix to the dialogue with Nicodemus and the discourse which grows out of it" (C. H. DODD, *op. cit.*, 311) or as a "footnote" (so D. DEEKS, see 2.[10]) or as part of the Nicodemus-episode (e.g. I. DE LA POTTERIE takes 2,23-3,36 as forming one unit "Nicodemus Judaeus in Jerusalem": see 2.[18]3; so also PASQUETTO: see 2.[21]).

[306] See 3.18.
[307] See 3.122.
[308] See 3.114,4-5.
[309] See 3.132,8.
[310] See 3.15.

of the temple (2,13-22) takes place during the *feast* of Passover (*to pascha tôn Ioudaiôn*: 2,13)[311]. The bridge-verses (2,23-25) between the second and third pericopes are joined to the Nicodemus-episode by means of *hook-words* (*anthrôpos*: 2,25; 3,1)[312]. The second Cana-sign (4,46-54) contains a clear *cross-reference* (4,46) to the first Cana-sign (2,1-11), and the signs that Jesus did in Jerusalem during the feast of Passover mentioned at 2,23 are recalled at 4,45[313]. The *literary genre* of each successive subsection (except the central ones) is different: the first pericope (2,1-11) is basically a miracle-narrative; the second subsection (2,13-22) is essentially a conflict-narrative; the central episodes (3,1-21; 3,22-36) are a combination of dialogue (3,2b-10; 3,26-30) and discourse (3,11-21; 3,31-36) with brief introductory narratives (3,1-2a; 3,22-26a); the Samaritan episode (4,4-42) is fundamentally a triple dialogue (between Jesus and the Samaritan woman [4,7-26], between Jesus and the disciples [4,31-38], and between the woman and the Samaritans [4,39-42]), introduced by a short narrative (4,4-6); the last pericope (4,46-54), like the first one (2,1-11), is essentially a miracle-narrative[314].

The division of Jn 2-4 into six subsections is supported also by the presence of some *dramatic techniques* such as the *change of scenes* or of *dramatis personae*[315]. Thus, while we have a wedding-scene at Cana in 2,1-11, we see Jesus driving the merchants and animals from the temple in 2,13-22. Again, whereas 3,1-21 presents Jesus engaged in a dialogue with a Jewish rabbi (Nicodemus) at night, the main scene in 3,22-36 consists of a dialogue between John the Baptist and his disciples about Jesus[315a]. Similarly, while the main action of 4,4-42 takes place at Jacob's well at Sychar, the scene changes back to Cana in 4,46-54 which contains two successive scenes of an anxious father pleading with Jesus to heal his dying son (4,46-50) and the father's meeting with his servants who come with the good news of the cure of his son (4,51-53). In

---

[311] See 3.17.
[312] See 3.1[10].
[313] See ch. 3, n. 25.
[314] See 3.1[12].
[315] See 3.21 and 3.25.
[315a] Some take 3,30 as the last word of the Baptist and therefore as the end of the Baptist-episode (3,22-30) and regard 3,31-36 as the words of Jesus or of the Evangelist. Thus they transpose the text and join it with the Nicodemus-discourse (so BERNARD [I, xxiii] and BULTMANN [160] place 3,31-36 after 3,16-21, while SCHNACKENBURG puts it between 3,12 and 3,13). BROWN considers it as "an isolated discourse of Jesus" added by the editor (I, 159-60). But whether it was originally an independent discourse or not, in the actual order and structure of Jn 3, the vv. 31-36 are intended to be a continuation of the Baptist's disourse in 3,27-30, since no change of speaker has been indicated at 3,31 and since 3,31-36 can be understood as the reason for the statement of the Baptist at 3,30: "He must increase and I must decrease". This may be an attempt at "baptizing" the Baptist and making him a Christian witness to Christ (cf. 1,6-8.15.19-36; 3,26-28; 5,33; 10,40-42). In any case, it is better not to separate what the Evangelist has joined together! We shall show below that 3,1-21 and 3,22-36 are parallel to each other (see 4.312,3).

short, the scenes and the secondary characters (Jesus being the protagonist in most episodes) are different in the six subsections we have detected in 2,1-4,54.

4.312 *Parallelism between the subsections of 2,1-4,54*

4.312,1 Parallelism between 2,1-12 and 4,43-54

Comparing the first and the last subsections (2,1-12; 4,43-54) we find that they have many *similarities*. First of all, they describe Jesus' first and second sign at Cana of Galilee. At the beginning of the second sign the first is explicitly recalled (4,46: *êlthen oun palin eis tên Kana tês Galilaias, hopou epoiêsen to hydôr oinon*). Notice also that the first verse of 2,1-11 and that of 4,46-54 mention "Cana of Galilee" (2,1; 4,46). Again, both the Cana-signs end with strikingly similar statements:

2,11a: *tautên* **epoiêsen** *archên* tôn **sêmeiôn** *ho Iêsous*
4,54 : *touto* de palin *deuteron* **sêmeion epoiêsen** *ho Iêsous*

2,11a: en Kana **tês Galilaias**
4,54 : elthôn... eis **tên Galilaian**

2,11c: **kai episteusan** eis auton *hoi mathêtai autou*
4,53d: **kai episteusan** *autos kai hê oikia autou holê*.

We have seen above that the *literary genre* of both the pericopes is the same (*miracle-narrative*) and that there is no other pericope in Jn 2-4 which has this literary genre [316].

Furthermore, it is interesting to observe that the second sign at Cana (4,46-54) has the same general *pattern* as the first Cana-sign (2,1-11) [317], which may be schematically represented as follows:

a) the setting of the sign (2,1-2; 4,46)
b) suggestion/request by a person (2,3; 4,47)

---

[316] See 3.1[12] and 4.311.
[317] In the words of R. E. BROWN:

> The general pattern of the two miracles is the same: Jesus has just come back into Galilee; someone comes with a request; indirectly Jesus seems to refuse the request; the questioner persists; Jesus grants the request; this leads another group of people (the disciples; the household) to believe in him. In neither story are we told exactly how the miracle was accomplished. There are even similarities in context... the two Cana miracles are the only two Johannine signs that do not lead immediately into a discourse. After each Cana miracle Jesus goes up to Jerusalem and the Temple (I, 194).

C. H. GIBLIN finds a triple pattern ("suggestion, negative response and positive action") not only in 2,1-11 and 4,46-54 but also in 7,2-14 and 11,1-44 ("Suggestion, Negative Response, and Positive Action in St. John's Portrayal of Jesus", *NTS* 26 [1980] 197-211). But such a minimal pattern applicable to all the four passages is obtained by not taking seriously the difference in the literary genre of the texts in question (e.g. while 2,1-11 and 4,46-54 are basically miracle stories, 7,2-14 is essentially a dialogue (7,2-9) and a transition (7,10-14). Again, the Cana-signs are much more similar to each other than to the other passages.

c) negative response of Jesus (2,4; 4,48)
d) positive reaction/request by the person (2,5; 4,49)
e) positive command by Jesus (2,7ab.8abc; 4,50ab)
f) execution of the command (2,7c.8d; 4,50f)
g) verification of the miracle (2,9-10; 4,51-53c)
h) positive faith response (2,11; 4,53d).

Such a strikingly identical pattern in all the eight steps in the two Cana-miracle-narratives and the presence of the same or similar expressions, as we have seen above, could not have been the result of chance but the fruit of careful planning on the part of the Evangelist who intended the two extreme pericopes of the section of Jesus' Initial Signs and Encounters (Jn 2-4) to be parallel to each other [317a].

Therefore, if the first Cana-sign (2,1-11) is represented by the letter *a*, the second Cana-sign (4,46-54) may be denoted by *a'*. Or if, for convenience, we take *a* (2,1-11) together with the transition *à* (2,12) and represent the whole of the first subsection (2,1-12) by A, then the entire last subsection (4,43-54) consisting of a transition *à'* (4,43-45) and *a'* (4,46-54) may be denoted by A'.

4.312,2 Parallelism between 2,13-25 and 4,1-42

While the two Cana-signs (2,1-11; 4,46-54) may be regarded as an instance of synonymous parallelism between two pericopes, the cleansing of the temple (2,13-22) and the Samaritan episode (4,4-42) seem to be a case of antithetical parallelism between two episodes, since the deeds and words of Jesus produce opposite effects on the Jews in Jerusalem in 2,13-22 and on the woman and people of Samaria in 4,4-42. For, whereas the former question his authority to drive the merchants and animals from the temple and demand a sign to authenticate his claim (2,18: *ti sêmeion deiknyeis hêmin hoti tauta poieis?*) and are bewildered by his enigmatic words about the destruction and restoration of the temple (2,19-20), the Samaritan woman gradually recognizes Jesus as a prophet (4,19: *kyrie, theôrô hoti prophêtês ei sy*) and the Christ (4,25: *oida hoti Messias erchetai ho legomenos Christos..*; 4,29: *mêti houtos estin ho Christos?*), and the Samaritans acknowledge him as the Saviour of the world (4,42: *oidamen hoti houtos estin alêthôs ho sotêr tou kosmou*).

There are also some (synonymous) parallel elements in 2,13-22 and 4,4-42. For example, in both the scenes Jesus refers to the temple in Jerusalem and speaks about the worship of the Father (2,16: *mê poieite ton oikon tou patros mou oikon emporiou*; 4,21: *erchetai hôra hote oute en tô[i] orei toutô[i] oute en Hierosolymois proskynêsete tô[i] patri*).

[317a] Whether the common pattern of the two Cana-signs reflects oral narrative tradition or not, does not affect our conclusion concerning their parallelism.

It is remarkable that in both the pericopes Jesus makes a cryptic reference to his death-resurrection (2,19: *lysate ton naon touton kai en trisin hêmerais egerô auton*; 4,34: *emon brôma estin hina... teleiôsô autou to ergon*; cf. 17,4; 19,28.30)[318].

Another element of similarity between the two pericopes is the double mention of the disciples of Jesus (*hoi mathêtai autou*: 2,17.22; 4,8.27-38). While the unbelieving Jewish authorities (*hoi Ioudaioi*: 2,18.20) in Jerusalem may be contrasted with the believing woman of Samaria (cf. 4,21.25.29.39), the disciples who believe Jesus' word (2,22: *kai episteusan... tô[i] logô[i] hon eipen ho Iêsous*) may be compared to the Samaritans who believe because of Jesus' word (4,42: *ouketi dia tên lalian pisteuomen; autoi gar akêkoamen...*).

We may also note two factual (not terminological) similarities and a contrast between 2,23-25 and 4,1-42. Both the passages speak of Jesus' superhuman knowledge of the human heart, for in 2,24-25 Jesus is said "to know all men" and every man's heart (*ti ên en tô[i] anthrôpô[i]*: 2,25) and in 4,17-18 Jesus is presented as knowing the irregular life of the Samaritan woman who has had five husbands and is now living with another man. Again, just as Jesus did not trust himself to the Jews of Jerusalem (2,24), at 4,1-3 he seems to be distrustful of the Pharisees, since he leaves Judea when they hear about his baptizing and making disciples. This lack of trust on the part of Jesus in the Jews of Jerusalem and in the Pharisees is in striking contrast with his trusting attitude to the woman of Samaria to whom he reveals the mystery of true worship (*pisteue moi, gynai,... en pneumati kai alêtheia[i] dei proskynein*: 4,21-24) and his Messianic identity (*egô eimi, ho lalôn soi*: 4,26). Thus, while Jesus refuses to reveal his identity as the (hidden) Messiah to the Jerusalemites (2,24)[319], he manifests himself openly to the Samaritan woman (4,25-26) and eventually to the people of Sychar (4,42), whose invitation to stay with them he accepted (4,40). While Jesus leaves Judea probably to get away from the Pharisees (4,1-3), he stays with the Samaritans willingly (4,40).

Because of the numerous similarities and contrasts mentioned above, 2,13-25 and 4,1-42 are parallel to each other and may be represented by the letters B and B' respectively. Since the major part of each pericope deals with Jesus' dialogue with the Jews and the Samaritan woman respectively, B (2,13-25) may be called "the cleansing of the Jerusalem-temple and dialogue with the Jews

---

[318] Probably *kataphagetai me* at 2,17 too points to Jesus' death, since the Evangelist seems to have deliberately changed the past tense of the quotation from Ps 69,9 (LXX 68,9 has the aorist *katephage*) into the future *kataphagetai* to which *hê graphê* at 2,22 seems to refer.
It is also interesting to note that *kataphagein* at 2,17 has the same root as *phagein* at 4,31-34, though in the first case the zeal for his Father's house will "consume" (*kataphagein* which literally means "to eat up") Jesus (2,17), while in the second case he is asked to "eat" (*phagein*).

[319] E. STAUFFER, "*Agnostos Christos*: Joh ii 24 und die Eschatologie des vierten Evangeliums", in: *The Background to the New Testament and Its Eschatology*, ed. W. D. Davis & D. Daube, (Festschrift C. H. Dodd) (Cambridge 1956) 281-99 especially 292.

on the new temple", and B' (4,1-42) may be entitled "dialogue with the Samaritan woman on living water and true (temple) worship"[320].

4.312,3 Parallelism between 2,23-3,21 and 3,22-4,3

Though at first sight the two episodes seem to be quite different, since the principal characters in the first scene are Jesus and Nicodemus, while those in the second are John the Baptist and his disciples, the Nicodemus-episode may be considered as parallel to the Baptist-episode, since the latter contains many close parallels to the former:

3,2	: houtos **êlthen pros** *auton*... **kai eipen autô[i]**: *Rhabbi*
3,26	: kai **êlthen pros** *ton Iôannên* **kai eipen autô[i]**: *Rhabbi*
3,3ab	: **apekrithê** *Iêsous* **kai eipen** autô[i]
3,27ab	: **apekrithê** *Iôannês* **kai eipen**
3,3de	: **ean mê** *tis* gennêthê[i] *anôthen*, **ou dynatai** idein tên basileian tou theou.
3,27cd	: **ou dynatai** *anthrôpos* lambanein oude hen **ean mê** ê[i] dedomenon autô[i] *ek tou ouranou*.
3,7c	: dei hymas gennêthênai **anôthen**
3,31a	: ho **anôthen** erchomenos epanô pantôn estin.
3,8ab	: **to pneuma** hopou thelei pnei (cf. also 3,5.6.8.8)
3,34c	: ou gar ek metrou didôsin **to pneuma**.
3,8c	: kai **tên phônên** autou *akoueis*
3,29b	: kai *akouôn* autou chara[i] chairei dia **tên phônên**...
3,11cd	: ho heôrakamen *martyroumen*
3,32abc	: ho heôraken kai êkousen touto *martyrei*
3,11e	: *kai tên martyrian* hêmôn ou **lambanete**
3,32d	: *kai tên martyrian* autou oudeis **lambanei**.
3,12a	: ei ta epi**geia** *eipon* hymin
3,31c	: kai ek tês **gês** *lalei*.
3,13	: **ho ek tou ouranou** *katabas*
3,31d	: **ho ek tou ouranou** *erchomenos*
3,15	: hina **pas ho pisteuôn** en autô[i] *echê[i] zôê aiônion*.
3,16c	: hina **pas ho pisteuôn** eis auton... *echê[i] zôên aiônion*.
3,36a	: **ho pisteuôn** eis ton hyion *echei zôên aiônion*.

---

[320] These titles are not intended to include the whole content of each episode (which a short title can seldom do) but only to indicate the literary genre ("dialogue") and the main thematic content of each passage. It must also be admitted that the parallelism between 2,13-25 and 4,1-42 is only partial, since many elements do not have parallels.

3,16ab : houtôs gar **êgapêsen** *ho theos* ton kosmon,
hôste *ton hyion* ton monogenê **edôken**
3,35ab : *ho patêr* **agapa[i]** *ton hyion*
kai panta **dedôken** en tê[i] cheiri autou.
3,17a : ou **gar apesteilen ho theos** *ton hyion...*
3,34a : hon **gar apesteilen ho theos**...
3,18ab : **ho pisteuôn eis** *auton* **ou krinetai**;
ho de mê pisteuôn êdê **kekritai**...
3,36ab : **ho pisteuôn eis** *ton hyion echei zôên aiônion*;
ho de apeithôn *tô[i] hyiô[i] ouk opsetai zôên* [321].

The parallels between the two passages are so numerous and so striking that it is unnecessary to comment on them, and we may regard the two episodes (3,1-21; 3,22-36) to be certainly parallel to each other [322].

Notice also that both in 2,23-3,21 and 3,22-36 a short narrative (2,23-3,1; 3,22-25) is followed by a dialogue (3,2-10; 3,26-30) and a discourse (3,11-21; 3,31-36).

We may describe the Nicodemus-episode as "Jesus' dialogue with Nicodemus on birth from above and discourse on eternal life", and the Baptist-episode as "John the Baptist's dialogue with his disciples on the groom from above and discourse on life". And these two parallel episodes may, therefore, be designated by the letters C and C' respectively.

4.31z From the above discussions it follows that the section of "Jesus' Initial Signs and Encounters" (2,1-4,54) consists of six subsections which are *chiastically* structured (1ABCC'B'A'), which may be schematically represented as follows:

JESUS' INITIAL SIGNS AND ENCOUNTERS (from Cana to Cana) (2,1-4,54)

A (2,1-12) : The beginning of the signs at Cana in Galilee:
the changing of water into wine.
(Transition: 2,12)
  B (2,13-25+) : The cleansing of the Jerusalem-temple and
dialogue with the Jews on the new temple.
(Bridge-verses: 2,23-25)+
    C (2,23-3,21) : Dialogue with Nicodemus on birth from above
and discourse on eternal life.
    C' (3,22-4,3+): Dialogue of J.B. with his disciples on the groom
from above and discourse on life.
(Bridge-verses: 4,1-3)+
  B' (4,1-42) : Dialogue with the Samaritan woman on living water
and true temple worship.
(Transition: 4,43-45)
A' (4,43-54) : The second sign at Cana in Galilee:
the healing of the royal official's son.

---

[321] BROWN mentions also the "dualistic contrasts like flesh/Spirit in [v.] 6 (earthly/heavenly in [v.] 12), and 'from above'/'of earth' in [v.] 31" as parallels (I, 160).

[322] Note that there are parallels not only between 3,11-21 and 3,31-36 but also between 3,1-10 and 3,25-30.

4.32 The Structure of "Jesus' Works, Signs and Discussions" (Jn 5-10)

As in the case of the first section, we shall first determine the division of 5,1-10,42 into subsections and then their structural relationship.

4.321 *Division of 5,1-10,42 into subsections*

The first three subdivisions of Jn 5-10 are clearly marked by the *literary-chronological* device *meta tauta* with which they begin (5,1; 6,1; 7,1)[323], and which, unlike *meta touto* (cf. 2,12), indicates an indefinite interval of time.

At the beginning of these three subsections the names of different *geographical* locations are mentioned (5,1.2: Jerusalem; 6,1: the other side of the Sea of Galilee; 7,1: Galilee; cf. also 7,1.4: Judea)[324].

Three different Jewish *feasts* too are spoken of in the initial verses of these episodes (5,1: an unnamed "feast of the Jews" [cf. also 5,9: "Sabbath"]; 6,4: "the Passover"; 7,2: "Tabernacles")[325]. Similarly, the feast of "Dedication" is explicitly mentioned in the first verse (10,22) of the last episode of Jn 5-10. A second "Sabbath" (9,14) is mentioned in connection with the healing of the man born blind.

While 5,1; 6,1-2 and 7,1 may be regarded as "transitional introductions" to the episodes (like 3,22-24 to the Baptist-episode), the verses immediately following (5,2-5; 6,3-4; 7,2-5) serve as the *introduction* proper to the first pericope in each episode (5,2-9c; 6,3-15; 7,2-9)[326]. Furthermore each initial pericope may be looked upon as an introduction to the whole episode (Jn 5; Jn 6; Jn 7-8). For instance, the curing of the cripple at the pool at Bethzatha on a Sabbath (5,2-9) triggers off the discussion and discourse that follow (5,9d-47). Similarly, the sign of the feeding of the five thousand (6,3-15) functions as an introduction to the discourse on the bread of life (6,22-59).

Notice also that Jn 5 and Jn 6 are distinguished not only by the change in place and time but also by the *change of dramatic characters*. Thus, while in Jn 5 we have Jesus, the paralytic and the Jewish authorities in Jerusalem, in Jn 6 the actors are Jesus, his disciples, the Twelve, and the Galilean crowd. Note that, whereas the disciples play a prominent part in the initial and final pericopes of Jn 6 (6,3-15.16-21.60-66.67-71), they are not mentioned at all in Jn 5.

Because of the above reasons we may take Jn 5 and Jn 6 to be the first two subsections of Jn 5-10[327].

Jn 2,23-25 and 3,22-24 serve as introductions to the dialogue/discourses that follow. Notice also that many believed in Jesus' name in 2,23 and many became his disciples in 4,1.

[323] See 3.161. It is true that *meta tauta* is found also at 5,14. But as we saw earlier (see 3.161 and n. 34a there), its occurrence at 5,14 with an historical present (*heuriskei*) indicates the division of an episode (5,1-47) and not the beginning of an episode as at 5,1; 6,1 and 7,1.

[324] See 3.15.

[325] See 3.17.

[326] See 3.122.

[327] Most Johannine scholars and commentators accept the distinction between Jn 5 and Jn 6 e.g. BROWN, I, 201; SEGALLA, 134.

4.3 THE STRUCTURE OF THE SECTIONS

Many Johannine experts agree that a new (sub)section begins with the first verses of Jn 7, but there is hardly any agreement among them about the end of the (sub)section [327a].

That Jn 7-8 is a literary unit (which forms the third subsection of Jn 5-10) is indicated by a number of literary, structural and dramatic criteria.

First of all, there is unity of *time* (the feast of Tabernacles: cf. 7,2.8. 10.11.14.37) and *place* (the temple: cf. 7,14.28; 8,20.59) [328].

[327a] Thus 7,1-52 (so KAMMERSTÄTTER, PRETE, RAU) or 7,1-8,59 (so BROWN, DEEKS, DODD, GOURGUES) or 7,1-9,41 (so BOISMARD, SEGALLA) or 7,1-10,21 (so CABA, MOLLAT, PUIGDOLLERS) or 7,1-10,42 (so VAN DEN BUSSCHE, DE LA POTTERIE) is taken as a literary unit (see ch. 2 above for these divisions and our critical evaluation of them). A. VANHOYE has suggested to me the possibility of a division at 7,52 because of the variation in vocabulary and literary genre of Jn 7 and Jn 8. We shall see below that these partial differences can be accounted for by the spiral structure and the dramatic development of Jn 7-8.

We may mention here also that S. SABUGAL (whom PASQUETTO follows) advances the following reasons for regarding 7,1-11,54 as a literary unit (*Christos. Investigación exegética sobre la cristologia joannea* [Barcelona 1972] 235-42):

(1) 7,1 and 11,53-54 are said to form inclusions (*peripatein* at 7,1 and 11,54; *en tê[i] Ioudaia[i]* at 7,1 and *en tois Ioudaiois* at 11,54; *apokteinai* at 7,1 and 11,53).

However, there are many reasons to doubt whether these are inclusions. Jesus' *peripatein* is mentioned not only at 7,1 and 11,54 but also elsewhere between these two verses (e.g. 10,23). In fact, not only the verb *peripatein* but also the very order of words in the expression of 7,1 (*periepatei ho Iêsous*) is found in 10,23. *En tois Ioudaiois* at 11,54 probably corresponds better to *eis tên Ioudaian* at the beginning of the Lazarus-episode (11,7) than to *en tê[i] Ioudaia[i]* mentioned many episodes earlier (7,1). Regarding *apokteinai* at 7,1 and 11,53 it must be noted that, while the latter refers to the Sanhedrin's decision to kill Jesus (*ebouleusanto hina apokteinôsin auton*: 11,53), the former is a back-reference to the Jews' seeking to kill him mentioned in Jn 5 (note the verbatim repetition of 5,18 at 7,1: *ezêtoun auton hoi Ioudaioi apokteinai*) and which will be frequently discussed in Jn 7-8 (cf. *apokteinai* at 7,19.20.25; 8,37.40). Furthermore, the mere repetition of the same words at the beginning and end respectively of two distant chapters (Jn 7 and Jn 11) does not automatically guarantee that they are intended as inclusions, unless there are other literary criteria (like the unity of time, place and action) which confirm the unity of the section (see below).

(2) It is said that 7,1-11,54 has a unity of place (Judea). But this is not quite true, since the scene of 10,40-11,16 is "beyond the Jordan" (cf. 10,40) and since Jesus says at 11,8: "Let us go into Judea again".

(3) 7,1-11,54 is affirmed to have a unity of time. But this is not true, since two different feasts (Tabernacles and Dedication) are explicitly mentioned at 7,2 and 10,22 respectively.

(4) It is said that the action in 7,1-11,54 takes place alternately inside and outside the temple. But this is a tour de force, since the Lazarus-episode, for instance, has nothing to do with the "inside" or "outside" of the temple in Jerusalem!

(5) It is said that the same revelatory formula *egô eimi* + predicate is used in Jn 6-11 ("the bread of life": 6,35.41.48.51; "the light of the world": 8,12; 9,5; "the door": 10,7.9; "the good shepherd": 10,11-14; "the resurrection and the life": 11,25). But this does not prove the literary unity of Jn 7-11, since the same formula is found also in Jn 6, as Sabugal himself admits. Furthermore, whereas in Jn 6-10 *egô eimi* is followed by a single predicate, in Jn 11 there is a double predicate, which distinguishes it from the earlier *egô eimi* formulas.

Because of these valid objections we do not think that 7,1-11,54 is intended by the Evangelist to be a single large literary unit.

[328] M. GOURGUES, *op. cit.*, 88. It is true that Jesus' dialogue with his unbelieving brothers (7,1-9) takes place in Galilee, but since it deals with Jesus' going up to Jerusalem for the feast of

Secondly, *en kryptô[i]* (7,4.10) in the introduction (7,1-13) and *ekrybê* (8,59) in the conclusion of the episode may be considered as forming an *inclusion* [329]. This is reinforced by the explicit mention of Jesus' going up to the temple at 7,14 (*anebê Iêsous eis to hieron*) and his going out of the temple at 8,59 (*exêlthen ek tou hierou*).

Thirdly, Jn 7-8 has its own characteristic vocabulary. For instance, there are about thirty different terms, names and expressions, which occur three or more times in Jn 7-8 but never in Jn 9 [329a]:

Galilaia: 7,1.9.41.52.52
zêteô: 7,1.4.11.18.18.19.20.25.30.34.36; 8,21.27.40.50.50
apokteinô: 7,1.19.20.25; 8,22.37.40
heortê: 7,2.8.8.10.11.14.37
adelphoi: 7,3.5.10
parrêsia: 7,4.13.26
kairos: 7,6.6.8
martyreô/ria: 7,7; 8,13.13.14.14.17.18.18
anabainô: 7,8.8.10.10.14
ochlos: 7,12.12.20.31.32.40.43.49
hieron: 7,14.28; 8,20.59
ginôskô: 7,17.26.27.49.51; 8,27.28.32.43.52.55
emautou: 7,17.28; 8,13.18.28.42.54
alêthês/eia/ôs: 7,18.26.40; 8,13.14.17.26.31.32.32.40.44.44.45.46
nomos: 7,19.19.23.49.51; 8,17
daimonion echô: 7,20; 8,48.49.52
krinô: 7,24.24.51; 8,15.15.16.26.50
piazô: 7,30.32.44; 8,20
hypêretês: 7,32.45.46
logos: 7,36.40; 8,31;37.43.51.52.55
doxazô: 7,39; 8,54.54
patêr [sing]: 8,16.18.19.19.19.27.28.38.38.39.41.41.42.44.44.44.49.53.54.56
apothnêskô: 8,21.24.24.52.53.53
Abraam: 8,33.37.39.40.52.53.56.57.58
amên amên legô hymin: 8,34.51.58
ton logon têreô: 8,51.52.55 [329b].

Tabernacles (cf. 7,2-4.6-8), these verses and 7,10-13 may be regarded as an introduction to the controversies between Jesus and the Jews in the temple (7,14-8,59).

We are not explicitly told where the Pharisees and high priests who sent officers to arrest Jesus were (7,45-52), but it may be presumed that they were in the temple precincts, since they heard the crowd murmur about Jesus (7,32) and since they are mentioned at 8,13 as being present at the temple treasury where Jesus was teaching (8,20).

[329] C. H. DODD says: "the words *en kryptô[i]* - *ekrybê* may be taken as clamping this entire series of dialogues into dramatic unity, with the Feast of Tabernacles to provide a significant background to the whole" (*op. cit.*, 348).

[329a] There are also a number of terms which are frequently found in Jn 9 but never in Jn 7-8 (see the table "*Vocabulary of Jn 9,1-41*" below) and others which are common to both (which accounts for the parallelism between Jn 7-8 and Jn 9 [see 4.322,1 below]).

[329b] Note that the last five items in the list are found only in Jn 8 (and not in Jn 7), though Jn 7 and Jn 8 have also numerous terms in common. The spiral structure of Jn 7-8 will account for this phenomenon (see below).

Fourthly, the unity of Jn 7-8 is confirmed by its *literary structure*. Its main divisions, namely, **a** (7,1-13), **b** (7,14-36), and **c** (7,37-8,59), are indicated by the explicit references to the feast of Tabernacles (7,2: *ên de engys hê heortê tôn Ioudaiôn hê skênopêgia*; 7,14: *êdê de tês heortês mesousês*; 7,37: *en de tê[i] eschatê[i] hêmera[i] tê[i] megalê[i] tês heortês*). Besides, the middle section **b** (7,14-36) is enclosed in an inclusion (*didaskein*: 7,14.35).

The Main Divisions of the Structure of Jn 7-8
a: Introduction (7,1-13)
b: Jesus' revelation in the middle of the feast (7,14-36)
c: Jesus' revelation on the last day of the feast (7,37-8,59).

The introduction **a** (7,1-13) may be subdivided into two smaller units (*a*: vv.1-9 and *b*: vv.10-13), the first of which is clearly demarcated by two inclusions (*en tê[i] Galilaia[i]*: 7,1.9; *hê heortê*: 7,2.8). Secondly, while 7,1-9 describes Jesus' dialogue with his unbelieving brothers in Galilee, 7,10-13 mentions Jesus' going up to Jerusalem secretly (7,10) and depicts the dramatic situation there (the Jews' frantic search for Jesus: 7,11; the crowd's division of opinion about him: 7,12; the people's fear of the Jewish authorities: 7,13), thus setting the stage for what is to come.

Jesus' self-manifestation "in the middle of the feast" and the mixed reactions it provokes (**b**: 7,14-36) are described in three connected units (*a'*: the divine origin of Jesus' teaching and work [7,14-24]; *b'*: division among the people about his Messianic mission [7,25-31]; and *c*: officers sent by the chief priests and Pharisees to arrest him [7,32-36]). Note that the central unit (7,25-31) is demarcated by a double inclusion (*houtos*: 7,25.26.31; *ho Christos*: 7,26.31).

The self-revelation of Jesus "on the last day of the feast" and the diverse reactions of the Jews (**c**: 7,37-8,59) are given in a number of fast-moving scenes (*a"*: Jesus as the source of living water [7,37-39]; *b"*: division among the people about his Messianic origin [7,40-44]; *c'*: return of the officers to the chief priests and the Pharisees without arresting Jesus [7,45-52]; *d*: Jesus, the light of the world, and the truth of his testimony and judgement [8,12-20]; *e*: the unknown destination and identity of Jesus [8,21-30]; *f*: the Jews, Abraham and Jesus [8,31-59]). Notice that the stuctural unity of 8,12-20 is underscored by an *inclusion* (*elalêsen*: 8,12.20) [329c]. Similarly, the mention of Abraham at the beginning and end of 8,31-59 (cf. vv.33.57.58) clamps the unit together.

From what has been said above the detailed structure of Jn 7-8 may be represented as follows:

[329c] Regarding the unity of 8,12-20 BROWN rightly remarks: "these verses seem to constitute a structural unit; not only because 20 marks a pause in the action and 21 is another heading, but also because there is a minor inclusion between 12 and 20, formed by the repetition of the verb 'spoke' in the opening words of these two verses" (I, 342).

Jesus, the Source of Living Water and the Light of the World (at Tabernacles) (7,1-8,59)

a: Introduction (7,1-13)
    a (7,1-9)   : discussion between Jesus and his brothers in Galilee
                    about his revelation through works
    b (7,10-13) : Jesus goes up to Jerusalem secretly and the crowd's
                    division of opinion about him

b: Jesus' revelation in the middle of the feast (7,14-36)
    a' (7,14-24): the divine origin of Jesus' teaching and work
        b' (7,25-31): division among the crowd about Jesus' Messianic identity
            c (7,32-36) : officers sent by the chief priests and the Pharisees
                  to arrest Jesus

c: Jesus' revelation on the last day of the feast (7,37-8,59)
    a" (7,37-39): Jesus, the source of living water
        b" (7,40-44): division among the crowd about Jesus' Messianic identity
            c' (7,45-52): officers' return to the chief priests and the Pharisees
                  without arresting Jesus
            d (8,12-20) : Jesus, the light of the world, and the truth of his
                  testimony and judgement
              e (8,21-30) : the unknown destination and divine identity of Jesus
                f (8,31-59): the Jews, Abraham and Jesus.

Note the parallelism between *a*, *a'* and *a"* (cf. *hê heortê*: 7,2.8.8.14.37; *ergon poiein*: 7,3.21; *zêtein apokteinai*: 7,1.19.20), between *b*, *b'* and *b"* (cf. *ochlos*: 7,12.31.40.43; *parrêsia[i] lalein*: 7,13.26; *ho Christos*: 7,26.27.31.41.41.42; *houtos estin ho Christos*: 7,26.41; *ho Christos erchetai*: 7,27.31.41.42; *piasai auton*: 7,30.44; *oudeis epebalen ep' auton tên/tas cheira/s*: 7,30.44), between *c* and *c'* (cf. *hoi Pharisaioi*: 7,32.32.45.47.48; *hoi archiereis*: 7,32.45; *hypêretai*: 7,32.45.46). Observe also the new elements (*d, e, f*) in **c**, which do not have corresponding elements in **b**. In short, Jn 7-8 has a *spiral structure*, which confirms the unity of the subsection.

Fifthly, the unity of Jn 7-8 is supported by its *literary genre*: *trial* of Jesus by the Jews, which, however, turns out to be a trial of the Jews by Jesus! (cf. the divergent views of the crowd about Jesus [7,12.26-27.31.40-43], the differences of opinion between the Pharisees and the officers sent to arrest Jesus [7,45-49], between the former and Nicodemus [7,50-52], the insistence on *martyrein* [7,7; 8,13.14.18.18] and *martyria* [8,13.14.17], *krinein* [7,24.24.51; 8,15.15.16.26.50] and *krisis* [7,24; 8,16]).

Finally, the motif of conflict and the polemical tone, so conspicuous in Jn 7-8, highlight the *dramatic unity* of this episode[330]. From the point of view of

---

[330] "The tone of the whole is markedly polemical... There are of course other controversial passages in this gospel, but scarcely another where the controversial note is so sharp and so sustained; and this in itself gives a certain unity to the whole episode" (*ibid.*, 346).

the *dramatic development* of the Johannine plot[331], if we compare Jn 7-8 with the preceding episodes in Jn 5 and Jn 6, we find that there is progress both in "the mission of Jesus" and in "the reaction" of the Jews to him, since he reveals that his presence and mission on earth are coming to a close (7,33: *eti chronon mikron meth' hymôn eimi kai hypagô pros ton pempsanta me*; cf. also 8,21), and the Jews' unbelief and opposition to Jesus reach a crescendo, manifested in their repeated attempts to arrest (7,30.32.44; 8,20), kill (7,1.19.20.25; 8,37.40) or stone him (8,59)[332].

Because of the convergence of the many reasons (criteria) given above, we may conclude that 7,1-8,59 forms a distinct literary unit or the third subsection of Jn 5-10[333].

The healing of the man born blind (9,1-41) forms the fourth subsection of Jn 5-10. Its delimitation is clearly marked by two *inclusions* (*typhlos*: 9,1.2.40.41; *hamartanô/hamartia*: 9,2.3.41.41)[334]. It is noteworthy that the episode both begins and ends with a question and an answer about "blindness" and "sin". Seeing the man born blind the disciples ask Jesus: "Rabbi, who sinned, this man or his parents, that he was born blind?" (9,2). And Jesus answers them: "It was not that this man sinned, or his parents..." (9,3). Again, at the end of the episode the Pharisees ask Jesus: "Are we also blind?" (9,40). And Jesus' answer is: "If you were blind, you would have no sin; but now that you say, 'we see', your sin remains" (9,41).

The literary unity of Jn 9 is highlighted by the dramatic development of the episode in *seven scenes* (9,1-7.8-12.13-17.18-23.24-34.35-38.39-41)[335].

Note also that Jn 9 is distinguished from the preceding episode by means of a *change of place*, since, unlike Jesus' teaching and controversy with the Jews in Jn 7-8, his finding and healing the blind man does not happen in the temple but elsewhere (though the exact place is not indicated: *kai paragôn eiden...*)

Jn 9 has also its own *characteristic vocabulary* which distinguishes it from the immediately preceding and following subsections. We provide below a chart with all the terms which occur three or more times in Jn 9 (from the first verse of ch. 9 to its last verse) and compare them with their occurrence in 7,1-8,59 and 10,1-21[336]:

---

[331] See 3.2[11].

[332] M. GOURGUES, *op. cit.*, 88-89.

[333] The spiral structure of Jn 7-8 accounts for the similarities (cf. *a, a', a''; b, b', b''; c, c'*) as well as the differences (cf. *d, e, f*) in the vocabulary of **a, b** and **c**.

[334] See 3.138.

[335] See 3.28.

[336] For the sake of easy comparison, the first column gives the occurrences in 7,1-8,59 (leaving out 7,53-8,11) and the third column those in 10,1-21.

4. THE LITERARY STRUCTURE OF THE FOURTH GOSPEL

Vocabulary of Jn 9,1-41

Terms	7,1-8,59	9,1-41	10,1-21
anthrôpos	7,22.23.23.46.51; 8,17.28.40	1.11.16.16.24.24.30.35	—
typhlos	———	1.2.13.17.18.19.20.24.25.32.39.40.41	21
erôtaô	———	2.15.19.21.23	—
mathêtês	7,3; 8,31	2.27.28.28	—
apokrinomai	7,16.20.21.46.47.52; 8.14.19.33.34.39.48.49.54	3.11.20.25.27.30.34.36	—
goneis	———	2.3.18.20.22.23	—
gennaô	8,41	2.19.20.32.34	—
erchômai	7,27.28.30.31.34.36.37.41.42.50; 8,14.14.20.21.22.42	4.7.39	8.10.10.12
dynamai	7,7.34.36; 8,21.22.43	4.16.33	21
kosmos	7,4.7; 8,21.22.43	5.5.39	—
poieô	7,3.4.4.17.19.21.23.31.51; 8,28.29.34.38.39.40.41.44.53	6.11.14.16.26.31.33	—
pêlos	———	6.6.11.14.15	—
ophthalmos	———	6.10.11.14.15.17.21.26.30.32	21
anoigô (″)	———	10.14.17.21.26.30.32	21
niptô	———	7.7.11.15	—
blepô	———	7.15.19.21.25.39.39.39.41	—
anablepô	———	11.15.18.18	—
oida	7,15.27.28.28.29; 8,14.14.19.19.19.37.55.55.55	12.20.21.21.24.25.29.30.31	4.5
Pharisaioi	7,32.32.45.47.48; 8,12	13.15.16.40	—
theos	7,17; 8,40.41.42.42.47.47.54	3.16.24.29.31.33	—
hamartôlos	———	16.24.25.31	—
hamartia	8,21.24.24.34.34.46	34.41.41	—
pisteuô	7,5.31.38.39.48; 8,24.30.31.45.46	18.35.36.38	—
Ioudaioi	7,1.2.11.13.15.35; 8,22.31.48.52.57	18.22.22	19
hyios	8,28.35.36	19.20.35	—
laleô	7,13.17.18.26.46; 8,12.20.25.26.26.28.30.38.40.44.44	21.29.37	6
akouô	7,32.40.51; 8,26.38.40.43.47.47	27.27.31.31.32.35.40	3.8.16.20

Looking at the chart we find that there are at least ten important terms which occur three or more times in Jn 9 but never in Jn 7-8 (*typhlos* [13x], *ophthalmos* [10x], *anoigô tous ophthalmous* [7x], *blepô* [9x], *anablepô* [4x], *goneis*

[6x], *pêlos* [5x], *erôtaô* [5x], *niptô* [4x], *hamartôlos* [4x])[337]. This suggests that the curing of the man born blind in Jn 9 is not intended as a continuation of Jesus' controversies with the Jews in Jn 7-8[338].

Similarly, the vocabulary of Jn 9 distinguishes it also from 10,1-21, since 18 of the 27 terms which occur three or more times in Jn 9 are totally absent from 10,1-21[339] and since three other terms or expressions which are found 13 times (*typhlos*), 10 times (*ophthalmos*), and 9 times (*anoigô tous ophthalmous*) respectively in Jn 9 are referred to only once (10,21) in 10,1-21[340]. Furthermore, 14 terms and expressions which are employed three or more times in 10,1-21 are completely absent from 9,1-41[341].

Vocabulary of 10,1-21

Terms	9,1-41	10,1-21	10,22-42
eiserchomai	—	1.2.9.9	—
thyra	—	1.2.7.9	
probaton	—	1.2.3.3.4.7.8.11. 12.12.13.15.16	26.27
kleptês	—	1.8.10	—
poimên	—	2.11.11.12.14.16	
phônê	—	3.4.5.16	27
akouô	27.27.31.31. 32.35.40	3.8.16.20	27
idios	—	3.4.12	
ginôskô	—	6.14.14.15.15	27.38.38
egô eimi (+ predicate)	—	7.9.11.14	—
erchomai	4.7.39	8.10.10.12	41
kalos	—	11.11.14	32.33
tithêmi psychên/autên	—	11.15.17.18.18	—
ho patêr	—	15.15.17.18	25.29.29.30.32. 36.37.38.38
lambanô	—	17.18.18	—

---

[337] *Gennaô* which is found five times in Jn 9 occurs only once in Jn 7-8 (at 8,41).

[338] This does not mean that Jn 7-8 and Jn 9 are not at all related. The giving of sight to the man born blind is a striking illustration of Jesus being "the light of the world" (8,12; 9,5). There are also a number of common terms in Jn 7-8 and Jn 9 (see the chart). All these account for their parallelism (see 4.322,1 below).

[339] See the chart ("*Vocabulary of Jn 9,1-41*").

[340] This cross-reference ("to open the eyes of the blind": 10,21) has led some to conclude that 9,1-10,21 forms a literary unit. But note that there is another cross-reference to the same at 11,37.

We may also mention that *oida* which is used 11 times in Jn 9 is employed only twice in 10,1-21 (vv.4.5).

[341] See the next chart ("*Vocabulary of 10,1-21*"). Besides the formulae (*tithêmi psychên*: 5x; and *egô eimi* + predicate: 4x), we may also mention the solemn introductory formula *amên amên legô hymin* which occurs twice (10,1.7) in 10,1-21 but not in Jn 9.

The radical difference in the characteristic vocabulary between Jn 9 and 10,1-21 indicates that they should be taken as two distinct literary units. This distinction is confirmed by the diverse internal structures of each passage, since the episode of the cured blind man has a dramatic seven-scene structure, while 10,1-21 consists of a diptych of parabolic discourses (10,1-6.7-21) which have a parallel structure (xyz // x'y'z') [342].

Notice also the difference in the literary genre of Jn 9 (which consists mainly of dialogue with some narrative) and 10,1-21 (which is primarily discourse [10,1-5.7-18] with a brief narrative [10,6] or narrative-dialogue [10,19-21] which describes the reaction of the audience to the discourse) [343].

Thus on the basis of the characteristic vocabulary of Jn 9 and 10,1-21, the dramatic technique of seven scenes in Jn 9, the parallel structural pattern of 10,1-21, and finally the change in the dialogue-narrative genre in Jn 9 to the discourse genre in 10,1-21, we conclude that 9,1-41 and 10,1-21 should be understood as two distinct literary units or subdivisions of Jn 5-10 [344].

Since the feast of the Dedication is mentioned at 10,22 [345], a new specific location ("in the temple, in the portico of Solomon") [346] is indicated at 10,23 and the Jews surround Jesus with an urgent request ("if you are the Christ, tell us plainly") at 10,24, these three verses introduce a new scene.

This scene comes to an end when Jesus escapes from (literally "went out from" [*exêlthen ek*]) the hands of the Jews who want to arrest him in the temple (10,39). This is followed by a short scene (Jesus goes away across the Jordan and stays there among those who believe in him: 10,40-42) which functions as a sort of conclusion to Jn 5-10 [347].

---

[342] See 3.31.

[343] See 3.1[12].

[344] Two objections to this may be raised by those who take 10,1-21 to be a continuation of Jn 9: (1) there is no interruption between the last verse of Jn 9 and the first verse of Jn 10; (2) "the emphatic words *amên amên legô hymin* serve, as elsewhere, to mark the transition from dialogue to monologue" (C. H. DODD, *op. cit.*, 358).

It must be admitted that these are true difficulties, since generally the Evangelist clearly marks the beginning of a new episode and normally the *amên amên legô hymin/soi* formula is used to stress and develop an idea already mentioned (e.g. 5,19 takes up 5,17). But these are not absolute rules which the Evangelist blindly follows. For instance, in Jn 15 he makes Jesus begin a new discourse on the vine and branches without any introductory formula at 15,1, which shows that the emphatically abrupt beginning (with an *egô eimi* or an *amên amên* saying) of a discourse on a new theme seems to be intended to catch the attention of the readers/listeners. The *amên amên* saying at 15,1 may be compared to that at 12,24, which is also found at the beginning of a discourse. In any case, the distinction between Jn 9 and 10,1-21 is supported by different (literary, dramatic and structural) criteria and so we believe our position is reasonable.

[345] See 3.17.

[346] See 3.15.

[347] See 4.221,2.

4.3 THE STRUCTURE OF THE SECTIONS

Notice also that the discourse of Jesus in 10,25-38, enclosed between the setting (10,22-24) and the conclusion (10,39) of the episode, may be said to form multiple inclusions [348]:

10,25: eipon hymin kai ou PISTEUETE;
   TA ERGA ha egô **poiô** en tô[i] onomati *TOU PATROS MOU*
   tauta martyrei peri emou;
10,26: alla hymeis ou PISTEUETE...
10,37: ei ou **poiô TA ERGA** *TOU PATROS MOU*,
   mê PISTEUETE moi;
10,38: ei de **poiô**, kan emoi mê PISTEUETE,
   TOIS ERGOIS PISTEUETE...

It is remarkable that these four verses contain four inclusions (PISTEUETE, **TA ERGA**, **poiô**, *TOU PATROS MOU*), which highlight the unity of the pericope. This is confirmed by the characteristic vocabulary of 10,22-42 [349].

Vocabulary of 10,22-42

Terms	10,1-21	10,22-42
Ioudaioi	19	24.31.31
apokrinomai	—	25.32.33.34
pisteuô	—	25.26.37.38.38.42
ergon	—	25.32.32.33.37.38
poieô	—	25.33.37.38.41
ho patêr	15.15.17.18	25.29.29.30.32.36.37.38.38
ginôskô	6.14.14.15.15	27.38.38
cheir	—	28.29.39
lithazô	—	31.32.33
theos	—	33.34.35.35.36

We may note that only three of the ten terms which occur three or more times in 10,22-42 are found in 10,1-21 (*ho patêr*, *ginôskô* and *Ioudaioi*). It is true that Jesus' words in 10,27 ("My sheep hear my voice, and I know them, and they follow me") recall his parabolic discourses in 10,1-21. This shows that though 10,1-21 and 10,22-42 are distinct, they are related to each other (see a similar phenomenon in Jn 5 and Jn 6 which have "life" [*zôê*] as one of their common themes).

---

[348] Though 10,25-26 is not the very beginning of the episode (10,22-39), since 10,25-26 and 10,37-38 contain the beginning and end of Jesus' discourse, the common terms there may be thought of as forming inclusions.
[349] See the chart below.

4.321z From our discussion it follows that the section of "Jesus' Works, Signs and Discussions" (5,1-10,42) divides itself, like the first section of "Jesus' Initial Signs and Encounters" (2,1-4,54), into six subsections (5,1-47; 6,1-71; 7,1-8,59; 9,1-41; 10,1-21; 10,22-42).

4.322 *Parallelism between the subsections of 5,1-10,42*

We shall first compare the central subsections (Jn 7-8 and Jn 9), then the end-sections (5,1-47 and 10,22-42), and finally the second and fifth subsections (6,1-71 and 10,1-21).

4.322,1   Parallelism between 7,1-8,59 and 9,1-41

Just as in Jn 7-8 Jesus himself refers to the curing of the cripple on a Sabbath (5,1-9) as a "work" which he did (*hen ergon epoiêsa*: 7,21; cf. also 7,3), so in Jn 9 he prefaces his healing of the blind man on a Sabbath as one of the "works" of God who sent him (*ta erga tou pempsantos me*: 9,4).

Again, the giving of sight to a man born blind is intended as an illustration of Jesus as the light of the world, especially since he repeats his revelatory words of 8,12 (*egô eimi to phôs tou kosmou*) before curing the blind man (*phôs eimi tou kosmou*: 9,5).

"Knowing" the "origin" (*pothen*) of Jesus is an important issue in both Jn 7-8 and Jn 9. Compare, for instance, the following statements:

7,27: *touton* **oidamen pothen estin**
9,29: *touton* de ouk **oidamen pothen estin**.

7,28: kame oidate kai **oidate pothen eimi**!
8,14: hymeis de ouk **oidate pothen** erchomai...
9,30: hymeis ouk **oidate pothen estin**.

In both the subsections the crowd or the blind man confesses that Jesus is the/a prophet (7,40: *houtos estin alêthôs ho prophêtês*; 9,17: *prophêtês estin*). Furthermore, while some in the crowd acknowledge Jesus as "the Christ" (*houtos estin ho Christos*: 7,41; cf. the same formula at 7,26, where it is not a confession but only a question), "confessing him to be Christ" (*homologein Christon*) is mentioned at 9,22. Notice that just as the crowd in Jn 7 does not dare to speak openly of Jesus "for fear of the Jews" (*dia ton phobon tôn Ioudaiôn*: 7,13), so the parents of the cured blind man are afraid of the Jews (*ephobounto tous Ioudaious*: 9,22).

It should also be noted that only in these two subsections (Jn 7-8 and Jn 9) of the section under study (Jn 5-10) do the "Pharisees" (*Pharisaioi*) appear (7,32.32.45.47.48; 8,13; 9,13.15.16.40), whereas in other subsections "the Jews" (*Ioudaioi*) are mentioned (as sometimes also in Jn 7-8 and Jn 9).

Both in Jn 7-8 and in Jn 9 Jesus passes judgement on the unbelieving Pharisees that they will die in their sin(s) (8,21.24) or that their sin remains (9,41).

We may also mention that the question of being or becoming disciples of Jesus is brought up during the dispute between Jesus and the Jews in Jn 7-8 (*alêthôs mathêtai mou este*: 8,31) and that between the healed blind man and the Pharisees (*sy mathêtês ei ekeinou*: 9,28; cf. also 9,27: *mê kai hymeis thelete autou mathêtai genesthai?*)³⁵⁰.

4.322,2 Parallelism between 5,1-47 and 10,22-42

First of all, the episodes described in 5,1-47 and 10,22-39 happen on the occasion of a Jewish *feast* (5,1: *ên heortê tôn Ioudaiôn*; 10,22: *egeneto tote ta enkainia*) in Jerusalem (*en tois Hierosolymois*: 5,2; 10,22).

The dialogue-discourses in 5,1-47 and 10,22-39 take place "in the temple" (*en tô[i] hierô[i]*: 5,14; 10,23). The central issue in both the episodes is Jesus' claim to have a unique relationship with God, the Father:

5,17 : **ho patêr** mou heôs arti *ergazetai* **kagô** *ergazomai*
10,30: **egô kai ho patêr** hen esmen.

This claim to divinity ("making oneself equal to God" or "making oneself God") is explicitly stated to be the cause of the Jews' inimical reaction to Jesus:

5,18 : hoti... **patera** idion **elegen** *ton theon*
            ison heauton **poiôn** *tô[i] theô[i]*.
10,33: hoti sy anthrôpos ôn **poieis** seauton theon.
10,36: hoti **eipon**: hyios tou theou eimi.

It is instructive to note that Jesus refers to God very frequently as "the Father" (**ho patêr**) in the two discourses (14 times in 5,17-47 and 9 times in 10,25-38, that is, on an average about once in every two verses)³⁵¹. Besides, Jesus calls himself "[the] Son of God" (*[ho] hyios tou theou*) both at 5,25 and 10,36³⁵².

The "works" (*erga*) that Jesus does are an important theme in both the discourses (5,20.36.36; 10,25.32.32.33.37.38; cf. also *ergazomai* at 5,17). Some of

---

³⁵⁰ See other parallel elements in the vocabulary chart.
³⁵¹ Jn 5,17.18.19.20.21.22.23.23.26.36.37.43.45; 10,25.29.29.30.32.36.37.38.38. It is not so frequent elsewhere in Jn 5-10 (see n. 215 above).
³⁵² Furthermore Jesus frequently refers to himself as "the Son" (*ho hyios*) in 5,17-47 (vv.19. 19.20.21.22.23.23.26), which is "Jesus' designation of himself... when speaking of his relationship to God" (SCHNACKENBURG, II, 172). Although *ho hyios* is not used absolutely in 10,25-38, equivalent expressions (besides *hyios tou theou* at 10,36) which indicate Jesus' unique relationship to God the Father abound in the dialogue/discourse. For instance, Jesus affirms: *egô kai ho patêr hen esmen* (10,30) and *en emoi ho patêr kagô en tô[i] patri* (10,38). Again, there are similar statements about the power of Jesus and of the Father to protect the sheep (the believers), for Jesus says in the two successive verses:
10,28: kai *ouch* **harpasei** *tis* auta **ek tês cheiros** *mou*
10,29: kai *oudeis* dynatai **harpazein ek tês cheiros** *tou patros*.

the expressions used by Jesus in the two passages are also identical or strikingly similar:

5,36 : auta **ta erga ha poiô** *martyrei peri emou...*
10,25: **ta erga ha egô poiô**... *martyrei peri emou* [353].

5,20 : **ho** gar **patêr** philei ton hyion
kai panta *deiknysin* autô[i] ha autos poiei,
kai meizona toutôn *deixei* autô[i] **erga**...
10,32: polla **erga** kala *edeixa* hymin ek **tou patros**.

It must be noted here that neither the "showing of the works" (*deiknynai* **erga**)[354] nor the "witnessing of works" (**ta erga** *martyrei peri emou*) occur anywhere else in the whole section of "Jesus' Works, Signs and Discussions" (Jn 5-10), although "works" and "witnessing" are separately mentioned elsewhere in Jn 5-10.

We may mention also another interesting similarity between Jesus' dialogue-discourse in 5,14-47 and in 10,25-38. In both the places Jesus speaks about "hearing (his) voice" (**akouein tês phônês**) in relation to "living" (*zên*) or receiving "eternal life" (*zôê aiônios*):

5,25 : hoi nekroi **akousousin tês phônês** *tou hyiou tou theou*
kai hoi **akousantes** *zêsousin*.
5,28 : pantes hoi en tois mnêmeiois **akousousin tês phônês** *autou*
kai ekporeusontai... eis anastasin *zôês*...
10,27: ta probata ta ema **tês phônês** *mou* **akousousin**...
10,28: kagô didômi autois *zôên aiônion*...[355].

Notice also that towards the end of his discourses in 5,14-47 and 10,25-38 Jesus appeals to the testimony of "the Scriptures" (5,39: *hai graphai*; 10,35: *hê graphê*[356]; cf. also 5,46-47: *egrapsen... grammasin*; 10,34: *gegrammenon en tô[i] nomô[i] hymôn*), and asks the Jews to "believe him" (*pisteuein* + dat. of the person: 5,38.46; 10,37.38) or his "words" (*tois emois rhêmasi*: 5,47) or his "works" (*tois ergois*: 10,38)[357], which testify that the Father has sent him (*ho*

---

[353] Notice also that 5,36bc expresses the same idea as 10,25d:
5,36bc: **ta gar erga** *ha dedôken moi* **ho patêr** *hina teleiôsô auta*
10,25d: **ta erga** *ha egô poiô en tô[i] onomati* **tou patros** *mou*...

[354] The word *deiknyein* does not occur at all between 5,20 and 5,32.

[355] It is true that *tês phônês (autou/mou) akouein* occurs also at 10,3.16 to which 10,27 primarily refers. But neither in 10,3 nor in 10,16 is the relation between "hearing the voice" and having "eternal life" or "living" mentioned as in 5,25.28 and 10,27-29. Hence these verses may be regarded as parallel passages.

[356] *Hê graphê* is mentioned twice between 5,39 and 10,35, namely, at 7,38.42, that is, in the central subsection of Jn 5-10 (which, we shall see below, has a chiastic structure [2BCDD'C'B'], in which the central and extreme elements often have some points in common: see 3.32 above).

[357] Although the term *pisteuein* is found many times in the intermediary chapters, *pisteuein* + dative occurs only four times (6,30; 8,31.45.46), of which only the last two are the words of Jesus. This can be explained by the chiastic structure of Jn 5-10 (see n. 356 above).

patêr me apestalken: 5,37; cf. also *hon apesteilen ekeinos*: 5,38; *hon ho patêr hêgiasen kai apesteilen*: 10,36)[358]. But all his appeals appear to have fallen on hostile ears, since they continue to seek (**ezêtoun**) to kill or arrest him:

5,18 : **ezêtoun auton** hoi Ioudaioi *apokteinai*
10,39: **ezêtoun** [oun] palin **auton** *piasai*.

Thus the section of "Jesus' Works, Signs and Discussions" (Jn 5-10) begins with a subsection (5,1-47) which mentions explicitly for the first time the Jews' "seeking to kill him" (5,18) and ends with a subsection (10,22-42) which describes another attempt "to arrest him" (10,39), so much so that Jesus has to go away from Jerusalem across the Jordan (10,40) in order to escape from their murderous hands (10,39).

Because of the above-mentioned numerous and undeniable parallels between 5,1-47 and 10,22-42, these are to be understood as parallel passages in the section of "Jesus' Works, Signs and Discussions" (Jn 5-10).

4.322,3 Parallelism between 6,1-71 and 10,1-21

It must be admitted at the outset that, if we compare only the vocabulary in the two subsections (6,1-71 and 10,1-21), the parallelism between them would not be as evident as in the central subsections (7,1-8,59 and 9,1-47) and in the end-subsections (5,1-47 and 10,22-42), although there are some interesting correspondences. Compare, for instance, 6,2 and 10,4:

6,2 : **êkolouthei** de *autô[i]* ochlos polys, **hoti** etheôroun...
10,4: kaí ta probata *autô[i]* **akolouthei, hoti** oidasin...

Again, at the end of Jesus' discourse in 6,22-59 and in 10,1-18 there is a division among the disciples (6,60-71) or among the Jews (10,19-21), the cause of the division being in both the cases his "words" (*ho logos houtos*: 6,60; *dia tous logous toutous*: 10,19), which are too hard to listen to (6,60: *tis dynatai autou akouein?* 10,20: *ti autou akouete?*). While many of his disciples (*polloi ek tôn mathêtôn autou*: 6,60.66) are scandalized (6,61) and many of the Jews (*polloi ex autôn*: 10,20) are convinced that Jesus has a demon and is mad (10,20), the Twelve (6,67-71) acknowledge that he has the words (*rhêmata*) of eternal life (6,68) and some Jews admit that his words (*rhêmata*) are not of one who has a demon (10,21).

---

[358] Just as 5,32-33 refers back to the Jewish delegation sent to John the Baptist (1,19-28) and his true (*alêthês*) testimony to the truth (*alêtheia*), so 10,40-41 recalls 1,28 and affirms that whatever John said about Jesus was true (*alêthês*):

5,32 : **alêthês** *estin hê martyria hên martyrei* **peri emou**
5,33 : hymeis apestalkate pros **Iôannên**, kai *memartyrêken* tê[i] **alêtheia[i]**
10,41: *panta de hosa eipen* **Iôannês peri toutou alêthê** *ên*.

Jesus' giving of bread in abundance (*perisseuô*: 6,12.13) to the crowd in Jn 6 seems to be a symbolic anticipation of the life in abundance (*perisson*: 10,10) that he has come to give all men: *egô êlthon hina zôên echôsin kai perisson echôsin* (10,10)[359].

In fact, the expression *echein zôên (aiônion)* which occurs four times in 6,1-71 (vv.40.47.53.54) and once in 10,1-21 (v.10), is not found elsewhere between Jn 6 and Jn 10,1-21[360].

It may be also worth mentioning that, while the "disciples" (*mathêtai*) of Jesus have an important role to play in Jn 6 (and especially in 6,1-15. 16-21.60-66.67-71), the "sheep" (*probata*) and the shepherd are the topics of the parabolic discourses in 10,1-18. Since the "sheep" are symbols of the believing "disciples", the latter in 6,68, like the sheep in 10,4 which follow him (*kai ta probata autô[i] akolouthei, hoti oidasin tên phônên autou*: 10,4), refuse to go away (6,68: *pros tina apeleusometha?*) and continue to follow him because they know (*egnôkamen*) his identity (6,69). Note that the same verb *ginôskein* is used both at 6,69 (to denote the disciples' knowledge of Jesus) and at 10,14 (to describe the sheep's knowledge of the shepherd).

Because of the reasons given above we may regard 6,1-71 and 10,1-21 as parallel passages.

4.32z From what has been said so far, it is clear that the section of "Jesus' Works, Signs and Discussions" (5,1-10,42) consists of six subsections which are *chiastically* arranged (2BCDD'C'B')[361]. This may be represented in a schema as follows:

---

[359] These are the only two passages (6,12-13; 10,10) where the verb *perisseuô* and the related adjective *perissos* occur in the entire Gospel of John. This abundance of bread which Jesus gave (6,12-13) seems to have been the reason why the crowd saw in Jesus the *Prophet-like-Moses* and the *Shepherd-like-David*, since the Galilean crowd's words (*houtos estin alêthôs ho prophêtês ho erchomenos eis ton kosmon*: 6,14) most probably reflect Deut 18,15.18 (*prophêtên... hôs eme, anastêsei soi Kyrios ho theos sou... prophêtên anastêsô autois..., hôsper se*) but their attempt at making him king because he fed them probably refers back to Ez 34,23; 37,24 where God promises to raise up a "Shepherd-like-David" who will be "a ruler in the midst of them" and who "will tend/feed them" (34,23: *kai anastêsô ep' autous poimena hena, kai poimanei autous, ton doulon mou Dauid, kai estai autôn poimên..., kai Dauid archôn en mesô[i] autôn, estai poimên heis pantôn*). If this explanation is accepted, the problem of many scholars like R. E. BROWN who finds it "difficult" to understand "the seeming identification of the Prophet and the (messianic) king" (I, 235) at 6,14-15 would disappear. If this Shepherd-like-David imagery is present in 6,15, then the parallelism between the feeding of the five thousand by Jesus (the Shepherd), the bread of life, in Jn 6 and the discourse on Jesus, the life-giving Shepherd, in 10,1-21 becomes all the more evident. (Note that *heis poimên* of Jn 10,16 probably refers back to the prophecy Ez 37,24 which also speaks of *poimên heis*.)

[360] Between 6,68 and 10,10 even the word *zôê* occurs only once (8,12: *hexei to phôs tês zôês*, where *echein* refers primarily to *phôs*).

[361] Jn 5,1-47 is represented by the letter 'B' (rather than the first letter 'A' of the alphabet) to show the parallelism between 5,1-47 and 2,13-25 (which has been denoted above by the letter 'B' in the structure of the first section [Jn 2-4]).

JESUS' WORKS, SIGNS AND DISCUSSIONS (at Jewish Feasts) (5,1-10,42)

B (5,1-47)	:	The work of curing the cripple by Jesus, the Son of God (on a Sabbath).
C (6,1-71)	:	The sign of feeding the five thousand by the bread of life (before Passover).
D (7,1-8,59)	:	Jesus, the source of living water and the light of the world (at Tabernacles).
D' (9,1-41)	:	The giving of sight to the blind man by the light of the world (on a Sabbath).
C' (10,1-21)	:	The parables of the sheepfold, the door, and the life-giving, good shepherd.
B' (10,22-42)	:	The works and identity of Jesus, the Christ, the Son of God (at Dedication).

4.33 The Structure of "the Climactic Sign and the Coming of Jesus' Hour" (Jn 11-12)

4.331 *Division of 11,1-12,50 into subsections*

The main division of Jn 11-12 is clearly marked by introductions and conclusions.

The first two verses of Jn 11 serve as an *introduction* to the Lazarus-episode, since they mention for the first time new characters (Lazarus, Martha and Mary) and a new place (Bethany).

Again, 11,54 appears to be a *transitional conclusion* to the Lazarus-episode (11,1-53), namely, the raising of Lazarus (11,1-45) and the consequent decision of the Sanhedrin to put Jesus to death (11,46-53), since mention is made of Jesus' departure to Ephraim and his stay there (*ho oun Iēsous... apēlthen ekeithen... eis Ephraim... kakei emeinen meta tōn mathētōn.* 11,54) [362].

The literary unity of 11,1-54 is supported by its *dramatic unity and development*. When Jesus hears the news of his friend's sickness, he remains in the place (11,1-6) but after Lazarus' death he decides to go to Bethany at the risk of his own life (11,7-16). Then come the moving scenes of the meeting of Martha and Mary with Jesus (11,17-37), which build up dramatic tension and expectation in the reader. The climax is reached when Jesus raises the dead Lazarus to life again by a mere word (11,38-44). The consequences of this miraculous action are described in 11,45-53. (Some believe in him, while others report the matter to the Pharisees, and the Sanhedrin decides to put to death Jesus who raised a dead man to life!).

---

[362] P. MOURLON BEERNAERT takes 11,54 and 11,55-57 to be the introduction to the next episode in Jn 12 ("Parallelisme entre Jean 11 et 12. Étude de structure littéraire et théologique", in: *Genèse et Structure d'un Texte du Nouveau Testament. Étude Interdisciplinaire du Chapitre 11 de l'Évangile de Jean*, A.-L. Descamps et al. [ed.] [Paris 1981] 123-49 especially 132). But whereas 11,55 mentions the nearness of the feast of Passover, 11,54 reports Jesus' going away to Ephraim and remaining there; and therefore it serves as a transitional conclusion rather than as an introduction.

The second subsection of Jn 11-12 begins with a *transitional introduction* (11,55-57) which describes the nearness of the Passover (*ên de engys to pascha tôn Ioudaiôn*: 11,55a) and the pilgrims' going up to Jerusalem (*kai anebêsan polloi eis Hierosolyma...*: 11,55b), while the high priests and the Pharisees are planning to arrest him (11,57). Thus 11,55-57 provides the *dramatic setting* for the events to be described in Jn 12.

All the events narrated in Jn 12 (the anointing at Bethany, the triumphal entry into Jerusalem and the coming of the Greeks) are linked together by means of the frequent mention of the *feast of Passover* (*pascha/heortê*: 12,1.12.20) [363].

There is a *chronological specification* with reference to the Passover at 12,1 (*pro hex hêmerôn tou pascha*) and a *literary-chronological indication* at 12,12 (*tê[i] epaurion*; cf. also 1,29.35.42; 6,22) [364].

We saw in ch. 3 that 12,37-43, which contains the Evangelist's explanation of the unbelief of the Jews, serves as a conclusion to the Book of Jesus' Signs (Jn 2-12) [365]. But in these verses the new theme of the fulfilment of the Scriptures, which recurs frequently in the Book of Jesus' Hour (12,38; 13,18; 15,25; 17,12; 18,9.32; 19,24.36), is introduced [366]. Even the very construction of the clause containing the verb *plêroô* (which is used always in the aor. subj. pass. [*plêrôthê[i]*] preceded by *hina*) is often identical. Thus 13,18; 17,12; 19,24.36 have *hina hê graphê plêrôthê[i]*. At other times *hê graphê* is replaced by a phrase or clause containing *ho logos* (the spoken word of Jesus or of a prophet or the written word of the Law):

12,38: **hina ho logos** *Esaiou tou prophêtou* **plêrôthê[i]** *hon eipon*.
15,25: **hina plêrôthê[i] ho logos** *ho en tô[i] nomô[i] autôn gegrammenos...*
18,9 : **hina plêrôthê[i] ho logos** *hon eipen...*
18,32: **hina ho logos** *tou Iêsou* **plêrôthê[i]** *hon eipen...*

The introduction of this important theme in what is normally taken by scholars as only the conclusion (12,37-43) of the first part of the Fourth Gospel (Jn 1/2-12) [367] confirms our judgement that even this conclusion forms part of the bridge-section (Jn 11-12), since it both concludes the Book of Jesus' Signs and introduces an important theme on which the Evangelist will insist in the Book of Jesus' Hour [367a].

---

[363] See 3.17.
[364] See 3.162.
[365] See 3.113.
[366] PANIMOLLE, III, 139.
[367] See ch. 3 above.
[367a] Notice that except for the names (*Esaiou tou prophêtou* and *tou Iêsou*) the construction of 12,38 and 18,32 is identical. Similarly, but for the qualifying phrase (*ho en tô[i] nomô[i] autôn gegrammenos*) or clause (*hon eipon*), the construction of 15,25 and 18,9 is the same (*hina plêrôthê[i] ho logos...*).

The limits of 12,37-43 are marked by an *inclusion* (*pisteuein eis auton*: 12,37.42) which also indicates the theme of the pericope, namely, the Jews' refusal to believe (*ouk episteuon*: 12,37) or to confess (*ouch hômologoun*: 12,42).

After 12,37-43 there appears a revelatory discourse of Jesus (12,44-50), although at 12,36 it was said that he hid himself (*apelthôn ekrybê ap' autôn*). Whether 12,44-50 was added by the Evangelist himself or by a redactor [368], its actual place in the plan of the Gospel can be correctly understood, if we take this discourse of Jesus as being spoken from behind the stage where he has disappeared. *Speaking invisibly from behind the stage* was common in ancient Greek tragedies. For instance, in the final scene (*exodos*) of *Hippolytus* by Euripides the goddess Artemis makes a long discourse to Theseos (Hippolytus' father) who is on the stage [369]. Thus making Jesus "cry out" (*ekraxen*: 12,44) after he has disappeared from the stage (cf. *ekrybê*: 12,37) is a good *dramatic technique* the author has used to create a mysterious atmosphere (as of an invisible voice) to make the reader reflect deeply on the last public discourse of Jesus. If this dramatic setting is admitted, there is no need to invoke a displacement-hypothesis to account for the actual place of this kerygmatic discourse [370].

4.331z Thus we come to the conclusion that the Bridge-Section ("the Climactic Sign and the Coming of Jesus' Hour") (11,1-12,50) consists of two main blocks of texts or subsections: the first centred around the Lazarus-episode (11,1-54) and the second around events that lead up to the arrival of "the hour" of Jesus, followed by a conclusion and a revelatory discourse of Jesus from behind the stage (11,55-12,50).

4.332 *Parallelism between 11,1-54 and 11,55-12,50*

P. Mourlon Beernaert says that there are "more than fifty elements of ch. 11" which are parallel to corresponding elements of ch. 12 [371]. We have found

---

[368] Johannine scholars are not agreed on this issue. M.-É. BOISMARD regards it as an addition by a redactor ("Le caractère adventice de Jo., XII, 45-50", *Sacra Pagina* II (Paris 1961) 189-92. (Cf. SCHNACKENBURG, II, 420-21 for an evaluation of Boismard's position).

[369] Cf. C. DIANO (ed.), *Il Teatro Greco. Tutte le Tragedie* (Firenze 1970) 491-93.

[370] *Pace* BERNARD (II, 445-48), BULTMANN (344-47) and others who transfer 12,44-50 to other places in the Gospel.

This discourse of Jesus not only *sums up* what has been revealed in Jn 2-12 but also *points to* what is to be manifested during his farewell discourse(s) and prayer in Jn 13-17 (e.g. compare 12,45: "he who sees me sees him who sent me" and 14,9: "he who has seen me has seen the Father"; the Father's commandment to Jesus in 12,49-50 and in 15,10). This confirms our view that 12,44-50 functions as part of the bridge-section (Jn 11-12).

[371] Cf. n. 362 above. He has also proposed (on pp. 133-34) a parallel internal structure for Jn 11 (ABC) and Jn 12 (A'B'C'), taking 11,1-16 (A) as parallel to 12,1-11 (A'), 11,17-32 (B) as parallel to 12,12-19 (B'), 11,33-44 (C) as parallel to 12,20-36 (C'), and 11,45-53 (Epilogue) as parallel to 12,37-43 (Epilogue).

about seventy (Greek) terms and names common to 11,1-54 and 11,55-12,50 (which we give below in the form of a chart for the sake of ready reference, following the order of the verses of 11,1-54):

Terms/Names Common to 11,1-54 and 11,55-12,50

Terms/Names	11,1-54	11,55-12,50
Lazaros	1.2.5.11.14.43	1.2.9.10.17
Bêthania	1.8	1
Maria	1.2.19.20.28.31.32.45	3
Martha	1.5.19.20.21.24.30	2
aleiphô	2	3
kyrios	2.3.12.21.27.32.34.39	13.[21].38
myron	2	3.3.5
ekmassô	2	3
pous	2.32.44	3.3
thrix	2	3
ide	3.36	19
phileô	3.36	25
agapaô	5	43
akouô	4.6.20.29.41.42	12.18.29.34.47
thanatos	4.13	33
apothnê[i]skô	14.16.21.25.26.32.37.50.51	24.24.33
doxa	4.40	41.43.43
doxazô	4	16.23.28.28
meneô	6.54	24.34.46
ho hyios (tou theou/anthrôpou)	4.27	23.34.34
hêmera	6.9.9.17.24.53	1.7.48
mathêtês	7.8.12.54	4.16
zêteô	8	56
hoi Ioudaioi	8.19.31.33.36.45.54	55; 9.11
hypagô	8.31.44	11.35
hôra	9	23.27.27
peripateô	9.10.54	35.35.36.36.46
kosmos	9.27	19.25.31.31.31.46.47.47
sôzô	12	27.47

While it cannot be denied that there are certain similarities between A and A' (e.g. the meeting of Martha/crowd with Jesus at 11,20 and 12,12-13), between C and C' (e.g. Jesus' being troubled at 11,33 and 12,27; Jesus' prayer to the Father at 11,41-42 and 12,27-28), from the point of view of the number of scenes in 11,1-54 and 12,1-50, the former has nine scenes (11,1-6.7-16.17-27.28-31.32-37. 38-44.45-46.47-53.54), while the latter has only five or six scenes or pericopes (12,1-8.9-11.12-19. 20-36.37-43.44-50) whose structural organization does not always correspond to that of 11,1-54. This, however, does not rule out the overall similarity between the two episodes in Jn 11 and Jn 12 (see below).

4.3 THE STRUCTURE OF THE SECTIONS

Terms/Names	11,1-54	11,55-12,50
dokeô	13.31	56
pisteuô	15.25.26.26.27.40.42.45.48	11.36.37.38.39.42.44.46
erchomai	17.19.20.27.29.30.32.34.38. 45.48	56; 1.9.12.12.13.15.22.22. 27.46.47
heuriskô	17	14
mnêmeion	17.31.38	17
Hierosolyma	18	55; 12
polloi	19.45	55; 11.42
hypantaô	20.30	18
kathizô	20	14
oida	22.24.42.49	35.50
didômi	22	57; 5.49
zôê/zaô	25.25.26	25.50
eis ton aiôna	26	34
ho Christos	27	34
phôneô	28	17
phônê	43	28.30
egeirô	29	1.9.17
oikia	31	3
eidon	31.32.33.34	9.21.40.41
exerchomai	31.44	13
akoloutheô	31	26
piptô	32	24
tarassô	33	27
pou	34	57; 39
pôs	36	34
dynamai	37	39
ophthalmos	37.41	40.40
poieô	37.45.46.47.47	2.16.18.37
pater [voc.]	41	27.28
ochlos	42	9.12.17.18.29.34
kraugazô	43	13
aphiêmi	44.48	7
Pharisaios	46.47	57; 19.42
archiereus	47.49.51	57; 10
anthrôpos	47.50	23.34.34.43
sêmeion poieô	47	18.47
apollymi	50	25
apokteinô	53	10
bouleuomai	53	10

Although some of these parallels may be chance occurrences, so many of them cannot be accounted for, unless we admit that the Evangelist intended 11,1-54 and 11,55-12,50 to be parallel to one another. This is confirmed by the fact that the two passages contain not only individual words in common but whole phrases and even sentences which are the same or strikingly similar. For instance, at 11,41 Jesus tells Martha that if she believes she "will see the glory of God" (*opsê[i] tên doxan tou theou*; cf. also 11,4) and at 12,41 the Evangelist speaks, in the context of the Jews' refusal to believe in Jesus, about Isaiah's "seeing his glory" (*eiden tên doxan autou*). Mary is introduced at 11,2 by using the same expressions to be employed in describing her action of anointing Jesus' feet with ointment and wiping them with her hair:

11,2: ên de *Mariam* hê **a l e i p s a s a** ton kyrion *myrô[i]*
kai **ekmaxasa** *tous podas autou* **tais thrixin autês**.

12,3: hê oun *Mariam* labousa litran *myrou* nardou pistikês polytimou **ê l e i p s e n** *tous podas tou Iêsou* kai **exemaxen tais thrixin autês** *tous podas autou*.

We may note also the similarity in the description of Martha's going to meet Jesus (11,20) and that of the crowds in Jerusalem (12,2-3):

11,20: *hê oun Martha hôs* **êkousen hoti Iêsous erchetai**
h y p ê n t ê s e n   a u t ô [i].

12,12: *ho ochlos polys...* **akousantes hoti erchetai ho Iêsous** eis Hierosolyma,

12,13: exêlthen eis **h y p a n t ê s i n   a u t ô [i]**...

Observe also the explicit reference to the miracle of raising Lazarus from the dead in 12,9 (*Lazaron... hon êgeiren ek nekrôn*) and its result in 12,11 (cf. 11,45):

11,45: *polloi oun ek tôn Ioudaiôn...* **episteusan eis auton**.

12,11: *polloi di' auton hypêgon tôn Ioudaiôn* kai **episteuon eis ton Iêsoun**.

Notice also the striking parallel relationship between 11,53 and 12,10 (which describe the decisions of the high priests to kill Jesus and Lazarus respectively):

11,53: **ebouleusanto hina apokteinôsin** *auton*.

12,10: **ebouleusanto...** **hina** kai *ton Lazaron* **apokteinôsin**.

4.33z Since 11,1-54 describes the climactic sign of raising Lazarus from the dead, which manifests Jesus as the resurrection and the life, and which leads to the Jewish Sanhedrin's decision to do away with him, and since 11,55-12,50 contains the anointing of Jesus at Bethany, his triumphal entry into Jerusalem, the coming of the Greeks and of "the hour"[372], and the Evangelist's reflection on the Jews' refusal to believe in Jesus, and since there are about seventy parallels in vocabulary and expressions[373], we may conclude that 11,1-54 is parallel to 11,55-12,50 and may be schematically represented as follows:

---

[372] Note that Jesus interprets this anointing by Mary as a symbolic anointing of his body for burial (12,7), which points to the imminence of his hour, and he understands the arrival of the Greeks seeking to see him as a sign of the arrival of his hour (12,20-24).

[373] Cf. P. MOURLON BEERNAERT, *art. cit.*, 134-35.

THE CLIMACTIC SIGN AND THE COMING OF JESUS' HOUR
(Bridge-Section) (11,1-12,50)

C (11,1-54) : The sign of raising Lazarus to life by Jesus, the resurrection and the life, and the Sanhedrin's decision to kill him.

C' (11,55-12,50) : The anointing at Bethany, the triumphal entry into Jerusalem, the coming of the Greeks and of Jesus' "hour", and the Jews' refusal to believe in him.

4.34 The Structure of "Jesus' Farewell of the Hour" (Jn 13-17)

4.341 *Division of 13,1-17,26 into subsections* [374]

The last subsection of Jn 13-17 begins at 17,1, since Jesus (after the discourses) is here described as raising his eyes to heaven and praying to the Father. Since the whole of Jn 17 consists of Jesus' uninterrupted prayer, which has a *different literary genre* from the preceding chapters 13-16 (narratives, dialogues and discourses), 17,1-26 may be understood as a distinct literary unit of Jn 13-17. There is unanimous agreement among Johannine scholars on this point [375].

Since Jesus begins the prayer of Jn 17 with the words: *Pater, elêlythen hê hôra* (17,1), it may be entitled "the prayer of the hour" [376]. This title is all the more appropriate as this prayer concludes the section (Jn 13-17) which begins with a verse which highlights the arrival of the hour of Jesus (*eidôs ho Iêsous hoti êlthen autou hê hôra...*: 13,1).

It is quite evident that the first subsection begins with the *introductory verse* at 13,1. But there is little agreement among scholars about the *end* of this subsection. Many take 13,30 to be the end, since it mentions Judas' departure from the supper room [377]. Besides, there seems to be a break between 13,30 and 13,31, since a new literary genre (direct discourse) is begun in 13,31, while the

---

[374] Cf. Y. SIMOENS, *op. cit.*, 1-51, for a critical evaluation of the different structures of Jn 13-17 proposed by various scholars, and 52-80 for his own concentric structure with 15,12-17 at the centre. The two principal criteria used by the author are inclusions and parallelisms. While many of his observations are valid, the term "inclusion" is often not used in the strict sense of the term (e.g. *doxazô* at 13,31-32 and at 17,1-5 is taken as an inclusion, although 13,31-32 comes at the end of the first unit (13,1-38) (in his structural division) and 17,1-5 at the beginning of the last unit (17,1-26).

Cf. also H. ZIMMERMANN, "Struktur und Aussageabsicht der johanneischen Abschiedsreden", *BiLeb* 8 (1967) 279-90.

[375] In the words of S. MIGLIASSO: "non ho trovato alcun autore, che dal punto di vista della divisione di questi capitoli [13-17], non consideri il c. 17 come unità indipendente" (*op. cit.*, 44).

[376] PANIMOLLE, III, 337.

[377] Thus SCHNACKENBURG writes: "The first section [13,1-30] that we have to consider is clearly marked off by the departure of Judas Iscariot (13:30)" (III, 6). For a detailed explanation of the unity of 13,1-30 see G. RICHTER, *Die Fusswaschung im Johannesevangelium. Geschichte ihrer Deutung* (Biblischer Untersuchungen 1) (Regensburg 1967) 285-320.

previous pericope is a narrative[378]. But there are many dissenting voices against this view. For instance, Segalla understands 13,31-35[379] as belonging to 13,1-30, mainly because of the *inclusions* between 13,1 and 13,34-35 (*agapaô/ agapê*) and between 13,3 and 13,33 (**hypagô**):

13,1 : *agapêsas* tous idious en tô[i] kosmô[i] eis telos *êgapêsen* autous.
13,3c: kai pros ton theon **hypagei**
13,33: hopou egô **hypagô** hymeis ou dynasthe elthein.
13,34: entolên kainên didomi hymin, hina *agapate* allêlous,
 kathôs *êgapêsa* hymas hina kai hymeis *agapate* allêlous.
13,35: en toutô[i] gnôsontai pantes hoti emoi mathêtai este,
 ean *agapên* echête en allêlois.

These inclusions, in Segalla's view, indicate that the first verses of Jn 13 are closely linked to 13,33-35 and signal the limit of the first subsection[380]. But the dialogue between Peter and Jesus (13,36-38) is also *closely connected* to 13,33, since Peter, taking up Jesus' words about his "going away" (13,33), asks him where he is going (13,36) and Jesus reaffirms his earlier statement about his "going away" to a place where Peter cannot now follow him:

13,33de: **hopou egô hypagô** hymeis **ou dynasthe** *elthein*.
13,36b : Kyrie, **pou hypageis?**
13,36d : **hopou hypagô ou dynasai** moi nyn *akolouthêsai*...

Because of these interconnections between 13,31-35 and 13,36-38 they should not be separated from one another[381]. On account of this link and the *conclusive* character of 13,31-38, these verses are taken by some authors as the last part of 13,1-38[382].

---

[378] S. MIGLIASSO is emphatic in affirming a break between 13,30 and 13,31:

Indubbiamente con Gv. 13,31 c'è un cambiamento di forma letteraria: da una narrazione (Gv. 13,1-10 [sic!]) si passa col v. 31b ad un discorso diretto, che viene introdotto da una forte locazione temporale di distacco: "Dopo che" (v. 31a), cui segue il riagganciamento al fatto già accaduto, la partenza (o, uscita) di Giuda (*op. cit.*, 45).

[379] Thus SEGALLA takes 13,31-35 as the third part of 13,1-35 and calls it "un commento interpretativo... ad interpretare l'avvenimento precedente" and gives the following reasons:

a) il tema della gloria (13,31-32) spiega e conchiude quello dell'ora (13,1); b) il tema della dipartita (13,33) chiarisce e richiama gli accenni di 13,1.3; c) quello in fine del comandamento dell'amore (13,34-35) dovrebbe essere una risposta all'amore supremo di Gesù e forma inclusione con l'inizio del capitolo sul tema dell'amore (13,1)... (362-63).

[380] *Ibid.* But without the help of other criteria, one cannot decide if the common terms in 13,1 and 13,34-35 form inclusions (indicating the beginning and end of a subsection) or parallelisms between two beginnings (see below).

[381] *Pace* SEGALLA who separates 13,36-38 from 13,31-35 in such a way that 13,36-38 is considered only "una breve introduzione" to the first discourse which follows (*ibid.*, 361).

[382] In the words of B. LINDARS: "John's narrative of the Last Supper *concludes*... with two short paragraphs [13,31-35.36-38], which correspond with the two preceding sections on Jesus as the model of discipleship (1-20) and on failure in discipleship (21-30)" (460) [my italics]. Cf. also LAGRANGE, 365-70; MARSH, 481; Y. SIMOENS, *op. cit.*, 61-62.

But many authors regard 13,31-38 as an *"introduction"* to the first farewell discourse[383] or to the whole of the last discourse[384]. Certainly some *key terms* of 13,31-38 are found in 14,1-31. For instance, Jesus' *hypagein* mentioned at 13,33.36 is taken up again in 14,4-5 (*hopou egô hypagô*: 14,4; *ouk oidamen pou hypageis*: 14,5) and in 14,28 (*êkousate hoti egô eipon hymin: hypagô...*). Again, the "glorification" (*doxazein*) of God/the Father (mentioned at 13,31-32) is repeated at 14,13[385]. Furthermore, the theme of love (*agapan/agapê*: 13,34.34. 34.35) is developed in 14,15-31 (*agapan*: 14,15.21.21.21.21.23.23.23.28.31).

Therefore, on the one hand, 13,31-38 is linked to 13,1-30 (cf. 13,1.3.33.34-35) and, on the other hand, it is connected to the discourse in Jn 14 through common vocabulary. Hence the problem concerning the end of the first subsection can be satisfactorily solved if we admit that 13,31-38 are *"bridge-verses"*[386], which simultaneously conclude the first subsection and introduce the second (cf. also the hook-word *exêlthen* at 13,30 and 13,31a).

Thus the first unit of Jn 13-17 consists of 13,1-38, which describes Jesus' washing of the disciples' feet, the symbolic act of the hour (13,1-17), the prediction of betrayal (13,18-30) and denial (13,36-38), and the parting love-commandment (13,31-35).

Since 13,31-38 are bridge-verses, the second subsection *begins* with 13,31 (*hote oun exêlthen...*) and its *end* is clearly distinguishable by Jesus' words to the disciples: *egeiresthe, agômen enteuthen* (14,31). That 14,31 is intended to be the limit of 13,31-14,31 is indicated also by means of two *quasi-inclusions* between the bridge-verses and the last verse (*entolê*: 13,34 & *entellomai*: 14,31; *agapaô*: 13,34; 14,31)[386a].

Since such vocabulary is normally found in the literary genre of "farewell speech"[387], 13,31-14,31 may be rightly called the *first farewell discourse*.

Jn 15,1 is admitted by all to be the *beginning* of a new division of Jn 13-17[388]. But there is little agreement among scholars as to the *extent* of this literary unit. Many are of the opinion that Jn 15-16 forms a single major

---

[383] BROWN, II, 608-9; SCHNACKENBURG, III, 48. Cf. S. MIGLIASSO, *op. cit.*, 55, n. 74, for a long list of authors who consider 13,31-38 to be an introduction or prologue to the discourse(s) that follow. However, S. MIGLIASSO himself takes only 13,31-32 as the introduction, while 13,33-38 is regarded as the first part of the discourse (*op. cit.*, 73-86; 169-70).

[384] BARRETT, 449; J. SCHNEIDER, "Die Abschiedsreden Jesu", in: *Gott und die Götter* (Festschrift E. Fascher) (Berlin 1958) 103-12 especially 106. Cf. BROWN, II, 608-9 for a critical evaluation of the above view.

[385] PANIMOLLE takes this recurrence of *doxazein* to be an inclusion (III, 203-4).

[386] See 3.191.

[386a] These are called "quasi-inclusions", since 13,34 is not, strictly speaking, the beginning of the bridge-verses (13,31-38), which, however, not only conclude the previous subsection (13,1-38) but also introduce the following one (13,31-14,31).

[387] Cf. BROWN, II, 597-601.

[388] See the various structures studied in ch.2 above and in Johannine commentaries.

division[389]. Others are of the view that 15,1-16,4a is "a single, connected discourse"[390], while still others regard 15,1-17[391] as a literary unit. The main reason why many scholars judge that the whole of Jn 15-16 is one large literary unit is their theory of composition, according to which Jn 15-16(17) is a redactional addition[392]. But even these authors admit that 15,1-17 is a literary unit. For example, R. E. Brown says: "Generally xv 1-17 is recognized by scholars to be a unit; for the last mention of the imagery of vine ('bear fruit') appears in [v.] 16, and there does seem to be a change of subject between [v.] 17 and [v.] 18"[393].

The main arguments R. Schnackenburg gives for the unity of 15,1-16,4a are: 1) the frequent use of *tauta lelalêka hymin*, which is regarded as "a structural element", in 15,1-16,4a; 2) the contrasts and connections between 15,1-17 and 15,18-16,4a (e.g. "love-hate", "disciples-world" and the choosing of the disciples out of the world mentioned at 15,16 and 15,19); and 3) "Jesus is, in both, the inner reason for the community of the disciples or their separation from the world"[394]. But these connections and contrasts do not necessarily demonstrate the unity of 15,1-16,4a, since precisely on account of the *antithetical parallelism* (or contrast) between 15,1-17 and 15,18-16,4a, these could be considered as two literary units.

That 15,1-17 is to be regarded as a literary unit is seen from "the break between 15,17 and 15,18"[395]. Not only is there a change of subject matter at 15,18 but there are also *inclusions* and *parallelisms* which indicate the limits of 15,1-17 and 15,18-16,4d. Thus *karpon pherein* at 15,2 and 15,16 and *patêr* at 15,1 and 15,16 form inclusions. Again, not only the world's hatred of the

---

[389] LAGRANGE (398-99), LINDARS (486), SEGALLA (390), and PANIMOLLE (III, 151) call Jn 15-16 the second discourse. BROWN (II, 546) prefers to see Jn 15-16 as "division 2" of "the Last Discourse" (13,31-17,26), "division 1" being 13,31-14,31 and "division 3" being Jn 17 (cf. 2.[23] above). LAGRANGE, BROWN and SEGALLA regard 15,1-17; 15,18-16,4a; 16,4b-33 as three subsections of Jn 15-16 and admit that the last subdivision (16,4b-33) is parallel to 13,31-14,31. PANIMOLLE, however, proposes 15,1-11 as a subunit distinct from 15,12-17 (III, 261-62).

[390] So SCHNACKENBURG, III, 91-92. Y. SIMOENS takes 15,1-16,3 as a unit (*op. cit.*, 130-32).

[391] BARRETT, 470; BULTMANN, 529; BECKER, II, 477-78.

[392] See, for instance, BROWN, II, 586-88; H. ZIMMERMANN, "Struktur und Aussageabsicht der johanneischen Abschiedsreden (Jo 13-17)", *BiLeb* 8 (1967) 279-90.

[393] BROWN, II, 665.

[394] SCHNACKENBURG, III, 92. *Tauta lelalêka hymin* is found also in 16,4e-33 (e.g. at 16,6.25.33).

[395] BECKER compares the break between 14,31 and 15,1 to that between 15,17 and 15,18 and says:

> Dass der Text nach 14,31 und mit 15,1 ganz unvermittelt einsetzt, steht selbstverständlich fest. Ähnlich gravierend wirkt der Bruch zwischen 15,17 und 15,18: mit 15,17 endet das voher verhandelte Thema vom Bleiben in Christus und vom Fruchtbringen durch Bruderliebe, der Blick auf die nur internen Gemeindeverhältnisse verändert sich danach zur Darstellung des Hasses der Welt gegenüber der Gemeinde und der Tröstung der Gemeinde in dieser Not (II, 478).

disciples mentioned at the beginning of 15,18-16,4d corresponds to the Jews' persecution of the disciples foretold at the end (16,2-3) but also 15,20ab (*mnêmoneuete tou logou hou egô eipon hymin*) corresponds to 16,4cd (*mnêmoneuête autôn hoti egô eipon hymin*).

Furthermore, just as 15,1-17 consists of *three subunits* (15,1-8.9-11.12-17) demarcated by *inclusions* (*ho patêr mou*: 15,1.8; *karpon pherein*: 15,2.2.2.8; *polys*: 15,2.8; *entolê/entellomai*: 15,12.17; *hina agapate allêlous*: 15,12.17), 15,18-16,4d too is composed of *three subunits* (15,18-25.26-27; 16,1-4d) marked by *inclusions* (*misein*: 15,18.25; *tauta lelalêka hymin hina*: 16,1.4)[396].

It is also noteworthy that the last subunit (15,12-17: the commandment of love) of 15,1-17 is *antithetically parallel* to the first subunit (15,18-25: the world's hatred) of 15,18-16,4d. Similarly, the first subunit (15,1-8: union with Jesus) of 15,1-17 may be *contrasted* with the last subunit (16,1-4d: persecution because of Jesus) of 15,18-16,4d. Note also that the middle subsections (15,9-11; 15,26-27) may be said to *correspond* to each other, since the disciples' keeping the commandments of Jesus and remaining in his love, patterned on Jesus' keeping the commandments of the Father and remaining in His love (15,9-10), may be considered as parallel to the disciples' bearing witness to Jesus, patterned on the Paraclete's testimony to Jesus (15,26-27).

Hence the *mashal* of the vine and the branches and the commandment of love (15,1-17) form a literary unit in which some important aspects are antithetically parallel to the passage on the world's hatred and persecution and the disciples' witnessing (15,18-16,4d).

Many scholars agree that 16,4e-33 is another literary unit which is parallel to the first farewell discourse in 13,31-14,31[397].

Some, however, take 15,26-16,15 as a pericope on the Paraclete[398]. The main arguments for regarding 15,26-16,15 as one literary unit are: 1) *to pneuma tês alêtheias* is found at 15,26 and 16,13, which is understood to be an inclusion; 2) 15,26-16,15 deals with the theme of coming (and/or the mission) of the Holy Spirit[399].

---

[396] Y. SIMOENS who argues for the central position of 15,12-17 in Jn 13-17 because of the inclusion between 15,12 and 15,17 (the commandment of love) (*op. cit.*, 58-61) has not noticed a similar inclusion between 15,18 and 15,25 (hatred) and others which we have seen above (between 15,1-2 and 15,8; between 16,1 and 16,4). One fails to understand how the whole of 15,1-5a and 15,8-11 can be called an "inclusion in the first unit", since "remaining in me (Jesus-vine)" (*op. cit.*, 147) is mentioned for the first time in v.4 (and not in the first verses). Similarly, "faire cela" (*tauta poiein*) found towards the middle of 15,18-25 (or according to the author's division, at the end of 15,18-21) cannot be said to form an inclusion with "faire cela" (*tauta poiein*) at 16,3. The author seems to use the term "inclusion" for any correspondence between two elements anywhere in a literary unit!

[397] So BROWN, II, 588-94; SCHNACKENBURG, III, 123-25; LAGRANGE, 417; SEGALLA, 403; Y. SIMOENS, *op. cit.*, 151.

[398] So PANIMOLLE, III, 304-5; MATEOS & BARRETO, 677.

[399] *Ibid.*

It is true that "the Spirit of truth" occurs at 15,26 and 16,13 but this recurrence of the same expression is not enough to decide whether it is intended as an inclusion or merely as a parallel. The *immediate context* of 15,26-27 is certainly one of hatred of the world (*misein*: 15,18.18.19.23.23.24.25) and persecution by the Jews (*diôkein*: 15,20.20; *aposynagogous poiein*: 16,2; *apokteinein*: 16,2). The "Spirit of truth" is spoken of by Jesus in connection with the disciples' witnessing to him in the midst of opposition and persecution. Hence 15,26-27 is a *continuation* of 15,18-25, as Panimolle admits[400], and therefore they are an integral part of 15,18-16,4d. Secondly, "the Spirit of truth" was mentioned also at 14,17, which is parallel to 16,13, since the whole of 13,31-14,31 is parallel to 16,4e-33[401].

Since a *new literary genre* (prayer) begins at 17,1, it is clear that 16,33 is the *end* of the literary unit which begins at 16,4e. While at the beginning of the first farewell discourse (13,31-14,31) the denial of Peter was predicted (13,36-38), at the end of the second farewell discourse (16,4e-33) the *desertion* of the disciples is foretold (16,32).

4.341z Thus we conclude that 13,1-17,26 consists of *six subsections* (13,1-38+; 13,31-14,31; 15,1-17; 15,18-16,4d; 16,4e-33; 17,1-27).

4.342 Parallelism between the subsections of 13,1-17,26

4.342,1 Parallelism between 15,1-17 and 15,18-16,4d

We have already seen above the ways in which the central subsections (15,1-17 and 15,18-16,4d) are *antithetically parallel* to each other. Note the following antithetical and/or identical terms and expressions: *agapan/agapê* (15,9.9.9.10.10.12.12.13.17), *misein* (15,18.18.19.23.23.24.25), *philos* (15,13.14.15), *philein* (15,9), *doulos* (15,15.15.20), *egô exelexamên hymas* (15,16.19), *to onoma mou* (15,16.21), *ouk oida* (15,15.21), *tauta lelalêka hymin* (15,11; 16,1.4), *ho patêr* (15,1.8.9.10.15.16.23.24.26.26; 16,3).

4.342,2 Parallelism between 13,31-14,31 and 16,4e-33

Since R. E. Brown has already given in a well-prepared chart more than two dozen parallels between 16,4e-33 and 13,31-14,31[402], we think it unnecessary to prepare another list of vocabulary common to both the farewell discourses.

---

[400] "Gv 15,26s costituisce *la continuazione* logica del brano immediatamente precedente, al quale si ricollega letterariamente con la tematica delle persecuzioni dei cristiani (Gv 15,20; 16,1ss), formando con esso una grande unità" (PANIMOLLE, III, 303) [my italics].

[401] See the "Chart I: The Parallels between xvi 4b-33 and xiii 31-xiv 31" given by BROWN (II, 589-91). [*Tauta de hymin ktl* of 16,4 is denoted as xvi 4b by BROWN but as 16,4e by us].

[402] *Ibid.*

Not only are numerous terms and expressions the same or strikingly similar in the two discourses, but there is similarity even in the structural organization of the two. In the words of Brown:

> By way of general parallels, we note that the over-all structure of the two is roughly the same. Both begin with the theme of Jesus' imminent departure. The question of where he is going and the motif of the sorrow of the disciples soon appear. Each unit has two Paraclete passages; each promises that shortly the disciples will see Jesus again and that the Father will love the disciples; each assures the disciples in Jesus' name that whatever is asked will be granted. In each Jesus is interrupted by questions from the disciples, and in each there appears the theme of the infidelity of the disciples to Jesus during the passion [402a].

4.342,3 Parallels between 13,1-38 and 17,1-26

Besides the *inclusion* between the first verse of 13,1-38 and the last verse of 17,1-26 (*agapan/agapê*: 13,1.1; 17,26.26)[403], there are also some *parallels* between the first and the last subsections. For example, towards the end of both the passages there are frequent occurrences of *agapan/agapê* (13,34.34.34.35; 17,23.23.24.26). Again, the "coming of the hour" of Jesus is underlined in the very first verse of both the pericopes (13,1: *êlthen autou hê hôra*; 17,1: *elêlythen hê hôra*). Furthermore, the "glorification" of God/the Father and of Jesus is emphasized at the end of the first subsection and at the beginning of the last (*doxazein*: 13,31.31.32.32; 17,1.1.4.5; cf. also 17,10; between 13,32 and 17,1 *doxazein* is found only thrice, namely, at 14,15; 15,8; 16,14). Jesus' "going from this world to the Father" is highlighted in both the subsections (13,1: *hina metabê[i] ek tou kosmou toutou pros ton patera*; 13,2: *pros ton theon hypagei*; 17,11: *kai ouketi eimi en tô[i] kosmô[i]... kagô pros se erchomai*; 17,13: *nyn de pros se erchomai*). Again, the Father's giving of everything into the hands of Jesus or conferring power over all flesh to the Son, is underlined at the beginning of both the washing of the feet and the prayer (13,2: *panta dedôken autô[i] ho patêr eis tas cheiras*; 17,2: *edôka autô[i] exousian pasês sarkos, hina pas ho edôken autô[i]...*)[404].

4.34z Since Jn 13-17 consists of *six subsections* (13,1-38; 13,31-14,31; 15,1-17; 15,18-16,4d; 16,4e-33; 17,1-26) in which the end-subsections (13,1-38 and 17,1-26) partially correspond to each other, the central subsections (15,1-17 and 15,18-16,4d) are in many respects antithetically parallel, and the second and

---

[402a] *Ibid.*, 588; 594.
[403] Y. SIMOENS, *op. cit.*, 55-56.
[404] Notice also an indirect reference to Judas, the betrayer (13,2.11.18.21.26.29) at 17,12 (*ho hyios tês apôleias*) and the reference to the fulfilment of the Scripture both at 13,18 and 17,12 (*hina hê graphê plêrôthê[i]*).

It must be admitted, however, that since there are also many differences between 13,1-38 and 17,1-26, the parallelism between them is only partial.

the fifth subsections (13,31-14,31 and 16,4e-33) are two parallel farewell discourses, the section of "Jesus' Farewell of the Hour" (13,1-17,26) may be said to have a *chiastic structure* (CDEE'D'C'). This may be presented in the form of the following schema:

JESUS' FAREWELL OF THE HOUR (at the Last Supper) (13,1-17,26)

  C (13,1-38+) : The symbolic act of the hour (the feet-washing) and the prediction of betrayal and denial.
    D (13,31-14,31) : The prediction of Peter's denials and the first farewell discourse.
      E (15,1-17) : The allegory of the wine and the branches and the commandment of love.
      E' (15,18-16,4d) : The hatred and persecution by the world, and the disciples' witnessing.
    D' (16,4e-33) : The second farewell discourse and the prediction of the disciples' desertion.
  C' (17,1-26) : The prayer of the hour [of Jesus' passion-death-resurrection].

4.35 The Structure of "Jesus' Hour of the Passion-Death-Resurrection" (Jn 18,1-20,29)

4.351 *Division of 18,1-20,29 into subsections*

The narrative of the Passion-Resurrection can be easily divided into subsections according to the different *geographical indications* given by the Evangelist[405]. Thus at 18,1 a garden (*kêpos*) across the Kidron valley (*peran tou cheimarrou tou Kedrôn*) is mentioned, where Jesus and his disciples enter. It is there that he meets the arrest-party led by Judas (18,2-11) and is arrested by the Roman soldiers and Jewish officers (18,12). At the court of the high priest (*aulê tou archiereôs*: 18,15) Jesus is questioned by the high priest (18,19-24) and denied by Peter (18,15-18.25-27). The praetorium (*to praitôrion*) is mentioned at the beginning of Jesus' trial before Pilate (18,28). The Hebrew name *Golgotha* is indicated as the place where Jesus is crucified (19,17) and later buried (19,41). In 20,1-18 we have two scenes at the tomb (*to mnêmeion*) of Jesus which Mary Magdalene and two disciples find to be empty and where Jesus appears to Mary. Jn 20,19-29 describes two appearances of the risen Jesus to his disciples behind locked doors (*tôn thyrôn kekleismenôn*: 20,19.26). Thus already the geographical indications at the beginning of the different episodes help us to distinguish the various subsections of Jn 18-20.

Some of these divisions are further supported by *literary-chronological indications* at the beginning and/or end of the episodes. For example, Jesus is said to have been brought from the house of Caiaphas to Pilate in the "early

---

[405] See 3.15.

morning" (*prôï*: 18,28) and he is condemned to death "about the sixth hour" (*hôra ên hôs hektê*: 19,14). Again, Mary Magdalene is reported to have come to the tomb of Jesus "early morning" (*prôi*) "on the first day of the week" (*tê[i] de mia[i] tôn sabbatôn*) (20,1). Similarly, Jesus is described at 20,19 as appearing to the disciples "on the evening of that day" (*ousês oun opsias tê[i] hêmera[i] ekeinê[i]*) [406].

The limits of many of the episodes described in Jn 18-20 are marked by *introductions* [407], *conclusions* [408], *inclusions* [409], *bridge-verses* [410], and different *dramatic techniques* [411].

The garden-scene of the betrayal and arrest of Jesus is *introduced* by 18,1 which describes his entering the garden across the Kidron valley with his disciples. The garden-scene *ends* with his arrest (18,12). Note also the occurrence of *speira* and *hypêretai* at 18,3 and 18,12 which may be thought of as forming a sort of *inclusion* for the first subsection. The *scene changes* to the palace of the high priest at 18,15. But immediately after the arrest we are told: "And first they led him to Annas; for he was the father-in-law of Caiaphas, who was high priest that year" (18,13). And both "Annas" and "high priest Caiaphas" are again mentioned at the end of the trial-scene (18,24: "Annas [had] sent him bound to Caiaphas the high priest"). In other words, 18,12-14 function as *bridge-verses* which conclude the garden-scene of Jesus' betrayal and arrest (18,1-14) and introduce the palace-scene of his trial and denial (18,15-27) [412].

Besides indicating a change of scene at 18,15 (from the garden to the palace of the high priest), 18,12-27 employs the dramatic technique of *double-stage action*, since, while Jesus is tried by the high priest (18,19-24), Peter is questioned by others (18,15-18.25-27) [413]. There is a striking contrast between the courageous conduct of Jesus before the high priest and the cowardly denials of Peter before the high priest's servants.

Notice also that some of the characters in the garden-scene (Judas, the soldiers and the group of disciples) are not seen in the interrogation-scene, in which some *new characters* appear (Annas, Caiaphas and the door-keeper). We may also note that Peter plays a more prominent part in the interrogation-scene than in the garden-scene, since he is now presented as denying Jesus three times.

---

[406] See 3.16.
[407] See 3.12.
[408] See 3.11.
[409] See 3.13.
[410] See 3.191.
[411] See 3.2.
[412] See 3.191. BROWN calls 18,12-13 "a transitional passage between the scene in the garden and the scene in the palace of the high priest" (II, 817; cf. also II, 785). In our terminology they are bridge-verses.
[413] Regarding 18,15-18 and 18,25-27 in their relation to 18,19-24 BROWN remarks: "The Johannine writer surrounds the interrogation of Jesus with two halves of a scene where Peter denies Jesus (15-18 and 25-27)" (II, 813).

Because of the above reasons we prefer to regard 18,1-14 and 18,12-27 as *two* distinct, though related, subsections rather than as a single literary unit as proposed by A. Janssens de Varebeke and R. E. Brown [414].

Jesus' trial before Pilate is a highly dramatic unit consisting of *seven alternating scenes* (18,28-32.33-38b.38c-40; 19,1-3.4-7.8-11.12-16b) [415] placed *outside* and *inside* the praetorium (marked by Pilate's "going out" [*exêlthen*] and "going in" [*eisêlthen*]), as A. Janssens de Varebeke has convincingly demonstrated [416]. Observe that in each of these seven scenes the *law of stage-duality* is observed [417]. There is, besides, an "*overall progression*" from the first scene to the last, as C. H. Giblin has suggested [417a]. Furthermore, the mention of "the Passover" (*to pascha*) in the first and the last scenes (18,28; 19,14) may most probably form an *inclusion* for the whole episode (18,28-19,16b). It is also worth noting that in the initial scene the Jews openly admit to have "handed over"/ "*betrayed*" Jesus to Pilate (*soi paredôkamen auton*: 18,30d) and in the final scene Pilate is spoken of as having "handed over"/ "*betrayed*" Jesus to the Jews (*paredôken auton autois*: 19,16a) [418].

While 19,16ab (*tote ou paredôken auton autois hina staurôthê[i]*) concludes Jesus' trial before the Roman governor, 19,16c (*parelabon oun ton Iêsoun*) introduces the next literary unit which describes the events on Golgotha (19,16c-42). That the Evangelist intends the whole of 19,16c-42 to be a large unit is indicated by the *inclusions* between 19,16c-18 and 19,40-42:

19,16c: par*elabon* oun **ton Iêsoun**.
19,40a: *elabon* oun to sôma tou Iêsou...
19,42b: ethêkan **ton Iêsoun**.

19,17a: exêlthen eis ton legomenon Kraniou *topon*
19,18a: *hopou* auton **estaurôsan**.
19,41a: ên de en tô[i] *topô[i]*
   b: *hopou* **estaurôthê[i]** kêpos.

---

[414] A. JANSSENS DE VAREBEKE, "La structure des scènes du récit de la passion en Joh., xviii-xix", *ETL* 38 (1962) 504-12; BROWN, II, 802-3. See also the latter's criticism of the former's sevenfold division of 18,1-27 (II, 813-14).

[415] Here the dramatic techniques of "alternating scenes" and "seven scenes" are masterfully combined (see 3.22 and 3.28).

[416] A. JANSSENS DE VAREBEKE, *art. cit.*, 504-22 especially 521.

[417] See 3.216.

[417a] C. H. GIBLIN, "Confrontations in John 18,1-27", *Bib* 65 (1984) 212, n. 7.

[418] Normally *paradidômi* in these verses (18,30d and 19,16a) is translated as "hand over". While this meaning is certainly there, probably the further deeper meaning "betrayal" is also intended by the Evangelist, since the same verb *paradidômi* has, until 18,30, always been used only to describe the betrayal of Jesus by Judas (cf. 6,64.71; 12,4; 13,2.11.12; 18,2.5; cf. also 21,20). This double meaning of *paradidômi* ("hand over"/ "betray") seems to be present throughout this episode, where the verb *paradidômi* is used with acc. and dat. (cf. 18,30d.35.36; 19,11.16a). Cf. O. CULLMANN, "Der johanneische Gebrauch doppeldeutiger Ausdrücke als Schlüssel zum Verständnis des vierten Evangeliums", *TZ* 4 (1948) 360-72, for other Johannine terms with double-meaning. (The Synoptics use *paradidômi* with acc. and dat. to refer to the betrayal of Jesus by Judas: Mt 26,15; Mk 14,10; Lk 22,4.6; cf. also Mt 20,18; Mk 10,33 where the verb is employed in the passive voice with dat.)

Furthermore, the events on Calvary (19,16c-42), like the trial before Pilate (18,28-19,16b), are arranged beautifully in *seven scenes*[419]:

1) the crucifixion of Jesus (19,16c-18)
2) the inscription "the king of the Jews" (19,19-22)
3) Jesus' outer garments and seamless tunic (19,23-24)
4) the mother of Jesus and the Beloved Disciple (19,25-27)
5) Jesus' thirst and giving (up) the Spirit (19,28-30)
6) the piercing of Jesus' side (19,31-37)
7) the burial of Jesus (19,38-42).

The next two subsections of Jn 18-20 consist of two diptychs[420]. The *first diptych* (20,1-18) depicts the discovery of the empty tomb of Jesus by Mary Magdalene, the Beloved Disciple and Peter (20,1-10) and the risen Jesus' appearance to Mary Magdalene there (20,11-18). The *second diptych* consists of two appearances of Jesus to the disciples in a locked room (20,19-23.26-29), which are joined together by means of "bridge-verses" (20,24-25) which describe the disciples' report to Thomas about their having seen the Lord and Thomas' skeptical reaction to it (20,25)[421].

The unity of 20,1-18 is created not only by the *place* (the tomb of Jesus)[421a] and *time* (in the morning) but also by the *inclusions* between 20,1-2 and 20,18:

---

[419] See 3.28. Our sevenfold subdivision of 19,16c-42 is somewhat different from that of A. JANSSENS DE VAREBEKE (*art. cit.*). His divisions are vv.17-22.23-24.25-27.28-30.31-37.38-40.41-42. Note that he combines the crucifixion (19,17-18) and the inscription on the cross of Jesus (19,19-22) into one scene (19,17-22), although the discussion between Pilate and the high priests apparently does not take place on Calvary. (Although Pilate is not present at Calvary also in 19,31 and 19,38, the same objection is not valid for our division, since 19,31 and 19,38 do not describe, unlike 19,19-22, a dialogue but only mention a request made to Pilate. These verses serve only as introductions to the episodes in 19,31-37 and 19,38-42 respectively.) Again, Janssens de Varebeke divides the burial scene (19,38-42) into two (19,38-40: "l'onction" and 19,41-42: "la sépulture": cf. *art. cit.*, 522), although the anointing is an integral part of the burial scene.

[420] See 3.29.

[421] Most Johannine scholars and commentators take 20,24-25 to belong to 20,26-29 (e.g. D. MOLLAT, "La foi pascale selon le chapitre 20 de l'évangile de saint Jean. Essai de théologie johannique", in: E. Dhanis, ed., *Resurrexit* [Rome 1974] 316-39; L. DUPONT, C. LASH & G. LEVESQUE, "Recherche sur la structure de Jean 20", *Bib* 54 [1973] 482-98; SCHNACKENBURG, III, 328). While DUPONT, LASH & LEVESQUE propose a concentric structure for Jn 20,1-31: A (20,1-10), B (20,11-18), C (20,19-23), B' (20,24-29), A' (20,30-31), MOLLAT suggests a chiastic structure for 20,1-29: A (20,1-10), B (20,11-18), B' (20,19-23), A' (20,24-29).

I. DE LA POTTERIE, however, regards 20,24-25 as belonging to 20,19-23 ("Genèse de la foi pascale d'après Jn 20", *NTS* 30 [1984] 26-49) and proposes a different chiastic structure for Jn 20,1-29: A (20,1-10), B (20,11-18), B'(20,19-25), A' (20,26-29) (*ibid.*, 28).

Probably it would be better to take 20,24-25 as bridge-verses concluding 20,19-23 and introducing 20,26-29 (thus reconciling the two differing positions mentioned above).

[421a] Strictly speaking all the actions described in 20,1-18 do not occur at the tomb, for 20,2-3 tells us about Mary's running to Simon Peter and the Beloved Disciple and their coming to the tomb, and 20,18 reports Mary's going to the disciples after having seen the risen Jesus. But the main actions happen at the tomb (20,1.4-8.11-17).

20,1 : **Maria hê Magdalênê** ERCHETAI prôï...
20,2 : ERCHETAI pros Simôna Petron kai pros ton allon *mathêtên*...
 kai legei autois: êran *TON KYRION*...
20,18: ERCHETAI **Maria hê Magdalênê** angellousa tois *mathêtais*
 hoti heôraka *TON KYRION*...

Notice also the remarkable parallelism between the words of Mary Magdalene to the disciples in 20,2 and to the angels in 20,13:

20,2 : *legei autois*: **êran ton kyrion** ek tou mnêmeiou
 kai ouk oidamen *pou ethêkan auton.*
20,13: *legei autois* hoti **êran ton kyrion** mou
 kai ouk oida *pou ethêkan auton.*

There are many other parallel elements in 20,1-10 and 20,11-18, for the following common terms and expressions are found in these two pericopes: *mnêmeion* (20,1.1.2.3.4.6.8.11.11), *parakyptô* (20,5.11), *keimai* (20,5.6.7.12), *theôrei* (20,6.12.14), *kephalê* (20,7.12), *horaô* (20,8.18), *oudepô/ouk ê[i]dei/san* (20,9.14). Notice also that in both the episodes Mary Magdalene plays an important role.

Because of the above reasons we believe that 20,1-18 is intended by the Evangelist as a unit (diptych) consisting of two parallel episodes.

The unity of 20,19-29 (the two appearances of Jesus to the disciples) is evident from the unmistakable parallelism and link between the two episodes:

20,19: ousês oun opsias tê[i] *hêmera[i]* ekeinê[i]...
 kai **tôn thyrôn kekleismenôn** hopou *êsan* **hoi mathêtai**...
 êlthan ho Iêsous kai estê eis to meson
 kai *legei* autois: e i r ê n ê h y m i n
20,26: kai meth' *hêmeras* oktô palin *êsan* esô **hoi mathêtai** autou...
 erchetai ho Iêsous
 tôn thyrôn kekleismenôn kai estê eis to meson
 kai *eipen:* e i r ê n ê h y m i n.

20,25: ho de *eipen* autois:
 ean mê **idô** en **tais chersin autou** ton typon hêlôn
 kai balô *ton daktylon mou* eis ton typon tôn hêlôn
 kai *balô* **mou tên cheira** eis tên pleuran autou,
 o u m ê p i s t e u ô.
20,27: eita *legei* tô[i] Thôma[i]:
 phere *ton daktylon sou* hôde kai **ide tas cheiras mou**
 kai phere **tên cheira sou** kai *bale eis tên pleuran mou,*
 kai m ê ginou a p i s t o s alla p i s t o s.

Because of the *numerous parallel elements* between 20,19 and 20,26 and between 20,25 and 20,27 on the one hand, and because of the *bridging* character of 20,24-25 (which concludes Jesus' first appearance to the disciples in 20,19-23 and prepares for his second appearance to them in 20,26-29) on the other hand, the two pericopes (20,19-25; 20,24-29) form a unit.

4.351z From the above discussion it is clear that the section of "the Hour of Jesus' Passion-Death-Resurrection" (18,1-20,29) consists of *six subsections* (18,1-14; 18,12-27; 18,28-19,16b; 19,16c-42; 20,1-18; 20,19-29).

4.352 *Parallelism between the subsections of 18,1-20,29*

4.352,1   Parallelism between 18,28-19,16b and 19,16c-42

The kingship of Jesus, which is the central theme of 18,28-19,16b (cf. *basileus*: 18,33.37.37.39; 19,3.12.14.15.15; *basileia*: 18,36.36.36), is highlighted also in 19,16c-42 by means of the trilingual inscription on the cross (*ho basileus tôn Ioudaiôn*: 19,19.21.21), the portrayal of his crucifixion as his enthronement and his burial as royal[422]. Many of the characters in both the dramatic episodes are the same e.g. Pilate (*Pilatos*: 18,29.31.33.35.37.38; 19,1.4.6.8.10.12.13.15 and 19,19. 21.22.31.38.38)[423], the Jews (*hoi Ioudaioi*: 18,31.33.35.36.38.39; 19,3.7.12.14 and 19,19.20.21.21.31.38.40.42), the high priests (*hoi archiereis*: 18,35; 19,6.15 and 19,21), soldiers (*stratiôtês*: 19,2 and 19,23.23.25.32.34). There is the repeated reference to crucifying Jesus in both the passages (*stauroô*: 19,6.6.6.10.15.15.16 and 19,18.20.23.41)[424]. Thus we conclude that the two central subsections (18,28-19,16b; 19,16c-42) of 18,1-20,29 are parallel to each other.

4.352,2   Parallelism between 18,12-27 and 20,1-18

In both the episodes (Simon) Peter (*Simôn Petros*: 18,15.25; 20,2.6; *Petros*: 18,16.16.17.18.26.27; 20,3.4) plays a prominent role, for in the first he denies Jesus (18,15-18.25-27) and in the second he comes to and examines the tomb of Jesus (20,1-10). Besides, in both the passages Peter is accompanied by "another disciple" (*allos mathêtês*: 18,15.16; 20,2.3.4.8)[425], which does not occur in the intervening episodes. Furthermore, discipleship is a common theme of both

---

[422] BROWN, II, 912; 960.
[423] The name "Pilate" does not occur anywhere else in the entire Gospel.
[424] This verb is found only in these two episodes in the Fourth Gospel.
[425] In 20,2 this "other disciple" (*ho allos mathêtês*) is identified as the Beloved Disciple (*hon ephilei ho Iêsous*), whereas in 18,15-16 we are not told explicitly that the second disciple was the Beloved Disciple but that there was "another disciple" (*allos mathêtês*) who was "known to the high priest". But since there is a literary relationship between 18,15-16 and 20,1-10 through the common expression *allos mathêtês* and since Peter is often presented in the Fourth Gospel in the company of the Beloved Disciple (13,23-24; 20,2-10; 21,7.20-23), it is probable that the unnamed disciple at 18,15-16 is the Beloved Disciple. Notice also that the latter is the first to enter the court of the high priest (18,15), just as he is the first to reach the empty tomb (20,4), to believe in the resurrection (20,8) and to recognize the risen Jesus at the Sea of Tiberias (21,7).

18,12-27 and 20,1-18 (*mathêtês*: 18,15.15.16.17.19.25; 20,2.3.4.8.10.18)[426], since the high priest questions Jesus about his disciples (18,19), the high priest's servants ask Peter whether he is one of Jesus' disciples (18,17.25), and the persons to whom Mary Magdalene goes with the news of both the empty tomb and the resurrection are the disciples (20,2.18).

4.352,3   Parallelism between 18,1-14 and 20,19-29

Both these episodes underline the divinity and sovereignty or lordship of Jesus. In 18,1-14 he, "knowing (*eidôs*) all that was to befall him" (18,4), goes to meet his armed adversaries (the arrest-party led by Judas), and when Jesus says "I am" (*egô eimi*: 18,5; cf. Ex 3,14), they fall to the ground as at a theophany or like the vanquished before the victorious king (18,6); and in 20,19-29 the risen Jesus appears to his frightened disciples gathered behind locked doors (20,19.26), who acknowledge and proclaim him to be the Lord and God (*ho kyrios*: 20,20.25.28; *theos*: 20,28)[427]. Notice also that both narratives describe the mutual relations/reactions of Jesus and his disciples as a group (*mathêtai*: 18,1-2; 20,19-20.26) and as individuals (Judas: 18,2.5; Peter: 18,10-11; Thomas: 20,27-28).

4.35z   Since 18,1-20,29 consists of six subsections (18,1-14; 18,12-27; 18,28-19,16b; 19,16c-42; 20,1-18; 20,19-29) in which the first subsection (18,1-14) is parallel in many respects to the last (20,19-29), the second (18,12-27) to the fifth (20,1-18), and the third (18,28-19,16b) to the fourth (19,16c-42), we may conclude that the section of "the Hour of Jesus' Passion-Death-Resurrection" (18,1-20,29) has a *chiastic* structure (5CDEE'D'C') similar to that of the section of "Jesus' Farewell of the Hour" (4CDEE'D'C')[428]:

---

[426] *Mathêtês* is found only four times in Jn 19 (thrice with reference to the Beloved Disciple: 19,26.27.27 and once referring to Joseph of Arimathea: 19,38).

[427] It is also worth noting that the Lord Jesus knows what the unbelieving Thomas has said to the other disciples during his absence (compare 20,25 and 20,27). Such divine or superhuman knowledge on the part of Jesus was underlined also in 18,4.

It is to be admitted, however, that these parallels are not, strictly speaking, literary but theological. While Jesus' divinity is only hinted at in 18,4-9 (cf. his foreknowledge of the future events of his life: 18,4; his use of the divine name *egô eimi*: 18,5; the arrest-party's falling to the ground: 18,6), it is explicitly confessed by Thomas in 20,28: *ho kyrios mou kai ho theos mou*. This certainly forms an inclusion with 1,1c: *kai theos ên ho logos*. Hence the Evangelist seems to have been more concerned about establishing the above inclusion between the Prologue (C*) and the last episode of the (original) Gospel (5C') than to highlight the parallelism between 18,1-14 (5C) and 20,19-29 (5C').

[428] See 4.34. As an answer to a possible objection that the corresponding elements of the chiastic structure of Jn 18-20 are dissimilar in some important aspects, it must be remembered that perfect parallelism of members is not necessary for chiasm; some significant similarities between the corresponding subsections are sufficient to conclude to the chiastic development of a large section like Jn 13-17 or Jn 18-20.

4.3 THE STRUCTURE OF THE SECTIONS

THE HOUR OF JESUS' PASSION-DEATH-RESURRECTION (18,1-20,29)

C (18,1-14+) : The sovereign Jesus before Judas, the betrayer, and the arrest-party.
  D (18,12-27) : Jesus' trial before the high priest and Peter's denials of Jesus.
    E (18,28-19,16b) : The trial and condemnation of Jesus, the king of the Jews, by Pilate.
    E' (19,16c-42) : The crucifixion, death and burial of the king of the Jews on Golgotha.
  D' (20,1-18) : Peter and the B.D. at the empty tomb and Jesus' appearance to Mary Magdalene.
C' (20,19-29) : The Lord Jesus' appearances to the disciples and the unbelieving Thomas.

4.36 The Structure of the Appendix (Jn 21)

We saw above that Jn 21 is an appendix consisting of an "epilogue" (21,1-23) and a "second (editorial) conclusion" (21,24-25)[429].

4.361 *Division and structure of the epilogue* (21,1-23)

The "epilogue" (21,1-23) divides itself into three pericopes (21,1-14.15-19. 20-23). The first pericope, which describes the risen Jesus' appearance to the seven disciples at the Sea of Tiberias, is enclosed within a *triple inclusion* (*phaneroô*: 21,1.1.14; *Iêsous*: 21,1.14; *tois mathêtais*: 21,1.14) between the first introductory verse (21,1) and the last concluding verse (21,14):

21,1 : meta tauta **ephanerôsen** heauton palin ho *Iêsous tois mathêtais*...
       ephanerôsen de houtôs.
21,14: touto êdê triton **ephanerôthê** *Iêsous tois mathêtais*...

While the first pericope has painted the picture of the risen Jesus' self-manifestation to a group of seven disciples through a miraculous catch of fish and breakfast (21,1-14), the next pericope (21,15-19) presents Jesus and Simon Peter engaged in a moving *dialogue* on the latter's personal love for Jesus (*agapaô*: 21,15.16; *phileô*: 21,15.16.17.17.17), his pastoral care for Jesus' sheep (*boske ta arnia mou*: 21,15; *poimane ta probata mou*: 21,16; *boske ta probatia mou*: 21,17) and the fate of Peter (21,18-19). The third pericope (21,20-23) deals with the destiny of the Beloved Disciple (*ho mathêtês hon egapa ho Iêsous*: 21,20; *ho mathêtês ekeinos*: 21,23; *ean auton thelô menein heôs erchomai, tí pros se?*: 21,22.23; *ouk apothnê[i]skei*: 21,23.23). Since the vocabulary and content of these units are different, they may be considered as distinct though connected pericopes (*hote oun eristêsan* of 21,15 is linked to *aristêsate* of 21,12, just as

---

[429] See 4.14.

akolouthein of 21,19 is connected to *akolouthein* of the next verse). Besides, whereas only Jesus and Simon Peter appear in 21,15-19, the Beloved Disciple also enters the scene in 21,20-23. Furthermore, while Peter is given a pastoral mission which will lead him to martyrdom (21,15-19), the Beloved Disciple has a different role and destiny, namely, to "remain" bearing witness to Jesus' risen presence (21,20-23) as he did at 21,7 ("It is the Lord")[430].

Thus the epilogue (21,1-23) may be said to consist of three distinct but connected pericopes (21,1-14.15-19.20-23). These may be represented by the letters C,D and C' respectively, since 21,1-14 is called the third manifestation of the risen Jesus to the disciples (21,14), similar to the first (20,19-23) and the second (20,26-29) which forms part of 5C' (20,19-29), since the triple confession of love by Peter in 21,15-19 certainly corresponds to his triple denial in 5D (18,12-27), and since the Beloved Disciple is mentioned together with Peter in 21,20-23 (cf. vv.20-21) as in 6C (21,1-14; cf. v.7) and in 4C (13,1-38; cf. vv.23-25 to which explicit reference is made in 21,20).

4.362 *Division and structure of the "second (editorial) conclusion"* (21,24-25)

The "second (editorial) conclusion" (21,24-25) consists of two parts: 1) a "testimonial conclusion" which testifies to the identity and veracity of the disciple who wrote the Gospel (21,24), and 2) a "hyperbolic conclusion" (21,25) which states that the whole world would be too small to contain the books that would be necessary to record all the deeds of Jesus[431]. The "testimonial conclusion" (21,24) may be compared to the "Christological conclusion" (Bz = 20,31abc) which is the author's written testimony to Jesus, the Christ, the Son of God (cf. *tauta de gegraptai* of 20,31a and *grapsas tauta* of 21,24)[432], and the

---

[430] See 5.27 below.

[431] Such hyperbolic statements are found in Biblical and non-biblical writings. For instance, Jochanan b. Zaddai (who died c. A.D. 80) says: "If all the sky were parchment, and all the trees were writing pens, and all the seas were ink, there would not be enough to write down my wisdom which I have learned from my teachers; and yet I have had the pleasure of only as much of the wisdom of the wise as a fly who [sic!] plunges into the ocean, takes away" (Str-B, II, 587, as translated and cited by Morris, 881, n. 67).
Cf. Bultmann, 697, n. 2 for other examples.

[432] The "testimonial conclusion" (21,24) is somewhat similar also to the "testimonial introduction" (1,19-34) which, in turn, is parallel to 1,6-8 and 1,15:

1,7 : **HOUTOS** *êlthen* eis **martyrian**, hina **martyrêsê[i] peri** tou *phôtos*...
1,15 : Iôannês **martyrei peri** autou kai *kekragen legôn*, **houtos ên** hon *eipon*...
1,19 : kai **hautê** *estin* **hê martyria** *tou Iôannou*...
1,34 : kagô heôraka kai **memartyrêka** hoti **houtos estin** ho hyios tou theou.
21,24 : **HOUTOS** *estin* ho mathêtês ho **martyrôn peri** toutôn kai *grapsas* tauta,
kai oidamen hoti alêthês *autou* **hê martyria** *estin*.

If John the Evangelist was one of the disciples of John the Baptist who became disciples of Jesus (cf. 1,35-40), then it is interesting to note that, just as the mission of John the Baptist is described by his former disciple in terms of his spoken testimony to Jesus (cf. 1,6-8.15.19), so the mission of John the Evangelist is described by his disciples in terms of his written testimony to Jesus Christ (cf. 21,24; cf. also 19,35bcd).

"hyperbolic conclusion" is somewhat similar to the "historical sign-conclusion" (Az = 20,30)[433]:

20,30: *polla* men oun *kai alla sêmeia epoiêsen ho Iêsous...*,
    ha ouk estin **gegrammena** en tô[i] ***bibliô[i]*** toutô[i].
21,25: **estin de** *kai alla polla* ha *epoiêsen ho Iêsous*,
    hatina ean **graphêtai** kath' hen, oud' auton oimai
    ton kosmon chôrêsai ta **graphomena** *biblia*.

4.36z Our conclusions on the structure of the appendix (21,1-25) may be summed up in the form of the following structural schema:

APPENDIX (21,1-25)

EPILOGUE: THE RISEN JESUS AND THE DISCIPLES (at the Sea of Tiberias) (21,1-23)

   C (21,1-14)   : The risen Jesus' manifestation to the seven disciples.
   D (21,15-19) : Jesus and Peter's confession of love, pastoral commission and destiny.
   C' (21,20-23) : Jesus, Peter and the destiny of the Beloved Disciple.

SECOND (EDITORIAL) CONCLUSION (20,24-25)

   Bz' (21,24): Testimonial conclusion.
Az' (21,25): Hyperbolic conclusion.

4.3z Applying the various criteria established in chapter 3 we have found that the Gospel of John consists of two major parts: 1) **the Book of Jesus' Signs** (2,1-12,50) and 2) **the Book of Jesus' Hour** (11,1-20,29), preceded by a **Christocentric introduction** (1,1-2,11) and followed by a **Christocentric conclusion** (20,30-31) and an **appendix** (21,1-25).

The Book of Jesus' Signs (2,1-12,50) is composed of *three sections*: 1) *Jesus' Initial Signs and Encounters (from Cana to Cana)* (2,1-4,54), 2) *Jesus' Works, Signs and Discussions (at Jewish Feasts)* (5,1-10,42), 3) *the Climactic Sign and the Coming of Jesus' Hour (Bridge-Section)* (11,1-12,50).

---

[433] See 3.112. According to I. DE LA POTTERIE 20,30-31 and 21,24-25 form a chiasmus (A = 20,30; B = 20,31; B' = 21,24; A' = 21,25) (cf. "Le témoin qui demeure: le disciple que Jésus aimait", *Bib* 67 [1986] 347). Although 20,30 is parallel to 21,25, and 20,31abc parallel to 21,24, they cannot, strictly speaking, be said to form a "chiasmus", since 20,30-31 and 21,1-25 do not form one literary unit. Furthermore, 20,31d (Cz) has no corresponding element in 21,24-25. (It is also surprising to see that later DE LA POTTERIE takes 21,24 and 21,25 as parallel to each other [A and A'] [*ibid.*, 350].)

Likewise **the Book of Jesus' Hour** (11,1-20,29) is made up of *three sections* (the first of which is identical with the last section of the Book of Jesus' Signs and is therefore a bridge-section): 1) *the Climactic Sign and the Coming of Jesus' Hour (Bridge-Section)* (11,1-12,50), 2) *Jesus' Farewell of the Hour (at the Last Supper)* (13,1-17,26), and 3) *the Hour of Jesus' Passion-Death-Resurrection* (18,1-20,29).

Furthermore, the first two sections of the Book of Jesus' Signs and the last two sections of the Book of Jesus' Hour have *chiastic structures*: 1ABCC'B'A' (2,1-4,54); 2BCDD'C'B' (5,1-10,42); 4CDEE'D'C' (13,1-17,26); 5CDEE'D'C' (18,1-20,29). And the Bridge-Section has a *parallel structure*: 3CC' (11,1-12,50).

It should also be noted that the three parts of the Christocentric *introduction* (hymnic-testimonial introduction: 1,1-18; testimonial-kerygmatic introduction: 1,19-51; historical sign-introduction: 2,1-11) *correspond chiastically* to the three parts of the Christocentric *conclusion* (historical sign-conclusion: 20,30; Christological conclusion: 20,31abc; soteriological conclusion: 20,31d): $C^*B^*A^+$ $A_z B_z C_z$.

4.z To sum up this chapter we give below 1) "The Main Divisions" and 2) "the Schema of the Literary Structure of the Fourth Gospel".

THE MAIN DIVISIONS OF THE LITERARY STRUCTURE OF THE FOURTH GOSPEL

0. CHRISTOCENTRIC INTRODUCTION (1,1-2,11)

I. THE BOOK OF JESUS' SIGNS (2,1-12,50)

1. *JESUS' INITIAL SIGNS AND ENCOUNTERS (from Cana to Cana)* (2,1-4,54)
2. *JESUS' WORKS, SIGNS AND DISCUSSIONS (at Jewish Feasts)* (5,1-10,42)
3+. *THE CLIMACTIC SIGN AND THE COMING OF JESUS' HOUR (Bridge-Section)*+ (11,1-12,50)+

II. THE BOOK OF JESUS' HOUR (11,1-20,29)

3+. *THE CLIMATIC SIGN AND THE COMING OF JESUS' HOUR (Bridge-Section)*+ (11,1-12,50)+
4. *JESUS' FAREWELL OF THE HOUR (at the Last Supper)* (13,1-17,26)
5. *THE HOUR OF JESUS' PASSION-DEATH-RESURRECTION* (18,1-20,29)

Z. CHRISTOCENTRIC CONCLUSION (20,30-31)

X. APPENDIX (21,1-25)

6. *EPILOGUE: THE RISEN JESUS AND THE DISCIPLES (at the Sea of Tiberias)* (21,1-23)
Z'. *SECOND (EDITORIAL) CONCLUSION* (21,24-25)

THE SCHEMA OF THE LITERARY STRUCTURE OF THE FOURTH GOSPEL

0. CHRISTOCENTRIC INTRODUCTION (1,1-2,11)

    C* (1,1-18) : Hymnic-testimonial introduction (Prologue).
    B* (1,19-51) : Testimonial-kerygmatic introduction.
    A+ (2,1-11)+ : Historical sign-introduction.

I. THE BOOK OF JESUS' SIGNS (2,1-12,50)

1. JESUS' INITIAL SIGNS AND ENCOUNTERS (from Cana to Cana) (2,1-4,54)

    A (2,1-12) : The beginning of the signs at Cana in Galilee: the changing of water into wine.
    B (2,13-25+) : The cleansing of the Jerusalem-temple and dialogue with the Jews on the new temple.
    C (2,23-3,21) : Dialogue with Nicodemus on birth from above and discourse on having eternal life.
    C' (3,22-4,3+) : Dialogue of J.B. with his disciples on the groom from above and discourse on life.
    B' (4,1-42) : Dialogue with the Samaritan woman on living water and true (temple) worship.
    A' (4,43-54) : The second sign at Cana in Galilee: the healing of the royal official's son.

2. JESUS' WORKS, SIGNS AND DISCUSSIONS (at Jewish Feasts) (5,1-10,42)

    B (5,1-47) : The work of curing the cripple by Jesus, the Son of God (on a Sabbath).
    C (6,1-71) : The sign of feeding the five thousand by the bread of life (before Passover).
    D (7,1-8,59) : Jesus, the source of living water and the light of the world (at Tabernacles).
    D' (9,1-41) : The giving of sight to the blind man by the light of the world (on a Sabbath).
    C' (10,1-21) : The parables of the sheepfold, the door, and the life-giving, good shepherd.
    B' (10,22-42) : The works and identity of Jesus, the Christ, the Son of God (at Dedication).

3+. THE CLIMACTIC SIGN AND THE COMING OF JESUS' HOUR (Bridge-Section)+(11,1-12,50)+

    C (11,1-54) : The sign of raising Lazarus to life by Jesus, the resurrection and the life, and the Sanhedrin's decision to kill him.
    C' (11,55-12,50) : The anointing at Bethany, the triumphal entry into Jerusalem, the coming of the Greeks and of "the hour", and the Jews' refusal to believe in Jesus.

II. THE BOOK OF JESUS' HOUR (11,1-20,29)

3+. THE CLIMACTIC SIGN AND THE COMING OF JESUS' HOUR (Bridge-Section) +(11,1-12,50)+

    C (11,1-54)   : The sign of raising Lazarus to life by Jesus, the resurrection and the life, and the Sanhedrin's decision to kill him.
    C' (11,55-12,50) : The anointing at Bethany, the triumphal entry into Jerusalem, the coming of the Greeks and of "the hour", and the Jews' refusal to believe in Jesus.

4. JESUS' FAREWELL OF THE HOUR (at the Last Supper) (13,1-17,26)

    C (13,1-38+) : The symbolic act of the hour (feet-washing) and the prediction of betrayal and denial.
    D (13,31-14,31) : The prediction of Peter's denials and the first farewell discourse.
    E (15,1-17) : The allegory of the wine and the branches and the commandment of love.
    E' (15,18-16,4d) : The hatred and persecution by the world, and the disciples' witnessing.
    D' (16,4e-33) : The second farewell discourse and the prediction of the disciples' desertion.
    C' (17,1-26) : The prayer of the hour [of Jesus' passion-death-resurrection].

5. THE HOUR OF JESUS' PASSION-DEATH-RESURRECTION (18,1-20,29)

    C (18,1-14+) : The sovereign Jesus before the betrayer Judas and the arrest-party.
    D (18,12-27) : Jesus' trial before the high priest and Peter's denials of discipleship.
    E (18,28-19,16b) : The trial and condemnation of Jesus, the king of the Jews, by Pilate.
    E' (19,16c-42) : The crucifixion, death and burial of the king of the Jews on Golgotha.
    D' (20,1-18) : Peter and the B.D. at the empty tomb and Jesus' appearance to Mary Magdalene.
    C' (20,19-29) : The Lord Jesus' appearances to the disciples and the unbelieving Thomas.

Z. CHRISTOCENTRIC CONCLUSION (20,30-31)

    Az (20,30)   : Historical sign-conclusion.
    Bz (20,31abc) : Christological conclusion.
    Cz (20,31d)   : Soteriological conclusion.

X. APPENDIX (21,1-25)

6. *EPILOGUE: THE RISEN JESUS AND THE DISCIPLES (at the Sea of Tiberias)* (21,1-23)

      C (21,1-14) : The risen Jesus' manifestation to the seven disciples.
      D (21,15-19) : Jesus and Peter's confession of love, pastoral commission and destiny.
      C' (21,20-23) : Jesus, Peter and the destiny of the Beloved Disciple.

Z'.*SECOND (EDITORIAL) CONCLUSION* (21,24-25)

    Bz' (21,24) : Testimonial conclusion.
    Az' (21,25) : Hyperbolic conclusion.

5
THE LITERARY STRUCTURE AND THE CHRISTOCENTRIC THEOLOGY OF THE FOURTH GOSPEL

In the preceding chapter we have established the literary structure of the Gospel of John by applying a number of different criteria. In this chapter we would like to outline the theology of the Johannine Gospel in the light of its literary structure. In other words, here we examine the *relation between the structure and the theology of the Gospel*, for "research must not only clarify what the formal patterns are but also demonstrate their relation to the theological perspective of a writing"[1].

But it must be noted that it is impossible, within the brief space of a single chapter, to develop in detail the different aspects of Johannine theology. Our scope is more modest, namely, to see whether the literary structure we have detected helps us to discover the *theological axis* around which all the other theological themes are developed.

We shall develop this chapter in two stages: 1) we shall briefly examine the development of the *major theological themes* in their relationship to the literary structure, and 2) we shall *sketch* the progressive unfolding of the *Christocentric theology* in the structural development of the Gospel, which will illustrate how the literary structure helps us to a better understanding of the Johannine theological perspective.

5.1 MAJOR THEOLOGICAL THEMES AND THE LITERARY STRUCTURE

Immediately the *problem* arises as to which of the themes are truly important for the Evangelist and how to detect them objectively. For what a reader regards as important depends much on his cultural and theological background, his prejudices and preconceptions, his presuppositions and problems. Hence what one considers as a central theme may be regarded by another as marginal.

High frequency in the occurrence of a term can be an indicator of its importance in the Gospel of John. For example, God is called "Father" (*patêr*) 120 times, which shows that the Fatherhood of God is a major Johannine

---

[1] C. H. TALBERT, *Literary Patterns, Theological Themes and the Genre of Luke-Acts* (Montana 1974) 12, n. 40.

theological theme. But low frequency of a term does not necessarily mean that it is less important. For instance, the Christological titles *ho hyios tou theou* and *ho hyios* occur only 9 times and 17 times respectively, from which, however, one cannot conclude that they are less important than the term *patêr* for the Evangelist [2].

A *comparison between the Johannine and Synoptic vocabulary* is suggested by some as another solution to the problem. For example, since the word *zôê* occurs 36 times in Jn as compared to 7 times in Mt, 4 times in Mk, and 5 times in Lk, it may be considered as a central Johannine theme. It must be remembered, however, that the relatively high frequency of a term is not always a sure criterion to decide whether it is Johannine or not, since such reasoning is based on the presupposition that the Johannine and the Synoptic authors could not have stressed some common themes. For example, because *mathêtês* is used more or less an equal number of times in Mt (73 times) and Jn (78 times), it does not follow that "discipleship" is not a major Johannine theme [3].

Without denying the utility of the absolute and relative frequency of occurrence of a term to determine its importance, a third solution, based on the *structure of the Gospel*, may be suggested: the themes which are found *both* in the *introduction* (1,1-2,11) and in the *conclusion* (20,30-31) are of capital importance for the correct discernment of the fundamental themes of the Gospel [4].

The conclusion (20,30-31) explicitly mentions Jesus' actions ("Now Jesus did many other *signs*"), his identity ("Jesus is *the Christ, the Son of God*"), his soteriological significance ("that you may have *life* in his name"), and the importance of believing in him ("that you may *believe* that Jesus is the Christ, the Son of God, and that *believing* you may have life in his name") [5]. We saw in the last chapter that all these theological themes of the conclusion are found also in the introduction [6]. This clearly underscores the Christocentric character of the Fourth Gospel and implicitly tells us that all the other theological themes must be seen in relation to the Christocentric themes given in the introduction and the conclusion. Hence in this section we will concentrate on the Christological-soteriological themes which are found both in 1,1-2,11 and 20,30-31, and which have also a high (absolute and/or relative) frequency of

---

[2] See 4.22 above.

[3] Notice that *mathêtês* is not included in the list of Johannine terms prepared by BARRETT, 5-6. Similarly, *sêmeion* which is one of the significant terms for John (cf. his conclusion in 20,30-31) is not found in BARRETT's list, while *ergon* is given as a Johannine term. Likewise he leaves out *pisteuein* which occurs 98 times in the Fourth Gospel!

[4] SCHNACKENBURG remarks about the key role of Jn 20,30-31:

> Because, at the end, the evangelist himself states the object of his work, this concluding statement represents something of a *key* for the basic understanding of his unique gospel, so the interpretation up to this point has to prove its worth *in relation to it* (III, 335) [my italics].

[5] Jesus' disciples (*mathêtai*) are also mentioned in 20,30.

[6] See 4.112,1.

occurrence in the Fourth Gospel. In other words, we combine the three solutions proposed by scholars to determine which are the most important theological themes for John. As we survey the development of these themes, we shall also examine some others which are closely connected to them (e.g. "the Son of Man", "the Son" and "the Father", in connection with "the Son of God"; "works" in relationship with "signs").

In short, we want to survey the following theological themes in the structure of the Fourth Gospel: 1) "Christ"/"Messiah", 2) "the Son of God", "the Son", "the Father" and "the Son of Man", 3) "signs" and "works", 4) "disciples", 5) "believing", and 6) "(eternal) life" [7].

5.11 Christ/Messiah (*Christos/Messias*)

We must preface the study of the title *Christos* with a word about the use of the name *Iêsous* in the Gospel of John. It occurs 238 times in Jn, which is much more frequent than in Mt (150x), Mk (81x) or Lk (88x). Furthermore it is found not only in the introduction and the conclusion but also in every one of the five sections and the appendix [7a]. In fact, the name "Jesus" is explicitly mentioned in all the subsections except two (15,1-17; 15,18-16,4d). This points to the historical character and the concreteness of the Johannine Jesus.

The title *Christos* occurs 17 times and *Messias* twice in Jn, which is much more than in any of the Synoptic Gospels [8]. The compound name *Iêsous Christos* is found only twice in the Fourth Gospel (1,17; 17,3) and in their context it characterizes Jesus as the revealer who brings salvation/life.

The importance of the title "Christ" in the Gospel of John is seen not only from the high (absolute and relative) frequency of its occurrence and the fact that Jn is the only NT book which has preserved the Hellenized form *Messias* (1,41; 4,25) of the original Aramaic $m^e shiha'$ or Hebrew $mashiah$ [9] but also from the prominent position it occupies in the structure of the Gospel. Thus *Christos* is found both in the introduction (1,20.25. 41) and in the conclusion (20,31) and in all the three sections of the Book of Jesus' Signs, which can be seen from the table on the next page.

It is certainly significant that the title *Christos/Messias* occurs 4 times (*Christos*: 1,20.25.41; *Messias*: 1,41) in the "testimonial-kerygmatic introduction" (B* = 1,19-51) and once in the "Christological conclusion" (Bz = 20,31abc),

---

[7] This list of Johannine themes is not intended to be exhaustive. Because they occur both in the introduction and in the conclusion and are frequently found in the body of the Fourth Gospel, they are very important for the Evangelist. This does not mean, however, that there are not other important Johannine themes (e.g. "love").

[7a] See the table on the next page.

[8] The title *Christos* occurs 10 times in Mt, 5 times in Mk and 12 times in Lk; the rest of the times the term is used as the proper name of Jesus (cf. S. SABUGAL, *Christos. Investigación exegética sobre la cristologia johannnea* [Barcelona 1972] 126 and n. 183 there). *Messias* is not found in the Synoptic Gospels. In fact, it does not occur in any book of the NT except in Jn (1,41; 4,25).

[9] BARRETT, 70.

Distribution of *Iêsous/Christos/Messias/Iêsous Christos* in Jn.

Title	INTR. (1,1-2,11)	BOOK OF JESUS' SIGNS (2,1-12,50)			BOOK OF JESUS' HOUR (11,1-20,29)		CONCL. (20, 30-31)	APPX. (21, 1-25)
		First Sect. (2,1-4,54)	Second Sect. (5,1-10,42)	Bridge Sect. (11,1-12,50)	Fourth Sect. (13,1-17,26)	Fifth Sect. (18,1-20,29)		
Iêsous	1,29. 36.37. 38.42. 42.43. 45.47. 48.50; 2,1+. 2+.3+. 4+.7+. 11+	2,1.2. 3.4.7. 11.13. 19.22. 24; 3,3.5. 10.22; 4,1.1. 2.6.7. 10.13. 17.21. 26.34. 44.47. 48.50. 50.53. 54	5,1.6.8.13. 14.15.16.17. 19; 6,1.3.5.10. 11.15.17.19. 22.24.24.26. 29.32.35.42. 43.53.61.64. 67.70; 7,1.6.14.16. 21.28.33.37. 39; 8,12.14.19. 25.28.31.34. 39.42.49.54. 58.59; 9,3.11.14. 35.37.39.41; 10,6.7.23. 25.32.34	11,4. 5.9. 13.14. 17.20. 21.23. 25.30. 32.33. 35.38. 39.40. 41.44. 46.51. 54.56; 12,1. 1.3.7. 9.11. 12.14. 16.21. 22.23. 30.35. 36.44	13,1. 7.8. 10.21. 23.23. 25.26. 31.36. 38; 14,6. 9.23; 16,19. 31; 17,1	18,1.2.4. 5.7.8.11. 12.15.15. 19.20.22. 23.34.36. 37; 19,1.5.9. 9.11.13. 16.18.19. 20.23.25. 26.28.30. 33.38.38. 40.42; 20,2.12. 14.14.15. 15.17.19. 21.24.26. 29	20,30. 31	21,1. 4.4.5. 7.10. 12.13. 14.15. 17.20. 21.22. 23.25.
Christos	1,20. 25.41	3,28; 4,25. 29	7,26.27.31. 41.41.42; 9,22; 10,24	11,27; 12,34	—	—	20,31	—
Messias	1,41	4,25	—	—	—	—	—	—
Iêsous Christos	1,17	—	—	—	17,3	—	—	—

which are parallel to each other (B* // Bz)[10]. The explicit mention of "the Christ" both in the introduction and in the conclusion forms a sort of inclusion for the whole Gospel, which highlights its importance, since Jesus is presented as the Messiah already in the introduction, and faith in his Messiahship is explicitly stated in the conclusion to be one of the purposes of writing the Gospel (*tauta de gegraptai hina pisteu[s]ête hoti Iêsous estin ho Christos*). The title *Christos* has a deeper significance in the conclusion than in the introduction, for in the latter it means mostly the Messiah of the Jewish expectations (1,20.25.41) and only implicitly the Christ of Christian faith, whereas in the conclusion it denotes the Saviour of Christian confession (cf. 1 Jn 5,1; Ac 9,22).

The first testimony of John the Baptist (1,19-28) begins with a reference to "the Christ". When the Baptist is questioned by the official delegation from the Jewish authorities in Jerusalem: "Who are you?" (*sy tis ei?*: 1,19), he answers emphatically (cf. 1:20: "he confessed, he did not deny, but confessed") that he is not the Christ (*egô ouk eimi ho Christos*). His reply implies that the questioners were wondering whether he was perhaps the long awaited Jewish Messiah. The Messianic implication of the question the Jewish delegation from Jerusalem put to the Baptist in B* (1,19: *sy tís ei?*) is explicitated in the question the Jews in Jerusalem would later ask Jesus himself in a parallel passage 2B'(10,24: *ei sy ei ho Christos eipon hêmin parrêsia[i]* [as John the Baptist had done in 1,19-20]; cf. Lk 3,15).

That the Baptist's categorical denial of being himself the Christ is implicitly a testimony to Jesus, the Messiah, is clear from the following facts: 1) the emphatic *egô* in *egô ouk eimi ho Christos* implies: "It is not I who am the Messiah" (but another who is the Messiah)[11]; 2) the denial is emphatically stated to be a "confession" (cf. the repetition of *hômologêsen* in 1,20), which elsewhere in the Johannine Gospel refers to publicly acknowledging Jesus as the Christ (cf. 9,22; 12,42)[12]; 3) the denial (confession) is introduced as "the testimony of John" (*kai hautê estin hê martyria tou Iôannou*: 1,19), which, as we have seen earlier, forms an inclusion with 1,34 (*kai memartyrêka hoti houtos estin ho hyios tou theou*); 4) in the parallel passage in the Prologue (b* = 1,6-8) John's mission was described in terms of bearing witness to Jesus, the light (*houtos êlthen eis martyrian, hina martyrêsê[i] peri tou phôtos*: 1,7.8); 5) the negation that John was the light in 1,8 (*ouk ên ekeinos to phôs*) is similar to his own denial in 1,20 that he is the Christ (*egô ouk eimi ho Christos*); 6) towards the end of the pericope in question the Baptist points to a mysterious person who is to come after him, the straps of whose sandals he is unworthy to untie (1,27; cf. Lk 3,16-17) and whom the Jews do not know though he is in their midst (1,26), probably a reference to the hidden Messiah (cf. 7,27); 7) two days later Andrew and his companion, two

---

[10] See "the Schema of the Literary Structure of the Fourth Gospel".
[11] SCHNACKENBURG, I, 228; BARRETT, 172.
[12] S. SABUGAL, *op. cit.*, 184-86.

of the Baptist's disciples whom he persuaded to follow Jesus (1,35-37), would announce their discovery of the Messiah (*heurêkamen ton Messian*: 1,41); 8) later the Baptist would remind his other disciples of his unambiguous denial at 1,20 of any Messianic claims for himself (*autoi hymeis moi martyreite hoti eipon hoti ouk eimi egô ho Christos*: 3,28). From this data it follows that the Baptist's denial that he is the Christ is indirectly a testimony to Jesus' Messiahship.

At the same time it must be granted that the stress on John the Baptist not being the Christ may be part of the Evangelist's polemic against the Baptist sectarians who might have held their master to be the Messiah[13]. But it must be remembered that this polemical aspect is only secondary in 1,19-28 and must not be overstressed, since the Baptist's refusal of the Messianic title could well be an historical reminiscence (cf. Lk 3,15-16; Ac 13,25). It may also be the Evangelist's way of "baptizing" the Baptist (cf. *homologein* at 1,20) in order to woo other followers of his to confess Jesus as the Christ, just as Andrew and his companion (the Evangelist?) did (cf. 1,35-41).

One may wonder why the Baptist does not openly say that Jesus is the Messiah. The probable reasons why he does not reveal the identity of the Messiah immediately are to strengthen the Messianic expectation in the hearts of the people, and to make them actively *seek* the Messiah (cf. 1,38), which is part of his mission of "making straight the way of the Lord" (1,23). Furthermore, from the dramatic point of view, the cryptic language helps to create curiosity in the readers of the Gospel to find out who is the Messiah.

The Messianic identity of Jesus is explicitly proclaimed by Andrew in 1,41, when he joyfully tells his brother Simon Peter about the discovery of the Messiah: *heurêkamen ton Messian*.

But we may ask what kind of a Messiah Andrew announces to Simon when he gives him the good news of his sudden discovery? Since the Evangelist has preserved the Hellenized form (*Messias*) of the very Aramaic term (*mˤshiḥa'*) and has translated it into Greek using *Christos*, he must have been aware of its original meaning associated with "anointing"[14] and its OT and Judaic background. Therefore most probably Andrew uses the title to denote the long awaited national Messianic king, "*the ideal, political king of the future*"[15]. But since, in contrast to the Synoptic Gospels, Jesus is never called "the Son of David" in the Johannine Gospel, *Messias* at 1,41 must not be simply identified with the Davidic Messiah (cf. 7,42, which is probably an instance of Johannine irony). This is supported by the fact that, though Jesus' kingship is stressed in

---

[13] So most of the commentators e.g. BARRETT, 172-73; BROWN, I, 46-47; BULTMANN, 88; SCHNACKENBURG, I, 228; cf. also S. SABUGAL, *op. cit.*, 186-93.

[14] S. SABUGAL, *op. cit.*, 197.

[15] *Ibid.*, 64: "El Mesías veterotestamentario y judaico es, ante todo, un rey: *El rey ideal y político del futuro.*"

the Fourth Gospel (1,49; 12,13; 18,28-19,22), Jesus runs away from the Galilean crowd which wants to crown him king (6,15) and affirms unambiguously during his trial before Pilate: "My kingdom is not of this world" (19,36). The meaning of "the Messiah" at 1,41 must not be determined by taking it to be simply synonymous with "the king of Israel" at 1,49 [16], since kingship is only one of the aspects of Jesus' Messiahship. In fact, Jesus is presented in 1,19-51 not only as the royal Messiah ("You are the king of Israel": 1,49) but also as the eschatological prophet or the prophetic Messiah (cf. Philip's words to Nathanael in 1,45: "We have found him of whom Moses in the law and also the prophets wrote, Jesus of Nazareth, the son of Joseph") and the hidden Messiah implied in the Baptist's words ("among you stands one whom you do not know": 1,26; "I myself did not know him; but for this I came baptizing with water, that he might be revealed to Israel": 1,31) and in the disciples' question to Jesus: *pou meneis?* (1,38). Hence the meaning of "the Messiah" must not be too narrowly specified at 1,41. It is probably meant to be an open-ended term, whose full significance will gradually become clearer as one reads through the Gospel (see, for instance, how Jesus reveals himself to be the prophetic Samaritan Messiah [*Ta'eb*?] in the parallel passage 1B' at 4,25-26, which we shall examine below).

The spiral structure of 1,35-51 (b c d e / c'd'e'f) confirms the above conclusion, for we have seen in chapter 3 that Andrew's announcement *heurêkamen ton Messian* at 1,41 corresponds to Philip's proclamation *hon egrapsen Môüsês en tô[i] nomô[i] kai hoi prophêtai heurêkamen...* at 1,45 [17], which is most probably an allusion to Deut 18,15.18 where a Moses-like prophet is promised (cf. 1,21; 6,14; cf. also Ac 3,22), which gave rise to the rabbinic maxim: "As the first redeemer (Moses), so shall be the last (the Messiah)" [18]. Note that the addition *kai hoi prophêtai* at 1,45 makes Jesus the fulfilment not only of the writings of Moses (cf. 5,46) but also of the prophets (e.g. the prophecies of Zecharia and Isaiah mentioned in Jn 12,16.41). Thus Jesus is rendered the fulfilment of all the Scriptures (cf. 5,39; 19,24.28.36) and not merely of those which speak of a future Messianic king (e.g. Is 9,2-7; 11,1-9; Zech 9,9). It is only by allowing such elasticity in the meaning of the title *Messias/Christos* that 1,41 can be said to contain implicitly, at the redactional level, the Christian confession and kerygma: "Jesus is the Christ" (e.g. Mk 8,29; Ac 9,22; 17,3; 18,5.28; 1 Jn 5,1).

---

[16] *Pace* S. SABUGAL, *op. cit.*, 199.

[17] See 3.34.

[18] "Como el primer redentor así el último redentor; como se dice del primer redentor: 'Moisés tomó a su mujer e hijos y los condujo en un asno' (Éx 24,10), así el último redentor 'humilde y cabalgando sobre un asno' (Zac 9,9); como el primero hizo descender el maná: 'Ved, os haré llover pan del cielo' (Éx 16,4), así el último redentor hara descender el maná: 'Habrá pan de trigo en la tierra' (Sal 72,6: sic midr.); como el primer redentor hizo brotar el agua (Núm 20,11), así el último redentor hara brotar el agua: 'Una fuente manará de la casa de Yahveh que regará el valle de las acacias' (Jl 4,18)" (MidrQoh 9b [a 1,9], cited by S. SABUGAL, *op. cit.*, 61, n. 156; cf. also p. 261).

Notice how the concept of Messiahship is widened in Jn 1. When the Baptist tells the Jewish delegation that he is not the expected Messiah (1,20), he is asked if he is Elijah or the prophet (1,21; cf. also 1,25). This fact shows that the Jews in Jerusalem made a distinction between the eschatolgical figures "the Messiah" and "the prophet" (cf. also 7,40-41 where the crowd in Jerusalem during the feast of Tabernacles distinguishes "the prophet" from "the Messiah"). But the first disciples of Jesus announce him to be both the Messiah (1,41) and the eschatological prophet foretold in the Scriptures (1,45). (It may be recalled that 1,41 and 1,45 are parallel units [d and d'] in the spiral structure [b c d e/c'd'e'f] of 1,35-51.) Again at the end of Jn 1 Nathanael acknowledges Jesus as the royal Messiah by combining in his confession the titles *ho hyios tou theou* and *basileus tou Israel* (1,49). Thus the concept of the Messiah in the "testimonial-kerygmatic introduction" (B* = 1,19-51) is gradually expanded so as to present Jesus as the hidden, prophetic, royal and divine Messiah.

All the above-mentioned Messianic aspects of Jesus are taken up and further developed or transformed, and others are added in the Book of Jesus' Signs (Jn 2-12), which contains the title *Christos* in each of its three sections (Jn 2-4; 5-10; 11-12). We shall now briefly examine these sections in the light of the literary structure.

While in B* (1,19-51) Jesus is revealed as the fulfilment of Jewish Messianic expectations, in 1B' (4,1-42) he manifests himself as the fulfilment of Samaritan Messianic hopes (cf. 4,25-26). Note that the same Aramaic title *Messias*, with its Greek translation *Christos* as used at 1,41, occurs at 4,25. Again, just as Andrew's announcement of the discovery of the Messiah comes as the climax of the first disciples' encounter with Jesus (1,35-42), so Jesus' self-revelation as the Samaritan Messiah (*Ta'eb?*) (*egô eimi ho lalôn soi*: 1,26) occurs as the climax of the conversation between Jesus and the Samaritan woman. She had first taken him for an ordinary "Jew" (*sy Ioudaios*: 4,9), then began to address him with more respect as "Sir" (*kyrie*: 4,11.15), later acknowledged him as a "prophet" (*kyrie, theôrô hoti prophêtês ei sy*: 4,19), and finally expressed her hope in the imminence of a Messiah (*oida hoti Messias erchetai, ho legomenos Christos*: 4,25).

In order to interpret correctly the meaning of the title *Messias/Christos* on the lips of the Samaritan woman it is necessary to examine the Samaritan Messianic expectations, focussed on the eschatological figure called *Ta'eb*. He is, as the word itself indicates, "the one who returns" and "the one who restores". In the light of Deut 18,15-18 he is described as the "new Moses, Moses *redivivus*," who basically has the prophetic and religious mission of revealing the hidden plan, authentic worship and true law of God not only to the Samaritans and the Jews but also to the whole world. But sometimes he is regarded both as a religious and as a political restorer (a king), who would reestablish the eschatological kingdom inaugurated by Moses and Joshua.

However, this act would include not only the kingdom of Israel but that of the whole world [18a].

Note that in the Johannine context of 4,25-26 it is primarily as the prophetic, religious revealer (and not as the political restorer) that Jesus manifests himself to be the (Samaritan) Messiah (*Ta'eb*?) [19], for it is only when the woman expresses the Samaritan conviction about the coming of the Messiah/Christ who "will announce to us all things" (*anangelei hêmin hapanta*: 1,25) about salvation (4,22) and the place and nature of true worship of God (4,20-24) that Jesus tells her: *egô eimi, ho lalôn soi* (1,26). Both the verbs *anangellein* and *lalein* are revelatory terms.

It is enlightening to note that while in B* (1,19-51) Jesus was presented primarily as the Jewish, royal, prophetic, Messiah (1,20.41.45.49), in 1B' (4,1-42) he is manifested as the Samaritan, revelatory, prophetic, Moses-like-Messiah (*Ta'eb*?). In other words, Jesus is the fulfilment not only of the Jewish Messianic hopes but also of the Samaritan eschatological expectations, for he is "the Saviour of the world" (4,42). Thus we see how the meaning of the Messiah of B* is modified and expanded in 1B'.

The concept of the Johannine Messiah is further enriched in another parallel passage 2B' (10,22-42). The Jewish authorities in Jerusalem ask Jesus during the feast of the Dedication to tell them unambiguously if he is the Christ or not (*ei sy ei ho Christos, eipe hêmin parrêsia[i]*: 10,24). Unlike his reaction to the Samaritan woman to whom he revealed himself clearly (*egô eimi*...: 4,26), he does not manifest his Messianic identity "plainly" to the unbelieving Jews, but his reply *eipon hymin kai ou pisteuete* (10,25bc) implies that he is the Messiah. And yet nowhere in the Gospel has Jesus told the Jews explicitly that he is the Christ! The rest of Jesus' reply in 10,25de-30 hints at a solution to this problem, for he tells them: "The works that I do in my Father's name, they bear witness to me... I and the Father are one" (10,25de.30). In other words, Jesus is more than the

---

[18a] *Ibid.*, 226-28. It is true that *Ta'eb* is not attested in the first century A.D. The oldest Samaritan document (*Memar Markah*) which mentions this figure does not date earlier than the third century. This does not, however, mean that the Samaritan Messianic expectations did not have earlier roots, although no Samaritan document attests the use of *Messias/Christos*. But Justin writes: *Ioudaioi de kai Samareis... aei prosdokesantes ton Christon* (*Apol*. I, 53, 6). Furthermore, the prophetical, political, religious, Samaritan "pseudomessiah", about whom Flavius JOSEPHUS writes (*Ant. Jud.* XVIII, 85-87), seems to have many of the characteristics of the Samaritan *Ta'eb*. In the words of S. SABUGAL: "los rasgos de esa figura revolucionaria del relato flaviano concuerdan, substancialmente, con la concepción de la literatura samaritana sobre el Ta'eb, reflejando, al mismo tiempo, algunas de las características que definen la figura del *Messias-Christos* del relato joanneo" (*op. cit.*, 229).

[19] *Ibid.*, 229-30. It is to be noted that the Johannine text (1,25) does not use the Samaritan title *Ta'eb* but the Hebrew title *Messias* (on the lips of the Samaritan woman). Again, Jesus does not explicitly say "I am *Messias*" or "I am *Ta'eb* but simply "I am" (*egô eimi*), followed by *ho lalôn soi*. This may be the Johannine way of suggesting that Jesus is the fulfilment of the Messianic expectations of both the Jews and the Samaritans, for he is later confessed by the Samaritans as "the Saviour of the world" (4,42).

Messiah of Jewish expectations, for he is the Son of God (cf. 20,31); or rather, he is the Messiah precisely because he is the Son of God. It is to be recalled that the Johannine Jesus had plainly told the Jews in Jerusalem about his divine Sonship earlier in 2B (5,1-47; cf. especially vv.17.19-30.37-47), which is parallel to 2B' (10,22-42) in the chiastic structure (2B C D D'C'B') of Jn 5-10.

Notice how the concept of Jesus' Messiahship is transformed. In B* (1,19-51) it seems that Jesus is confessed as "the [adopted] Son of God" because he is the royal Messiah ("the king of Israel": 1,49), whereas in 2B' (10,22-42) Jesus presents himself as the Messiah because he is "the [divine] Son of God" (cf. also 10,36). In the light of the latter the former has to be reinterpreted.

As is to be expected in any chiastic structure, the theme (of Jesus' Messianic and divine identity) of the last structural element (2B' = 10,22-42) has already been discussed in the central elements (2D = 7,1-8,59; 2D' = 9,1-41). To begin with, note that the title *Christos* occurs 6 times in Jn 7 (vv.26.27.31.41.41.42) and once in 9,22.

In 7,25-31 the question whether Jesus is the Christ is raised by the Jerusalemites during the most popular Jewish feast of Tabernacles brimming with Messianic expectations (7,26: *mêpote... houtos estin ho Christos?*). But they come to the conclusion that he cannot be the Christ, since they know his (geographical or human) origin (*touton oidamen pothen estin*: 7,26ab; cf. 6,42; 7,52), whereas the origin of the (hidden) Messiah will be unknown to all (*ho de Christos hotan erchêtai oudeis ginôskei pothen estin*: 7,27cde). Jesus' answer implies that they do not know his true origin because they do not know the Father who has sent him (*hon hymeis ouk oidate*: 7,28). The implication is that Jesus is truly the (hidden) Messiah, since his divine origin (the Father) is unknown to them.

Jesus' Galilean origin (*mê gar ek tês Galilaias ho Christos erchetai?*: 7,41; cf. 7,52) is a stumbling block to some in Jerusalem on the last day of the feast of Tabernacles, since they believe in the Scriptures which have foretold that the Messiah will be a descendant of David (2 Sam 7,12; Ps 89,3-4) and will come from the Davidic town of Bethlehem (Mic 5,2; cf. Mt 2,5-6). Possibly this is another instance of Johannine irony which hints at the truth through an objection, if it can be presumed that the Evangelist knew about Jesus' birth in Bethlehem. The silence about Christ's birthplace may be part of the Evangelist's presentation of Jesus as the hidden Messiah whose place of origin no one knows (7,27). It may also be that such a fact is not important for his understanding of Jesus as the royal Messiah whose kingdom is not of this world (cf. 18,36). Note that Jesus is never called "the Son of David" in Jn, although his kingship is highlighted in many places (1,49; 12,13.15; 18,28-19,16; 19,19-22).

Two other aspects of Jesus' Messiahship are hinted at in Jn 7. In 7,31 we are told that many believed in him as the Messiah because of the many signs he did (cf. 20,30-31). We shall see later that the Johannine signs have a revelatory

Messianic function[20]. According to 7,40-41 some believe in Jesus as the eschatological prophet or the expected Christ because of his revelatory words (cf. *akousantes tôn logôn toutôn* at 7,40) about his gift of the Spirit. That this gift is symbolized by the living water flowing from his side (7,37-39; cf. 4,10.14; 19,34) implies that Jesus is the Spirit-filled Messiah (cf. 1,32-34).

It is worth noting that in Jn 7 different types of Jewish Messianic expectations (the hidden, the prophetic, and the royal Messiah) are mentioned, and Jesus is presented as the fulfilment of all these eschatological hopes[21].

Some of these Messianic aspects are discussed again in the dramatic episode in 2D' (Jn 9), which is parallel to 2D (Jn 7-8). For instance, the cured blind man confesses Jesus as a prophet (*prophêtês estin*: 9,17) come from God (*para theou*: 9,33), since he has opened his eyes blind from birth (9,32). His defence of Jesus before the unbelieving Pharisees seems to have been equivalent to confessing him to be the Christ (*auton homologein Christon*: 9,22), since he was thrown out of the synagogue (9,34) according to the decision of the Jewish authorities mentioned in 9,22. Since this refers to the situation of the Jewish Christians at the end of the first century[22], the title *Christos* in this passage most probably has not only a Messianic but also a Christian meaning (cf. *homologein* at 12,42; 1,20; Rom 10,9)[23].

Unwittingly the unbelieving Pharisees once again acknowledge their ignorance of Jesus' origin (*touton de ouk oidamen pothen estin*: 9,29), thus unknowingly admitting that he is the hidden Messiah whose origin no one knows (cf. 7,27)! This seems to be part of the Johannine irony (cf. 11,50-52; 12,34).

Another interesting characteristic of the Johannine presentation of Jesus, the Messiah, is the description of him as the bridegroom. Using the matrimonial allegory of the bridegroom and the bride (*ho echôn tên nymphên nymphios estin*: 3,29), the Baptist manifests Jesus, the Messiah, as the bridegroom of those who "go to him" and enter into a covenantal relationship with him through faith and baptism. Note that 3,28-29 is the Baptist's answer to his disciples' complaint in 3,26 that Jesus "is baptizing and all are going to him" (*ide houtos baptizei kai pantes erchontai pros auton*). Here the phrase *erchesthai pros auton* is to be understood not only in the sense of movement towards Jesus but also in the symbolic sense of believing in him (cf. 7,37-38), though the Baptist's disciples must have used the expression only in the first sense. The above interpretation is supported by the Baptist's implicit reference to "those who go to him" as "what is given from heaven" (*dedomenon... ek tou ouranou*: 3,27). This is another way of saying that they are God's gift to Jesus (cf. 6,37; 17,6). Thus the presentation

---

[20] See 5.13 below.

[21] The Messianic discussions in Jn 7-8 probably reflect the discussions between Jesus and the Jews on the one hand and those between the Johannine community and the Jews on the other (see the next note).

[22] J. L. MARTYN, *History and Theology in the Fourth Gospel*, 2 ed. (Nashville 1979) 37-62.

[23] BARRETT, 361.

of Jesus as the Messianic bridegroom and of those who believe him as the bride (3,28-29), a truth which seems to have been hinted at already in the first Cana-sign (where Jesus is the "bridegroom" who has given "the good wine" in abundance: 2,9-10), indicates the intimacy between Jesus and the believers. This intimacy is similar to that existing between Jesus, the good shepherd, and the disciples, the sheep, which will be described in detail in a parallel passage (2C' = 10,1-21) later in the Gospel. Since the matrimonial imagery had been often used by the prophets to describe the covenantal relationship between Yahweh and the people of Israel (e.g. Is 5-8; Jer 2,2; Ez 16,62; Hos 2,19-20), it is possible that the designation of Jesus as the *nymphios*, similar to the application of *Kyrios* at 1,23, may be an implicit affirmation of Jesus' divine dignity [24] and the covenantal relationship between him and the new people of Israel conceded to him by God the Father (3,27; cf.3,35) who out of love has likewise given Jesus, his only Son, to the believers so that they may share in his divine life (3,16.36).

In two parallel passages 3C (11,1-54) and 3C' (11,55-12,50) in the bridge-section (Jn 11-12) Jesus is confessed or referred to as "the Christ" (11,27; 12,34) in the context of his soteriological significance.

Thus at the end of Martha's meeting with Jesus (11,17-27) who reveals himself as "the resurrection and the life" (11,25) she confesses her faith in him as "the Christ" (*egô pepisteuka hoti sy ei ho Christos ho hyios tou theou ho eis ton kosmon erchomenos*: 11,27). It is to be observed that the three Christological titles ("the Christ", "the Son of God", "he who is coming into the world") in the climactic confession of Martha are to be interpreted not only in the light of each other but at two levels, namely, at the historical and the post-resurrectional levels (cf. 20,31). While at the historical level the three titles refer to the Jewish Messiah, after the resurrection of Jesus the title "the Son of God" would signify his divine Sonship in the full sense of the term and hence the combined expression ("the Christ, the Son of God, he who is coming into the world") would have the deeper Christological significance that Jesus is the eschatological divine Messiah [25].

Furthermore, when Jesus speaks to the crowd in Jerusalem about the salvific significance ("drawing all men to myself") of his being "lifted up from the earth" (12,32; cf. 3,14) on the cross (12,33), the people express their expectation of an eternal Messiah ("the Christ remains for ever": 12,34), which corresponds to the oracle of Nathan in 1 Chron 17,14. Just as "the Christ" was combined with "the Son of God" in Jn 11,27, here in 12,34 this same title is joined to "the Son of Man". The implication for the Evangelist is that in Jesus, the Christ and the Son of Man, who is lifted up (on the cross and in heaven through his resurrection), the Jewish expectation of an eternal Messiah is profoundly fulfilled, "but not in the sense that the Messiah is exempt from death" [26].

---

[24] S. SABUGAL considers this as certain (*op. cit.*, 177).
[25] *Ibid.*, 347-51.
[26] C. H. DODD, *The Interpretation of the Fourth Gospel*, 228.

5.1 MAJOR THEOLOGICAL THEMES AND THE LITERARY STRUCTURE

It is surprising that the title *Christos* is absent from the Book of Jesus' Hour except in the bridge-section (Jn 11-12), which describes, besides Martha's Messianic confession of Jesus (11,27) and the people's hope of a Messiah who would never die (12,34), the Hosanna-singing crowd's acclamation of Jesus as "the king of Israel" (*ho basileus tou Israêl*: 12,13) during his triumphal entry into Jerusalem before his passion begins. Jesus' kingship is given unexpected prominence in the passion-narrative (cf. the trial before Pilate where Jesus' kingship is the crucial issue [18,33-38; 19,12-16]; the acts of being crowned and proclaimed as "the king of the Jews" [*ho basileus tôn Ioudaiôn*: 19,3.14]; and the attribution of the title on the cross: "Jesus of Nazareth, king of the Jews" [19,19-22]) where his kingship is shown to be "not of this world" (18,36). In these passages the title *basileus* seems to substitute for the title *Christos*, thus modifying the Jewish idea of the Messiah as a this-worldy king (cf. 6,14-15)[27].

Finally, the Evangelist utilizes the title *Christos* in combination with *ho hyios tou theou* in the conclusion in which he states the purpose of his writing the Gospel (20,31). Here the two titles mutually interpret each other. Together they seem to comprise the complete Christian confession of faith in Jesus, a résumé, as it were, of what Christians believe him to be.

"Jesus Christ" (*Iêsous Christos*) is used not as a Christological title but as a personal name in 1,17 and 17,3[28]. The fact that *Christos* has become part of Jesus' personal name demonstrates the tremendous importance the early Christians attached to his being the Christ.

5.11z The high frequency (17 times) of the title *Christos* in the Fourth Gospel indicates that it is one of the most important Christological titles[29]. This is supported by the presence of *Messias*, the hellenized form of the original Aramaic term, in the Gospel of John and in none of the other NT books. Moreover, the prominence of the title *Christos* is highlighted by the significant places in the plan of the Gospel at which the title occurs (e.g. in the introduction: 1,20.25.41.41; in the conclusion: 20,31)[30] and in the bridge-section (11,25; 12,34). Furthermore, it is found in all the three sections (Jn 2-4; 5-10; 11-12) of the Book of Jesus' Signs (Jn 2-12)[31]. The chiastic structures of the first two

---

[27] *Ibid.*, 229.

[28] It may not be purely accidental that the compound name "Jesus Christ" occurs in an introductory hymn to Jesus (1,1-18) and in a concluding prayer of Jesus (17,1-26), which are parallel to each other (C* // 4C').

[29] S. SABUGAL says that "el empleo de ese título [*Christos*] sobrepasa [17 veces] el respectivo de los demás títulos mesiánicos: *basileus tou Israêl* (2 veces), *(ho) basileus* (5 veces), *basileus tôn Ioudaiôn* (9 veces), *(ho) hyios tou theou* (5 veces), *ho hyios tou anthrôpou* (13 veces), *ho sotêr tou kosmou* (1 vez)" (*op. cit.*, 395). We may note here, however, that the Christological title *ho hyios* also occurs 17 times in the Fourth Gospel (see 5.122 below).

[30] Note that the title *Christos* occurs in the parallel parts of the introduction (B* = 1,19-51) and the conclusion (Bz = 20,31abc).

[31] See the schema given below. It is worthy of note that most of the times the title "Christ" occurs in parallel passages in the literary structure: cf. B* (1,19-51) // 1B' (4,1-42) // 2B' (10,22-42) // Bz (20,31abc); 3C (11,1-54) // 3C' (11,55-12,50); 2D (7,1-8,59) // 2D' (9,1-41).

sections and the parallel structure of the third, in which the different aspects of Messiahship is developed, help us to have a better understanding of the Johannine interpretation of Jesus' Messiahship.

It is remarkable that the Johannine Jesus is presented as the perfect fulfilment of all the different Jewish and Samaritan Messianic expectations of a royal/prophetic/hidden/eternal Messiah. By integrating all these Messianic aspects in the title *Christos*, the concept of Messiahship is enlarged, enriched and transformed. For instance, Jesus is a kingly Messiah but not a this-worldly king; Jesus is a hidden Messiah, not in the sense that his place of origin is unknown, but in the deeper sense that his divine origin from the Father is hidden until it is revealed. The meaning of "Christ" is also transformed by its combination with other titles like "the Son of God" and "the Son of Man" (which we shall examine below). It must also be remembered that only at the post-resurrectional level would the title "Christ" have the transformed Christian meaning mentioned above (20,31), while at the historical level it would have meant only the Jewish/Samaritan Messiah.

5.12 The Son of God, the Son, the Father, and the Son of Man

Besides the Christological title *ho hyios tou theou*, we shall examine two other connected titles involving *hyios*, namely, *ho hyios* and *ho hyios tou anthrôpou*. Since *ho hyios* is closely connected to *ho patêr*, we shall also include the latter in our study.

5.121 "The Son of God" (ho Hyios tou Theou)

The full title *ho hyios tou theou* is found 9 times in Jn, which is much in comparison with the other books of the NT [32]. Many of its occurrences in Jn are at prominent places in the structure of the Gospel such as the introduction, the conclusion and bridge-section, as can be seen from the table given on the next page [32a].

---

[32] The title *(ho) hyios (tou) theou* (in the singular) applied to Jesus occurs only 47 times in the entire NT (Mt = 9x; Mk = 4x; Lk = 7x; Jn = 9x; Ac = 2x; Rom = 1x; 2 Cor = 1x; Gal = 1x; Eph = 1x; Heb = 4x; 1 Jn = 7x; Rev = 1x). The plural *hyioi (tou) theou* applied to Christians is found 5 times in the NT (Mt = 1x; Rom = 3x; Gal = 1x) but never in Jn, where *tekna (tou) theou* is used to denote Christian believers (1,12; 11,52).

[32a] At 3,18 the title is part of the phrase *to onoma tou monogenous hyiou tou theou*. At 1,34 some manuscripts read *ho eklektos tou theou* or *ho eklektos hyios tou theou* instead of *ho hyios tou theou*. But the latter reading is to be preferred "on the basis of age and diversity of witnesses" (TCGNT, 200). The definite article *ho* is missing at 10,36; some manuscripts also leave out *tou* before *theou* there (cf. GENT at 10,36). The articles are missing at 19,7.

Ho hyios ho monogenês at 3,16 is included in the table under *ho hyios*. (The variant reading *monogenês hyios* at 1,18 is not given in the list, since we prefer the reading *monogenês theos*; cf. TCGNT at 1,18.)

5.1 MAJOR THEOLOGICAL THEMES AND THE LITERARY STRUCTURE

Distribution of *ho Hyios tou Theou* and *ho Hyios* in Jn

Title	INTR. (1,1-2,11)	BOOK OF JESUS' SIGNS (2,1-12,50)			BOOK OF JS' HOUR (11,1-20,29)		CONCL. (20, 30-31)	APPX. (21, 1-25)
		First Sect. (2,1-4,54)	Second Sect. (5,1-10,42)	Bridge Sect. (11,1-12,50)	Fourth Sect. (13,1-17,26)	Fifth Sect. (18,1-20,29)		
ho hyios tou theou	1,34. 49	(3,18)	5,25; 10,36	11,4. 27	—	19,7	20,31	—
ho hyios	—	3,(16) 17.35. 36.36	5,19.19. 20.21.22. 23.23.26; 6,40; 8,35.36	—	14,13; 17,1	—	—	—
sou ho hyios	—	—	—	—	17,1	—	—	—
(monogenês)	1,14. 18	3,16. 18	—	—	—	—	—	—

In the "testimonial-kerygmatic introduction" B* (1,19-51) the Baptist concludes his testimony to Christ (1,19-34) with a public declaration: "I have borne witness that this is the Son of God" (1,34). Here the Christological title "the Son of God" seems to sum up the whole content of the Baptist's testimony to Jesus, since *memartyrêka* at 1,34 (whose object is *hoti houtos estin ho hyios tou theou*) forms a literary inclusion with *hê martyria* at 1,19. (Note that, according to 1,6-7 and 1,31, the very purpose of the Baptist's mission was "to bear testimony" to Jesus and "to reveal him to Israel"; this is done best by proclaiming him as "the Son of God" at 1,34).

Likewise, towards the end of the second part of the "testimonial-kerygmatic introduction" (1,35-51) the title "the Son of God" occurs in the climactic confession of Nathanael: "You are the Son of God" (1,49); this is the last of a series of confessions by the disciples (cf. 1,41.45).

It must be recalled that the title *ho hyios tou theou* in the "testimonial-kerygmatic introduction" B* (1,34.49) forms a sort of inclusion with the same title in the parallel "Christological conclusion" Bz (20,31abc)[33]; this fact underscores the importance of the title in our Gospel. We may also note that even the construction of the confessional formula at

---

[33] See "the Schema of the Literary Structure".

1,34.49 and 20,31 is the same (namely, subject + verb *einai* + complement *ho hyios tou theou*):

1,34: houtos *estin*   ho hyios tou theou
1,49: sy   ei   ho hyios tou theou
20,31: Iêsous *estin*... ho hyios tou theou.

The meaning of the title "the Son of God" at 1,34 and 1,49 must be understood at two levels. At the "redactional-historical" level, on the lips of the Baptist and Nathanael, it would have been understood in the Messianic sense (cf. the combination of "the Son of God" with "the king of Israel" in Nathanael's confession)[34]; at the post-resurrectional level "the Son of God" would have the deeper "metaphysical" meaning of divine Sonship[35]. It is in the latter sense, and not in a mere Messianic sense, that the title is used in the conclusion (20,31), since it follows immediately after Thomas' confesssion in the divinity and lordship of the risen Jesus ("My Lord and my God": 20,28). In other words, the statement at 20,31 that "Jesus is the Son of God" is a confession of Christian belief in the divine Sonship of Jesus Christ (cf. 1 Jn 4,15; 5,5). The inclusion of this Christological title in the very statement which reveals the purpose of writing the Gospel indicates the importance the Evangelist attached to it.

Whereas in the introduction B* (1,19-51) the Baptist testifies and one of the first disciples of Jesus (Nathanael) proclaims that Jesus is "the Son of God" (1,34.49), in 2B (5,1-47) and 2B' (10,22-42), two parallel passages in the chiastic structure (B C D D'C'B') of the second section (Jn 5-10) of the Book of Jesus' Signs, Jesus himself reveals his identity as "(the) Son of God" (5,25; 10,36). This is all the more significant, since the title "(the) Son of God" does not occur anywhere between 5,25 and 10,36.

In 2B (Jn 5) Jesus applies the title "the Son of God" implicitly to himself (5,25) in the context of a controversy with, and in the face of the murderous persecution by, the Jewish authorities on account of his (apparent) violation of the Sabbath in curing a cripple and on account of his (blasphemous) claim to divine status by calling God his own Father (5,16-18). The apologetic context and the chiastic structure (A B C D D' C' B' A') of Jesus' ensuing discourse (5,19-30), at the centre of which the title *ho hyios tou theou* is found (5,25 =

---

[34] PANIMOLLE, I, 179-80. We are not concerned here with the historical question whether or not "the Son of God" was a Messianic title in pre-Christian Judaism (which is still a point debated by scholars; cf. C. H. DODD who mentions IV Ezra [which is contemporary with Jn] which clearly and explicitly alludes to 'My son the Messiah' [*op. cit.*, 253]) and therefore whether or not Nathanael *de facto* used such a title in his confession (cf. Mk 14,61; Mt 16,16). Our question is: what does the Evangelist want us to understand when he makes Nathanael confess Jesus as "the Son of God, the king of Israel" in their first encounter? The combination of the two titles shows that "the Son of God" is understood in a Messianic sense.

[35] SCHNACKENBURG, I, 306.

D')[36], make it quite clear that the title is used here to denote Jesus' divine Sonship. He shares in the Father's life in a unique manner (5,26) and therefore mediates divine life for those who believe in him (5,24-25).

In 2B' (10,22-39) a similar situation of hostility is manifested in the attempt of the Jews to stone Jesus (10,31) because of his claim to perfect unity with the Father (*egô kai ho patêr hen esmen*: 10,30); this claim seems to the Jews a clear blasphemy (10,33: *hoti sy anthrôpos ôn poieis seauton theon*). Here too Jesus defends his divinity and demonstrates from the Scriptures, by using an *a fortiori* argument, that he has not blasphemed in calling himself "(the) Son of God" (10,34-36). Jesus also appeals, as in 5,36, to the testimony of the Father's "works" which manifest the mutual immanence of the Father and the Son (*en emoi ho patêr kagô en tô[i] patri*: 10,38). It follows from what has been said that here, as in 5,25, Jesus employs the title "(the) Son of God" to reveal both his divine identity as the Son of the Father and his unique union with Him. In other words, here Jesus manifests himself as more than the Jewish Messiah (about which he was asked by the Jews at the beginning of the pericope: "If you are the Christ, tell us plainly": 10,24), for he is the divine "Son of God" intimately united and in constant communion with the Father.

Towards the end of his dialogue with Nicodemus Jesus implicitly refers to himself as "the Son of God" for the first time in the Fourth Gospel (3,18)[37]. Since it is part of the full title "the only begotten Son of God" (3,18) and is immediately preceded both by "the only-begotten Son" (3,16) and by "the Son" (3,17), it certainly refers to Jesus' unique divine Sonship. But the context and content of 3,16-18 make it clear that the stress is on soteriology, namely, on salvation or condemnation, on sharing in the divine life through faith in the only beloved Son of God or condemning oneself by refusing to believe in the divine Son of God, the saviour and giver of life[38].

The title "the Son of God" is found twice in the Lazarus-episode (Jn 11), once on the lips of Jesus (11,4) and once in the confession of Martha (11,27). It is interesting to note that 11,4 is the last instance of Jesus' implicit reference to himself as "the Son of God", and 11,27 is the last confession of faith in Jesus as "the Son of God" in the Book of Jesus' Signs (2,1-12,50).

---

[36] See 3.32 where the chiastic construction of 5,19-30 (A B C D D' C' B' A') is discussed. As we saw there, the central elements DD' of the chiasmus are structurally very important. Hence the occurrence of the title "the Son of God" in D' (5,25) seems to be specially significant.

[37] In the Prologue Jesus is called *monogenês para patros* (1,14) and *monogenês theos* (1,18). Jesus' divine Sonship is only implicit in his reference to the temple as "the house of my Father" at 2,16.

Some scholars regard 3,13-21 (e.g. SCHNACKENBURG, I, 380-81) or 3,16-21 (e.g. BERNARD, I, 117; LAGRANGE, 86-87) as the theological reflections of the Evangelist rather than the words of Jesus. But since a change of speaker is not indicated at 3,13 or 3,16, we prefer to consider 3,11-21 as a discourse of Jesus (cf. BROWN, I, 149 for other reasons for this view).

[38] MCPOLIN, 69.

Although the same expression "the Son of God" is used both by Jesus (11,4) and by Martha (11,27), a different depth in meaning is to be discerned in the two cases. While Jesus would have utilized the title to refer to his divine Sonship (11,4), Martha would have used it as a Messianic title (11,27), since "the Son of God" is preceded by the Messianic title "the Christ" and followed by the expression "he who is to come into the world" (11,27)[39]. But note that in both the cases the title is applied to Jesus not only in his filial relation to God but also in his saving role as life-giver (notice the insistence on "death" and "life" in 11,4 and 11,23-27 and especially 11,25: "I am the resurrection and the life") and Jesus' question to Martha at 11,26: "Do you believe this?", which emphasizes the relation between "life" and "faith" in Jesus as the mediator of divine life, which is similar to 3,16-17).

During Jesus' trial before Pilate the Jews accuse him of having made himself "Son of God" and hence of deserving death (19,7) for blasphemy (cf. 5,18; 10,33). It is therefore clear that the Johannine Jesus dies on account of his claim to divine Sonship[40]. It must be observed that he is also accused of "making himself king" (19,12.21), and is condemned as "the king of the Jews" (19,19.21). The irony is that by rejecting Jesus, "the Son of God", as their king, the Jews, the people of God, have rejected God as their king (19,15).

5.121z In Jn the title *ho hyios tou theou* is applied only to Jesus. A different expression involving *teknon*, namely, *(ta) tekna (tou) theou*, is used to denote Christians in the Johannine Gospel (1,12; 11,52)[41], in contrast to many other NT books which employ *hyioi theou* to refer to Christian believers (e.g. Mt 5,9; Lk 20,36; Rom 8,14.19; 9,26; Gal 3,26). The Johannine usage underscores the Christocentric character of this title. Although it occurs only 9 times, it is found at key-places in the structure of the Gospel, such as in the introduction (1,34.49) and the conclusion (20,31), in the bridge-section (11,4.27), and at the beginning (5,25) and end (10,36) of the middle section (Jn 5-10) of the Book of Jesus' Signs (Jn 2-12). Whenever the title is found on the lips of Jesus, it refers to his divine Sonship (3,18; 5,25; 10,36; 11,4), whereas it may have a double-level meaning (Messiah/divine Son) when it forms part of a confession of faith in Jesus (1,34.49; 11,27). The meaning depends on whether we look at the title in the

---

[39] Martha's confession in the bridge-section ("you are the Christ, the Son of God, he who is coming into the world": 11,27) is similar to Nathanael's confession in the introduction ("you are the Son of God; you are the king of Israel": 1,49). Both these confessions of faith in Jesus as "the Son of God" must be understood at two levels, namely, at the time of Jesus' ministry and at the time of the Evangelist, that is, after Jesus' glorification. The same combination of the titles "the Christ, the Son of God" as in 11,27 is also found in the conclusion of the Gospel (20,31).

[40] We have seen in the last chapter that the trial of Jesus before the Roman Procurator (18,28-19,6b) is one of the two central elements of the chiastic construction (5C D E E' D' C') of Jn 18-20. Therefore the Jews' accusatory designation of Jesus as "the Son of God" in this central episode of the passion-resurrection seems to underline the importance of this title in the Gospel.

[41] Christian believers are called *tekna (tou) theou* (and not *hyioi [tou] theou*) also in 1 Jn (3,1.2.10; 5,2).

historical context of the persons who make the confession or in the post-resurrectional context of the Christian community (cf. 1 Jn 4,15; 5,5). During Jesus' passion (19,7) and after his resurrection (20,31) "the Son of God" stands for his divinity. It must also be remembered that the Johannine "Son of God" indicates not only Jesus' unique filial relation to God (1,34.49; 10,36; 11,4; 19,7; 20,31) but also his role as mediator of eternal life to those who believe in him (5,25; 11,27; 20,31; cf. 1 Jn 5,11.12). In other words, "the Son of God" is a Christological title with a soteriological significance. This will become clearer when we examine the title "the Son" in Jn.

5.122 *"The Son" (ho Hyios)*

Ho hyios is used absolutely as a title for Jesus 17 times in Jn [42]. If we look at its distribution, we find that it is used 15 times in the Book of Jesus' Signs (Jn 2-12) and only twice in the Book of Jesus' Hour (Jn 11-20). Furthermore, it is found only in three sections (Jn 2-4; 5-10; 13-17), while it is absent from three others (Jn 11-12; 18-20; 21) [43]. Again it is concentrated in the section of "Jesus' Works, Signs and Discussions" (for it occurs 11 times in Jn 5-10) and especially at its beginning (for it is used 8 times in Jn 5). It is found four times in the middle (Jn 3) of the section of "Jesus' Initial Signs and Encounters" (Jn 2-4) [44]. It is also worth noting that the title is used almost exclusively by Jesus himself in the course either of his discourses or of the prayer of the hour [45].

Since the greatest concentration of *ho hyios* is in 5,19-30 (vv.19.19.20. 21.22.23.23.26), we shall start our study of "the Son" with a brief discussion of this discourse of Jesus. Its context is the following: Jesus has cured a cripple on a Sabbath (5,1-9) and as a response to the adverse reaction of the Jews has made the self-defensive statement: *ho patêr mou heos arti ergazetai kagô ergazômai* (5,17). This setting already indicates that the key issue of the ensuing discourse is Jesus' special filial relationship to God, his Father (cf. *ho patêr mou*

---

[42] See the table on the "Distribution of *ho hyios tou theou* and *ho hyios* in Jn". (*Sou ho hyios* at 17,1d is not included in the list under *ho hyios* but is given separately in the table. *Ho hyios ho monogenês*, which is found in 3,16, is not counted among the 17 occurrences of the absolute use of *ho hyios*. *Monogenês* occurs also at 1,14.18 and 3,18). The absolute use of "the Son" occurs only thrice in Mt (11,27; 24,36; 28,19) and once each in Mk (13,32), Lk (10,22), Paul (1 Cor 15,28) and Heb (1,8; four other times without the article: 1,2; 3,6; 5,8; 7,28). (It is found 5 times in 1 Jn and once in 2 Jn.) Cf. Schnackenburg, II, 172.

[43] See the table. If, however, "the Son" is combined with "the Son of God", we find that all the five sections, the introduction and the conclusion contain one or the other or both of the titles.

[44] See the table.

[45] The only exception is its triple occurrence in 3,35-36, where John the Baptist seems to be the speaker, since there is no indication of a change of speaker from 3,27-30 (when the Baptist was talking to his disciples about Jesus) (so Barrett, 224), though some scholars take 3,31-36 as a continuation of Jesus' discourse to Nicodemus in 3,11-21 (so Brown, I, 159-60. Schnackenburg inserts 3,31-36 between 3,12 and 3,13 [I, 380-81], whereas Bernard [I, xxiii] and Bultmann [160-61] transpose 3,31-36 and join it to 3,21. Others like Lagrange (92) regard the Evangelist as the speaker in 3,31-36.

in 5,17)[46], which authorizes him "to work", like God Himself, even on the Sabbath. Since this claim of equality with God is understood by his hostile audience as blasphemous (5,18; cf. 10,33)[47], Jesus explains the meaning of his Sonship in 5,19-30.

That the central interest of the discourse is the nature, quality and role of Jesus' Sonship is seen not only from the occurrence of "the Son" 8 times and of "the Son of God" once in just 12 verses (5,19-30) but also from the inclusion between 5,19 (*ou dynatai ho hyios poiein aph' heautou ouden*) and 5,30 (*ou dynamai egô poiein ap' emautou ouden*) and the chiastic structure of 5,19-30 (A B C D D' C' B' A')[48].

Jesus begins the discourse with what appears to be a parable of the apprentice-son (e.g. the son of a professional carpenter learning a skill from his father) who imitates his father in whatever he does (5,19) and to whom the father shows everything because he loves the son (5,20). But from the context (cf. 5,17) and the rest of the discourse it is evident that Jesus is speaking about the unique relationship between God the Father and himself, for he shares in the very life of the Father (5,26) and in the divine prerogatives of giving life (*zô[i]opoiein*: 5,21; cf. Deut 32,39; 1 Sam 2,6; 2 Kgs 5,7; Hos 6,2) and judgement (*krisis*: 5,22.27.30; cf. Ac 10,42; Hen 69,27)[49]. In the words of C. H. Dodd: "It is in this unity with the Father in exercising the divine prerogatives of vivifying and judging that the unique sonship of Christ is manifested"[50]. This unity between the Father and the Son is so great that later Jesus would say in a parallel passage: "I and the Father are one" (10,30) and "the Father is in me and I am in the Father" (10,38)[51].

The discussion of Jesus' divine status and authority as the unique Son of God in 5,19-30 is taken up again in 8,35-36[52]. Here Jesus uses the metaphor of the son and the slave to show the radical difference between the permanent

---

[46] See a similar reference to "my Father" (*ho patêr mou*) at 2,16 in the parallel passage 1B (2,13-25).

[47] Note the striking parallelism between Jesus' statements in 5,17 and 10,30 on the one hand, and between the alleged reasons for the Jews' hostile reactions to him in 5,18 and 10,33 on the other:

5,17 : **ho patêr mou** heos arti ergazetai *kagô* ergazomai.
10,30: *egô* kai **ho patêr** hen esmen.

5,18 : alla kai **patera idion** elegen **ton theon**
ison heauton poiôn **tô[i] theô[i]** (cf. 5,12: *anthrôpos*)
10,33: alla peri blasphêmias kai hoti sy *anthrôpos* ôn
poieis seauton **theon**.

[48] See 3.32.

[49] Regarding the discourse in 5,17-30 C. H. DODD observes: "the two supreme prerogatives of God as Creator and Ruler of the universe are vested in the Son, namely, zôopoiêsis and krisis" (*op. cit.*, 255).

[50] *Ibid.*, 257.

[51] This occurs in 2B' (10,22-42) which is parallel to 2B (5,1-47).

[52] This is to be expected, since Jn 5-10 has a chiastic structure (2B C D D' C' B'), in which Jn 5 and Jn 7-8 form the first (B) and third (D) episodes (see 4.32).

status of the son and the temporary status of the slave in the house ("The slave does not continue in the house for ever; the son continues for ever": 8,35). Furthermore, he underscores the authority of the Son to liberate those in slavery ("So if the Son makes you free, you will be free indeed": 8,36). This authority is a manifestation of the power of giving life or judgement which the Father has shared with the Son, as was spoken of in 5,21-22.27.30.

Observe that, just as at 8,35 Jesus spoke of "the house" (*hê oikia*) in which the Son stays perpetually, he tells the disciples during the first farewell discourse about his Father's "house" (*en tê[i] oikia[i] tou patros mou*: 14,2) where he would take them so that they may be where he is (*hina hopou eimi egô kai hymeis ête*: 14,3). In other words, the disciples are to live in constant communion with Jesus, the divine Son (cf. *paralêmpsomai hymas pros emauton*: 14,3), who abides in continuous union with the Father ("I am in the Father and the Father in me": 14,11). One of the consequences of this communion of the disciples with Jesus is that he would grant them the prayers they make in union with him (*en tô[i] onomati mou*: 14,13.14) "that the Father may be glorified in the Son" (14,13), since the Son seeks always the Father's glory (7,18) and not his own (8,50)[53].

During the prayer of the hour Jesus refers to himself as "the Son" for the last time (17,1). Here he prays for his own glorification so that he may glorify the Father (*doxason sou ton hyion hina ho hyios doxasê[i] se*: 17,1). Both from the context and from the concentric structure of 17,1-5 (a = vv.1-2; b = v.3; a' = vv.4-5)[54] it is clear that the Son and the Father are simultaneously glorified by the gift of eternal life (17,1-2) to the believers given to the Son by the Father (17,2; cf. 6,37. 39). It is the Father's will that believers should have eternal life (6,40) through Jesus' glorifying passion-death-resurrection (17,4-5). At the centre of the concentric structure (17,3), the description of eternal life in terms of knowing God the Father and Jesus Christ implies that the believers will have this life-giving knowledge especially through Jesus' passion-death-resurrection. This event will reveal to them the depth not only of the Father's love which made Him give His only Son (3,16) but also of Jesus' love which made him lay down his life for them (15,13).

The salvific significance of the Son's mission in the world was stressed the very first time Jesus used the title *ho hyios* to refer to himself: "For God sent the Son into the world, not to condemn the world, but that the world may be saved through him" (3,17). This salvation mediated through the Son is described in terms of eternal life: "For God so loved the world that He gave His only Son, that whoever believes in him should not perish but have eternal life" (3,16). It is enlightening to note that the very first time Jesus applies the title "the Son" to himself it is done to emphasize the Father's love for mankind as manifested in the gift of His only Son with the salvific scope of granting eternal life to those

---

[53] BARRETT, 461. Observe that these verses (7,18; 8,50; 14,13) occur in parallel passages 2D and 4D in the literary structure of Jn.
[54] See 3.33.

who believe in him (3,16-17). The unique filial relationship of Jesus to God the Father is stressed in 3,16-18 through the application to Jesus of the compound titles "the only-begotten Son" (*ho hyios ho monogenês*: 3,16) and "the only-begotten Son of God" (*ho monogenês hyios tou theou*: 3,18) in the context of his saving or life-giving mission. In order to appropriate this eternal life human persons must believe in the Son (3,16). This is reiterated in the parallel passages 3,36 and 6,40 [55]. Because the Father loves the Son and has entrusted everything into his hands (3,35), it is the will of the Father that only those who are united with the Son through a personal, active, committed faith in him may share in the divine life (6,40).

5.122z Unlike the title "the Son of God" (which, as we have seen above, is sometimes used as a Messianic title), the absolute title "the Son" (*ho hyios*) usually indicates the unique divine Sonship of Jesus to God the Father. This fact is confirmed by the close connection between the sayings on "the Son" and those on "the Father" (which we shall examine below). The divine Sonship of Jesus is inextricably related to his mission of revealing the Father and of saving men by enabling them to share in the divine life of the Father and the Son through faith in him [56].

5.123 *"The Father" (ho Patêr)*

God is referred to as the "Father" (*patêr*) 120 times in Jn, that is, almost twice as often as in all the Synoptic Gospels [57]. Its distribution in Jn can be seen from the table given on the next page.

---

[55] Note that these verses are found in parallel passages (namely, in 2C and 1CC') in the chiastic structures of Jn 5-10 and Jn 2-4 (see "the Schema of the Literary Structure").

It is remarkable that 3,16-18 and 3,34-36 contain many common theological themes such as Jesus' divine mission (*apesteilen ho theos*: 3,17.34), his divine Sonship (*ho hyios [ho monogenês/tou theou]*: 3,16.17.18.35.36.36), the Father's love (*êgapêsen*: 3,16; *agapa[i]*: 3,35), divine gift (*edôken*: 3,16; *dedôken*: 3,35), "believing in the Son" (*ho pisteuôn eis auton/ton hyion*: 3,16.18.36) and "having eternal life" (*echein zôên aiônion*: 3,16.36). Also the judgement of those who do not believe in the Son (3,18) corresponds to the wrath of God which rests upon those who disobey the Son (3,36). See 4.312,3 for numerous other parallel elements in 2,23-3,21 and 3,22-4,3 which are the central subsections (C C') of the chiastic structure (1A B C C' B' A') of the first section (Jn 2-4) of the Book of Jesus' Signs.

[56] SCHNACKENBURG sums up the results of his overview of the sayings on "the Son" as follows:

> Surveying these passages, we see that all the essential aspects of Jesus' revealing and saving work come out in them: his mission into the world, his revealing activity in the world, his doing of works, 'signs', which manifest his life-giving power, and finally his way into glory and his saving work as the glorified one. The uniqueness of Jesus' mission and the saving significance of his words and deeds are expressed through the uniqueness of his relation to God, that is his Son-relationship (II, 174).

[57] Mt = 45x; Mk = 5x; Lk = 17x.

Distribution of *Patêr* Applied to God in Jn

INTR. (1,1-2,11)	BOOK OF JESUS' SIGNS (2,1-12,50)		BOOK OF JESUS' HOUR (11,1-20,29)			CONCL. (20, 30-31)	APPX. (21, 1-25)
	First Sect. (2,1-4,54)	Second Sect. (5,1-10,42)	Bridge Sect. (11,1-12,50)	Fourth Sect. (13,1-17,26)	Fifth Sect. (18,1-20,29)		
1,14. 18	2,16; 3,35; 4,21. 23.23	5,17.18.19.20. 21.22.23.23.26. 36.36.37.43.45; 6,27.32.37.40. 45.46.46.57.57. 65; 8,16.18.19.19. 19.27.28.38.38. 42,49.54; 10,15.15.17.18. 25.29.29.30.32. 36.37.38.38	11,41; 12,26. 27.28. 49	13,1.3; 14,2.6.7.8.9.9. 10.10.10.11.11. 12.13.16.20.21. 23.24.26.28.28. 31.31; 15,1.8.9.10.15. 16.23.24.26.26; 16,3.10.15.17. 23.25.26.27.28. 28.32; 17,1.5.11.21. 24.25	18,11; 20,17. 17.17. 21	—	—

Regarding its distribution it must be observed that the term occurs in the introduction (1,14.18) and in all the five sections (Jn 2-4; 5-10; 11-12; 13-17; 18-20). Its occurrence in the different sections, however, is quite uneven, for it is found 51 times in Jn 5-10 and 52 times in Jn 13-17 but only 6 times in Jn 11-12 and 5 times each in Jn 2-4 and 18-20 [58]. This shows that the revelation of the Father is stressed more in the second and fourth sections than in the others. Notice that this revelation is made mainly to the (unbelieving) Jews in Jn 5-10 and to the (believing) disciples in Jn 13-17. It is also noteworthy that in 112 out of the 120 uses Jesus himself speaks of God as "the Father" (*ho patêr*) or "my Father" (*ho patêr mou*), "the Father who sent me" (*ho patêr ho pempsas me* or *ho pempsas me patêr*) or addresses God as "Father" (*pater*) [59]. This already focuses

---

[58] See the table above.

[59] *Ho patêr mou*: 2,16; 5,17.43; 6,32; 8,19.19.49.54; 10,18.25.29.37; 14,2.7.20.21.23; 15,1.8. 10.15.23.24; 20,17.

Ho patêr ho pempsas me or *ho pempsas me patêr*: 5,23.37; 6,44; 8,16.18; 12,49; 14,24.

Pater (voc.): 11,41; 12,27.28; 17,1.5.11.21.24.25.

Patêr hymôn is used at 8,42 (without the article) and at 20,17. In 8,42 the Jews' claim that God is their Father (8,41) is called into question by Jesus but in 20,17 the risen Jesus sends Mary Magdalene to the disciples ("my brethren") with the news: "I am ascending to my Father and your Father...", which means that the Father of Jesus has now become the Father of the disciples.

our attention both on the Father-Son relationship between God and Jesus and on the Son's mission from the Father [60].

The first time the "Father" is mentioned is in connection with the incarnation of the Logos which manifested the glory of an "only Son from (the) Father" (*monogenous para patros*: 1,14); this usage underlines the uniqueness of Jesus' divine Sonship (*monogenês*; cf. also 1,18; 3,16.18) and hints at his mission of revealing the Father, which is explicitly stated in 1,18: "No one has ever seen God; the only Son-God (*monogenês theos*) who is in the bosom of the Father has made [him] known" [61]. The figurative expression *ho ôn eis ton kolpon tou patros* indicates the intimate, dynamic and filial relationship of Jesus with the Father, and gives the reason why he was able to reveal the invisible God (cf. 6,46).

In a parallel passage at 3,35 we are explicitly told that the Father has a loving, trusting relationship to His Son for "the Father loves the Son and has given all things into his hands". The Father's love (*agapan*) for the Son is explicitly stated by Jesus himself in other parallel pericopes (10,17; 17,23.24.27) [61a]. This loving Father-Son relationship may also be expressed through mutual experiential knowledge (*ginôskein*: 10,15).

In many places the Father is spoken of as the *Sender* of Jesus (*ho pempsas me*: 5,23.37; 6,44; 8,16.18; 12,49; 14,24). This underlines the fact that the Father is the source of Jesus' mission of revelation and salvation. Jesus is constantly aware that he has come from the Father and goes to the Father (13,1; 16,28) [62]. The Father has not only sent the Son but He is always with him (16,32) and within him (10,38; 14,10.11; 17,21). Their union and communion is so intimate that Jesus can say: "I and the Father are one" (10,30; cf. 17,11.22). This is more than any prophet could claim.

That God the Father is first and foremost the Father of Jesus is repeatedly and emphatically stated by Jesus himself (cf. the numerous instances of his reference to "my Father" [*ho patêr mou*]) [62a]. This unique relationship is also revealed by his familiar form of addressing God in prayer as *pater* (11,41; 12,27.28; 17,1.5.11.21.24.25), which probably stands for the original Aramaic *Abba* (Mk 14,36) [63].

The Father is frequently presented as the *Giver*, for He has given Jesus life (5,25) and glory (17,22.24), words (17,8) and works (5,36), power to give life

---

[60] It is not possible, within a short space, to examine all the passages which speak about the Father. For our purpose it is enough to outline the important motifs connected with God, the Father, as a complement to our study of "the Son" (of God).

[61] The meaning of *monogenês theos* at 1,18 can be best understood by translating it as the "only Son-God".

[61a] Note that 3,35; 10,17 and 17,23.24.27 occur in 1C', 2C' and 4C' respectively in the structure of Jn.

[62] SCHNACKENBURG, II, 174-77.

[62a] See n. 59 above.

[63] MLAKUZHYIL G., "*Abba*, the Christian *Mantra*", *The Clergy Monthly* 38 (1974) 391-97.

(17,2) and to pass judgement (5,22.27), and, in short, everything (3,35; 13,3; 17,7). While the believers are the Father's gift to Jesus (6,37.39; 10,29; 17,6.9.24; 18,9), Jesus himself is His best gift to humanity (3,16).

By receiving this gift of the Father in faith human beings become children of God (1,12-13) and thus the Father of Jesus, the divine Son, also becomes the Father of the believing disciples (cf. *ho patêr mou kai patêr hymôn* at 20,17). They thus become Jesus' brethren (cf. *hoi adelphoi mou* at 20,17) whom the Father loves (16,27; 17,23) just as He loves Jesus (17,23.26).

5.123z The sayings about "the Father" and "the Son" are so closely interrelated that one cannot speak of the Son without speaking of the Father and *vice versa*. The Johannine Father-Son passages underline "the loving unity of Father and Son, their common work, their communion in all things, their complete oneness in being"[63a].

5.124 *"The Son of Man" (ho Hyios tou Anthrôpou)*

Since the Christological title "the Son of Man" is closely associated with "the Son" in Jn[64], we shall rapidly examine it[65].

The title *ho hyios tou anthrôpou* occurs 13 times in our Gospel[66]. It is found once in the introduction (1,1-2,11) twice in "Jesus' Initial Signs and Encounters" (Jn 2-4), 6 times in "Jesus' Works, Signs and Discussions" (Jn 5-10), thrice in "the Climactic Sign and the Coming of Jesus' Hour" (Jn 11-12) and once in "Jesus' Farewell of the Hour" (Jn 13-17)[67].

We may note that the most frequent occurrences are found in parallel subsections, namely, twice in 1C (2,23-3,21), thrice each in 2C (6,1-71) and 3C' (11,55-12,50)[68]. In 12 out of the 13 times Jesus himself uses the expression *ho hyios tou anthrôpou*[69] Both connection and progression mark these "Son of Man" sayings as the Gospel develops, as we shall see below[70].

[63a] SCHNACKENBURG, II, 177.

[64] *Ibid.*, 185.

[65] Notice that the expression *ho hyios tou anthrôpou* contains the term *hyios* as in *ho hyios tou theou*. This is one of the reasons for its inclusion here.

[66] Pilate presents Jesus as *ho anthrôpos* to the Jews at 19,5, which has not been included. The Synoptic occurrences are: Mt = 30x; Mk = 14x; Lk = 26x.

[67] See the table below on the next page.

[68] See "the Schema of the Literary Structure".

[69] The only exception to this is found in 12,34 where the crowd takes up Jesus' saying about the lifting up of the Son of Man (cf. 12,23.32) and asks about his identity.

[70] Cf. F. J. MOLONEY, *The Johannine Son of Man* (Roma 1976), whose titles of the chapters indicate the interrelationship and development of the "Son of Man" sayings in Jn (cf. especially XI-XII):

THE PROMISE OF THE SON OF MAN: John 1,51.
THE UNIQUE REVEALER WHO MUST BE 'LIFTED UP': John 3,13-14.
THE SON OF MAN AS JUDGE: John 5,27.
THE SON OF MAN AS THE GIVER OF LIFE: John 6,27.53.62.
THE CROSS: THE REVELATION OF THE SON OF MAN AS 'EGO EIMI': John 8,28.
BELIEF IN THE SON OF MAN: John 9,35.
THE CROSS AND THE GLORIFICATION OF THE SON OF MAN: John 12,23.34.
NOW IS THE SON OF MAN GLORIFIED: John 13,31; 19,5.

Distribution of *(ho) Hyios tou Anthrôpou* in Jn

INTR. (1,1- 2,11)	BOOK OF JESUS' SIGNS (2,1-12,50)			BOOK OF JESUS' HOUR (11,1-20,29)		CONCL. (20, 30-31)	APPX. (21, 1-25)
	First Sect. (2,1- 4,54)	Second Sect. (5,1- 10,42)	Bridge Sect. (11,1- 12,50)	Fourth Sect. (13,1- 17,26)	Fifth Sect. (18,1- 20,29)		
1,51	3,13.14	5,27; 6,27.53.62; 8,28; 9,35	12,23. 34,34	13,31	—	—	—

In the introduction Jesus promises Nathanael a heavenly vision of "the angels of God ascending and descending upon the Son of Man" (1,51). This "emphasizes the Son of Man's close and continual contact with heaven, hinting at his origin and goal, admirably introducing the reader to the Johannine Son of Man, the unique revealer" [71].

Next we find Jesus manifesting himself as the heavenly Son of Man, the singular revealer (3,13), who must be "lifted up" (3,14) like Moses' bronze serpent in the desert (cf. Num 21,9); this image hints at Jesus' future revelatory and salvific crucifixion. Moloney describes the link between 1,51 and 3,13-14: "What has been promised by the first use of the title in 1,51 - the future revelation of God in the Son of Man - has now been further specified: the Son of Man is the unique revealer and his revelation will save all those who believe in him" [72]. Furthermore, it must be noted that both the passages speak of an "ascending" (*anabainein*) and "descending" (*katabainein*) movement but in 3,13-14 the movement is attributed to the Son of Man rather than to the angels (cf. 1,51). This means that the saving revelation takes place through the *hypsôsis* of the Son of Man.

Jesus talks about the "lifting up" of the Son of Man not only at 3,14 but also at 8,28 and 12,34 (cf. also 12,32-33). These may be called the Johannine passion predictions, since they are similar to the Synoptic ones (cf. Mk 8,31; 9,31; 10,33 and par.) [73]. While 3,14 and 12,34, which are part of parallel subsections (1C and 3C') [74], seem to stress the divine necessity of being lifted up

---

[71] *Ibid.*, 41.

[72] *Ibid.*, 67. It may be also observed that some of the words used in 3,13 are the same as those in 1,51 (e.g. *ouranos, anabainein, katabainein, ho hyios tou anthrôpou*), although the subjects of the verbs of "ascending" and "descending" are different in the two verses.

[73] *Ibid.*, 136. It is remarkable that one of these three predictions of the Son of Man is found in each of the three sections (Jn 2-4; 5-10; 11-12) of the Book of Jesus' Signs.

[74] See "the Schema of the Literary Structure".

(cf. *dei* followed by the aor. inf. passive *hypsothênai* in the two verses), 8,28 hints at the human instrumentality in lifting up the Son of Man (cf. *hypsôsête*). The *hypsôsis* of the Son of Man is presented in 3,13-15 as the necessary condition for the believer to have eternal life, and in 8,28 as the moment when (*hotan... tote*) Jesus, the Son of Man, will be known as *egô eimi*, the divine being in union with the Father whom he reveals. His being lifted up on the cross will enable him to draw all men to himself (12,32).

At 5,27 Jesus reveals himself as the "Son of Man" to whom the Father has given the power to be the "judge of those who repudiate the revelation"[75]. But to those who receive his revelation in faith, Jesus, the Son of Man, gives a "food which endures to eternal life" (6,27). In fact, eating his flesh and drinking his blood are the conditions for having eternal life (6,53). It is interesting to observe that there is some verbal similarity between 3,13 and 6,62 (both the verses mention the Son of Man's ascending [*anabainein*]). There is also a similarity between 3,14-15 and 6,53-54 (since "eternal life" becomes a reality [3,15; 6,54] for any one who believes in the Son of Man [3,35] and who eats his flesh and drinks his blood [6,54])[76].

Christ's question to the cured blind man: "Do you believe in the Son of Man?" (9,35) occurs at the critical moment when the cured one is expelled from the synagogue for having defended Jesus as a "prophet" (9,17) "from God" (9,33) and as the Christ (implied in 9,22.34). His expulsion from the synagogue (9,22) and his believing and adoring response (9,38) reflect a post-Paschal situation, namely, the period after the "lifting up" of the Son of Man (8,28)[77].

Finally, in two parallel passages Jesus speaks of the "glorification of the Son of Man" (12,23; 13,31)[78]. The mention of "the hour" (*hê hôra*) at 12,23.27 makes it clear that "the lifting up from the earth" spoken of at 12,32 is an allusion to the crucifixion of the Son of Man (12,33). That this is part of Jesus' glorification is a mystery which the crowd fails to comprehend (12,34). Jesus reveals to the disciples that it is in and through the glorification of the Son of Man that God the Father is going to be glorified (13,31; cf.12,23.28).

---

[75] W. H. CADMAN and G. B. CAIRD, *The Open Heaven. The Revelation of God in the Johannine Sayings of Jesus* (Oxford 1969) 34.

[76] We have seen in the last chapter that 2,23-3,21 and 6,1-71 are parallel to each other (1C and 2C) in the successive sections (Jn 2-4; 5-10).

[77] Notice that *hotan hypsôsête* (aor. subj.) at 8,28 implies that the "lifting up of the Son of Man" must precede the knowledge of him as *ego eimi*. It is also worthy of note that the immediate context of both the Son of Man sayings at 8,28 and 9,35 speaks of revelation (*lalein*: 8,26.26.28; 9,37) and judgement (*krinein*: 8,26; *krima*: 9,39). This confirms our conclusion in the preceding chapter that the two episodes (Jn 7-8 and Jn 9) are parallel to each other (see 4.322,1).

[78] F. J. MOLONEY, *op. cit.*, 201. Jn 12,23 and 13,31 are the only two passages which speak about the "glorification" of "the Son of Man". It is remarkable that they occur in the "bridge-section" (Jn 11-12) and in the "bridge-verses" (13,31-38) between 13,1-30 and 14,1-31 (see 4.23 and 4.341).

5.124z Although the Christological title "the Son of Man" occurs only 13 times in the Fourth Gospel, it is an important one, since it is employed at the end of the "testimonial-kerygmatic introduction" (1,51) and at significant places in the body of the Gospel, namely, in the central discourse of Jesus in 1C (3,13.14) of the first section (Jn 2-4), in the first four subsections 2B (5,27), 2C (6,27.53.62), 2D (8,28), 2D' (9,35) of the second section (Jn 5-10), and in the bridge-passages (12,23.34.34; 13,31).

Summing up our short study of the Son of Man sayings, we can say that the Johannine "Son of Man" stands for Jesus as a human being with a mysterious heavenly origin (3,13; 6,62) who has come down from heaven both to reveal God by going up to Him (3,13; cf. also 1,51) and to give life (6,27.53; cf. also 3,14-15) to those who believe in him (3,15; 9,35) (and judgement to those who refuse to believe: 5,27; 9,39). In order to go up to God Jesus must be "lifted up" on the cross (3,14; 8,28; 12,34) and be "glorified" (12,23; 13,31)[79].

5.12z Comparing the titles "the Son of God", "the Son" and "the Son of Man" in the Johannine Gospel, we find that all of them refer to Jesus, but they often differ in the aspects they underline[80]. While *ho hyios tou theou* may sometimes be used as a Jewish Messianic title for Jesus (e.g. 1,49; 11,27) or (in the deeper theological sense) as a Christian designation of Jesus as the true divine Son (e.g. 19,7; 20,31), the absolute *ho hyios* in relation to *ho patêr* always refers to Jesus' divine Sonship (e.g. 3,17; 5,19-30; 14,13; 17,1), whereas *ho hyios tou anthrôpou* points to the human Jesus[81]. This is clear from the fact that though both "the Son (of God)" and "the Son of Man" are said to be "glorified" (11,4; 17,1 and 12,23; 13,31 respectively), the former is never spoken of as "being lifted up" as is the latter (3,14; 8,28; 12,34)[82]. Again, though both the titles are used to refer to Jesus as the unique revealer of God, the title "the Son of Man" suggests the incarnation (3,13), whereas "the Son (of God)" points to the unique union and communion with the Father (5,19-26) as the reason for Jesus' being the divine revealer[83]. But because "the Son of Man" has a

---

[79] F. J. MOLONEY concludes his study as follows: "The Johannine Son of Man is the human Jesus, the incarnate Logos; he has come to reveal God with a unique and ultimate authority and in the acceptance or refusal of this revelation the world judges itself" (*ibid.*, 220; cf. also 214-219 for a comparison between the Johannine and the Synoptic Son of Man).

The humanity of Jesus is highlighted also by the frequent Johannine use of *(ho) anthrôpos* to designate Jesus (4,29; 5,12; 7,46; 8,40; 9,11.16.24; 10,33; 11,47.50; 18,14.17.29; 19,5).

[80] *Ibid.*, 211-13.

[81] "There is a concentration on the human figure of Jesus in the use of the title "the Son of Man". It is a title which is entirely dependent upon the incarnation. The Son of Man reveals the truth to men because he is man - because of the incarnation... The Son of Man revealed God to men and brought judgement to men through his presence, as a man, among them. The high point of this revelation and judgement took place on the cross... There is a very important distinction between this idea and John's use of "the Son (of God)". The latter speaks of the basis of Jesus' existence and purpose - his union with the Father before, during and after the incarnation" (*Ibid.*, 213).

[82] *Ibid.*, 212.

[83] *Ibid.*

mysterious heavenly origin (3,13; 6,62), this Christological title may be considered a theological bridge between the Messianic title "the Christ" and the divine title "the Son" (of God).

5.13 "Signs" and "Works" [84]

Since the miracles of Jesus are sometimes called "signs" (e.g. 2,11; 4,54; 6,14; 9,16) and at other times "works" (e.g. 7,21; 9,4), we have to examine both the terms, although only the first is found explicitly in the conclusion of the Fourth Gospel (20,30-31).

The Johannine terms *sêmeion* and *ergon* occur 17 and 27 times respectively in Jn [85]. We shall first study them separately, and then compare them in order to note the similarities and differences.

5.131 "Sign" (Sêmeion)

It must be observed at the outset that 16 out of the 17 occurrences of the term *sêmeion* in Jn refer explicitly to Jesus' signs. (The only exception is 10,41 where it is said: "John [the Baptist] did no sign", a phrase which in its context implies that Jesus did.)

The importance of *sêmeion* is seen not only from the number of times the term is found but also from the role it has in key places in the plan of the Gospel. Thus in the final conclusion Jesus' life is described in terms of the "many signs" that he did (20,30). A similar conclusion which mentions Jesus' "many signs" is found at the end of his public ministry (12,37). In the introduction of the Gospel Jesus' first miracle of changing water into wine is called the "beginning of the signs" (*archê tôn sêmeiôn*: 2,11). This may be thought of as forming inclusions with the "many signs" (*sêmeia*) mentioned in the conclusions (12,37; 20,30) [86]. Besides, many of the major miracles in the Gospel are designated as "signs" (e.g. the healing of the royal official's son: 4,54; the multiplication of the loaves: 6,14; the curing of the man born blind: 9,16; the raising of Lazarus: 11,47; 12,18) [87]. Furthermore, many of the main characters

---

[84] Cf. BROWN, I, 525-32; R. H. RENGSTORF, *Sêmeion*, in : *TDNT*, VII, 243-57; SCHNACKENBURG, I, 515-27. (Cf. also the bibliography given by BROWN, I, 531-32).

[85] They are found less often in the Synoptic Gospels: *sêmeion*: Mt = 13; Mk = 7; Lk = 11; *ergon*: Mt = 6; Mk = 2; Lk = 2. We may also mention the frequency of the related verbs *sêmainein* (Mt = 0; Mk = 0; Lk = 0; Jn = 3) and *ergazesthai* (Mt = 4; Mk = 1; Lk = 1; Jn = 8).

It is possible that the final redactor responsible for the addition of Jn 21 added the parenthetical verses 12,33 and 18,32 in which the stereotype expression *sêmainôn poiô[i] thanatô emellen apothnê[i]skein* appears, since *sêmainôn poiô[i] thanatô[i]* is found also in 21,19 (though the first two references are to Jesus' death, while the last one is to Peter's).

[86] We have seen in the last chapter that the "historical sign-introduction" (A+ = 2,1-11) corresponds to the "historical sign-conclusion" (Az = 20,30) (see "the Schema of the Literary Structure").

[87] It is interesting to recall the structural location of these signs. The two Cana-signs (2,1-11; 4,46-54) occur in the first and the last subsections which are parallel to each other (1A and 1A') in

in the Johannine drama talk about the "signs" (Jesus: 4,48; 6,26; the Jews: 2,18; Nicodemus: 3,2; the crowd: 6,30; 7,31; 10,41; the Pharisees: 9,16; the high priests and the Pharisees: 11,47). The Evangelist himself speaks about the "signs" in his summaries, comments and conclusions (2,11.23; 4,54; 6,2.14; 12,18.37; 20,30). These references show the importance he attached to the "signs" in his Gospel. In fact, the theme of "signs" runs through the Gospel (and especially in the first part: Jn 2-12) like a leading thread[88]. This can be seen from the chart on the next page.

It is interesting to note that, although the term "sign" occurs in the first three sections (Jn 2-4; 5-10; 11-12) and in many of their subsections (1A, 1B, 1C, 1A', 2C, 2D, 2D', 2B'; 3C, 3C'), the four "signs" that are described are placed in parallel subsections (1A and 1A'; 2C and 3C). It is also remarkable that the two Cana-signs in 1A (2,1-11) and 1A' (4,46-54) do not contain any discourse which explains their significance, whereas the sign of feeding the five thousand in 2C (6,1-15) is followed by the bread-of-life discourse (6,22-59) and the sign of raising Lazarus to life in 3C (11,43-44) is preceded by the dialogue-discourse on Jesus, the resurrection and the life (11,1-42).

Concerning the meaning of the term *sêmeion* it must be remarked at the outset that rather than a univocal sense it has many aspects and levels of meaning[89].

To begin with, a "sign" may be (mis)taken merely as a miracle. This is what Jesus complains about when he says: "Unless you see signs and wonders, you will not believe" (4,48)[90]. This is the lowest level of understanding the signs of Jesus which is reached by the crowds in Jerusalem and Galilee as well as by the high priests and the Pharisees, for many of them see him merely as a won-

---

the chiastic structure of Jn 2-4 (1A B C C' B'A'). The feeding of the five thousand (6,1-71) and the raising of Lazarus (11,1-54) are found in parallel passages of Jn 5-10 and Jn 11-12, namely, in 2C and 3C respectively (see "the Schema of the Literary Structure").

[88] In the words of D. MOLLAT: "La notion de *sêmeion* est profondément engagée dans la trame du quatrième évangile. Depuis l'*archê tôn sêmeiôn* qui, aux noces de Cana, donne naissance a la foi des disciples, on peut l'y suivre jusqu'à l'épilogue (xx, 30s.) *comme un fil conducteur*" ("Le sêmeion johannique", in: *Sacra Pagina*, Vol. II, ed. J. Coppens & A. Descamps & É. Massaux, [Paris 1959] 209).

Similarly, according to BARRETT, "the stress on signs done by Jesus and beheld by his disciples is important and illustrates the structure and method of the gospel as a whole" (575).

[89] This is true of most of the important Johannine themes. In the words of W. GROSSOUW:

Ces termes semblent dotés d'une sorte d'élasticité, rendant possibles des glissements de pensée. On se ferait illusion si on voulait fixer leur sens à l'aide d'un ou deux textes. L'interprétation serait à tout le moins unilatérale. L'évangéliste aime explorer toute l'échelle de leurs significations possibles et ne dévoiler leur richesses que progressivement" ("La glorification du Christ dans le quatrième évangile", in: *L'Evangile de Jean. Recherches bibliques* [Bruges 1958] 133, cited by MOLLAT, *art. cit.*, 210).

[90] The expression *sêmeia kai terata* is used in the OT (LXX) to denote extraordinary miraculous events especially those of the Exodus (e.g. Ex 7,3; 11,9; Deut 34,11; Wis 8,8). Since the Greek phrase meant for the non-Jews marvelous omens in times of crisis (so H. RENGSTORF, "Sêmeion", in: *TDNT*, VII), if the royal official in 4,46-54 was a Gentile, Jesus might have been challenging him to go beyond the superficial faith based on the miraculous occurrences.

5.1 MAJOR THEOLOGICAL THEMES AND THE LITERARY STRUCTURE

Distribution of *Sêmeion* and *Ergon/Ergazesthai* in Jn

Terms	INTR. (1,1-2,11)	BOOK OF JESUS' SIGNS (2,1-12,50)			BOOK OF JESUS' HOUR (11,1-20,29)		CONCL. (20, 30-31)	APPX. (21, 1-25)
		First Sect. (2,1-4,54)	Second Sect. (5,1-10,42)	Bridge Sect. (11,1-12,50)	Fourth Sect. (13,1-17,26)	Fifth Sect. (18,1-20,29)		
Sêmeion	2,11+	2,11. 18.23; 3,2; 4,48. 54	6,2.14.26.30; 7,31; 9,16; 10,41	11,47; 12,18.37	—	—	20,30	—
Ergon	—	(3,19. 20.21); 4,34	5,20.36.36; 6,(28).29; 7,3.(7).21; (8,39.41); 9,3.4; 10,25.32.32. 33.37.38	—	14,10.11. 12; 15,24; 17,4	—	—	—
Erga-zesthai	—	(3,21)	5,17.17; 6,27.(28).30; 9,4.(4)	—	—	—	—	—

der-worker (cf. 2,23; 6,2; 9,16; 11,47). By presenting different groups of people as (mis)understanding the meaning of the signs in all the three sections of the Book of Jesus' Signs, the Evangelist implicitly invites the reader to go deeper (cf. 4,48).

A "sign" may mean a miracle that authenticates one's mission from God[91]. Such a sign is demanded from Jesus by the Jewish authorities in 1B (2,18; cf. also 6,30), a request which shows their lack of faith; in 1C Nicodemus concludes from the "signs" done by Jesus that he must have "come from God" (3,2). Likewise in 2C and 3C the crowds in Galilee and Jerusalem get an inkling of the prophetic and Messianic mission of Jesus from the signs of the multiplication of the loaves (6,1-14) and of the raising of Lazarus (11,43-45; 12,18), for they acclaim him as the eschatological Moses-like prophet (6,14) and the expected Messianic king (12,13). That the "signs" served as credentials of Jesus' Messianic mission is suggested by the observation of the crowds in 2D: *ho Christos hotan elthê[i] mê pleiona sêmeia poiêsei hôn houtos epoiêsen?* (7,31)[92].

---

[91] In this sense the word *ôth* or *sêmeion* is often used in the OT, about which MOLLAT remarks: "Il désignera le signe qui confirme la parole, qui appuie le geste, qui authentique la mission d'un envoyé de Dieu" (*art. cit.*, 211). (Cf. Ex 3,12; 4,19).

[92] *Ibid.*, 211-12.

The Evangelist himself underlines the Messianic nature of the "signs" in the conclusion of the Gospel (20,30-31: "Now Jesus did many other signs... that you may believe that Jesus is the Christ..."). This assertion is supported by the thematic affinities between the "signs" in the Exodus and those in the Gospel of John, since many of the latter recall those of the former (e.g. the manna in the desert in Ex 16 and the multiplication of the loaves in Jn 6). Mollat's observation in this connection is worth citing:

> Ce caractère messianique des "signes" johanniques se révèle dans leur parenté avec ceux de l'Exode. Selon la pensée juive, l'âge messianique devait reproduire, en plus grandiose encore, les merveilles de l'épopée mosaïque. Or cette idée paraît avoir guidé saint Jean dans le choix de ses *sêmeia*. Plusieurs au moins reprennent ceux de l'Exode: signe de l'eau, signe de la manne, signe de la lumière, signe de la vie... [93].

In connection with the thematic affinity between the first signs of Moses in the Book of Exodus and those of Jesus in the Gospel of John we may mention that the first plague (the changing of water into blood: Ex 7,14-24) is somewhat similar to the first "sign" in Jn (the changing of water into wine: 2,1-11), since both deal with the changing of water into something else; the last plague (the death of the first-born of the Egyptians while the Israelite first-born were spared: Ex 11,1-12,32) has some similarity with the last "sign" in the first section of the Fourth Gospel (Jn 2-4) (the saving of the royal official's son from death: 4,46-54), since both deal with the themes of death and life. (It may be objected that while Ex 7-12 describe ten plagues, Jn 2-4 narrate only two signs. This remark is true [since John had to select some signs: cf. 20,30], but note that other signs are mentioned [2,23; 3,2; 4,45], yet not described, between the two Cana-signs in 1A and 1A' which begin and end the chiastic structure [1A B C C' B' A'] of Jn 2-4.) The scope of the Exodus-plagues and the Johannine signs is also somewhat similar, namely, the manifestation of God as the Lord (cf. Ex 7,5) and of Jesus as the Messiah (cf. Jn 20,30-31) respectively [94]. This thematic relationship between the Johannine "signs" and the "signs" of the Exodus is confirmed by some literary characteristics common to both [95]. For example, compare the following passages:

---

[93] *Ibid.*, 214. Cf. also G. ZIENER, "Weisheitsbuch und Johannesevangelium", *Bib* 38 (1957) 396-418; 39 (1958) 37-60; "Johannesevangelium und urchristliche Passafeier", *BZ*, NF, 2 (1958) 263-74. According to Ziener the choice and order of the Johannine signs are patterned on those of the Exodus as narrated in the Book of Wisdom.

[94] "Quelle est la portée du signe dans Jean?", asks H. VAN DEN BUSSCHE. And he answers:
> La désignation tient son origine de l'Ancien Testament et vise surtout *les prodiges de l'Exode*. Par leur réapparition à l'époque du Christ, les signes annoncent les temps messianiques et révèlent *la fonction messianique* de celui qui les fait. ("La structure de Jean I-XII", in: *L'Evangile de Jean. Etudes et Problèmes* [Recherches Bibliques III] [Desclée De Brouwer 1958] 80 [my italics].

After surveying all the Johannine "signs" H. VAN DEN BUSSCHE concludes: "Nous pouvons donc admettre que *les signes* dans le quatrième évangile *désignent Jésus comme Messie*" (*ibid.*, 82) [my italics].
Cf. also L. CERFAUX, "Les miracles, signes messianiques de Jésus et oeuvres de Dieu selon l'Evangile de saint Jean", in: *L'Attente du Messie* (Recherches Bibliques I) 131-38.

[95] D. MOLLAT, *art. cit.*, 214-15.

Ex 11,10 : **epoiêsan** panta ta **sêmeia** kai ta terata tauta en gê[i] Aigyptô[i] *enantion Pharaô* (cf. also Ex 7,3; 10,1-2).

Jn 12,37 : tosauta de autou **sêmeia pepoiêkotos** *emprosthen autôn* o u k e p i s t e u o n eis auton.

Num 14,11: heôs tinos o u p i s t e u o u s i moi epi pasi tois **sêmeiois**, hois **epoiêsa** *en autois*?

One of the most important aspects of the Johannine "signs" is their symbolical and soteriological significance[96]. They symbolically reveal the supernatural reality that Christ has come to communicate to humanity. Thus the changing of water into wine in 1A (2,1-11) symbolically represents his new revelation (2,10: "you have kept *the good wine* until now"); the healing of the official's son in 1A' (4,46-54) highlights the life-giving power of his revelatory word (4,50.53); the multiplication of the loaves in 2C (6,1-15) symbolizes Jesus, the bread of life (6,35.48); the raising of Lazarus from the dead in 3C (11,1-44) reveals Jesus as the resurrection and the life (11,25)[97].

5.131z Thus we see that the word "sign" is an important term with many shades of meaning. "Signs" may mean merely miraculous actions, or miracles which authenticate the prophetic or Messianic mission of Jesus, or miracles which symbolize his gift of eternal life and therefore reveal him as the giver of life. By integrating all these elements we may describe the Johannine "signs" as miracles which manifest the Messianic mission of Jesus, symbolize his gift of eternal life and thus reveal his soteriological significance[98]. Some of these aspects are highlighted by the parallel positions occupied by the four signs in the structure of the sections of the Book of Jesus' Signs (namely, 1A // 1A'; 2C // 3C). There is also a deepening of the meaning of the signs when we move from 1A and 1A' to 2C and 3C, which reveal more clearly Jesus' gift of life to those who believe in him (cf. 6,35.48-51; 11,25-26; cf. also 20,30-31).

Jesus' "signs" can be understood as soteriological symbols of eternal life only after seeing them as "works". Hence we must examine the terms *ergon/erga/ergazesthai* in Jn.

---

[96] "In John" says BROWN, "the primary function of the miracles seems to be one of symbolism..." (I, 526). SCHNACKENBURG states quite emphatically that "the Christological significance proves to be the most important element of the Johannine "signs", the most characteristic of their properties and the heart of their theology" (I, 525).

[97] D. MOLLAT, *art. cit.*, 212.

[98] According to this descriptive definition of "signs", Jesus' non-miraculous actions like the cleansing of the temple (2,13-17) are not included, since the Evangelist does not call them "signs". It is true that Jesus' cleansing of the temple is somewhat similar to some of the OT prophetic signs (e.g. Jeremiah's breaking of an earthen flask: Jer 19,1-11 or his carrying a yoke on his neck: 27,2) but the Jews do not seem to have taken it for a "sign", since they demand a "sign" from Jesus in 2,18 (so BROWN, I, 528, while others like H. VAN DEN BUSSCHE understand it as a Messianic sign [*art. cit.*, 80-1]). Jesus himself seems to take it more as a "work" (*ergon*) which reveals his divine Sonship (see 5.13 above) than as a "sign", since he refers to his Father's house (2,16: *mê poieite ton oikon tou patros mou oikon emporiou*), which implies that he is the Father's Son.

5.132 *"Work"/"works"/"to work"* (*ergon/erga/ergazesthai*) [99]

The noun *ergon* is found in the singular 6 times and in the plural 21 times in Jn; the related verb *ergazesthai* occurs 8 times [100]. It is most remarkable that almost always these terms are found on the lips of Jesus [101]. It is also noteworthy that 17 times Jesus is said to be the one who does the work(s), and God the Father is associated with the work(s) 15 times [102]. Men are mentioned to be doers of works 8 times [103].

If we leave aside the Johannine text 3,19-21 which speaks about the works of men, we find that all the "Christological" *erga*-passages (in which Jesus speaks about his "works") are enclosed between his two *ergon*-sayings in 4,34 and 17,4, the only two verses in which he describes the entire work of his earthly life as "*the work*" (*to ergon*) [104]. During his ministry Jesus is so inseparably united with the Father that he can say: "My food is to do the will of him who sent me and to accomplish his work" (4,34) [105]. When "the hour" of his death-resurrection arrives (17,1), Jesus can truly affirm that he has accomplished the work which the Father gave him to do (17,4) [106]. This life-work, which is brought to its final completion and perfect fulfilment in his death-resurrection, is gradually realized in his individual "works" (*erga*) and "working" (*ergazesthai*) [107].

---

[99] Cf. J. RIEDL, *Das Heilswerk Jesu nach Johannes* (Freiburg 1973); A. VANHOYE, "L'oeuvre du Christ, don du Père (Jn 5,36 et 17,4)", *RechSR* 47 (1960) 377-419.

[100] *Ergon*: 4,34; 6,29; 7,21; 10,32.33; 17,4. *Erga*: 3,19.20.21; 5,20.36.36; 6,28; 7,3.7; 8,39.41; 9,3.4; 10,25.32.37.38; 14,10.11.12; 15,24. *Ergazesthai*: 3,21; 5,17.17; 6,27.28.30; 9,4.4.

[101] The only exceptions are 6,28.30; 10,33. At 6,28 and 10,33 the crowd/Jews take up what Jesus has said in the immediately preceding verses (6,27 and 10,32).

[102] *Jesus*: 4,34; 5,17.36.36; 6,30; 7,3.21; 9,4; 10,25.32.32.33.37.38; 14,12; 15,24; 17,4. *God (the Father)*: 4,34; 5,17.20.36; 6,28.29; 9,3.4; 10,25.32.37.38; 14,10.11; 17,4.

[103] Jn 3,19.20.21; 6,28; 7,7; 8,39.41; 9,4.

[104] J. RIEDL, *op. cit.*, 43: "Wie schon wiederholt festgestellt wurde, finden sich alle "christologischen" *erga*-Stellen zwischen den zwei Rahmenversen Joh 4,34 und Joh 17,4. In zusammenfassender Einzahl bezeichnet dort Jesus selbst sein ganzes irdisches Wirken als *to ergon*, als *das* Werk schlechthin." Cf. also *ibid.*, 43-186.

[105] *Ibid.*, 44-68 and especially 63:

> Jesus steht also nicht nur unter dem gebietenden Willen des ihn sendenden Vaters. Er ist auch mit dem Wirken dieses Sendenden aufs innigste verbunden, so dass sein Werk also Gottes Werk entsteht. Das Werk ist also dann das Werk beides, des sendenden Vaters und des gesandten Sohnes. Gottes Wirken in und durch Jesus und die Jesus aufgetragene Wirksamkeit sind also eins... Da das Tun des Vaterwillens und das Vollenden des Werkes "Speise" Jesu ist, lebt Jesus durch das Tun des Vatervillens."

In the words of A. SCHLATTER: "Dieses Einssein mit dem göttlichen Willen, das ihn dem göttlichen Willen dienstbar macht, ist der Grund seines Lebens und der Quell seiner Kraft" (*Der Evangelist Johannes, wie er spricht, denkt und glaubt. Ein Kommentar zum 4. Evangelium*, 2 ed. [Stuttgart 1948] 130, quoted by J. RIEDL, *op. cit.*, 63).

[106] J. RIEDL, *op. cit.*, 69-182.

[107] J. RIEDL remarks: "Dieses Werk [Jesu] ist zwar keine einmalige Tat, sondern eine Serie von Wort- und Tat-Werken, gipfelt aber in einer einzigen Tat, im Sterben Jesu" (*ibid.*, 187; cf. also 244-45). Similarly, SCHNACKENBURG says: "The individual works form an integral part of the total work of revelation and salvation which Jesus has to accomplish on earth (*to ergon* 4:34; 17,4)" (II, 123).

If we examine the "Christological" *erga*-passages, we find that there is a concentration of the "work"-vocabulary in certain pericopes[108]. The most striking examples are 5,14-47 (*erga*: vv.20.36.36; *ergazesthai*: v.17.17) and 10,22-42 (*erga/on*: vv.25.32.32.33.37.38), which are parallel (2B and 2B') subsections (the first and the last) of the chiastic structure (2B C D D'C' B') of the section of "Jesus' Works, Signs and Discussions" (Jn 5-10)[109]. After curing the cripple at the pool of Bethzatha on a Sabbath (5,1-9), Jesus defends his action before the Jews (who persecute him) by declaring: "My Father is working still, and I am working" (5,17). "In claiming the right to work [on the Sabbath] even as his Father worked, Jesus was claiming a divine prerogative"[110]. To the Jews who accuse him of making himself equal to God by calling Him his Father (5,18) Jesus explains his divine Sonship in terms of his complete unity in action and being with the Father (5,19-30) which is manifested by his doing the works which the Father has given him to accomplish (5,36). This double theme of divine works and divine Sonship is taken up again and highlighted during the feast of the Dedication in Jerusalem (10,22-42), for Jesus tells the Jews: "The works that I do in my Father's name, they bear witness to me" (10,25). When they take up stones to stone him (10,31), he asks: "I have shown you many good works from the Father; for which of these do you stone me?" (10,32). When they accuse him of blasphemy, he defends his divine Sonship by declaring that he does the works of the Father: "If I am not doing the works of my Father, then do not believe me [that 'I am the Son of God': cf. 10,36]; but if I do them, even though you do not believe me, believe the works, that you may know and understand that the Father is in me and I am in the Father" (10,37-38). In short, the "works" that Jesus does bear witness both to his divine Sonship and to the mutual immanence of Jesus and the Father. The role of "works" in revealing the unity and mutual indwelling of Jesus and the Father is discussed again during the Farewell Discourse (14,10-11). We may conclude, therefore, that the "works" which Jesus does reveal that he is the Son of God and not a second God independent of Yahweh; it is precisely as the Son who depends totally on the Father (5,19), whom the latter loves and to whom He reveals everything that He does (5,20), that Jesus carries out the works of the Father (10,37)[111]. The unity of Jesus and the Father is so complete that Jesus can also say: "the Father who dwells in me does his works" (14,10).

---

[108] See the "Distribution of *Sêmeion* and *Ergon/Ergazesthai* in Jn".
[109] See "the Schema of the Literary Structure".
[110] BROWN, I, 217.
[111] The evidence for Jesus' divine Sonship is his doing the "works" of his Father. This is the case with all true children. Thus Jesus tells the Jews who claim to have Abraham as their father: "If you were children of Abraham, you would do the works of Abraham" (8,39). Jesus accuses those who seek to kill him to be the children of their father, the devil (8,44), since they do his murderous works (8,41) and desires (8,44). Thus the "works" one does show the true origin and nature of one's sonship, just as the fruits produced by the branch of a tree reveal unmistakably the type of tree to which the branch belongs. This does not mean, however, that the "works" of Jesus necessarily led men to believe in his divine Sonship. In fact, the unbelieving brothers of Jesus seem to have seen nothing in his "works" apart from their sensational aspect as marvels (cf. 7,3).

Some of the "works" of Jesus are clearly miraculous. For instance, Jesus refers to his healing the paralytic (5,1-9) as a "work" that he did (*hen ergon epoiêsa*: 7,21); Jesus' unbelieving brothers refer to his miracles as "the works you are doing" (7,3); again Jesus tells the disciples before healing the blind man: "we must do the works of him who sent me" (9,4). Other "works", however, do not seem to be miracles. For example, during the Farewell Discourse Jesus tells the disciples: "Truly, truly, I say to you, he who believes in me will also do the works that I do; and greater works than these will he do, because I go to the Father" (14,12). This does not mean that the disciples will work miracles more marvelous than those done by Jesus, but that in the post-Easter period they will bring to humanity a share in Jesus' life, or judgement (cf. 5,20)[112].

5.132z Keeping in mind the different elements we have discussed above, we may describe the "works" (*erga*) of Jesus as the deeds which disclose both his divine Sonship and his unity of being and action with the Father[113]. This is highlighted in Jn 5-10 and, in a special manner, in the first and last parallel elements (2B = Jn 5; 2B' = 10,22-42) of the chiastic structure of the section (2B C D D' C' B')[114].

5.133 *Comparison between "Signs" and "Works"*

While *sêmeia* and *erga* are both employed for miracles, the term *erga* seems to be wider in application than *sêmeia*, since the former includes also non-miraculous "works" (cf. 14,12), whereas the latter (*sêmeia*) refers only to miracles[115]. Secondly, while both "signs" and "works" have an authenticating or revelatory function, the "signs" manifest Jesus as the Messiah (7,31), while the "works" reveal his divine Sonship and union with the Father (10,25.37-38)[116].

---

[112] According to Brown, "in John there is less emphasis on the marvellous character of the 'greater works' that the disciples will do: the 'greater' refers more to their eschatological character" (II, 633). Connecting the *meizona toutôn* of 14,12 with the *meizona toutôn* of 5,20 Schnackenburg concludes: "The disciples will go further than Jesus by giving his 'greater works' - raising to life and judgement - an even greater effect, since Jesus goes to the Father and continues to act through the disciples. It is not until after his glorification that he is able to reap the full fruit of his life and death (see 12:24,32; 17:2)" (III, 71-72). Cf. also J. Riedl, *op. cit.*, 284-90 and especially 288-89.

[113] Cf. H. van den Bussche, *art. cit.*, 81. Cf. also n. 111 above.

[114] See "the Schema of the Literary Structure".

[115] The verb *sêmainein* is used thrice to refer to a prophetic statement by Jesus about his own death (12,33; 18,32) or that of Peter (21,19), and because of this some scholars are tempted to include "words" in the Johannine concept of "signs". For instance, Brown says: "even words may be signs, e.g. in xii 33 (xviii 32) and xxi 19 there is a statement which serves as a sign (*sêmainein*) of how Jesus or Peter is to die" (I, 528). Yet it is doubtful whether the Evangelist himself employed the verb *sêmainein* with the meaning "to serve as a sign" as Brown understands it, since "words" are never called "signs". Cf. n. 85 above for the suggestion that the parenthetical sentences with *sêmainein* at 12,33; 18,32; 21,19 may be additions by a redactor.

[116] H. van den Bussche says concerning the significance of the "signs" in Jn: "les *signes* annoncent les temps messianiques et révèlent *la fonction messianique* de celui qui les fait" (*art. cit.*, 80) [my italics]. Comparing "signs" and "works" he affirms: "Les signes, garants de la mission divine du Messie, établissent *en tant qu'oeuvres l'unité de l'action et d'existence entre Dieu et son Fils*" (*ibid.*, 81) [my italics].

There is also a difference in the use of the singular forms *sēmeion* and *ergon*. While both can be used to denote an individual miracle (e.g. *sēmeion*: 4,54; *ergon*: 7,21), *to ergon*, unlike *sēmeion*, is employed to designate Jesus' entire ministry or life-work (4,34; 17,4)[117]. This shows that the idea of "work" is wider than that of "sign", and in a sense the former contains the latter, in as much as the "signs" form part of the total "work" of Christ.

It is also clear from Jn 9 that the same miracle may be seen as either a "work" or a "sign" by different people. Thus Jesus understands and wants his disciples to understand his giving of sight to the man born blind as a "work" of God (9,3-4), while some of the Pharisees see it only as one of the miraculous "signs" (9,16).

It may be also remarked that the deeper meaning of Jesus' "signs" (as soteriological symbols of eternal life) can be understood only when they are seen not only as Messianic miracles (e.g. 2,11; 4,54; 6,14; 7,31) but also as the saving, life-giving "works" of the Son of God. For no mere human Messiah but only the divine Son has, like the Father, life in himself (5,26), and hence can give life to whom he will (5,21). The disciples understood the deeper symbolic significance of the "signs" only after Jesus' death-resurrection, since only after Easter did they come to believe in his divinity (cf. the confession of Thomas: "My Lord and my God": 20,28). Thus the disciples' understanding of the "signs" seems to have undergone a "Johannine somersault" as a result of the resurrection of Jesus and under the guidance of the Spirit of truth (16,13). The "signs" of the Messiah became the "works" of the Son of God, and the "works" again became the "signs" (soteriological symbols) of eternal life. We may therefore propose that the Evangelist has used the term "signs" in this deep theological sense in the conclusion of the Gospel (20,30-31), and this usage is an invitation to his readers to contemplate all the miracles of Jesus in this perspective of faith [118].

5.14 Disciples *(Mathētai)* [119]

The importance of *mathētēs* in Jn can be easily seen from the high frequency of its occurrence (78 times)[120]. There are only three other nouns (*Iēsous*, *patēr*, *theos*) in the Fourth Gospel which occur more often than *mathētēs* [121].

---

[117] BROWN, I, 528.

[118] Perhaps this would throw some new light on the much discussed problem of the content and meaning of "signs" in 20,30.

[119] Cf. R. MORENO, "El discípulo de Jesucristo, según el evangelio de S. Juan", *EstBib* 30 (1971) 269-311; H. RENGSTORF, *mathētēs*, *TDNT*, IV, 415-61; SCHNACKENBURG, III, 203-17; A. SCHULZ, *Nachfolgen und Nachahmen. Studien über das Verhältnis der neutestamentlichen Jüngerschaft zur urchristlichen Vorbildethik* (München 1962) 137-44; M. VELLANICKAL, "'Discipleship' according to the Gospel of John", *Jeevadhara* 10 (1980) 131-47.

[120] It is found less often in the Synoptic Gospels (Mt = 73; Mk = 46; Lk = 37) than in Jn. *Synmathētai* occurs only in Jn (11,16).

[121] *Iēsous*: 237; *patēr*: 137; *theos*: 83. (Note that we are speaking here about *nouns*. The following verbs, for instance, occur more than 83 times: *legein + eipein* = 470x; *einai* = 442x; *erchesthai* = 156x; *poiein* = 110x; *pisteuein* = 98x; *echein* = 86x; *oida* = 84x.)

It is also noteworthy that 74 out of the 78 times the term *mathêtês* refers to the disciples of Jesus. Four times, when it refers to the disciples either of John the Baptist (1,35.37; 3,25) or of Moses (9,28), the term is used in connection with some of them becoming Jesus' disciples (1,35.37) or being hesitant (3,25) or being opposed to doing so (9,28). This is a clear indication of the Evangelist's exclusive interest in the disciples of Jesus.

The importance of the "disciples" is also shown by their presence in all the sections [122] and at prominent places in the plan of the Fourth Gospel.

Distribution of *Mathêtês* in Jn

INTR. (1,1-2,11)	BOOK OF JESUS' SIGNS (2,1-12,50)			BOOK OF JESUS' HOUR (11,1-20,29)		CONCL. (20, 30-31)	APPX. (21, 1-25)
	First Sect. (2,1-4,54)	Second Sect. (5,1-10,42)	Bridge Sect. (11,1-12,50)	Fourth Sect. (31,1-17,26)	Fifth Sect. (18,1-20,29)		
1,35.37; 2,2+. 11+	2,2. 11.12. 17,22; 3,22. 25; 4,1.2. 8.27.	6,3.8.12.16. 22.22.24.60. 61.66; 7,3; 8,31; 9,2.27.28.28	11,7.8. 12.54; 12,4.16	13,5. 22.23. 35; 15,8; 16,17. 29	18,1.1.2. 15.15.16. 17.19.25; 19,26.27. 27.38; 20,2.3.4. 8.10.18. 19.20.25. 26	20,30	21,1.2. 4.7.8. 12.14. 20.23. 24

Notice that the disciples of Jesus are explicitly mentioned both in the "historical sign-introduction" A+ (2,1-11; cf. vv.2.11) and in the "historical sign-conclusion" Az (20,30), which therefore form an inclusion. The disciples are also spoken of in the "bridge-section" (Jn 11-12) [123]. Furthermore, there is an entire section in which Jesus is alone with his disciples (Jn 13-17) [124]. The last section (Jn 18-20) before the conclusion (20,30-31) begins and ends with pericopes in which the disciples play a prominent part and are frequently

---

[122] See the chart on the "Distribution of *Mathêtês* in Jn".

[123] See 3.19. Cf. *mathêtai* at 11,7.8.12.54; 12,4.16. We may recall here that 2,1-11 is a bridge-pericope and therefore the presence of *mathêtai* there (2,2.11) is all the more significant.

[124] Also the Appendix (Jn 21) exclusively deals with (the risen) Jesus and his disciples. It may also be noted that, besides 2,1-11 in which the disciples of Jesus as a group are mentioned for the first time, a part of the introduction (1,35-51) deals with the Messianic discovery of five individual disciples (Andrew, Simon Peter, Philip, Nathanael, and an anonymous disciple [probably the Beloved Disciple]) some of whom are mentioned also in the Appendix (Simon Peter, Nathanael and two unnamed disciples one of whom is probably the Beloved Disciple).

mentioned (18,1-14.12-27; 20,1-18.19-29)[125]. Similarly, the disciples have an important function in the initial and final pericopes of Jn 6 (vv.1-15.16-21. 60-66.67-71). Again, the words *mathētai* at the beginning and end of some pericopes form inclusions (e.g. 2,2.11 in 2,1-11; 21,1.14 in 21,1-14). Besides those mentioned above, there are some pericopes in which the presence of the disciples is explicitly stated at the beginning (e.g. 3,22 in 3,22-36; 9,2 in 9,1-41) or in the middle (e.g. 2,17 in 2,13-22; 12,16 in 12,12-19; 19,26.27 in 19,16c-42). Apart from the Farewell Discourses (Jn 13-17), there are some typically Johannine dialogues between Jesus and his disciples (4,31-38; 9,2-5; 11,7-16) which have no Synoptic counterparts[126]. Thus the disciples occupy prominent places in the overall plan and in many of the pericopes of the Fourth Gospel[127].

But when it comes to the question of the number and identity of the disciples involved in the different pericopes, it is often difficult to decide. It may be noted that *hoi mathētai autou* occurs 32 times and *hoi mathētai* is used absolutely 16 times to refer to the disciples [of Jesus][128]. While the first phrase is found in most chapters of Jn, the second occurs only in five chapters and, except for two occurrences (4,31.33), it is found only in Jn 11-21 (11,7.8.12.54; 13,5.22; 20,10.18.19.20; 21,1.4. 12.14). It is true that "it often stands for the disciples *already mentioned*"[129] (e.g. 4,31.33; 11,8.12; 20,10.20; 21,4.12) but one is surprised to see it especially at the beginning of a pericope (e.g. 11,7; 13,5; 20,19; 21,1). At times it may be used to denote the Twelve (e.g. 13,5.22)[130], but the fact that the Evangelist presents them as *hoi mathētai* rather as *hoi dōdeka* shows that "discipleship is the primary Christian category for John"[131], and

---

[125] Notice the numerous instances of "disciple(s)" in these pericopes (18,1.1.2.15.15.16.17. 19.25; 20,2.3.4.8.10.18.19.20.25.26).

[126] SCHNACKENBURG, III, 205-6.

[127] It may be also noted here that in a number of pericopes different individual disciples are mentioned by name (e.g. Andrew: 1,40.44; 6,8; 12,22; (Simon) Peter: 1,40.41.42; 6,8.68; 13,6.9.24.36; 18,10.15.25; 20,2.6; 21,2.3.7.11.15.16.17; Philip: 1,43.44.45.46.48; 6,5.7; 12,21.22; 14,8; Nathanael: 1,45.46.47.48.49; 21,2; Judas (Iscariot): 6,71; 12,4; 13,2.26.29; 18,2.3.5; Jude: 14,22; Thomas: 11,16; 14,5; 20,24.26.27.28; 21,2; Joseph of Arimathea: 19,38). The Beloved Disciple, however, is spoken of without mentioning his name in Jn 13-21 (13,23; 18,15.16; 19,26.26; 20,2.3.4.8; 21,7.20.23.24).

[128] *Hoi mathētai autou*: 2,2.11.12.17.22; 3,22; 4,2.8.27; 6,3.8.12.16.22.22.24.60.61.66; 9,2; 12,4.16; 13,23; 16,17.29; 18,1.1.2.19.25; 21,2. The reading of 20,30 is not certain (cf. *TCGNT* at 20,30).

Hoi mathētai: 4,31.33; 11,7.8.12.54; 13,5.22; 20,10.18.19.20; 21,1.4.12.18.

[129] BERNARD, I, 73. This is supported by the absolute *ho mathētēs* (singular) in 19,27 (twice) to refer to the Beloved Disciple mentioned in the previous verse.

[130] *Ibid.* One can reach this conclusion only by comparing the Johannine account of the Last Supper with the Synoptic one (Mt 26,20; Mk 14,17) where "the Twelve" are explicitly mentioned. According to BERNARD (*ibid.*) *hoi mathētai* at 20,19.20 refers to (the) "ten" of "the Twelve" but one cannot be certain that only members of "the Twelve" were present, when the risen Jesus appeared to "the disciples" (cf. Lk 24,33: "the eleven and those who were with them").

[131] R. E. BROWN, *The Community of the Beloved Disciple* (London 1979) 191, and "Other Sheep Not of This Fold", *JBL* 97 (1979) 17.

that even those who belong to the group of the Twelve are first and foremost "disciples" [132].

That there is a vagueness about the use of *mathêtai* in the Gospel is evident from the divergent conclusions of various Johannine scholars about the identity and the number of the "disciples" in the pericopes [133]. But the very vagueness seems to be intended for an internal reason, namely, "the concept [of "disciples"] has already been used, extended and applied to a new situation" [134], the situation of the Johannine community and of all the later believers, since the "disciples" in the Johannine Gospel represent not only "those who are made believers by Jesus through his word and his signs" but also "the later community in contrast to the unbelieving Jews" and "the later believers in that they are challenged and tempted and their faith is inadequate" [135]. In other words, in Jn the "disciples are firstly Jesus' close companions, secondly his serious adherents and finally all later believers" [136]. That the later believers are included in the *mathêtai* is especially clear in those passages in which Jesus himself talks about discipleship. Thus he tells the Jews in Jerusalem who believed in him: "If you remain in my word, you are truly my disciples" (8,31). Similarly, during the Farewell Discourse he tells his disciples: "By this all men will know that you are my disciples, if you have love for one another" (13,35), and again: "By this my Father is glorified, that you bear much fruit, and so prove to be my disciples" (15,8). Now it is clear that these sayings are applicable not only to Jesus' companions but also to all Christians, since faith, fraternal love and fruit-bearing are the requirements or characteristics of all true disciples or believers of all times. Because of this polyvalent or multilevel use of the "disciples", *mathêtai* in Jn may be said to be a link between the Synoptic understanding of *mathêtai* as companions of Jesus and the Acts' concept of *hoi mathêtai* as Christians [137].

---

[132] One must also remember that, unlike Mark, John does not give much prominence to "the Twelve", since *hoi dôdeka* is mentioned only four times (6,67.70.71; 20,24), that is, only in two episodes.

[133] For example, R. MORENO maintains that, after the defection of the disciples during the Galilean crisis (6,60-71), those disciples who accompanied Jesus in the later episodes were most probably only the Twelve, for he says: "A partir de este momento son ellos [*hoi dôdeka*], con toda probabilidad, los que acompañan a Jesús en los restantes episodios en que aparecen los "discípulos" (*mathêtai*): curación del ciego de nacimiento (9,2), estancia en Perea y resurrectión de Lázaro (11,7.8.12)" (*art. cit.*, 272).

Now compare this view with that of BERNARD according to whom *hoi mathêtai* at 11,7.8.12.54 "indicates only the disciples present on the occasion, whose number is not specified" (I, 74). Whether *hoi mathêtai* in Jn 11 refers, historically speaking, to "the Twelve" or not, the designation "the disciples" underscores the Johannine emphasis on discipleship.

[134] SCHNACKENBURG, III, 208.

[135] *Ibid.*, 206-7.

[136] *Ibid.*, 208.

[137] A. SCHULZ says: "Das vierte Evangelium weist nämlich in seinen verschiedenen Bestimmungen vom Wesen des *mathêtês* ein deutliches Kontinuum begrifflicher Entwicklung von dem ursprünglich rabbinisch-synoptischen Verständnis des Terminus zu der mit der Ag gemeinsamen Vorstellung des 'Jüngers' als Christenbezeichnung auf" (*op. cit.*, 137). Cf. also H. RENGSTORF, *art. cit.*, 457-59.

5.1 MAJOR THEOLOGICAL THEMES AND THE LITERARY STRUCTURE

The more frequent use of the absolute *hoi mathētai* in the Book of Jesus' Hour (Jn 11-20)[138] may be an indication of the superimposition of the later Christian believers (cf. *hoi mathētai* in Ac 6,1-21,16) on to the companions of Jesus (*hoi mathētai autou*). This seems to be confirmed by the use of *hoi mathētai* in Jn 21,1.14 where it refers to the group of seven disciples, who probably symbolize the Christian community[139].

Now it is not possible within a few paragraphs to develop in detail the meaning and characteristic features of "discipleship" in Jn. What we shall do is only mention some of the salient points that emerge from the study of the structure of the Gospel.

We have already observed the prominence given to the disciples in the introduction, where a bird's eye-view of their path of discovering Jesus, the Christ, the Son of God, is given[140].

The disciples' accompanying Jesus or their presence with him is often explicitly mentioned by the Evangelist (e.g. 1,39; 2,2.12; 3,22; 6,3; 9,2; 11,54; 13,5; 18,1-2) or is implied, since often the disciples' words, actions or reactions are mentioned during an episode, though their presence may not have been explicitly recorded at the beginning of the event (e.g. 2,17.22; 11,7; 12,16). During the last supper Jesus himself tells the disciples: "you have been with me from the beginning" (15,27)[141].

The disciples not only accompany Jesus but also take care of his needs like that of food (4,8.31), and help him in his ministry (4,2.38). This aspect, however, is not highlighted in Jn.

One of the fundamental traits of true discipleship is faith in Jesus (1,50; 6,69; 14,10-11; 16,30; 17,8) which involves a personal commitment to him (2,11; 14,1), a theme which we shall examine later[142]. But here we may mention an interesting insight derived from the structure of the Gospel, namely, all those who truly believe in Jesus, and not merely those who accompany him, are to be regarded as his authentic disciples. This is suggested by the following facts: 1) the royal official who believed Jesus' word (4,50) and whose faith was confirmed by the second Cana-sign (4,53-54) is placed parallel to the first disciples who were confirmed in their faith in Jesus (1,41.45.49.50) by the first Cana-sign (2,11), since the two Cana-signs (1A and 1A') are parallel to each other in the chiastic structure of Jn 2-4 (1A B C C' B'A')[143]; 2) the Samaritans who came to

---

[138] See ch. 4 for the division of the structure of Jn.

[139] This view seems to be supported by the images and figures used by the Johannine Jesus to refer simultaneously to the disciples and to the later Christian believers. Such symbolic images are 1) *ta probata* (10,1-18.26-30; 21,15-17), 2) *ta klēmata* (15,1-8), 3) *(hoi) philoi (mou)* (15,13-15) and 4) *hoi adelphoi (mou)* (20,17; 21,23).

[140] See 3.34. Cf. 5.212 for the stages in the disciples' Messianic discovery (based on the spiral structure of Jn 1,35-51).

[141] According to Mk 3,14 one of the reasons why Jesus chose the Twelve is "that they may be with him" (*hina ōsin met' autou*). This seems to be true of the "disciples" in Jn.

[142] See 5.15 below.

[143] See "the Schema of the Literary Structure".

believe in Jesus through a direct experience of him and confessed him as the Saviour of the world (4,42) in 1B' (4,1-42) are comparable to the first disciples who discovered Jesus' Messianic identity through a personal encounter with him and confessed their faith in him as the Messiah, the Son of God and the king of Israel (1,41.49), in B* (1,19-51)[144]; 3) Martha, who makes her confession of faith in Jesus (*egô pepisteuka hoti sy ei ho Christos ho hyios tou theou ho eis ton kosmon erchomenos*: 11,27) in spite of the death of her brother Lazarus whom Jesus could have prevented from dying (cf. 11,21), is placed in a structural position (3C = 11,1-54) parallel to that of Peter (in 2C = 6,1-71) who proclaims his faith in Jesus publicly (*hêmeis pepisteukamen kai egnôkamen hoti sy ei ho hagios tou theou*: 6,69) in spite of the desertion of many disciples (cf. 6,66); 4) Jesus' definition (in 2D = 7,1-8,59) of genuine disciples (*alêthôs mathêtai mou este*) as those who remain in his word and who will know the liberating truth (8,31-32) is verified in the case of the cured blind man (in 2D' = 9,1-41) who, acting on Jesus' word (to go and wash in the pool of Siloam: 9,7.11.15), was liberated not only from his physical blindness but also from spiritual darkness by becoming Jesus' disciple (*sy mathêtês ei ekeinou*: 9,28) and came to know the enlightening truth concerning who Jesus is (9,17.31.35-38).

One of the things repeatedly underlined in Jn is the disciples' difficulty in understanding the deeper significance of Jesus' words, deeds and identity during his life-time, that is, before his resurrection. Thus they are surprised to see Jesus talking with a (Samaritan) woman (4,27), and misunderstand his words both about the mysterious food he lives on (4,32-33) and about Lazarus' "sleep" and need to be awakened (11,11-13). Again, during the triumphal entry of Jesus into Jerusalem we are told: "His disciples did not understand this at first" (12,16). Even during the Last Supper they are slow to grasp the significance both of his symbolic actions like the washing of their feet (13,7) and of his words about "the way" (14,4-5) or about "a little while" (16,16-18). Even when they affirm that they understand his plain words and know for certain (*oidamen*) that his superhuman knowledge about all things demonstrates his origin from God (16,29-30), he tells them that their desertion of him would prove the shallowness of their claim (16,31-32).

This does not mean that the disciples did not come to know Jesus at all. For in 2C (6,1-71) Simon Peter speaks of the disciples' experiential knowledge of Jesus as "the holy one of God" (*egnôkamen hoti sy ei ho hagios tou theou*: 6,69). In the parallel passage 2C' (10,1-21) Jesus himself speaks of the mutual experiential knowledge of the good shepherd (Jesus) and the sheep (the disciples) (*ginôskô ta ema kai ginôskousi me ta ema:* 10,14), which is applicable not only to his disciples during his life-time but to Christian believers of all times. And in another parallel pericope 4C'(17,1-26) Jesus prays to the Father: "Now they know... (*nyn egnôkan...*) that I came from thee" (17,7-8) and "these have come to know (*egnôsan*) that it was you who sent me" (17,25).

---

[144] *Ibid.*

A better and deeper understanding of Jesus on the part of the disciples after his glorification is mentioned both by the Evangelist (2,22; 12,16) and by Jesus (13,7; 14,20). This is attributed to the guidance of the Holy Spirit, the Spirit of truth (14,26; 16,13-14), whom they would receive at Jesus' glorification (cf. 7,39; 19,30; 20,22).

Not only the disciples' faith in and knowledge of Jesus but also their love for him are spoken of in the Fourth Gospel. In fact, Jesus himself speaks of love in the two parallel farewell discourses 4D (13,31-14,31) and 4D' (16,4e-33)[145]. In the first he gives the disciples a criterion to judge whether they truly love him: "If you love me, you will keep my commandments" (14,15). Acquiescing to the least desire of the beloved is the sure sign of genuine love. This is the language only lovers can understand. This is so important that Jesus repeats it 4 times in just 10 verses (14,15-24). Notice the striking similarity among them:

14,15: **ean agapate me**, *tas entolas tas emas têrêsete*.
14,21: *ho echôn tas entolas mou kai têrôn autas* ekeinos estin
 ho agapôn me...
14,23: **ean tis agapa[i] me** *ton logon mou têrêsei*...
14,24: **ho mê agapôn me** *tous logous mou ou têrei*...

It is clear from the above observations that the disciples' love for Jesus is not manifested so much in sentimental feelings as in carrying out the desires he expressed in his "word(s)" or "commandments"[146], just as Jesus' love for the Father is revealed in his doing the will of the Father as expressed in His comandments (4,34; 14,31; 15,10).

The disciples who love Jesus in deeds, he assures them, will be loved by him and the Father *(ho de agapôn me agapêthêsetai hypo tou patros mou, kagô agapêsô auton*: 14,21; cf. 13,1.34; 15,9.11; *ean tis agapa[i] me... kai ho patêr mou agapêsei auton*: 14,23; cf. 17,23) and the proof of this divine love is that Jesus will manifest himself to them *(kai emphanizô autô[i] emauton*: 14,21) and he together with the Father will come and dwell with them *(kai pros auton eleusometha kai monên par' autô[i] poiêsometha*: 14,23).

In 16,27 Jesus tells the disciples that the Father himself loves them tenderly *(philei)* because they love Jesus affectionately as a friend *(pephilêkate)* as he loves them as his friends *(philoi*: 15,15; cf. 11,3: *philein* and 11,11: *philos*)[147].

---

[145] Note also that in 2D (7,1-8,59) Jesus denies the Jews' claim to have God as their Father since they do not love him who has come from God (8,41-42), whereas in 5D' (20,1-18) Jesus will refer to the disciples who love him (cf. 16,27) as his brothers who have his Father as their Father (20,17). In 6D (21,15-19) Jesus asks Peter thrice: "Do you love me?" (21,14.16.17).

[146] We shall see below that the most important commandment of Jesus to the disciples is that of mutual love (13,34-35; 15,12-17).

[147] *Pace* BERNARD (II, 702-4), BULTMANN (711, n. 5), BARRETT (584), BROWN (I, 497-99) who hold *agapan* and *philein* to be mere synonyms, the Johannine *philein* seems to stress the affectionate aspect of love (e.g. of the Father for the Son [5,20] or of a friend for his friend [11,3.11; 21,15.16.17])

Love of one another is to be the most distinguishing characteristic of Jesus' disciples: "By this will all men know that you are my disciples, if you have love for one another" (13,35). And this mutual fraternal love is to be patterned on the love Jesus has for them ("love one another as [*kathôs*] I have loved you": 13,34; 15,12) which is altruistic ("I have loved you that you also may love one another": 13,34). In other words, the reason why he has loved them is not that they may love him in return (Jesus never asks the disciples to love him) but that they may love one another [148]. This altruism is part of the newness of Jesus' commandment of love (*entolê kainê*). And the extent of this altruistic love is shown by laying down one's life for one's friends (*meizona tautês agapên oudeis echei hina tis tên psychên autou thê[i] hyper tôn philôn autou*: 15,13), as Jesus has done (cf. 11,11.15-16.50-52; 13,1: *eis telos êgapêsen autous*). This is the type and measure of selfless, self-giving, self-sacrificing and other-oriented love and friendship that Jesus commands his disciples to have for one another (15,12-17). This is the kind of abiding fruit that he desires his disciples should produce (15,16); this is the kind of abundant fruit by which they should glorify his Father (15,8); this is the kind of altruistic love which should be the distinguishing mark of Jesus' true disciples (13,35). This is highlighted by the commandment of Christ-like love given both in the first element 4C (13,1-38; cf. vv.34-35) and in the central element 4E (15,1-17; cf. vv.12-17) of the chiastic structure of "Jesus' Farewell of the Hour" in Jn 13-17 (4C D E E' D' C').

---

while *agapan* emphasizes the active aspect of love. Therefore they are not two forms of love, one higher than the other as some scholars maintain (e.g. R. C. TRENCH, *Synonyma des Neuen Testaments*, is of the opinion that *philein* is higher than *agapan*, while the opposite view is held by WESTCOTT, 303), just as *oida* and *ginôskô* are not two forms of knowledge one higher than the other but rather they underline two aspects (*oida*: certainty; *ginôskô*: dynamism) of knowledge (Cf. G. MLAKUZHYIL, *The Phenomenology of the Verbs of Knowing in the Gospel of John* [A Licentiate Dissertation in Biblical Theology, Pontificia Università Gregoriana, Rome, 1976]).

[148] In our opinion, whereas the first *hina*-clause in 13,34 is epexegetic, the second is final which indicates the ultimate scope of Jesus' loving the disciples. In other words, Jesus has loved them so that they may love one another. And the "new" (*kainê*) measure of their mutual love is his love for them (*kathôs êgapêsa hymas*: 13,34c; cf. 15,12.13). Hence no major punctuation mark must be put between the first *allêlous* and *kathôs*, as is done in *RSV* which has a semi-colon. We give below the text and the correct translation (in our opinion) of 13,34:

Entolên kainên didômi hymin,		**A new commandment I give you,**
hina agapate allêlous	(a)	*that you love one another*
kathôs êgapêsa hymas	(b)	**as I have loved you**
hina kai hymeis agapate allêlous.	(a')	*that you also may love one another.*

The "newness" of Jesus' commandment of love consists in the "new" criterion or yardstick of his love which makes him lay down his life for them (15,13). This is certainly new compared to the commandment of love in the OT: "Love your neighbour as yourself" (Lev 19,18; cf. Mt 19,19; Mk 12,31), since one who loves another only as oneself need not die for the other. In other words, one who loves like Jesus loves others more than oneself. In short, Christ's love is the criterion of Christian love (13,35).

Now we may rapidly note a few parallelisms between the themes connected with the disciples in the different sections of the Book of Jesus' Hour (Jn 11-20). In the parallel subsections (3C and 3C') of the bridge-section (Jn 11-12) the disciples fail to understand the meaning of Jesus' actions (going to Judea: 11,7-10; triumphal entry into Jerusalem: 12,16) and words (about Lazarus' sleep: 11,11-13) and words of Scripture about Jesus (12,14-16). This may be compared to the disciples' misunderstanding of the washing of their feet by Jesus and his words to Peter and to Judas in 4C (13,6-9.27-29). Their difficulty in understanding Jesus' cryptic words about the "little while" and the "going away" are reported in 4D (13,33.36) and 4D' (16,16-17). Similarly, just as the denial by one of the disciples is foretold in 4D (13,38; note also that Peter's denial is reported in 18,17.25.27, that is, in 5D), so the desertion of the disciples is foretold in 4D' (16,32). Moreover, there are similarities between the parallel passages of Jn 18-20. Thus in 5C Jesus comes to the garden with his disciples (18,1-2) and protects them from the armed arrest-party of the Jews (18,8), and in 5C' he comes to them remaining behind locked doors for fear of the Jews (20,19.26). In 5D and 5D' Peter and another disciple (most probably the Beloved Disciple in both the episodes) either follow Jesus to the place of his trial (18,15-16) or come to the place of his burial (20,3-10).

5.14z Our brief discussion of the term *mathētai* makes it evident that discipleship is of great importance in Jn because Jesus' disciples are mentioned frequently at significant places in the overall plan of the Gospel, such as the introduction, the conclusion and the bridge-section, and play a prominent role in many episodes in all the sections. The historical disciples, with their qualities and defects, seem to be presented as types of Christian believers of all times. The most fundamental characteristic of discipleship in Jn is its Christocentrism. Dynamic, committed faith in Jesus is its most essential quality. True disciples also grow in their personal knowledge of Jesus. Their experience of Jesus' love generates love for him, which, in turn, leads to greater union and more intimate communion with him. The fruit of this loving union is a Christlike fraternal love. To use an Indian metaphor, a true disciple of Christ is like a coconut tree whose roots are faith in Jesus, whose trunk and leaves are knowledge of Jesus, whose flowers are love for Jesus and whose fruits (coconuts) are (Christlike) fraternal love. A good coconut tree is known by the coconuts it produces.

5.15 Believing *(Pisteuein)*

That *pisteuein* is one of the key-terms in Jn is seen not only from its high frequency (98 times)[149] but also from its occurrence in the introduction (1,1-2,11) and conclusion (20,30-31), its repeated use (18 times) in the bridge-section (Jn 11-12) and its presence in all the sections (except the

---

[149] While *pisteuein* is found 98 times in Jn, it occurs only 11 times in Mt, 14 times in Mk and 9 times in Lk.

Distribution of *Pisteuein* in Jn

INTR. (1,1-2,11)	BOOK OF JESUS' SIGNS (2,1-12,50)			BOOK OF JESUS' HOUR (11,1-20,29)		CONCL. (20, 30-31)	APPX. (21, 1-25)
	First Sect. (2,1-4,54)	Second Sect. (5,1-10,42)	Bridge Sect. (11,1-12,50)	Fourth Sect. (13,1-17,26)	Fifth Sect. (18,1-20,29)		
1,7. 12.50; 2,11+	2,*11* 22.*23.* 24; 3,12. 12.15. *16.18.* 18.*18.* 36; 4,21. *39.*41. 42.48. 50.53	5,24.38.44. 46.46.47.47; 6,29.30.35. 36.*40.*47.64. 64.64.69; 7,5.*31.*38. *39.*48; 8,24.*30.*31. 45.46; 9,18.35.36. 38; 10.25.26.37. 38.38.*42*	11,15. 25.*26.* 26.27. 40.42. 45.48; *12,11.* 36.37. 38.39. 42.44. 44.46	13,19; 14,*1.1.* 10.11 11.*12.* 29; 16,9. 27.30. 31; 17,8. 20.21.	19,35; 20.8. 25.29. 29	20,31. 31	—

Appendix) and in most of the episodes in them (and particularly in those of the Book of Jesus' Signs), as can be seen from the table above [150].

It is worthy of note that the noun *pistis* is never used in Jn, although the verb *pisteuein* is found 98 times. This already indicates the active character of Johannine faith. The participial phrase *ho pisteuôn* to describe "the believer" (3,16.18.36; 6,35.47; 7,38.39; 11,25; 12,44.46; 14,12; 17,20; cf. also 5,24; 6,40; 11,26) also points in the same direction [151].

The most striking feature of the Johannine understanding of faith is its radical Christocentric character, for "faith" in Jn means essentially faith in Jesus; faith in God is spoken of very rarely (5,24; 12,44; 14,1) and that too in the context of believing in Jesus. The very purpose of writing the Gospel is to lead the readers to "believe that Jesus is the Christ, the Son of God" (20,31). That Christ is the centre of Johannine faith is seen also from the insistence on "believing" (*pisteuein* + dative) Jesus (4,21; 5,38.46; 6,30; 8,31.45.46; 10,37.38; 14,11) or his words (2,22; 4,50; 5,47) or works (10,38) and more especially on

---

[150] The numbers in *italics* indicate the occurrences of *pisteuein eis*. There are only very few episodes or subsections in which "believing" is not explicitly mentioned (10,1-21; 15,1-17; 15,18-16,4d; 18,1-14; 18,12-27; 18,28-19,16b; 21,1-25). Note that all these texts (except the first) belong to the second part of the Gospel (see the "Distribution of *Pisteuein* in Jn" given above).

[151] BROWN, I, 512.

"believing in" (*pisteuein eis*) Jesus[152], which consists in an active commitment to the person of Jesus[153]. The Christological content of faith is often indicated by *pisteuein* followed by a *hoti*-clause which describes his identity (e.g. "the holy one of God": 6,69; "the Christ, the Son of God": 11,27; 20,31; "I am": 8,24; 13,19), his origin and mission from the Father ("I came from the Father": 16,27; 17,8; "you have sent me": 11,42; 17,21) and their mutual immanence ("I am in the Father and the Father in me": 14,10). While all these constructions occur throughout the Gospel, *pisteuein* with the dative is found more frequently in Jesus' discussions with the unbelieving Jews in 2B (5,24.38.46.46.47.47), 2B' (10,37.38.38; cf. 10,25.26) and 2D (8,31.45.46) than elsewhere. This fact indicates that "believing Jesus" is the first stage of faith (cf. also 4,21; 14,11). The second stage seems to consist in believing in Jesus' identity and mission as described by *pisteuein hoti*, which occurs relatively more often in C's (cf. 6,69 in 2C; 11,17.42 in 3C; 13,19 in 4C; 17,8.21 in 4C') than in the other subsections. Finally, "believing in" Jesus (*pisteuein eis*) appears to be the final stage of faith, which occurs very often in 1C (3,16.18.18), 2C (6,29.35.40), 3C (11,25.26.45.48), 3C' (12,11.36.37.42.44.44.46), 2D (7,5.31.38.39.48; 8,30) and 4D (14,1.1.12). Such faith is frequently spoken of as the condition for "having eternal life" (*echein zôên aiônion*: 3,16.36; 6,40; cf. also 1,12; 11,25-26)[154].

The importance the Evangelist attaches to the theme of faith can also be seen from the way he has redacted many episodes and particularly from the concluding redactional remarks at the end of many events. Thus at the end of the first and second Cana-signs the Evangelist tells us explicitly that the disciples believed in Jesus (2,11) and that the royal official and his household became believers (4,53). Similarly, we are told that many believed in Jesus during the first Passover feast in Jerusalem (2,23) and during his stay at Bethany beyond the Jordan after the feast of Dedication (10,42). Likewise the Evangelist concludes the Samaritan and the Lazarus episodes by stating that many (Samaritans or Jews) believed in Jesus (4,39.42; 11,45; cf. also 12,11). Looking back at the whole public ministry of Jesus, John makes the following concluding remarks: "Though he had done so many signs before them, yet they did not believe in him" (12,37).

Besides underlining "believing" in the concluding redactional passages of many episodes, as we have seen above, the Evangelist dramatically ends a number of important events with a confession of faith in Jesus. For instance, the Samaritans of the city of Sychar tell the woman: "It is no longer because of your words that we believe, for we have heard for ourselves, and we know that this is indeed the Saviour of the world" (4,42). Again, at the end of the discourse on the bread of life when many of Jesus' disciples desert him, Peter makes the famous profession of faith: "You have the words of eternal life; and we have

---

[152] Out of the 36 occurrences of *pisteuein eis* in Jn (cf. the verse numbers in italics in the table above) 35 refer to Jesus, the only exception being 14,1 (cf. also 12,44).
[153] BROWN, I, 513.
[154] See 5.16 below.

believed, and have come to know, that you are the Holy One of God" (6,68-69). Likewise, towards the end of Jn 9 the cured blind man professes his faith in Jesus, the Son of Man: "Lord, I believe" (9,38). Martha's encounter with Jesus outside the village of Bethany ends with her confession: "I believe that you are the Christ, the Son of God, he who is coming into the world" (11,27)[155]. At the end of the Farewell Discourse the disciples confess: "We believe that you came from God" (16,30). Finally, the Fourth Gospel comes to its climax with the confession of Thomas: "My Lord and my God" (20,28) and Jesus' blessing on all those who believe ("Blessed are all those who have not seen and yet believe": 20,29).

The importance attached to faith can be perceived also from the number of times Jesus engages in dialogues, discourses, discussions and debates on the need, types, qualities and consequences of believing or not believing in him. There is also the significant fact that at the two most crucial moments in his life (namely, before raising Lazarus to life, an act which would eventually cost him his own life, and at the hour of his passion-death-resurrection) he prays to the Father that the people/world may believe that He has sent him (11,42; 17,21)[156].

Finally we may also mention here that "believing" is often spoken of in connection with many other important Johannine themes such as "signs" (2,11.23; 4,48.53; 6,30; 7,31; 10,41-42; 11,47-48; 12,37; 20,30-31) and "works" (10,25-26.37-38; 14,11-12)[157], "word" (2,22; 4,39.41.41.50; 6,69; 17,20; cf. also 3,12; 8,30; 10,25) and "witnessing" (1,7; 4,39; 10,25-26; 19,35), "seeing" (1,50; 2,23; 4,38; 6,30.36.40; 11,40.45; 20,8.25.29), "knowing" (2,24; 4,42.53; 6,69; 10,38; 16,30) and "having eternal life" (3,15.16.36; 5,24; 6,40.47; 11,25; 20,31)[158].

5.15z From our brief discussion of *pisteuein* in Jn we can conclude that Christocentric faith is one of the most prominent Johannine themes. This is particularly true in the introduction (1,1-2,11), the conclusion (20,30-31) and the Book of Jesus' Signs (Jn 2-12). The different facets and stages of faith are shown

---

[155] Although Martha's confession does not occur at the end but in the middle of the Lazarus-episode, yet they are her last words during her meeting with Jesus outside the village of Bethany (11,17-27).
Nathanael too makes a similar confession at the end of his first encounter with Jesus: "Rabbi, you are the Son of God; you are the king of Israel" (1,49).
It may also be mentioned that many of the episodes present a gradual progress in faith in those who are receptive to Jesus' revelation (e.g. Nathanael: 1,45-51; the Samaritan woman: 4,7-30; the royal official: 4,46-54; the cured blind man: 9,1-41; Martha: 11,17-27; Mary Magdalene: 20,11-18).

[156] Observe that these two prayers are found in parallel passages 3C (11,1-54) and 4C' (17,1-26). The third prayer of Jesus in Jn occurs at 12,27-28, that is, in 3C' (11,55-12,50) which is parallel to 3C.

[157] See 5.13.

[158] The link between faith and eternal life will be examined below (see 5.16). Cf. F.-M. BRAUN, *Jean le Théologien*, III (Paris 1966) 107-12; 119-33; 153-82. F. MUSSNER, *Zôê* (München 1952) 48-188; SCHNACKENBURG, II, 352-61; S. ZEDDA, "Le realtà escatologiche presenti: la vita eterna", in: *L'Escatologia Biblica*, II (1975) 303-67.

in many carefully constructed episodes. Faith and unbelief are often spoken of in connection with the signs and works of Jesus, and are the topics of his dialogues and discourses, discussions and debates, with friends and foes, individuals and crowds, Jews and Samaritans, disciples and Gentiles. All this evidence shows how necessary it is not only to believe Jesus' words and works and to acknowledge him as the Christ and the Son of God but also to commit oneself actively to his person.

5.16 "(Eternal) Life" *(Zôê [Aiônios])*

"Life" is another major theological theme of Jn. This is evident from the relatively high frequency of the term *zôê* (36 times) and of the related verbs *zên* (17 times) and *zô[i]opoiein* (13 times)[159]. There is also the fact that "life" is explicitly mentioned both in the introduction (1,4.4) and in the conclusion (20,31), which forms an inclusion for the whole Gospel. Besides, it is present in all the sections (except the last one and the Appendix)[160].

It must be noted that the distribution of *zôê*, *zaô* and *zô[i]opoieô* is not uniform. Most of the occurrences are in the Book of Jesus' Signs (*zôê*: 30 times out of 36; *zaô*: 15 times out of 17; *zô[i]opoieô*: all the three times). *Zôe* and *zaô* are found only rarely (thrice and twice respectively) in Jn 13-17, and never in the narrative of the passion-resurrection (Jn 18-20).

"Life" is introduced already in the Prologue, where the Logos is presented as the source of "life" (*ho gegonen en autô[i] zôê ên*: 1,3-4)[161], and the "life" is described as "the light of men" (*kai hê zôê ên to phôs tôn anthrôpôn*: 1,4). Thus at the beginning of this hymnic introduction the divine Word (1,1-2) is revealed not only as the mediator of creation (1,3) but also as the source of life and light for all human beings (1,4-5). The nature of this life is later specified as the divine life of those who welcome the revealed Word of God in faith, and thus become the children of God through birth from God (1,12-13).

How this divine life is imparted to human beings is explained in two parallel passages 1C (cf. 3,15-16) and 1C' (cf. 3,36)[162]. The ultimate explanation of man's participation in God's life is found in the Father's love for humankind, which alone accounts for the sending of His only Son to save the world (3,16-17). This divine mission of God's only Son (*monogenês*: 1,14.18; 3,16.18) included not only his incarnation (1,14) but also his being "lifted up" on the cross. The lifting up of the Son of Man is stated to be a divine "must" (*dei*) so that believers may have eternal life (3,15). As we see in the parallel passage, man also has a role to

---

[159] *Zôê* and *zaô* are found much less frequently in the Synoptic Gospels (*zôê*: Mt = 7; Mk = 4; Lk = 5; *zaô*: Mt = 6; Mk = 3; Lk = 9; *zô[i]opoieô* does not occur at all in the Synoptic Gospels).
[160] See the "Distribution of *Zôê*, *Zaô* and *Zô[i]opoieô* in Jn" given on the next page.
[161] *TCGNT*, 195-96 and I. DE LA POTTERIE, "De interpunctione et interpretatione versuum Joh. 1,3.4", *VD* 33 (1955) 193-208, for the reasons why *ho gegonen* is joined with *en autô[i] zôê ên* of v. 4.
[162] It may be recalled that the discourses in which these verses occur are parallel to each other, namely, 1C (2,23-3,21) and 1C' (3,22-4,3).

Distribution of *Zôê, Zaô* and *Zô[i]opoieô* in Jn

Terms	INTR. (1,1-2,11)	BOOK OF JESUS' SIGNS (2,1-12,50)			BOOK OF JESUS' HOUR (11,1-20,29)		CONCL. (20, 30-31)	APPX. (21, 1-25)
		First Sect. (2,1-4,54)	Second Sect. (5,1-10,42)	Bridge Sect. (11,1-12,50)	Fourth Sect. (13,1-17,26)	Fifth Sect. (18,1-20,29)		
zôê	1,4.4	3,15. 16.36; 4,14. 36	5,24.24. 26.26.29. 39.40; 6,27.33. 35.40.47. 48.51.53. 54.63.68; 8,12; 10,10.28	11,25; 12,25. 50	14,6; 17,2.3	—	20,31	—
zaô	—	4,10. 11.50. 51.53	5,25; 6,51.51. 57.57.57. 58; 7,38	11,25. 26	14,19. 19	—	—	—
zô[i]opoieô	—	—	5,21.21; 6,63	—	—	—	—	—

play in order to have this divine life: he must believe in Jesus, the Son of God (*ho pisteuôn eis ton hyion echei zôên aiônion*: 3,36; cf. almost the identical words in 3,16: *hina pas ho pisteuôn eis auton... echê[i] zôên aiônion*). Since believing in Jesus is the condition for having eternal life, disobeying him excludes one from "seeing life" (3,36). The reason why an active faith in the Son is necessary so as to share the divine life is because "the Father loves the Son and has given all things into his hands" (3,35), which include eternal life (17,2). In short, in order to have eternal life man must believe in the beloved Son of God whom He has sent to save man from death and impart eternal life. Note also that this "life" is qualified as "eternal" in 3,15.16.36a (and in 14 other places in Jn), a qualifier which indicates not only an infinite duration as opposed to the temporary length of natural life that ends with death (cf. 5,24) but also a qualitatively new life which even death cannot destroy, namely, the life of the Father and the Son (cf. 5,26), a theme which will be developed later. We may also mention here that even when "life" is not modified by the adjective "eternal", it denotes the same reality of "eternal life" as is suggested by the parallelism between 3,36a (*zôê aiônios*) and 3,36b (*zôê*) (cf. also 5,24 and 6,53.54).

That the very purpose of his mission is to give life in abundance is unambiguously affirmed by Jesus himself in a parallel parabolic discourse in 2C' (cf. 10,10: "I have come that they may have life and have it in abundance", a text which is similar to 3,16 where the ultimate purpose of God's sending his only Son is said to be: "that whoever believes in him should not perish but have eternal life")[163]. It follows from 10,10 and 10,14-15 that the life which Jesus has come to give consists in a mutual, loving, intimate knowledge of Jesus and the disciples (the sheep), patterned on that of the Father and Jesus.

In fact, in another parallel passage (4C' = the prayer of the hour) Jesus describes eternal life in terms of knowing him and the Father: *hautê estin hê aiônios zôê, hina ginôskôsin se ton monon alêthinon theon kai hon apesteilas Iêsoun Christon* (17,3). This knowledge is, in the final analysis, a communion of life with Christ and through him with the Father[164]. This is the eternal life that the Father has authorized the Son to communicate to all men and women (17,2). This life of fellowship with the Father and the Son is made possible especially by the glorification of Jesus through his death-resurrection. This fact is corroborated by the connection between "the coming of the hour" (*elêlythen hê hôra*: 17,1), "the glorification of the Son" (cf. the inclusion between *doxazon ton hyion* in 17,1 and *doxason me sy, pater* in 17,5) and the "giving of eternal life" (*hina... dôsê[i] autois zôên aiônion*: 17,2). The importance of eternal life is also supported by the structural position of 17,3 at the centre of the concentric structure (A B A') of 17,1-5[165].

That Jesus is not only the mediator of eternal life but also its constant sustenance is manifested in the parallel discourse in 2C (Jn 6), which has the greatest concentration of *zôê* (11 times) and *zaô* (6 times) in Jn[166]. Here Jesus tells the crowd (which came to Capernaum looking for him after the multiplication of the loaves) to "work for the food which endures to eternal life" (6,27), the bread from heaven which "gives life to the world" (6,33). When the crowd asks for this bread (6,34), Jesus presents himself as "the bread of life" (*egô eimi ho artos tês zôês*: 6,35.48) and assures them that "he who believes in him has eternal life" (6,40.47). This faith is concretized in, and this life is sustained and nourished by, the eating and drinking of his body and blood (6,51.53.54). Furthermore, Jesus has "the words of eternal life" (6,68); in fact, his words are "Spirit and life" (6,63), for they convey the "life-giving" (*zô[i]opoioun*) Spirit (6,63; cf. 20,22). In short, in Jn 6 Jesus is revealed as the source and sustenance of eternal life for those who believe in him.

---

[163] Note that the Greek text of 3,16 and 10,10 contains the same expression *hina zôên echôsin* (though the two verses have a different word order) and the same verb *apollymi* (though it means "perish" in 3,16 and "destroy" in 10,10). Notice also that 6,27 and 12,25 too contain the terms *zôê* and *apollymi*. We have seen in the last chapter that the discourses in which these verses (3,16; 6,27; 10,10; 12,25) occur are parallel to one another (1C, 2C, 2C', 3C').

[164] Cf. F. MUSSNER, *op. cit.*, 171-76.

[165] See 3.3.

[166] See the distribution of *zôê* in the table given above.

After the death of Lazarus Jesus reveals himself to Martha as "the resurrection and the life" (*egô eimi hê anastasis kai hê zôê*: 11,25) and this claim is demonstrated by raising Lazarus to life (11,43-44). That the self-revelatory words of Jesus in 11,25 mean more than his power to bring a dead person back to physical life is made clear by the addition of *kai hê zôê* (which always refers to eternal life in Jn) to *hê anastasis*, and by the couplet which follows [167]:

11,25cd: *ho pisteuôn eis eme* kan **apothanê[i] zêsetai**,
11,26a : kai pas **ho zôn** kai *pisteuôn eis eme*
        ou mê apothanê[i] eis ton aiôna.

Here every believer in Jesus is assured that he will live (*zêsetai*) beyond physical death (*kan apothanê[i]*) and that he will not die for ever (*ou mê apothanê[i] eis ton aiôna*). "The saying contrasts natural existence with eternal life, and shows that the barrier of physical death is broken in faith and the earthly life acquires a new dimension through Jesus" [168]. Here in 3C (cf. 11,25-26), as in earlier parallel passages 1C (cf. 3,16), 1C' (cf. 3,36), and 2C (cf. 6,40.47), faith in Jesus is required as an essential condition for living or not dying for ever.

Another condition for having eternal life is stated by Jesus at 12,25ab in the parallel discourse in 3C'. Here "hating one's life" is said to be the way of gaining eternal life. Note the antithetical parallelism of the two parts of 12,25ab, which makes the meaning of the enigmatic statement clear:

ho philôn **tên psychên autou** *apollyei* **autên**,
kai *ho misôn* **tên psychên autou** en tô[i] kosmô[i] toutô[i]
eis z ô ê n   a i ô n i o n   *phylaxei* **autên**.

He who loves (*phileî*) his physical life (*psychê*) selfishly, loses (*apollyei*) it with his death, but he who hates (*misôn*) or loves less his life in this world, so as to be willing to die to self like the grain of wheat that falls to the ground and dies (12,24), will preserve it for eternal life (*eis zôên aiônion phylaxei autên*: 12,25) [169]. Thus death to self is the path to life. It may be noted that 12,25 is the first text in which *psychê* and *zôê* are explicitly linked together, although they might have been implied in the parallel parabolic discourse on the good shepherd in 2C' (10,10-11: "I have come that they may have life [*zôê*]... The good shepherd lays down his life [*psychê*] for the sheep") [170].

---

[167] SCHNACKENBURG, II, 331.
[168] *Ibid.*
[169] BROWN remarks: "We might say that vs. 25 explains the way in which the new grain produced by the seed of [vs.] 24 gains a life of its own" (I, 474).
[170] Whereas at 10,10-11 Jesus speaks about laying down *his psychê* so that the disciples (sheep) may have *zôê*, at 12,25 he talks about their loving or hating *their psychê* and about their having *zôê*.

Jesus concludes his revelatory discourse in 12,44-50 with two verses which reveal the relation between eternal life and the words which he speaks at the command of the Father:

A 49a: hoti e g ô ex emautou ouk e l a l ê s a,
   b: all' ho pempsas me *patêr* autos moi *entolên* dedôken
  cd: ti eipô kai ti l a l ê s ô.

B 50ab: kai oida hoti hê *entolê* autou **zôê aiônios** estin.

A' 50c: ha oun e g ô l a l ô,
   d: kathôs eirêken moi ho *patêr*,
   e: houtôs l a l ô [171].

It is clear from both the structure and the context of these verses that their central idea may be expressed as: "The words which Jesus speaks at the Father's command are a source of eternal life to those who accept them"[172]. Jesus' statement at 12,50ab ("I know that his commandment is eternal life") is similar to Peter's confession at 6,68 ("You have the words of eternal life"), although the Father's "commandment" is connected with eternal life in 12,50, while Jesus' "words" are linked to eternal life in 6,68[173].

So far we have examined (eternal) life in the parallel passages C* (1,1-18), 1C (2,23-3,21), 1C' (3,22-4,3), 2C (6,1-71), 2C' (10,1-21), 3C (11,1-54), 3C' (11,55-12,50), 4C' (17,1-26), all of which reveal Jesus as the life-giver and insist upon the need of believing in him in order to have eternal life. This explains why the Evangelist mentions in the conclusion Cz that "believing you may have life in his name" (20,31d).

Now we shall briefly analyze the rest of the passages which speak of life and examine them from the structural point of view.

During the dialogue with the Samaritan woman in 1B' (4,1-42) Jesus promises to give her "living water" (*hydôr zôn*: 4,10.11) which will become a "spring of water welling up to eternal life" (4,14). Whether the "living water" here is a symbol of the Spirit or of Jesus' revelation or of both[174], it is clear that it is a "gift of God" (*dôrea tou theou*) which Jesus "gives" (*didômi*: 4,10). It

---

[171] Observe that the concentric structure (ABA') of 12,49-50 with many parallels (*egô* of v.49a and v.50c; *elalêsa* of v.49a & *lalêsô* of v.49d and *lalô* of v.50ce; *patêr* of v.49b and v.50d). The central verse contains the important statement: *hê entolê autou zôê aiônios estin*.

[172] SCHNACKENBURG, II, 424.

[173] Although 12,50 has "the commandment" (*hê entolê*) whereas 6,68 has "the words" (*ta rhêmata*), they have essentially the same meaning, since what Jesus speaks is what the Father has commanded him to say (cf. 12,49). It may be also noted that the same term *ta rhêmata* used in Peter's profession of faith (6,68) is also found in the verses which immediately precede 12,49-50, namely, in 12,47-48. (We have seen in the last chapter that there are many other parallel elements in 6,60-71 and 12,44-50.)

[174] So BROWN, I, 178-79; SCHNACKENBURG, I, 426-27; F. J. MCCOOL, "Living Water in John", in: *Bible in Current Catholic Thought*, ed. J. L. McKenzie, (New York 1962) 226-33.

becomes "an inner principle of spiritual life which is not bound by the limits of earthly existence"[175] but which issues inexhaustively into eternal life (4,14). Note that Jesus mentions "living water" and "eternal life" in order to lead the woman to recognize who he is (*tis estin*: 4,10; *egô eimi*: 4,26; cf. also 4,29)[176]. In other words, the Evangelist hints at the fact that, if Jesus can give "living water that wells up to eternal life", he must be the (divine) Messiah, the true Saviour of the world (4,42). Similarly, the saving of the royal official's son from death (4,46-54) through Jesus' life-giving word that the child "lives" (*zê[i]*: 4,50.51.53)[177] insinuates that Jesus is the life-giver and therefore the Saviour.

What is only hinted at in Jn 4 about Jesus' identity is explicitated in 2B (Jn 5) where the terms *zôê*, *zaô* and *zô[i]opoieô* are employed 7 times, once and twice respectively[178]. It must be observed that most occurrences are in Jesus' discourse on his divine Sonship (5,19-30: vv.21.24.24.25.26.26.29), a fact which underlines the unity of action between the Son and the Father. Compare, for instance, the first and the last verses which form an inclusion:

5,19: **ou dynatai** h o   h y i o s   *poiein aph' heautou ouden*
5,30: **ou dynamai** e g ô   *poiein ap' emautou ouden*.

The common activity of the Father and the Son is specified in 5,21 in terms of "making alive" (*zô[i]opoiei*): "For as the Father raises the dead and gives them life (*zô[i]opoiei*), so also the Son gives life (*zô[i]opoiei*) to whom he will". This giving presupposes, of course, that, "as the Father has life in himself, so he has granted the Son also to have life in himself" (5,26). Jesus' possession of life is the reason why those who hear the voice of the Son of God will live (5,25; cf. also 5,29). Thus we see that, although the terminology on "life" is frequently used in 5,19-30, its primary function is to highlight the divine Sonship of Jesus[179]. Finally, during the discourse on his witnesses (5,31-47) Jesus tells the Jews: "You search the Scriptures, because you think that in them you have eternal life; and it is they that bear witness to me; yet you refuse to come to me that you may have life" (5,39-40). Here Jesus accepts the testimony of the Scriptures concerning himself, but presents himself (not the Scriptures) as the source of eternal life (cf. 5,21.26).

In the parallel episode during the feast of Dedication in 2B' (10,22-42) Jesus contrasts the unbelieving Jews with his sheep which listen to his voice and follow

---

[175] LINDARS, 183.
[176] A similar phenomenon is found also in Jn 5 (see below).
[177] John employs the verb *zên* sometimes to denote physical life (4,50.51.53; 11,26), sometimes spiritual life (5,25; 6,51.57.58; 11,25; 14,19); sometimes the participle *zôn* is used symbolically to qualify "water" (4,10.11; 7,38) and "bread" (6,51).
[178] See the table given above.
[179] This is supported by the chiastic structure of 5,19-30 (A B C C' B'A') (see 3.32).

him (10,27; cf. 10,3-4), and affirms that he gives them eternal life (10,28)[180] and declares: "I and the Father are one" (10,30), and asks the Jews to "believe the works that you may know and understand that the Father is in me and I am in the Father" (10,38). These sayings of Jesus reveal his divine identity and unity with God. In other words, the argument seems to be similar to that of the parallel discourse in 2B (Jn 5; cf. vv.17.19-30.36.39), namely, because he has a unique relationship with the Father (10,30.38; cf. 5,26), does His works (10,32. 37.38; cf. 5,36) and gives eternal life (10,28; cf. 5,21), he must be the Son of God (10,36; cf. 5,17.19-30).

On the last day of the feast of Tabernacles Jesus promises to those who come to him in faith "rivers of living water" (*potamoi hydatos zôntos*: 7,38)[181] which the Evangelist interprets as a reference to the glorified Jesus' gift of the life-giving Spirit to the believers (7,39)[182].

In the context of the feast of Tabernacles Jesus reveals himself as "the light of the world" and promises those who follow him "the light of life" (*to phôs tês zôês*), the life-giving light, the light that liberates them from the sphere of darkness and death and brings them to the divine sphere of eternal life (8,12)[183].

That Jesus is the revelation of life is disclosed to the disciples during the first Farewell Discourse in 4D (13,31-14,31), for Jesus manifests himself to them as "the way, the truth and the life" (*egô eimi hê hodos kai hê alêtheia kai hê zôê*: 14,6). From the immediate context of this verse (cf. Jesus' statement in v.4: *kai hopou [egô] hypagô oidate tên hodon*; Thomas' question in v.5: *pôs dynametha tên hodon eidenai?* and Jesus' answer in the second part of v.6: *oudeis erchetai pros ton patera ei mê di' emou*), it is evident that what is emphasized in Jesus' "I am" saying in v.6 is "the way" (*hê hodos*), although it is connected by *kai* to "the truth and the life"[184]. The first *kai* (between *hê hodos* and *hê alêtheia*) is epexegetic or explanatory and therefore the saying can be translated as "I am the way, that is, the truth and the life"[185]. In other words, Jesus is the way because

---

[180] This statement about "giving life" (*didômi zôên*) at 10,28 may be regarded as parallel to the similar statement about the Son's "giving life" (*zô[i]opoiei*) at 5,21, although the Greek verbs used are not the same.

[181] Cf. SCHNACKENBURG, II, 152-55; BROWN, I, 320-21 for the discussion whether Jesus or the believer is the source of the rivers of living water.

[182] This promise of the gift of the Spirit in 2D (7,38-39) is comparable with Jesus' repeated promises of sending the Spirit in the parallel passages in 4D (14,16-17.26) and 4D' (16,7-15).

[183] BROWN, I, 344; SCHNACKENBURG, II, 191. The occurrence of *zôê* at 8,12 may be compared to a similar occurrence of it at 14,6 (in 4D) (see below).

[184] In the words of I. DE LA POTTERIE: "È chiaro che l'elemento principale del v.6 deve trovarsi nella prima dichiarazione di Gesù: *"io, sono la via"*, mentre il resto del versetto ha solo una funzione esplicitante di questa metafora" (*Gesù Verità* [Roma 1973] 108).

[185] SCHNACKENBURG, III, 65. I. DE LA POTTERIE remarks about the meaning of 14,6: "Le vérset ne signifie donc pas que Jésus est un chemin *vers* la vérité; le sens doit être que Jésus est le chemin vers le Père, *précisément en* tant qu'il est la vérité et la vie; *alêtheia* et *zôê* expliquent son rôle de médiateur: c'est parce que Jésus est la vérité et la vie qu'il peut nous conduire au Père" (*La Vérité dans S. Jean*, I [Rome 1977] 253).

he is the truth and the life. This interpretation is confirmed by the verses which follow v.6, for vv.7-9 explain how Jesus is the way because he is the truth, namely, the revelation of the Father (cf. Philip's request to Jesus in 14,8: *kyrie, deixon hêmin ton patera* and Jesus' reply in 14,9: *ho heôraken me heôraken ton patera*). That Jesus is the mediator of life seems to be implied in his promise to the disciples in 14,19: *hymeis de theôreite me hoti egô zô kai hymeis zêsete.* Ultimately it is the life of the Father shared by Jesus which he gives to the disciples (14,20)[186].

Since the close relationship between the hour of glorification and the gift of eternal life is explained in Jn 13-17 and especially in 17,1-5, as we have seen above, the absence of the terms *zôê* and *zaô* from the narratives of the passion-death-resurrection (Jn 18-20) is quite understandable.

5.16z From what has been said so far we may conclude that for the fourth Evangelist eternal life means not only everlasting life as opposed to temporary life which ends with death but also a qualitatively new life, the life of the Age to Come which has already become a reality with the coming of Christ. The divine life of the Father and the Son is shared by the believers here and now through the mediation of Jesus, the incarnate divine Son[187]. The present possession of eternal life through an active faith in Jesus is insisted upon by the frequent repetition of *ho pisteuôn (eis ton hyion/auton) echei zôên aiônion* (3,15.16.36; 5,24; 6,40.47; 20,31). The Christocentric character of the eternal life of the believers is underscored also by presenting Jesus as the life (11,25; 14,6).

5.1z We have rapidly surveyed the theological themes which are stressed both in the introduction and in the conclusion, and which occur frequently in the body of the Gospel (namely, "the Christ"/ "Messiah", "the Son of God", ["the Son", "the Father", and "the Son of Man"], "signs" [and "works"], "disciples", "believing" and "eternal life"). After having examined them in the light of the literary structure, we can conclude that most of them are Christocentric in character, since they deal with the person, mission and salvific significance of Jesus. For they reveal to us who Jesus is (namely, "the Christ/Messiah", "the Son of Man", "the Son of God", "the Son" of "the Father"), what he does ("signs" and "works"), and what he gives to "believing" "disciples" (namely, "eternal life"). Notice that the "disciples" in Jn are almost exclusively those of Jesus and what is most emphasized in discipleship is a personal relationship to him. "The Father" whom Jesus reveals is basically his Father who has sent him and with whom he is totally united in being and action. Faith in Jn essentially means faith in Jesus. Eternal life is the divine life that is mediated by Jesus to those who believe in him. In short, the Johannine themes we have examined point to a Christocentric theological perspective, which we also detected in the literary structure of the Gospel.

---

[186] BROWN, II, 646; SCHNACKENBURG, III, 78.
[187] Cf. C. H. DODD, *op. cit.*, 144-50 and especially 149.

5.2 CHRISTOCENTRIC THEOLOGICAL SKETCH IN THE LITERARY STRUCTURE

In ch. 4 we saw that the Gospel of John divides itself into two major parts: the Book of Jesus' Signs (Jn 2-12) and the Book of Jesus' Hour (Jn 11-20), preceded by an introduction (1,1-2,11) and followed by a conclusion (20,30-31) and an appendix (Jn 21). The first part (Jn 2-12) deals with the signs and works, dialogues and discourses, disputes and discussions of Jesus during his public ministry, all of which reveal his person and mission. The second part (Jn 11-20) speaks of "the hour" of Jesus, namely, his passion-death-resurrection and its salvific significance. Thus both the main parts of the Gospel are Christocentric in character. Besides, the conclusion of the Gospel states its Christocentric purpose, since it mentions the many signs that Jesus did before his disciples which reveal him as the Messiah, the Son of God and the giver of life to the believers (20,30-31). Furthermore, the reader's attention is dramatically drawn to Jesus Christ already in the introduction (1,1-2,11), for he is the centre of the Prologue (1,1-18), which is a hymn to the incarnate Logos; John the Baptist bears witness to him and the first disciples proclaim him as the Messiah and the Son of God (1,19-51); the first Cana-sign (2,1-11) reveals his glory (2,11). Thus we find that Jesus Christ is the central axis around which the Fourth Gospel is developed from the introduction to the conclusion. In other words, the Johannine Gospel is Christocentric in nature, since its primary concern is the revelation of the person, mission and salvific significance of Jesus Christ (cf. 20,30-31). If the Fourth Gospel can be compared to a circle, its centre is Christ. If it can be thought of as a spiral, Jesus is its axis. It must be remembered, however, that the "Christocentric" character of the Fourth Gospel does not mean that John stops with Christ; the Johannine Jesus is not the end but the way to the Father (14,6). If Jesus is the axis of the Fourth Gospel, the Father is the apex of the axis and therefore the summit of the spiral as well.

We shall now briefly examine how the divisions and subdivisions of the literary structure of the Gospel throw light on its Christocentric theology. The structure functions as a winding staircase around the priceless treasures of Johannine theology, which may be contemplated from the steps of the structural staircase.

Since our scope is only to *sketch* the Christocentric theology of the Gospel based on its literary structure, we shall follow the plan of the Gospel itself instead of outlining its theology thematically. It must be remembered that the Johannine author does not develop his theology logically but contemplatively. Just as one would contemplate the beauty of a crown by looking at its multi-coloured jewels arranged in definite patterns, so John contemplates Christ through various episodes (consisting of Jesus' deeds and words) organized in beautiful symmetrical patterns (e.g. the chiastic structures of Jn 2-4; 5-10; 13-17 and 18-20).

5.21 The Christocentric Theological Sketch in the Introduction (1,1-2,11)

We saw in the last chapter that 1,1-2,11 consists of a triple introduction to Jesus Christ ("hymnic-testimonial introduction": 1,1-18; "testimonial-kerygmatic introduction": 1,19-51; "historical sign-introduction": 2,1-11), which corresponds chiastically to the triple division of the conclusion ("historical sign-conclusion": 20,30; "Christological conclusion": 20,31abc; "soteriological conclusion": 20,31d), which may be represented as C*B*A$^+$ AzBzCz [188].

5.211 *Jesus, the divine, creative, revelatory, regenerative, incarnate Word, in 1,1-18 (C*)*

"The spiral structure of the Prologue" [189] makes it clear that this Christological hymn describes the different aspects and roles of the Word such as his divinity (*theos*: vv.1c.18) and humanity (*sarx*: v.14; *skênoô*: v.14), his mediation in creation (*panta di'autou egeneto, kai chôris autou egeneto oude hen*: v.3), regeneration (*edôken autois exousian tekna theou genesthai... hoi... ek theou egennêthêsan*: vv.12-13) and revelation (*logos*: vv.1.1.1.14; *phôs*: vv.4.5.7.8.8.9; *alêtheia*: vv.14.17; *exêgeomai*: v.18) [190].

Many of the important theological themes developed in the body of the Gospel are already introduced in the Prologue [191]. For instance, the (incarnate) Logos' pre-existence (1,1 = 17,5.24), his divinity (*theos*: 1,1.18 = 20,28) [192], his unique relation to God the Father as the only Son (*monogenês*: 1,14.18 = 3,16.18) [193] who alone sees Him (1,18 = 6,46) [194] and shares in His glory (1,14

---

[188] See 4.11.

[189] See 3.34. Notice that four of the five sections of the Prologue (a*, b*, c*, c**) contain the term "revelatory" in their titles.

[190] VAN DEN BUSSCHE remarks: "Le Logos personifié ouvre majesteusement l'oeuvre entière et indique l'aspect le plus important de la personnalité du Christ, décrite ensuite dans l'évangile: sa fonction de révélation" (53).

[191] In the words of T. E. POLLARD: "The Prologue provides a summary of the Gospel, or perhaps rather an overture in which the stage is set and the atmosphere created for the drama of the Gospel, and the main themes of the Gospel are announced" (*Johannine Christology and the Early Church* [Cambridge 1970] 14). Cf. also J. A. T. ROBINSON, "The Relation of the Prologue to the Gospel of St. John", *NTS* 9 (1962-63) 120-29.

[192] Note that these verses, which alone call Jesus "God" (*theos*), form an inclusion and are found in parallel passages in the literary structure of the Fourth Gospel, namely, in C* (1,1-18) and 5C' (20,19-29). Concerning the use of the term *theos* to designate Jesus at 1,1.18 and 20,28 B. A. MASTIN affirms that "in the construction of the Fourth Gospel prominence is given to the designation of Jesus as *theos*... These three verses are placed at strategic points in the gospel, and this underlines the significance of what they say" ("A Neglected Feature of the Christology of the Fourth Gospel", *NTS* 22 [1975-76] 34; 42). Cf. also G. REIM, "Jesus as God in the Fourth Gospel: the Old Testament Background", *NTS* 30 (1984) 158-60, who agrees with Mastin's view and suggests Ps 45,7 (= LXX Ps 44,7: *echrisen se ho theos ho theos sou*) as the OT background for designating Jesus, the Messiah, as God.

[193] It is noteworthy that *monogenês* occurs only in these verses in the entire Fourth Gospel and that the subsections in which it occurs are parallel to each other, namely, in C* (1,1-18) and 1C' (2,23-3,21).

[194] These verses occur in parallel passages C* (1,1-18) and 2C (6,1-71) respectively (see "the Schema of the Literary Structure").

= 12,41)¹⁹⁵ are underscored in the Prologue. The emphasis on the pre-existence and the divinity of the Word is balanced by the stress on the Word's becoming truly and fully human (*kai ho logos sarx egeneto*: 1,14a) and dwelling among men (*kai eskênôsen en hêmin*: 1,14b)¹⁹⁶. Similarly, his revelatory relation to humanity as "the light of the world" (1,4.9 = 8,12; 9,5; cf. also 3,19) and his saving function as "the life" of believers (1,4.12-13 = 11,25-26)¹⁹⁷ are insisted upon in the hymnic introduction. Likewise the fact of the rejection of Jesus by his own people through unbelief (the development of which is dramatically described in Jn 2-12 and explicitly stated in the conclusion: 12,37)¹⁹⁸ is hinted at already in the Prologue (cf. 1,11). The testimony of John the Baptist to Jesus Christ is introduced in the Prologue (1,6-8.15); this is described more in detail in 1,19-35 and in 3,22-4,3 (cf. also 5,33.36; 10,40-41). Thus Jesus Christ, truly divine (1,1.18) and fully human (1,14), the mediator of divine revelation (1,17) and regeneration (1,12-13), is manifested in the Prologue. Notice also that the Prologue indicates what the right response of a person to this grace of revelation (1,14.16-17) in Jesus Christ should be, namely, faith in his name (1,12: *tois pisteuousin eis to onoma autou*). That is to say, the soteriology of the Prologue is also Christocentric in nature. Likewise its ecclesiology is Christ-centred, for what the disciples/Christian community contemplated is the glory of the incarnate Word as the only Son of the Father (1,14) and the grace they received is from his fulness (1,16) of "grace and truth" (1,14), the grace of divine revelation (1,17-18). In short, the theology of the Prologue is through and through Christocentric. This does not mean that God the Father is not important in the Prologue. He is often mentioned there (1,1.2.14.18). But it must be observed that the Father (*ho theos* and *ho patêr*) is always referred to in order to reveal the personal relation of Christ to God and his revelatory role (1,1.2.14.18)¹⁹⁹.

5.212 *Jesus, the Messiah, the Son of God, the lamb of God, the king of Israel and the Son of Man, in 1,19-51 (B*)*

We saw in chapter 4 that B* (1,19-51) is a "testimonial-kerygmatic introduction" to Jesus²⁰⁰. It consists of two connected sections B̊ (1,19-34: the

---

¹⁹⁵ These verses are found in C* (1,1-18) and 3C' (11,55-12,50) which are parallel to each other (see "the Schema of the Literary Structure").

¹⁹⁶ Cf. D. MOLLAT, *Introduction a l'Etude de la Christologie de Saint Jean* (Rome 1970) 17-31; 32-40, where the themes of "*Jesus-Anthrôpos*" and "*Sarx*" in Jn are studied.

¹⁹⁷ The passages in which these verses occur are parallel (C* // 3C). Notice also that *tekna (tou) theou* are also mentioned both in C* (1,12) and 3C (11,52). Similarly, *ex theou gennêthênai*, mentioned in the Prologue (1,13), is taken up and developed in 3,3-8 (that is, in 1C which is parallel to C*) (see "the Schema of the Literary Structure").

¹⁹⁸ Note that 12,37 forms part of 3C' which is parallel to C* (see "the Schema of the Literary Structure").

¹⁹⁹ The unique and intimate relationship of the Logos/Jesus to God (the Father) is indicated by the expressions *ên pros ton theon* (1,1b.2), *monogenês para patros* (1,14c), *monogenês theos ho ôn eis ton kolpon tou patros* (1,18b).

²⁰⁰ See 4.112,2.

Baptist's testimony to Jesus) and C° (1,35-51: the disciples' discovery of Jesus). B° is composed of two parallel pericopes, b° (1,19-28: the Baptist's negative testimony to himself) and b°° (1,29-34: the Baptist's positive testimony to Jesus). Similarly, C° consists of two parallel pericopes, c° (1,35-42: the Messianic discovery of Jesus by the first disciples) and c°° (1,43-51: the Messianic discovery of Jesus by Philip and Nathanael). It must also be noted that b° and b°° take up the testimony of the Baptist introduced in b* (1,6-8) and b** (1,15) respectively. For instance, it was said in the Prologue that John was sent from God "to bear testimony to the light" (1,6-8) and 1,19-28 begins with the statement: "And this is the testimony of John..." (1,19). Again, 1,30 is almost a verbatim repetition of 1,15:

1,15: **houtos ên** *hon eipon*: **ho opisô mou erchomenos**
emprosthen mou gegonen, hoti prôtos mou ên.

1,30: **houtos estin** *hyper hou egô eipon*, **opisô mou erchetai** anêr
hos emprosthen mou gegonen, hoti prôtos mou ên [201].

The negative testimony that the Baptist bears to himself in 1,19-21 (that he is neither the Messiah nor Elijah nor the prophet) is indirectly a testimony to Jesus, since he is presented elsewhere in the Gospel as the expected Messiah (1,41; 11,27) and the eschatological prophet (6,14; cf. also 1,45). The Baptist describes his role as preparing the way of the Lord (1,23), the unknown Messiah (1,26), whose sandals he is unworthy to untie (1,27). In other words, all that the Baptist is, does and says, is directed to Jesus (cf. 1,7-8.15.23-27.28-30).

The positive testimony of John to Jesus as described in 1,29-34 confirms the above conclusion concerning the Christocentric character of his witnessing, for he states unambiguously that the purpose of his baptizing ministry is to reveal Jesus to Israel (1,31). And the content of his testimony is Christ, the Lamb of God (1,29.36), the Son of God (1,34)[202], who exists and ranks before him (1,30), the one on whom the divine Spirit descended and remained (1,32-33), and who baptizes not with water but with the Holy Spirit (1,33).

The next two pericopes c° (1,34-42) and c°° (1,43-51), which are externally parallel to each other (c° c°°) but have an internal spiral structure (b c d e, c' d' e' f)[203], sketch the disciples' discovery of Jesus' Messianic identity and the essential features of discipleship.

The stages in the Messianic discovery and discipleship outlined in 1,35-42 may be summed up in 12 points: 1) others' testimony to Jesus (cf. *emblepsas tô[i] Iêsou... legei: ide ho amnos tou theou*: v.36); 2) listening to the testimony (*akouein*: v.37); 3) following Jesus (*akolouthein*: vv.37-38); 4) seeking [him] (*zêtein*: v.38); 5) coming and seeing for oneself (*erchesthai kai idein*: v.39);

---

[201] These parallels indicate the intimate connection of b* (1,6-8) and b** (1,15) with b° (1,19-28) and b°° (1,29-34), since the latter develop the themes introduced in the former (e.g. *martyrein/martyria* at 1,7.7.8.15.19.32.34).

[202] See 5.121.

[203] See 3.34.

6) remaining with Jesus (*par' autô menein*: v.39); 7) discovering Jesus' Messianic identity (*heurêkamen ton Messian*: v.4l); 8) finding others (*heuriskein*: v.41); 9) announcing Jesus to others (*legein*: v.4l); 10) leading others to Jesus (*agein auton pros ton Iêsoun*: v.42); 11) discovery of being known by Christ (*sy ei Simôn ho hyios Iôannou*: v.42); 12) transformation of oneself (indicated by the change of name: *sy klêthêsê[i] Kêphas*: v.42)[204]. It is evident that most of these themes are directly or indirectly related to Jesus Christ. That is, they are Christocentric in nature.

Many of the themes in 1,35-42 are taken up in 1,43-51 and some new stages in the disciples' progressive discovery of Jesus are introduced there. Thus the themes of following Jesus (*akolouthei moi*: v.43), discovering him (*heurêkamen*: v.45) by coming and seeing (*erchou kai ide*: v.46) and discovering oneself to be known by Jesus (*ide alêthôs Israêlitês en hô[i] dolos ouk estin*: v.47) are found not only in 1,35-42 but also in 1,43-51. One should note that Jesus' initiative in finding and calling Philip to follow him is highlighted in 1,43 (cf. *êthelêsen exelthein... kai heuriskei Philippon kai legei autô[i] ho Iêsous: akolouthei moi*). The new stages in the disciples' discovery of Jesus which are introduced in 1,43-51 are: 1) Jesus' initiative and authority in calling them to follow him (1,43); 2) deeper insight of faith into Jesus as the fulfilment of the Scriptures (*hon egrapsen Môysês en tô[i] nomô[i] kai hoi prophêtai heurêkamen*: v.45) and as the Son of God and the king of Israel (*sy ei ho hyios tou theou, sy basileus ei tou Israêl*: v.49); 3) still greater vision of Jesus (*meizô toutôn opsê[i]*: v.50) as the Son of Man, the revelatory presence of God (v.5l).

The Christocentric character of 1,35-42 and 1,43-51 is also made clear by the numerous Christological titles given to Jesus in these carefully constructed pericopes: "the lamb of God" (*ho amnos tou theou*: v.36), "Rabbi/teacher" (*rhabbi/didaskale*: vv.38.49), "Messiah/Christ" (*Messias/Christos*: v.41), "the one of whom Moses in the Law and also the prophets wrote" (v.45), "the Son of God" (*ho hyios tou theou*: v.49), "the king of Israel" (*basileus tou Israêl*: v.49) and "the Son of Man" (*ho hyios tou anthrôpou*: v.51)[205].

5.212z Although John the Baptist and the disciples play a prominent role in 1,19-34 and 1,35-51 respectively, what they bear witness to and announce is what they have experienced and discovered in Jesus Christ. Notice also that 1,35-51 gives a synopsis of the Johannine understanding of discipleship which is centred on Christ, because it basically consists in a deepening of the faith-experience and progressive discovery of Jesus Christ. In other words, the theological thrust of these introductory pericopes is Christological, a factor which corresponds to the Christological conclusion: "these things are written that you may believe that Jesus is the Christ, the Son of God" (20,31abc)[206].

---

[204] Some of these stages are mentioned by M. VELLANICKAL, "'Discipleship' according to the Gospel of John", *Jeevadhara* 10 (1980) 131-47 and especially 134-40.

[205] Many of these Christological titles will appear again in the subsequent sections of the Gospel (see 5.22; 5.23; 5.24; 5.25; 5.26 below).

[206] See 4.111 and 4.112,3.

5.213 *Jesus, the Messiah, in 2,1-11 (A+)*

It has been established earlier that the first Cana-sign (2,1-11) is a bridge-pericope which forms part of both the Christocentric introduction (1,1-2,11) and the Book of Jesus' Signs (2,1-12,50)[207].

We have also seen that 2,1-11 has a chiastic structure (a b c c' b' a')[208] all the elements of which have something to do directly or indirectly with Jesus. Thus the name of "Jesus" is explicitly mentioned 6 times (vv.1.2.3.4.7.11) in four subunits (a, b, c', a'). He is introduced in v.2 (a) as having been invited to the marriage at Cana. When the shortage of wine is brought to his notice, he makes an enigmatic reference to his "hour" (*oupô hêkei hê hôra mou*: v.4). In v.5 Mary instructs the servants to do whatever he would tell them. In vv.7-8 it is Jesus who tells them to fill the jars with water and to take it to the steward of the feast. Though Jesus is not explicitly mentioned in vv.9-10 (b'), the bridegroom who is praised by the steward for keeping the good wine till the end (v.10) is a symbolic figure of Jesus, the Messianic bridegroom (cf. 3,29), who gives the best wine of Messianic blessings. This is confirmed by the structural parallelism (bb') between *oinon ouk echousin* (v.4) and *ton kalon oinon* (v.10), whose origin the steward did not know (*ouk ê[i]dei pothen estin*)[209].

Finally, the Evangelist explains the significance of this miracle as "the beginning of the signs" (*archê tôn sêmeiôn*: v.11a)[210], which manifested Jesus' glory (*ephanerôsen tên doxan autou*: v.11b). This explanation clearly underlines the Christocentric (cf. "his glory"), revelatory (cf. "manifested") character of the first Cana-sign[211]. It would have revealed his glory to the disciples because the

---

[207] See 3.192; 4.112 and 4.121. The bridging nature of 2,1-11 is described by SCHNACKENBURG as follows:

> The story of this first "sign" by which Jesus reveals his glory (v.11) is *both the climax of the foregoing*, which pressed on towards a visible manifestation of the Messiah acclaimed but not fully known by his first disciples (cf. 1:50,51) *and the starting-point for the whole self-revelation of Jesus which is given through "signs"* (cf. 12:37; 20:30). This is indicated by the final remark of the evangelist, v.11, particularly valuable after the brief narrative, since it points forward to other "signs" to come (11a) and rounds off at the same time the story of the winning of the first disciples (11c) (I, 323; my italics).

[208] See 3.32.

[209] Jesus' (mysterious) origin is often referred to in the Gospel by means of the expression *pothen einai* (cf. 7,27.28; 9,29.30; 19,9).

[210] See 5.131 for the meaning of the Johannine "sign".

[211] SCHNACKENBURG comments on the primary theological meaning of the first Cana-sign: "the main interest of the evangelist is concentrated on the Messianic and Christological self-revelation of Jesus..." (I, 339).

The ecclesiological (cf. *mathêtai* at 2,2.11) aspect of 2,1-11 is subordinated to its Christological significance (cf. the conclusion at 2,11). In fact, the *ecclesiology* itself of the first Cana-sign is *Christocentric*. First of all, the group of disciples, which may be thought of as representing the future Christian community, is referred to as "his disciples" (*hoi mathêtai autou*: 2,2.11), which shows that it is only by belonging to Jesus that they become "disciples". This union with Jesus is indicated even by the Greek grammatical construction of 2,2, which consists of a *plural subject* (*kai ho Iêsous kai hoi*

context of the wedding (*gamos*: vv.1.2), and the quality (*ho kalos oinos*: v.10) and abundance (about 120 gallons: v.6) of the wine given by Jesus could have been understood symbolically by the disciples as signaling the inauguration of the Messianic times when there would be an abundance of grain and wine [212]. In other words, in the historical setting painted by the Evangelist, the disciples would have interpreted the Cana-sign Messianically and thereby confirmed their faith in him as the expected Messiah (*kai episteusan eis auton hoi mathētai autou*: v.11). For the Christian reader who knows the Johannine theme of replacement, the Cana-sign could also reveal Jesus' glory in another way, because the water for Jewish purification was replaced by choice wine as a sign of the best gift of Jesus to the believers, namely, eternal life (cf. 10,10: "I have come that they may have life and have it in abundance"), which would be given when he would be "lifted up" (cf. 3,14-15) during his "hour" (2,4) of glorification (cf. 17,1-3) [213].

5.21z Looking at the triple introduction (1,1-2,11) from the theological point of view we find it to be through and through Christocentric [214]. In the hymnic Prologue both the divine (cf. *theos*: 1,1.18) and the human (cf. *sarx*: 1,14) aspects of the incarnate Word are emphasized. His mediation in creation (1,3),

---

mathētai autou) and a *singular verb* (*eklēthē*). Secondly, the disciples' commitment to Christ in faith is underscored in the concluding statement that they "believed in him" (*episteusan eis auton*: 2,11c).

The Johannine *Mariology* of 2,1-11 is also *Christocentric*, for Mary is never mentioned by her name; she is introduced and always referred to as "the mother of Jesus" (*hē mētēr tou Iēsou/autou*: 2,1.3.5). Again, what she tells the servants ("Do whatever he tells you": 2,5) indicates that her role is to dispose the hearts of men to do Jesus' will. His addressing his mother as "woman" (*gynai*: 2,4) and his reference to his "hour" (*hē hōra mou*: 2,4) show that "she is to receive a role when *the hour* of his glorification comes..." (BROWN, I, 109). This is confirmed by an interesting detail in the Johannine narrative, namely, Mary seems to be primarily concerned about the disciples of Jesus who have no wine to drink, for her words ("they have no wine": 2,3) may refer to "his disciples" (*hoi mathētai autou*) mentioned at the end of the immediately preceding verse. This is supported by the fact that nothing is said about the reaction of the bridegroom or the wedding guests to Jesus' sign of changing water into wine, whereas his disciples are said to have "believed in him" because of the revelatory sign (2,11). Thus Mary's intervention seems to have resulted in the deepening of the disciples' faith in Jesus. In short, the incipient Johannine Mariology in 2,1-11 is closely linked to its ecclesiology which is Christ-centred.

[212] "Through such symbolism the Cana miracle could have been understood by the disciples as a sign of the Messianic times and the new dispensation, much in the same manner that they would have understood Jesus' statement about the new wine in the Synoptic tradition. The reference in vs.11 to Jesus' revealing his glory fits into this theme, for the revelation of divine glory was to be a mark of the last times" (BROWN, I, 105).

Here Jesus seems to be implicitly presented as the Bridegroom-Messiah (cf. 3,29). Cf. J.-P. MICHAUD, "Le signe de Cana (Jean 2,1-11)", in: *Maria in Sacra Scriptura* V (1967) 37-97, especially 86-87; PANIMOLLE (I, 218-19).

[213] See 5.213.

[214] Regarding 2,1-11 PANIMOLLE says: "L'interesse principale e il significato più profondo del racconto del segno operato a Çana è certamente di carattere cristologico" (I, 217). Cf. also BROWN, I, 103; SCHNACKENBURG, I, 339; M.-É. BOISMARD considers the Cana-sign as a manifestation of Jesus, the Messiah (*Du Baptême à Cana*, 135).

revelation (1,17-18) and regeneration (1,12-13) is highlighted. In other words, he is not only the Son of God become man so as to reveal God to men but also the giver of eternal life to all. In order to have a share in his life (1,4) or to be born of God (1,13), men must welcome the incarnate Word of God by believing in his name (1,12). This is similar to the soteriological conclusion, according to which it is by believing in Jesus, the Christ, the Son of God, that we can have a share in his divine life (*hina pisteuontes zôên echête en tô[i] onomati autou*: 20,31d).

In short, in the Prologue the reader is taken to the summit of a high hill, from which he can have a panoramic view of most of the Johannine theological mountain consisting of a range of hills revealing the person, mission and salvific significance of Jesus Christ. The light of the Prologue is like lightning that illuminates the theological horizon of the Gospel of John. Or rather, for one who reads it carefully and meditates it prayerfully, it is like the beautiful, inexpressible and unforgettable sunrise (which I was privileged to see) which gradually lights up the long Himalayan range with everchanging kaleidoscopic colours. It not only dispels the surrounding darkness (1,5) but also reveals the snow-covered chain of mountain peaks, calling all to come and contemplate its majestic glory (1,14). It also discloses the dark threatening clouds forming in the distant horizon (1,10-11) and yet renders them radiant by placing a silver lining around them (1,12-13). Praises of the rising sun (Son) surge in our grateful hearts for the graces of light (1,4.5.9), truth (1,14.16-17) and life (1,4.12-13).

The Prologue may be compared also to the Synoptic accounts of the transfiguration of Jesus (Mt 17,1-8; Mk 9,2-8; Lk 9,28-36) which reveals his divine glory. Just as Jesus takes James, John and Peter to a high mountain (Mt 17,1; Mk 9,2) to pray (Lk 9,28) and to manifest his divine metamorphosis (Mt 17,2; Mk 9,2; Lk 9,29), so John takes us, in the spirit of prayer, to the top of a hymnic mountain to contemplate Jesus' divine glory in the flesh (1,14). Just as Elijah and Moses appear to the privileged disciples in the Synoptic transfiguration (Mt 17,3; Mk 9,4; Lk 9,10), so John the Baptist (1,6-8.15) and Moses (1,17) are named in the Prologue. And the disciples in the Prologue (we), like the privileged apostles in the Synoptic transfiguration, see the glory of the Son of God (Jn 1,14: *etheasametha tên doxan autou, doxan hôs monogenous para patros*; cf. Lk 9,32: *eidon tên doxan autou*). But instead of seeing Jesus' "face shining like the sun" or "his garments becoming white as light" (Mt 17,2; Mk 9,3), we see him as "the true light that enlightens every man" (Jn 1,9). Again, instead of Peter making a "tent" (*skênê*) for Jesus (Mt 17,4; Mk 9,5; Lk 9,33), we are told that the divine Word "has pitched his tent among us" (*eskênôsen en hêmin*: Jn 1,14). And instead of a voice from the cloud declaring: "This is my beloved Son" (Mt 17,5; 9,7; Lk 9,35), we hear the voice of John the Baptist crying out: "He who comes after me ranks before me, for he was before me" (Jn 1,15), and the Christian community's confession of Jesus as the "only Son from the Father" (1,14) and the "only Son-God who is in the bosom of the Father" (1,18).

From the pinnacle of the Prologue we descend to a lower level of the hill, when we come to 1,19-51 which deals basically with Jesus' Messianic identity (cf. the many Christological titles such as "the Messiah/Christ", "the Lamb of God", "the Son of God", "the king of Israel", "the Son of Man"). The fundamental theological thrust of this "testimonial-kerygmatic introduction" (B*) is the same as that of the "Christological conclusion" (Bz), namely, to present Jesus as the Messiah (1,20.25.41; 20,31) and the Son of God (1,34.49; 20,31). Note that the title "the Son of God" at 1,34.49 receives deeper meaning in the light of the Prologue which presented Jesus as "God" (1,1.18) and the "only Son from the Father" (1,14.18), truths which John the Baptist and the first disciples could not have known when they proclaimed him "the Son of God".

We descend to the foot of the theological mountain when we come to the first Cana-sign (2,1-11). The sign of changing water into wine points to Jesus as the Messiah, although this is not explicitly stated. This "historical sign-introduction" (A+) is connected to the "historical sign-conclusion" (Az). In fact, the latter ("Now Jesus did many other signs before the disciples...": 20,30) could form a fitting conclusion to the former (2,1-11), which ends with the Evangelist's observation that this Cana-sign was the beginning of Jesus' signs which manifested his glory and confirmed the faith of his disciples (2,11).

To sum up, while A+ (2,1-11) and Az (20,30) imply that Jesus is the Messiah because of the sign(s) he has done, B* (1,19-51) and Bz (20,31abc) explicitly testify, proclaim or state that Jesus is "the Christ" and "the Son of God". This human-divine Jesus Christ is confessed in C* (1,1-18) and Cz (20,31d) as the source of eternal life for those who believe in him. Thus the triple introduction (1,1-2,11) contains in a nutshell the basic theological message of the entire Gospel, the Christocentric scope of which is stated by the Evangelist himself in the conclusion (20,30-31).

5.22 The Christocentric Theological Sketch in "Jesus' Initial Signs and Encounters" (Jn 2-4)

In the following paragraphs we shall sketch the Johannine theology of the parallel pericopes/episodes (1AA', 1BB', 1CC') in the chiastic structure (1A B C C' B' A') of "Jesus' Initial Signs and Encounters" (Jn 2-4).

5.221 *Jesus, the Messiah, the life-giver, in 2,1-12 (1A) and 4,43-54 (1A')*

We have already seen that the first Cana-sign (2,1-11) is presented Christocentrically. This is equally true of the second Cana-sign (4,43-54), at the beginning and end of which the first is recalled (4,46.54) and which has the same general pattern as that of the first [215].

---

[215] See 4.312,1.

The sign of healing the royal official's dying son calls our attention to Jesus' life-giving power. This is stressed by mentioning twice that the child was "about to die" (*êmellen gar apothnê[i]skein*: 4,47; *prin apothanein*: 4,49) and thrice that he "lives" (*ho hyios sou zê[i]*: 4,50.53; *ho pais autou zê[i]*: 4,51). Just as in the first Cana-sign the faith of the disciples in Jesus, the Messiah (cf. 1,41), was confirmed or deepened (*episteusan eis auton*: 2,11), so in the second Cana-sign the fragile faith of the royal official is gradually strengthened. For when he at first comes to Jesus with the request to come down to Capernaum and heal his son (4,47), he seems to believe in Jesus only as a wonder-worker (which is implied in Jesus' complaint in 4,48: "unless you see signs and wonders, you will not believe"). Next we find him believing Jesus' word (*episteusen ho anthrôpos tô[i] logô[i]*: 4,50) that his son lives. Finally, we are told that he and his whole household became believers (*episteusen autos kai hê oikia autou holê*: 4,53), when he realized that his son was cured at the very moment when Jesus told him that his son was alive (4,53).

By means of the parallel presentation of the two Cana-signs in which the Christocentric faith of the disciples (2,11) is similar to that of the royal official (4,53), the Evangelist inculcates the importance of faith in Christ. What matters for the Evangelist is not whether one is a Jew (like the first disciples) or a Gentile (like probably the royal official), but whether one believes in Jesus or not.

Just as the first Cana-sign could be theologically interpreted at two levels, so also the second. In the historical setting envisaged by the Evangelist, the sign of healing the dying child would have made his father and his household believe in Jesus as a powerful prophet (cf. 9,17) or as the Messiah sent by God (cf. 7,31). But at the post-resurrectional level the sign of saving the life of a dying child would have pointed to Jesus as the giver of eternal life (cf. 5,21.26; 10,10). Note that at both the levels the sign is described and interpreted Christologically (4,48. 53.54; cf. 2,11). We are told neither how the water in the jars was changed into wine nor how the royal official's son was cured from a distance, but it is quite clear that the miraculous signs were produced by the transformative and saving power of the word of Jesus (2,7-9; 4,50.53). In short, both the Cana-signs are Christocentric in character.

5.222 Jesus, the prophet, the Messiah, the Son of God, the temple of God, the Saviour of the world, in 2,13-25 (1B) and 4,1-42 (1B')

The Christological significance of the prophetic action of the cleansing of the temple was understood by the disciples at two levels. At the historical level they interpreted it Messianically in the light of Ps 69,9 (= LXX Ps 68,9: "the zeal for thy house has consumed me"). But by changing the past *katephagen me* of Ps 68,9 (LXX) into the future *kataphagetai me* (Jn 2,17), the Evangelist hints at the future death of Jesus[216]. His death and resurrection are intended by his

---

[216] SCHNACKENBURG, I, 347 and n. 17 which mentions the Messianic application of Ps 69 by the early Church as reflected in Jn 15,25; 19,29; Mk 15,36 par.; Mt 27,34; Ac 1,20; Rom 11,9-10; 15,3.

enigmatic saying to the Jews: *lysate ton naon touton kai en trisin hêmerais egerô auton* (2,19)[217]. "The explanation given in 2:21 gives the saying about the destruction and rebuilding of the temple a... supremely Christological significance. Jesus freely surrenders his body to destruction; but within three days he will deliver it again from death (cf. 10:18)"[218]. Besides presenting Jesus as the Messiah who would be killed and raised up again on the third day (2,17-22), the sayings of Jesus also indicate at least indirectly that he is the Son of God (for he calls the temple the house of "my Father" [*tou patros mou*]: 2,16)[219], who has divine power to raise his dead body to life again (for he says: "I will raise it up [*egerô auton*] in three days": 2,19). The cleansing of the temple reveals Jesus not only as the Messiah and the Son of God but also as the new temple of God (2,21: *naos tou sômatos autou*)[220]. This was grasped by the disciples only after the resurrection of Jesus, as the Evangelist himself tells us in 2,22.

We saw in ch. 4 that the cleansing of the temple (1B = 2,13-25) is in many ways parallel to the Samaritan episode (1B' = 4,1-42)[221]. In this dramatic episode the mystery of Jesus' person and mission is gradually revealed. First he is presented as a human being who is tired (*kekopiakôs*: 4,6) and thirsty (cf. Jesus' request for a drink at 4,7) after a long journey. The Samaritan woman takes him for an ordinary Jew (*sy Ioudaios ôn*: 4,9), who, however, does not follow the Jewish custom of not associating with the Samaritans (4,9). Jesus then suggests that he is the one who gives "living water" (4,10), at which point the woman asks ironically whether he is greater than Jacob who gave the Samaritans the well at Sychar (4,12). This question implicitly contains the theological truth that Jesus is greater than the patriarchs (cf. a similar ironical question by the Jews in Jerusalem at 8,53: "Are you greater than our father Abraham who died?" and Jesus' answer at 8,58: "Before Abraham was, I am"). Because of his superhuman knowledge of the irregular life the woman was

---

[217] Notice that the words *naos, lyein* and *egeirein* can refer both to the temple and to the body of Jesus. This intended double meaning leads to the misunderstanding of the Jews who take the words to refer only to the temple (*Ibid.*, 349).

[218] *Ibid.*, 352.

[219] This is the first time that Jesus himself calls God "my Father". This will be repeated frequently and developed in Jn 5-10 (e.g. 5,17.43; 10,29.37).

[220] The very action of cleansing the temple may point to Jesus' divinity. "Con il gesto dell'espulsione dei mercanti Gesù si è presentato come un personaggio divino, come il figlio di Dio, realizzando in tal modo la profezia di Mal 3,1ss che parla della venuta del Signore nel suo tempio per purificarlo" (PANIMOLLE, I, 244). Cf. also F.-M. BRAUN, "L'expulsion des vendeurs du Temple (Mt. XXI,12-17,23-27; Mc. XI,15-19,27-33; Lc. XIX,45-XX,8; Jo. II,13-22)", *RB* 38 (1929) 178-200, especially 189.

It may be noted here that already Nathan's messianic oracle had connected the construction of the temple with divine filiation (2 Sam 7,13-14: "He shall build a house for my name... I will be his father and he shall be my son"). The newness in Jn is that Jesus himself is the new temple of God (2,19-21).

[221] See 4.312,2.

leading, Jesus is recognized by her as a prophet (4,16-19). At the end of his discussion with her about the place and nature of worship (4,20-24) Jesus reveals himself to her as the Samaritan Messiah (*Ta'eb*?) who would reveal everything (4,25-26.29).

Similarly, Jesus manifests himself to the disciples as the one who does the will of God who sent him (4,34) and as the one who has sent them to reap the harvest (4,38). In other words, Jesus is the Apostle par excellence of God and the disciples are Jesus' apostles who continue his mission (17,18; 20,21).

Finally, the episode comes to a climactic conclusion with the Samaritans' acknowledgement of Jesus as "the Saviour of the world" (4,42). Furthermore, a Christic worship of the Father is hinted at both in the cleansing of the temple (cf. 2,19.21: the new temple of God is the risen body of Jesus) and in the dialogue with the Samaritan woman on the place of worship (cf. 4,21-23: the Father is to be worshipped not in Jerusalem nor in Gerizim but "in Spirit and in truth", the latter of which terms refers to the revelation in Jesus who is "the truth" [cf. 14,6]). Since Jesus is the new temple of God, the Father can be truly worshipped only in Christ.

5.222z In both the cleansing of the temple and the Samaritan episode Christ is the central figure who reveals himself as a prophet and/or the Messiah, who is truly human (for he is hungry, thirsty and tired and can be killed like any other human being) and yet as one possessing superhuman knowledge and power which point to his divine origin and mission as the Saviour of the world. The aspect of his unique divine Sonship, which will be taken up and developed later (e.g. in 5,19-30), is only hinted at here (2,16; 4,21-23). Although in both the episodes (2,13-25; 4,1-42) Jesus reveals himself, the response of men is not the same. The blind unbelief of the Jewish authorities in Jerusalem (2,18.20) is probably to be contrasted with the gradual growth in the faith-vision of the Samaritan woman (4,7-30); similarly, the superficial faith of the Jerusalemites based on the marvelous aspect of the miracles of Jesus (2,23-25) seems most probably to be contrasted with "the deeper faith of the Samaritans based on the word of Jesus"[222]. In short, the theology of both the Johannine episodes is primarily Christocentric, since the two themes that dominate them are the self-revelation of Jesus and the human response of unbelief or faith in him[223].

---

[222] BROWN, I, 185.
[223] SCHNACKENBURG, I, 343-44; 420-21; PANIMOLLE, I, 244-46; 248-52; 404-410; 417-19.
The theme of the revelation of who Jesus is, we have seen, is the central theme both of 1,19-51 (B*) and 20,31abc (Bz), which may therefore be thought of as being parallel to 2,13-25 (1B) and 4,1-42 (1B'). Notice also that just as the reaction of the Jewish delegation to the indirect revelation of Jesus through the testimony of the Baptist was negative (1,24-25), so the response of the Jewish authorities to Jesus' revelation through the cleansing of the temple is negative (2,18), whereas Jesus' revelation is received in faith both by the first disciples (1,35-51) and by the Samaritan woman and people (4,1-42). The revelation of Jesus as the Son of God and the hostile response of the Jews in Jerusalem is further focussed in 5,1-47 (2B) and 10,22-42 (2B'), as we shall show below (see 5.231).

5.223 *Jesus, the Messiah, the bridegroom, the Son of Man, the Son of God, the mediator of the Holy Spirit and eternal life, in 2,23-3,21 (1C) and 3,22-4,3 (1C')*

Many of the major themes of the Prologue (1,1-18 = C*) are taken up and developed in the parallel dialogue-discourses in 2,23-3,21 (1C) and 3,22-4,3 (1C').

Thus "birth from God" (*ek tou theou gennêthênai*), which was mentioned at 1,13 in connection with "becoming children of God" (*tekna theou genesthai*: 1,12), becomes the basic theme of Jesus' dialogue proper with Nicodemus (3,1-10) which repeatedly stresses the need of "being born from above/Spirit" (*gennêthênai anôthen/ek tou pneumatos*: 3,3.5.6.7.8) in order to see or enter the kingdom of God (3,3.5), an expresssion which means to experience eternal life (3,16.36; note the parallelism between *idein tên basileian tou thou* at 3,3 and *idein zôên* at 3,36).

Jesus Christ was presented in the Prologue as the unique revealer of God because of the unique place he occupies in the bosom of the Father, which enables him to know the Father more intimately than any one else and to communicate this loving knowledge to others (1,18). This unique revelatory role of Jesus is restated in different words in 3,11-13 and 3,31-34 by emphasizing the truth that only Jesus can reveal heavenly mysteries to humanity because only he has seen and heard them and knows them for certain, and so can bear witness to them [224].

A personal commitment in faith to the revealed person of the (incarnate) Word (*pisteuein eis to onoma autou*) was indicated at 1,12 as the necessary condition for becoming children of God. A similar faith in the person of the only begotten Son of God (*pisteuein eis to onoma tou monogenous hyiou tou theou*) is stated at 3,18 to be the sine-qua-non condition for avoiding "judgement", for only the one who believes in the Son (*ho pisteuôn eis auton/ton hyion*) can have eternal life (*echei zôên aiônion*: 3,16.36) [225]. Notice that faith (*pisteuein*), which is mentioned twice in the Prologue (1,7.12), is spoken of many times in 2,23-3,21 (cf. 2,23; 3,12.12.15.16.18.18.18), so much so that many scholars consider faith in Jesus Christ as the most fundamental theme of the pericope [226].

Although both the Nicodemus-episode and the Baptist-episode mention God the Father (*ho theos*: 3.16.17; 3,33.34; *ho patêr*: 3,35), He is spoken of in

---

[224] It is also worth mentioning that the related revelatory terms "light" (*phôs*) and "truth" (*alêtheia*) are found both in the Prologue (1,4.5.7.8.8.9; 1,14.17) and in the discourse to Nicodemus (3,19.19.20.20.21; 3,21).

[225] Note that the theme of "life" (*zôê*) was introduced already in the Prologue (1,4.4).

[226] G. C. GAETA, *Il dialogo con Nicodemo* (Brescia 1974) 143; PANIMOLLE, I, 294; 301. Faith is mentioned also in 3,22-36 (v.36). Not receiving the testimony as indicative of lack of faith is spoken of both at 3,11 (*kai tên martyrian hêmôn ou lambanei*) and at 3,32 (*kai tên martyrian autou oudeis lambanei*). The refusal of his own to receive the Logos was mentioned already in the Prologue (*kai hoi idioi auton ou parelabon*: 1,11).

connection with His sending of the Son into the world. Similarly, the pneumatology of the two episodes is Christocentric, since it is Christ who gives the Spirit without measure (3,34; cf. 7,39; 19,30; 20,21), and since birth from the Spirit (3,5.6.8) will become a reality only when Jesus, the Son of Man, will be lifted up (3,14) on the cross, the place from which he will bestow the Spirit (19,30). In short, the primary theological emphasis in both 2,23-3,21 and 3,22-36 is Christocentric.

5.22z Looking at the theological development in the literary structure of Jn 2-4 as a whole, we find that the two Cana-signs (at the beginning and end of the chiastic structure) point to Jesus as the Messiah. That he is more than the expected eschatological Messiah is hinted at in the cleansing of the temple and in the dialogue with the woman of Samaria, since he calls God "my Father" or "the Father". The intimate Father-Son relationship and the co-related themes of faith in the Son and eternal life are further developed in the dialogue-discourses in 3,1-21 and 3,22-36, which are the central episodes (1C and 1C') in the chiastic structure (1A B C C' B' A') of Jn 2-4. In other words, there is a widening and a deepening of the Christocentric theology as we move from the extreme episodes (1A and 1A'), whose signs manifest Jesus as the Messiah, to the second and fifth episodes (1B and 1B'), which not only reveal Jesus' Messiahship but also hint at his divine Sonship, to the central episodes (1C and 1C'), which underline the mediation of the Messianic bridegroom, the Son of Man, the Son of God, in revelation and salvation (eternal life) to those who believe in him [227].

It must also be mentioned that there is a progress from the first Cana-sign (1A) to the second (1A'). The second sign deals with death (*apothnê[i]skein*: 4,47.49) and (physical) life (*zên*: 4,50.51.53) and therefore is related to the central subsections (1C and 1C') which speak of (eternal) life (*zôê [aiônios]*: 3,15. 16.36.36). Thus the sign of Jesus' reviving the dying child in 1A' becomes, in the light of 1C and 1C', a symbol of Jesus' gift of eternal life. Again, what was only implicit in 1A is explicitated in 1C', namely, Jesus is the Messianic bridegroom (cf. *nymphios* at 2,9 and at 3,29). Thus there is not only parallelism but also thematic development in the chiastic structure of Jn 2-4.

We may note also that 1A and 1A' correspond to Az (20,30), since they describe the signs which Jesus did; 1B and 1B' to Bz (20,31abc), since they present Jesus as the Christ and the Son of God; 1C and 1C' to Cz (20,31d), since they speak about eternal life for those who believe in him.

5.23 The Christocentric Theological Sketch in "Jesus' Works, Signs and Discussions" (Jn 5-10)

When we pass from the section of "Jesus' Initial Signs and Encounters" (Jn 2-4) to the section of "Jesus' Works, Signs and Discussions" (Jn 5-10), we reach

---

[227] See 4.31.

a new stage not only in the dramatic but also in the theological development of the Fourth Gospel. For example, while Jesus' miracles are referred to mostly as "signs" in Jn 2-4, often they are designated as "works" in Jn 5-10. Again, whereas both the signs (2,1-11; 4,46-54) described in Jn 2-4 are performed by Jesus at the request of someone pleading for his help (2,3; 4,47.49) and that even after an apparent refusal (2,4; 4,48), all the miracles narrated in Jn 5-10 are done on Jesus' own initiative (5,1-9; 6,1-15.16-21; 9,1-7). This fact already indicates a difference in emphasis in the presentation of Jesus, that is to say, it is in the nature of the Son of God to do the works of the Father in favour of the sick and the hungry, the helpless and the hopeless (cf. 5,6.17; 6,5.19; 9,4; 10,32). Many of the theological themes mentioned in passing or dealt with up to a certain point in the first section are taken up and developed more fully in the second (e.g. the divine Sonship of Jesus and the Fatherhood of God; the themes of life, light and judgement). There is also a certain correspondence in the themes of the parallel passages in the chiastic structure (2B C D D' C' B') of Jn 5-10 [228], as we shall see below.

5.231 *Jesus, the Christ, the Son of God, in 5,1-47 (2B) and 10,22-42 (2B')*

We have already seen that the Jews in Jerusalem were scandalized by Jesus' cleansing the temple in 1B (2,13-22) and his implicit claim that he is the Son of God (cf. *ho patêr mou*: 2,16). In 2B (Jn 5) Jesus cures a cripple on a Sabbath (5,1-9) and affirms explicitly: "My Father (*ho patêr mou*) is working still and I am working" (5,17). Because of his violation of the Sabbath [229] and his claim that God is his own Father (*patera idion elegen ton theon*: 5,18), which means that he is the Son of God, the Jews in Jerusalem persecute him and seek to kill him (5,16.18). Similarly, in 10,22-42 (2B') the Jews in Jerusalem attempt to stone him (10,31) because of his claim: "I and the Father are one" (10,30) [230], for they consider it a blasphemy for him as for any man to make himself God (10,33) or equal to God (5,18). In both these instances Jesus defends himself through a discourse (5,19-47; 10,34-38) which demonstrates that he is the Son of God. These factors make it evident that the theological emphasis in both the episodes is Christocentric.

---

[228] See 4.32 for the chiastic structure (2B C D D' C' B') of this section.

[229] Healing the sick on the Sabbath was considered by the Jews to be a work forbidden by the Law of Moses (cf. 7,23) and therefore Jesus was branded as a sinner (9,16.24).

[230] Similarly the Jews in Jerusalem pick up stones to throw at Jesus (8,59) when he says: "Before Abraham was, I am" (8,58), because it was a blasphemy for them.

Notice that the accusations of breaking the Sabbath (5,18; 7,23) which shows that Jesus is a sinner (9,16.24) and of blaspheming (10,33) because of his claim to divine pre-existence (8,58) and unique union with God, the Father (5,17; 10,30), occur in the two extreme (2B and 2B') and central (2D and 2D') elements of the chiastic structure of Jn 5-10 (2B C D D' C' B').

The primary purpose of the entire pericope 5,19-30 is to present Jesus as "the Son"[231]. This is clear from the repeated use of the title *ho hyios* (8 times) in 5,19-30 and the inclusion between 5,19 and 5,30. The chiastic structure (*a b c d d'c'b'a'*) of the pericope itself underscores the unique divine Sonship of Jesus[232]. The total dependence of the Son on the Father in everything he does is emphatically stated in *a* (5,19) and *a'* (5,30). But this dependence is not one of a servant but of a Son whom the Father loves tenderly and to whom He lovingly reveals everything that He does (5,20 = *b*) and whom He empowers even to call the dead from their tombs and raise them to eternal life or judgement (5,28-29 = *b'*). The Son, like the Father, can raise the dead and give life to anyone he likes (5,21 = *c*) because the Son shares in the very life of the Father (5,26 = *c'*). Similarly, the Father has given the Son, who is also Son of Man, the divine privilege and power to judge (5,22.27 = *c c'*), which entitles him to be honoured like the Father (5,23 = *c*). Therefore, in order to have eternal life and escape condemnation, all must listen to the Son (5,24.25 = *d d'*). Clearly both the soteriology and eschatology of this discourse are Christocentric since they follow from the Son-Christology[233], according to which there is perfect union of action and being between the Father and the Son (cf. also 10,25.30: "I and the Father are one").

Jesus' claim to be the divine Son is supported by many witnesses like John the Baptist who bore testimony to Jesus, the truth (5,33; cf. 14,6), the works that Jesus, the Son, does in his Father's name (5,36; cf. 10,25.37-38), the Father who sent him (5,37; 10,36) and the Scriptures which testify to him (5,39; cf. 10,34-35).

It is to be noted that, besides the similarities between 2B and 2B', there is also a certain progress both in Jesus' self-revelation and in the adverse reaction of the Jews in the two subsections. For instance, while in 5,17.19 Jesus states that the Son can do only what the Father does (cf. also 5,30), in 10,30 and 10,38 he affirms his total unity with the Father and their mutual indwelling. In other words, there is a progress from "doing" in 2B to "being" in 2B' (besides mentioning "doing" as in 2B). Similarly, whereas 5,18 tells us that the Jews were seeking (*ezētoun*) to kill Jesus because of a blasphemous statement, in 10,31 they actually pick up stones to put him to death then and there for blasphemously making himself God (cf. 10,33).

In short, the central theological message of both 2B (5,1-47) and 2B' (10,22-42) is that Jesus is the Son of God who is intimately and uniquely united with the Father in action and being[234].

---

[231] PANIMOLLE, II, 65-66; cf. also *L'evangelista Giovanni*, 164-67.

[232] See 3.32.

[233] F. MUSSNER, *Zôê. Die Anschauung vom "Leben" in vierten Evangelium unter Berücksichtigung der Johannesbriefe* (München 1952) 48-188; SCHNACKENBURG, II, 352-61, especially 355-56; 426-37; J. BLANK, *Krisis*, 120-82.

[234] Notice that both the dialogue-discourses in 5,1-47 and 10,22-42 begin with a question about Jesus' identity ("Who is the *man* who told you, 'Take up your pallet and walk'?": 5,12: "How long will you keep us in suspense? If you are the *Christ*, tell us plainly: 10,24). Note also that Jesus' words reveal that he is more than a mere man and the Christ, namely, he is the Son of God. Notice that this is parallel to the statement in Bz (20,31abc), namely, that Jesus is not only the Christ but also "the Son of God".

5.232 *Jesus, the prophet-king, the Son of God, the bread of life, the life-giving shepherd, in 6,1-71 (2C) and 10,1-21 (2C')*

Just as in the healing of the paralytic in Jn 5, so in Jn 6 Jesus takes the initiative in feeding the five thousand (6,4-13)[235]. And the crowd recognizes the miraculous multiplication of the loaves as a sign of the expected eschatological prophet-king (6,14-15)[236]. Furthermore, Jesus' walking on the stormy sea (6,16-19) and his reassuring, revelatory *egô eimi* saying to the frightened disciples (6,20; cf. Ex 3,14) manifest his divinity[237]. The Christocentric character becomes much more prominent in the discourse that follows (6,22-59). First of all, Jesus reveals himself as "the bread of life" (*egô eimi ho artos tês zôês*: 6,35.48), the divine revelation that gives life to men[238], the life-giving bread from heaven which is the Father's gift to them (6,32-33)[239]. In order to have this bread of life which bestows eternal life man must believe in Jesus, the Father's emissary (6,29.35.40.47)[240], and eat his flesh and drink his blood (6,53.54.57.58). Peter's profession of faith in Jesus as "the Holy One of God" who has "the words of eternal life" (6,68-69) points in the same Christocentric direction that he is the source of life for those who believe in him as the divine Messiah (compare *ho hagios tou theou* in Jn 6,69 and *ho hosios sou* in Ac 2,27; 13,35)[241].

In the parallel parabolic discourse in 10,1-21 (2C') Jesus presents himself as the Messianic shepherd (10,2-4), the door of the sheep (10,7.9) and the life-giving

---

[235] In the Synoptics it is the disciples who tell Jesus to send the crowd away so that it may go and buy food (Mt 14,15; Mk 6,35; Lk 9,12) and who distribute the loaves and the fish to the crowd (Mt 14,19; Mk 6,41; Lk 9,16); in Jn it is Jesus himself who asks Philip about buying food to feed the crowd (6,5), distributes the food to the reclining crowd (6,11) and asks the disciples to collect the left-overs (6,12).

[236] W. A. MEEKS, *The Prophet-King. Moses Traditions and the Johannine Christology* (SNT 14) (Leiden 1967) 17-29; 87-99.

[237] "Il Verbo incarnato, camminando sulle acque e proclamando: Io sono, si rivela come vero Dio, a somiglianza di Jahvé, la cui via passava sul mare e i cui sentieri sono nelle grandi acque (Sal 77,20)" (PANIMOLLE, II, 174). Cf. also MAGGIONI, 1451; PH. B. HARNER, *The "I AM" of the Fourth Gospel* (Philadelphia 1970) 47-48.

[238] PANIMOLLE states: "nel discorso di Cafarnao il Verbo incarnato è presentato come la manifestazione piena e perfetta della vita divina, sotto l'immagine del pane vivente disceso dal cielo" (II, 197-98). Cf. also BROWN, I, 272-74.

[239] Note the similarity between 6,32-33 and 3,16 (which are found in parallel subsections, namely, in 2C = 6,1-71 and 1C = 2,23-3,21):

3,16: houtos gar êgapêsen *ho theos* **ton kosmon**
hôste *ton hyion ton monogenê* **edôken**,
hina pas ho pisteuôn eis auton... echê z ô ê n aiônion.
6,32: *ho patêr* mou **didôsin** hymin
ton arton ek tou ouranou ton alêthinon;
6,33: *ho gar artos tou theou* estin... z ô ê n **didous** *tô[i] kosmô[i]*.

[240] Notice that the necessity of an existential faith in Jesus for having eternal life was mentioned already in the parallel passages 1C (3,16) and 1C' (3,36) of the first section (Jn 2-4).

[241] McPOLIN, 109.

shepherd (10,11.15) who has come so that they may have life in abundance (10,10) and for whom he voluntarily lays down his life (*tên psychên autou tithêsin hyper tôn probatôn*: 10,11.15.17.18)[242]. Jesus is not only the Moses-like shepherd sent by God to lead, liberate and feed His people (10,2-4; cf. 6,11.14; Ex 3,10) but also the divine good shepherd (10,11.14-16) promised by God through Ezechiel (cf. especially 34,15: "I myself will be the shepherd of my sheep" and 37,23: "And I will set up over them one shepherd"), a pastor who will know and love, feed and guide, protect and care for the sheep. Jesus, the good shepherd, fulfils this prophetic promise beyond all expectations, for he lays down his life for the sheep (10,11.15.17.18) and allows them to share in his divine life (10,10). In order to have this life they must listen to his voice and follow him (10,3.4.16), which is another way of saying that men must believe in him in order to have communion of life with him. Thus we come to the conclusion that both 6,1-71 (2C) and 10,1-21 (2C') are Christocentric subsections which reveal Jesus not only as the Messiah and the Son of God (emphasized in 2B and 2B') but also as the giver of life to those who enter into a personal relationship with him through an active faith. This will be further developed in the parallel Lazarus-episode in 3C (11,1-54), as we shall see below.

5.233 *Jesus, the prophet, the Messiah, the Son of Man, the Son of God, the light of the world, the judge, in 7,1-8,59 (2D) and 9,1-41 (2D')*

We saw in ch. 4 that the section of "Jesus' Works, Signs and Discussions" (Jn 5-10) is constructed chiastically (2B C D D' C' B')[243]. It is to be expected in a chiastic structure that the extreme and the central elements will have some important themes in common. This is found to be true in the case of Jn 7-8 (2D) and Jn 9 (2D')[244].

Jn 7 (2D) begins with the Evangelist's remark that Jesus would not go about in Judea because the Jews were seeking to kill him (7,1), which is a reference back to 5,18 (2B). Their attempt to kill him is recalled later by Jesus himself (7,19; 8,37.40) and by some of the Jerusalemites (7,25).

Furthermore, the Sabbath healing of the paralytic reported in Jn 5 (2B) is discussed again by Jesus in 7,21-23 (2D)[245]. Notice that the curing of the cripple on the Sabbath (5,9.11.16; 7,23) is designated as a "work" which Jesus has done (*ergon epoiêsa*: 7,21) in imitation of what his Father does (*ho patêr mou heôs arti ergazetai, kagô ergazomai*: 5,17; cf. also 5,19.20.30), just as the Jews who try to kill Jesus (8,40) do the works of their father (8,41), the devil, who is a

---

[242] A similar *hyper* with a soteriological significance is found also in 2C (6,51: *kai ho artos de hon egô dôsô hê sarx mou estin hyper tês tou kosmou zôês*), which hints at Jesus' death, explicitly stated in 2C' (10,11.15.17.18).

[243] See 4.32.

[244] Many scholars who have failed to see the chiastic structure of Jn 5-10 have been tempted to displace part of Jn 7 (especially 7,14-24) to the end of Jn 5 (see 1.21).

[245] BROWN, I, 315.

murderer (8,44). In other words, the works that Jesus does bear witness to who he is (5,36), namely, the divine Son (5,19). Just as his actions are not from himself (5,19.30) but from the Father who lovingly shows him everything that He Himself does (5,20), so his teaching is not from himself but from the Father who sent him (7,16-17), for he speaks only of what he has seen, heard and learnt from the Father (8,28.38.40). It is also noteworthy that the Father Himself is presented as the best witness of Jesus both in 5,32.37 and 8,18. Notice also that Moses' testimony to Jesus is recalled both in 5,46 and in 7,19.23. Similarly Jesus' authority to judge, which he has received from the Father, is mentioned both in 5,22.27 and in 8,16.

Just as in Jn 5 (2B) Jesus told the Jews that only those who do not seek the glory of man (5,41.44) but the glory of God (5,44) and who have the word of God (5,38) and the love of God (5,42) dwelling in them, can believe, recognize and receive the one who comes in the name of the Father (5,38.43), so in 7,17 (2D) the Jews are told by Jesus that only those who are willing to do the will of God can recognize the divine origin of the teaching of Jesus, who seeks not his own will (5,30) and glory (7,18) but the will and glory of the Father who sent him. In other words, only the person who is attuned to God can receive the one whom He has sent, just as a transistor radio has to be tuned in order to receive a particular program broadcast from a transmitter.

Thus we find that Jn 5 (2B) and Jn 7-8 (2D) have many theological themes in common, but the most important ones seem to be the divinity and Sonship of Jesus. This is made clear by Jesus' own statement in 5,17 ("My Father is working still, and I am working"), which is explained in the apologetic discourse that follows (5,19-47), and by his concluding, climactic, revelatory, solemn statement in 8,58: "Amen amen I say to you, before Abraham was, I am". Note also the progress from "doing" (*ergazomai*: 5,17) in 2B to "being" (*ego eimi*: 8,58) in 2D.

One of the major themes of Jn 7-8 (2D) is that Jesus is "the light of the world" (*egô eimi to phôs tou kosmou*: 8,12) by following whom one "will not walk in darkness but will have the light of life" (8,12). This truth is illustrated by the episode in Jn 9 (2D'), in which a man born blind receives physical sight from and spiritual insight into Jesus. For, before healing the blind man Jesus repeats the revelatory statement of 8,12 that he is the light of the world (9,5), and the episode comes to a climax in the cured blind man's confession of faith in and worship of Jesus, the Son of Man (9,35-38). In this dramatic episode the gradual growth in the faith of the blind man is contrasted with the growing blindness of the Pharisees. Jesus' concluding statement reveals what has already happened both to the proud Pharisees and to the blind man: the man who was blind has gained sight and insight but the presumptuous Pharisees who claimed to see have become blind ("For judgement I came into this world, that those who do not see may see, and that those who see may become blind": 9,39). The stages in the faith of the cured blind man are indicated by what he himself says about or to Jesus: "the man called Jesus" (9,11), "a prophet" (9,17), "a worshipper of

God" (9,31), a man "from God" (9,33), "Lord" (9,36) and "Lord, I believe" (9,38). Similarly, the deepening unbelief of the Pharisees is shown by the statements they make about Jesus. The initial hesitation on the part of some Pharisees that Jesus may not be a sinner who violates the Sabbath, since he does many signs (9,16), becomes eventually a unanimous certitude (*oidamen*) that he is a sinner (9,24), whose origin they do not know (*ouk oidamen pothen estin*: 9,29). As they become hardened in their unbelief in Jesus, they revile (9,28) and excommunicate the man who believes in Jesus as the Messiah (9,22.34). Finally, their blindness becomes so acute that they do not even realize that they are blind (9,40), but remain in the darkness of the sin of unbelief (9,41)[246].

5.23z Looking back at the whole section of "Jesus' Works, Signs and Discussions" (Jn 5-10) we find that its major theological focus is on the divine Sonship of Jesus (stressed in 2B = 5,1-47 and 2B' = 10,22-42), which can be understood only when his divine origin (*pothen estin/erchetai*, emphasized in 2D = 7,1-8,59 [cf. 7,27.28; 8,14] and in 2D' = 9,1-41 [cf. 9,29.30]) is known[247]. Though the main emphasis in these subsections is on the divinity of Jesus, his humanity is also sufficiently highlighted in Jn 5-10, for Jesus is often referred to as a "man" (*anthrôpos*: 5,12; 7,46; 8,40; 9,11.16.24; 10,33) and as "the Son of Man" (*ho hyios tou anthrôpou*: 6,27.53.62; 8,28; 9,35; cf. also *hyios anthrôpou* at 5,27), which, as we have seen above, underscores in Jn the human nature of Jesus[248]. In other words, the Christological mystery of the human and divine identity of Jesus is revealed in Jn 5-10 (and especially in Jn 5; 7-8; 9; 10,22-42). That this human-divine Jesus or "Godman" is the source of life for the believers, is the main issue in 6,1-71 (2C) and 10,1-21 (2C'), for Jesus reveals himself as the bread of life (6,35.48.51) and as the good shepherd who lays down his life for the sheep (10,11.15.17.18) so that they may have life in abundance

---

[246] A similar phenomenon of deepening unbelief on the part of the Jewish authorities in Jerusalem during the feast of the Dedication is noticed also in 10,22-39. For first they ask Jesus to tell them plainly if he is the Christ (10,24). When he does, they refuse to believe (10,25). And when he reveals his unity with God the Father ("I and the Father are one": 10,30), they pick up stones to stone him as a blasphemer (10,31.33). When he proves his claim to be the Son of God by Scriptural support (10,34-36) and asks them to believe at least on the evidence of the works of the Father that he does (1037-38), they try to arrest him (10,39). (This confirms the chiastic structure of Jn 5-10 we established in the last chapter.)

It is also worth recalling that there is an emphasis on Jesus' "works" (*erga*) not only in the central elements (2D and 2D') but also in the extreme elements (2B and 2B') of the chiastic structure of Jn 5-10 (2B C D D' C' B') (cf. 5,17.20.36; 7,3.21; 9,3.4; 10,25.32.33.37.38).

[247] Where Jesus is/comes from will be understood only when the place where he is going to is known. In other words, his divine origin will become clear only when his ultimate destination is revealed. This is not understood by the Jews in Jn 7-8 (cf. 7,33-36; 8,21-22). But his final destination (through his death-resurrection-ascension) will be revealed to his disciples during the parallel farewell discourses in 4D (13,31-14,21 cf. 13,33.36; 14,3-6.28) and 4D' (16,4e-33 cf. 16,5.27-30). Note that Jesus himself reminds the disciples in 4D (13,33) what he had told the Jews in 2D (7,33-34; 8,21) about his "going away" (*hypagein*).

[248] See 5.124.

(10,10)²⁴⁹. Jn 7-8 (2D) is a sort of trial of Jesus, the Messiah, the Son of God, by the Jews but it turns out to be a trial of the murderous Jews by Jesus, which explains the polemical aspect of this subsection. Similarly, in Jn 9 the Jews/ Pharisees who try the cured blind man who believes in Jesus and defends him are found guilty by Jesus (cf. 9,39-41).

Comparing Jn 2-4 with Jn 5-10 we find that we are at a higher theological level in "Jesus' Works, Signs and Discussions" than in "Jesus' Initial Signs and Encounters", though there are many theological themes in common. Thus Jesus is spoken of as the prophet and the Messiah both in Jn 2-4 (cf. *prophêtês*: 4,19.44; *Christos/Messias*: 3,28; 4,25.29) and in Jn 5-10 (cf. *prophêtês*: 6,14; 7,40; 9,17; *Christos*: 7,26.31.41; 9,22; 10,24). Some of his "signs" are described in the second section as in the first, but their salvific significance is discussed more in detail in the second section (e.g. in Jn 6). Besides "signs", some of Jesus' "works" which reveal him as "the Son of God" are described and discussed in Jn 5-10 (e.g. the healing of the paralytic and the discourse that follows). The theme of Jesus' divine Sonship which was touched upon in the first section is developed much more in detail in the second (e.g. in 5,17-47; 10,22-39). The Jews' opposition to Jesus' revelation is greater in Jn 5-10 than in Jn 2-4 (cf. the many attempts to arrest him, to stone him, to kill him in Jn 5-10). The conflict between light and darkness, between revelation and unbelief, becomes intense in the second section. The central issue of discussion and dispute is who or what Jesus is. In short, the primary purpose of Jn 5-10 is to show "that Jesus is the Christ, *the Son of God*" (20,31), the emphasis being on "the Son of God", whereas the stress in Jn 2-4 is on "Christ".

5.24 The Christocentric Theological Sketch in "the Climactic Sign and the Coming of Jesus' Hour" (Jn 11-12)

We have seen that Jn 11-12 functions as a bridge between the Book of Jesus' Signs (Jn 2-12) and the Book of Jesus' Hour (Jn 11-20), and that it consists of two parallel subsections (3C = 11,1-54 and 3C' = 11,55-12,50)²⁵⁰, whose theological outlines we shall now successively examine.

5.241 *Jesus, the Christ, the Son of God, the Lord, the resurrection and the life, the life-giving lover, in 11,1-54 (3C)*

The Lazarus-episode (namely, the raising of Lazarus and the Sanhedrin's decision to do away with Jesus: 11,1-54 = 3C) forms a dramatic theological climax in the Johannine Gospel not only because of Martha's climactic confession of Jesus as "the Christ, the Son of God" in 11,27 (which is similar to

---

²⁴⁹ This theme of Jesus as the life-giver will be further developed and demonstrated in 3C (11,1-54) and 3C' (11,55-12,50), as we shall see below.
²⁵⁰ See 4.33.

the Christian confession of faith in 20,31) [251] and the repeated reference to Jesus as "the Lord" (*Kyrios*: 11,2.3.12.21.27.32.34.39) but also because the sign of raising Lazarus dramatically brings out the theological truth that Jesus is "the resurrection and the life" (11,25) and the paradox that his gift of life to a dead man (11,38-44) brings about his own death (11,45-53) [252]. Furthermore, the death-resurrection of Lazarus points forward to Jesus' own death-resurrection, through which the believers (those whom he loves) will be raised from death to eternal life (11,25-26).

It is also noteworthy that for the first time in the Fourth Gospel Jesus is explicitly mentioned (in 3C) as *loving*. Martha and Mary inform Jesus about their brother's sickness in the words: "Lord, he whom you love (*hon phileis*) is ill" (11,3). Again, when Jesus weeps (11,35), the Jews standing by remark: "See how he loved him" (*ide pôs ephilei auton*: 11,36). The Evangelist himself states that Jesus loved (*êgapa*) Martha, Mary and Lazarus (11,5). Finally, Jesus himself refers to Lazarus as "our friend" (*ho philos hêmôn*: 11,11). In fact, the raising of Lazarus to life demonstrates the truth of Jesus' own later statement to the disciples: "Greater love has no man than this, that a man lay down his life for his friends" (15,13) and the Evangelist's penetrating observation in 4C that "having loved his own who were in the world, he loved them to the end" (*eis telos êgapêsen autous*) (13,1).

That Jesus was knowingly and willingly risking his own life for his friend is made clear in the conversation between Jesus and his disciples before he goes to Bethany (11,7-16) for, when he tells them: "Let us go into Judea again" (11,7), they try to dissuade him from doing so by reminding him of the Jews' recent attempt to stone him (11,8; cf. 10,31). Yet he insists on going to his friend Lazarus who "has fallen asleep" (died) (11,11.14.15), in order to "awaken him"

---

[251] While "the Son of God" on the lips of Martha at 11,25 may be understood at the historical level as synonymous with "the Christ", the deeper divine significance is intended in 20,31 (cf. also Jesus' use of the title "the Son of God" at 11,4).

[252] BROWN's observations in this connection are worth citing:

All Jesus' miracles are signs of what he is and what he has come to give man, but in none of them does the sign more closely approach the reality than in the gift of life. The physical life that Jesus gives to Lazarus is still not in the realm of the life from above, but it is so close to that realm that it may be said to conclude the ministry of signs and inaugurate the ministry of glory. Thus, the raising of Lazarus provides an ideal transition, the last sign in the Book of Signs leading into the Book of Glory. Moreover, the suggestion that the supreme miracle of giving life to man leads to the death of Jesus offers a dramatic paradox worthy of summing up Jesus' career (I, 429).

Furthermore, the "glorification" (*doxazein*) of the Son of God spoken of by Jesus at 11,5 (cf. also 12,23) links Jn 11-12 with Jn 13-17 (cf. 13,31-32; 17,1). Besides, the Sanhedrin's decision to kill Jesus because of the mighty miracle of raising Lazarus (11,47-53) is recalled during the trial of Jesus before the high priest in Jn 18 (cf. 11,50 and 18,14). Again, the death, burial and resurrection of Lazarus symbolize those of Jesus himself narrated in Jn 19-20 (cf. *apothnê[i]skein*: 11,14.44; 19,33; *mnêmeion*: 11,17.38; 19,41.42; 20,1.2.3.4.6.8.11; *pou tetheikate/ethêkan auton*: 11,34; 20,2.13.15; *airein ton lithon*: 11,39.41; 20,1; *dein*: 11,44; 19,40; *soudarion*: 11,44; 20,7; *anistêmi*: 11,23.24; 20,9). This confirms our position in ch. 4 that Jn 11 (together with Jn 12) forms a "bridge-section".

(raise him to life) (11,11), even if it costs Jesus his own life (cf. 11,16). That Jesus is the good shepherd who lays down his life freely for his sheep was stated already in 2C' (cf. 10,11.15.17-18)[253].

The salvific nature of Jesus' death is underlined by the unconscious prophecy of the high priest Caiaphas: "it is expedient for you that one man should die for the people (*hina heis anthrôpos apothanê[i] hyper tou laou*), and that the whole nation should not perish" (11,50). The salvific scope of Jesus' laying down his life (*tên psychên mou/autou tithêmi/tithêsin*) in favour of the sheep (*hyper tôn probatôn*) was mentioned by Jesus himself during the parabolic discourse on the good shepherd (10,11.15)[254]. The Evangelist's comment in 11,51-52 on the high priest's prophecy (11,50) widens its scope to include also the Gentiles among those for whom Jesus would die. The universality of salvation hinted at here (3C) will later be explicitly stated by Jesus himself: "when I am lifted up from the earth, I will draw *all men* to myself" (12,32) (3C')[255], a statement which the Evangelist explains as a reference to Jesus' death on the cross (12,33)[256].

The Christocentric character of the Lazarus-episode is seen also from the fact that Lazarus' sickness, death and resuscitation will lead to Jesus' glorifying death (11,4.50-51) in and through which the scattered children of God will be gathered into one (11,52). Again, a Christocentric faith (that is, faith in the person of Jesus, the Christ, the Son of God, the resurrection and the life) is needed to escape permanent death and to have immortal, eternal life not only after the resurrection on the last day but already here and now (11,24-27). Thus future eschatology becomes realized eschatology because of Christ, the resurrection and the life.

5.241z The whole of the Lazarus-episode presents Jesus, the Christ, the Son of God, as the human-divine lover and the Lord of life, for he raises a dead friend to life even risking his own life. This is a symbol of his gift of eternal life through his salvific, glorifying, life-giving death. In other words, the most prominent feature of the Christology and soteriology of Jn 11 is the presentation of the loving Jesus, the Christ, the Son of God, as the resurrection, the life and immortality, for the believers whom he loves and for whom he lays down his life[257]. In short, Jesus is the life-giving lover and the loving life-giver.

---

[253] We may recall that 10,1-21 (2C') and 11,1-54 (3C) are parallel to each other (see "the Schema of the Literary Structure").

[254] See the last footnote. Cf. also 6,51 for the gift of his "flesh for (*hyper*) the life of the world" (in 2C parallel to 3C). Note also the presence of *synagein* at 6,12.13 (2C) and 11,52 (3C) (and *Didachê* 9,4). Cf. BROWN, I, 248; 443; PANIMOLLE, I, 57-58.

[255] BROWN, I, 442-43.

[256] This is one of the many parallels between 11,1-54 (3C) and 11,55-12,50 (3C') (see 4.332).

[257] PANIMOLLE, III, 33-35.

5.242 *Jesus, the anointed Messiah-king of Israel and the Son of Man about to be lifted up and glorified during his "hour", but rejected by the people, in 11,55-12,50 (3C')*

The anointing of Jesus by Mary at Bethany (12,1-8) described between the two transitions (11,55-57; 12,9-11), which mention the high priests' decision to arrest him (11,57) and to kill not only him but also Lazarus (12,10; cf. also 11,53), prophetically symbolizes his anointing for burial. This is made clear by Jesus' answer to the hypocritical question of the greedy Judas concerning why the precious ointment was not sold and the large sum given to the poor (12,5): "that she might keep it for the day of my burial"[258]. This phrase indicates the imminence of the death and burial of Jesus.

Jesus' triumphal entry into Jerusalem manifests him as the king-Messiah. This is evident both from the cries of the crowd which sings: "Hosanna! Blessed is he who comes in the name of the Lord, even the king of Israel!" (12,13) and from the Scriptural application of the prophecy of Zach 9,9 to Jesus' sitting on an ass (12,14): "Fear not, daughter of Zion; behold your king is coming, sitting on an ass's colt!" (12,15).

The placing of Jesus' triumphal entry immediately after his anointing is important for the correct interpretation of the Johannine understanding of Jesus' Messiahship and kingship[259]. Whereas the Fourth Evangelist has been reluctant to present Jesus as the royal Messiah (for the Johannine Jesus is never called "the Son of David" and he runs away from the crowd which would like to crown him king: cf. 6,15), now that he is anointed for burial (12,7), he is publicly proclaimed as the kingly Messiah or the Messianic king of Israel (12,13-15), which seems to insinuate that Jesus' anticipated burial-anointing is his Messianic or kingly anointing. This is confirmed by the emphasis given to Jesus' kingship during his passion and particularly during his trial before Pilate (18,28-19,16b) and during his crucifixion (cf. the title on the cross "the king of the Jews": 19,19-22). McPolin's words in this connection are worth quoting:

> Just as the anointing at Bethany prefigures his burial in death, so also his entry into the city and his acclamation by the crowd as king look ahead to his enthronement or exaltation as king on the cross where he manifests God's love which draws believers to Jesus (3:14-16; 12:32). Thus through his death he becomes the king or the Lord of life for all believers (18,37)[260].

---

[258] This is my own translation of *hina eis tēn hēmeran tou entaphiasmou mou tērēsē[i] auto* (12,7c). This elliptical *hina*-clause is Jesus' answer to Judas' question *dia ti* ("why?": 12,5), *aphes autēn* ("Leave her alone!") being an independent imperative (interjection). In other words, Jesus tells Judas that the reason why the ointment was not sold and given to the poor was that she might keep it for anointing his body for burial, which she did though unconsciously. (If this interpretation of 12,7 is correct, then Jesus was not asking her to keep some of the ointment for the day of his embalming.)

[259] Note that the Synoptic Gospels describe Jesus' triumphal entry into Jerusalem (Mt 21,1-11; Mk 11,1-11) much before his anointing (Mt 26,6-13; Mk 14,3-9).

[260] McPolin, 167.

The universality of Jesus' kingship is unconsciously acknowledged even by the unbelieving Pharisees: "behold the world has gone after him!" (12,19). This universality is also highlighted by the coming of the gentile Greeks who desire to "see" Jesus (12,20-21), and who are "the vanguard of mankind coming to Jesus in faith"[261].

The coming of the Greeks is a clear signal to Jesus of the arrival of his "hour" of glorification (12,23) when he will be "lifted up" on the cross and will "draw all" men and women to himself (12,32-33) through the manifestation of his immense love for them. It is this love which impels him to die for them on the cross (15,13). Therefore he is ready to die like the grain of wheat which falls to the ground so that it may bear much fruit (12,24). Hence in an agonizing prayer to the Father ("Now is my soul troubled": 12,27) he welcomes "the hour" that will "glorify" the Father (12,28)[261a] by revealing the breadth and depth of His saving love for humanity (3,16) and his triumph over the powers of darkness and unbelief (12,31). The lifted up Son of Man, the crucified Christ, will be like a powerful magnetic pole that draws all soft iron filings to itself (12,32) but repels all opposing forces. The spiritual magnetisation of human beings takes place by their adhering to Christ through faith in him and allowing themselves to be transformed by him (12,36).

It is enlightening to note that precisely at this juncture the Evangelist pauses to reflect on the negative response of the people to Jesus' revelation through numerous signs ("Though he had done so many signs before them, yet they did not believe in him": 12,37). Thus like the Servant of God in Is 53,1 Jesus is rejected by his people (Jn 12,38). This regrettable fact not only refers to the unbelief and rejection he experienced during his ministry (cf. 11,47-53) but also points forward to his total rejection during his passion[262] when his own people will disown him ("we have no king but Caesar": 19,15; cf. 1,11) and cry out for his crucifixion (19,6.15). Apparently this very rejection forms part of the plan of God for the glorification of Jesus (12,40-41; cf. Is 6,1.10).

Thus as Jesus disappears from the scene ("he hid himself from them": 12,36) and as the curtain falls at the close of the third act (Jn 11-12), the voice of Isaiah lamenting over the unbelief (12,38) and blindness of the people (12,40) is heard. This is followed by the dramatic cry of Jesus, as it were from behind the curtain[263], summing up his revelatory salvific message and summoning all to believe in him (12,44-50). This short and straightforward discourse, which both

---

[261] *Ibid.*, 169.

[261a] This may be compared to the Synoptic scene of the agony in Gethsemane (Mt 26,38), which is not recounted in the garden scene in Jn 18,1-11. In this Johannine anticipation of the agony-scene Jesus' soul is troubled (12,27) (cf. Mt 26,37-38) and he turns to the Father in prayer and prays that the Father may be glorified through the hour of his passion-death-resurrection (Jn 12,27-28).

[262] See 4.351.

[263] See 4.331.

discloses the revelatory and saving mission of Jesus (12,45-47.49-50) and invites the audience (readers) to believe in him (12,44) in order to have eternal life and to avoid judgement by his word (12,48), has many thematic echoes of the earlier passages (especially Jesus' discourses) and a number of theological resonances with the farewell discourse in Jn 13-17 (e.g. faith in Jesus and the Father: 5,24; 12,44; 14,1; seeing Jesus and the Father: 6,40; 12,45; 14,9; Jesus' coming into the world: 1,9; 3,19; 6,14; 12,46; 16,28; 18,37; Jesus as the light of the world: 1,4.9; 3,19; 8,12; 9,5; 12,46; Jesus' saving, not condemnatory, mission: 3,17; 12,47; judgement: 3,18; 12,48; 16,11; the last day: 6,39.44.54; 11,24; 12,48; the commandment or will of the Father connected with eternal life: 6,40; 12,50; 17,2). Thus this discourse of Jesus, which is often branded by scholars as a disconnected redactional addition [264] functions well as a bridge-discourse in the bridge-section (Jn 11-12) between the Book of Jesus' Signs (Jn 2-12) and the Book of Jesus' Hour (Jn 11-20).

5.24z Looking at the whole of Jn 11-12 we find that the theological emphasis is on Jesus as the loving life-giver, as is illustrated by the raising of his friend Lazarus from the dead even at the risk of his own life. This is a symbol of the eternal life he would give those who believe in him. This he does through his death-resurrection at "the hour" (11,25-26.50-53; 12,32) which would glorify him and the Father (12,23.28). New significance is therefore given to the Christological titles such as the Christ, the Son of Man, the Son of God and the Lord applied to Jesus in the bridge-section. The salvific significance of the life-giving and glorifying death-resurrection of Jesus is be further elaborated in the next section (Jn 13-17).

5.25 The Christocentric Theological Sketch in "Jesus' Farewell of the Hour" (Jn 13-17)

Since Jn 13-17 contains the nucleus of Johannine theology, to try to summarize it in a few pages is a Herculean task. What we shall do is only to highlight a few theological points which emerge from the chiastic structure of Jn 13-17 which we established in ch. 4.

5.251 *Jesus, the exemplar of loving service, the Son of Man, the Son of God, the revealer of the Father, the mediator of divine life and love, about to be betrayed by Judas but glorified by the Father at "the hour", in 13,1-38 (4C) and 17,1-26 (4C')*

Jesus' awareness of the arrival of the hour of his departure from this world to the Father (13,1) which is the hour of his glorification (17,1) through his passion-death-resurrection is stressed right at the start of Jn 13 and Jn 17. The first verse of Jn 13 emphasizes Jesus' limitless love for his own and the last verse

---

[264] See 1.12; 1.13; 1.23.

of Jn 17 highlights the foundational love of the Father for Jesus and the disciples (17,26). This love-inclusion indicates that all the intervening passages are to be interpreted in the light of and as a revelation of this divine love.

It is in this context of "the hour" of Jesus (*eidôs ho Iesous hoti êlthen autou hê hôra*: 13,1) and of the revelation of Jesus' immense love for his own (*agapêsas tous idious tous en tô[i] kosmô[i] eis telos êgapêsen autous*: 13,1) that his washing the disciples' feet must be interpreted. In order to underscore the significance of this symbolic action we are once again reminded of Jesus' awareness not only of his divine origin and the destination of his departure ("that he had come from God and was going to God": 13,3) but also of the unlimited divine power received from his Father ("knowing that the Father had given all things into his hands": 13,3; cf. 3,35). The significance of this simple, symbolic, salvific act of the almighty Son of God holding, washing and wiping the dusty, dirty feet of the disciples who would deny, desert and betray him is explained by G. O'Collins as follows: "Within and through the life of the Trinity, all things were in his hands, and yet he took into those hands our feet - to wash them. After that he stretched out those same hands to be nailed to a cross"[265]. In fact, the washing of the disciples' feet is a prophetic prefiguration of the death of Jesus, an act that not only "washes" us from the dust and dirt of "all sin" (cf. 1 Jn 1,7) but also enables us to inherit eternal life with him (cf. *echein meros met' emou*: 13,8), for the power to give eternal life to those who adhere to him in faith is part of the power the Father has given the Son through his glorifying death- resurrection (17,1-2; cf. 3,14-15; 5,21.25-26)[266]. The washing of the disciples' feet by Jesus, who is their teacher and Lord (13,13-14), is also an example of humble and loving service to be followed: "For I have given you an example, that you also should do as I have done to you" (13,15). This "as I have done to you" refers not simply to the feet-washing but also to his life-giving death which it symbolised. Hence the disciples are asked to be at the service of one another (13,14) to the extent of laying down their lives as Jesus did. Such "doers" are called "blessed" (*makarioi*) by Jesus (13,17). This demand to render selfless, life-giving service to one another is similar to Jesus' command to the disciples to "love one another as I have loved you" (13,33; cf. 15,12.13.17). The "newness" of his commandment consists precisely in loving like him (*kathôs êgapêsa hymas*), loving to the end (*eis telos*: 13,1). It is by such mutual love that true disciples of Jesus are to be known (13,34).

The footwashing, the symbol of the supreme, loving and life-giving sacrifice of Christ on the cross, is prefaced by a sad reference to the devilish decision of

---

[265] G. O'COLLINS, *Finding Jesus. Living through Lent with John's Gospel* (New York 1983) 61.

[266] It is possible that Jesus' death and resurrection are hinted at also by the use of *tithêmi* and *lambanô* at 13,4 and 13,12 in connection with the "laying aside" and "taking" his "garments" (*himatia*), since the same verbs were used together with "life" (*psyche*) to describe the Son's "laying down" his "life" and "taking it up" again (10,17). The "garments" seem to have a symbolic significance also at 19,23-24.

Judas to betray Jesus (13,2). The crime of betrayal shows its ugly, unclean face also at the end ("you are not all clean": 13,11). The thought of betrayal by a chosen disciple and close friend who enjoyed the intimacy of his table-fellowship and the realization of the ingratitude and insult implied in the act of betrayal ("He who ate my bread has lifted his heel against me": 13,18; Ps. 41,10) disturbs Jesus deeply (13,21; cf. 11,33; 12,27). His sad but solemn statement: "Amen amen I say to you, one of you will betray me" (13,21) is another attempt of Jesus to touch the heart of the betrayer [267]. In the parallel subsection 4C' (during the prayer of the hour) Jesus recalls his loss of Judas, "the son of perdition" (17,12), and interprets it as part of the plan of God foretold in the Scriptures (*hina hê graphê plêrôthê[i]*: 17,12; cf. also 13,18). In fact, Jesus regards the betrayal as the beginning of the passion through which he is glorified, for "when he had gone out, Jesus said: 'Now is the Son of Man glorified, and in him God is glorified'" (13,31).

The intimate friendship of Jesus, to which all disciples are called (13,18), is symbolically represented by the Beloved Disciple "lying in the bosom of Jesus" (*anakeimenos... en tô[i] kolpô[i] tou Iêsou*: 13,23), which is similar to the communion of love enjoyed by the only Son-God "who is in the bosom of the Father" (*ho ôn eis ton kolpon tou patros*: 1,18). In fact, Jesus prays to the Father that all believers may share in this divine union and constant communion between the Father and the Son ("that they may all be one, even as you, Father, are in me, and I in you, that they also may be in us": 17,21; "I in them and you in me, that they may become perfectly one": 17,23).

Just as Jesus revealed the identity of the betrayer only to the Beloved Disciple (13,26), so also love and friendship impel him to reveal to the disciples his "family secrets", for he tells the Father in 4C': "I have given them the words which you gave me" (17,8; cf. 15,15). Not only through his words but also through his deeds (cf. 5,17) Jesus has made the Father known (*ephanerôsa sou to onoma*: 17,6; *egnôrisa autois to onoma sou*: 17,26). And Jesus' passion-death-resurrection is going to be a further revelation (*gnôrisô*: 17,26) of the Father and His immense love for Jesus and the believers (17,23.26). It is through the revelation of the supreme love manifested in the passion culminating on the cross that Jesus is going to glorify the Father and be glorified by Him (*doxazô*: 13,31-32; 17,1.5; cf. 12,26). The final scope of the revelation of the Father and His love is "that the love with which you have loved me may be in them and I in them" (17,26), so that the disciples may love one another as Jesus has loved them (13,33). And it is through such mutual love patterned on the mutual love of the Father and the Son that the world will know that they are the true disciples of Jesus (13,34) whom the Father has sent (17,23).

---

[267] Jesus' giving a morsel to Judas during the meal might have been his last loving attempt to win him over (13,26; cf. Ruth 2,14) (cf. BROWN, II, 578).

5.251z All the events narrated in 4C (13,1-38) and the prayer of Jesus in 4C' (17,1-26) are interpreted in the light of "the hour" (13,1; 17,1), the hour of his glorification (13,31-32; 17,1.5). For instance, the washing of the feet is primarily the prophetic prefiguration of his life-giving death (13,2-11), which is also an example of loving service (13,12-17). The prediction of the betrayal reveals not only Jesus' knowledge of the betrayer but also his sensitive human heart which is deeply troubled at the prospect of being betrayed by a friend. But his heart is so attuned to his Father's will, is so keen to accomplish the work of revelation and salvation the Father has entrusted to him (17,4) and is so ready to glorify the Father (17,1.5) that he can see even the betrayal by a chosen disciple as forming part of the plan of God for his glorification (13,31-32).

The prayer of Jesus in Jn 17 is essentially the prayer of the hour (17,1). His awareness of the time of his return to the Father which was mentioned at 13,1.3 pervades the whole prayer (17,1.5.11.13.24). The limitless love of Jesus for his own (*eis telos*) stressed in 13,1 is revealed in 17,23.26 to be the flow of the Father's love for him and the believers. While this life-giving love for the disciples was manifested in the action of his washing their feet, which was the symbol of his life-giving death (13,2-11), and which he explains also as an example of loving service to be followed in the community of his disciples (13,12-17), his prayer presents the intimate union between him and the Father as the model of loving fellowship among his disciples (17,11.21.22.23).

5.252 *The departure and return of Jesus, the way to the Father and the mediator of the Spirit of truth, in 13,31-14,31 (4D) and 16,4e-33 (4D')*

The numerous parallels between 13,31-14,31 and 16,4e-33 have been mentioned in the preceding chapter [268]. One of the prominent themes of both the farewell discourses is Jesus' imminent departure and its soteriological significance for the disciples. For he tells them repeatedly that he is going to the Father (13,33; 14,28; 16,5.17.28) to prepare a place for them (14,2), to manifest to them the Father more openly (16,25), and to send them another Paraclete, the Spirit of truth (14,16-17.26; 16,7-15).

As Jesus had earlier told the Jews in 7,33-34 and 8,21 (which occur in a parallel passage 2D) [269], so now the night before his death he talks to the disciples about his imminent departure (cf. 13,33; 16,5.16-22). There are a number of similarities between Jesus' words to the Jews and to the disciples (as he himself explicitly reminds the latter: "as I said to the Jews so now I say to you": 13,33): 1) he is going to be with them only a little while (7,33; 13,33; 16,16); 2) for he is about to go away (to the one who sent him) (7,33; 8,21; 16,5); 3) they will seek him (7,34; 8,21; 13,33); 4) but where he is going they cannot come (7,34; 8,21;

---

[268] See 4.342,2.
[269] Note that 7,33-34; 8,21 occur in 2D (Jn 7-8) which is parallel to 4D (13,31-14,31) and 4D' (16,4e-33).

13,33). There are also some remarkable differences: 1) whereas Jesus' statements about his going away in Jn 7-8 are made in the context of a controversy with the unbelieving Jews, his words to the disciples are spoken in the context of bidding farewell to his own, which is indicated by the endearing way he addresses them as "little children" (*teknia*: 13,33); 2) whereas he tells the Jews that, in spite of their search for him, they would not find him (7,34) and that they would die in their sin (of unbelief) (8,21), in the case of the disciples he limits the impossibility of following him to the present moment and affirms the future possibility (13,36). In fact, at 16,16 he promises them that after a short interval of absence they would see him again (cf. also 14,3).

The reactions of the Jews and those of the disciples to Jesus' enigmatic words about his departure are also quite different. While both the groups are puzzled by his words (7,36; 8,22; 16,17-18), the Jews (mis)understand them or wonder whether he plans to go and teach the Diaspora Jews (7,35) or to commit suicide (8,22), whereas the disciples fail to understand (but do not misunderstand) their master's mysterious words (13,36; 16,17-18; cf. also 14,4). Again, while Jesus leaves the unbelieving Jews in their misunderstanding, he explains the enigma to his receptive disciples in two parallel discourses (14,1-7; 16,19-28): his departure is a return to his Father (14,2; 16,28) to prepare a place for them in his home (14,2) and to send them another Paraclete (16,7).

Furthermore, Jesus promises the disciples that he would come back to them (*erchomai*: 14,3.18; 16,22). This refers not only to his post-resurrectional appearances to them (cf. *êlthen*: 20,19; *erchetai*: 20,26; cf. also the disciples' joy at seeing the risen Jesus at 20,20 as he had foretold at 16,22) but also to his coming to them and entering into a deeper communion with them ("and I will take you to myself": 14,3) in and through the Spirit (14,16-17.25-26; 15,26-27; 16,7-15; 20,22) and with the Father (14,23).

In fact, through his departure to the Father and return to the disciples (14,23), Jesus reveals that he is the way (*hê hodos*: 14,6) to the Father[270], the only mediator between men and the Father ("no one comes to the Father except through me": 14,6), the truth (*hê alêtheia*: 14,6), the perfect revelation of the Father ("he who has seen me has seen the Father": 14,9). Thus knowing Jesus one comes to know the Father (14,7), because he is in constant communion with the Father ("I am in the Father and the Father is in me": 14,10.11) so much so that the words spoken by Jesus are truly the words of the Father, and the works done by Jesus are actually done by the Father Himself who remains in him (14,10).

---

[270] Jesus, the way, may be compared (not to a path that leads to a house but) to a mountain-path. Just as by walking along the path one can contemplate the beauty and majesty of the mountain, so by following Jesus, the path, one can have an experiential knowledge of the Father (14,6-9).

We may recall here that earlier in a parallel passage (2D = Jn 7-8) Jesus spoke of the unbelieving Jews' utter ignorance of him and the Father (*oute eme oidate oute ton patera mou; ei eme ê[i]deite kai ton patera mou an ê[i]deite*: 8,19), whereas in 14,7 he tells his disciples that they know both him and the Father (*ei egnôkate me, kai ton patera mou gnôsesthe; kai ap' arti ginôskete auton kai heôrakate auton*)[271]. Jesus, the Son, is the face of the Father; by seeing the Son they see the Father (14,9), because Jesus is in the Father and the Father is in him (14,10-11). In short, Jesus is the transparency or the reflection of the Father.

Such knowledge of the intimate interrelationship and communion between Jesus and the Father will become a reality in the lives of the disciples when Jesus returns to them (14,18-20) with the Father so as to dwell with them (14,23). Then Jesus will reveal the Father "plainly" (*parrêsia[i]*: 16,25) and they will experience the Father's love and affection for them (14,21; 16,27).

Another consequence of Jesus' departure-return (death-resurrection) is that the disciples' prayers made in union with him ("in his name": 14,13.14; 16,23.24) will be granted by him and the Father (14,13-14; 16,23-24.26-27). Furthermore, precisely because he is going to the Father, the believers will be empowered to continue the works of Jesus (14,12)[272].

Another benefit (*sympherein hymin*: 16,7) of Jesus' "going" to the Father is the "giving" (14,16; cf. 7,39) or the "sending" (16,7) of another Paraclete, the Spirit of truth[273], who will remain with them and within them for ever (14,16-17), will teach them everything, will remind them of and help them grasp the message of Jesus (14,26) and will guide them into all the truth (16,13), which is the revelation in Jesus Christ (16,13-15; cf. 14,6). Besides helping and guiding the believers to interiorize the message and meaning of Jesus, the Paraclete will prove to them, and through them to the world (cf. 15,26-27), 1) that it is guilty of the sin of unbelief, 2) that Jesus, whom the world condemned, is just, since he is glorified by the Father, and 3) that, by putting Jesus to death, the world itself is judged (16,8-11)[274]. This forensic activity of the Paraclete forms part of his guidance of the disciples into all the truth (16,13) and of his bearing witness to Jesus (15,26)[275].

---

[271] Note that 8,19 contains an unreal condition (*ei ê[i]deite* with an *an* in the apodosis: cf. M. ZERWICK, *Biblical Greek* [Rome 1963] 313), whereas 14,7 contains a real condition (*ei egnôkate*). (Here at 14,7 the reading *egnôkate* is to be preferred to *egnôkeite*: cf. TCGNT at Jn 14,7).

[272] "The paradox presented by Jesus' promise that his work on earth will be continued because he is going to the Father is "solved" by his return in the person of the Paraclete" (J. L. MARTYN, *History and Theology in the Fourth Gospel* [1968] 140 [in the first edition]).

[273] Comparing 16,7 with 7,39 BARRETT observes: "The thought is identical with that of 7,39: the coming of the Spirit waits upon the glorifying of Jesus" (486). We may recall that 7,39 and 16,7 occur in parallel passages 2D (Jn 7-8) and 4D' (16,4e-33) in the structure of the Fourth Gospel.

[274] Cf. BROWN, II, 705-6; 712-14.

[275] The forum of the forensic activity of the Paraclete is not merely internal (that is, "in the mind and understanding of the disciples": BROWN, II, 712) nor primarily external (that is, in the world: BARRETT, 487-88) but primarily internal and secondarily external, since the disciples,

Jesus' death-resurrection is also a confrontation with Satan, the prince of this world (14,31), in which the latter will be conquered (*nenikêka*: 16,33; cf. "cast out" in 12,31) and condemned (*kekritai*: 16,11). Jesus' victory over the forces of evil should give the disciples courage and confidence to face tribulation in the world (16,33), and so he invites them to "arise and go forth" (14,31) with him to meet death and the devil, to demonstrate to the world, through his willing obedience to the Father, that he loves Him (14,31; cf. 14,15.21).

5.252z We find that the two parallel "farewell discourses" (13,31-14,31 and 16,4e-33) contain many theological themes in common and that they complement and interpret one another. The fundamental theme that pervades all of them is Jesus' departure-return, in and through which Jesus' intimate relationship with the Father will be made manifest and a closer communion with the disciples will be established. This underlines the Christological and soteriological significance of his death-resurrection, and highlights the Christocentric character of these discourses.

Note that the pneumatology of these passages is also very Christ-centred. Even the names given to the Spirit are significant in this connection. He is "the Spirit of truth" (14,17; 16,13; cf. also 15,26) and therefore the Spirit of Jesus because he is "the truth" (14,6). The Spirit is called "another Paraclete" (14,16; cf. 14,16; 15,26; 16,7), which implies that Jesus is the first Paraclete. Besides, the Spirit is given only when Jesus is glorified through his death-resurrection (7,39; 19,30; 20,22). In fact, he is sent by Jesus (15,26; 16,7) or by the Father "in the name" of Jesus (14,26). The Spirit-Paraclete, like Jesus, is to be with and within the believers. He is to teach them, as Jesus has taught them, and is to remind them of all that Jesus had taught them and help them to interiorize his teaching. He is to guide them in all the truth related to revelation and salvation in Jesus and is to glorify him. In short, the Spirit-Paraclete may be said to be the (physically) absent Jesus' (spiritual) presence with and within the believers. One must have the eyes of faith in (14,1) and love for (14,15) Jesus in order to recognize him in his Spirit (cf. 14,16-17) and allow oneself to be led by him (16,13).

5.253 *Jesus the vine, and disciples the branches, the commandment of love, and the world's hatred, in 15,1-17 (4E) and 15,18-16,4d (4E')*

We have seen in ch. 4 that the two antithetical subsections 4E (15,1-17) and 4E' (15,18-16,4d) consist of three small connected units each (15,1-8.9-11.12-17; 15,18-25.26-27; 16,1-4d)[276]. We shall now study briefly the key theological themes of these units and indicate their interrelationships.

---

enlightened by the testimony of the Paraclete about the sin of unbelief of the world, the justice of Jesus who is exalted by the Father and the judgement of the world, are to bear witness to Jesus (15,26-27).

[276] See 4.341.

5.2 CHRISTOCENTRIC THEOLOGICAL SKETCH

We saw in ch. 3 that 15,1-8 has a concentric structure (*a b c d c' b' a'*)[277] with v.5 (*d*) as its centre: "I am the vine and you are the branches. He who abides in me, and I in him, he it is that bears much fruit, for apart from me you can do nothing". It underlines the central theme of the need of union between Jesus and the disciples in order to produce much fruit. It must be observed that the emphasis is on "fruit-bearing" union (note the triple repetition of *karpon pleiona/polyn pherein* in the beginning [v.2], middle [v.5], and end [v.8], that is, in the first, central and last elements of the concentric structure; cf. also *karpon pherein* in vv.2ab.4b). The need of constant communion with Jesus in order to produce fruit is insisted upon both positively (*meinate en emoi, kagô en hymin*: v.4a; *ho menôn en emoi kagô en autô[i]*: v.5b; *ean meinête en emoi kai ta rhêmata mou en hymin meine[i]*: v.7ab) and negatively (*ean mê menê[i] en tê[i] ampelô[i]... ean mê en emoi menête*: v.4cd; *ean mê tis menê[i] en emoi*: v.6a). The consequence of not abiding in Jesus, the vine, is that such a branch will be barren (v.4bc) and will be cut off (v.2a), cast out and burnt (v.6bcde). Whereas the barren branches are chopped off (*airei*: v.2a), the fruit-bearing branches are pruned (*kathairei*: v.2b) by the Father (the farmer: *geôrgos*) through His word (*logos*: v.3b) spoken by Jesus. In fact, it is Jesus' word or revelation that cleanses the disciples (*êdê hymeis katharoi este dia ton logon hon lelalêka hymin*: v.3; cf. 13,10). The permanent presence or indwelling (*menein*) of his words (*ta rhêmata*) in the disciples is a condition for their prayers to be heard (v.7) because it is the revelation of Jesus received in the hearts of the disciples which transforms their hearts and attunes them to the hearts of Jesus and the Father, so that their petitions in prayer will be conformed to the will of the Father[278]. Such disciples, like healthy branches that constantly draw life-giving sap from the vine, will produce abundant fruit and glorify the Father (15,8), the farmer (15,1). In short, the image of the vine and the branches (15,1-8) indicates the intimate indwelling and constant communion between Jesus and his true disciples and underscores its intrinsic connection with bearing fruit. (The nature of this mutual "abiding" and the kind of the fruit to be produced are described in the following units: vv.9-11.12-17.)

Jesus explains in 15,9-11 that the "abiding" (*menein en*) dealt with in 15,1-8 is truly an "abiding in love" (*meinate en tê[i] agapê[i] tê[i] emê[i]*: 15,9c), the divine love that has descended from the Father through the Son to the disciples (*kathôs êgapêsen me ho patêr, kagô hymas êgapêsa*: 15,9ab). The Father's love for the Son (15,9-10; cf. 3,35; 17,23.24.26) is the source and model of Jesus' love for the disciples (*kathôs... kagô*: 15,9; cf. 20,21). And the kind of response Jesus gave to the Father's love must be the model for the disciples' response to Jesus' love. "Keeping the commandments" (*tas entolas têrein*) is the surest expression and the concrete criterion of "remaining in love" (*menein en tê[i] agapê[i]*). A lover who accomplishes the least wish of the beloved is a true lover and is genuinely "in love".

---

[277] See 3.3 and n.123 there.
[278] McPOLIN, 209.

The reward of such active, other-oriented love is love itself or rather the joy of loving and being loved. The reason why Jesus has revealed to the disciples the mutual joyful love that binds him and the Father is that the disciples too may share in this divine joy of loving and being loved (15,11). This is why Jesus gives his followers "the commandment of love" (15,12-17).

While the image of the vine and the branches (15,1-8) stresses the necessity and quality of the disciples' union with Jesus, his commandment of love (15,12-17) highlights the need and nature of mutual fraternal love [279]. The two are linked together by means of 15,9-11 which describes the connection between his loving union with the Father and doing His will expressed in His commandments.

That the main theme of 15,12-17 is the commandment of mutual love is clearly indicated by the inclusion between vv. 12 and 17:

15,12: hautê estin *hê entolê hê emê*, **hina agapate allêlous**
kathôs **êgapêsa** hymas.

15,17: tauta *entellomai* hymin, **hina agapate allêlous**.

It is enlightening to note that this is the only commandment of the Johannine Jesus, which underlines its supreme importance. It is described as "my" commandment (cf. the position of *hê emê* at the end of the principal clause in 15,12). It is his commandment not only because it is he who commands his disciples to love one another but also because his love for them is the cause and criterion of their mutual love, for they are to love one another "as I have loved you" (*kathôs êgapêsa hymas*: 15,12; cf. 13,34). And Jesus himself explains the *kathôs* in the following verses. First of all, he loves them as his "friends" ("I have called you friends": 15,15). There is no greater love than Jesus' love for them, for he has loved them "to the end" (*eis telos*: 13,1), to the extent of "laying down his life" (*tên psychên tithêmi*: 15,13; cf. 10,11.15.17.18) for them. The supreme sacrifice of his life is not the only way he has shown his love and friendship for them, for it was he who chose them to be his disciples and close friends (15,16.19; cf. 6,70; 13,18). Besides his initiative in choosing them, he took them into confidence by revealing to them all the divine "family secrets", "for all what I have heard from my Father I have made known to you" (15,15). His love for them is so deep that he can manifest to them the intimate life of love between him and the Father and draw them into that immense, intense, divine love (cf. 17,26).

---

[279] The "fruit" spoken of in 15,1-8 is defined in 15,12-17 as fraternal "love". Jn 15,1-8 and 15,12-17 may be compared to the two sides of the same "Christian" coin which has on one side the picture of Jesus and the disciples (the vine and the branches) and on the other side the picture of the disciples who love one another. The two sides are held together by the thickness of the coin (the mutual love of Jesus and the Father: 15,9-11) which gives solidity to the coin. Just as there is no coin without two sides, so no one can be a true Christian unless he is united with Jesus and unless he has brotherly love. The material of which the Christian coin is made (e.g. gold) is the divine love (of the Father and the Son).

If Jesus has loved the disciples freely, generously and intensely as an intimate friend, they are to respond to this love and friendship and prove to be his true friends by doing his deepest desire, expressed in his last testament or commandment at the end of his life ("You are my friends, if you do what I command you": 15,14), and what he commands them is to "love one another as I have loved you" (15,12.17). In other words, they are to love one another as friends freely, intimately, generously and to the extent of laying down their lives for one another. They are, like Jesus, to take the initiative in loving; they are, like Jesus, to share everything they have; they are, like Jesus, to live and die for others. In short, Jesus-like love is the fruit that is expected of the friends of Jesus (15,16). Such Christ-like, selfless, self-giving, fraternal love is the distinguishing mark of the true disciples of Christ or the test of authentic Christians (cf. 13,35), just as the taste of the wine is the test of the vine.

It follows from what has been already said that the above discourse on the vine and the branches and the commandment of mutual love (15,1-17) is through and through Christocentric, because the disciples are to remain in Christ, like the branches in the vine, in order to produce fruit, and they are to love one another as Christ has loved them.

The counterpart of the Christians' communion with Christ and Christ-like fraternal love (15,1-17) is the world's hatred and persecution (15,18-16,4d). The fate of friends or the destiny of the disciples and the master is identical (15,18-20). If Jesus was the object of the world's hatred, opposition and persecution, their lot will not be any different from his (15,18.20; 17,14). The forces of darkness and hatred cannot stand the light of love revealed in Jesus (*to onoma mou*: 15,21) and reflected in his chosen disciples (15,19; cf. 15,16; 17,26). The ultimate reason for the world's hatred and persecution of Jesus and his faithful followers is the wilful unbelief and sinful ignorance of Jesus and the Father (15,21; 16,3; cf. 17,25) in spite of the revelation of divine love manifested in the mission, words and deeds of Jesus (15,22-24).

It is in this context of opposition, oppression and persecution that the disciples are to bear witness to Christ in the world (15,27). They will be enlightened, supported and strengthened in this witnessing mission by the Paraclete, the Spirit of truth, who testifies to Christ (15,26) in their hearts (14,26; 16,13-15) and, in and through their testimony, in the world (16,8-11). This shows that, just as Christ's communion with the Father led him to Calvary, communion with the crucified Christ and the consequent Christ-like love of one another will lead loyal Christians to the cross.

Jn 15,1-16,4d has a number of similarities with the "commissioning" discourse (and the election narratives) in the Synoptic Gospels (Mt 10,5-42; Mk 3,13-15; 6,7-11; Lk 9,1-5). Just as, according to Mk 3,14, Jesus chose the Twelve "to be with him and to be sent out", according to the Johannine discourse we are examining, Jesus has chosen the disciples (*egô exelexamên hymas*: 15,16.19) not only to be with him like the branches of the vine (15,1-8) but also "to go and bear fruit" (*kai ethêka hymas hina hymeis hypagête kai karpon pherête*: 15,16). Again, just as the Matthean Jesus instructs the Twelve about the persecutions they will have to suffer in order to bear witness to him under the guidance of the Holy Spirit (Mt 10,16-25), so the Johannine Jesus foretells that the disciples, like Jesus himself, will be hated and persecuted by the world as they bear witness to him under the inspiration of the Spirit of truth (15,18-16,4d):

Jn 15,18: eï ho kosmos hymas *misei*... (cf. also 15,19)
    15,21: alla tauta panta poiêsousin eis hymas **dia to onoma mou**...
Mt 10,22: kai esesthe *misoumenoi* hypo pantôn **dia to onoma mou**...

Jn 16,2 : **aposynagôgous** poiêsousin **hymas**;
          all' erchetai hôra hina pas ho *apokteinas* hymas...
Mt 10,17: kai en tais **synagôgais** mastigôsousin **hymas**.
    10,21: paradôsei de adelphos adelphon eis *thanaton*...

Jn 15,20: *ouk estin doulos* meizôn **tou kyriou autou**...
Mt 10,24: *ouk estin* mathêtês hyper ton didaskalon
          oude doulos hyper **ton kyrion autou**.

Jn 15,26: **to pneuma**... ho para *tou patros* ekporeuetai,
          ekeinos m a r t y r ê s e i peri *e m o u*;
    15,27: kai *hymeis* de m a r t y r e i t e...
Mt 10,18: ...heneken *e m o u* eis m a r t y r i o n...
    10,20: ou gar *hymeis* este hoi lalountes
          alla **to pneuma** *tou patros* hymôn to laloun en hymin.

But there are also some remarkable differences between the Synoptic and Johannine versions of choosing and commissioning the disciples. Whereas according to Mk 3,14 the Twelve were elected by Jesus "to be with him" (*hina ôsin met' autou*), according to Jn they are not only "to be with him" (*ap' archês met' emou este*: 15,27) but also "to abide in him" (*menein en emoi*: 15,4.5.7) like the branches in a vine. Secondly, they are not sent so much "to preach" and "to cast out demons" as in Mk 3,14-15 as "to bear witness" (15,27) to Jesus through their Christ-like mutual love (15,16). While the Synoptic Jesus gives the disciples detailed directions as to what should or should not be done (Mt 10,5-15; Mk 6,8-11; Lk 9,3-5), the Johannine Jesus gives them only one commandment, the commandment of Christ-like love (15,12-17), to guide them in their witnessing mission.

5.253z If 13,31-14,31 and 16,4e-33 form essentially a "farewell" discourse, 15,1-17 and 15,18-16,4d contain basically a "commissioning" discourse, in which Jesus explains to the disciples the Christocentric nature, the necessary prerequistes and the crucial consequences of their mission. The disciples are chosen by Christ to be united with him (like the branches of the vine: 15,1-8) and to bear the fruit of Christ-like fraternal love (15,12-17), in and through which they are to bear witness to him in the world. This will inevitably lead to their persecution by the forces of evil opposed to Christ and his message of love (15,18-16,4d). But the Paraclete, the Spirit of truth, whom the glorified Christ will send from the Father, will be by their side to enlighten and support them in their mission of witnessing to Christ (15,26-27). In short, Christ must be the centre of their spiritual life, the criterion of their fraternal love and the scope of their witnessing mission.

5.25z The section of "the Farewell of the Hour" (Jn 13-17) is basically a theological interpretation of "the hour" of Jesus' passion-death-resurrection (to be narrated in the next section: Jn 18-20) in the context of bidding "farewell" to his disciples. The whole of Jesus' passion-death-resurrection and the giving of the Holy Spirit are considered as one event of Jesus' passover from this world to the Father and return to his own, that is, a journey from his own to the Father and back to his own. And the entire event is considered the greatest revelation of the love of the Father and Jesus for his own (13,1; 17,26).

Jesus' washing the feet of his disciples' (when one of them has already decided to betray him) symbolically represents his salvific passion-death-resurrection which reveals the extent of his love and enables them to have a share in his divine life (13,8; 17,2). Not only Jesus and the Father are going to be glorified through the hour (13,31-31; 17,2.4-5) but also those who believe in Jesus are going to contemplate and experience that divine glory (17,22.24). As a result of the hour of Jesus the believers will enter into a deeper union and communion with him, the Father and the Holy Spirit. The Spirit-Paraclete will be sent by the crucified-glorified Christ or given in his name by the Father. Under the guidance of the Spirit of truth the believers will discover the depths of the mystery of God's life of love and will be drawn more and more into that stream of loving life and living love. Intimately united with Jesus like the branches of a vine and constantly drawing on the sap of eternal life and love, they will be able to live a life of Christ-like love and bear testimony to Jesus and his love in a world that hates and persecutes them. The Christocentric character of this theology (e.g. of revelation, salvation, the Holy Spirit, the Church) is therefore evident, for Christ is the mediator of divine revelation and eternal life, the sender of the Spirit-Paraclete and the centre of the community of the faithful.

5.26 The Christocentric Theological Sketch in the Section of "the Hour of Jesus' Passion-Death-Resurrection" (18,1-20,29)

As in the previous sections we shall briefly examine the prominent Christocentric features of the parallel episodes in the chiastic structure (5C D E E'D'C') of 18,1-20,29 [280].

---

[280] See 4.35.

5.261 Jesus of Nazareth, "I am", the life-giving shepherd, the sovereign Spirit-giving Lord and God, in 18,1-14 (5C) and 20,19-29 (5C')

The Johannine Jesus in the garden of Gethsemane is not a man in agony as in the Synoptic Gospels (Mt 26,36-46; Mk 14,32-42; Lk 22,40-46) but the sovereign, human-divine Jesus of Nazareth at whose self-revelation "I am" (*egô eimi*: 18,5) his armed adversaries led by Judas the betrayer fall upon their faces as at a divine ephiphany (18,6; cf. Ez 1,28). The combination of the human name "Jesus of Nazareth" (18,5.7) and the divine name "I am" (18,5.6.8; cf. Ex 3,14) points paradoxically to the mystery of Jesus' human-divine person[281]. This mystery of his divinity and humanity was introduced already in the Prologue (1,1: "In the beginning was the Word... and the Word was God [*theos*]"; 1,14: "And the Word became flesh [*sarx egeneto*]"). If he is the divine Son-God (*monogenês theos*: 1,18) who always existed (*ên*: 1,1) even before the creation of the world (17,24) and has, in time and space, become truly and fully human (1,14), with a human body and soul, subject to hunger and thirst, fatigue and fear, suffering and death, then he is the human "Jesus of Nazareth" who is, at the same time, the divine "I am".

Again, the garden-scene manifests Jesus as the good shepherd (10,11.15.17.18) who protects his sheep (18,8-9; cf. 17,12) and sacrifices his own life to save their lives. For he not only prevents the disciples from being arrested by ordering the soldiers to let them go (18,8) but also allows himself to be taken and bound. "No doubt the evangelist saw this as one more acted out parable of the whole passion (like the washing of the feet)"[282].

Jesus' command to Simon Peter to sheath the sword (18,11) and his words: "shall I not drink the cup which my Father has given me?" (18,11) show his willingness to suffer and die for the sake of the sheep in accordance with the salvific plan of the Father (cf. 10,17-18).

The risen Jesus' sovereignty and Lordship, his humanity and divinity, are manifested to the disciples in the parallel post-resurrectional appearances in 20,19-29. For though the doors of the room are closed and bolted from inside, the risen Jesus comes to the disciples (20,19.26), dispels the darkness of fear and doubt, fills their hearts with peace and joy (20,19-20.26), faith (20,29) and a forgiving Spirit (20,22). While his Lordship and divinity are confessed by the

---

[281] "Jesus asks the Jews: 'Who is it you are looking for?' They reply with his human name, and he replies with a divine name which is a vehicle of power, and it overwhelms them. Probably, therefore, we should link this incident with another mysterious phrase in the prayer of chapter 17: 'So long as I was with them I preserved them in (or with) your Name which you have given to me' (v.12)" (J. BLIGH, *The Sign of the Cross. The Passion and Resurrection of Jesus according to St. John* [Slough 1974] 18.

Note that 17,12 and 18,5 occur in parallel pericopes 4C' and 5C respectively in the Literary Structure of the Fourth Gospel. We may also recall another use of a similar *egô eimi* in connection with the prediction of the betrayal in 3C (13,19).

[282] *Ibid.*, 17.

disciples through the use of the titles *ho kyrios [mou]* (20,20.25.28) and *ho theos mou* (20,28), his crucified humanity is revealed by the risen Jesus himself by showing them his pierced hands and side (20,20.27; cf. 19,18.34; 20,25). It is theologically significant that it is the crucified Christ, bearing the marks of the crucifixion on his risen body, that Thomas confesses as his Lord and God (20,28). The climactic Christian confession consists in the cry of faith in the Lordship and divinity of the crucified Christ.

It is this crucified-risen Jesus, the human-divine Lord, who bestows the forgiving, life-giving Spirit (19,30; 20,22; cf. 7,39) and commissions the disciples to continue his revelatory-salvific mission on earth ("As the Father has sent me, even so I send you": 20,21).

Now comparing Jesus' appearances to the disciples (20,19-29) with his confrontation with his arrest-party (18,1-14), we find that the glory of the risen Lord pervades already the Gethsemane-scene. Just as the risen Jesus is aware of the disciples' fear (20,19) and Thomas' doubt (20,25.27), so Jesus in the garden of Gethsemane has the superhuman knowledge of all that is going to happen to him (18,4). Similarly, he is the sovereign Lord of the situation not only in 20,19-29 but also in 18,1-14, for at this self-revelation *egô eimi* (18,5) the arrest-party falls to the ground and they arrest him only when he freely allows them, after having ordered the soldiers to let the disciples go away. In short, the glory of the risen Lord is reflected already in the garden of Gethsemane like the first rays of the rising sun which illuminate and redden the cluster of clouds in the eastern horizon, announcing a glorious dawn (even before the sun itself becomes visible). In other words, the Johannine Gethsemane-scene is the beginning of a "glorious" passion [283].

5.261z From what has been said above it follows that the theology of 18,1-14 and 20,19-29 is conspicuously Christocentric because of the stress on Jesus' sovereignty and Lordship, humanity and divinity, superhuman knowledge of and filial submission to the salvific plan of the Father, human concern for and divine protection of his disciples, correcting those who oppose the will of the Father but succouring those who succumb to doubt, commissioning those who have experienced his peace to continue his revelatory-salvific mission and breathing on them the forgiving, life-giving Spirit. The Johannine passion and resurrection illuminate one another, for the glory of the risen Lord shines through the face of the arrested Jesus of Nazareth, and the marks of the passion (begun in Gethsemane) are still visible in the risen body of the Lord.

---

[283] A. DAUER, *Die Passionsgeschichte im Johannesevangelium* (München 1972) 236-49; I. DE LA POTTERIE, "La passione secondo il quarto evangelista", *PAF* 19 (1970) 41-59; J. RIAUD, "La gloire et la royauté de Jésus dans la passion selon Saint Jean", *BVC* 56 (1964) 32-34.

5.262 *Jesus, the man and teacher, tried and denied, but risen as the Lord, lover and brother, in 18,12-27 (5D) and 20,1-18 (5D')*

One of the theological points highlighted in Jesus' trial before the high priest and denial by Peter is Jesus' humanity, for he is twice referred to as "(this) man" (18,14.17). Caiaphas' prophecy that "it is expedient that one man (*anthrôpos*) should die for the people" (11,50) is explicitly recalled in 18,14. Again, the first question put to Peter (by the high priest's door-keeper) is: "Are you also one of this man's (*tou anthrôpou toutou*) disciples?" (18,17). Jesus is here presented as a true human being who, like anybody else, can be bound (18,12), struck (18,22), and killed (18,14). Peter seems to be "ashamed of" such a Jesus and therefore he denies that he is a disciple of "this fellow" (18,17)[284].

That even after the resurrection Jesus remains human is seen from the facts that he can be taken for a gardener (20,15) and held in loving embrace by Mary Magdalene (20,17). Besides, he himself refers to God as "my God and your God" (20,17). On the other hand, Jesus is twice referred to as "the Lord" (*ho kyrios*: 20,2.18) and once as "my Lord" (*ho kyrios mou*: 20,13) by Mary Magdalene. This points to the Christological mystery of the human Jesus being the divine Lord.

Jesus is presented also as a teacher both during his trial before the high priest and during his appearance to Mary Magdalene. For he is questioned by the high priest about his "teaching" (*didachê*: 18,19); Jesus himself admits having taught in the synagogues (cf. 6,59) and in the temple (18,20; cf. 7,14.16.17.28); Mary Magdalene addresses him as *Rabbouni* ("teacher": 20,19). He teaches not only through his revelatory words (*parrêsia[i] lelalêsa*: 18,20; cf. 7,26; *elalêsa*: 18,20.23; cf. 7,46) but also through his courageous conduct. For he is bold enough to question the hypocritical high priest (18,20-21) and to protest against the official who slapped him (18,22-23). This is in stark contrast to the cowardly conduct of Peter who denies his discipleship when questioned by the servants of the high priest.

The mutual love of Jesus and the disciple, subtly hinted at in 18,15 (two disciples follow him) and 18,19 (Jesus protects the disciples through his silence about them), is magnificently manifested in 20,1-18. In fact, the love of Mary Magdalene and Jesus may be compared to that of the beloved and the lover in the Song of Songs[285]. Mary's arrival at Jesus' tomb even before daybreak

---

[284] Though the danger to Peter's life was not great, "yet he denied his association with Christ - probably more through shame than through fear. He was ashamed of Jesus, now that he had so tamely submitted to his enemies" (J. BLIGH, *op. cit.*, 26). Here we are not concerned about the historical reason why Peter denied Jesus; we are interested only in the Johannine presentation of the denial. The words of the maid *ho anthrôpos houtos* (18,17) seem to have a derogatory meaning ("this fellow") as on the lips of the arrogant Pharisees in 9,24. Note that, while the cured blind man defends Jesus, who is branded a sinner by the Pharisees, and openly acknowledges himself to be his disciple (9,25-28), Peter, who proclaimed his readiness even to die for his master (13,37), is ashamed of being one of his disciples (18,17.25.26-27).

[285] A. FEUILLET, "La recherche du Christ dans la nouvelle alliance d'après la Christophanie de Jo. 20,11-18", in: Mél. H. de Lubac (1963) 102-4.

(20,1), her running in despair to the disciples (20,2), her broken-hearted weeping (20,11.13.15), her repeated lamentation at the loss of her beloved Lord (20,2.13.15), her incessant search for him (20,15), her endearing address *Rabbouni* (20,16), her attempt to hold him in her arms for ever (20,17), are all signs of her intense love and affection for him. And he seems to enjoy playing, as it were, hide and seek with her. For he appears to her as a gardener (20,14-15); he asks her why she is weeping and whom she is seeking (20,15), as if he did not know! Finally, he reveals his identity by calling her affectionately by her name "Mary".

The mutual love of Jesus and the other disciples is also evident in 20,1-18. His love for the Beloved Disciple is explicitly recalled in 20,2. Even though one of the disciples had denied him and the others had deserted him (cf. 16,32), he calls them his "brothers" (*hoi adelphoi mou*: 20,17) and sends Mary with the message that his Father has become their Father (20,17). He had already left a simple but significant sign (the rolled up napkin: 20,7) to help his loved ones to see and believe in his resurrection (20,8). The disciples' love for him is revealed in their race to his tomb (20,4).

5.262z The Johannine narratives of the Jewish trial and the Petrine denial of Jesus, the discovery of the empty tomb and his appearance to Mary Magdalene disclose the mystery of his true humanity and Lordship, the nature of his teaching, his relationship to his disciples as their teacher, brother and lover, and the various responses to his revelation and love. There may be also a contrast between Peter who denies his master and the risen Jesus who recognizes his disciples to be "my brothers".

5.263 *Jesus, the man, the Son of God, the king of the Jews, crucified and glorified, the fulfilment of the Scriptures, and the giver of the Spirit, in 18,28-19,16b (5E) and 19,16c-42 (5E')*

The highly dramatic episodes of the trial of Jesus before Pilate (18,28-19,16b) and of the crucifixion, death and burial (19,16c-42), highlight a number of Christological-soteriological points mentioned earlier in the Gospel, such as his humanity, divinity, kingship, crucifixion, Scriptural fulfilment, gift of the Spirit.

To begin with, the first question Pilate puts to the Jews regarding Jesus is: "What accusation do you bring against this man (*ho anthrôpos houtos*)?" (18,29; cf. 18,17) and after scourging him Pilate proclaims to them: "Behold the man!" (*ide ho anthrôpos*: 19,5). When he is crucified, his human name ("Jesus of Nazareth") is affixed to the cross (19,19; cf. 18,5.7). Like any other man he is crucified (19,18) and buried (19,40). The reality of his death is certified by the flow of blood and water from his pierced side (19,34). That Jesus was truly a human being has been repeatedly mentioned starting from the Prologue (1,14; 4,29; 5,12; 6,42; 7,46; 8,40; 9,11.16.24; 10,33; 11,50) and admitted by Jesus himself (cf. 8,40) and by his friends and foes. Like other human beings he is hungry and thirsty (4,7; 19,28); he gets tired (4,6), troubled (11,33; 12,27; 13,21) and tearful (11,35). Again, we have seen above that one of the aspects underlined by the title "the Son of Man" (*ho hyios tou anthrôpou*) is Jesus' humanity [286]. The revelation of Jesus as the man reaches its climax in Pilate's proclamation in 19,5: "Behold the man!".

It is interesting to note that the first time the Jews cry out for Jesus' crucifixion (*staurôson staurôson*: 19,6) is when he is presented by Pilate as "the man" (19,5) [287]. But Jesus himself had hinted at it a number of times, especially in connection with the "lifting up of the Son of Man" (3,14; 8,28; 12,32), which the Evangelist has explained is a reference to Christ's crucifixion (12,33; 18,32). The ultimate reason for the Jewish demand for crucifixion is Jesus' claim to be the Son of God (19,7; cf. 5,18; 10,33.36).

But the Christological motif that is most dominant in the Roman trial is Jesus' kingship [288]. He who had run away from the enthusiastic Galilean crowd that wanted to crown him king (6,15) now seems to admit to be a king (18,37) and is proclaimed by the Roman governor to be "the king of the Jews" (18,39; 19,14.15.19). In fact, the first question Pilate asks Jesus is: "Are you the king of the Jews?" (18,33). In the ensuing dialogue the non-worldly nature of his kingship is made amply evident: "My kingdom is not of this world" (18,36bcf). He is not a political king who comes to power or wins his earthly kingdom through the use of force or political intrigue and remains on the throne through the wars he wages (18,36). His royal mission and role is to bear witness to the truth (18,37), the revelation of God, which he does through his words, deeds and person, since he himself is the truth (14,6). Hence he is the king of those who welcome the revelation of God in him. He is the king of the true Israelites like Nathanael (1,47) who confessed him to be "the king of Israel" (1,49; cf. 12,13). The meaning of the Messianic kingship of Jesus, acknowledged by Nathanael and proclaimed by the Passover crowds in Jerusalem (12,13), is illuminated by what is said about his kingship and done to him as "the king of the Jews" in 18,28-19,42. Jesus' own words about the nature of his kingship make it clear that it has nothing to do with politics, though he is called "the king of the Jews" both by Pilate (18,39; 19,14.15.19) and by the mocking soldiers who crown him with thorns and array him with a royal purple robe (19,2-3). Though this was done in mockery, the Evangelist seems to see it as the coronation of Jesus and the crucifixion as his enthronement. Jesus is a crucified king and it is from the cross that he reigns. It is when he is "lifted up" on the cross that he draws all men to himself (12,32). The universality of his kingship seems to be implied in the trilingual title on the cross (19,19-22).

---

[286] See 4.124.

[287] The last cry of the Jewish crowd for Jesus' crucifixion is heard (19,15) when Pilate proclaims him their "king" (19,14).

[288] J. BLANK, "Die Verhandlung vor Pilatus: Joh 18,28-19,16 im Lichte johanneischer Theologie", *BZ* 3 (1959) 60-81 and especially p. 62.

The gift par excellence that Jesus, the crucified king, gives is his Spirit, for his death is described as an act of "giving the Spirit" (*paredôken to pneuma*: 19,30). Unlike Lk 23,46 which records Jesus' prayer: "Father, into your hands I commit my spirit" (*pater, eis cheiras sou paratithemai to pneuma mou*), Jn 19,30 does not specify the Spirit as "my Spirit", nor does it indicate to whom "the Spirit" is given or handed over (*paredôken*)[289]. But what is underscored is that, according to the Johannine understanding, Jesus' death on the cross is a Spirit-giving death (19,30). Just as the risen Jesus breathes the Spirit on the disciples (20,22), the dying Jesus gives the Spirit (19,30). Thus the Johannine Pentecost coincides with Jesus' death-resurrection, just as the crucifixion of Jesus is already his exaltation or glorification. The lens of "the hour" of Jesus focuses the mysteries of Jesus' death, resurrection, ascension and giving of the Spirit into one concentrated mystery of his glorification (12,23; 13,31; 17,1.5).

It is also probable that the flow of blood and water from the pierced side of Jesus (19,34), besides denoting his death, symbolizes his gifts of life (life was supposed to reside in blood) and the Spirit (water is a symbol of the Holy Spirit: cf. 4,10; 7,38-39). This interpretation of 19,34 does not go against the sacramental understanding of water and blood as symbols of Baptism and Eucharist, since Jesus spoke of the need of being born of (water and) the Spirit in 3,5-8 in order to enter the kingdom of God (3,5) and later revealed the Spirit as "life-giving" (*zô[i]opioun*: 6,63) in connection with Jesus' gift of the Eucharist (6,51-58). It is the life-giving activity of the Holy Spirit that energizes the elements of water, bread and wine and makes them sacramental channels of divine life.

Jesus' gift of the life-giving Spirit to the believers (cf. 7,39) seems to be symbolized also by the gift of his own mother to the Beloved Disciple as his mother ("Behold your mother!": 19,27)[290]. Though many understand Jesus' mother as a symbol of the Church[291] and the Beloved Disciple as that of the Christian[292], while the latter symbolism is evident enough from the way he is presented in Jn, the Church-symbolism of Jesus' mother is not without difficulty, because the Church is never designated in Jn as a mother of whom Christians are

---

[289] *Paradidômi* is used elsewhere in Jn to denote Judas' betrayal of Jesus (6,64.71; 12,4; 13,2.11.21; 18,2.5; 21,20), the Jews' handing him over (betrayal?) to Pilate (18,35), and Pilate's handing him over (betrayal?) back to the Jews (18,36; 19,16). The expression *paradidômi to pneuma* at 19,30 to describe dying is unique. Since the Spirit is the gift of the glorified Jesus to the believers (7,39) and since he is glorified already in his crucifixion and death (cf. "lifting up" at 3,14; 8,28; 12,32-33), *paredôken to pneuma* at 19,30 has most probably the theological meaning that through his death on the cross "he handed over the Spirit".

[290] Cf. BROWN, II, 922-27 for the various interpretations of the theological import of this episode and especially of the symbolism of the mother of Jesus (e.g. as Israel, Jewish Christianity, the Church) and of the Beloved Disciple (e.g. as Christians, Gentile Christians, the individual Christian).

[291] *Ibid.*, 924-27.

[292] Regarding the symbolism of the Beloved Disciple BROWN affirms: "There is little doubt that in the Johannine thought the Beloved Disciple can symbolize the Christian" (II, 924).

born (in fact, the "Church" is never mentioned at all). Though the Spirit is also never explicitly called a mother in Jn, the necessity of being born from the Spirit is unambiguously affirmed by Jesus himself during his discourse on new birth from above (3,3-8). If believers in Jesus are children of God (*tekna theou*) because they are "born of God" (*ek theou egennêthêsan*) (1,12-13), which is later specified as a birth from the Spirit (3,5-8), the mother of Jesus (19,26-27) may be suggested as a symbol of the Holy Spirit who gives birth to the brothers of Jesus (*hoi adelphoi mou*: 20,17). This would also explain why Jesus entrusts first the Beloved Disciple to his mother ("Behold, your son!": 19,26) and "then" (*eita*) his mother to the Beloved Disciple ("Behold, your mother!": 19,27). The disciple's taking her *eis ta idia* from that "hour" also makes better sense if Jesus' mother is the symbol of the Spirit who is to remain with and within the disciples for ever (14,16-17)[293].

Another important theological motif that is emphasized in the events on Calvary is Jesus' fulfilment of the Scripture (*hina hê graphê plêrôthê[i]*: 19,24.36; *hina teleiôthê[i] hê graphê*: 19,28). Thus the division of Jesus' garments and the casting of lots for his tunic by the soldiers (19,23-24), his thirst on the cross (19,28), his bones not being broken but his side being pierced (19,33-36), are all explained as part of the plan of God foretold in the Scriptures which Jesus brings to perfect fulfilment.

5.263z Thus the Johannine dramatic presentation of Jesus' trial before Pilate and the symbolic episodes connected with his crucifixion, death and burial underscore the Christocentric motifs of his kingship, humanity, sovereignty, Scriptural fulfilment and gift of the Spirit.

5.26z The theological profile of Jesus that is painted in the Johannine passion-resurrection narrative highlights not so much his sufferings during the passion and then his glory after his resurrection but rather a human-divine Christ glorified already during his appearance before his arrest-party, during his Jewish and Roman trials, and on the cross, and bearing the marks of the passion even as the risen Lord. His divinity and sovereignty, kingship and Lordship, are revealed already during the passion, and his human care and love for his own are made manifest not only in the passion narrative but also in the episodes connected with the resurrection. The passion and the resurrection illuminate and interpret one another so much that Jesus is glorified already in and through the passion and crucifixion (e.g. the "lifting up" on the cross is already an exaltation) and the risen glorified Lord is still fully human and humane. In other words, the Jesus of the Johannine passion-resurrection is not a hyphenated man-God or God-man but a Godman who reveals the mystery of his person that is both divine and human and manifests best and brings to perfect completion his revelatory and salvific mission. All that happens in Jn 18-20 belongs to the *t-etelestai* (19,30) of Jesus, the Man and God, the Revealer and Saviour, the King and Brother, the Teacher and Spirit-giver, the Lord and Lover.

---

[293] The mother of Jesus as the symbol of the Holy Spirit is only a suggestion. Space does not permit us to persue the matter further.

5.27 The Christocentric Theological Sketch in the Appendix (Jn 21,1-25)

We saw in ch. 4 that the appendix (Jn 21), added at the end of the Fourth Gospel, consists of an epilogue (21,1-23) and a second (editorial) conclusion (21,24-25).

The epilogue (21,1-23), which describes the disciples' miraculous catch of fish and breakfast (21,1-14), the pastoral commission and destiny of Peter (21,15-19), and the fate of the Beloved Disciple (21,20-23), contains mostly a Christocentric ecclesiology.

The group of seven disciples staying together (*êsan homou*: 21,2) and acting in unison (*erchometha kai hêmeis syn soi*: 21,3) is a symbol of the Christian community. But the fact that, though they labour the whole night, they catch nothing (21,3) demonstrates the truth of Jesus' saying: "without me you can do nothing" (15,5). The risen Jesus' "standing" (*estê*: 21,4; cf. 20,14.19.26) on the shore early in the morning points to his presence even when the disciples do not recognize him (21,4; cf. 20,14). He seems to have appeared to them under the guise of a customer (as he did to Mary Magdalene under the guise of the gardener [20,15] or to the disciples on the way to Emmaus as a stranger [Lk 24,18]) come to inquire if they have any fish (21,5). (Even later when they come close to him, they seem to have some difficulty recognizing his identity from his appearance, for 21,12 tells us: "Now none of the disciples dared ask him, 'Who are you?', knowing that it was the Lord"). This seems to imply that the disciples are to recognize the risen Jesus' presence not so much from his external appearance but from his efficacious words and caring deeds (21,5-6.9-12). Like the Beloved Disciple, who intuited the identity of the risen Lord (21,7; cf. 20,8) from the miraculous catch of fish by following his instructions (21,6), the believers who have experienced his love and who are attuned to his love will be able to recognize his presence in the Christian mission guided by his directives, which is bound to bear abundant fruit (cf. 15,7-8) like the enormous quantity of fish caught by the disciples at his word (21,6.11). The large catch of fish (153 of them: 21,11) symbolizes the universal nature of the Christian mission and the unbroken (*ouk eschisthê*: 21,11) net, like the untorn (*mê schisômen*: 19,24) tunic of Jesus (19,23-24), the unity of the Christian community [294]. The "hauling" (*helkein*: 21,6.11) of the net full of fish ashore may also symbolize the risen Jesus' "drawing" (*helkein*: 12,32) of all men to himself in and through the missionary activity of his disciples.

Most probably the meal provided by the risen Jesus to the disciples at the Sea of Tiberias (21,9-13), which resembles the multiplication meal in Jn 6 with its Eucharistic overtones (compare especially 6,11 and 21,13), is a symbol of the Eucharistic meal in which the Christian community experiences Jesus' intimate loving communion [295].

---

[294] BROWN, II, 1097; PANIMOLLE, III, 483-84.

[295] This is the position of many Johannine scholars e.g. PANIMOLLE, III, 489; cf. also the authors mentioned there in n. 50.

Through the triple profession of love, Peter, who had denied Jesus thrice (18,15-18.25-27), is rehabilitated and through the triple commission he is entrusted with the flock of Jesus (21,15-17). It is interesting to note that the primacy of Peter here is based on the primacy of his love for Jesus [296], for he commissions Simon to feed his lambs (*boske ta arnia mou*: 21,15) only after asking him if he loved him more than the other disciples (*agapa[i]s me pleon toutôn*: 21,15). The love that Jesus speaks about is *agapê*, a love that is generous, self-giving, self-sacrificing. After having denied Jesus, Peter does not dare to compare his *agapê* for Jesus with that of the other disciples, but he affirms his affectionate love (*philein*) as a friend (*philos*) [297]. His greater affection for Jesus than that of the other disciples was demonstrated by his springing into the water and swimming across the lake to come to Jesus first (21,7), while the other disciples came in the boat (21,8). When Peter publicly confesses his genuine affection for Jesus as a friend (*philô se*: 21,15), Jesus asks him to feed his "lambs" (*arnia*: 21,15), which probably refers to the leaders in the Christian community. In other words, in Jn 21,15 Jesus seems to commission Peter to feed the leaders (shepherds) of his sheep [298]. Love for Jesus is a prerequisite for shepherding his sheep as his question and commission to Peter make clear in 21,16 (*agapas me?...poimaine ta probata mou*). The presupposition here is that if Peter loves Jesus, he would love also the sheep whom Jesus loves and for whom he has laid down his life. Shepherding or tending includes feeding, guiding and guarding the sheep. "My sheep" (*ta probata mou*) here stands for all the believers in Jesus, while "my little sheep" (*ta probatia mou*) at 21,17 [299] probably refers to the new

---

[296] According to Mt 16,16-19 the primacy of Peter seems to be a primacy of faith in Jesus, since he promises to give him the keys of the kingdom (16,19) after he has confessed his faith in Jesus as "the Christ, the Son of the living God" (16,16). It is true that in Jn 6,69 Peter makes a profession of faith in Jesus as "the holy one of God". But there Jesus did not commission Peter to shepherd his flock.

[297] Pace BROWN who regards *agapan* and *philein* as synonyms (II, 1103), the self-giving aspect of love seems to be stressed in *agapan* while the affectionate aspect is underlined in *philein*. (Notice that when Jesus weeps at 11,35 the Jews say: *ide pôs ephilei autón* (Lazarus) whom Jesus himself had called a "friend" [*philos*: 11,11].)

[298] The word *arnion* does not occur anywhere else in Jn. In fact, the only other NT book which contains the tern *arnion* is Rev (in which it is found 29 times). Rev 7,17 describes the Lamb (*arnion* as one who will tend (*poimanei*) and guide (*odêgêsei*) the sheep as a shepherd. *Arnia* in Jn 21,15 too may have such a symbolic significance. This meaning of *arnia* lends support to the interpretation of Jn 21,15-17 (and Mt 16,16-19) by the First Vatican Council in connection with the dogmatic definition of Petrine primacy: "Peter the apostle was constituted by Christ the Lord as *chief of all the apostles* and as visible head of the Church on earth" (DB, 3053-55, as translated and cited by BROWN, II, 1116). Vatican I, which has stressed the Petrine authority over the other apostles and the entire Church, has not perhaps emphasized sufficiently the basis of that authority on Peter's greater love for Jesus which will lead him to love and give his life for Jesus' flock, as is made absolutely clear in Jn 21,15-19.

[299] With BROWN (II, 1105) we prefer the reading *probatia* (of Codex Alexandrinus and Codex Vaticanus) at 21,17, since the reading *probata* (of Codex Sinaiticus) may be a scribal attempt at harmonization with *probata* at 21,16 and in Jn 10 and since, if *probata* were the original reading,

Christians or neophytes; Peter is given a special charge to nourish (*boske*) them with personal affection for Jesus (*philein*). In short, Peter, the friend of Jesus, is given a pastoral commission over all his flock. This does not, however, mean that Peter now replaces Christ as the chief Shepherd or that the sheep now belong to Peter. The flock still belongs to Jesus and Peter is to keep that constantly in mind. As St. Augustine correctly comments: "Tend my sheep as mine, not as yours"[300].

And tending Jesus' sheep will lead Peter to lay down his life for Jesus and his sheep (21,18-19), as Jesus, the Good Shepherd, did (10,11.15.17). It is to "follow" him in laying down his life for the sheep that Jesus invites Peter in 21,19 (*akolouthei moi*), thus fulfilling his promise in 13,38 (*akoloutheseis de hysteron*) and Peter's desire to die for Jesus (13,37).

While Peter bears witness to Jesus through the loving pastoral care of the Christian community and through his martyrdom, the Beloved Disciple is to "remain" (*menein*: 21,22.23) as a witness to Jesus in the community of his disciples and brothers (cf. 21,7: "It is the Lord"). The Gospel that he has written is part of his perennial testimony to Jesus in the community of faith and fraternal love (21,24; cf. 19,35; 20,31). Thus like John the Baptist, the friend of the Messianic bridegroom (3,29), who came to reveal Jesus to Israel (1,31) through his testimony (1,7), so the Beloved Disciple continues to manifest the mystery of Jesus' person and his saving love for men. The inexhaustible riches of that mystery is hinted at in the hyperbolic editorial conclusion (21,25).

5.27z The most important theological contribution of Jn 21 is its rich *Christocentric ecclesiology*. First of all, the Christian community is constituted of the disciples of Jesus, his brothers, his friends, his sheep, whom he guides and feeds and to whom he reveals himself. The universality of the ecclesial community is symbolically represented by the 153 fish and its unity by the untorn net (like the untorn tunic of Jesus). The fishing expedition of the seven disciples of Christ under the leadership of Peter manifests the missionary endeavours of the Christian community which, however, can bear fruit only when the risen Jesus is efficaciously present and only when his directives are followed in faith. It is also a Eucharistic community gathered around the table of the Lord and sharing the meal that he has prepared himself as a symbol of his love and self-gift. In short, it is a Christocentric community. In this community there are also various types of persons with different functions like the pastoral function of the "loving" Peter and the witnessing function of the "remaining" Beloved Disciple. Love for Christ and fulfilling his will must be the sole motives for doing whatever has been entrusted by the Lord to each one in the Christ-centred community of brothers.

---

there would be no special reason for a scribe to change it to the rare *probatia*. But *pace* BROWN who sees no difference in the meaning of *arnia*, *probata* and *probatia*, a distinction in meaning is required to account for the unique occurrence of *arnia* and *probatia* here in Jn.

[300] *Joh.* CXXIII 5; PL 35: 1967.

5.z Our examination of the major theological themes and our sketch of Johannine theology in the structural development of the Gospel have both demonstrated the close connection between *structure and theology*. As the Evangelist himself has stated in the conclusion (20,30-31), he has chosen the material carefully and composed the Gospel for a specific purpose, namely, so that the readers may believe that Jesus is the Messiah and the divine Son of God, and that through their personal, existential faith in him they may have eternal, divine life. In other words, the Fourth Gospel has a *Christocentric* theological scope. The Evangelist has combined beautifully the high Christo centric theology with a fascinating artistic literary structure [301]. Or rather, he has conveyed the profound Christ-centred theology through the medium of a well-organized, dramatic, literary structure.

The *five-act theological drama* (Jn 2-4; 5-10; 11-12; 13-17; 18-20) preceded by a triple introduction (1,1-2,11) magnificently manifests the *salvific mission* and the *human-divine person of Jesus* and the human response of *faith* or *unbelief* provoked by his revelation. His words (dialogues, discourses, discussions and debates) and deeds (symbolic actions, signs and works), death and resurrection, reveal not only who Jesus is and what his mission consists in but also the divine *life* which he shares with the Father and which he has come to communicate to those who believe in him.

The central *theological themes* mentioned above are introduced already in 1,1-2,11, *developed progressively* in the chiastic structures of the first (Jn 2-4), second (Jn 5-10), fourth (Jn 13-17) and fifth (Jn 18-20) sections and in the parallel structure of the bridge-section (Jn 11-12) and finally recalled in the conclusion (in the inverse order of the introduction). Taking the risk of simplification we may say that the two Cana-signs in 1A (2,1-11) and 1A' (4,43-54) manifest Jesus as the Messiah; the cleansing of the temple in 1B (2,13-2,25) and the Samaritan episode in 1B' (4,1-42) reveal Jesus as the prophet/Messiah and hint at his being the Son of God, which is further explicitated and developed in the dialogue/discourse following the "work" of curing the cripple in 2B (5,1-47) and in the dialogue/discourse in 2B' (10,22-42). That Jesus is not only the Christ, the Son of Man, the Son of God, but also the life-giver is revealed in the Nicodemus-episode in 1C (2,23-3,21), the Baptist-episode in 1C' (3,22-4,3), the bread-of-life-episode in 2C (6,1-71), the life-giving good shepherd-discourse in 2C' (10,1-21), the Lazarus-episode in 3C (11,1-54), the coming of the Greeks and "the hour" of Jesus in 3C' (11,55-12,50), the washing of the feet as a symbol of Jesus' life-giving death in 4C (13,1-38), the prayer of the hour in 4C' (17,1-26), and his appearances to the disciples in 5C' (20,19-29). The true identity of Jesus

---

[301] "Il vangelo di Giovanni si rivela senza alcun dubbio come uno dei piu profondi e affascinanti scritti del NT. In questo libro la più fine arte letteraria è fusa mirabilmente con la più alta Cristologia" (S. A. PANIMOLLE, *L'evangelista Giovanni, pensiero e opera letteraria del quarto vangelo* [Roma 1985] 7).

can be understood only when his origin (whence he has come) is grasped. This, besides revealing Jesus as the light of the world, is one of the important issues discussed in the dialogues, discourses and controversies in 2D (Jn 7-8) and 2D' (Jn 9). Jesus' true origin (the Father) can be perceived only when his destination in death-resurrection is known. This is explained in the Farewell Discourses in 4D (13,31-14,31) and 4D' (16,4e-33). The life of love and communion between Jesus and the believers and among themselves, revealed to an extent already in the earlier passages, reaches the height of its revelation in the parabolic allegory of the vine and the branches and the commandment of mutual love in 4E (15,1-17), a consequence of which is the hatred and persecution by the world spoken of in 4E' (15,18-16,4d). The world's hatred reaches its climax in the trial of Jesus before Pilate in 5E (18,28-19,16b) and in his death on the cross in 5E' (19,16c-42). His Spirit-bestowing, life-giving death on the cross is at the same time the greatest revelation of Jesus' limitless love for his own (cf. 15,13). Thus we find that there is a progressive development of the Christocentric theology from 'A's to 'E's in the literary structure of the Fourth Gospel[302].

---

[302] This does not mean that historically the disciples of Jesus understood the depth of his revelation during his life-time (even during the last discourse). For instance, Jesus was confessed as truly divine ("My Lord and my God": 20,28) only after the resurrection. But under the guidance of the Spirit of truth the Evangelist has dramatically and theologically interpreted the life, death and resurrection of Jesus and has communicated it in and through the medium of an orderly and artistic literary structure, which shows that he is both a theological and a literary genius.

CONCLUSION

Since we have given appropriate conclusions at the end of each chapter and of each section and subsection, we do not intend to repeat them all here but only to recapitulate the major results of our investigation and to indicate the modest but hopefully original contribution of our doctoral dissertation.

The major contribution of our investigation consists, we believe, in the **new literary structure of the Fourth Gospel** that we have proposed in chapter 4. There we saw that the Gospel of John consists of a triple **Christocentric introduction** (hymnic-testimonial: 1,1-18; testimonial-kerygmatic: 1,19-51; historical-sign: 2,1-11), two major divisions, namely, **the Book of Jesus' Signs** (2,1-12,50) and **the Book of Jesus' Hour** (11,1-20,29), a **Christocentric conclusion** (20,30-31) and an **appendix** (21,1-25). The introduction and the Book of Jesus' Signs are linked through the first Cana-sign (2,1-11) which functions as a *bridge-pericope*; the Book of Jesus' Signs and the Book of Jesus' Hour are closely connected by means of a *bridge-section* (Jn 11-12). Both the Book of Jesus' Signs and the Book of Jesus' Hour contain three sections each (2,1-4,54: *Jesus' Initial Signs and Encounters*; 5,1-10,42: *Jesus' Works, Signs and Discussions*; 11,1-12,50: *the Climactic Sign and the Coming of Jesus' Hour*; 13,1-17,26: *Jesus' Farewell of the Hour*; 18,1-20,29: *the Hour of Jesus' Passion-Death-Resurrection*), the bridge-section (Jn 11-12) being common to both the books. In other words, the body of the Gospel (2,1-20,29) is constituted of *five sections* in all, which may also be thought of as corresponding to *five acts* in the *Johannine drama*. Furthermore, the *first two sections* and the *last two* sections are *chiastically structured* (1A B C C'B'A'; 2B C D D' C' B'; 4C D E E' D' C'; 5C D E E' D' C') and the central *bridge-section* has a *parallel structure* (3C C'). There are similarities between the episodes represented by the corresponding letters not only in the same section (e.g. 1A and 1A' or 1B and 1B') but also in the other sections (e.g. 1B, 1B', 2B, 2B'; 1C, 1C', 2C, 2C', 3C, 3C', 4C, 4C', 5C, 5C'; 2D, 2D', 4D, 4D', 5D, 5D'). There is also a gripping *dramatic development* of the plot from section to section (and often in the same section, subsection or episode). In other words, the Fourth Evangelist has structured the Gospel very artistically and dramatically using a number of **literary devices, dramatic techniques** and **structural patterns**, which we have described in chapter 3. Since our detection of the literary-dramatic structure of the Fourth Gospel is based on the **convergence** of numerous (about 30) and different kinds of **criteria**, we believe it to be objective.

Our structure has also **integrated** many of the **positive points** and **insights** of the Johannine scholars who have proposed various literary or dramatic structures, which we critically examined in chapter 2. The structure we have suggested is proposed not as the last word but as one based on a large number and different types of criteria culled from the Fourth Gospel itself, and which can **account for** many of the **apparent aporias** and **peculiarities** of the Johannine Gospel, such as the so-called interruptions and inconsistencies in sequence and repetitions of similar passages, which we mentioned in chapter one. For instance, the repetitions (e.g. 3,11-21 &3,31-36; 13,31-14,31 &16,4e-33) have a meaningful function in the chiastic or parallel structures of the sections. The structure we have proposed does not depend on any hypothetical theory of accidental displacements or of multiple sources, but highlights the **literary and dramatic unity** of the Johannine Gospel as we have it today.

In the light of our structure, we can also give some **reasons for the divergence in the divisions** of the Gospel of John as suggested by different scholars. First of all, many of the structures they have proposed are based on a *single* or *only a few criteria* rather than on the convergence of a number of and different kinds of criteria. Secondly, many have *failed to see* the close *connection* between the major divisions through the *bridge-passages* (2,1-11; 11,1-12,50), the *chiastic* construction of the first, second, fourth and fifth sections, the *parallel* structure of the bridge-section (Jn 11-12) and the *dramatic development* of the Johannine plot, while others have looked at the Gospel only from the dramatic point of view and *not* from the *literary structural* angle.

Finally, we believe that the literary-dramatic structure we have proposed helps us to understand the theological message of the Fourth Gospel. This we have tried to show in the fifth chapter: **"the literary structure and the Christocentric theology of the Fourth Gospel"**. We have shown how the *major Johannine themes* such as the *Messiahship* and the *divine Sonship* of Jesus, his *signs (and works)*, *discipleship*, *faith* and *eternal life*, which are mentioned in the conclusion of the Gospel of John (20,30-31), are *Christocentric* in character and they have been gradually and artfully developed in the literary structure of the Gospel. *Sketching the theological message* of the successive sections in the structure of the Fourth Gospel, we have found that the *Christocentric scope of the Gospel* as enunciated in its conclusion is magnificently realized in and through the medium of the literary structure, for there is a *progressive revelation of Jesus, the Christ, the Son of God and the life-giver* (20,30-31) in the dramatic and organic development of the Gospel. Participation in the divine life through faith in, love of and communion with Jesus, the Messiah, the divine Son of the Father and the mediator of eternal life, culminates in the mutual *indwelling* of Jesus Christ and the believers, which manifests itself in *mutual fraternal Christ-like love* and in *witnessing* to Christ in the midst of persecutions. All this is reflected in the structural development of the Gospel. In short, the *literary structure* we have established reveals the *Christocentric theology* of the Fourth Gospel.

Studying scientifically the structure of the Fourth Gospel and meditating prayerfully on the mystery of Christ mediated through it may be compared to a scientific exploration of a tropical forest by contemplative mountaineers who, walking along the low valleys and climbing up the high hills, not only make a map of the mountain but also marvel at its immeasurable majesty and enjoy its inexpressible beauty. May the *structural map* we have made of the Fourth Gospel help the reader to trek through the Christocentric forest and contemplate the mystery of the mission and person of Jesus, the Christ, the Son of God, the giver of life.

BIBLIOGRAPHY

N.B. 1) The *acronyms* of *Periodicals* and the Sigla of Series are as in *Elenchus Bibliographicus Biblicus* 63 (1982) 6-24.
2) The *Greek text* of the NT that we have used is NESTLE-ALAND's *Greek-English New Testament*, [GENT] 2 ed. (Stuttgart 1985), whose text is the same as that of the United Bible Society's *The Greek New Testament*, [GNT] 3 ed., K. Aland, M. Black, C. M. Martini, B. M. Metzger, and A. Wikgren (Stuttgart 1983).
3) Biblical quotations in *English* are from the *Revised Standard Version*, 2 ed. (1971), unless otherwise noted.

A. BIBLIOGRAPHY OF BIBLIOGRAPHY ON THE GOSPEL OF JOHN

N.B. The bibliography of Johannine bibliography given below does *not* include that *before 1964/65*, since MALATESTA gives a "cumulative and classified bibliography" on the Gospel of John from 1920-1965 (see below).

— *Elenchus Bibliographicus Biblicus* 45 (1964) - 64 (1983).
— *ETL: Elenchus Bibliographicus* 41 (1965) - 61 (1985).
— *IZBG* 11 (1964-65) - 31 (1984-85).
BECKER J., "Aus der Literatur zum Johannesevangelium", *TRu* NF 47 (1982) 279-84; 51 (1986) 3-7.
LANGEVIN P.-É., *Bibliographie Biblique, Biblical Bibliography, Biblische Bibliographie, Bibliografia Biblica, Bibliografía Bíblica I (1930-70)* (Québec 1972) 336-72; *II (1930-75)* (Québec 1978) 731- 81; *III (1930-83)* (Québec 1985) 925-68.
MALATESTA E., *St. John's Gospel 1920-1965. A Cumulative and Classified Bibliography of Books and Periodical Literature on The Fourth Gospel* (AnBib 32) (Rome 1967).
MODA A., "Quarto Vangelo 1966-1972", *RivB* 22 (1974) 53-86.
THYEN H., "Aus der Literatur zum Johannesevangelium", *TRu* NF 39 (1974) 1-44.
WAGNER G., *An Exegetical Bibliography on the Gospel of John* (Bibliographical Aids 8) (Rüchlikon/Zürich 1975).

B. COMMENTARIES ON THE GOSPEL OF JOHN

N.B. An *asterisk* * before the SURNAME of a commentator (e.g. *BERNARD) indicates that the *literary structure* of the Fourth Gospel proposed in the commentary is discussed in ch. 2 of this book.

BARCLAY W., *The Gospel of John*, I-II, 2 ed. (The Daily Study Bible) (Edinburgh 1975).
BARRETT C. K., *The Gospel according to St John. An Introduction with Commentary and Notes on the Greek Text*, 2 ed. (London 1978).

BAUER W., *Das Johannesevangelium erklärt*, 3 ed. (Tübingen 1935).
BECKER J., *Das Evangelium nach Johannes*: I, *Kapitel 1-10*; II, *Kapitel 11-21* (Ökumenischer Taschenbuchkommentar zum Neuen Testament 4/1; 4/2) (Würzburg 1979; 1981).
*BERNARD J. H., *A Critical and Exegetical Commentary on the Gospel according to St John*, I-II (International Critical Commentary) (Edinburgh 1929).
BLANK J., *Das Evangelium nach Johannes*, I-II (Geistliche Schriftlesung 4) (Düsseldorf 1977).
BOEHMER J., *Das Johannesevangelium nach Aufbau und Grundgedanken* (Eisleben 1928).
BOICE J. M., *The Gospel of John. An Expositional Commentary*, I-V (Grand Rapids 1975-79).
*BOISMARD M.-É. & LAMOUILLE A., *Synopse des quatre Évangiles en français*, Tome III, *L'Évangile de Jean* (Paris 1977).
BOUYER L., *Le quatrième Évangile - Introduction et commentaire*, (Paris 1955).
BRAUN F.-M., "L'Évangile selon Saint Jean traduit et commenté" in: *La Sainte Bible*, Tome X: *Les Saints Evangiles, S. Luc - S. Jean*, ed. L. Pirot & A Calmer, (Paris 1950) 293-484.
*BROWN R. E., *The Gospel according to John. Introduction, Translation, and Notes*, I, *i-xii*; II, *xiii-xxi* (AnchorB 29; 29A) (Garden City 1966; 1970).
BÜSCHEL F., *Das Evangelium nach Johannes*, 2 ed. (Das Neue Testament Deutsch 4) (Göttingen 1964).
BULTMANN R., *The Gospel of John. A Commentary*, tr. G. R. Beasley-Murray (Oxford 1971).
DE BOOR W., *Das Evangelium nach Johannes*, 1. Teil (Kap. 1-10); 2. Teil (Kap. 11-21) (Wuppertal 1968; 1970).
DURAND A., *L'Évangile selon Saint Jean*, 2 ed. (Verbum Salutis 4) (Paris 1938).
EDWARDS R. A., *The Gospel according to St. John* (London 1954).
FENTON J. C., *The Gospel according to John in the Revised Standard Version* (New Clarendon Bible: New Testament 4) (Oxford 1970).
GHIBERTI G., "Vangelo secondo Giovanni", in: *La Bibbia: parola di Dio scritta per noi*, III (Torino 1980) 327-457.
GNILKA J., *Johannesevangelium* (Die neue Echter Bibel. Kommentar zum Neuen Testament mit der Einheitsübersetzung 1) (Würzburg 1984).
GRANT F. C., *The Gospel and Epistles of John* (Harper's Annotated Bible Series) (New York 1956).
GRUNDMANN W., *Das Evangelium nach Johannes* (THandkNT), ed. E. Fascher (Berlin 1968).
GUTHRIE D., "John", in: *The New Bible Commentary Revised*, ed. D. Guthrie et al. (Grand Rapids 1970) 926-67.
HAENCHEN E., *John 1. A Commentary on the Gospel of John: Chapters 1-6; John 2. A Commentary on the Gospel of John: Chapters 7-21*; tr. R. W. Funk (Hermeia) (Philadelphia 1984).
HENDRIKSEN W., *Exposition of the Gospel according to John*, I-II (Grand Rapids 1953).
HIBBERT G., *John* (Scripture Discussion Commentary 9) (London 1972).
HIRSCH E., *Das vierte Evangelium in seiner ursprünglischen Gestalt verdeutet und erklärt* (Tübingen 1936).
HOBBS H. H., *An Exposition of the Gospel of John* (Grand Rapids 1968).
HOSKYNS E. C., *The Fourth Gospel*, 2 ed. (London 1947).
HULL W. E., *John* (The Broadman Bible Commentary 9) (Nashville 1970).

B. COMMENTARIES ON JOHN

HUNTER A. M., *The Gospel according to John* (Cambridge Bible Commentary: New English Bible) (Cambridge 1965).
JENSEN J. L., *John* (Chicago 1970).
JEREMIAS J., *Das Evangelium nach Johannes. Eine urchristliche Erklärung für die Gegenwart* (Chemnitz 1931).
KEALY S. P., *That You may Believe. The Gospel according to John* (Slough 1978).
KIRK A. & OBACH R. E., *A Commentary on the Gospel of John* (New York/Toronto 1981).
LAGRANGE M.-J., *Évangile selon Saint Jean*, 5 ed. (Études Bibliques) (Paris 1936).
LIGHTFOOT R. H., *St. John's Gospel. A Commentary* (London 1956).
LINDARS B., *The Gospel of John* (New Century Bible) (London 1972).
LION A., *Lire Saint Jean* (Lire la Bible 32) (Paris 1972).
LOISY A., *Le quatrième Évangile. Les épitres dites de Jean*, 2 ed. (Paris 1921).
MACGREGOR G. H. C., *The Gospel of John* (Moffatt Commentary) (London 1928).
MAGGIONI B., *I Vangeli* (Assisi 1975).
MACRAE G. W., *Invitation to John. A Commentary on the Gospel of John with Complete Text from the The Jerusalem Bible* (Garden City 1978).
MARSH J., *The Gospel of St. John* (The Pelican Gospel Commentaries) (London 1968).
*MATEOS J. & BARRETO J., *El Evangelio de Juan. Analisis Lingüistico y Comentario Exegetico* (Madrid 1979).
MCPOLIN J., *John* (New Testament Message 6) (Wilmington 1979).
MEYER F. B., *The Gospel of John. The Life and Light of Man, Love to the Uttermost* (Lakeland Series Reprint) (London 1970).
MOLLA C. F., *Le quatrième évangile* (Geneva 1977).
*MOLLAT D. "L'Évangile selon Saint Jean", in: *L'Évangile et les Épitres de Saint Jean*, D. Mollat & F.-M. Braun, (La Sainte Bible [= Bible de Jérusalem]), 2 éd. (Paris 1960); 3 éd. (Paris 1973).
MORRIS L., *The Gospel according to St. John. English Text with Introduction, Exposition and Notes* (The New International Commentary on the New Testament) (London 1971).
NEWBIGIN L., *The Light has Come. An Exposition of the Fourth Gospel* (Grand Rapids 1982).
NIXON R. E., *St. John* (Bible Study Books) (Grand Rapids 1968).
PACK F., *The Gospel according to John. Part I, 1:1-10:42* (The Living Word Commentary 5) (Austin 1975).
PANIMOLLE S. A., *Lettura Patorale del Vangelo di Giovanni*, I, *Gv 1-4*; II, *Gv 5-10*; III, *Gv 11-21* (Bologna 1978; 1980; 1984).
*PASQUETTO V., *Da Gesù al Padre. Introduzione alla lettura esegetico-spirituale del vangelo di Giovanni* (Collana "Sussidi" Teresianum, 1) (Roma 1983).
PERKINS P., *The Gospel according to St. John. A Theological Commentary* (Herald Scriptural Library) (Chicago 1978).
*PRETE B., "Vangelo secondo Giovanni", in: *Il Messaggio della Salvezza*, VIII, 4 ed. (Torino 1978) 797-870.
REUSS J., ed., *Johannes-Kommentare aus der griechischen Kirche. Aus Katenenhandschriften gesammelt und herausgegeben* (Berlin 1966).
RICHARDSON A., *The Gospel according to Saint John* (Torch Bible Commentary) (London 1959).
RUSSEL R., *St. John* (A New Catholic Commentary on Holy Scripture) (London 1969).
SANDERS J. N. & MASTIN B. A., *A Commentary on the Gospel according to St. John* (Black's New Testament Commentaries) (London 1968).

SCHLATTER A., *Der Evangelist Johannes. Wie er spricht, denkt und glaubt. Ein Kommentar zum 4. Evangelium*, 2 ed. (Stuttgart 1948).
SCHNACKENBURG R., *The Gospel according to St. John*, I, *Introduction and Commentary on Chapters 1-4*, tr. K. Smyth; II, *Commentary on Chapters 5-12*, tr. C. Hastings, F. McDonagh, D. Smith, & R. Foley; III, *Commentary on Chapters 13-21*, tr. D. Smith & G. A. Kon (New York 1968; 1980; 1982).
" *Das Johannesevangelium*, IV. Teil. *Ergänzende Auslegungen und Exkurse (HerdTKom, NT, Band IV) (Freiburg 1984)*.
SCHNEIDER J., *Das Evangelium nach Johannes* (THandkNT) (Berlin 1976).
SCHULZ S., *Das Evangelium nach Johannes* (NTDt 4) (Göttingen 1972).
SCHWANK B., *Das Johannesevangelium*, I-II (Düsseldorf 1966; 1968).
SCOT J., *Commentaire de l'Évangile de Jean* (Paris 1972).
*SEGALLA G., *Giovanni. Versione, Introduzione, Note* (Nuovissima Versione della Bibbia) (Roma 1976).
SMITH D. M., Jr., *John* (Proclamation Commentaries) (Philadelphia 1976).
SPÖRRI G., *Das Evangelium nach Johannes*, I-II (Zürich 1950).
STRACHAN R. H., *The Fourth Gospel. Its Significance and Environment*, 3 ed. (London 1946).
STRACK H. L. & BILLERBECK P., *Kommentar zum Neuen Testament aus Talmud und Midrasch*, II, *Das Evangelium nach Markus, Lukas und Johannes und die Apostelgeschichte* (München 1924).
STRATHMANN H., *Das Evangelium nach Johannes*, 11 ed. (Göttingen 1968).
SWAIN L., *The Gospel according to St. John* (New Testament for Spiritual Reading 4) (London 1978).
TASKER R. V. G., *The Gospel according to St. John* (Tyndale New Testament Commentaries) (Grand Rapids 1971).
*TENNEY M. C., *John, the Gospel of Belief. An Analytic Study of the Text* (London 1954).
TENNEY M. C. & LONGENECKER R. N., *The Expositor's Bible Commentary with The New International Version of the Holy Bible*, IX, *John - Acts*, ed. F. E. Gaebelein (Grand Rapids 1981).
*VAN DEN BUSSCHE H., *Jean. Commentaire de l'Évangile Spirituel* (Bruges 1967).
VAWTER B., "The Gospel according to John", in: *Jerome Biblical Commentary* II (Englewood Cliffs 1968) 414-66; 828-39.
WELLHAUSEN J., *Das Evangelium nach Johannes* (Berlin 1908).
*WESTCOTT B. F., *The Gospel according to St. John. The Authorized Version with Introduction and Notes, and a new Introduction by Adam Fox* (London 1958).
WIKENHAUSER A., *Das Evangelium nach Johannes*, 2 ed. (RNT 4) (Regensburg 1957).
ZEVINI G., *Vangelo secondo Giovanni*, I (Commenti spirituali del Nuovo Testamento) (Roma 1984).

C. LITERARY UNITY AND STRUCTURE OF THE GOSPEL OF JOHN

N.B. See the *Commentators* with an *asterisk* * in B above.

ALLO E. B., "Jean", in: *Dictionnaire de la Bible, Supplement*, IV, ed. L. Pirot & A. Robert, (Paris 1949) 817-21.
BARROSSE T., "The Seven Days of the New Creation in St. John's Gospel", *CBQ* 21 (1959) 507-16.

BALMFORTH H., "The Structure of the Fourth Gospel", in: *Studia Evangelica*, II, ed. F. L. Cross (Texte und Untersuchungen 87) (Berlin 1964) 25-33.
BECKER H., *Die Reden des Johev. und der Stil der gnostischen Offenbarungsrede*, ed. R. Bultmann, (Göttingen 1956).
BECKER J., "Aufbau, Schichtung und theologiegeschichtliche Stellung des Gebets in Johannes 17", *ZNW* 60 (1969) 56-83.
" "Wunder und Christologie", *NTS* 16 (1969-70) 130-48.
" "Aus der Literatur zum Johannesevangelium", *TRu* NF 47 (1982) 294-301.
BOISMARD M.-É., "Le chapitre xxi de saint Jean: essai de critique littéraire", *RB* 54 (1947) 473-501.
" "L'évangile à quatre dimensions", *LumièreV* 1 (1951) 94-114.
" "*Le Prologue de Saint Jean* (LDiv 11) (Paris 1953) 99-108.
" *Du Baptême à Cana (Jean 1,19-2,11)* (LDiv 18) (Paris 1956) 13-24.
" "Le caractère adventice de Jo., XII,44-50", in: *Sacra Pagina* II, ed. J. Coppens & A. Descamps & É. Massaux, (Paris 1959) 190-92.
BORGEN P., "Observations on the Targumic Character of the Prologue of John", *NTS* 16 (1969-70) 288-95.
BOYLE J. L., "The Last Discourse (Jn 13,31-16,33) and Prayer (Jn 17): Some Observations on their Unity and Development", *Bib* 56 (1975) 210-22.
BOWEN C. R., "The Fourth Gospel as Dramatic Material", *JBL* 49 (1930) 292-305.
BÜHNER J.-A., "Denkstrukturen im Johannesevangelium", *TBei* 13 (1982) 224-31.
BURCH V., *The Structure and Message of St. John's Gospel* (London 1928).
BUZY D., "Un procédé littéraire de saint Jean", *BLitEc* 39 (1938) 61-75.
CABA J., *Dai Vangeli al Gesù Storico* (Roma 1974) 337-55. [Though the whole book is not on the Gospel of John, it is included here, since the literary structure of Jn is given on pp. 343-49.]
CHARLIER C., *Jean l'évangeliste. Structure dramatique du quatrième évangile, méditation liturgique du prologue* (Bible et vie chrétienne 5) (Paris 1978) 11-20.
CLARK D. K., "Signs in Wisdom and John", *CBQ* 45 (1983) 201-9.
CLAVIER H., "La structure du quatrième évangile", *RHPR* 35 (1955) 174-95.
CONNICK C. M., "The Dramatic Character of the Fourth Gospel", *JBL* 67 (1948) 159-69.
COTHENET É., "Le quatrième Évangile", in: *Introduction à la Bible*, Tome III: *Introduction Critique au Nouveau Testament*, Vol. IV: *La tradition johannique*, ed. A. George & P. Grelot (Paris 1977) 131-37.
CULPEPPER R. A., "The Pivot of John's Prologue", *NTS* 27 (1980) 1-31.
" *Anatomy of the Fourth Gospel. A Study in Literary Design* (Philadelphia 1983).
DEEKS D., "The Structure of the Fourth Gospel", *NTS* 15 (1968-69) 107-29.
DEFOURNEY P., "Au sujet de la composition du quatrième évangile", *Collectanea Mechliniensa* 11 (1937) 359-67.
DE LA POTTERIE I., "L'evangelo di san Giovanni", in: *Introduzione al Nuovo Testamento*, 2 ed., G. Rinaldi & P. de Benedetti (Brescia 1971) 876-912, especially 893-98.
" "Structura primae partis Evangelii Johannis (Cap. III et IV)", *Verbum Domini* 47 (1969) 130-40.
" "Dialogus Jesu cum Nicodemo", *Verbum Domini* 47 (1969) 141-50.
" *Exegesis Quarti Evangelii. Capita III-IV* (Romae, PIB, 1972-73).
" *Exegesis Quarti Evangelii. De Matre Iesu in IV Evangelio* (Romae, PIB, 1976-77).
" *De narratione Passionis et Mortis Christi: Ioh 18-19* (Romae, PIB, 1978-79).
" "Genèse de la foi pascale d'après Jn 20", *NTS* 30 (1984) 26-49, especially 27-30.

DE LA POTTERIE I., "Structure du Prologue de Saint Jean", *NTS* 30 (1984) 354-81.
" "Le témoin qui demeure: le disciple que Jésus aimait", *Bib* 67 (1986) 343-59.
DODD C. H., *The Interpretation of the Fourth Gospel* (Cambridge 1953) 289-443.
DOMERIS W. R., "The Johannine Drama", *JThSAfr* 42 (1983) 29-35.
DUPONT L., LASH C., & LEVESQUE G., "Recherche sur la structure de Jean 20", *Bib* 54 (1973) 482-98.
FEUILLET A., "L'heure de Jésus et le signe de Cana. Contribution à l'étude de la structure du quatrième évangile", *ETL* 36 (1960) 5-22 = "The Hour of Jesus and the Sign of Cana. A Contribution to the Study of the Structure of the Fourth Gospel", in: *Johannine Studies* (New York 1964) 17-37.
" "La signification théologique du second miracle de Cana (Jo. IV,46-54)", in: *Études Johanniques* (Paris 1962) 34-46 = "The Theological Significance of the Second Cana Miracle", in: *Johannine Studies* (New York 1964) 39-51.
" "The Composition of Chapters IX-XII", in: *Johannine Studies* (New York 1964) 129-47.
" *Le prologue du quatrième évangile* (Paris 1968) 137-57.
FLANAGAN N., "The Gospel of John as Drama", *BToday* 19 (1981) 264-70.
FLOWERS H. J., "Interpolations in the Fourth Gospel", *JBL* 40 (1921) 146-58.
FORTNA R. T., *The Gospel of Signs* (Cambridge 1970).
GÄCHTER P., "Der formale Aufbau der Abschiedsrede Jesu", *ZkT* 58 (1934) 155-207.
" "Strophen im Johannesevangelium", *ZkT* 60 (1936) 99-120; 402-23.
GAETA G. C., *Il dialogo con Nicodemo. Per l'interpretazione del capitolo terzo dell'evangelio di Giovanni* (StBib 26) (Brescia 1974).
GALBIATI E., "Nota sulla struttura del 'Libro dei Segni' (Gv. 2-4)" *Eunt Doc* 25 (1972) 139-44.
GAMBINO G., "Stuttura, composizione e analisi letterario-teologica di Gv. 6,26-51b", *RivBib* 24 (1976) 337-58.
GEOLTRAIN P., "Les noces à Cana. Jean 2,1-12. Analyse des structures narratives", *FoiVie* 73 (1974) 83-90.
GIBBS J. M., "Mark 1,1-15, Matthew 1,1-4,16, Luke 1,1-4,30, John 1,1- 51. The Gospel Prologues and their Function", *Studia Evangelica* 6 (1973) 154-88.
GIBLIN C. H., "Suggestion, Negative Response, and Positive Action in St. John's Portrayal of Jesus", *NTS* 26 (1980) 197-211.
" "Confrontations in John 18,1-27", *Bib* 65 (1984) 210-32.
" "John's Narration of the Hearing before Pilate (John 18,28-19,16a)", *Bib* 67 (1986) 221-39.
GIRARD M., "La structure heptapartite du quatrième évangile", *SR* 5 (1975-76) 350-59.
" "La composition structurelle des sept 'signes' dans le quatrième évangile", *SR* 9 (1980) 315-24.
" "Analyse structurelle de Jn 1,1-18: l'unité des deux Testaments dans la structure bipolar du prologue de Jean", *ScEsp* 35 (1983) 5-31.
GLUSMAN E. F. Jr., "Criteria for the Study of the Outlines of Mark and John", in: *Society of Biblical Literature 1978 Seminar Papers*, II, ed. P. J. Achtemeier, (Missoula 1978) 239-49.
GOULDER M. D., "The Liturgical Origin of St. John's Gospel", in: *Studia Evangelica*, VII, ed. E. A. Livingstone, (Berlin 1982) 205-21.
GOURGUES M., *Pour que vous croyiez. Pistes d'exploration de l'évangile de Jean* (Paris 1982) 73-101.

GRANSKOU D. M., *Structure and Theology in the Fourth Gospel. A Study of Literary Features in the Fourth Gospel and their Relation to its Theology* (Diss. Princeton Theological Seminary 1960).
GREGORY A. M., Jr., *A Study of the Literary Structure of the Fourth Gospel in Relation to its Message* (Diss. Southern Baptist Seminary, Louisville 1955).
GRUNDMANN W., *Zeugnis und Gestalt des Johannesevangeliums. Eine Studie zur denkerischen und gestalterischen Leistung des vierten Evangelisten* (ArbT 7) (Stuttgart 1961).
" "Verkündigung und Geschichte in dem Bericht vom Eingang der Geschichte Jesu im Johannesevangelium", in: *Der historische Jesus und der kerygmatische Christus*, ed. H. Ristow & K. Matthiae, (Berlin 1961) 289-309.
GUILDING A., *The Fourth Gospel and Jewish Worship* (Oxford 1960) 46-54.
HAACKER K., *Die Stiftung des Heils. Untersuchungen zur Struktur der johanneischen Theologie* (ArbT 47) (Stuttgart 1972).
HAENCHEN E., "Probleme des johanneischen 'Prologs'", *ZTK* 60 (1963) 305-34.
HANHART K., "The Structure of John I 35-IV 54", *Studies in John* (Fs. J. N. Sevenster = SuppNT 24) (Leiden 1970) 22-46.
HIRSCH E., "Stilkritik und Literaranalyse im vierten Evangelium", *ZNW* 43 (1950) 129-43.
HOWARD W. F., *The Fourth Gospel in Recent Criticism and Interpretation*, rev. 4 ed., C. K. Barrett (London 1955) 95-127.
INFANTE L., "L'amico dello sposo. Figura del ministero di Giovanni Battista nel Quarto Vangelo", *RivB* 31 (1983) 3-19, esp. 4-5.
" *L'amico dello sposo. Figura del ministero di Giovanni Battista nel Vangelo di Giovanni* (Roma 1984) 28-31.
JANSSENS DE VAREBEKE A., "La structure des scènes du récit de la passion en Joh., xviii-xix", *ETL* 38 (1962) 504-22.
JAUBERT A., "La comparution devant Pilate selon Jn 18,28-19,16", *FoiVie* 73 (1974) 3-12.
JOHNSTON G., *The Spirit-Paraclete in the Gospel of John* (Cambridge 1970) 155-161.
KAMMERSTÄTTER J., *Zur Struktur des Johannesevangeliums. Seine zentrierte Symmetrie als Träger des kerygmatischen Aktualismus* (Diss. Wien 1970).
KERN W., "Der symmetrische Gesamtaufbau von Jo. 8,12-58", *ZkT* 78 (1956) 451-54.
KIEFFER R., "Rum och tid i johannesevangeliets teologiska struktur" ["Space and Time in the Theological Structure of the Gospel of John"] *SvEx* 49 (1984) 109-25.
KNOX T. M., "The Computer and the NT" (and A. Q. Morton on the Structure of John), *SvEx* 28-29 (1963-64) 111-16.
KYSAR R., "The Source Analysis of the Fourth Gospel. A Growing Consensus?" *NT* 15 (1973) 134-52.
" *The Fourth Evangelist and His Gospel* (Minneapolis 1975) 13-37.
LEE E. K., "The Drama of the Fourth Gospel", *ExpTim* 65 (1953-54) 173-76.
LÉON-DUFOUR X., "Trois chiasmes johanniques", *NTS* 7 (1960-61) 249-55.
LOHMEYER E., "Über Aufbau und Gliederung des vierten Evangeliums", *ZNW* 27 (1928) 11-36.
MACGREGOR G. H. C. & MORTON A. Q., *The Structure of the Fourth Gospel* (London 1961).
MALATESTA E., "The Literary Structure of John 17", *Bib* 52 (1971) 190-214.
MARZOTTO D., "Stuttura letteraria e teologia di Gv 19,23-42", in: *La Sapienza della Croce Oggi*, I (Torino 1976) 163-68.
MAYNARD A. H., "Common Elements in the Outlines of Mark and John", in: *Society of Biblical Literature 1978 Seminar Papers*, II, ed. P. J. Achtemeier, (Missoula 1978) 251-60.

McDowell E., "The Structural Integrity of the Fourth Gospel", *Baptist Review and Expositor* 34 (1937) 397-416.
Menoud P.-H., *L'Évangile de Jean d'après les recherches récentes*, 2 ed. (Paris 1947).
" "L'Évangile de Jean d'après les recherches de Bultmann à Barrett", *Recherches Bibliques*, III (Bruges 1958) 11-40.
Migliasso S., *La presenza dell'Assente. Saggio di analisi letterario-strutturale e di sintesi teologica di Gv 13,31- 14,31* (Roma 1979).
Minear P. S., "The Original Functions of John 21", *JBL* 102 (1983) 85-98.
Mollat D., "La foi pascale selon le chapitre 20 de l'évangile de saint Jean. Essai de théologie johannique", in: *Resurrexit*, ed. E. Dhanis, (Rome 1974) 316-39.
Morris L., "The Composition of the Fourth Gospel", in: *Scripture, Tradition and Interpretation. Essays presented to Everett F. Harrison by His Students and Colleagues in Honor of His Seventy-fifth Birthday*, ed. W. W. Gasque & W. S. Lasor (Grand Rapids 1978) 157-175.
Morton A. Q., "The Structure of the Fourth Gospel", in: *Studia Evangelica* II (Texte und Untersuchungen 87), ed. F. L. Cross, (Berlin 1964) 85-90.
Mourlon Beernaert P., "Parallelisme entre Jean 11 et 12. Étude de structure littéraire et théologique", in: *Genèse et Structure d'un Texte du Nouveau Testament. Étude Interdisciplinaire du Chapitre 11 de l'Évangile de Jean*, ed. A.-L. Descamps et al., (Paris 1981), 123-49.
Newman B. M. Jr., "Some Observations regarding the Argument, Structure and Literary Characteristics of the Gospel of John", *BTrans* 26 (1975) 234-39.
Niccacci A., L'unità letteraria di Gv 13,1-38", *EuntDoc* 29 (1976) 291-323.
Nicol W., *The Sêmeia in the Fourth Gospel* (Leiden 1972).
Olsson B., *Structure and Meaning in the Fourth Gospel. A Text-Linguistic Analysis of John 2,1-11 and 4,1-42* (ConBibNT 6) (Lund 1974).
O'Rourke J. J., "Asides in the Gospel of John", *NT* 21 (1979) 210-19.
Panimolle S. A., *Il Dono della Legge e la Grazia della Verità* (Roma 1973) 71-105.
Paul A., "La résurrection de Lazare (Jean 11), in: *Le fait biblique* (Paris 1979) 187-222.
Puigdollers R., "Notas sobre la estructura del cuarto evangelio", *NatGrac* 19 (1972) 123-151.
Quiévreux F., "La structure symbolique de l'évangile de St. Jean", *RHPR* 33 (1953) 123-65.
Rau C., *Struktur und Rhythmus im Johannesevangelium. Eine Untersuchung über die Komposition des vierten Evangeliums* (Stuttgart 1972).
Rissi M., "Der Aufbau des vierten Evangeliums", *NTS* 29 (1983) 48-54.
Ruckstuhl E., *Die literarische Einheit des Johannesevangeliums* (Studia Friburgensia N.S. 3) (Freiburg 1951).
" "Johannine Language and Style. The Question of Their Unity", in: *L'Évangile de Jean*, ed. M. de Jonge, (Leuven 1977) 125-48.
Sabugal S., *Christos. Investigación exegética sobre la cristologia joannea* (Barcelona 1972) 235-55.
Sahlin H., *Zur Typologie des Johannesevangeliums* (Uppsala 1950) 8-58.
Schenke L., "Die formale und gedankliche Struktur von 6,26-58", *BZ* 24 (1980) 21-41.
Schnackenburg R., "Das Anliegen der Abschiedsrede in Joh 14", in: *Wort Gottes in der Zeit* (Fs. Karl Herrmann Schelkle), ed. H. Feld & J. Nolte, (Düsseldorf 1973) 95-110.
" "Strukturanalyse von Joh. 17", *BZ* 17 (1973) 67-78; 196-202.
" "Aufbau und Sinn von Johannes 15", in: *Homenaje a Juan Prado. Miscelanea de estudios biblicos y hebraicos*, ed. L. Alvarez Verdes & E. J. Alonso Hernandes, (Madrid 1975) 405-20.

Schulz S., "Die Komposition des Johannesprologs und die Zusammensetzung des 4. Evangeliums", in: *Studia Evangelica* I (TU 73), ed. K. Aland et alii, (Berlin 1959) 351-62.
" *Komposition und Herkunft der Johanneischen Reden* (Stuttgart 1960) 11-213.
Schwartz E., "Aporien im vierten Evangelium", *Nachrichten von der königlichen Gesellschaft der Wissenschaften zu Göttingen. Philologisch-historische Klasse* (Berlin 1907) 342-72; (Berlin 1908) 115-48; 149-88; 497-570.
Schweizer E., *Egô Eimi. Die religionsgeschichtliche Herkunft und theologische Bedeutung der joh. Bildreden, zugleich ein Beitrag zur Quellenfrage des vierten Evangeliums* (Göttingen 1939).
Segalla G., "La struttura chiastica di Giov 15,1-8", *BibOr* 12 (1970) 129-31.
" "La struttura cirolare-chiastica di Gv. 6,26-58 e il suo significato teologico", *BibOr* 13 (1971) 191-98.
" *La preghiera di Gesù al Padre (Giov. 17). Un addio missionario* (StBib 63) (Brescia 1983) 17-32.
Segovia F. F., "The Structure, *Tendenz*, and *Sitz im Leben* of John 13:31-14:31", *JBL* 104 (1985) 471-93.
Simoens Y., *La gloire d'aimer. Structures stylistiques et interprétatives dans le Discours de la Cène* (AnBib 90) (Rome 1981).
Smith D. M., *The Composition and Order of the Fourth Gospel. Bultmann's Literary Theory* (New Haven 1965).
Staley J., "The Structure of John's Prologue: Its Implications for the Gospel's Narrative Structure", *CBQ* 48 (1986) 241-64.
Strachan R. H., "Development of Thought within the Fourth Gospel", *ExpTim* 34 (1922-23) 228-32; 246-49.
Talbert C. H., "Artistry and Theology. An Analysis of the Architecture of Jn 1,19-5,47", *CBQ* 32 (1970) 341-66.
Teeple M., *The Literary Origin of the Gospel of John* (Evanston 1974).
Temple S., "A Key to the Composition of the Fourth Gospel", *JBL* 80 (1961) 220-32.
" *The Core of the Fourth Gospel* (London 1975).
Tenney M. C., "The Footnotes of John's Gospel", *BS* 117 (1960) 350-64.
" "Literary Keys to the Fourth Gospel. The Symphonic Structure of John", *BS* 120 (1963) 117-25.
Thomas W. H. G., "The Plan of the Fourth Gospel", *BS* 125 (1968) 313-23.
Thompson J., "The Structure of the Fourth Gospel", *Exp* 10 (1915) 512-26.
Thyen H., "Aus der Literatur zum Johannesevangelium", *TRu* NF 40 (1975) 289-330.
" "Entwicklungen innerhalb der johanneischen Theologie und Kirche im Spiegel von Joh. 21 und der Lieblingsjüngertexte des Evangeliums", in: *L'Évangile de Jean. Sources, rédaction, théologie* (BiblETL 44), ed. M. de Jonge (Leuven 1977), 275-87.
" "Aus der Literatur zum Johannesevangelium", *TRu* NF 43 (1978) 329-36.
Tragan P.-R., "Le discours sur le pain de vie: Jean 6,26-71. Remarques sur sa composition littéraire", in: *Segni e Sacramenti nel Vangelo di Giovanni*, ed. P.-R. Tragan, (Roma 1977) 89-119.
Trudinger L. P., "The Seven Days of the New Creation in St. John's Gospel: Some Further Reflection", *EvQ* 44 (1966) 154-58.
Tsuchido K., "The Composition of the Nicodemus-Episode, John II,23-III,21", *Annual of the Jap.Bibl.Inst.* 1 (1975) 91-104.

VAN BELLE G., *Les Parenthèses dans l'Évangile de Jean. Aperçu historique et classification. Texte Grec de Jean* (Leuven 1985) 105- 112; 156-210.
VAN DEN BUSSCHE H., "De structuur van het vierde evangelie", *CollBrGand* 2 (1956) 23-42; 182-99.
" "La Structure de Jean I-XII", in: *L'Évangile de Jean, études et problèmes*, ed. M.-É. Boismard, F.-M. Braun, et al., (Recherches Bibliques 3) (Brouwer 1958) 61-109.
" *Het Vierde Evangelie* I *Het Boek der Tekens. Verklaring van Johannes 1-4* (Tielt 1961) 61-74.
VANHOYE A., "La composition de Jn 5,19-30", in: *Mélanges Bibliques. En hommage au R. R. Béda Rigaux*, ed. A. Descamps & A. de Halleux (Duculot 1970) 259-74.
WEBSTER E. C., "Pattern in the Fourth Gospel", in: *Art and Meaning: Rhetoric in Biblical Literature*, ed. D. J. A. Clines, D. M. Gunn & A. J. Hauser, (JStOT Supplement Series 19) (Sheffied 1982) 230-57.
WEISE M., "Passionswoche und Epiphaniewoche im Johannesevangelium. Ihre Bedeutung für Komposition und Konzeption des vierten Evangeliums", *KerDo* 12 (1966) 48-62.
WELLHAUSEN J., *Erweiterungen und Änderungen im vierten Evangelium* (Berlin 1907).
WILKENS W., *Zeichen und Werke* (Zürich 1969) 141-55.
WILLEMSE J., *Het vierde evangelie. Een onderzoek naar zijn struktuur* (Antwerpen 1965).
ZIENER G., "Weisheitsbuch und Johannesevangelium", *Bib* 38 (1957) 396-418; 39 (1958) 37-60.
ZIMMERMANN H., "Struktur und Aussageabsicht der johanneischen Abschiedsreden (Jo 13-17)", *BiLeb* 8 (1967) 279-90.

D. OTHER LITERATURE ON THE GOSPEL OF JOHN

ABBOTT E. A., *Johannine Vocabulary* (London 1905).
" *Johannine Grammar* (London 1906).
BARON M., "La progression des confessions de foi dans les dialogues de S. Jean", *Bible et Vie Chrétienne* 82 (1968) 32-44.
BARRETT C. K., "John and the Synoptic Gospels", *EvT* 85 (1973-74) 228-33.
" "Christocentric or Theocentric? Observations on the Theological Method of the Fourth Gospel", in: *La notion biblique de Dieu. Le Dieu de la Bible et le Dieu des philosophes* (BiblETL 41), ed. J. Coppens (Leuven 1976) 361-84.
BRAUN F.-M., "In Spiritu et veritate", *RevThom* 52 (1952) 245-74.
" *Jean le théologien et son évangile dans l'Eglise ancienne*, I, (Paris 1959).
" *Jean le théologien*, II, *Les grandes traditions d'Israël et l'accord des Écritures selon le quatrième Évangile* (Paris 1964).
" *Jean le théologien*, III, *Sa théologie. Le Mystère de Jesus-Christ* (Paris 1966).
BRAUN P., *La Mère des Fidèles. Essai de théologie johannique*, 2 ed. (Paris 1954).
BROWN R. E., *The Community of the Beloved Disciple* (London 1979).
" "Other Sheep Not of This Fold", *JBL* 97 (1978) 5-22.
CERFAUX L., "Les miracles, signes messianiques de Jésus et oeuvres de Dieu, selon l'évangile de saint Jean", in: *L'Attente du Messie* (Recherches Bibliques) (Bruges 1958) 131-38.
COOK W. R., *The Theology of John* (Chicago 1979).
CREHAN J., *The Theology of St. John* (London 1965).
CROSSAN D., *The Gospel of Eternal Life. Reflections on the Theology of St. John* (Milwaukee 1967) 41-44.

D. OTHER LITERATURE ON JOHN

CULLMANN O., "Der johanneische Gebrauch doppeldeutiger Ausdrücke als Schlüssel zum Vertändnis des vierten Evangeliums", *TZBas* 4 (1948) 360-72.
" *The Johannine Circle*, tr. J. Bowden, (London 1976).
DE LA POTTERIE I., "De interpunctione et interpretatione versuum Joh. 1,3.4", *Verbum Domini* 33 (1955) 193-208.
" *Gesù Verità. Studi di cristologia giovannea*, tr. A Milanoli et al. (Torino 1973).
" *La Verité dans S. Jean*, I-II, (AnBib 73-74) (Rome 1977).
" *La passion de Jésus selon l'Évangile de Jean. Texte et esprit* (Lire la Bible 73) (Paris 1986).
DUPONT J., *Essais sur la Christologie de Saint Jean. Le Christ, Parole, Lumière et Vie. La Gloire du Christ* (Bruges 1951).
FERRARO G., *L'"Ora" di Cristo nel Quarto Vangelo* (Roma 1974).
FESTUGIÈRE A.-J., *Observations Stylistiques sur l'Évangile de S. Jean* (Paris 1974).
FEUILLET A., *Études Johanniques* (Paris 1962).
" "L'heure de la femme (Jn 16,21) et l'heure de la Mère de Jésus (Jn 19,25-27)", *Bib* 47 (1966) 169-84; 361-80; 557-73.
GÄCHTER P., *Maria im Erdenleben* (Innsbruck 1954).
GOEDT M. DE, "Un schème de révélation dans le quatrième évangile" *NTS* 8 1961-62) 142-50.
GROSSOUW W., "La glorification du Christ dans le quatrième évangile", in: *L'Évangile de Jean. Études et problemes* (Recherches Bibliques III) (Bruges 1958) 131-45.
JONGE M. DE., ed., *L'Évangile de Jean* (Leuven 1977).
KIM S., *The "Son of Man" as the Son of God* (Tübingen 1985).
LINDARS B., *Behind the Fourth Gospel* (London 1971).
LOHSE E., "Wort und Sakrament im Johnnesevangelium", *NTS* 7 (1960-61) 110-25.
MARROW S. B., *John 21: An Essay in Johannine Ecclesiology* (Rome 1968).
MARTYN J. L., *History and Theology in the Fourth Gospel*, 2 ed. (New York 1979).
MCCOOL F. J., "Living Water in John", in: *Bible in Current Catholic Thought*, ed. J. L. McKenzie, (New York 1962) 226-33.
MEEKS W. A., *The Prophet-King. Moses Traditions and the Johannine Christology* (SNT 14) (Leiden 1967).
MLAKUZHYIL G., *The Phenomenology of the Verbs of Knowing in the Gospel of John* (A Licentiate Dissertation in Theology, Pontificia Università Gregoriana, Rome, 1976).
MOLLAT D., "Le sêmeion johannique", in: *Sacra Pagina*, II, ed. J. Coppens & A. Descamps & É. Massaux, (Paris 1959).
MOLONEY F. J., *The Johannine Son of Man*, 2 ed. (Rome 1978).
MORENO R., "El discípulo de Jesucristo según el evangelio de S. Juan", *EstBib* 30 (1971) 269-311.
MUSSNER F., *Zoê* (München 1952).
NEIRYNCK F., "John and the Synoptics", in: *L'Évangile de Jean*, ed. M. de Jonge, (Leuven 1977) 73-106.
" *Jean et les Synoptiques. Examen critique de l'exégése de M.-É. Boismard* (BiblETL 49) (Leuven 1979).
PANIMOLLE S. A., *Evangelista Giovanni. Pensiero e opera letteraria del quarto evangelista* (Roma 1985).
POLLARD T. E., *Johannine Christology and the Early Church* (Cambridge 1970).
RICHTER G., *Die Fusswaschung im Johannesevangelium. Geschichte ihrer Deutung* (BibUnt 1) (Regensburg 1967).

RIEDL J., *Das Heilswerk Jesus nach Johannes* (Freiburg 1973).
ROVIRA BELLOSE J. M., *Revelación de Dios, Salvación del Hombre* (Salamanca 1979).
SCHNEIDER J., "Die Abschiedsreden Jesu", in: *Gott und die Götter* (Fs. E. Fascher) (Berlin 1958) 103-12.
SEGALLA G., *Gesù pane del cielo per la vita del mondo. Cristologia ed Eucaristia in Giovanni* (Padova 1976).
SEYNAEVE J., "Le Thème de 'l'Heure' dans le Quatrième Évangile", *RAfrT* 7 (1983) 29-50.
SIDEBOTTOM E. M., *The Christ of the Fourth Gospel in the Light of First Century Thought* (London 1961).
SOARES-PRABHU G. M., ed., *Wir werden bei ihm wohnen. Das Johannesevangelium in indischer Deutung* (Theologie der Dritten Welt 6) (Freiburg 1984).
STAUFFER E., "*Agnostos Christos*: Joh ii 24 und die Eschatologie des vierten Evangeliums", in: *The Background to the New Testament and Its Eschatology*, ed. W. D. Davis & D. Daube, (Fs. C. H. Dodd) (Cambridge 1956) 281-99.
THÜSSING W., *Die Erhöhung und der Verherrlichung Jesu im Johannesevangelium* (NTA XXI 1/2) (Münster 1959).
VANHOYE A., "Témoignage et Vie en Dieu selon le 4e Évangile", *Christus* 2,6 (1950) 155-71.
" "L'oeuvre du Christ, don du Père (Jn 5,36 et 17,4)", *RechSR* 48 (1960) 377-419.
" "Notre foi, oeuvre divine, d'après le quatrième évangile", *NRT* 86 (1964) 337-54.
" "Interrogation johannique et exégèse de Cana (Jn 2,4)", *Bib* 55 (1974) 157-67.
VELLANICKAL M., "'Discipleship' according to the Gospel of John", *Jeevadhara* 10 (1980) 131-47.
" *The Divine Sonship of Christians in the Johannine Writings* (AnBib 72) (Rome 1977).
ZEDDA S., "Le realtà escatologiche presenti: la vita eterna", in: *L'Escatogia Biblica*, II (Brescia 1975), 303-67.
ZIENER G., "Johannesevangelium und urchristliche Passafeir", *BZ* NF 2 (1958) 263-74.

E. OTHER BOOKS AND ARTICLES CONSULTED

AESCHYLUS, *Suppliants* (cf. C. DIANO, ed., *Il Teatro Greco: Tutte le Tragedie* [Le voci del mondo 11] [Firenze 1970] 62-85).
ALAND K., *Synopsis of the Four Gospels. Greek-English edition of the Synopsis Quattuor Evangeliorum* (On the basis of the Greek Text of Nestle-Aland 26th edition and Greek New Testament 3rd edition), 6 ed. (Stuttgart 1983).
" *Vollständige Kondordanz zum griechischen Neuen Testament, Band I*: Teil I; Teil II. *Band II: Spezialübersichten* (Berlin 1978-83).
ALTER R., *The Art of Biblical Narrative* (New York 1981).
BAUER W. & GINGRICH F. W. & DANKER F., *A Greek-English Lexicon of the New Testament and Other Early Christian Literature*, 2 ed. (London 1979).
BLAND K. P., "Rabbinic Lectionary Cycle", in: *Interpreter's Dictionary of the Bible, Supplementary Volume* (Nashville 1976) 537-38.
BRECK J., "Biblical Chiasmus: Exploring Structure for Meaning", *BTB* 17 (1987) 70-74.
BROWN C., ed., *The New International Dictionary of New Testament Theology* I-III (Exeter 1975-78).
BULTMANN R., *History of the Synoptic Tradition*, tr. John Marsh (Oxford 1963).
BURNEY C. F., *The Poetry of Our Lord* (Oxford 1925).
BUTTRICK G. A., ed., *The Interpreter's Dictionary of the Bible. An Illustrated Encyclopedia* I-IV (New York/Nashville 1962); Supplementary Vol. (Nashville 1976).

CLARK D. J., "Criteria for Identifying Chiasm", *LingBib* 5 (1975) 63-72.
CORTES E., *Los Discursos de Adiós de Ge 49 a Jn 13-17* (Barcelona 1976).
CROISET M., *Histoire de la Littérature Grecque*, III, *Periode Attique: Tragédie - Comédie - Genres Secondaires*, 3 éd. (Paris 1913).
DAHOOD M., "Chiasmus", in: *The Interpreter's Dictionary of the Bible*, Supplementary Volume (Nashville 1976) 145.
DIANO C., ed., *Il Teatro Greco: Tutte le Tragedie* (Le voci del mondo 11) (Firenze 1970).
DI MARCO A., *Il Chiasmo nella Bibbia. Contributi di Stilistica Strutturale* (Ricerche e Proposte 1) (Torino 1980).
EURIPIDES, *Alcestis, Hippolytus, Children of Heracles, Andromache, Madness of Heracles, Ion, Electra, Iphigenia in Tauris, Phoenissae, Orestes, Rhesus, Iphigenia at Aulis* (cf. C. DIANO, ed., *Il Teatro Greco: Tutte le Tragedie* [Firenze 1970] 393-1091).
HARVEY P., *The Oxford Companion to Classical Literature* (Oxford 1937).
HOMEYER H., *Lukian. Wie man Geschichte schreiben soll*, Griechisch und Deutsch, herausgegeben, übersetzt und erläutert (München 1965).
HORATIUS FLACCUS, Quintus, *Ad Pisones epistola ad artis poeticae formam redacta* (apud F. Muguet) (Paris, 1674) [HORACE].
JOSEPHUS, Flavius, *History of the Jewish War* (Cf. Josephus, II-III, *The Jewish War*, Books I-III; Books IV-VII) (London 1927; 1928).
KAWIN F., *Telling It Again and Again: Repetition in Literature and Film* (Ithaca 1972).
KITTEL G. & FRIEDRICH G., ed., *Theological Dictionary of the New Testament*, I-IX, tr. G. W. Bromiley, (Grand Rapids 1964-74).
LAW R., *The Tests of Life. A Study of the First Letter of St. John* (Edinburgh 1909).
LIDDELL-SCOTT, *A Greek-English Lexicon*, 9 ed. (Oxford 1940).
LUCIAN, *Pôs dei historian syngraphein* [*How to Write History*] (Cf. H. HOMEYER, *Lukian. Wie man Geschichte schreiben soll*).
LUND N. W., *Chiasmus in the New Testament* (Chapel Hill 1942).
MALATESTA E., *The Epistles of John. Greek Text and English Translation Schematically Arranged* (Rome 1973).
MALLY E. J., "The Gospel according to Mark", in: *The Jerome Biblical Commentary*, II, ed. R. E. Brown & J. A. Fitzmyer & R. E. Murphy (London 1970) 21-61.
MARROU H. I., *A History of Education in Antiquity* (New York 1956).
METZGER B. M., *A Textual Commentary on the Greek New Testament* [TCGNT], corrected ed. (London 1975).
MEYNET R., "Comment établir un chiasme. A propos des 'Pèlerins d'Emmaus'", *NRT* 100 (1978) 233-49.
MIESNER D. R., "The Circumstantial Speeches of Luke-Acts: Patterns and Purpose", in: *Society of Biblical Literature 1978 Seminar Papers*, II, ed. P. J. Achtemeier (Missoula 1978) 223-37.
MLAKUZHYIL G., "Abba, the Christian Mantra", *The Clergy Monthly* 38 (1974) 391-97.
MOULTON W. F. & GEDEN A. S. & MOULTON H. K., *A Concordance to the Greek Testament*, 5 ed. (Edinburgh 1978).
MUNCK J., "Discours d'adieu dans le Nouveau Testament et dans la littérature biblique", in: *Aux sources de la traditon chrétienne* (Mélanges M. Goguel) (Neuchâtel 1950) 155-70.
NOACK B., "The Day of Pentecost in Jubilees, Qumran, and Acts", *Annual of the Jewish Theological Insitute* 1 (1962) 72-95.
PARUNAK H. VAN DYKE, "Oral Typesetting: Some Uses of Biblical Structure", *Bib* 62 (1981) 153-68.

" "Transitional Techniques in the Bible", *JBL* 102 (1983) 525-48.
" "Some Axioms for Literary Architecture", cf. *JBL* 102 (1983) 526, n. 6.
PETUCHOWSKI J., ed., *Contributions to the Scientific Study of Jewish Liturgy* (New York 1970) 179-302.
PIROT L., ed., *Dictionnaire de la Bible, Supplement*, I-X (Paris 1928-85).
RADDAY Y. T., "Chiasmus in Hebrew Biblical Narrative", in: *Chiasmus in Antiquity: Structures, Analysis, Exegesis*, ed. J. Welch, (Hildesheim 1981) 50-117.
RENGSTORF K. H., "*Mathêtês*", in: *Theological Dictionary of the New Testament*, IV, ed. G. Kittel & G. Friedrich, tr. G. W. Bromiley, (Grand Rapids 1967) 415-61.
" "*Sêmeion*", in: TDNT, III (Grand Rapids 1971) 200-69.
SCHULZ A., *Nachfolgen und Nachahmen. Studien über das Verhältnis der neutestamentlichen Jüngerschaft zur urchristlichen Vorbildethik* (SANT 6) (München 1962).
SOPHOCLES, *Electra, Trachiniae, Oedipus Tyrannus, Oedipus at Colonus* (cf. C. Diano, ed., *Il Teatro Greco: Tutte le Tragedie* [Firenze 1970] 223-382).
STADAERT B., *L'Évangile selon Marc. Composition et Genre Littéraire* (Bruges 1978).
STERNBERG M., "The Structure of Repetition in Biblical Narrative", *Ha-Sifrut* 25 (1977) 110-50.
STOCK A., "Chiastic Awareness and Education in Antiquity", *BibTB* 14 (1984) 23-27.
" "Hinge Transitions in Mark's Gospel", *BibTB* 15 (1985) 27-31.
STOCK K., *Le Pericopi Iniziali del Vangelo di San Marco* (Roma, PIB, 1976).
TALBERT C. H., *Literary Patterns, Theological Themes and the Genre of Luke-Acts* (SBL MS 20) (Montana 1974).
TAYLOR V., *The Gospel according to St. Mark*, 2 ed. (London 1966).
TRENCH R. C., *Synonyma des Neuen Testaments* (Tübingen 1907).
VAGANAY L., "Le plan de l'Épître aux Hébreux", in: *Mémorial Lagrange* (Paris 1940) 269-77.
VANHOYE A., *La Structure Littéraire de l'Épître aux Hébreux* (Paris 1963); 2 ed. (Paris 1976).
" & DE LA POTTERIE I. & DUQUOC C. & CHARPENTIER É., *La Passion selon les quatre Évangiles* (Lire la Bible 55) (Paris 1981).
VANNI U., *La Struttura Letteraria dell'Apocalisse*, 2 ed. (Brescia 1980).
WATSON W. G. E., "Chiastic Patterns in Biblical Hebrew Poetry", in: *Chiasmus in Antiquity: Structures, Analysis, Exegesis*, ed. J. W. Welch, (Hildesheim 1981) 118-68.
WEBSTER N., *Webster's New Collegiate Dictionary* (Springfield 1973).
WELCH J. W., ed., *Chiasmus in Antiquity: Structures, Analyses, Exegesis* (Hildesheim 1981).
ZERWICK M., *Biblical Greek. Illustrated by Examples by Maximilian Zerwick.* English edition adapted from the fourth Latin edition by J. Smith (Rome 1963).
" & GROSVENOR M., *A Grammatical Analysis of the Greek New Testament.* Unabridged, revised edition in one volume (Rome 1981).

INDEX OF AUTHORS

N.B. **Numbers** in **boldface** indicate the pages where there is an important discussion of the author in question.

Abrams M. H., 58
Aeschylus, 119, 120, 146, 189
Agathon, 120
Aland K., 87
Allo E. B., 19
Alter R., 108, 110
Aristotle, 120
Augustine St., 345

Barreto J., 17, **29-31**, 144, 150, 157, 158, 170, 225
Barrett C. K., 8, 9, 10, 13, 30, 42, 89, 167, 223, 224, 244, 247, 248, 253, 261, 263, 272, 285, 329
Barrosse T., 32
Bauer W., 28
Becker H., 131
Becker J., 9, 10, 139, 143, 224
Bengel J. A., 125
Bernard J. H., 5, 6, 9, 13, 15, 17, **18-19**, 30, 92, 139, 144, 167, 169, 194, 217, 259, 261, 281, 282, 285
Bland K. P., 23
Blank J., 314, 340
Bligh J., 336, 338
Boismard M.-É., 8, 11, 12, 14, 15, 17, **31-35**, 92, 144, 151, 158, 163, 167, 169, 170, 201, 217, 305
Bowen C. R., 112
Braun F.-M., 17, 20, 22, 35, 152, 163, 290, 309
Breck J., 129
Brown R. E., 5, 6, 7, 8, 9, 10, 11, 12, 13, 15, 16, 18, 22, 30, 35, **79-83**, 89, 92, 116, 122, 123, 124, 139, 140, 142, 144, 152, 153, 154, 156, 157, 161, 163, 164, 167, 169, 170, 171, 172, 173, 174, 176, 177, 178, 179, 181, 182, 183, 184, 185, 186, 192, 194, 195, 199, 200, 201, 203, 214, 223, 224, 225, 226, 227, 229, 230, 233, 248, 259, 261, 271, 275, 277, 278, 279, 281, 285, 288, 289, 294, 295, 297, 298, 305, 310, 315, 316, 320, 321, 326, 329, 341, 343, 344, 345
Bultmann R., 5, 8, 9, 10, 12, 13, 15, 62, 88, 89, 101, 115, 139, 143, 155, 167, 194, 217, 224, 236, 248, 261, 285
Burney C. F., 122

Caba J., 18, 20, 55, **69-71**, 92, 118, 144, 150, 152, 153, 155, 157, 161, 167, 170, 184, 185, 201
Cadman W. H., 269
Caird G. B., 269
Cerfaux L., 171, 274
Charpentier E., 186
Clavier H., 131
Clines J. A., 37
Cortes E., 183
Cothenet É., 64, 161, 162
Croiset M., 119, 120, 190, 191
Cullmann O., 10, 230
Culpepper R. A., 1, 18, **58-62**, 92, 118, 144, 151, 167, 169, 170, 184

Dahood M., 125
Dauer A., 337
de Boor W., 139
Deeks D., 17, **41-43**, 92, 144, 167, 169, 193, 201
Defourney P., 17, **28**, 92, 101, 102, 144, 151, 169, 170
de la Potterie I., 17, 18, 62, **67-69**, 92, 131, 144, 148, 149, 150, 152, 153, 155, 157, 161, 162, 166, 167, 169, 170, 171, 173, 174, 176, 180, 182, 184, 185, 186, 193, 201, 231, 237, 291, 297, 337
Diano C., 119, 120, 121, 146, 151, 189, 217

di Marco A., 125
Dodd C. H., 12, 13, 18, 37, **53-55**, 92, 117, 118, 144, 148, 152, 153, 155, 157, 161, 167, 169, 170, 172, 174, 178, 184, 185, 186, 187, 188, 193, 201, 202, 208, 254, 258, 262, 298
Domeris W. R., 112, 118, 119, 120
Dupont J., 231
Duquoc C., 186

Edwards H., 9
Euripides, 119, 120, 121, 146, 189, 217

Ferraro G., 82, 94, 162, 164, 165, 166
Festugière A.-J., 112, 123
Feuillet A., 163, 164, 166, 170, 171, 172, 338
Flowers H. J., 12
Fortna R. T., 9, 10, 11, 14, 15, 142
Fraenkel J., 125

Gächter P., 163
Gaeta G. C., 311
Ghiberti G., 62
Giblet J., 1
Giblin C. H., 195, 230
Girard M., 32
Goettmann J., 32
Goulder M. D., 17, 19, **23-25**, 169, 184
Gourgues M., 18, **71-74**, 92, 144, 152, 153, 155, 157, 161, 162, 169, 184, 201, 205
Grossouw W., 272
Guilding A. 17, 19, **21-23**, 25, 92, 144, 167, 169, 180
Gunn D. M., 137

Haenchen E., 12
Harner Ph. B., 315
Harvey P., 119, 120
Hauser A. J., 37
Homeyer H., 104, 168
Hönig W., 44
Horace, 189, 190
Hoskyns E. C., 140

Infante L., 192

Janssens de Varebeke A., 40, 113, 116, 230, 231

Jeremias J., 10
Jochanan b. Zaddai, 236
Jonge M. de, 10
Josephus, Flavius, 152, 251

Kammerstätter J., 17, 18, 28, 29, **49-51**, 92, 131, 144, 167, 169, 201
Kealy S. P., 87, 94
Keck L., 105
Kieffer R., 19
Koulomzine N., 26
Kysar R., 9, 10, 11, 131

Lamouille A., 12
Lagrange M.-J., 12, 13, 140, 155, 222, 224, 225, 259, 261
Langbrandtner W., 12
Lash C., 231
Law R., 131
Lee E. K., 112
Léon-Dufour X., 126, 130
Leroy H., 49
Levesque G., 231
Liddell-Scott, 191
Lightfoot R. H., 144, 152, 153, 154, 155, 167
Lindars B., 10, 11, 12, 15, 89, 139, 167, 222, 224, 296
Lohmeyer E., 17, **26-28**, 92, 105, 144, 150, 169, 170
Lohse E., 12
Lucian, 104, 168
Lund N. W., 125, 128, 129
Luthardt C. E., 44
Lyonnet S., 87

MacGregor G. H. C., 9
Maggioni B., 315
Malatesta E., 94
Mally E. J., 160
Marrow S. B., 167
Marsh J., 139, 222
Martyn J. L., 111, 115, 118, 253, 329
Mastin B. A., 111, 139, 300
Mateos J., 17, **29-31**, 144, 150, 157, 158, 170, 225
McCool F. J., 295
McPolin J., 259, 315, 322, 323, 331
Meeks W. A., 315

Menoud P.-H., 10
Meynet R., 125
Michaud J.-P., 305
Migliasso S., 155, 161, 184, 221, 222, 223
Minear P. S., **140-43**
Mlakuzhyil G., 266, 286
Mollat D., 17, **19-21**, 25, 144, 151, 158, 167, 169, 170, 201, 231, 272, 273, 274, 275, 301
Moloney F. J., 16, 267, 269, 270
Moreno R., 279, 282
Morris L., 236
Morton A. Q., 9
Mourlon Beernaert P., 158, 181, 215, 217, 220
Munck J., 183
Mussner F., 290, 293, 314

Neirynck F., 10, 11, 12
Nestle E., 87
Nicol W., 6, 9, 10, 11, 15, 141, 142
Nineham D. E., 105
Noack B., 22, 115

O'Collins G., 325

Panimolle S. A., 42, 132, 133, 184, 186, 216, 221, 223, 224, 226, 258, 305, 309, 310, 314, 315, 321, 343, 346
Parker P., 12
Parunak H. van Dyke, 105
Pasquetto V., 17, 18, 33, 53, **74-76**, 92, 144, 167, 169, 170, 173, 184, 185, 193, 201
Pesch R., 105
Pollard T. E., 146, 300
Porten B., 125
Prete B., 17, 18, 43, **51-53**, 92, 144, 152, 153, 157, 169, 170, 173, 176, 180, 184, 185, 201
Puigdollers R., 17, **35-37**, 92, 144, 151, 169, 170, 201

Quiévreux F., 26
Quintilian, 94

Radday Y. T., 125, 129
Rau C., 18, 44, **47-49**, 92, 101, 102, 144, 169, 201
Reim G., 300

Rengstorf K. H., 140, 271, 272, 279, 282
Riaud J., 337
Richter G., 221
Riedl J., 276, 278
Rissi M., 18, **83-85**
Robinson J. A. T., 300
Rovira Bellose J. M., 165
Ruckstuhl E., 10, 13, 15

Sabugal S., 201, 245, 247, 248, 249, 251, 254, 255
Sahlin H., 17, **28-29**
Sanders J. N., 111, 139
Schlatter A., 13, 276
Schnackenburg R., 5, 6, 8, 9, 10, 12, 13, 15, 22, 30, 89, 139, 152, 163, 167, 171, 194, 211, 217, 221, 223, 224, 231, 244, 247, 248, 258, 259, 261, 264, 266, 267, 271, 275, 276, 278, 279, 281, 282, 290, 294, 295, 297, 298, 304, 305, 308, 309, 310, 314
Schneider J., 152, 223
Schulz A., 279, 282
Schulz S., 12, 139, 152
Schwank B., 5
Schwartz E., 5, 12, 14
Schweizer E., 10
Segalla G., 18, **76-79**, 92, 139, 144, 155, 156, 167, 169, 170, 173, 176, 179, 182, 184, 185, 192, 200, 201, 222, 224, 225
Seynaeve J., 166
Simoens Y., 183, 221, 222, 224, 225, 227
Smith D. M., Jr., 1, 10, 12
Smith R. F., 125
Sophocles, 119, 120, 146, 189
Spitta F., 9, 12
Staley J., 43, 44
Stauffer E., 197
Stock A., 105, 125
Stock K., 105
Strack-Billerbeck, 89, 236
Strathmann H., 12, 13

Talbert C. H., 121, 243
Taylor V., 105
Teeple M., 5, 6, 7, 8, 9, 10, 12, 13, 14, 15
Temple S., 14, 15
Tenney M. C., 18, **55-58**, 92, 101, 102, 118, 144, 167, 169, 185, 188

Thüssing W., 163, 165, 166
Thyen H., 8, 12, 14
Trench R. C., 286

Vaganay L., 106
van den Bussche H., 18, 62, **64-66**, 92, 144, 149, 152, 155, 157, 161, 166, 167, 169, 170, 173, 175, 176, 177, 178, 179, 180, 182, 184, 185, 188, 201, 274, 275, 278, 300
Vanhoye A., 1, 87, 94, 105, 106, 126, 127, 163, 186, 276
Vanni U., 1, 87
Vellanickal M., 279, 303

Watson W. G. E., 125, 129
Webster E. C., 17, **37-40**, 92, 144, 169, 184, 185

Webster N., 152
Welch J. W., 125, 129
Wellhausen J., 12, 14
Westcott B. F., 13, 18, **62-64**, 92, 139, 144, 152, 153, 155, 157, 161, 169, 184, 185, 188
Wild A., 44
Wikenhauser A., 5, 6, 7, 9, 13, 152, 155, 167
Wilkens W., 11, 12, 13
Willemse J., 17, 18, 28, 29, **44-46**, 92, 144, 170, 178

Zedda S., 290
Zerwick M., 329
Ziener G., 29, 274
Zimmermann H., 221, 224

THE SCHEMA OF THE CHRISTOCENTRIC LITERARY STRUCTURE OF THE FOURTH GOSPEL

0. CHRISTOCENTRIC INTRODUCTION (1,1-2,11)

- C* (1,1-18) : Hymnic-testimonial introduction (Prologue).
- B* (1,19-51) : Testimonial-kerygmatic introduction.
- A+ (2,1-11) + : Historical sign-introduction.

I.

1. JESUS' INITIAL SIGNS AND ENCOUNTERS (from Cana to Cana) (2,1-4,54)

- T A (2,1-12)   : The beginning of the signs at Cana in Galilee: the changing of water into wine.
- H
- E B (2,13-25+)   : The cleansing of the Jerusalem-temple and dialogue with the Jews on the new temple.
-    O C (2,23-3,21) : Dialogue with Nicodemus on birth from above and discourse on having eternal life.
-    O C' (3,22-4,3+) : Dialogue of J.B. with his disciples on the groom from above and discourse on life.
- B B' (4,1-42)   : Dialogue with the Samaritan woman on living water and true (temple) worship.
- O K
- O A' (4,43-54)   : The second sign at Cana in Galilee: the healing of the royal official's son.
- K

J E 2. JESUS' WORKS, SIGNS AND DISCUSSIONS (at Jewish Feasts) (5,1-10,42)
S U
S'

- B (5,1-47)   : The work of curing the cripple by Jesus, the Son of God (on a Sabbath).
- C (6,1-71)   : The sign of feeding the five thousand by Jesus, the bread of life (before Passover).
- I D (7,1-8,59)   : Jesus, the source of living water and the light of the world (at Tabernacles).
- G
- N D' (9,1-41)   : The giving of sight to the blind man by the light of the world (on a Sabbath).
- S
-    C' (10,1-21)   : The parables of the sheepfold, the door, and the life-giving, good shepherd.
- J
- N B' (10,22-42)   : The works and identity of Jesus, the Christ, the Son of God (at Dedication).

2
– 3+ THE CLIMACTIC SIGN AND THE COMING OF JESUS' HOUR (Bridge-
1   Section) +(11,1-12,50)+
2

- C (11,1-54)   : The sign of raising Lazarus to life by Jesus, the resurrection and the life, and the Sanhedrin's decision to kill him.

II.

- C' (11,55-12,50)   : The anointing at Bethany, the triumphal entry into Jerusalem, the coming of the Greeks and of 'the hour', and the Jews' refusal to believe in Jesus.

T
H
E 4. JESUS' FAREWELL OF THE HOUR (at the Last Supper) (13,1-17,26)

- B C (13,1-38+)   : The symbolic act of the hour (feet-washing) and the prediction of betrayal and denial.
- O
- O D (13,31-14,31) : The prediction of Peter's denials and the first farewell discourse.
- K
-    E (15,1-17)   : The allegory of the wine and the branches and the commandment of love.
- O
- F E' (15,18-16,44) : The hatred and persecution by the world, and the disciples' witnessing.
-    D' (16,4e-33)   : The second farewell discourse and the prediction of the disciples' desertion.
- J
- E C' (17,1-26)   : The prayer of the hour [of Jesus' passion-death-resurrection].
- S
- U
- S'

5. THE HOUR OF JESUS' PASSION-DEATH-RESURRECTION (18,1-20,29)

- H C (18,1-14+)   : The sovereign Jesus before the betrayer Judas and the arrest-party.
- O
- U D (18,12-27)   : Jesus' trial before the high priest and Peter's denials of discipleship.
- R
-    E (18,28-19,16b) : The trial and condemnation of Jesus, the king of the Jews, by Pilate.
- J
- N E' (19,16c-42)   : The crucifixion, death and burial of the king of the Jews on Golgotha.
-    D' (20,1-18)   : Peter and the B.D. at the empty tomb and Jesus' appearance to Mary Magdalene.
-    C' (20,19-29)   : The Lord Jesus' appearances to the disciples and the unbelieving Thomas.

Z. CHRISTOCENTRIC CONCLUSION (20,30-31)

- Az (20,30)   : Historical sign-conclusion.
- Bz (20,31abc) : Christological conclusion.
- Cz (20,31d)   : Soteriological conclusion.

X. APPENDIX (21,1-25)

6. EPILOGUE: THE RISEN JESUS AND THE DISCIPLES (at the Sea of Tiberias) (21,1-23)

- C (21,1-14)   : The risen Jesus' manifestation to the seven disciples.
- D (21,15-19)   : Jesus and Peter's confession of love, pastoral commission and destiny.
- C' (21,20-23)   : Jesus, Peter and the destiny of the Beloved Disciple.

Z'. SECOND (EDITORIAL) CONCLUSION (21,24-25)

- Bz' (21,24)   : Testimonial conclusion.
- Az' (21,25)   : Hyperbolic conclusion.

```
C*       C.C'    D.D'     E.E'      E.E'     D.D'     C.C'     C*
B* B....B'   C....C'   D....D'    D....D'   C....C'  Bz  C.C'  D
A+...1...A'  ---2---   ---3+---   ----4----  ----5---   ---6---  Bz'
                                                              Az'
```

BS
2515.2
.M56   Mlakuzhyil, George.
1987   The Christocentric
           literary structure
           of the Fourth Gospel.

HIEBERT LIBRARY
Fresno Pacific College - M. B. Seminary
Fresno, Calif. 93702